FIRST DO NO HARM

For Ken, from all of us

'Character is like a tree and reputation like its shadow.
The shadow is what we think of it; the tree is the real thing'

Abraham Lincoln (1809-1865)

First Do No Harm

Law, Ethics and Healthcare

Edited by

SHEILA A.M. McLEAN
University of Glasgow, Scotland

ROUTLEDGE
Routledge
Taylor & Francis Group
LONDON AND NEW YORK

First published 2006 by Ashgate Publishing

Published 2016 by Routledge
2 Park Square, Milton Park, Abingdon, Oxfordshire OX14 4RN
711 Third Avenue, New York, NY 10017, USA

First issued in paperback 2016

Routledge is an imprint of the Taylor & Francis Group, an informa business

British Library Cataloguing in Publication Data
First do no harm : law, ethics and healthcare. - (Applied legal philosophy)
1.Medical law and legislation 2.Medical ethics
I.McLean, Sheila
344'.041

Library of Congress Cataloging-in-Publication Data
First do no harm : law, ethics and healthcare / edited by Sheila A. M. McLean.
p. cm. -- (Applied legal philosophy)
Includes index.
ISBN 0-7546-2614-8
1. Medical laws and legislation. 2. Human experimentation in medicine--Law and legislation. 3. Medical ethics. I. McLean, Sheila. II. Series.

K3601.F57 2006
344.04'1--dc22

20005035025

ISBN 13: 978-1-138-27750-2 (pbk)
ISBN 13: 978-0-7546-2614-5 (hbk)

Contents

Len Doyal Emeritus Professor of Medical Ethics, Queen Mary University of London, United Kingdom

Veronica English Medical Ethics Department, British Medical Association, United Kingdom

Pamela R. Ferguson Professor of Scots Law, Faculty of Law and Accountancy, University of Dundee, United Kingdom

Marie Fox Professor of Law, University of Keele, United Kingdom

Ian Freckelton Honorary Professor, Law Faculty, Department of Forensic Medicine, Department of Psychological Medicine, Monash University, Adjunct Professor, La Trobe Law, La Trobe University, Adjunct Professor, Law Faculty, Deakin University, Australia

Michael Freeman Professor of English Law, Faculty of Laws, University College London, United Kingdom

Lawrence O. Gostin Associate Dean and John Carroll Research Professor of Law, Georgetown University; Professor of Public Health, the Johns Hopkins University; Director, Center for Law & the Public's Health (WHO and CDC Collaborating Center), United States

Vivienne Harpwood Professor of Law, University of Cardiff, United Kingdom

John Harris Sir David Alliance Professor of Bioethics, Institute of Medicine Law and Bioethics, School of Law, University of Manchester, United Kingdom

Mark Henaghan Professor and Dean of Law, University of Otago, Dunedin, New Zealand

Søren Holm Professor, Cardiff Law School, United Kingdom and Section for Medical Ethics, University of Oslo, Norway

Emily Jackson Professor of Medical Law, Queen Mary, University of London, United Kingdom

John Keown Rose F. Kennedy Professor of Christian Ethics, Kennedy Institute of Ethics, Georgetown University, United States

Linda Kharaboyan Research Associate, Centre de recherche en droit public, Université de Montréal, Canada

Bartha Knoppers Canada Research Chair in Law and Medicine, Centre de recherche en droit public, Université de Montréal, Canada

Graeme Laurie Professor of Medical Jurisprudence and Co-Director AHRC Research Centre for Studies in Intellectual Property and Technology Law, University of Edinburgh, United Kingdom

Gerard Magill Executive Director and Department Chair, Center for Health Care Ethics, Saint Louis University, United States

Sandy McCall Smith Professor Emeritus of Medical Law, University of Edinburgh, United Kingdom

Jean McHale Professor, Faculty of Law, University of Leicester, United Kingdom

Sheila A.M. McLean International Bar Association Professor of Law and Ethics in Medicine, Director, Institute of Law and Ethics in Medicine, University of Glasgow, United Kingdom

David Meyers Member of the California Bar, visiting lecturer in Medical Jurisprudence at the University of Tasmania Law School, Australia and at the University of Edinburgh Law School, United Kingdom

Jonathan Montgomery Professor of Health Care Law, University of Southampton, United Kingdom

Derek Morgan Professor of Health Care Law and Jurisprudence, Law School, University of Cardiff, United Kingdom

Rebecca Mussell Medical Ethics Department, British Medical Association, United Kingdom

Christopher Newdick Reader in Health Law, University of Reading; member of the Berkshire Priorities Committee, United Kingdom

Kenneth McK. Norrie Professor of Law, University of Strathclyde, United Kingdom

Kerry Petersen Associate Professor, School of Law, LaTrobe University, Melbourne, Australia

Julian Sheather Medical Ethics Department, British Medical Association, United Kingdom

Loane Skene Professor of Law, Faculty of Law; Adjunct Professor, Faculty of Medicine, Dentistry and Health Sciences, University of Melbourne, Australia

Ann Sommerville Medical Ethics Department, British Medical Association, United Kingdom

Elaine E. Sutherland LL.B., LL.M., Professor of Child and Family Law, School of Law, University of Stirling, Scotland, and Professor of Law, Lewis and Clark Law School, Portland, Oregon.

Harvey Teff Professor Emeritus of Law, University of Durham, United Kingdom

Preface

Sheila A.M. McLean

A glance at the list of contributors to this festschrift to celebrate Ken Mason's contribution to Medical Law should be sufficient to show the reader just how much Ken is loved, respected and admired. His friends and fans in the biomedical law and ethics community are legion. His contribution is both personal and scholarly and it has been a great pleasure for me to bring all of these distinguished contributors together in editing this volume. I am grateful to them for finding time in their busy schedules to write these excellent chapters in lasting testimony to Ken's work.

When I started teaching Medical Law in 1976, the subject was small but fascinating. Over the years, its parameters have widened, its analysis has become more rigorous and multi-disciplinary and its importance to the lives of ordinary people – as well as healthcare professionals – has been widely recognised. Each of the contributors to this volume has made their own contribution; none more so than Ken Mason. This book, then, celebrates Ken's outstanding abilities, his humility and the affection we all have for him. It also, I believe, makes its own contribution to medical law and ethics. The range of subjects covered, the variety of approaches adopted and the quality of the individual chapters make this an important and compelling account of the issues currently challenging scholars in the field; that it is in honour of Ken Mason is the icing on the cake!

Sheila A.M. McLean

the patients and doctors individually concerned believe that such killing would be morally justified. It assumes the right to dictate to individuals a moral position. In a modern liberal democracy, this presents a major problem of legitimacy. What gives lawmakers, in Parliament or the courts, the right to promote or proscribe a particular course of action in the face of controversy?

The importance of the issue was starkly illustrated by the divisions between the majority and minority views set out by the House of Commons Committee on Science and Technology in its report *Human Reproductive Technologies and the Law.*[4] Unusually, the Committee was fundamentally divided on the approach to be taken and the report was issued only with the recognition that five members of the Committee disagreed with its conclusions.[5] The crux of the disagreement concerned the proper function of regulation in the context of medical advances. The majority view was characterised as 'an extreme libertarian approach' by the dissenters and said by them to pay insufficient regard to public opinion and the evidence submitted to the inquiry, to disregard ethical arguments against an extreme libertarian approach, and to lack balance in adopting libertarian interpretations of principles or propositions, which are subject to debate.[6]

The approach that was criticised in this way was based on the view that:

> assisted reproduction and research involving the embryo of the human species both remain legitimate interests of the state. Reproductive and research freedoms must be balanced against the interests of society but alleged harms to society, too, should be based on evidence … Many of the decisions about what to regulate or to legislate about depend on the approach taken with regard to the balance of harm and benefit or potential harm and potential benefit … alleged harms to society or to patients need to be demonstrated before forward progress is unduly impeded.[7]

On this analysis, there is a presumption of non-intervention into what are principally conceived as matters of individual freedom. It is legitimate to control the manner in which scientific advances are made in order to enable consideration of the risks that may be involved but not to rule out particular activities on the basis that they are otherwise unethical.

This can be seen to be similar to the framework that underpinned the decision of the European Court of Human Rights in *Pretty v. UK.*[8] The case concerned the compatibility with human rights of restrictions on assisted suicide. Diane Pretty contended that English law's prohibition of her chosen mode of death, killing by her husband at her request, breached her rights to determine how she died. Claims built on article 2 (the right to die) and article 3 (protection from inhumane and degrading

---

4 HC 7 2004-5.

5 *Eighth Special Report* HC 491 2004-5.

6 See the formal minutes of the Committee for Wednesday 23 March 2005, published with the *Eighth Special Report*.

7 HC 7 2004-5, paras 46-47.

8 *Pretty v. UK* [2002] 2 FCR 97.

treatment) were firmly rejected, as they had been in the House of Lords.[9] However, her rights under Article 8 of the European Convention on Human Rights required more careful scrutiny. A blanket ban on assisted suicide was acceptable only if there was a legitimate aim in restricting Mrs Pretty's personal autonomy and if the restrictions were proportionate to that aim so as to be 'necessary in a democratic society'. In the view of the European Court of Human Rights, the vulnerability of those who might be affected (although not Diane Pretty herself) and the risk of abuse if the law was relaxed were sufficient to permit States to prohibit assisted suicide.[10]

This argument is similar in structure to that used by the 'libertarian' majority in the Select Committee. The starting point was non-regulation of patients' choices, subject to interference only if a harm condition was met. The outcome of the application of this analysis was very different, in that the Court accepted that there was risk even though there was no direct evidence, while the majority of the Committee refused to accept claims of risk without proof. However, the assumption that the role of the law was to control harm resulting from the exercise of choices by patients and professionals, rather than determine the morality of the activities in question, was common to both decisions.

It was a very different approach to that put before the ECHR by the Catholic Bishops Conference of England and Wales. They contended that:

> Actions with the purpose of killing oneself or another, even with consent, reflected a damaging misunderstanding of the human worth. Suicide and euthanasia were therefore outside the range of morally acceptable options in dealing with human suffering and dying.[11]

This is an argument that the law should be shaped around the intrinsic morality of actions. Some actions should be proscribed even without evidence of specific harms because they are incompatible with human dignity. Even if safeguards could be put in place to ensure that the vulnerable were protected and abuse effectively controlled, suicide and euthanasia would remain immoral. This is a view that can be characterised as a 'sanctity of life' approach whose supporters Ken Mason once suggested 'may turn out to be major custodians of the human conscience'.[12]

This chapter explores the problem of the legitimacy of medical law and asks whether the close connection between law and morality that inspired Ken Mason's work can be maintained in an increasingly consumerist society. It uses some of the examples that he explored in *Human Life and Medical Practice* – which were terminal illness, euthanasia, suicide, brain damage and death, the neonate, abortion and embryocide – to explore how the context has changed since he discussed the issues and how medical lawyers can justify their right to seek to shape healthcare practice through the coercive force of the law. If law has no such right, then medical law is

9 *R (Pretty) v. DPP* [2002] 1 All ER 1.

10 See paragraphs 68-78 of the ECHR judgment.

11 See paragraph 29 of the ECHR judgment.

12 *Human Life and Medical Practice, supra cit*, at p. 124.

this type of issue when he discussed the wrongs of a policeman drinking while on duty – no person should be punished for being drunk, but a soldier or policeman who was drunk on duty ought to be punished because they would not be engaged in a purely 'self-regarding' activity. Rather, they would have disabled themselves from performing their duty to the public.[19] Particular conduct may be required from those in public roles even where as private citizens they should be free to act as they wish.

In so far as health professionals exercise authority that is legally recognised as peculiar to their status, such as permitting the use of prescription-only medicines, it can be said that there is a particular role the law permits them to play that they should not be allowed to undermine. An argument of this sort is sometimes offered by doctors who oppose physician-assisted suicide. It suggests that if doctors were known sometimes to take active steps to kill their patients, then it would undermine the trust that is essential to a therapeutic relationship. On this argument, the enterprise of healthcare has a moral content that it is permissible for the law to defend because it is essential to securing the future of health services. While it would not be permissible to prohibit patients and relatives from performing voluntary euthanasia, because their actions affect only those involved, when a professional participates, it impacts on the profession as a whole. Thus, physician-assisted suicide could legitimately be regulated.

The plausibility of this approach is enhanced by consideration of the codes of professional ethics under which doctors and others work. Continued registration and therefore licence to practise depends on adherence to such codes. Membership of the profession carries a commitment to a specific set of moral values that are additional, and possibly different, to the broader ethical requirements on citizens. No one is obliged to become a health professional, but if they do so they promise to follow the prescribed morality and can legitimately be held to their promises. Patients are not obliged to avail themselves of health services, but if they do they must accept that the people treating them are bound by their professional ethics.

There are at least two reasons why this approach seems unlikely to resolve the difficulties in justifying the enforcement of morality. The first is that we already accept the possibility of a more pluralistic professional morality than this account implies. The clearest evidence of this lies in the provision of a 'conscience clause' permitting those who object on moral grounds to participation in abortion services to opt out from their provision.[20] This heterogeneity of moral approach has not caused the destruction of medical and nursing ethics. In a less formal way, a similar recognition of the fact that ethical issues do not necessarily require a uniform solution can be seen in the decision in *Airedale NHS Trust v. Bland*.[21] In that case the House of Lords declared that it was permissible for doctors caring for a young man in a persistent

19 *On Liberty*, Chapter IV.

20 Abortion Act 1967, s 4.

21 [1993] 1 All ER 821. For a defence of this interpretation of the case, see Montgomery, J., *Health Care Law*, Oxford, Oxford University Press, 2003, chapter 20.

vegetative state to withdraw hydration and nutrition because that was a course of action regarded as acceptable by a responsible body of medical practitioners. It was not suggested, however, that to continue to administer such care would have been unlawful. This course of action too would have been regarded as acceptable by a responsible body of medical option. Thus, different views were equally acceptable to the law as being within the legitimate scope of clinical freedom.

The implication is that even if practising medicine is an inherently public activity, it can accommodate considerable divergence of ethical views. Consequently, the argument that the integrity of medical ethics needs to be maintained by the enforcement of common principles is undermined. More needs to be given by way of justification for the imposition of homogenous views.

The second reason why relying on the moral content of doctors' public role looks a weak justification for the legitimacy of medical law (as traditionally practised) can be seen in the case of *Burke v. GMC*.[22] The case concerned a challenge to guidance issued by the GMC on decisions about withholding life-sustaining treatment. Leslie Burke was concerned that treatment might be withheld from him when his health deteriorated (he had spino-cerebellar ataxia, a congenital degenerative brain condition) against his wishes. In one sense the arguments seemed hypothetical in that it was highly probable that doctors who followed the guidance would have cared for him in the way that he wished.[23] However, this was not guaranteed because the guidance allowed for clinical discretion as to what treatment was appropriate.

In the High Court, Munby J accepted the validity of Burke's challenge arguing that the GMC's guidance paid insufficient regard to patients' rights to require the treatment that they wanted. The Court of Appeal held that there was no such right, although in the particular circumstances in which Leslie Burke was likely to find himself the duty to preserve life was likely to guarantee that he would be treated. Nevertheless, as a strict matter of law, in the unlikely circumstances that doctors believed that artificial hydration would cause him harm, then they would not be obliged to provide it even if he requested it.[24]

The importance of this litigation for the question considered in this paper lies in three aspects. First of all, the moral code under which medicine operated was seen as a legitimate issue for legal challenge. If medical ethics were a private matter, then it would not matter whether it precisely matched the strict legal position. Leslie Burke's challenge to individuals caring for him might have breached his rights and be ripe for litigation, but there was no need to challenge the general guidance because it was merely guidance. Only if the issue became 'real' in relation to the actions of individuals would the rights become justiciable.[25] The acceptance of the case by the

22 [2004] EWHC 1879 (Admin); [2005] EWCA Civ 1003.

23 [2005] EWCA Civ 1003, para 13.

24 See paras 49-55, especially 55.

25 There is some indication that the Court of Appeal thought that he should have been advised in these terms, see paras 13-14.

courts implies that professional norms are seen as a component of the quasi-legal structure of medical law and therefore a public issue.

Secondly, the case demonstrates the controversial nature of the issues. The Court of Appeal sought to restrict the issue to matters directly affecting Leslie Burke and criticised the judge for elevating it into an exploration of general principle. Concern was also expressed about the way in which the case drew attention as talismatic of broader debates in society.[26] Interventions were made to the litigation by parties believing that they had a stake in the issues beyond the private matters concerning Leslie Burke's care. These included the Disability Rights Commission (contending that the issues exposed the devaluing by the health professions of the lives of those with disabilities), the Catholic Bishop's Conference of England and Wales and ALERT (concerned to protect the sanctity of human life). These interveners were seeking to promote a particular moral view in a way that Lord Devlin would have understood. In their view the case was more than a private matter affecting only patient and doctor.

Finally, the *Burke* case draws attention to the possibility of a drift away from the enforcement of morality into a consumerist rights based approach.[27] Munby J sought to move the concept of 'best interests' away from being an application of value judgment working through the traditional imperatives of medical ethics to do no harm and, if possible, do some good. Instead, in Munby's account, the issue became a more content-neutral question of autonomy and the right of patients to decide what happens, whether or not it was 'good' for them. He argued that the only circumstance in which life-sustaining treatment should be withheld was where it was subjectively 'intolerable' to the patient. This protects the right to choose irrespective of what is chosen.

While this approach was firmly rejected as a solution to the *Burke* case by the Court of Appeal, that Court recognised that this principle is significant in relation to refusal of treatment. Competent patients are entitled to choose to refuse treatment that is objectively good for them, even irrationally. This protection of their autonomy ensures that treatment is not imposed upon them 'for their own good' and is consistent with Mill's liberty principle as a bastion of individuality. In Millian terms it could be said that the reason why it does not work for demands for particular treatment is that requiring a health professional to act moves the question from being purely self-regarding (and private) to having an impact on others (public). This shift to the public domain could be the justification for moralistic regulation, but it seems unlikely that requiring health professionals to stand by and let patients whom they could save die has any less impact on them than requiring them to give treatment

26 This has been interestingly described as a 'stigmata' effect, see Lee, R. and Morgan, D., 'Regulating Risk Society; stigmata cases, scientific citizenship and biomedical diplomacy', (2001) *Sydney Law Review*, 297-318.

27 This is connected to a wider debate about the connection between law and morality in the regulation of medicine. See Montgomery, J., 'Law and the Demoralisation of Medicine', (2006) 26 *Legal Studies* 185-210.

they believe is inappropriate. Indeed it could be said to be more difficult for them to deal with.[28]

Most fundamentally, however, the problem with an argument for the legitimacy of medical law based on the public nature of the enterprise is unsatisfactory because it does both too much and too little. Too much, in that it would suggest that all moral issues in medicine can be resolved by enforcing a moral viewpoint. This flies in the face of the existing recognition of plurality in some areas. Too little, in that it cannot distinguish those aspects of the public choices where requiring a homogenous morality is permissible.

A second approach which could emerge out of the approach taken by Munby J, but with less extensive disruption to current legal approaches, would draw the legitimacy of medical law from its protection of a limited set of particularly important moral principles. The established legal acceptance that the value of autonomy prevails over the principles of best interests or the sanctity of human life is based on another possible solution to the enforcement of morality problem.[29] This operates by distinguishing between particular moral principles and regarding some of them as enforceable even though people do not personally hold them. This is, of course, what Hart actually argued in the debate over the enforcement of morality – that there was a 'critical morality' (in his case liberalism) that it was permissible to enforce. It is therefore necessary to see whether such an approach can be used to delineate the legitimate scope for medical law.

Status Claims – The Role of Rights?

The strongest candidate for such an approach would be based on human rights. Such rights have already been identified as deserving of special protection in law and medical law would be working through the implications of this prior commitment to preserve a fundamental morality. Whether or not you accept that human rights are objectively valid, they have been accepted by society and can draw their force from a contractarian basis of (implied or imputed) mutual consent. Legitimising medical law through this strategy can be seen as defensible on either the Hart or the Devlin account. In relation to the latter, human rights law could be said to represent the codification of those aspects of prevailing morality that are seen as essential to its common life and therefore properly protected against challenge. In Hartian terms, human rights can be said to describe those aspects of people's well-being where infringement is seen as causing the sort of harm that justifies intervention (in Millian terms, the 'assignable interests' of individuals).

28 Consider the difficulty members of the team had in accepting the patient's wish to die in *Re B* [2002] 2 All ER 449.

29 For an explanation of this prioritisation and some of the problems in applying it, see Montgomery, J., 'Health Care Law for a multi-faith society', in Murphy, J. (eds) *Ethnic Minorities, their Families and the Law*, Oxford, Hart Publishing, 2000, 161-179.

A human rights based approach to medical law would be able to accommodate the claim that healthcare decisions were largely private. It would be insufficient merely to show that others disapproved of actions, or that they were affected by them. Only if their human rights were compromised would be law be entitled to intervene. Rights claims would be privileged over other moral arguments and the general claims of society to cost-efficiency and homogeneity.[30] Medical law might be confined to a more limited scope, as it would need to build (for the UK) on the range of rights recognised in the European Convention of Human Rights (ECHR), but it could be confident of the moral high ground in doing so.

There are, however, a number of problems with this approach. The first concerns the difficulties of interpreting the documents. Early champions of medical law as a species of human rights law stressed the importance of the right to autonomy, yet it was only in the *Pretty* case (over 50 years after the European Convention on Human Rights was drafted) that the European Court of Human Rights finally recognised a right of autonomy implicit in Article 8 of the Convention. This suggests that reliance on human rights might not forestall the debate over legitimacy. So long as the interpretation of convention rights is controversial, the legitimacy debate is recast as an argument about what rights mean. Thus, the abortion issue remains hotly disputed as a human rights matter because it is not clear whether the fetus or unborn child is a 'life' in relation to Article 2.[31] If it is, then abortion is clearly a human rights issue and a legitimate matter for medical law to regulate. If not, then it may not be.

The second difficulty with the human rights strategy to provide medical law with legitimacy arises within the texts themselves. Human rights law can be a powerful tool in controlling medical power. One of the few areas of medical law that has seen significant challenge since the implementation of the Human Rights Act 1998 is mental health law. Of particular importance has been the development of jurisprudence that ensures that doctors cannot impose treatment merely because the criteria in the mental health legislation are met but must either secure consent or demonstrate medical necessity.[32] In general, however, the English courts have so far shown themselves reluctant to make major changes.[33] The reality is that the drafting of the European Convention is quite friendly to paternalistic medicine. Article 5 permits detention for the purposes of disease control. Most importantly, Article 8 sees privacy (now including autonomy) as needing to be balanced against 'public health and morals'. Applying this to abortion, while the law has shied away from dealing with the issue on the basis that the fetus has its life protected, it has not resolved the matter in terms of women's right to choose. It is perfectly possible to

30 This conception of the role of rights is explained in Montgomery, J., 'Patients first: the role of rights', in Fulford, K., Ersser, S. and Hope, T. (eds), *Patient Centred Health Care*, Oxford, Blackwell Scientific, 1996, 142-152.

31 *Vo v. France* App No 53924/00 [2004] 2 FCR 577.

32 *R (on the application of Wilkinson) v. Broadmoor Special Hospital Authority* [2001] EWCA Civ 1545, [2002] 1 WLR 419; *R (on the application of N) v. Doctor M* [2002] EWCA Civ 1789, [2003] 1 FCR 124.

33 *NHS Trust A v. M; NHS Trust B v. H* [2001] 1 FCR 406.

justify regulating abortion on the basis that the right to privacy under Article 8 needs to be balanced with the needs of public health and morals. Thus, the appeal to human rights has given some structure to the debate but it cannot legitimate an answer because the texts are too ambiguous.

The third concern about the human rights approach arises from the range of rights that are actually recognised. Many argue that the ECHR is a dated document and does not fully cover the needs of the twenty-first century. Supplementary human rights documents, such as the Oviedo Convention on Bioethics,[34] seem to be needed to cover the territory populated by medical law. Yet to look to such developments brings the problem that the UK has declined to sign the Bioethics Convention, so the argument that prior commitment to human rights justifies its subsequent enforcement breaks down. There has been no such commitment.

These issues highlight the risks of basing the legitimacy of medical law on human rights – it may force us to contract the scope of the subject to those areas where the texts are clear. Legitimacy at such cost may not be attractive. Indeed, some would argue that to look to human rights for a solution is inappropriate for matters that are properly part of public debate. The reluctance of the House of Lords in the *Pretty* case to hold that human rights were even engaged was partly fuelled by such concerns. To resolve the case by appeal to human rights law designed for a non-healthcare context was to exclude proper debate of the issues. As Lord Steyn put it:

> Any proposal that the Universal Declaration should require states to guarantee a right to euthanasia or assisted suicide (as opposed to permitting states by democratic institutions so to provide) would have been doomed to failure … in the field of fundamental beliefs the European Court of Human Rights does not readily adopt a creative role contrary to a European consensus, or virtual consensus. The fact is that among the 41 member states – north, south, east and west – there are deep cultural and religious differences in regard to euthanasia and assisted suicide. The legalisation of euthanasia and assisted suicide as adopted in the Netherlands would be unacceptable to predominantly Roman Catholic countries in Europe. The idea that the Convention *requires* states to render lawful euthanasia and assisted suicide (as opposed to allowing democratically elected legislatures to adopt measures to that effect) must therefore be approached with scepticism. That does not involve support for the proposition that one must go back to the original intent of the Convention. On the contrary, approaching the Convention as a living instrument, the fact is that an interpretation *requiring* states to legalise euthanasia and assisted suicide would not only be enormously controversial but profoundly unacceptable to the peoples of many member states.[35]

Such issues were for Parliament not the judges to determine. To hold that human rights dictated the outcome would be to extend the function of the Convention too far into the legitimate 'margin of appreciation' that states have to determine the nature

---

34 *Convention for the Protection of Human Rights and Dignity of the Human Being with regard to the Application of Biology and Medicine: Convention on Human Rights and Biomedicine*, signed at Oviedo, 4.4.1997, European Treaty Series – No. 164.

35 *R (Pretty) v. DPP* [2002] 1 All ER 1, para 56.

campaign for the imposition of particular moralities (for example on abortion) as it could give no account of why their moralism should be resisted. The other extreme view would be to accept that the legitimacy problem is insuperable and allow medical law to collapse into a combination of consumer law (in relation to private relationships) and public law (in relation to state spending). Neither leaves much scope for the approach that Ken Mason embodied of careful exploration of moral issues with recognition of the limits of the law.

Fortunately, it is not necessary to drift to either of these extremes. The key to the legitimacy problem in the modern context is to see medical law as a tool to ensure the recognition that its subject matter is morally charged and to protect the ability of individuals to grapple with the ethical issues that arise. It maintains the pre-conditions for moral agency. To impose a particular moral position will usually be to deny people who think differently the possibility of working through their own ethical responsibilities. It would consequently foster the view that the questions were not ethical so much as a matter of compliance with societal requirements. Medical law needs to make clear that its protagonists are morally accountable for their decisions and not merely following rules set down by others. In that sense the legitimacy of medical law lies in its attempt to preserve the possibility of morality, not to enforce a particular version of the 'good'.

The difference between this approach and consumerism can be seen in its implications for the relationship between patients and health professionals. In the *Burke* case, Munby J's acceptance of a right to require treatment would have subordinated the judgments of professionals to those of a patient. That would have compromised the ability of professionals to make moral choices. Equally, the moral independence of patients is protected by the requirement that treatment cannot be given without their consent (provided that they are competent). The resulting partnership is one of moral equals, neither of whom necessarily takes precedence. The assumption is that both will use the opportunity to grapple with their consciences. The expectation that health professionals will do this lies behind the generally benign judicial attitude to regulating healthcare.[40] No such assumption is made about patients, who may refuse treatment even for irrational reasons.[41] However, the Kantian tradition from which modern respect for autonomy is drawn would value choice as the expression of independent reason, not mere whim. The law's reluctance to explore patients' reasoning can perhaps be explained as an illustration of the limits of proof rather than a morally important feature in its own right.

On this understanding, the legitimacy of the Human Fertilisation and Embryology Act 1990 turns on its creation of a framework within which different decisions on morally significant matters are taken at different and appropriate levels.[42] The permissibility of some matters, such as cloning or keeping embryos alive in vitro for

40 This point is developed further in Montgomery, J., 'Law and the Demoralisation of Medicine', (2006) 26 *Legal Studies* 185-210.

41 *Sidaway v. Bethlem RHG* [1985] 1 All ER 643, per Lord Templeman.

42 See the account of the Act in Montgomery, J., note 37.

more than 14 days, was determined by Parliament. Others were within the gift of the Authority subject to Parliamentary oversight. Members are expected to exercise their judgment on difficult moral issues and be free to do so reasonably freely provided that they observe the legal limits to their powers. Those judgments can be exercised through licensing and also through guidance in the Code of Practice. Some things remain open for decision by individual clinicians and patients. At every level the framework makes moral judgment possible, while rarely resolving the moral issues definitively through law.

Adopting such a view of the proper function of medical law offers a more satisfactory solution to the problem of legitimacy, but it requires lawyers to be prepared to accept a significant degree of indeterminacy. Such uncertainty has sometimes been seen as a failure of legal regulation.[43] However, the more certain the legal requirements, the more likely the legitimacy problem is to be raised. If the job of medical law is to provide a structure for moral decision making, then the key questions will concern the allocation of the power to decide and the mechanisms for making decisions accountable. Failures in medical law would be identified not so much in relation to what is permitted to occur, but in the way key protagonists are disempowered. The law should protect both patients' and professionals' rights to exercise their judgment and prevent outsiders from dictating to them what should happen.

This is something different from consumerism because it recognises the moral integrity of health professionals as well as patients. It preserves a degree of private space, but is compatible with external regulation on the 'harm principle' in extreme cases where such harm can be clearly demonstrated and on the basis of human rights where those are clearly defined. However, where such regulation is based simply in imposing substantive moral views it would defeat the legitimate purpose of medical law because it would defeat its object. Moral decision making would be taken away from patients and professionals and consequently those claiming the moral high ground would also be destroying the basis of moral responsibility in giving care.

43 Miola, J., 'Medical law and medical ethics – complementary or corrosive?', (2004) 6 *Medical Law International* 251-274.

The 1970s saw the beginnings in the UK of medical ethics, a movement inspired by the already flourishing movement in the USA. Nowadays we find a whole range of activities sometimes called 'applied philosophy' or 'applied ethics', which discuss the environment, the treatment of animals, the problems of engineering, business, public policy and so on. What can philosophers contribute to these fields? To ask this is to ask for an account of the relationship between theory and practice.

Philosophers are thought of, and think of themselves, as creatures of reason. Nevertheless, they are influenced by images, analogies, or models and I hope to show that, historically speaking, there have been several images which have affected the perceptions which philosophers have had about the proper relationship between theory and practice. I shall briefly examine several of these.

The Razor

The first analogy or image can be found in the Greek world but it is most commonly associated with the work of the medieval philosopher William of Ockham. William of Ockham, is credited (perhaps wrongly) with forging what has come to be called 'Ockham's Razor': 'Entia non sunt multiplicanda', or 'Entites ought not to be multiplied'.[3] It is, of course, a matter for debate as to what he means by this slogan, but it has been used as a philosophical razor to cut out speculation and whatever cannot be verified. This macho image of the razor-wielding philosopher has been enormously influential in the development of perhaps a rather thin or shaved view of science, and more especially, a thin view of medicine. For example, doctors often tell us that what is wanted is 'established fact' and not 'opinion', as if facts and opinions exhausted the possibilities. More seriously, the over-emphasis on the randomised trial, cut off from the enormously powerful healing psychological factors in the doctor-patient relationship, is a legacy of the image of the fear of the razor. For example, in medicine there is the idea that you do not have real research unless you have fact and you do not have fact unless you can count something. So instead of asking the patient if he is feeling better on the pills he is asked to score how he is feeling on a scale of plus 10 to minus 10. In terms of the razor image, anything qualitative is asking to have its throat cut; only the quantitative will be recognised as real science. This theoretical image has therefore had a damaging effect on practice.

The Microscope

A second image or model which has exerted great influence on philosophers is that of the microscope. This image originates in David Hume. He tells us that he is providing a new philosophical microscope to make ideas clear.[4] This image might be

---

3 Moody, E.A., *The Logic of William of Ockham*, New York, Harvard University Press, 1935.

4 Hume, D. (1748), Selby-Bigge, L.A. (ed) *An Enquiry Concerning Human Understanding* (2nd ed), Oxford, Clarendon Press, 1902, section 1.

said to be one of the major influences on the whole analytic movement. It is indeed quite compatible with what I have called the two dogmas of ethics – that philosophy proper is not concerned with matters of fact and that it should be morally neutral. We find, for example, that in one of the seminal books of philosophical ethics of the twentieth century, G.E. Moore distinguishes the question, 'What does "good" mean?' from the question 'What kinds of things are good?'.[5] It is true that Moore answered the second question in the final part of his book, but most philosophers never make it to the end of the book, and moral philosophy subsequent to Moore concentrated on the question of meaning. In terms of this microscope analogy then, philosophy helps practice by making ideas clear.

The image is less obviously destructive than the razor and appealed to the desire of philosophers to have a quasi-scientific role in academic life. And there is no doubt that conceptual clarification is one central function of philosophy, and one which can have a bearing on practice. It is easy to make fun of the philosopher, who, when faced with a difficult question always begins, 'It depends what you mean by …'. The reality is that this is an important first step in many difficult problems. Nevertheless, the microscope analogy is open to some serious objections when viewed as a full account of the relationship between theory and practice. I shall mention two objections.

The first is that the philosophical microscope is not so objective as its scientific counterpart. Even in science it is notorious that the scientist tends to see what he hopes to see. In philosophy there is no doubt that the philosopher's eye will have a film of theory over it. This was true of Hume, and also of Moore, whose analysis of the concept of 'good' was skewed by his theory of language. The mistake is not that of seeing a problem or concept from a given point of view, it is in being unaware that you are doing so because you are misled by the microscope image into thinking that your analysis is more neutral or objective than it is. The second objection is that concepts are being looked at only one at a time through the microscope, whereas a full understanding of them requires seeing the links between them and also the links between the concepts and their total cultural context.

Maps

Various metaphorical images were associated with the idea that concepts are embedded in a cultural context, but the one which was (perhaps) most influential was that of cartography. The philosopher could help practice by mapping our concepts. Wittgenstein says that a philosophical problem has the form 'I do not know my way about'.[6] During the 1960s a large number of books were written by philosophers on every aspect of practical activity. The title often began 'The Concept of ...' or 'The Logic of ...'. One of the earliest of these books, which was still very influential in the

5 Moore, G.E., *Principia Ethica*, Cambridge, University Press, 1903.
6 Wittgenstein, L., *Philosophical Investigations*, Oxford, Blackwell, 1953, para 123.

1960s, was Gilbert Ryles' seminal work *The Concept of Mind.*[7] Once again, despite charges of triviality, there is no doubt that this movement was a help in clarifying and thus influencing practice. To mention Peters again, his distinctions, between education and training, or education and indoctrination, were hugely influential on educators in many areas, and Herbert Hart's *The Concept of Law*[8] was very influential in legal circles, outside of the narrowly philosophical area.

Many books influenced by the three images so far discussed could, with some squeezing, be fitted in between the two constraints I mentioned at the start – no facts and no direct attempt to influence practice. But as these constraints weakened in the 1970s, for reasons partly internal to philosophy, philosophy became bolder and increasingly philosophers got their hands dirty with the facts and cheerfully made recommendations to others with practical problems. The inspiration behind this was partly images in Greek philosophy. No one would nowadays have the nerve to adopt Plato's idea of the philosopher as a king, an absolute ruler, who determines every detail of social and political life. But some philosophers were and are much influenced by the more modest ideas of Aristotle, to whom I shall now turn.

Interpreters

Aristotle blurs the distinction on which many philosophers this century insist – between ethics as a synonym for ordinary morality, and ethics as a theoretical activity, an attempt to understand ethics in the first sense. As far as he is concerned, the point of ethics is not knowing but doing.[9] In other words, his ethics is really a practical guide to the good life. It is also true that he did not regard his ethics as philosophy in the strict sense. Nevertheless, although he does not regard his ethics as philosophy, it does not seem to be straight moralising either. His view is that the principles of the good life are embedded in our ordinary thinking, but they are hidden or overlaid by other inconsistent ideas. The job of the philosopher (or ethicist) then is to sift through our ordinary thinking and purge it of inconsistency. We might say that the philosopher is interpreting our ideas for us.

The idea of the philosopher who sifts through and interprets ordinary thought and comes out with guiding principles is a popular one in applied philosophy circles. In the sphere of medical ethics, for example, the position is stated by Professor Raanan Gillon, an influential philosopher/doctor working in this area in the UK:

> In brief, the four principles plus scope approach claims that whatever your personal philosophy, politics, religion, moral theory or life stance, you will find no difficulty in committing yourself to four *prima facie* moral principles, plus a concern for their scope of application. Moreover, these four principles plus a concern for their scope of application

7 Ryle, G., *The Concept of Mind*, London, Hutchinson's University Library, 1947.

8 Hart, H.L.A., *The Concept of Law*, London, Oxford University Press, 1961.

9 Aristotle, *Nicomachean Ethics*, Thomson, J.A.K. (trans), Harmondsworth, Penguin 1953, chapter 3.

> can be seen to encompass most, if not all, of the moral issues that arise in health care. (I am increasingly inclined to believe that the approach can, if sympathetically interpreted, be seen to encompass all moral issues, not merely those arising in health care.) The principles are respect for autonomy, beneficence, non-maleficence and justice. What the principles plus scope approach can provide is a common set of moral commitments, a common moral language, and a common set of moral issues to be considered in particular cases, before coming to your own answer, using your preferred moral theory or other approach to choosing between these principles when they conflict ...[10]

A great deal of current applied ethics works on this kind of model. The philosopher has interpreted ordinary moral thinking and has come up with what he considers to be consensus principles. The practitioners supply the facts which make up the minor premises of moral arguments and the philosopher may provide further guidance on how the principles apply to the cases. It should be noted that this approach can almost fit the constraints of the 'two dogmas of ethics' because the philosopher is dealing mainly with the principles and he is helping the practitioners (by an interpretative process) to come to their own conclusions, rather than moralising himself.

Now, there are various problems with this approach to the links between theory and practice, but one is that it does not seem to provide a very accurate account of how we reason in morality. People faced with a moral problem do not deduce a decision from the major premise of a principle coupled to the minor premise consisting of the facts of a particular problem. Rather they classify cases in the light of similar cases. This was in fact the method of casuistry in the early modern period.

Casuists and Judges

Casuistry has been defined as:

> the interpretation of moral issues, using procedures based on paradigms and analogies, leading to the formulation of expert opinion about the existence and stringency of particular moral obligations, framed in terms of rules or maxims that are general but not universal or invariable, since they hold good with certainty only in the typical conditions of the agent and circumstances of action.[11]

Casuistry has a bad name since it is associated with special pleading. As such it is totally rejected by many writers of the eighteenth century, such as Adam Smith.[12] Oddly enough, although Adam Smith rejects casuistry as a method of moral reasoning, he is happy with an activity he calls 'natural jurisprudence', which is for

10 Gillon, R., *The Principles of Health Care Ethics*, Chichester, John Wiley, 1994, p. xxii.

11 Jonsen, A., 'Casuistry as Methodology in Clinical Ethics', *Theoretical Medicine*, 1991, 12, 295-307.

12 Smith, A., *The Theory of Moral Sentiments* (1759), Oxford, Clarendon Press, 1976, VII, iv.

which Smith makes explicitly, and a third which might be raised nowadays on the basis of Smith's assumptions.

Objection from the Content of Obligation

This objection makes three connected points. First, that the casuists' 'attempted, to no purpose, to direct by precise rules what it belongs to feeling and sentiment only to judge of'.[17] Smith's point here is not that rules are never appropriate but that the casuists use them for the looser virtues where rules are inappropriate. Smith's second point is that in any event it is not possible to ascertain through rules what is required in many cases, for there cannot be rule-like dividing lines between, for example, a delicate sense of justice and a weak scrupulosity of conscience, or between reserve and dissimulation – 'what would hold good in one case would scarcely do so exactly in another'.[18] A third and connected point is that even although books of casuistry contain many cases, 'yet upon account of the still greater variety of possible circumstances'[19] it would only be a matter a chance if a case was found which was exactly parallel to the one being considered. Hence, Smith concludes that books of casuistry not only try to do the impossible, but are also useless. These connected criticisms concern the content of what we ought to do.

In reply, two points can made. First, Smith is surely wrong in thinking that any moral questions can be answered simply by appealing to our feelings and sentiments. Many moral situations are complex and immediate feelings can mislead. This is not to say that feelings are unimportant but rather that reason should lead in making moral decisions. The second point of reply is that Smith misunderstands casuistry if he thinks that casuists over-use rules. Perhaps indeed, in their stress on immersion in the details of particular cases, they under-use rules.

Objection from Moral Motivation

The second criticism which Smith makes is double-barrelled, and it concerns moral motivation. First, books of casuistry, because of their style do not 'tend to animate us to what is generous and noble – or soften us to what is gentle and humane'.[20] Secondly, and more dangerously, they 'tend rather to teach us to chicane with our own consciences, and by their vain subtleties serve to authorise innumerable evasive refinements with regard to the most essential articles of our duty'.[21] A very Kantian criticism! In view of these criticism it is not surprising that Smith concludes that 'casuistry ought to be rejected altogether' and that the 'two useful parts of moral philosophy, therefore, are Ethics and Jurisprudence'.[22]

17 Smith, *op. cit.*, VII, iv, 33.
18 *Ibid.*
19 *Ibid.*
20 *Ibid.*
21 *Ibid.*
22 *Ibid.*

The first barrel can be ducked. Casuists are not intending to 'animate' or motivate us. That perhaps is a job for poets, writers, preachers or social reformers. But the second barrel hits the mark. There is a danger, if you think every case is different, that you will 'chicane' with your conscience. Only if we underline the importance of the paradigm cases can that be avoided.

Objection to the Assumption of Moral Expertise

The third criticism emerges if we consider what Smith takes to be the two useful parts of moral philosophy – Ethics and Jurisprudence, or what he often calls 'natural jurisprudence'. By the time of Smith, lawyers had taken on the mantle of secular casuists. For example, they decided complex issues of property and rights. So why did Smith allow the practice of natural jurisprudence, which involves what he calls 'abstruse distinctions'[23] while rejecting casuistry? The answer is that law was seen as something external to the newly discovered individual self. Certainly there were problems of collisions between individual conscience and law, and an important aspect of the history of jurisprudence is that of recording successive attempts to keep law and conscience in harmony. But to the extent that law was perceived to be external to the self, it was regarded as legitimate for there to be 'experts' who considered precise applications of natural jurisprudence in systems of positive law.

But what of the modern casuist, the ethics consultant in medicine or business or the environment? Is such a person a moral expert? The third criticism of modern casuistry then is that it assumes that there can be the kind of expert we are willing to allow in law, but are not willing to allow in morality. Do the modern casuists in medicine or public affairs assume that they are moral experts? Can there be moral experts, and if so, where does that leave the autonomy of the individual conscience?

To take the first question, it is true to say that in the practice of casuistry, ancient or modern, some conception of expertise is being presupposed. If we consider the complexity of the issues which are faced in medical ethics, such as problems in surrogacy, the transplanting of foetal tissue, cloning and so on, it is apparent that we are dealing with problems where the technical and moral are inextricably entwined so that some conception of expert judgment is being presupposed. It might be argued that the complexity concerns the technical, empirical side to the problems and once the facts are sorted out then the purely moral element can kick in. This controversy first surfaced in the Scottish Enlightenment in the mid-eighteenth century. On the one hand it was argued by Hutcheson, Hume and Smith that in moral judgment we should first clarify the facts, what is the case, no matter how complex, and our awareness of the facts will then cause the appropriate moral sentiment to be activated. In other words, 'moral judgment' is strictly speaking an inaccurate description; the element of judgment is purely directed to sifting the facts, and the element of the moral is purely an emotional or attitudinal reaction. Thomas Reid, on the other hand,

---

23 *Ibid.*

held that the facts and values could not be separated and judgment was integral to the whole process. In a witty passage he observed that if Hutcheson and Hume were correct, then a judge should really be called a 'feeler'![24]

In my opinion, Reid has the better of them here. The sorting of the facts in a technical matter is not simply a morally neutral activity. The question of which facts are the important ones involves value judgments. Fact and value make up a seamless garment. What are the implications of taking this line?

One implication is that there is room for the moral expert. It does not of course follow that this expertise is generalisable. Someone may be considered a moral expert in one area but have no qualifications to speak on another. Nor does it follow that every moral problem needs an expert. If I see you drop a wallet on the way out of the room, there is no need for an expert to tell me what I ought to do. The main context in which moral expertise might be shown may be that of the expert committee set up to deal with a problem generated by the new technology. I shall not here go into what would be appropriate qualifications for membership of such a committee, or what might disqualify. Clearly, some knowledge of the technicalities and/or some analytical skills might count as qualifications (albeit not sufficient ones) and a vested interest might be a disqualification.

The second question here concerns individual autonomy. Am I suggesting that we should hand over our right to make some moral decisions for ourselves to an expert, or expert committee? The short answer is 'yes', but this must immediately be qualified. Firstly, it is only some moral questions which admit of an expert answer. Secondly, we are in a sense familiar with expertise in courts of law. Judges are trained to or are experienced in sifting through complexities, have a measure of detachment from their immediate feelings, and are able to see the wider implications for the public interest of decisions one way or the other. What I am suggesting is something similar for morality in a technical sphere. There is a continuum involved from a quasi-legal expert committee such as the BMA Ethics Committee – which from time to time issues booklets expressing the expert view of the committee on a matter such as the withholding or withdrawing of treatment at the end of life – to an individual doctor who explains a proposed treatment option, perhaps recommends one, but must obtain the consent of the patient. This kind of moral expertise was perhaps not needed in the time of Adam Smith – although even he recognises it in the sphere of 'natural jurisprudence' – but it is necessary to guide us through the moral complexities of the modern age.

Is Casuistry (as Natural Jurisprudence) a Branch of Moral Philosophy?

Finally, I raise the question of whether casuistry, granted that it is possible and can be desirable, is a branch of moral philosophy. This question must be raised because we began by looking at the different ways in which philosophy has been related

24 Reid, T., *Essays on the Active Powers* (1788), Lehrer, K. (ed), Indianapolis, Bobbs-Merrill, 1975, Essay V, Chap. 7.

to practice. If casuistry is a helpful approach to moral practice is it a branch of philosophy? A fortiori, are the many subsets of casuistry, such as medical ethics, branches of moral philosophy?

There is no one answer to this question because fashions change as to what is, or is not, a legitimate philosophical activity. There is however, one objection to the view that casuistry is a legitimate branch of moral philosophy. The objection is that the judgments of casuistry are directed at reaching decisions in particular cases, whereas moral philosophy is concerned with types of cases. Smith certainly held that moral philosophy was concerned with types of case, for it belonged to what he called 'didactic discourse'.[25] Didactic discourse was concerned with putting 'the arguments on both sides of the question in their true light, giving each its proper degree of influence, and has it in view to persuade no further than the arguments themselves appear convincing'.[26] This type of discourse is contrasted on the one hand with rhetoric, which attempts to persuade, and on the other hand, with 'narrative discourse' (such as historical discourse) which is concerned with particular events or actions. Philosophy, like the sciences, is a form of didactic discourse and is directed at types of event or action. 'In every case, therefore, Species or Universals, and not Individuals, are the objects of Philosophy'.[27] If we assume this view of philosophy, then it will follow that if casuistry is directed at reaching decisions in particular cases it cannot be a branch of moral philosophy.

Smith's argument here is rather like Aristotle's, when he says that his Ethics is not philosophy. Aristotle has two points: that philosophy is concerned with knowing, whereas ethics is concerned with doing; and that the objects of philosophy are universals of various sorts, whereas, the objects of ethics are individual actions. But even if we allow this assumed view of philosophy, it might still be the case that those trained in philosophy have something to contribute to the solution of practical problems, via the methods of casuistry or natural jurisprudence.

Conclusion

What, then, can an ethicist contribute to medicine? What methods are appropriate in dealing with ethical questions in medicine? Firstly, ethics can place concepts of medical discourse under a philosophical microscope. For example, a favourite term of medical discourse is 'quality of life'. What in a medical context does this mean? Is it used consistently? Does it make mathematical sense to have quality of life scales?

Secondly, moral philosophy can offer logical cartography. For example, a central term of medical discourse is 'evidence'. But how does the type of evidence preferred

25 Campbell, T.D., *Adam Smith's Science of Morals*, London, Allen and Unwin, 1971, Chap. 1.

26 Smith, A., *Lectures on Rhetoric and Belles Lettres*, Oxford, Clarendon Press, 1976, I, 149.

27 Smith, A., *Essays on Philosophical Subjects*, Oxford, Clarendon Press, 1976, p. 119.

foundation of modern medical practice as a global institution, with no serious challengers to its knowledge and expertise in health care.

The success of Hippocratic ideals in medicine today, however, is problematic. Although professional communication and collegiality are the guardians of medicine's evidence base and collective conscience, modern medical practice is part of a highly complex multi-professional enterprise, regulated by the state and resourced by it or other bodies such as insurance, pharmaceutical and publishing companies. The core activity of physicians still takes place in the individual doctor-patient relationship; and because each patient is different, evidence-based medicine does not remove the need either for clinical judgment or for care-motivated communication and treatment. But judgment by definition is fallible, and so inevitably are doctors, today as in the past. The problem today however, is that just because medicine has achieved so much, much more is expected, and fallibility is less well tolerated by society.

In these circumstances, moreover, modern medicine has often been tempted to over-feed unrealistic expectations. Medical scientists in pursuit of research funding have not always done all that they might to moderate media predictions of what they can deliver 'in five or ten years'. It is not impossible, of course, that stem cell therapy, for example, may eventually revolutionise medical practice, ushering in a whole new era in which failing or faulty organs and systems are repaired or regenerated by artificial means of imitating nature, and consigning the Hippocratic triad of poisoning, cutting and burning to the dustbin of medical history. But even if these broad sunlit uplands are at last achieved, and the morbidity of future generations is compressed to the limit, it is inconceivable that illness and disease, accident and trauma, sickness and suffering, will ever be abolished from a world that remains recognisably human, or that in such a human world physicians will cease to be fallible.

One practice of the Hippocratic physicians, which seems reprehensible to the modern mind, may be relevant to this, however. This was their refusal to continue treating a patient they judged to be incurable. The task of medicine, the author of *The Art* wrote, 'is to do away with the sufferings of the sick, to lessen the violence of their diseases, and to refuse to treat those who are overmastered by their diseases, realizing that in such cases medicine is powerless'.[7] The Hippocratic physicians' reasons for refusing were partly to protect patients from further interventions that might do more harm than good, and partly to protect the reputation of their rational art from accusations that it did not work; and this realism, it needs to be remembered, was what first set medicine on the road to scientific progress.

Physicians today, of course, particularly specialists in palliative medicine, rightly reject the old idea that 'nothing more can be done' for a patient with a terminal prognosis. But sometimes, as Auden reminded us, a doctor 'with a twinkle in his eye/ Will tell me that I have to die'.[8] Whether that is appropriate in the case of individual patients, of course, depends on when, where, how and to whom it is said; and the

7 Hippocrates, *The Art* III, in Jones, W.H.S. (trs), *Hippocrates,* Vol II. London, Loeb/ Heinemann, 1923, p. 269.

8 Auden, W.H., *Collected Shorter Poems 1927–1957*, London, Faber & Faber, 1966, p. 269.

cultural context also is ethically relevant. But in the case not of individuals but of society, a no less realistic message about the human limitations as well as the possibilities of medicine may need to be heard. It is still necessary to distinguish medicine from magic, and to appreciate that scientific uncertainty and human fallibility are an inevitable and indispensable aspect of medical advance. Unless or until that message is accepted by public opinion, the success of Hippocratic ideals in medicine will remain problematic.

Democratic Ideals in Society

Public opinion is the other side of the long view. The problematic success of democratic ideals in society also can be traced back to the age of Hippocrates, when religious and philosophical thinkers across the world – Confucius, Buddha, the Hebrew Prophets and Socrates – were all raising radical new questions about what it means to be an individual, and how individuals should live together in society. But again, it was not until around the seventeenth and eighteenth centuries that ideas of human rights and of society as a collaboration of free and equal individuals began to take hold and be worked through, eventually in the emancipation of slaves, votes for women and many other aspects of modern political constitutions. Across the world, of course, the realisation of democratic ideals is still patchy, and the forms it has taken in the West can no longer be seen as models for what it means to be modern elsewhere. But insofar as democratic ideals have been successful, in the West and elsewhere, they are an implicit presupposition of many contemporary public debates about medical ethics.

But this too is a *problematic* success. There are two sides to popular democratic ideals today. On the one hand, the autonomy of the individual should be respected. On the other, decisions should be reached by the general will of society expressed through due political and legal processes. But these two sides can come into conflict. A decision reached by the general will may make it difficult or impossible to respect the autonomy of the individual. For example: a patient with a rare degenerative condition asks for a treatment which will prolong and improve the quality of his life. But because the treatment is very expensive, and the needs of other patients also must be met, the health authority refuses to provide it, and the patient cannot afford to purchase it.

Such conflicts are compounded by the fact that modern democratic society is pluralist. On many ethical issues there may be no general will, but only a cacophony of conflicting voices. In a modern democratic society, the absence of a general will or commonly held coherent system of values creates enormous difficulties for government and the courts when they are called upon to legislate or interpret the law on such contentious issues. Once again therefore, public and philosophical debate about such ethical issues may seem simply to be a way of delaying difficult decisions.

What the long view adds to this, perhaps, is why these decisions are so difficult. What the long view – of the problematic success of Hippocratic ideals in medicine developed countries' populations age and the capacity for technological extension of lives become a serious drain on budgets.

Another aspect of the information age is a capacity on the part of investigative and monitoring agencies to assemble information about the patterns of health service provision by individual practitioners, comparing them against the mean and inquiring as to the reasons for departures from the statistically normal.[9] In the 1990s concerns commenced in a number of countries to form the basis for both criminal prosecutions and regulatory hearings in relation to over-servicing, inappropriate prescribing and self-prescribing.

Two consequences flow from the phenomena accompanying the health information age. The first is a preparedness, on the part of a percentage of patients, to lodge complaints with regulatory bodies and even to initiate civil litigation when they do not receive the information to which they consider they were entitled before submitting to a particular form of treatment. The second is an inclination on the part of organs of government, such as those administering public health programmes, to monitor practitioners' prescription patterns, especially in relation to narcotics and benzodiazepines, to oversee the potential for excessive service provision and to initiate investigations into practitioners' conduct.

Public Health Perspectives

An emerging perspective on the accountability of health professionals views adverse outcomes and iatrogenic harm as a public health risk. It attempts to document the incidence and nature of the expression of grievances as a means of identifying poor service provision and thereby to protect the public from the phenomenon of poorly performing and dangerous practitioners. Such an approach analyses patterns in the notification of complaints and classifies in a quasi-epidemiological way those factors which place members of the community at risk and which are over-represented amongst practitioners who are the subject of complaints, proven and not proven.

Thus, complaints are viewed as an opportunity to isolate patterns of practitioner behaviour[10] and characteristics which may be amenable to remediation or change; therefore complaints are seen as a form of health information that creates means of improving the quality of health service provision.

---

9 See Bell, R., 'Protecting Medicare Services: Trials of a Peer Review Scheme', (2005) 13 *Journal of Law and Medicine*, 29-105.

10 See e.g. Wilson, B., 'Health Disputes: A Window of Opportunity to Improve Health Services', in Freckelton, I. and Petersen, K. (ed), *Controversies in Health Law*, Sydney, Federation Press, 1999; Paterson, R., 'Complaints and Quality: Handle with Care!', (2004) *New Zealand Medical Journal*: http://www.nzma.org.nz/journal/117-1198/970/.

Emerging Phenomena in Regulation

Self-regulation and Peer Review

The dominant reference point for regulation of professionals has traditionally been peer review – the notion that those best able to evaluate professional conduct are colleagues of the practitioner.[11] It has been thought that peers are well-positioned to gauge the propriety of conduct because of themselves being in a comparable or the same area of practice and thus able to assess whether a professional has fallen below what is to be expected of a practitioner of good repute and competency. In addition, peers should be prepared to make adverse findings so as to demarcate between ethical and unethical conduct and thereby to be seen to be ready to police high standards of behaviour within their profession – by so doing they are upholding the integrity and standing of their profession.

However, experience with the 'club culture' identified by Professor Ian Kennedy in his inquiry into allegations by the anaesthetist Steven Bolsin in relation to paediatric cardiac deaths at the Royal Bristol Infirmary[12] has highlighted the potential for cultural resistance within traditional health care professions to modern notions of transparency and accountability. A similar phenomenon has been described in relation to the 'unfortunate experiment' of cervical cancer treatment at the National Women's Hospital in New Zealand[13] and the Canberra Hospital Neurosurgical Ward in Australia.[14]

Critics[15] have argued that a 'brotherhood ethic' has also led to a propensity on the part of peer review bodies to be unduly tolerant of unprofessional behaviour and a pattern of adopting 'tap on the shoulder' strategies for regulating unprofessional conduct rather than robust adverse findings at formal inquiries; sexual transgressions have been identified as a particular example of inappropriate leniency. It has also been asserted that the quality of decision making by peers has lacked the hallmarks which should characterise the determination of serious allegations of misconduct against members of a profession.

Further, it has been said that members of the public will not have confidence in a system which consists of complaints against health practitioners being resolved

---

11 See Daniel, A., *Medicine and the State: Professional Autonomy and Public Accountability*, Syndey, Allen & Unwin, 1990.

12 See e.g. Bristol Royal Infirmary Inquiry, 2001, available at: http://www.bristol-inquiry.org.uk accessed on 06/09/05.

13 See Cartwright, S., 'Revisiting the Cartwright Inquiry', (2002) 3(1) *New Zealand Bioethics Journal*, 3-10; Coney, S., *The Unfortunate Experiment*, Auckland, Penguin, 1988.

14 See Faunce, T., Mure, K., Cox, C. and Maher, B., 'When Silence Threatens Safety: Lessons from the First Canberra Hospital Neurosurgical Inquiry', (2005) 12 *Journal of Law and Medicine*, 112-118.

15 See e.g. Rogers, S., 'Culling Bad Apples: Blowing Whistles and the Health Practitioners Competence Assurance Act 2003 (NZ)', (2004) 12 *Journal of Law and Medicine*, 119-133; Thomas, *loc. cit*, 2004.

by persons likely to know and to have worked with the practitioners who are the subject of complaint. Some disciplinary systems have incorporated investigative, prosecutorial and arbitral functions within the same body.[16] Particular concerns have been identified in relation to such forms of peer regulation on the basis of the extent to which complainants might fear that they would not receive a full and dispassionate response to their grievances.

The international trend appears to be away from unfettered self-regulation of health practitioners. An example of this, discussed below, is the increasing role of non-practitioner members of regulatory bodies. Another is the fact that in a number of jurisdictions a statutory measure of unprofessional conduct is conduct of a lesser standard than is reasonably to be expected of a practitioner by members of the public.[17] This explicitly incorporates into the criteria for unsatisfactory professional behaviour an extra-professional measure – one that is reflective of contemporary community standards.

Lay participation on regulatory bodies is comparatively recent but is growing. Such a non-practitioner role reduces the extent to which decision making fully constitutes peer review bur it provides an external perspective which reduces the force of the criticism that regulatory bodies are 'old boys' clubs' looking after their own. In Victoria, Australia, the 11 regulatory bodies for health practitioners each have three non-practitioner participants out of between nine and 12 members. By contrast, the United Kingdom General Medical Council has 40 per cent lay membership[18] and on performance assessments of medical practitioners there must always be a non-medical participant. In Canada there is generally significant lay participation on disciplinary hearings, although lay involvement in performance assessments is not yet part of the process. The international trend is towards a greater role for non-practitioner contribution in assessment of practitioners and formal decision making; conversely there is attrition of the extent of peer review as the major paradigm.

Spreading the Ambit of Regulation

Forensic Functions Until comparatively recently work undertaken by health practitioners in a forensic capacity was largely exempt from evaluation by regulatory bodies. However, with a growing recognition that a substantial proportion of health practitioners are called upon to undertake some forensic work in the form of writing reports for courts and tribunals and occasionally giving evidence, regulatory bodies have confronted the criteria on the basis of which such work should be classified as

16 See Department of Human Services, *Review of the Regulation of Health Professions in Victoria: Options for Structural and Legislative Reform*, Melbourne, DHS, 2005, available at: http://www.dhs.vic.gov.au/pdpd/workforce/downloads/review_optionspaper_apr05.pdf

17 See e.g. *Medical Practice Act 1994* (Vic), s 3.

18 General Medical Council, 2005, *Developing Medical Regulation: A Vision for the Future*, available at: http://www.gmc-uk.org/call_for_ideas/developing_medical_regulation_200504.pdf, accessed on 07/09/05.

unprofessional and the consequences that should attach to such a designation. Three cases are particularly illustrative of the emerging approach.

In *Mustac v. Medical Board of Western Australia*,[19] the Western Australian Court of Appeal rejected an appeal by a psychiatrist against the decision of the Western Australian Medical Board to suspend his registration for six months for having engaged in improper conduct in a professional respect by reason of his methodology in writing two forensic reports. Dr Mustac was found by the Board to have applied a psychometric test, the Test of Memory Malingering ('the TOMM') impermissibly to questions of overall veracity in circumstances where it was not designed for that purpose. Largely on the basis of the results from the psychometric test, he was found to have concluded illegitimately that two patients whom he had assessed for workers' compensation purposes had exhibited an intention to deceive him.

The Court of Appeal accepted, on the basis of the manual for the TOMM, that the test itself only permitted a conclusion to be drawn that a subject is making a false or exaggerated claim of a memory deficit. It concluded that Dr Mustac's views about his subjects' false or exaggerated claims had not been open to him and that his conclusions about intentionality and motivation were illegitimate and unprofessional. Ultimately, it upheld the decision of the Board, holding that as the behaviour of the psychiatrist fell well short of indicating that his conduct was in accordance with a body of respectable of minority opinion, the suspension of the practitioner was justified.

In *Re Paterson*[20] the Professional Conduct Committee of the General Medical Council was called upon to evaluate the professional conduct of an expert medical witness in respect of two aspects of his conduct. The first related to a forensic report that he wrote and evidence that he gave before the Family Division of the High Court of Justice. Amongst other things, Dr Paterson was commissioned to give evidence as an expert on behalf of parents who were accused of causing non-accidental injury to their children. He submitted a report which expressed the view that more likely than not the fractures sustained by a child, X, were caused by bone disease, probably temporary brittle bone disease ('TBBD') which he described as a 'self-limiting osteogenesis imperfecta with spontaneous improvement, and with numerous fractures confined to the first year of life'.

The Professional Conduct Committee found that it is a practitioner's responsibility to ensure that any expert report they write is properly researched. The practitioner must also disclose and explain any departures from his or her published research. While it is permissible to modify a published view 'this must be made explicit in any report and any modifications must be fully explained and justified in language that is clear, comprehensive and non-ambiguous to the reader'. It concluded that Dr Paterson did not do this.

---

19 [2004] WASCA 156.

20 Professional Conduct Committee decision: available at: http://www.gmc-uk.org/probdocs/decisions/pcc/2004/PATERSON_20040304.htm.

The Committee acknowledged Dr Paterson's right to 'believe in TBBD and to share opinions with other physicians, conduct research and write papers in medical literature and to act as an expert witness'. It accepted that he did so sincerely but emphasised that providing expert evidence in courts 'carries a heavy responsibility': 'The Courts must be able to rely on the evidence of expert witnesses, evidence that must be properly researched, balanced and not misleading'. It emphasised that 'a profession's most valuable asset is its collective reputation and the confidence it inspires in members of the public'. Influenced by Dr Paterson's failure to accept that he had engaged in misconduct or to show willingness to change his ways, it concluded that 'it would be impossible to formulate appropriate and practical conditions' that would adequately protect the public. Because of what it termed Dr Paterson's 'persistent lack of insight' into the seriousness of his actions and potential consequences, in particular his failure to have regard to the guidance given to him by the judiciary and the General Medical Council, it declined 'merely' to suspend him and, instead, erased his name from the medical register.

In *Re Meadow*,[21] the United Kingdom Fitness to Practise Panel of the General Medical Council was called upon in 2005 to evaluate the professional conduct of a well known paediatrician who had written reports and give expert evidence in ways which it was alleged were misleading. The allegations arose from involvement as an expert by Professor Sir Roy Meadow in criminal proceedings against Sally Clark for the murder of her two children. Her conviction was later quashed by the Court of Appeal.[22]

The Panel found that Sir Roy had been engaged as a consultant paediatrician by the Cheshire Constabulary of Police to assist their investigation. He was ready, willing and considered himself able to give expert evidence as to child abuse and unnatural infant deaths, Sudden Infant Death Syndrome ('SIDS'), the probability of occurrence and recurrence of SIDS deaths within a family, and the statistical consideration of data on such matters. It found that he owed a duty to familiarise himself with all relevant data and published (or to be published) work, sufficient to provide competent, impartial, balanced and fair expert evidence of scientific validity:

> Insofar as you chose to use statistics to support your evidence it was your responsibility to only use them in accordance with good statistical principles and practice in relation to matters within your expertise. You owed a duty to identify relevant matters (including assumptions) on which your statistical evidence was based.

It found that he had failed in this duty and, while he should have refrained from giving expert evidence on matters beyond his competence, he had failed to do so. The Panel found that Sir Roy's evidence was misleading and erroneous, although that had not been his intention, his error lying in squaring odds of matters which

21 Fitness to Practise Panel, General Medical Council, 15 July 2005, available at: http://www.gmcpressoffice.org.uk/apps/news/latest/detail.php?key-180, accessed on 01/08/05.

22 *R v. Clark* [2003] EWCA 1020.

may have been associated and thus not amenable to the 'multiplication factor', as well as failing to have regard to dependent variables which would have substantially changed the statistics which he was citing. It found that his errors had been 'grave' and that his conduct had had serious implications and repercussions for many people, not least those working in the field of child protection. It concluded that his errors were so serious that in spite of his contributions to medicine and his international reputation it had no option but to strike his name from the medical register.

However, a new issue has arisen as a result of a decision on appeal from the Fitness to Practise Panel in Re Meadow.[23] Justice Collins has determined that the principle of witness immunity extends to disciplinary proceedings with the result that a significant level of immunity for forensic work is accorded to health practitioners – especially their oral evidence. However, the decision is controversial and under appeal.[24] To sequester forensic work from regulation would seem to be inconsistent with the general direction of regulation in the modern environment.[25] The decisions of the Western Australian Court of Appeal and of the General Medical Council provide a signal for what is likely to be the future in terms of regulation of forensic conduct – ethical and balanced practice should be the hallmark of forensic work, as well as in clinical.[26] Forensic work should be evidence-based and undertaken with meticulous care, ensuring that all relevant literature is known to the practitioner and that sound methodologies are employed. Assumptions should be articulated. Distinctions should be made between facts and opinion. Interpretation of data needs to be orthodox and in terms of literature published on the subject by the expert, unless there is good, articulated reason to the contrary. Finally, interpretation, whether statistical or otherwise, should be temperate and accurate, not exceeding the competence of the practitioner and not employing analogies which could induce prejudice or be misleading for a court or tribunal.

Personal Misconduct Uncertainty has long existed about whether and, if so to what extent, health practitioners may be found to have engaged in professional misconduct if they have committed disreputable or illegal acts in a private capacity – not directly connected with their discharge of professional duties.

In 1999 the Privy Council grappled with this vexed issue in *Roylance v. General Medical Council*[27] where it was asked to determine whether the District General

---

23 *Meadow v. General Medical Council* [2006] EWHC 146 (Admin).

24 See Freckelton, I., 'Immunity for Experts from Disciplinary Regulation' (2006) 13 *Journal of Law and Medicine*, 393-397.

25 See generally Rosen, R. and Dewar, S., *On Being a Doctor: Redefining Medical Professionalism for Better Patient Care*, King's Fund, London, 2004; Royal College of Physicians, *Doctors in Society: Medical Professionalism in a Changing World*, London, 2005, www.rcplondon.ac.uk/pubs/books/docinsoc/docinsoc.pdf (accessed on13/6/06); I. Freckelton, 'Regulation of Health Practitioners' in I. Freckelton and K. Petersen (ed), *Disputes and Dilemmas in Health Law*, Federation Press, Sydney, 2006).

26 See Freckelton, I., 'The Edges of Regulation' (2006) *Law in Context* (forthcoming).

27 [1999] UKPC 16.

Manager of the Bristol and Weston Health Authority was guilty of serious professional misconduct for having failed to take action during a time when concerns were being raised about the excessive mortality of infant patients and failing to take steps to prevent certain practitioners from undertaking cardiac operations on infants. The Privy Council held that for misconduct to be professional misconduct it must have a link with the profession of medicine but emphasised that certain behaviour may constitute professional misconduct even though it does not occur within the actual course of the carrying on of the person's professional practice, such as the abuse of a patient's confidence or the making of some dishonest private financial gain.[28] In addition, it held that:

> serious professional misconduct may arise where the conduct is quite removed from the practice of medicine, but is of a sufficiently immoral or outrageous or disgraceful character … One particular concern in such cases of moral turpitude is that the public reputation of the profession may suffer and public confidence in it may be prejudiced.[29]

It upheld the erasure of the District General Manager from the medical register.

The *Roylance* decision constitutes an important assertion of the jurisdiction of regulatory bodies over practitioners in circumstances separate and distinct from their clinical interface with patients. The decision reaffirms that the interests of the professions in terms of their standing and their reputation and of members of the public extend beyond the direct work undertaken by health practitioners.

Complementary Medicine The fact that such a considerable percentage of health service provision comes via practitioners of alternative or complementary medicine has brought with it the call for greater regulation of therapeutic products,[30] healthcare practices which are otherwise dependent upon the bringing of civil actions by aggrieved patients or the exclusion from professional associations of poorly performing practitioners.[31] An added fillip to extended regulatory arrangements has been the recognition that a percentage of complementary practitioners do not function as complementary practitioners – rather, they function separately and apart from orthodox medicine and do not cross-refer patients and may not be adequately aware of the potentiating or toxic effects of combined doses of complementary and orthodox medications.[32] This has been of particular concern in the context of treatments for cancer and other diseases which are potentially curable by orthodox medicine.

---

28 *Ibid.*, at 41.

29 *Ibid.*, at 42.

30 See Ellena, K.R., 'The Uncritical Enthusiasts Versus the Uninformed Sceptics: Regulation of Complementary and Alternative Medicines', (2005) 13 *Journal of Law and Medicine*, 105-124.

31 Bensoussan, A. and Myers, S.P., *Towards a Safer Choice: The Practice of Traditional Chinese Medicine in Australia*, MacArthur, University of Western Sydney, 1996.

32 See e.g. *Shakoor v. Situ* [2000] 4 All ER 181.

In Victoria a bold step was taken in relation to traditional Chinese medicine and is mooted in relation to naturopathy. The Chinese Medicine Registration Act 2000 (Vic) provided that the practice of Chinese medicine, defined to include any form of acupuncture or treatment with or dispensing of Chinese herbs, is illegal save by persons duly registered by the Chinese Medicine Registration Board. This led to complex grandfathering decisions in relation to long-time practitioners with qualifications not from Australian tertiary courses, but has provided a fillip for Chinese medicine to function in a more evidence-based way and as a genuine complement to orthodox western medicine. It has also encouraged practitioners of Chinese medicine to become better schooled in the effects and characteristics of orthodox pharmacotherapy as well as Chinese herbs, which also can have lethal toxicities.

It is likely that the recognition of the potentially dangerous nature of a number of the complementary therapies will lead to registration processes by formal bodies, rather than simply professional associations – principally as a mechanism for removing practitioners with inadequate qualifications and skill levels and also as a means of inducing practitioners to function in a complementary rather than competitive capacity. It is a further example of the broadening ambit of health practitioner regulation.

The Changing Legal Environment

Significant changes can be identified in the forms of disposition meted out to health practitioners found to have engaged in significantly unprofessional conduct since the 1980s. Most prominent amongst the changes have been the sanctions imposed for sexual misconduct, for conflict of interest and for lack of probity. This has been matched by a concomitant shift in decision makers' language – both at first instance before bodies such as the General Medical Council and Medical Practitioners Boards.

The significant change in approach by appellate courts and disciplinary tribunals has been characterised by an overt acknowledgment of the disempowerment generally present in the relationship between a patient and a healthcare practitioner; an imbalance prone to exploitation if the practitioner does not act ethically.[33] Robust critiques of abuse of power and predatory behaviour by health professionals published in professional literature[34] appear to have played a role in shifting the

33 See e.g. Freckelton, I., 'The Sexually Exploitative Doctor', (1994) 1 *Journal of Law and Medicine*, 203-204; *Re A Medical Practitioner* [1993] 2 Qd R 154 at 162.

34 See Walton, M., 'Sex and the Practitioner: The Predator', (2002) 34 *Australian Journal of Forensic Sciences*, 7-15; Gartrell, N.K *et al.*, 'Physician-Patient Sexual Contact: Prevalence and Problems', (1992) 157(2) *Western Journal of Medicine*, 139-143; Gutheil, T.G. and Gabbard, G.O., 'The Concept of Boundaries in Clinical Practice: Theoretical and Risk-Management Dimensions', (1993) 150 *American Journal of Psychiatry*, 188-196; Lucire, Y., 'Sex and the Practitioner: The Victim', (2002) 34 *Australian Journal of Forensic Science*, 17-

views of regulatory bodies. This has resulted in a pattern of firmer first instance decision making by regulatory bodies and tribunals in relation to crossing of sexual boundaries, especially by psychiatrists and psychologists. Latterly the tendency has been for these decisions to have been upheld by the appellate courts.

Thus, in *Council for the Regulation of Health Care Professionals v. General Medical Council*, Leveson J observed that formal guidance adopted by the GMC:

> identifies sexual misconduct and dishonesty, with specific reference to falsification of a curriculum vitae, as two of the most serious types of misconduct which may require erasure. It also provides that the public interest includes not only the specific risk to individual patients from doctors' misconduct, but also the maintenance of public confidence in the profession. In this regard, it is important that women are not deterred from seeking medical assistance because of a lack of confidence in doctors arising out of sexual misconduct.[35]

The Privy Council too in *Dare v. General Medical Council,* in the context of a relationship between a psychiatrist and his (medically qualified) patient observed that:

> Patients in therapy are extremely vulnerable regardless of their professional standing. Having initiated a relationship with a patient who was "functioning as a child" the appellant failed to stop the behaviour he displayed over a period of time. As a psychiatrist he should have known how to manage Miss A's feelings of transference without taking advantage of her in a dependent state. He should have sought advice, we have no doubt that he should have referred Miss A to another doctor at a time when he had insight into the way that the professional relationship was diminishing and his sexual feelings towards his patient were on the increase. Thus his judgment was seriously at fault in not recognising the danger signs. Their Lordships have no doubt that behaviour such as this seriously undermines the trust the public place in the profession and in particular in psychiatrists practising psycho-analysis and psycho-therapy. In their Lordships' view, the Committee having heard all the evidence were entitled to conclude that they regarded the appellant's behaviour as 'abhorrent', 'appalling ... a disgraceful abuse of the trust'.[36]

The issue of the incompatibility of dishonesty and ongoing registration of a healthcare practitioner has come before the health regulatory tribunals and the courts on a number of occasions. In the important decision of *Patel v. General Medical Council*,[37] a doctor appealed from a decision by the Professional Conduct Committee of the General Medical Council in the United Kingdom – ultimately to the Privy Council – against a decision that his name be erased from the practising register for various acts of dishonesty. The Council held that '[f]or all professional

---

24; Searight, H.R. and Campbell, D.C., 'Physician-patient Sexual Contact: Ethical and legal Issues and Clinical Guidelines', (1993) 36 *Journal of Family Practice*, 647-653.

35 [2004] EWHC 944 (Admin) at [46].

36 [2002] UKPC 54 at p.17.

37 [2003] UKPC 16.

persons including doctors a finding of dishonesty lies at the top end in the spectrum of gravity of misconduct'.[38]

What can be discerned is a readier response by first instance regulators to pronounce decisively that a variety of forms of conduct on the part of health professionals constitute behaviour that is *prima facie* incompatible with registered status. This compares with the more 'understanding' response of earlier generations of regulators.

Matters involving serious allegations against health practitioners have the potential to result in deregistration, suspension or the imposition of conditions upon registration. It goes without saying that such sanctions can be personally and professionally devastating for practitioners. It is apparent from the volume of appellate litigation in relation to health practitioners against whom adverse findings are made at first instance in the United Kingdom, Australia and Canada that the area of 'disciplinary law' is expanding for the legal profession. There is a tendency for more technical points to be argued on behalf of practitioners, for legal principles to be explored and challenged and for decisions adverse to practitioners to be appealed. In Australia there is no doubt that first instance hearings are becoming longer and more complex. The decisions of the Professional Conduct Committees of the General Medical Council in the United Kingdom and of the Victorian Medical Practitioners Board, the Psychologists Registration Board, the Dental Practice Board, the Chinese Medicine Registration Board and the Civil and Administrative Tribunal on *de novo* review are posted on the internet, enabling transparency of reasoning with the result that the shaming and the improprieties of practitioners are highly visible for their colleagues and even for current and potential patients.

This combination of factors has resulted in something of an impetus in the direction of adversarialism for matters that reach formal decision-making phase in Australia, New Zealand, the United Kingdom and Canada. In practice this has meant longer and more expensive hearings, the involvement of more senior lawyers, taking of more technical points,[39] lengthier and more complex reasons for decision, a proliferation of appellate judgments and escalating levels of attention from the media for decisions in relation to health practitioners, especially doctors.

In turn this has provided an incentive for regulatory authorities to reconfigure allegations of impropriety into matters of health, performance and competence in need of investigation, rather than conduct inquiries which are likely to lead to heavily contested and stigmatising hearings.

Awareness of Broader Causes for Adverse Outcomes

There is a growing recognition that there can be multiple causes for individual instances of unsatisfactory practitioner conduct. These include systems factors, health problems experienced by practitioners and deficiencies in skills and competence.

---

38 *Ibid*., at p.10.

39 See Searles, D., 'Professional Misconduct – Unprofessional Conduct. Is there a Difference?', (1992) *Queensland Law Society Journal*, 239-244.

Systemic Issues

Irvine has argued that:

> We got professional regulation the wrong way round. The emphasis was on reacting to serious events through central mechanisms, such as the GMC. Prevention, and the early recognition, diagnosis and action on problems, were not priorities. Hence, the *ad hoc* nature of the arrangements for supervising the quality of medical practice at the point of service delivery, and the highly variable informal systems to deal with problem doctors.[40]

Quite regularly errors and unsatisfactory outcomes for which particular practitioners are responsible can be the product of complex institutional and systems factors. Many examples can be advanced. For instance, diminished concentration on the part of a junior medical officer can be caused by his or her having worked a series of long shifts at the direction of hospital management. It accomplishes little to discipline the practitioner for an error brought about by exhaustion for which the practitioner bears little responsibility.

Likewise, hospital policy may require the discharge of certain categories of patients at an arbitrary time subsequent to surgery. The fact that a patient in the care of a surgeon or physician suffers complications which could have been identified and addressed had the patient continued to be an inpatient is technically the responsibility of the practitioner. However, resources issues which resulted in administrative decisions which in turn generated premature practitioner discharges constitute the background within which a clinical error in judgment may be identified.

Such matters are ill-addressed by disciplinary hearings and significant consequences for individual practitioners, much as such results may be palatable for adversely affected patients or patients' families.

Health Impairment

Another aetiology of unsafe practice by health practitioners can be their own state of health, ranging from cognitive impairment arising from age-related deterioration, brain injury or psychiatric illness to physical ailments, such as chronic pain or heart or other conditions to substance dependencies. A number of medical regulators in Australia, Canada and the United Kingdom have set up or facilitated health programmes for doctors so as to maximise the prospects of practitioners receiving the assistance they need to address their health problems and thereby render them fit once more for practice.

---

40 See Cruess, R.L., Cruess, S.L. and Johnston, S.E., 'Professionalism: an Ideal to Be Sustained', (2000) 356 *Lancet*, 156-159; Irvine, D., 'Time for Hard Decisions on Patient-centred Professionalism', (2004) 181 *Australian Medical Journal*, 271-274; Irvine, D.H., 'The Performance of Doctors I: Professionalism and Regulation in a changing world', (1997) 315 *British Medical Journal*, 1540-1542; Irvine, D.H., 'The Performance of Doctors II: Maintaining Good Practice, Protecting Patients from Poor Performance', (1997) 314 *British Medical Journal*, 314: 1613-1615.

Australian regulatory bodies tend to take a low key approach with health issues, eschewing formal hearings as often as possible, and encouraging practitioners to have breaks from work to address their health concerns and to return to practice subject to mutually agreed restrictions on practice for a period of time until medical reports suggest that the practitioner's condition has been adequately addressed. Thus, the approach is one of working with the practitioner in order to facilitate rehabilitation and provision of education to practitioners about the risks of not having a family doctor, working too hard, becoming too stressed and yielding to substance dependence.

Performance Deficits

One of the notable features of regulation of health professionals is that cross-pollination amongst international bodies and legislatures is resulting in a reduction in the disciplinary orientation of regulation. Part of what is taking place is a redefinition of the culture of professionalism. For instance, Donald Irvine, President of the General Medical Council, argued in 1997 that such a culture should be inclusive, involving all doctors and embracing continuing medical education, personal professional development, clinical audit and quality improvement methods. He contended that it would have six core components:

- A clear ethical framework and, where possible, the use of explicit professional and clinical standards;
- Effective local professional regulation for maintaining good practice;
- Regular publication by the royal colleges and others of data showing doctors' involvement in continuing medical education, audit, and other performance related activities;
- Sound local arrangements for recognising dysfunctional doctors early and for taking appropriate action;
- Well defined criteria and pathways for referral to the GMC when severely dysfunctional doctors cannot or should not be managed locally;
- At all stages, practical help and support so that doctors who get into difficulties can be restored to full practice wherever possible.[41]

From a generic perspective, the allegations made against health practitioners can be classified in a variety of ways, including as follows: sexual misconduct, blurring of boundaries between practitioner and client, dishonesty, breach of confidentiality, conflict of interest, unsatisfactory provision of treatment, conduct of procedures without suitable advice about options and potentially adverse consequences, and unsatisfactory communication generally. However, often particular instances of what might be classified as unprofessional conduct within these categories are indicative of deficits in skill or competence.

41 Irvine, *loc cit.*, (1997).

Starting with initiatives in Canada,[42] a new approach has been trialled in jurisdictions in North America,[43] the United Kingdom,[44] Australia[45] and New Zealand[46] whereby in appropriate cases an investigation is directed not to whether a practitioner has engaged in unprofessional conduct but into the practitioner's professional competence and skill levels. Such an assessment is generally peer dominated and conducted by reference to professional guidelines and practices – to evaluate whether the practitioner's performance is substandard by reference to accepted norms and procedures. If it is, the orientation of regulatory bodies is to address the deficits by mandated further education, counselling or supervision, or sometimes by restrictions on practice. As with the approach in relation to health-caused deficiencies of practice, the attempt is to draw upon the skills possessed by a practitioner and enhance the potential of the practitioner to practice safely and in accordance with professional standards. Where possible, this is done collaboratively by respected colleagues of the practitioner, at the aegis of the regulatory body, identifying deficits and setting out a roadmap toward remediation.

Weymouth described as the most common deficiencies identified in British Columbia insufficient medical records, lack of referral letters to consultants, inadequate sterilisation of equipment and lack of an emergency kit. He commented that '[p]hysicians with deficiencies have often developed habits characterised by inattention to details'.[47] Of the 1,434 primary or subsequent visits for performance assessment in British Columbia, 91.8 per cent of physicians were found to have no significant deficiencies in their medical practice.

The emerging focus on performance assessment and monitoring builds upon the trend toward mandatory continuing professional development ('CPD')[48] and

42 Weymouth, V., (1999) 'Office Medical Practice Peer Review: The British Columbia Experience', paper presented to the Parlons Qualité Conférence, Montréal, 17 June 1992, revised October 1999; Page, G.G. *et al.*, 'Physician-assessment and Physician-enhancement Programs in Canada', (1995) 153 *Canadian Medical Association Journal*, 1723-1728; Hall, W. *et al.*, 'Assessment of Physician Performance in Alberta', (1999) 161 *Canadian Medical Association Journal*, 52-57.

43 Norman, G.R. *et al.*, 'Competency Assessment of Primary Care Physicians as Part of a Peer Review Program', (1993) 270(9) *Journal of the American Medical Association*, 1046-1051.

44 See the work undertaken by the National Clinical Assessment Authority. However, the General Medical Council performance procedures rely upon the parameters of *Good Medical Practice*. See also McCaul, J., 'The Scottish Approach to Poorly Performing Doctors', (2002) available at: http://careerfocus.bmjjournals.com/chi/content/full/324/7334/S51?ct.

45 See e.g. Part 3, Division 3 of the Medical Practice Act 1994 (Vic); Reid, A., 'Poorly Performing Doctors', *Law in Context* (2006, forthcoming).

46 See Medical Council of New Zealand: http://www.mcnz.org.nz/Default.aspx?tabid=1084, accessed on 27/09/05.

47 Weymouth, V., 'Office Medical Practice Peer Review: The British Columbia Experience', paper presented to the Parlons Qualité Conférence, 17 June 1992, Montréal.

48 See Parboosingh, J., 'CPD and Maintenance of Certification in the Royal College of Physicians and Surgeons of Canada', (2002) 5 *The Obstetrician and Gynaecologist*, 43-49; Peck, C.M *et al.*, 'Continuing Medical Education and Continuing Professional Development:

potential re-accreditation on the basis of demonstrated ongoing competency.[49] In the United Kingdom, which leads the world in this regard, a precondition to ongoing registration is proof of participation in CPD and accreditation. This is a major shift away from the notion that mere possession of tertiary qualifications is sufficient for a lifetime licence to practise. It provides a means whereby the general community can have a measure of confidence that health practitioners are staying abreast of current developments, are not isolated from their colleagues and remain well regarded and competent from the informed perspective of their professional peers. A corollary of this approach, though, is that fewer matters are likely to be dealt with as instances of unprofessional conduct, the focus increasingly being not upon individual acts that are unsatisfactory but upon what is giving rise to substandard performance and behaviour likely to be indicative of defective skills, technique or knowledge.

However, the days are still relatively early in relation to performance-based resolution of complaints and notifications about practitioner performance. While the application of such an approach to the skills and competence of doctors and dentists is immediately plausible – at least in some areas of practice, such as anaesthesia and endodontics – the application is less clear in relation to general practice and psychiatry and a number of other areas of practice by other health professions, such as psychology and nursing. The boundary lines between conduct and performance also have to be worked through, so that it is clear whether a conduct or performance investigation will be triggered in given circumstances. In addition, the expense and delay ramifications of performance-based investigation have to be resolved as peer assessment tends to be time consuming and costly – who is to pay for such investigations? There is also the question of how acceptable such an approach is to aggrieved patients who may have suffered adverse consequences to what they perceive as practitioner misconduct. While many complainants cite as their reason for lodging complaints their hope that the practitioner will be prevented from behaving towards others as they have towards them, the behind-the-scenes mentoring and guidance directed toward returning the practitioner to practice may not provide a high level of satisfaction to complainants.

Moves Toward Revalidation

A significant development, likely little by little to be implemented internationally in varying forms[50] is that it is proposed that doctors in the United Kingdom will

International Comparisons', (2000) 320 *British Medical Journal*, 432-435; World Federation for Medical Education, 2003, *Continuing Professional Development of Medical Doctors WFME Global Standards for Quality Improvement: Result from Task Force Seminar, 25-27 October 2002*, WFME, 2003.

49 See Trunkey, D.D.T. and Botney, R., 'Assessing Competency: A Tale of Two Professions', (2001) 192 *Journal of the American College of Surgeons*, 385-395.

50 See Dauphinee, W.D., 'Validation of Doctors in Canada', (1999) 319 *British Medical Journal*, 1188-1190; Rogers, S., 'Culling Bad Apples: Blowing Whistles and the Health Practitioners Competence Assurance Act 2003 (NZ)', (2004) 12 *Journal of Law and Medicine*, 119-133; Newble, D., Paget, N. and McLaren, B., 'Revalidation in Australia and

need a licence to practise.[51] To retain their licence, doctors will have to 'revalidate', by demonstrating at regular intervals to the General Medical Council (GMC), that they remain up to date and fit to practice. Henceforth revalidation and licensing will constitute the cornerstone of medical practitioners' accountability to United Kingdom patients and the wider public. This is not a wholly new phenomenon; clinical governance previously was regarded as being based on principles of local oversight and accountability. Formal procedures were introduced into the National Health System from April 1999 which included annual appraisal for doctors, based on the guidance given by the GMC's *Good Medical Practice.*[52]

Historically, doctors were admitted to the register on qualification (or on assessment, if they qualified outside the United Kingdom). No further checks were done unless the doctor's performance gave rise to concerns that led to a referral to the fitness to practise procedures.[53] The change is that revalidation will shift the emphasis of regulation away from qualifications alone towards a regular assessment of whether the doctor remains up to date and fit to practise.[54] It will require all doctors to establish that they reflect meaningfully on their practice, using information gathered through audit and in other ways, and to seek the views of others on their performance, throughout their medical careers.

The GMC's draft guidance for doctors, current in September 2005, sets out a number of core requirements for revalidation, including:

- a description of the doctor's practice;
- evidence of participation in appraisal and completion of an agreed 'Personal Development Plan';
- a statement declaring eligibility for local certification;
- declarations relating to health and probity.[55]

New Zealand: Approach of Royal Australasian College of Physicians', (1999) 319 *British Medical Journal*, 1185-1188; Norcini, J.J., 'Recertification in the United States', (1999) 319 *British Medical Journal*, 1183-1185; Southgate, L. and Dauphinee, D., 'Maintaining Standards in British and Canadian Medicine: The Developing Role of the Regulatory Body', (1998) 316 *British Medical Journal*, 697-700; Southgate, L. *et al.*, 'The Assessment of Poorly Performing Doctors: the Development of the Assessment Programmes for the General Medical Council's Performance Procedures', (2001) 35 (Suppl 1) *Medical Education*, 2-8.

51 See Cunningham, J.P.W. *et al.*, 'Defensible Assessment of the Competency of the Practicing Physician', (1997) 72(1) *Academic Medicine*, 617- 9; McKinley, R., Fraser, R.C. and Baker, R., 'Model for Directly Assessing and Improving Clinical Competence and Performance in Revalidation of Clinicians', (2001) 322 *British Medical Journal*, 712-715.

52 General Medical Council, *Good Medical Practice*, available at: http://www.gmc_uk.org/med_ed/default.htm, accessed 07/09/05.

53 See Cunningham *loc cit.*

54 See McKinley *et al.*, *loc cit.*

55 See General Medical Council, 'Licencing and Revalidation', http://www.gmc-uk.org/revalidation/index.htm, visited 29 September 2005; see also General Medical Council, *Developing Medical Regulation: A Vision for the Future*, 2005, at para 130: http://www.gmc-uk.org/call_for_ideas/developing_medical_regulation_200504.pdf, visited 29 September 2005.

- In addition, doctors are required to submit for greater scrutiny their compliance with various topics outlined in the Guide to Medical Practice.

The revalidation process is intended also to ensure that doctors regularly reflect on their practice. For most doctors, the vehicle for delivering that regular reflection will be an annual appraisal but if a practitioner cannot participate in such an appraisal scheme, the GMC will call for the doctor's folder. The GMC will also require verifiable evidence that there are no significant local concerns about a doctor's practice. Suitable evidence, for a doctor who works in a managed environment, will be confirmation by a person with formal clinical governance responsibilities that there are no unresolved concerns about the doctor's practice. In the absence of this, the results of validated questionnaires, completed by professional colleagues and, where appropriate, patients also, may provide acceptable evidence.

If a doctor cannot produce an appropriate clinical governance certificate or results from validated questionnaires, the GMC will call for the doctor's folder. Finally, doctors will be required to provide evidence as to their good health and probity. All practitioners will be required to provide a personal declaration, certified by another doctor who is registered with the GMC.

Dame Janet Smith has argued that within the revalidation folder, there should be information for assessment by the GMC about:

- prescribing data and records of complaints or concerns;
- a record of continuing professional development activity;
- a patient satisfaction questionnaire;
- the results of a clinical audit and some significant audit events;
- a copy of an appraisal form; and
- a certificate to show the successful completion of a knowledge test.[56]

The GMC has commented that, for most medical practitioners in clinical settings working in GMC-approved environments, it expects that most of Dame Janet's suggestions will be met within the doctor's appraisal and/or clinical governance systems.[57]

What is being attempted in the United Kingdom is an extensive, monitored, mandated regime for ensuring medical practitioners' fitness to practise. It is open to criticism for its bureaucratisation, its dependence upon what are likely to be pro forma processes and the burden that it will impose upon practitioners to compile relevant documentation – more time on paperwork and less on practice. However, its aim to weed out practitioners who are lacking in core competencies, who are out of date, who are ill thought of by peers or whose health is declining will be politically attractive well beyond the United Kingdom.

---

56 General Medical Council, 2005, at para 131.

57 See General Medical Council, *Good Medical Practice*, available at: http://www.gmc-uk.org/med_ed/default.htm, accessed 07/09/05.

The Future

What can be discerned in terms of the past one and a half decades of evolution and even transformation of regulation of the healthcare professions is a substantial increase in its extent and sophistication. Practitioners' conduct is now subject to assessment in their personal and professional lives where it has the potential to impact upon community confidence in the standing and quality of health service delivery.

In addition, the culture of regulation has become more stringent in relation to a variety of key aspects of professional misfeasance – most particularly, transgression of permitted boundaries, exploitation of patients and dishonesty. Community wishes for patients to participate more effectively in decision making about their own health have also been reflected in regulatory enforcement of the need for practitioners to communicate effectively about treatment options and side effects.

Regulation is extending too into aspects of practice, such as management[58] and forensic work.[59] This is reflective of an awareness that health practitioners utilise their professional skills in areas outside the direct clinical interface and should be accountable broadly to those potentially adversely affected by the quality of their decision making and exercise of judgment.

Another impetus is toward more widescale regulatory regimes incorporating health practitioners who have previously functioned outside of the establishment. The reality is that those therapeutically utilising toxic substances and intrusive procedures have the potential to do serious harm if they intersect poorly with the orthodox practice of health care, if they are inadequately trained or knowledgeable, or if their levels of performance slip below that which the public and peers would reasonably expect. This recognition is likely to lead to the broadening of the regulatory net into a number of the 'alternative therapies' and to pressures for them to be regarded, at least for regulatory reasons, as complementary to traditional medicine. In turn, this will require greater levels of knowledge by orthodox and complementary practitioners about other modalities of health practice and preparedness to work co-operatively in patients' best interests.

Finally, it is apparent that a variety of new regulatory approaches will become the dominant paradigm. These will reduce the focus upon individual instances of misconduct and will construct mechanisms for measuring ongoing competence and skill levels. When specific notifications and complaints are made, the trend will be toward evaluation of the multifactorial causes of adverse outcomes. To the extent that they are identified as performance or skill-related, intervention (where possible, by agreement) will seek to remedy deficits. To the extent that they are systemic issues, there is likely to be more preparedness by regulators, armed with additional powers, to probe indirect causes of unsatisfactory outcomes and address them with less of a punitive focus upon individuals and more of an attempt to grapple with underlying issues which give rise to suboptimal practices and thereby risks to health and safety.

---

58 See *Roylance v. GMC* [1999] UKPC 16.

59 See e.g. *Mustac v. Medical Practitioners Board* [2004] WASCA 156.

Chapter 5

The International Health Regulations: A New Paradigm for Global Health Governance?

Lawrence O. Gostin

The international community joined together during the late twentieth century to form a world trade system. Although imperfect, the world trade system contains adjudicable and enforceable norms designed to facilitate global economic activity. Human health is at least as important as trade in terms of its effects on the wellbeing of populations. Moreover, health hazards – biological, chemical and radionuclear – have profound global implications. Whether the threat's origin is natural, accidental or deliberate, the harms, as well as the response, transcend national frontiers and warrant a transnational response. Despite its high importance, the global community has never come together to form a world health system. Notably, the International Sanitary Regulations, adopted in 1951, and later renamed the International Health Regulations (IHR), are antiquated, limited in scope and burdened by inflexible assumptions and entrenched power structures.[1]

On May 23, 2005, the World Health Assembly adopted a fundamental reform of the IHR – an historical development for international law and public health.[2] It may represent a nascent development of a coherent international law regime for global health. This chapter examines the origins of the IHR, describes the transformation in global governance embodied in the revised IHR, and proposes a new conception of global health governance.

The Historical Origins of the IHR

The origins of the IHR, the only global rules governing the international spread of infectious diseases, date back to the first International Sanitary Conference, held in Paris in 1851 to address the European cholera epidemics. During the latter half of the nineteenth century, ten sanitary conferences were held and eight conventions were

1 Gostin, L.O., 'International Infectious Disease Law: Revision of the World Health Organization's International Health Regulations', 291 *JAMA*, 2623 (2004).

2 World Health Assembly, 'Revision of the International Health Regulations', Resolution A58/55 (May 23, 2005).

negotiated (most did not come into force) to address the trans-boundary effects of infectious diseases. The International Sanitary Convention dealing with cholera was adopted in Venice in 1892, followed by another Convention dealing with plague in 1897.[3] In 1903, the International Sanitary Convention replaced the conventions of 1892 and 1897.[4]

At the turn of the twentieth century, the international community established regional and international institutions to enforce these conventions. American States set up the International Sanitary Bureau (ISB) in 1902, which became the Pan American Sanitary Bureau (PASB), a precursor to the Pan American Health Organization (PAHO).[5] European States developed their own multilateral institution in 1907, L'Office International d'Hygiène Publique (OIHP).[6] The Health Organization of the League of Nations (HOLN) was formed between the two world wars in 1923. Article XXIII of the League of Nations Covenant meekly stated that members would 'endeavor to take steps in matters of international concern for the prevention and control of disease'. The ISB, OIHP and HOLN were separate institutions, without harmonisation of goals or practices.

The United Nations was established after the horrors of World War II.[7] One of the UN's primary functions was the protection of global health. The World Health Organisation (WHO) was the first international agency established by the UN.[8] Its preamble expresses universal aspirations[9] stating that its 'principles are basic to the happiness, harmonious relations and security of all peoples'.[10] The WHO Constitution grants the agency the power to seek Member State adoption of conventions (Article

3 International Health Regulations Revision Project, 'World Health Organization, Global Crisis – Global Solutions: Managing Public Health Emergencies of International Concern Through the Revised International Health Regulations', WHO/CDS/CSR/GAR/2002.4 (2002), available at: http://www.who.int/csr/resources/publications/ihr/whocdsgar20024.pdf (accessed 01/06/05).

4 International Sanitary Convention, Dec. 3, 1903, 35 Stat. 1770, 1 Bevans 359.

5 'Agreement between the World Health Organization and the Pan American Health Organization', Res. WHA2.91 (June 30, 1949), in *World Health Organization Basic Documents* (44th ed), Geneva, World Health Organization, 2003.

6 Fidler, D.P., *International Law and Infectious Diseases*, New York, Oxford University Press, 1999.

7 Article 55 of the UN Charter states that a primary objective of the UN is to promote 'higher standards of living' and 'solutions of international ... health', U.N. Charter art. 55.

8 Arai-Takahashi, Y., 'The Role of International Health Law and WHO in the Regulation of Public Health', in Johnson, M.R. and Johnson, L. (eds), *Law and the Public Dimension of Health*, London, Cavendish Publishing, 2001: 113-141.

9 Frank, F.P., 'The Preamble of the Constitution of the World Health Organization', 80 *Bull. World Health Org.*, 981-983 (2002).

10 World Health Organization Constitution, July 22, 1946, pmbl., 62 Stat. 2679. 14 U.N.T.S. 185, 1896-187. See note, *supra*.

19),[11] promulgate regulations (Article 21) and make recommendations (Article 23).[12]

Pursuant to the agency's Article 21 power, WHO Member States adopted the International Sanitary Regulations (ISR) on July 25th, 1951. The ISR were renamed the International Health Regulations (IHR) in 1969.[13] The IHR initially applied to six diseases: cholera, plague, relapsing fever, smallpox, typhus and yellow fever. The IHR were slightly modified in 1973 (particularly for cholera) and again in 1981 (to exclude smallpox, in view of its global eradication). By the early 1980s the IHR applied only to cholera, plague and yellow fever – the same diseases originally discussed at the first International Sanitary Conference in 1851. Thus, before the 2005 revision, the IHR had not been significantly changed since the ISR's initial adoption in 1951.

Antiquated Global Health Governance

Why have Nation States historically resisted global health governance when they have acceded to global trade governance? The most plausible explanation is countries' outdated assumptions about sovereignty, horizontal governance and entrenched power.[14]

Sovereignty

Sovereignty, although often criticized, remains an influential idea in international relations, particularly in matters of health. Sovereignty has multiple dimensions, but

---

11 The only WHO Convention adopted pursuant to this power is the Framework Convention on Tobacco Control adopted in 2003. 'Framework Convention on Tobacco Control', WHO Doc A56/VR/4 (2003), available at: http://www.who.int/gb/ebwha/pdf_files/WHA56/ea56r1.pdf (last visited Jun. 1, 2005) (not yet in force).

12 Taylor, A.L. *et al.*, 'International Health Instruments: An Overview', in Detels, R. (ed), *Oxford Textbook of Public Health*, Oxford, Oxford University Press, 2002, 359-86.

13 The old IHR contained several broad requirements for Member States: (1) Notifications – Countries must report to the WHO any case of these diseases, occurring in humans in their territories, and give further notification when an area is free from infection. (2) Health Standards at Points of Arrival and Departure – Countries must adopt hygiene measures at ports, airports, frontier posts, and on international cargo, goods, baggage, containers, and other articles. Hygiene measures include providing potable water and wholesome food; conducting inspections of equipment, installations, and premises; and maintaining facilities for isolation and care of infected persons, and for disinfecting, disinsecting and deratting. (3) Health Documents – Countries may require health and vaccination certificates for travellers from infected to non-infected areas. (4) Maximum Measures – The health measures permitted by the IHR are 'the maximum measures applicable to international traffic, which a State may require for the protection of its territory'.

14 Fidler, D.P., 'SARS: Political Pathology of the First Post-Westphalian Pathogen', 31 *J.L. Med. & Ethics*, 485 (2003).

includes political authority over internal affairs, power to control border crossings and freedom from external interference.[15] The police power to protect the public's health and safety is a traditional prerogative of national sovereignty.[16] Assertions of sovereignty, of course, are not always detrimental. A nation's decision to impose scientifically based health regulations that are more stringent than required under international law is not simply a valid assertion of autonomy. Health regulations based on good science can provide increased protection for the Nation State and its neighbours.

When used to preserve a poorly regulated status quo, however, assertions of sovereignty can severely harm global interests in health. Consider the potential adverse health effects within each of the three main spheres of sovereignty. First, State power to control internal affairs enables political leaders to set low standards for public health surveillance and regulation. Given the cross-boundary effects of health threats, a State's failure to identify and respond promptly to domestic health threats poses substantial risks to both its own citizens and other nations. Second, a country's control over borders allows governments to ignore international health standards in regulating the flow of goods and people across their borders. The State may either set weak standards (facilitating the spread of disease) or overly strict standards (needlessly affecting travel and trade). Indeed, many international disputes arise from travel or trade restrictions imposed by international agencies or the States themselves. Finally, a State's assertion of non-interference provides an ostensible justification for failing to comply with international health norms. A country may delay notifying the WHO of an emerging health threat, prevent its scientists from sharing information, or refuse to cooperate with international agencies.[17]

Respect for sovereignty is particularly problematic because countries have built-in incentives for secrecy and inaction in the face of emerging health threats. Public notification of health hazards can adversely affect a country's economy and prestige. It can trigger media coverage or travel advisories affecting trade and tourism, and adversely affect the reputation and electoral prospects of political leaders. One need only look at the political and economic effects of SARS in Asia and North America to understand the potentially perverse incentives of transparency in matters of health.

Horizontal Governance

Connected to the problem of sovereignty is the preference for horizontal governance of health threats. Under horizontal governance, nations regulate health threats through bilateral or regional agreements, eschewing the imposition of rules by international

15 Jackson J.H., 'Sovereignty-Modern: A New Approach to an Outdated Concept', 97 *Am. J. Int'l. L.*, 782 (2003).

16 Gostin, L.O., *Public Health Law: Power, Duty, Restraint*, Berkeley, University of California Press, 2000.

17 Consider China's months-long failure to report the SARS outbreak. See Groopman, J., 'The SARS Epidemic: Global Warning', *Wall St. J.*, Apr. 23, 2003, at A22.

health agencies. Indeed, since the European sanitary conferences in the nineteenth century, governments have focused primarily on border controls to prevent health threats. Horizontal governance is not a particularly effective method of protecting global health. Border controls can rarely prevent the spread of disease, particularly if the threat is not detected promptly.

Vertical governance is likely to be far more effective by setting uniform standards for national health surveillance and regulation based on science. Vertical governance means that international health agencies can set minimum public health capacities at the regional and national levels. Yet countries exhibit deep reservations about yielding their sovereignty to multinational authorities. Vertical governance does not require countries to forego all autonomy, but greater devolution of power would enable the WHO to establish and enforce a system of global health preparedness that would make every country safer.

Entrenched Power

The current stagnation in global health governance may also be attributable to entrenched power structures. Economically and politically powerful countries, principally in Europe and North America, have had a disproportionate influence on the global health agenda.[18] This geopolitical imbalance results in multiple problems for world health.

First, geopolitical centres of power have acted as if it were possible to protect themselves from the endemic diseases of the developing world. The bilateral and multilateral agreements in nineteenth-century Europe could be understood as an attempt to seal the Western European frontier to prevent the movement of epidemics from Africa and Asia. It is possible to see a similar dynamic today with border and immigration policies designed to fend off diseases such as hemorrhagic fever, tuberculosis, and HIV/AIDS.

Second, the developed world has an abiding interest in continuing its economic vitality through free trade agreements. It is perhaps for this reason that the old IHR focused as much on commerce as health. The avowed purpose was 'to ensure the maximum security against the international spread of diseases with a minimum interference with world traffic'.[19] Yet the SARS outbreaks demonstrated the need for decisive public health action, sometimes at the expense of commerce and trade.[20] Developed countries have similarly insisted on furthering their economic interests through the creation and protection of intellectual property rights for pharmaceutical

18 Fidler, D.P., 'Microbialpolitik: Infectious Diseases and International Relations', 14 *Am. U. Int'l L. Rev*, 1, 21 (1998).

19 World Health Organization, International Health Regulations, July 25, 1969, foreword (3rd ann. ed. 1983).

20 Gostin, L.O. *et al*., 'Ethical and Legal Challenges Posed by Severe Acute Respiratory Syndrome: Implications for the Control of Severe Infectious Disease Threats', 290 *JAMA*, 3229 (2003).

companies, making lifesaving vaccines and drugs largely unaffordable in developing countries.[21] For example, although 95 per cent of the burden of HIV/AIDS is in the developing world, only eight per cent of those in need of antiretroviral treatments have access to them.[22]

Finally, developed countries have resisted systematic action to provide technical and financial assistance for health protection in poorer countries.[23] This failure to allocate resources equitably has powerful ramifications for world health. Resource-poor countries do not have the means to protect their own populations from the disproportionate burdens of endemic disease. The marked health disparities between the rich and poor regions of the world pose fundamental questions of fairness. At the same time, poor countries do not have the capacity for surveillance and response to emerging infections to prevent major outbreaks. This is not simply a problem in developing countries, but poses a major concern in the developed world. In the age of global travel and commerce, health hazards can move rapidly across the world.[24] Health protection is only as good as the weakest link, so low capacities in poor countries threaten every nation.

The International Health Regulations (2005): The Global Politics of Law Reform

Fundamental reform of the IHR would not have been possible were not for a confluence of events that raised infectious diseases into the realm of 'high politics'. The 1995 World Health Assembly (WHA) resolved in 1995 to revise the IHR in response to frightening outbreaks of cholera in Peru, plague in India, and Ebola hemorrhagic fever in Zaire.[25] This was also a time when the world was experiencing one of the greatest pandemics in global history – HIV/AIDS.[26] The IHR revision

---

21 Cornia, G.A., 'Globalization and Health: Results and Options', 79 *Bull. World Health Org.*, 834, 837 (2001) (noting that 'even in the cases in which [the Agreement on Trade-Related Aspects of Intellectual Property Rights] allows parallel imports of cheap generic drugs, trade pressures by [developed countries] limits access to affordable drug imports').

22 World Health Organization, 'Coverage and Need for Antiretroviral Treatment' (June 2004), at http://www.who.int/3by5/coverage/en/ (accessed on 01/06/05) (noting that only 8 per cent of those in the developing world and 4 per cent of those in Africa who require antiretroviral treatment were receiving antiretroviral treatment in June 2004).

23 Consider the difficulties encountered in gathering adequate contributions from developed countries for the Global Fund to Fight AIDS, Tuberculosis and Malaria. See McNeild, Jr., D.G., 'World's Anti-AIDS Donations Slow, Cutting US Contribution, Too', *N.Y. Times*, Aug. 19, 2004, at A18.

24 Garrett, L., *Betrayal of Trust: The Collapse of Global Public Health*, New York, Hyperion, 2000.

25 WHO, 'Revision and Updating of the International Health Regulations', WHA48.7 (May 12, 1995).

26 Gostin, L.O., *The AIDS Pandemic: Complacency, Injustice, and Unfulfilled Expectations*, University of North Carolina Press, 2004.

process received considerable 'push-back' particularly from the United States and the European Union. Concerns about the economic and security consequences of SARS,[27] avian influenza,[28] Marburg[29] and bioterrorism[30] made it politically difficult to oppose an ambitious reform of international infectious disease law.

The IHR (2005) contain 66 articles organized into ten parts, with 9 annexes (see Table 5.1).[31] The rules expand WHO jurisdiction beyond a narrow band of infectious diseases to the entire spectrum of public health risks of international importance. The IHR focus on key aspects of global preparedness ranging from surveillance and capacity building to public health response and border control. The cumulative effect could transform WHO's role and stature as well as establish a coherent structure for systematic detection and intervention in the face of global health threats.

Purpose, Scope, and Principles: Health, Trade and Human Rights

The IHR have an expansive scope covering 'public health risks'[32] and 'public health emergencies of international concern'.[33] A 'disease' is defined to include communicable and noncommunicable threats: 'an illness or medical condition, irrespective of origin or source, that presents or could present significant harm to humans (Art. 1).' Consequently, WHO has authority to act in virtually any context where an event has transnational dimensions, such as biological, chemical and radionuclear health risks. Since the source of the hazard is immaterial, WHO possesses jurisdiction for events that are naturally occurring, accidental and intentional. However, since WHO's new jurisdiction overlaps with several international

27 Gostin, L.O., Bayer, R. and Fairchild, A. L., 'Ethical and Legal Challenges Posed by Severe Acute Respiratory Syndrome: Implications for the Control of Severe Infectious Disease Threats', 290 *JAMA*, 3229-3237 (2003); World Health Organization. Severe Acute Respiratory Syndrome (SARS): Status of the Outbreak and Lessons for the Immediate Future. Geneva, Switzerland: World Health Organization, 2003.

28 Aldhous, P. and Tomlin, S., 'Avian Flu: Are We Ready?', 435 (7041) *Nature*, 399-402 (26 May 2005).

29 Ndayimirije, N. and Kindhauser, M.K., 'Marburg Hemorrhagic Fever in Angola – Fighting Fear and a Lethal Pathogen', 352 *New Eng. J. Med.*, 2155-2157 (2005).

30 Gostin, L.O. *et al.*, 'The Model State Emergency Health Powers Act: Planning and Response to Bioterrorism and Naturally Occurring Infectious Diseases', 288 *JAMA*, 622-628 (2002).

31 Fidler D.P. and Gostin L.O., 'The New International Health Regulations: An Historic Development for International Law and Public Health', 33(4) *J. Law, Med. & Ethics*, 85-94 (2006).

32 A 'public health risk' means 'a likelihood of an event that may affect adversely the health of human populations, with emphasis on one which may spread internationally or may present a serious and direct danger (Art. 1)'.

33 A 'public health emergency of international concern' means 'an extraordinary event which is determined: (i) to constitute a public health risk to other States through the international spread of disease and (ii) to potentially require a coordinated international response'.

organisations, it was necessary to harmonise the different roles (Arts. 6(1), 10(3), 14, 17(f)).[34] The IHR accomplishes this task by stating that its rules and other international agreements 'should be interpreted so as to be compatible'. The IHR 'shall not affect the rights and obligations of any state Party deriving from other international agreements (Art. 57)'.

The purpose of the IHR are 'to prevent, protect against, control and provide a public health response to the international spread of disease in ways that are commensurate with and restricted to public health risks, and which avoid unnecessary interference with international traffic and trade (Art. 2)'. The old IHR focused as much on the protection of trade as it did on the protection of health. The revision, however, stresses prevention, protection and control, with the admonition to avoid trade restrictions that are 'unnecessary'. The tipping point is where health measures go beyond those needed to avert or ameliorate the public health risk – a limit placed on State action based on science, which is a recurring theme in the revision (e.g., Art. 43(2) requires States Parties to base determinations on scientific principles and evidence). The IHR interact with international trade law in interesting, important ways, with both focusing on the legitimacy of State health measures that adversely affect international commerce.

The IHR not only balance health with trade, but also health with human rights. States Parties must have 'full respect for the dignity, human rights and fundamental freedoms of persons', guided by the UN Charter and in consultation with WHO. The IHR have 'universal application for the protection of all people of the world (Art. 3)' and health measures taken must be applied in a transparent and non-discriminatory manner (Art. 42). The IHR also contain provisions for health information privacy and data protection (Art. 45, see discussion below).

States Parties must, in particular, treat international travellers with 'respect for their dignity, human rights and fundamental freedoms and minimize any discomfort or distress' (Art. 32). Courteous and respectful treatment requires consideration of each traveller's gender, culture, ethnicity and religion. States Parties must assure travellers, especially if subjected to health measures, the necessities of life such as food, water, accommodation, clothing, medical treatment and means of communication (Art. 32). Travellers have the right to 'prior express informed consent' for medical examination, vaccination, prophylaxis or other health measures such as isolation, quarantine or

34 WHO is required to coordinate its activities with other intergovernmental organizations and international bodies including the U.N., International Labour Organization, Food and Agriculture Organization, International Atomic Energy Agency, International Civil Aviation Organization, International Maritime Organization and International Committee of the Red Cross. WHA 58/55, para 4. During the IHR reform process, WHO sought expert guidance on conflicts of law. See Center for Law and the Public's Health, *A Conflict Analysis of the Draft Revised International Health Regulations and Existing International Law: A Report to the World Health Organization*, Washington DC: Georgetown University Law Center, July 2004.

'public health observation'[35] (Art. 23(3)). If a traveller does not consent, the State Party can deny entry to the country or, if there is an imminent public health risk, resort to compulsion. Compulsory measures must be necessary to control the risk and, in the case of medical examination, be the least invasive and intrusive necessary to achieve the public health objective (Arts. 23 (2), 31(2)) (see further discussion of travellers below).

The balancing dynamic in the IHR, then, includes adherence to scientific methodologies, the flow of trade and travel, and respect for human rights. In each of these realms, there are hard tradeoffs: When can countries act in the face of scientific uncertainty? How much interference with economic freedom is tolerated in the name of health? When should personal autonomy, privacy and liberty yield for the sake of the public's health and safety?

National Public Health Legislation

Although the IHR mandates States Parties to act according to certain principles and dictates, it reserves the sovereign right of States Parties to legislate for the public good, upholding the purpose of the IHR and consistent with sound science (Art. 3). The State's exercise of public health powers must be consistent with the balancing dynamic suggested above. The legislation must achieve the same or greater level of health protection than WHO recommendations. Moreover, it must be 'no more restrictive of international traffic and not more invasive or intrusive to persons than reasonably available alternatives that would achieve the appropriate level of health protection' (Art. 43(1)).

Core National Capacities for Public Health Preparedness: Surveillance and Response

To facilitate communication, each State Party must designate an IHR Focal Point and WHO must designate IHR Contact Points (Art. 4). States Parties have the duty to develop, strengthen and maintain core public health capacities: (i) to detect, assess, notify and report events, and (ii) to respond promptly and effectively to public health risks and public health emergencies of international concern (Arts. 5(1), 13(1)). Global health protection relies on the ability of national and sub-national governments to engage in speedy and accurate surveillance and response to health threats. It is for that reason that the detailed requirements for capacity building contained in Annex 1, and future WHO guidelines, are critically important.

The mandate to build public health infrastructures is vacant without adequate resources for poor countries where, in some cases, the per capita annual spending on health is unconscionably low. It is for that reason that the World Health Assembly

35 'Public health observation' means the monitoring of the health status of a traveller over time for the purpose of determining the risk of disease transmission (Art. 1).

urged Member States to 'mobilise the resources necessary' and to provide support upon request 'in the building, strengthening and maintenance of the public health capacities required under the IHR (2005) (WHA 58/55, para. 5)'. Although the IHR ask state parties to provide financial and technical resources, these are either non-binding (Art. 13(5)) or weak (Art. 44(1)). Similarly, WHO duties to provide surveillance and response assistance (Arts. 5(3), 13(3), 13(6)) do not address WHO's own shortage of funds and personnel. Given the financial demands created by other global health problems, such as increasing access to HIV/AIDS treatment[36] and meeting the health-related Millennium Development Goals,[37] the IHR's silence on how the economic demands of the core capacity objectives will be met is a serious problem for which the IHR provide no apparent answers or strategies.

The IHR, cognisant of past recalcitrance of Member States to communicate promptly and fully, provide detailed requirements for data dissemination. The new approach is radical because it does not limit surveillance to a narrow list of diseases, uses a broad array of unofficial data sources, and empowers WHO to override State decisions. First, States Parties have an obligation to *notify* WHO within 24 hours of all events in their territory which may constitute a public health emergency of international concern (Art. 6).[38] To avoid ambiguity, a 'decision instrument' in Annex 2 provides detailed criteria for these determinations (See Figure 5.1).[39] Second, State Parties must *share all relevant public health information* during an unexpected or unusual public health event, irrespective of origin or source, which may constitute a public health emergency of international concern (Art. 7). This power implies a State obligation to share data about accidental or intentional health hazards, an obligation that became highly politicised in intergovernmental negotiations. Notably absent from the IHR were detailed specifications for information, lab specimens, and on-the-ground assistance in the event of a suspected terrorist event. Third, State Parties must *consult and keep WHO appraised* of events that may not be notifiable due to incomplete scientific information (Art. 8).

Notably, the IHR authorises WHO to take into account unofficial sources of information (e.g., non-governmental organisations and independent scientists),

36 World Health Organization, *The 3 by 5 Initiative*, available at: http://www.who.int/3by5/en/. Accessibility verified [June 1, 2005].

37 World Health Organization, *Achievement of Health-Related Millennium Development Goals: Report by the Secretariat*, A58/5, May 13, 2005.

38 States Parties have a similar duty to inform WHO of public health risks outside their territory (Art. 9(2)).

39 Listed diseases are automatically notifiable: smallpox, polio, SARS and a new subtype of influenza. For other listed diseases, States Parties must always use the algorithm (cholera, pneumonic plague, yellow fever, viral hemorrhagic fevers, West Nile fever and other diseases of special concern such as dengue fever, Rift Valley fever, and meningococcal disease). Finally, the algorithm must be used for any other event of potential international concern. The algorithm utilises criteria such as the seriousness of the public health impact, the unusual or unexpected character of the event, the risk of international spread and the risk of international travel or trade restrictions (Annex 2).

which must be assessed according to established epidemiological principles. WHO is required to inform the State Party, consult, and attempt to verify the accuracy of the data before taking action (Arts. 9, 10). This power enables WHO to utilise a broad network of potentially important surveillance data available in the age of the internet and other electronic information systems. The Global Outbreak Alert and Response Network, or GOARN (a collaboration of institutions and networks that pool human and technical resources for the rapid identification, confirmation and response to outbreaks of international importance), is centrally important to the functioning of the IHR.[40, 41]

The regulations require WHO to share non-governmental information with state parties 'and only where it is duly justified may WHO maintain the confidentiality of the source' (Art. 9.1). The general requirement on WHO to disclose the source of non-governmental information might deter non-state actors from supplying WHO with information, particularly in authoritarian regimes. The IHR provide no express guidance for determining under what circumstances WHO would be justified in maintaining the confidentiality of non-state sources.

The WHO Director General (DG) is empowered to determine whether an event constitutes a public health emergency of international concern. The DG must take into account data provided by the State Party, the decision instrument (Annex 2), the advice of the Emergency Committee,[42] scientific principles and evidence, and the risk to human health and interference with international traffic (Art. 12). In the event of a disagreement with the State Party, the DG must follow a defined procedure, but makes the final determination (Art. 49). Thus, under international law, WHO can override the judgments of sovereign States as part of a coherent governance system for global health.

Dissemination of Health Information: Privacy

WHO has a duty to send to all State Parties and, as appropriate, intergovernmental organizations, public health data received and which is necessary to enable States to respond to a public health risk. Such disclosures must be 'in confidence' (Art. 11(1)). However, WHO may not disclose specific information without the agreement of the State Party until certain findings are made about the high risk to the international community (Art. 11(2)). WHO is also empowered to disclose information to the public, if data about the same event has already become public and there is a need for authoritative and independent information. The statement that such data are

---

40 Fidler, D.P., 'Emerging trends in international law concerning global infectious disease control', *Emerging Infectious Diseases*, 2003; 9(3): 285-290.

41 World Health Organization, *Global Defence Against the Infectious Disease Threat*, Geneva, Switzerland: World Health Organization, 2002.

42 The DG must establish an Emergency Committee to provide views on public health emergencies of international concern and the issuance of temporary recommendations (Arts. 48-49).

'confidential' may be misplaced, for this is not a principled attempt to protect the privacy of named individuals, but a political compromise to protect the interests of governments.

The IHR do contain genuine provisions to protect personal privacy. States Parties must keep personally identified or identifiable information 'confidential and processed anonymously as required by national law' (Art. 45(1)). Many States and regional alliances have data protection laws, including the United States[43] and the European Union,[44] but many do not, which could considerably weaken the IHR's privacy mandate. States may disclose and process personal data where 'essential for the purposes of assessing and managing a public health risk', but must follow fair information practices. Personal data must be processed fairly and lawfully, relevant and not excessive, accurate and current, and not kept longer than necessary. WHO must also as far as practicable provide individuals with their personal data in an intelligible form and allow for correction of inaccuracies (Art. 45).

WHO Recommendations

WHO has the power to issue temporary and standing recommendations. The DG must issue temporary recommendations upon determining that a public health emergency of international concern is occurring (Art. 15). WHO may also make standing recommendations of appropriate health measures for routine or periodic application for specific, ongoing public health risks (Art. 16). Recommendations may include health measures to be implemented by State Parties to prevent or reduce the international spread of disease and avoid unnecessary interference with international traffic. Article 18 contains applicable health measures for persons (e.g., medical examinations, vaccination, contact tracing, isolation and exit screening) and baggage, cargo, containers, conveyances and goods (e.g., review manifest and routing, inspections, safe handling, seizure and destruction, and refusal of departure or entry). Criteria for issuing recommendations include consideration of the views of State Parties and the Emergency or Review Committee,[45] scientific evidence and international standards (Art. 17).

43 Gostin L.O., 'National Health Information Privacy: Regulations Under the Health Insurance Portability and Accountability Act', 285 *JAMA*, 3015-3021 (2001).

44 Symposium Issue, 'European Directive on Data Protection', 95/46/EC, 9 *European Journal of Health Law* (2002); Hervey, T. and McHale, J., *Health Law and the European Union*, Cambridge, Cambridge University Press, 2004; Beyleveld, D., Townend, D., Rouille-Mirza, S. and Wright, J. (eds), *The Data Protection Directive and Medical Research Across Europe*, Aldershot, Ashgate, 2005.

45 The DG must establish a Review Committee to give technical advice regarding IHR amendments, standing recommendations, and other advice (Arts. 50-53).

International Travellers, Health Documents and Charges

International travel is one of the primary means by which pathogens are spread across frontiers. A health measure directed at travellers can either be an effective means of containing an outbreak or it can overreach, causing adverse effects on trade, tourism and human rights. The IHR, therefore, contain special provisions for travellers (Arts. 23, 30-32, 43). States Parties must treat travellers with respect and minimise discomfort or distress as the discussion of human rights above explains (Art. 32). A 'suspect' traveller, who may have been exposed to infection,[46] and is placed under 'public health observation', can continue an international voyage if he or she does not pose an imminent public health risk (Art. 30). Despite the duty to be respectful and allow passage, States Parties possess a variety of powers over international travellers if they pose a public health risk.

Under Article 23, State Parties may require for public health purposes on arrival or departure: (i) information about the traveller's destination and itinerary, and (ii) a *non-invasive* medical examination that is the least intrusive necessary to achieve the public health objective (Art. 23(1)). Upon evidence of a public health risk, State Parties may conduct the least intrusive and invasive medical examination, or other health measure, necessary to achieve the objective of preventing the international spread of disease (Art. 23(2)). Travellers, or their parents or guardians, must be informed of any health risk associated with vaccination or other prophylaxis, and physicians must be educated about this requirement (Art. 23(4)). Similarly, medical examinations or procedures must conform to established national or international safety standards (Art. 23(5)).

International travellers have certain rights under the IHR. State Parties may not, as a condition of entry, compel travellers to undergo invasive medical examination, vaccination or other prophylaxis or proof of vaccination (Art. 31(1)).[47] Similarly, international travellers must give informed consent to medical examinations, vaccinations or other health measures (Art. 23(3)). If a traveller refuses to give consent to an authorised examination, vaccination or other prophylaxis, the State Party can deny entry. If there is evidence of an imminent public health risk, the State Party can override the traveller's wishes and *compel* medical examination,[48] vaccination or other prophylaxis, or additional health measures such as isolation or quarantine. State Parties must act in accordance with national law and to the extent necessary to control the risk (Art. 31(2)). State Parties may not charge travellers for

46 A 'suspect' is a person considered as having been exposed or possibly exposed to a public health risk capable of transmission (Art. 1).

47 State Parties, however, may require medical examination, vaccination or proof of vaccination: (i) when necessary to determine a public health risk; (ii) as a condition of entry for travellers seeking temporary or permanent residence; or pursuant to Article 23 (health measures on arrival and departure) or 43 (additional health measures), described above (Art. 31(1)).

48 As stated earlier, the medical examination must be the least invasive and intrusive necessary to achieve the public health objective.

health measures, except for those seeking temporary or permanent residence or for certain measures conducted primarily for the traveller's benefit (Art. 40).

No health documents can be required in international traffic other than those provided in the IHR or WHO recommendations (Art. 35). The documents that can be required include: questionnaires about the traveller's health and contacts (Art. 35); vaccination certificates that conform to the IHR (Art. 36); maritime and aircraft declarations of health (Arts. 37, 38); and ship sanitation certificates (Art. 39).

Points of Entry, Conveyances and Goods

The IHR contain detailed provisions about points of entry (Arts. 19-22: airports, ports, ground crossings), conveyances (Arts. 24-29: ships, aircraft, lorries, trains and coaches) and goods, containers and container loading areas (Arts. 33-34). State Parties must ensure that these venues for travel and border crossing have sufficient capacity, competent authorities and standards for surveillance, sanitation, disinfection, disinsection, deratting, decontamination, etc. These provisions were largely included in the old IHR and continue to apply.

A New Paradigm for Global Health Governance

To overcome the problems of sovereignty, horizontal governance and entrenched power, the international community should consider a new conception for global health based on the rule of international law. WHO's revision of the IHR, if expanded, could serve as a model for effective public health governance.

The Salience of Health Over Trade

The IHR should stress the salience of global health and the WHO's role in achieving that purpose. WHO should dedicate itself to the protection and promotion of global health. Wherever possible, health rules should respect travel and trade, while assuring that promoting global health remains the WHO's primary mission. That is the vision of the WHO Constitution, which does not mention the protection of trade or commerce.

Wide Jurisdiction

The narrow scope of the old IHR impeded the WHO in effectively dealing with modern health threats. The new IHR has a broad and expansive scope. This new approach is preferable because it is flexible, prospective and covers all hazards (radiological, chemical and biological), whether naturally occurring, accidental or intentional. It does not require amendment of the IHR each time a novel health threat emerges.

Comprehensive Data Collection

Rapid and comprehensive data collection is crucial to global health. Yet surveillance is hindered by the reluctance of countries to fully cooperate. Global surveillance can be dramatically improved by effective vertical governance. First, the WHO could establish criteria for uniform data sets, core informational requirements, and timely monitoring and reporting. These norms would help set a standard for national and global surveillance. Second, as is envisaged in the new IHR, the WHO should expand its data sources beyond official government channels. 'Small-world networks' consisting of scientists, health professionals, membership associations and non-governmental organisations could considerably broaden the sources of health information. Finally, the WHO should utilise modern technology for surveillance, including electronic health records and the internet, to gather and analyse surveillance data.

National Public Health Preparedness

Uniformly strong public health capacities at the national level offer the best prospect for global health. Prompt and efficient monitoring and response at the national level is critically important to prevent the proliferation of disease. To improve national competencies, WHO should set minimum standards for laboratories, data systems and response even beyond those in the revised IHR. By setting performance standards and measuring outcomes, WHO could continually help Member States evaluate their public health preparedness. Compliance with international health norms has been a serious problem that must be addressed by the WHO. This could be accomplished through a combination of hard and soft law: mediation, adjudication and incentives.

A related problem is that poor countries cannot meet minimum standards for public health preparedness. The international community, therefore, should substantially increase technical and financial assistance for health system improvement in developing countries. This commitment would not be open-ended; nor would it necessarily be sufficient to meaningfully reduce global health disparities. However, at a minimum, the developed world should help assure that all nations have core public heath capacities for surveillance and containment of emerging health threats of global importance. This kind of commitment not only allows progressive development of higher standards of health in resource-poor countries, but is also in the interests of the industrialised world.

Human Rights Safeguards

Many aspects of global health regulation affect human rights, including surveillance (privacy), vaccination and treatment (bodily integrity), travel restrictions (movement), and isolation and quarantine (liberty). Health measures may also be applied inequitably, leading to discrimination against unpopular groups, such as migrants and ethnic minorities. The revised IHR goes along way to respecting human rights, but leaves out important modern understandings. The WHO could demonstrate even greater respect for human rights by incorporating the internationally accepted norms contained in the Siracusa principles, which require health measures to be necessary, proportionate and fair.[49] Health measures should be based on the rule of law and provide due process for persons whose liberty is placed in jeopardy.

Good Public Health Governance

WHO Member States have not always followed basic principles of good public health governance. They have sometimes acted in ways that are insular and discriminatory, without adequate regard to science. WHO could set an example of good public health governance by complying with the principles of transparency, objectivity and fairness. The agency's policies and recommendations should be established in an open manner, based on scientific evidence and exercised equitably. The agency gains credibility by its adherence to science, the truthfulness of its disclosures, and its fair dealings with countries, rich and poor alike.

The Future of Global Health Governance

More effective monitoring and management of international health threats is undoubtedly a global public good. Yet the question arises whether international law is the most effective institutional vehicle to achieve this objective. After all, the WHO has been relatively impotent in enforcing the existing IHR. During the SARS outbreaks, moreover, the agency was active and effective without the need for formal international law.

Certainly, revised IHR will not assure capable leadership and sound governance by the WHO. Yet, the revision offers an opportunity for a renewed commitment by the international community to a shared vision of global health. The revision gives the WHO a clear mission, significantly enhanced jurisdiction and formal power to set standards and make recommendations. By assenting to a far-reaching revision of the IHR, Member States are ceding some control over health threats of international importance and grant to the WHO a measure of centralised authority.

International law can help forge a new conception of global health governance that assures:

- the salience of health over trade;
- broad jurisdiction over conditions of international public health importance;

49 United Nations, Economic and Social Council, UN Sub-Commission on Prevention of Discrimination and Protection of Minorities, Siracusa Principles on the Limitation and Derogation of Provisions in the International Covenant on Civil and Political Rights, Annex, UN Doc E/CN.4/1985/4 (1985), reprinted in 7 *Hum. Rts. Q.*, 3 (1985).

- global surveillance through core data requirements and 'small-world networks';
- national public health preparedness by enforcing standards, creating incentives, and cultivating developmental and technical assistance;
- human rights protection through incorporation of the Siracusa principles; and
- good public health governance through transparency, objectivity and fairness.

By adhering to the rule of law, the international community has taken a vital step toward better protection against the biological, chemical and radiological hazards posed in the modern age.

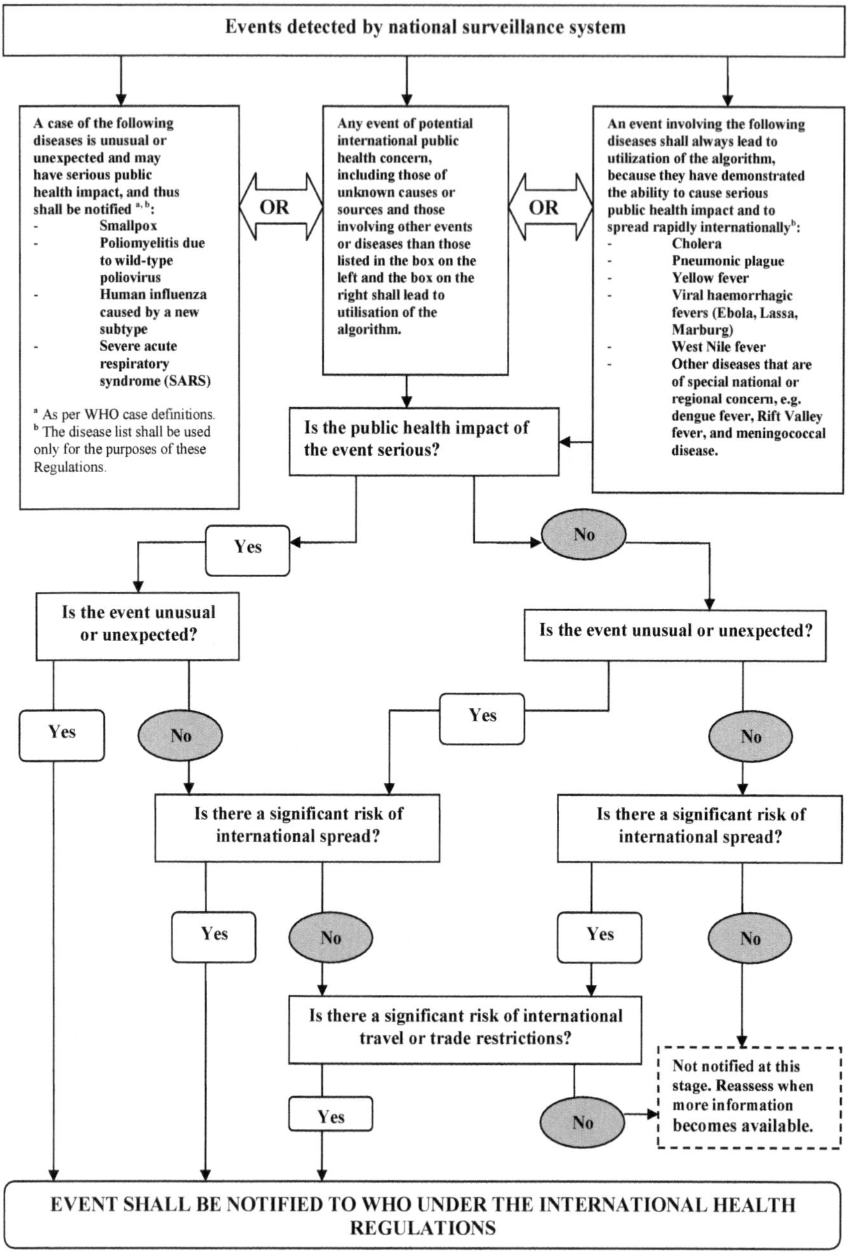
Events detected by national surveillance system
A case of the following diseases is unusual or unexpected and may have serious public health impact, and thus shall be notified a, b:
- Smallpox
- Poliomyelitis due to wild-type poliovirus
- Human influenza caused by a new subtype
- Severe acute respiratory syndrome (SARS)
a As per WHO case definitions.
b The disease list shall be used only for the purposes of these Regulations.
OR
Any event of potential international public health concern, including those of unknown causes or sources and those involving other events or diseases than those listed in the box on the left and the box on the right shall lead to utilisation of the algorithm.
OR
An event involving the following diseases shall always lead to utilization of the algorithm, because they have demonstrated the ability to cause serious public health impact and to spread rapidly internationally b:
- Cholera
- Pneumonic plague
- Yellow fever
- Viral haemorrhagic fevers (Ebola, Lassa, Marburg)
- West Nile fever
- Other diseases that are of special national or regional concern, e.g. dengue fever, Rift Valley fever, and meningococcal disease.
Is the public health impact of the event serious?
Yes
No
Is the event unusual or unexpected?
Is the event unusual or unexpected?
Yes
No
Yes
No
Is there a significant risk of international spread?
Is there a significant risk of international spread?
Yes
No
Yes
No
Is there a significant risk of international travel or trade restrictions?
Yes
No
Not notified at this stage. Reassess when more information becomes available.
EVENT SHALL BE NOTIFIED TO WHO UNDER THE INTERNATIONAL HEALTH REGULATIONS

Figure 5.1

Table 5.1

Parts and Articles of the IHR (2005)

PART I – DEFINITIONS, PURPOSE AND SCOPE, PRINCIPLES AND RESPONSIBLE AUTHORITIES
Article 1 Definitions
Article 2 Purpose and scope
Article 3 Principles
Article 4 Responsible authorities
PART II – INFORMATION AND PUBLIC HEALTH RESPONSE
Article 5 Surveillance
Article 6 Notification
Article 7 Information-sharing during unexpected or unusual public health events
Article 8 Consultation
Article 9 Other reports
Article 10 Verification
Article 11 Provision of information by WHO
Article 12 Determination of a public health emergency of international concern
Article 13 Public health response
Article 14 Cooperation of WHO with intergovernmental organizations and international bodies
PART III – RECOMMENDATIONS
Article 15 Temporary recommendations
Article 16 Standing recommendations
Article 17 Criteria for recommendations
Article 18 Recommendations with respect to persons, baggage, cargo, containers, conveyances, goods and postal parcels
PART IV – POINTS OF ENTRY
Article 19 General obligations
Article 20 Airports and ports
Article 21 Ground crossings
Article 22 Role of competent authorities
PART V – PUBLIC HEALTH MEASURES
Article 23 Health measures on arrival and departure
Article 24 Conveyance operators
Article 25 Ships and aircraft in transit
Article 26 Civilian lorries, trains and coaches in transit
Article 27 Affected conveyances
Article 28 Ships and aircraft at points of entry
Article 29 Civilian lorries, trains and coaches at points of entry
Article 30 Travellers under public health observation
Article 31 Health measures relating to entry of travellers

Disclaimer: Professor Gostin worked with WHO on the IHR revision process. He also directs the WHO and CDC Collaborating Center on Law and the Public's Health. The views in this essay do not necessarily reflect those of the WHO or the CDC.

Chapter 6

International Medical Research Regulation: From Ethics to Law[1]

Don Chalmers

Introduction

It is a challenging task to identify an area of medicine that has not attracted the scholarly attention of Professor Mason. His output in books[2] and other writings[3] has been prodigious and his unique and lively style has always eschewed the mundane and descriptive approach to legal scholarship. Amongst these extensive works stands the influential co-authored work, *Law and Medical Ethics.*[4] Apart from being one of the first common law texts on medical law (outside of the USA), it was also a pioneering work with chapters devoted to the subject of biomedical human research and experimentation.[5] The topic of research and experimentation is now

---

1 The funding support of the Australian Research Council (DP0559760) for this work is acknowledged with appreciation

2 Mason, J.K. and McLean, S., *Legal and Ethical Aspects of Healthcare*, London, Greenwich Medical Media, 2003; Mason, J.K., *Medicine for Lawyers*, London, Butterworths, 2001; Mason, J.K., McCall Smith, A. and Laurie, G.T., *Law and Medical Ethics* (6th ed), London, Butterworths, 2002; Mason, J.K. and Purdue, B.N., *The Pathology of Trauma*, London, Arnold, 2000; Mason, J.K., *Medico-legal Aspects of Reproduction and Parenthood*, Aldershot, Ashgate Publishing, 1998.

3 See, for example, Mason, J.K., 'Unwanted Pregnancy: A Case of Retroversion?', in McLean, S.A.M. (ed), *Medical Law and Ethics*, Aldershot, Ashgate Publications, 2002; Mason, J.K., 'Wrongful Pregnancy', *Stair Memorial Encyclopaedia*, Butterworths and the Law Society of Scotland, 1996 at pp. 198-202; Mason, J.K., 'Death and Dying: One Step at a Time?', in McLean, S.A.M. (ed), *Death, Dying and the Law*, Aldershot, Dartmouth, 1996; Mason, J.K., 'Contemporary Issues in Organ Transplantation', in McLean, S.A.M. (ed), *Contemporary Issues in Law, Medicine and Ethics*, Aldershot, Dartmouth, 1996 at pp. 117-141; Mason, J.K., 'Consent to Treatment and Research in the ICU', in Pace N. and McLean, S.A.M., *Ethics and the Law in Intensive Care*, Oxford University Press, 1996, at pp. 29-46.

4 Now in its 6th edition, Mason, J.K., McCall Smith, R.A. and Laurie, G.T., *Law and Medical Ethics*, London, Butterworths, 2002.

5 Mason, J.K. and McCall Smith, R.A., *Law and Medical Ethics* (1st ed), Butterworths, 1983, chapter 15, 'Biomedical Human Experimentation', at pp. 193-205 and chapter 16, 'Research on Children and Fetal Experimentation', at pp. 206-217

an established component of any discussion of medical law.[6] Medical research regulation has been at the forefront of international attention for the last decade. The continuing and steady increase in regulation of the medical research endeavour is the subject of this chapter.

This chapter will discuss the development of medical research ethics internationally and future directions for the regulation of medical research and its governance primarily through research ethics committees.[7] It may be a time for change[8] from current arrangements that still rely substantially on volunteerism. The focus is on the Australian experience that exemplifies trends in other countries[9] towards greater regulation. This chapter will refer to the Australian Law Reform Commission and the Australian Health Ethics Committee report entitled *Essentially Yours: The Protection of Human Genetic Information in Australia*, dealing with the protection of human genetic information,[10] and to its recommendations on genetic research and strengthening the ethics review system for human research.

Medical Ethics and Medical Research Ethics

Frequently, the Nuremberg Code and the later Declaration of Helsinki are treated as the starting points and sources for the principles governing research ethics involving humans. However, medical ethics themselves are sources of the core principles

6 See also Kennedy, I. and Grubb, A., *Principles of Medical Law*, Oxford University Press, 1998, chapter 13 (UK); Geisen, D., *International Medical Malpractice Law: A Comparative Law Study of Civil Liability Arising from Medical Care*, Dordrecht, Martinus Nijhoff, 1988, chapters 43-48 (EU and international); Breen, K., Plueckhahn, V. and Cordner, S., *Ethics Law and Medical Practice*, London, Allen and Unwin, 1997, chapter 16 (Australia); Furrow, B., Greaney, T.L., Johnson, S., Jost, T. and Schwartz, R., *Health Law* (2nd ed), St Paul, West Group Publishing, 2000, chapter 21 (USA).

7 The term 'Research Ethics Committee' is used generically to refer to committees that provide ethical approval for medical and health research projects and that have the primary duty to protect the research participants. They have a variety of national designations: Local Research Ethics Committees (UK); Human Research Ethics Committees (Australia); Institutional Review Boards (USA); Institutional Ethics Committees (New Zealand, though there are also regional health and disability ethics committees). They are distinguishable from hospital based 'clinical ethics committees' (called research ethics committees in the USA).

8 Prologue to the National Bioethics Advisory Commission Report, *Ethical and Policy Issues in Research involving Human Participants*, Vol. 1 Bethesda, Maryland, August 2001. See also Chalmers, D. 'Research ethics – A time for Change', (2004) 32 *Journal of Law and Medical Ethics*, 583-595.

9 Particularly the USA in the National Bioethics Advisory Commission Report, *Ethical and Policy Issues in Research Involving Human Participants*, Vols 1 & II Bethesda, Maryland August 2001, available at: http://www.georgetown.edu/research/nrcbl/nbac/human/overvol2.html.

10 Report 96 March 2003.

of research ethics. The Hippocratic Oath in its earliest formulation dealt with the fundamental idea of 'benefit' for the patient and required doctors to:

> keep this Oath ... for the benefit of my patients and abstain from whatever is deleterious and mischievous ... with purity and with holiness I will pass my life and practice my Art ... I will not divulge ... all such should be kept secret.

The Hippocratic Oath has been revised and restated in the Medical Associations of all nations, which in their modern statements, require the medical profession to:

(i) consider the well being of the patient;
(ii) honour the profession and its traditions;
(iii) recognise limitations in the prevention and treatment of disease;
(iv) protect patient secrets; and
(v) avoid abuse of the doctor/patient relationship.[11]

The central tenet of the Hippocratic Oath to do no harm to the patient has been a constant theme in the centuries of development of the core of medical ethics. This tenet underlies the histories of Jewish[12] and Islamic,[13] as well as Chinese and Indian medicine. The development of medical ethics, rather than research ethics, was enriched by the teachings of John Gregory at Edinburgh University in the eighteenth century. This Edinburgh connection extended to the work of Professor Benjamin Rush in the United States, who had earlier been a student of John Gregory, and the writings of Thomas Percival. Rush and others were involved with the formulation in 1847 of the American Medical Association's Code of Medical Ethics, which drew heavily from the writings of John Gregory (1725-1773), Thomas Percival (1740-1804) and Benjamin Rush (1747-1813).[14] There is an interesting debate as to whether the American Code of Medical Ethics was '... nothing more than self-serving professional etiquettes ... to disguise organised medicine's attempt to monopolize medical thought so that, by driving homeopaths and other "irregular" competitors from the medical market place, it could ultimately monopolize medical practice'.[15]

---

11 See, for example the *Code of Ethics* of the Australian Medical Association; Canadian Medical Association and American Medical Association. D Giesen, *op cit.*, pp. 669-672.

12 See Mendelson, D., 'The Medical Duty of Confidentiality in the Hippocratic Tradition and Jewish Medical Ethics', (1998) 5 *J of Law and Med*, 227.

13 See Rahman, F., 'Health and Medicine in the Islamic Tradition: Change and Identity', New York, Crossroads Publishing USA, 1987 (Kazi Publications USA, 1997).

14 See Baker, R., *The Codification of Medical Morality Vol 2: Anglo-American Medical Ethics and Medical Jurisprudence in the 19th Century*, Dordrecht, Kluwer Academic Publishers, 1995, pp. 1-6 and in the same volume see Baker, R., 'The Historical Context of the American Medical Association's 1847 Code of Ethics', Chapter 2 and Reiser, S.G., 'Creating a Medical Profession in the United States: The First Code of Ethics of the American Medical Association', Chapter 3.

15 *Ibid.*, p. 2.

The rich contribution of Islamic physicians and philosophers to the history of medicine and medical ethics is increasingly appreciated. The major work of Abd Allah ibn Sina known as Avicenna (988-1037), the *Canon of Medicine*, was used not only in the Middle East, but also in Europe. Translations of his works were used in Europe for centuries after his death. The first of the five books of the *Canon* sets out general medical principles and includes guidance on the relationship of the doctor and patient and the duties of the doctor.[16] Avicenna was one of many great Muslim physicians who contributed to Islam's development of medicine in hygiene, hospital care, medical training, pharmacy, patient records and respect for the physician.[17] The current Islamic Code of Medical Professional Ethics,[18] for example, sets out guidelines for the personal and professional conduct, behaviour and attitude of the doctor, some dealing specifically with the patient relationship, such as '[b]ased on sound logic and clear Islamic teachings, the physician has no right to recommend or administer any harmful material to his patients', and '[t]he humanitarian aspect of the medical profession must never be neglected. The physician must render the needed help regardless of the financial ability or ethnic origin of the patient'.

The modern re-statements of national codes of medical ethics are often modeled on the Declaration of Geneva prepared by the World Medical Association in 1948.[19]

> … the health of my patient will be my first consideration. I will respect the secrets, which are confined in me. I will maintain by all the means in my power to honour and the noble traditions of the medical profession … I will not permit considerations of religions, nationality, race, party politics or social standing to intervene between my duty and my patient. I will maintain the utmost respect for human life … I will not use my medical knowledge contrary to the laws of humanity.

This Declaration of Geneva became the basis for the International Code of Medical Ethics later the following year. However, the principles of medical ethics were largely directed to the doctor/patient relationship and the delivery of ethical medical services, rather than research. The modern researcher is surrounded, like the modern doctor, with considerably more regulators, ethicists and auditors.[20]

The Nuremberg Code was developed in direct response to the inhumane and cruel experimentation conducted in Nazi concentration camps.[21] This Code goes beyond

---

16 See http://www.footnotenml.nih.gov/hmd/arabic/F8.html, accessed on 18/11/04.

17 See E. Abouleish, MD *Contributions of Islam to Medicine*, http://www.islam-usa.com/im3.html, accessed on 23/11/04.

18 See Shahid Athar MD (ed), *Islamic Medicine*, http://www.islam-usa.com/iml.html, accessed on 23/11/04.

19 Amended in Sydney in 1968 and in Venice in 1983.

20 Pace D. Rothman, *Strangers at the Bedside*, New York, Basic Books, 1991.

21 See Annas, G. and Grodin, M. (eds), *The Nazi Doctors and the Nuremberg Code: Human Rights in Human Experimentation*, London, Oxford University Press, 1992; Winkler, D. and Barondess, J. 'Bioethics and Anti-Bioethics in Light of Nazi Medicine: What we must remember?', (1993) *Kennedy Inst of Ethics Journal* 3(1), 39-55.

any conception of doctor/patient etiquette or professional monopoly and deals with 'matters of ethical significance to humanity'.[22] In summary, the Nuremberg Code laid down ten principles as follows:

1. Voluntary consent of the human subject is absolutely essential.
2. The experiment should yield 'fruitful' results.
3. The experiment should be designed and based on the results of animal experimentation or natural history as such as anticipatory results justify the experiment.
4. The experiment should avoid all unnecessary physical and mental suffering and injury.
5. No experiment should be conducted where there is an a priori reason to believe that death or injury will occur.
6. The degree of risk should never exceed the importance of the problem to be solved.
7. Proper preparations and adequate facilities should be provided to protect the subject.
8. The experiment should be conducted only by scientifically qualified persons.
9. The subject should be at liberty to end the experiment.
10. The scientist must terminate an experiment where there is probable cause to believe that injury, disability or death will result.[23]

The Declaration of Helsinki was introduced as an initiative of the World Medical Association and was a significant watershed in the progress towards regulation of human experimentation. The Declaration of Helsinki was an amplification of the Nuremberg Code and was first formally adopted by the eighteenth World Medical Assembly in Helsinki in June 1964. This Declaration has been amended on many occasions subsequently.

The Declaration of Helsinki confirmed and established the *key pillars* for ethical review of medical research, namely:

- voluntary consent of the research participant;
- independent review of the project;
- assessment of the risk;
- involvement of competent researchers of integrity, and
- research merit.

---

22 Leake, C., *Percival's Medical Ethics*, Baltimore, Williams and Wilkinson, 1927, p. 57 cited in Baker, R. *op cit*, p. 4.

23 Judgment of Beals, Sebring and Crawford JJ in *United States v. Karol Brandt and Others* (1947-48). Nuremberg Military Tribunals Vols 1-ii (the Medical Case), Washington, US Government Printing Office, 1948-49.

Events in the United States were to have significant impact on the international development of medical research ethics. The Tuskegee Syphilis Study[24] was one of a number of publicised and highly questionable examples of the absence of research standards. Following these revelations, the United States Congress enacted the National Research Act, 1974, which established the National Commission for the Protection of Human Subjects of Biomedical and Behavioral Research and, equally importantly, required each institution conducting federally supported research involving human subjects to establish Institutional Review Boards (IRBs). Shortly after this Act, the Department of Health, Education and Welfare issued its *Policy for the Protection of Human Research Subjects* in 1975 when '... virtually every University, Medical School and Research Hospital had established IRBs that operated within the requirements of both federal and state regulations'.[25] These regulations have been revised regularly.[26] The IRBs are the cornerstones of the Federal regulatory process,[27] and are required to review the ethical aspects of all research protocols within the Institution where research is funded wholly or partly by the Federal Department. The Federal regulations require each IRB to follow written procedures with the conduct of initial and monitoring review of the research. The Federal regulations also establish reporting requirements for the IRB to the researcher and to the Institution. The regulations also set up a number of other detailed operational requirements such as annual review of research projects, approval of any changes to a research protocol and strict requirements for reporting of any immediate hazard to a human subject enrolled in a project. The FDA also requires that the IRB report any unanticipated problems involving risk to human subjects or any serious or continuing non-compliance with Federal regulations. Where there are any threats to human subjects the project must be suspended or terminated or reported to the FDA.

The regulations also allowed some procedures to be considered, not by the full committee, but by a majority through a process of *expedited review*. The development of IRBs was by no means uniform and different institutions reported differences of size, professional composition, meetings, review procedures, access to records and other differences.[28] Nevertheless, the early formalisation of the American IRB was influential in the development of ethics committees in other parts of the world.[29]

24 Furrow, B., Greaney, T.L., Johnson, S., Jost, T. and Schwartz, R., *op cit*, p. 979 (USA).

25 *Id.*

26 See 45 *Code of Federal Regulations*, s 46.101 (a)-(f). The Food and Drug Administration (FDA) has correlative regulations paralleling the Department of Health and Human Services Policy.

27 Furrow, B., Greaney, T.L., Johnson, S., Jost, T. and Schwartz, R. *op cit*, p. 981 *et seq* (USA).

28 *Ibid.*, at pp. 981-982 (USA).

29 For example, in Australia, the *Statement on Human Experimentation*, the first Code on Human Research, was amended in 1982 to introduce ethics committees.

Arguably, the Federal constitutional form has been the most influential American legal export but the regulation of ethical review through the IRB cannot be discounted.[30]

The 1980s and 1990s saw the steady introduction of research ethics committees into research-active countries. Generally, these committees reviewed only medical and health research on humans and were composed of researchers but also lay, legal and religious members. They were institutionally based with guidelines from some government or professional body. These developments were broadly uniform. The Declaration of Helsinki had a significant influence on the development of research ethics at the national level. The 1980s and 1990s witnessed the steady expansion of ethics review of research. Many national authorities introduced codes of ethical research practice based on the Declaration of Helsinki. Australia was an early acolyte of the ethics review process. In Australia, for example the Declaration was ratified in 1967 by the peak medical research-funding agency, the National Health and Medical Research Council (NHMRC), which introduced a code of practice for medical research, the *Statement on Human Experimentation*, which was based on the Declaration. At this time, the NHMRC introduced one of the key features of ethical codes of research practice; compliance with the *Statement* and ethical approval were made pre-conditions of funding by the NHMRC. However, like the USA, these conditions only applied to institutions receiving NHMRC funding that were usually public.

More significantly, breach of an ethical research guideline is subject to enforcement procedures. Although leading journals and regulatory authorities require assurance of ethical approval before publication and drug registration respectively, the non-enforcement of research guidelines remains a feature of the ethics review system in most countries. Another key pillar was established with the formal introduction of research ethics committees in 1982. In 1992 the Australian Health Ethics Committee (AHEC) was established with sole responsibility for the formulation of guidelines dealing with medical research[31] and overseeing the developing national system of research ethics review committees. The *Statement on Human Experimentation* was replaced with a significantly more detailed and broader *National Statement on*

30 The Institutional Review Board is separate from the American Ethics Committees, which advise doctors and families on decisions about withdrawing life support treatment; provision of advice on withholding treatment from newborn infants with birth defects; policy making through drafting of guidelines for hospital personnel on controversial areas of medical practice; education through their organisation of seminars on the areas of controversy; and provision of advice on specific ethical dilemmas in the treatment of specific patients. See Annas, G., 'Ethics Committees in Neo-natal; Substantive Protection of all Procedural Diversion?', (1984) 74 *Am J Pub Health*, 843 and President's Commision Report, *The Study of Ethical Problems in Medicine and Biomedical and Behavioural Research Deciding to Forego Life Sustaining Treatment*, Washington, 1983.

31 National Health and Medical Research Council Act 1992 (Cth) s 8. However, these guidelines must be drawn up following a unique two-stage public consultation process under s 14.

Ethical Conduct in Research Involving Humans[32] in 1999 (*National Statement*). The *National Statement* also included, for the first time, chapters on the required standards of ethical conduct in human genetic research, research involving human tissue and research involving persons highly dependent on medical care.[33]

Most nations report a two-tier review system. On the first tier, the ethical 'health' of the research review system is dependent on the researchers' primary responsibilities under the codes of research practice. Researchers have the primary responsibilities for the integrity of research design and respect for participants.[34] Essentially research ethics committees, on the second tier, review and approve but never police the system.[35] An increasing number of countries have introduced a third tier, like Australia,[36] with a national committee (examples include the Health Research Council Ethics Committee, New Zealand; National Consultative Committee for Health and Life Sciences, France; Bioethics Advisory Committee, Singapore; National Ethics Committee for Health Research, Lao PDR; National Ethics Review Committee for Research, Pakistan; National Commission for Ethics in Health Research, Indonesia). In the end, the ethics review system will always rely heavily on the integrity of the researchers and the scrutiny of ethics review committees rather than on the oversight of any national committee.

Research Ethics and International Instruments

The last two decades have also witnessed an expanding number of international instruments, conventions and declarations relating to medical research and to the functions of ethics review committees. In the latest edition of *Law and Medical Ethics*, for example, Mason, McCall Smith and Laurie note the draft additional Protocol that was prepared to the Council of Europe's Convention on Human Rights and Biomedicine.[37] This Protocol sets out the broad general principles applying to research on human subjects. The international documents, in the same fashion as international conventions and declarations, vary in their influence on national

32 *National Statement on Ethical Conduct in Research Involving Humans*, prepared by the Australian Health Ethics Committee under the relevant provisions of the National Health and Medical Research Council Act, 1992 (Cth) and endorsed by the Australian Vice Chancellors' Committee, the Australian Research Council and the Learned Academies in 1999. It is a national research code of practice governing social as well as biomedical research.

33 *Ibid.* Chapter 6 – emergency, intensive, neo-natal and terminal care; and impaired capacity and unconscious patients.

34 *Ibid.* Principles 1.1, 1.2, 1.3 and 1.4 in particular.

35 See Chalmers, D. and Pettit, P., 'Ethics Towards a Consensual Culture in the Ethical Review of Research', (1998) *Med J of Aust*, (for the AHEC) 168(2), 79-82.

36 See Chalmers, D., 'Research Ethics in Australia' commissioned paper for National Bioethics Advisory Commission, USA available at: http://www.georgetown.edu/research/nrcbl/nbac/human/overvol2.html.

37 Mason, J.K., McCall Smith and Laurie (6th ed), *op cit*, p. 572.

codes of research practice. They may be divided into two classes of the *direct* or the *referential*.

In the *direct* category are the *Guidelines for Good Clinical Practice*[38] published by the International Conference of Harmonisation that brings together the regulatory authorities of Europe, Japan and the United States. These guidelines have been recommended for adoption by the regulatory bodies of all countries with the aim of providing '... public assurance that the rights, safety and well-being of trial subjects are protected, consistent with the principle that have their origin in the *Declaration of Helsinki*, and that the clinical trial data are credible'.[39] Also of considerable direct influence is the Council of the European Union's Directive relating to research in the development of medicinal products, which emphasise good medical practice as:

> a set of internationally recognised ethical and scientific quality requirements which must be observed for designing, conducting, recording and reporting clinical trials that involve the participation of human subjects. Compliance with this good practice provides assurance that the rights, safety and well-being of prior subjects are protected, and that the results of the clinical trial are credible.[40]

Increasingly, National Codes are being revised by reference to developing international standards. The UNESCO *Declaration on the Human Genome and Human Rights*,[41] as an example, states that '[n]o research ... concerning the human genome ... should prevail over respect for the human rights, fundamental freedoms and human dignity of individuals or ... groups of people'.[42] The Declaration does not create binding national legal obligations. Similarly, the code of good manufacturing practice issued by the various therapeutic goods administration organisations in different countries are based on international standards.

In the larger *referential* category are the myriad of international documents that are referred to and may be considered in revisions of National Codes, such as the International *Ethical Guidelines for Biomedical Research Involving Human Subjects*, published by the Council of International Organisations of Medical Sciences (CIOMS) and the World Health Organisation in 1993.[43] Apart from these international documents there also is a fair degree of national copycatting from the national research ethics codes of other countries. For example, the Australian

38 CPMP/ICH, *Note for Guidance and Good Clinical Practice*, and the EU Directive on Good Clinical Practice.

39 Guideline E6: 1996.

40 European Parliament and Council of Europe Directive 201/20/EC, 4 April 2001, Art. 1(2).

41 Promulgated by the General Conference, UNESCO, 29th Session on 11 November 1997.

42 Art. 10

43 These Guidelines were some of the first to include ethical guidelines in relation to research conducted in developing countries. These particular guidelines were carefully considered by the Australian Health Committee in its publication of the current *National Statement on Ethical Conduct in Research Involving Humans*.

National Statement on Ethical Conduct in Research Involving Humans was developed with close reference to the content, wording and ideas in the United States Code of Federal Regulations dealing with research involving humans, the Canadian Code of Ethical Conduct for Research Involving Humans[44] and guidelines applying in the United Kingdom[45] and New Zealand.[46]

Research Ethics: Future Directions

The national biotechnology policies of developed countries have been supported generally with burgeoning increases in funding and investment in medical and health research. Increased research activity has brought pressures, many of them common internationally, that suggest increased regulation and accountability is the direction for the future evolution of the ethics review system. In addition to the increased volume of research, there have been major shifts in research practices resulting from greater emphasis on commercialisation, multi-centre collaborations, databases and genetic research. Many of these issues were considered in a joint report by the Australian Health Ethics Committee and the Australian Law Reform Commission published in 2003, titled *Essentially Yours: A Report into the Protection of Genetic Information in Australia*[47] (ALRC/AHEC Report). Dr Francis Collins[48] described the report as 'a truly phenomenal job, placing Australia ahead of what the rest of the world is doing'.[49]

The ALRC/AHEC Report makes recommendations across the spectrum of activities touching on human genetics, including health care, genetic testing, discrimination in employment and insurance, DNA fingerprinting and parentage testing. Importantly, the recommendations ranged over the regulation of human genetic research, in general and of human genetic databases and tissue collections in particular. However, it is the specific recommendations about genetic research and research governance that will be considered in the wider context of the future development of research ethics.

44 The Medical Research Council, the Natural Sciences and Engineering Research Council and the Social Science developed this Tri-Council document and Humanities Research Council of Canada was published in 1997.

45 Royal College of Physicians, *Guidelines on the Practice of Ethics Committees on Medical Research Involving Humans*, London, 1996.

46 Health Research Council of New Zealand, *Ministry of Health Review of the Ethical Review Structure in New Zealand*, September 1997.

47 Report 96 of 2003.

48 Head of the United States National Human Genome Research Institute and Chair of the Human Genome Project and its successor the International Haplotype Mapping Project.

49 News release XIX International Congress of Genetics Melbourne July 5-9 2003.

Research Ethics Committees

Broadly, research ethics committees are required to review and approve research Protocols by ensuring the free and informed consent of research participants and that the expected benefits of the Protocol do not take precedence over the rights of the individual. However, it was perhaps inevitable that a system based originally in institutions, rather than organised at a national level, would develop idiosyncratic characteristics. In Australia,[50] by the mid 1990s an Inquiry was established to investigate a number of issues within the ethics review system – workload pressures, lack of scientific expertise, absence of training opportunities, members' potential legal liability, non-pharmaceutical company sponsored clinical trials, lack of coordination between ethics committees dealing with multi-centre research, project monitoring and the over-representation of researcher and institutional membership on research ethics committees. Some years later, the US National Bioethics Advisory Committee Report,[51] echoed a number of these concerns and identified 'a time for change' in protecting research participants in the United States. In particular, the Report noted the need for Federal legislation to protect participants in both publicly and privately sponsored research with a single independent Federal Office for Human Research Oversight; requirements for education, certification and accreditation of Committees; review of IRB membership with the inclusion of members who represent perspectives of participants unaffiliated with the institution; emphasising the informed consent process rather than editorialising documentation; improving and strengthening privacy; investigating the need for compensation programs and better resourcing of IRBs.[52] These concerns about research ethics committees are common in the United Kingdom,[53] New Zealand[54] and Canada.[55]

Criticisms are often leveled against the ethics review system – in many jurisdictions – particularly that it lacks traditional enforcement mechanisms to ensure compliance. In Australia, for example, research ethics committees are not accredited and are not restricted in the types of research they may review.[56] There are no ethics training requirements for members of these committees. The national committee, the Australian Health Ethics Committee (AHEC), has no power to sanction researchers

50 See *Report of the Review of the Role and Functions of Institutional Ethics Committees*, Report to the Commonwealth Minister for Health and Family Services AGPS, May 1995 (Chair, Professor D. Chalmers).

51 National Bioethics Advisory Commission Report, *supra cit.*

52 *Ibid.*, Recs 2.1, 2.2; 3.1-3.4; 3.9, 3.10; 5.1, 5.3; 5.4; 6.6 and 7.1 respectively.

53 See McLean, S.A.M., 'Regulating Research and Experimentation: A View from the UK', 2004, 32 *J of Law Med & Ethics*, 604-612.

54 Dawson, J. and Peart, N., *The Law of Research: A Guide*, U. of Otago Press, 2003 pp. 47-60.

55 Downie, J., 'Protecting health research subjects: a jurisdictional analysis', (2003) Special Edition *Health L J*, 207-242.

56 In practice, however, large-scale international clinical research trials are generally considered by a limited number of large hospital-based committees.

breaching the guidelines in the *National Statement* nor committees that fail adequately to monitor their approved projects, beyond threats to withdraw public funding or naming the institution in the Annual Report to Parliament. The National Bioethics Advisory Commission echoed these concerns in the United States and recommended a range of initiatives to improve the research review system including education for IRB members; accreditation of IRBs; independent risk-benefit assessment; investigator disclosure of interests; additional protections for vulnerable groups; compensation for participants suffering direct harm; review of multi-site research; and, reduced threats to privacy.[57] The NBAC concluded that 'a comprehensive and effective oversight system is essential to uniformly protect the rights and welfare of participants while permitting ethically and scientifically responsible research to proceed without undue delay'.[58]

In Australia, the ALRC/AHEC Report recommended a range of ways to strengthen the ethics review system by balancing membership of research ethics committees, improving expertise and advice; monitoring the conduct of research approved (e.g. by random checks on research institutions); improving resources, education and training, and, accountability in reporting. The Report recommended that the NHMRC should review the need for an *accreditation* system for committees that are involved in the ethical review of human genetic research projects.[59] Secondly, the Report recommended that the mechanisms for compliance and enforcement of the *National Statement* should be strengthened,[60] particularly, to ensure private research bodies, involved in commercialisation of human genetic research, comply. Finally, the Report recommended that the code of research practice, the National Statement, be enforceable through legislation. These recommendations were directly aimed at improving the consistency, efficiency, transparency and accountability of research ethics committees.

Some countries have already revised their research ethics review arrangements. In New Zealand, institutional research ethics committees continue, but health and disability research approvals in the regions were transferred to Health and Disability Ethics Committees (HDECs). Regional HDECs and institutional ethics committees are accredited by the national Health Research Council Ethics Committee (HRCEC)[61] and are required to comply with the Operational Standards for Ethics Committees issued by the Minister of Health. If an institutional ethics committee, public or private, applies for accreditation by the HRCEC, it is also required to comply with the Operational Standards.[62] In the UK, Local Research Ethical Committees (LRECs) are set up by Health Authorities and are regulated by guidelines and standards issued

57 National Bioethics Advisory Commission Report Vol 1, *supra cit.*

58 *Ibid.*, at Rec. 2.2 at 28.

59 Rec 17-2.

60 Rec 14-1.

61 See s 25 Health Research Council Act 1990 (NZ) for the other functions of the Committee.

62 See Dawson, J. and Peart, N., *The Law of Research: A Guide,* U. of Otago Press, 2003 Chapter 3 'Research Ethics Committees', pp. 47-60.

through the Central Office for Research Ethics Committees in the Department of Health.[63] There is a discernable trend to increased regulation.

Ethics in Genetic Research

Since the publication of the human genome sequence in 2001[64] the volume and intensity of genomic research has increased. This research is moving from the sequencing of the gene to an understanding of 'full systems biology'.[65] There has been a correlative increase in commercial activity to translate research into profitable diagnostic and therapeutic products. Pharmaceutical companies are looking beyond the single-fits-all blockbuster drug discovery strategy to personalised therapies through pharmacogenomic approaches to develop new drugs and therapeutic applications through genetic research. The two approaches are SNPs or gene expression profiling but there are reliability limits to RNA microarrays for the latter.[66] Others cautiously suggest that pharmacogenomics is a genetic variation on the theme of patient stratification.

Genetic research involves the traditional balance between the value of scientific freedom and protection of research participants' rights, in an increasingly privatised commercial research environment, but with an additional essential aspect. Genetic research can uncover information, not only about an individual, but also about that person's parents, siblings, children and even more distant blood relations. This prophetic potential has prompted many counties to develop codes of practice for ethical conduct in human genetic research. Australia was one of the first countries to establish such guidelines. The National Statement sets out a regime for human genetic research and contains the basic pillars of *consent* and *review*. Research ethics committees should satisfy themselves that no contestable or dubious ethical values are assumed by the research protocol; confidentiality and privacy of stored genetic information is assured for identified or potentially identifiable participants; future research and communication of research results is considered; identifying information must not be released or transferred without written consent of the individual. There are also some 12 considerations that ought to be addressed by researchers and the ethics committee *before* approval for the research involving the prospective collection genetic material and information.[67]

---

63 See Department of Health, *Arrangements for NHS Research Ethics Committees*, 2001 discussed in Mason, McCall Smith and Laurie, *op cit*, at paras 19.14-19.18, pp. 576-578.

64 *Science: Special Issue* (2001) Vol 291 1145-1344 and *Nature: Special Issue* (2001) Vol 409 745-964.

65 Genetic research has diversified into new scientific pathways of *transcriptomics* (DNA transcribing for mRNA, gene expression monitoring), *proteomics* (protein function, protein structure and protein interactions) and *metabolomics* (study of metabolism function).

66 See 'Personalized Arthritis Therapy', (2005) 25:4 *Genetic Engineering News*, pp. 13-14.

67 Including that they are free to refuse consent without giving reasons; arrangements to ensure the privacy and confidentiality; if the research may reveal information of potential

Commendable as these guidelines may be, the ALRC/AHEC Report recommended further regulation of human genetic research recognising the complexities and sensitivities of such research. The Report recommended a review of the circumstances and grounds for approving use of genetic material without individual consent. Any such waiver of consent should be reported to the AHEC[68] and the National Statement amended to provide clear guidelines about obtaining consent to unspecified future human genetic research.[69] The Report also made recommendations to further improve ethical standards with respect to developing: mechanisms for coding DNA identifying samples in different research contexts; promoting the use of *independent intermediaries* between the researcher and the sample holder to hold the codes linking the genetic samples to the individual identifiers; ensuring that participants are fully informed of the implementations of testing of genetic samples; and policies for full disclosure of all commercial arrangements.[70]

Privacy in Research and Tissue Samples

The various national codes of research practice generally include guidelines to assure the confidentiality and privacy of research information. Broadly, distinctions are drawn between information that *identifies* or *potentially identifies* a research participant (sometimes referred to as 'coded') and information that is *de-identified* and cannot be linked to an individual research participant (sometimes referred to as 'anonymised'). Privacy guidelines focus on the former. These distinctions are critical in the design, conduct and reporting of research in general and human genetic research and research on human tissue, in particular.

Privacy legislation in many countries is often based on the influential OECD Information Privacy Principles published in 1980. These principles[71] brought a measure of consistency to the national approaches to privacy by setting standards for the collection, storage, release, access and accountability for personal information. Later EU privacy directives, particularly the Directive on Data Protection on trans-border data flow[72] maintained this principled approach. In Australia, for example, the Commonwealth Privacy Act 1988 introduced Information Privacy Principles

---

importance to their own or family future health; if it is proposed to approach relatives, and if so the protocol and consent requirements before such an approach; that genetic material and information may have uses unrelated to the ethics approved; and, if their genetic material is to be disposed of on completion of the research or after a further period of storage; and.(Chapter16.10).

68 Rec 15-1.

69 Rec 15-2.

70 Rec 16-1.

71 Collection Limitation Principle; Data Quality Principle; Purpose Specification Principle; Use Limitation Principle; Openness Principle; Individual Participation Principle; Accountability Principle.

72 95/46/EC, see also *Directive on Telecommunications Privacy* (97/66/EC now 2002/58/EC).

(IPPs), covering the collection, storage, release, access to and challenge to personal information but was limited to federal agencies. Section 95 of this Act required special guidelines to be drafted by the AHEC to cover privacy of personal information in research involving federal agencies. The remit of this Act was extended significantly by the introduction of National Privacy Principles governing private sector privacy.[73] However, the application of these provisions was unclear in relation to research, particularly genetic research, on human tissue samples.

The ALRC/AHEC Report[74] recommends the harmonisation of all federal and state health privacy legislation applying to genetics in Australia.[75] The most interesting and unique recommendation of the Report centres on the proposal that genetic samples should be included in the general definition of 'Personal Information'.[76] This recommendation recognises the widely accepted view that bodily tissue samples, when subjected to genetic analysis, provide *information* on that person and their family. By treating the results of a genetic test carried out on a bodily sample as information attracts the existing protections, regulatory regime and enforcement procedures of the privacy legislation.

Research Ethics and Conflicts of Interest

Health research is conducted in an increasingly commercialised environment. Many developed nations have issued biotechnology strategies that include medical research as one of the key drivers of commercial and knowledge-based[77] development. The earlier distinctions between public and private interests are becoming increasingly blurred as governments promote and fund public and private partnerships and collaborations.[78] These developments are challenging the core values of science, described by Robert Merton as 'universalism, collegiality, disinterestedness and organised scepticism'.[79] Patents and licences are more common in the commercialised research environment and are replacing the traditional peer-reviewed publication outcomes of research.[80] Many small start-up companies rely on these symbiotic

---

73 See Privacy (Private Sector) Amendment Act 2001 (Cth).

74 ALRC/AHEC *Essentially Yours: The Protection of Human Genetic Information in Australia*, Report 96 March 2003.

75 *Ibid.*, Rec 7-1.

76 Commonwealth *Privacy Act* 1988, s 6.

77 Sakaiya, T., *Knowledge-Value Revolution*, New York, Kodansha American Inc. 1992.

78 See Chalmers, D. and Nicol, D., 'Commercialisation of Biotechnology: Public Trust and Research', (2004) 6 *Int. J. Biotechnology*, 116-133.

79 *The Sociology of Science*, University of Chicago Press, Chicago 1973; see also Nicol D., Otlowski M. and Chalmers D. 'Consent, Commercialisation and Benefit Sharing', (2001) 9 *Journal of Law and Medicine* 80.

80 Nicol, D. and Neilsen J., 'An invitation to participate in an enquiry: assingnment and licensing of biotechnology patents', (2002) *Australasian Biotechnology*, 12(2), 35-37; see also 'How human geneticists in US view commercialization of the HGP', (2001) 29 *Nature Genetics* 15.

partnerships with larger companies as a source for their research funding. These partnerships will include profit sharing arrangements between the parties. Closer affiliations and changing research practices are raising sceptical concerns about the independence and disinterestedness of researchers. The National Institutes for Health in the USA has taken a tougher stand on conflicts of interest and recently published stricter ethical regulations on extracurricular activities and interests of their staff.[81] This builds on guidance to assist IRBs in assessing conflicting financial interests of researchers seeking ethical approval for their project. This is an increasingly complex area in the mixed public and private research environment.[82]

Greater commercialisation has placed additional responsibilities on research ethics review committees. The traditional role of protection of the participants in research now extends to overseeing the ethical integrity of the commercial research relations. In many cases, Ethics Review Committees have been placed in an invidious situation. They are left, in some cases, to review the declaration and decide on a course of action. Most countries have avoided introducing hard-line conflict of interest rule, but rather, have preferred the *soft-touch* approach. For example, in Australia, a researcher is *not* required to disclose every interest to research participants. Rather, the researcher is required to declare any business or other similar association with a supplier of a drug, surgical or other device to be used in a trial. The Ethics Committee must examine the budget and should be satisfied that:

> (a) payment in money or kind would not cause researchers to apply pressure to an individuals so as to obtain their consent to participate, (b) payment in money or kind could not influence the findings of the research, (c) there will be disclosure to the research participants of relevant aspects of those budgets; and (d) funding is sufficient to conduct and complete the trial so that participants are not disadvantaged by premature cessation.[83]

Interestingly many Australian research ethics committees have gone beyond the National Statement and require disclosure of commercial arrangements[84] without creating difficulties. Leaving the conflict of interest for adjudication by an ethics committee is a weak response. The National Bioethics Advisory Commission did not take a hard line to the avoidance of conflicts of interest but rather use the euphemism '*managing* conflicts of interests' (emphasis added) in recommending that sponsors

---

81 *Supplemental Standards of Ethical Conduct and Financial Disclosure Requirements for Employees of the Department of Health and Human Services*, February 3, 2005 see: http://a257.g.akamaitech.net/7/257/2422/01jan20051800/edocket.access.gpo.gov/2005/pdf/05-2029.pdf, accessed on 16/05/05. These new regulations have been described as 'punitive and draconian' see (2005) 25:5 *Genetic Engineering News*, pp. 1, 14-16.

82 US Department of Health and Human Services, in (2004) 198 *Bull Med Ethics* (May) 9.

83 See *National Statement for Ethical Conduct in Research Involving Humans*, *supra cit*, chapters 12.5 and 12.6.

84 For example, the ARC Blood Service HREC requires disclosure of commercialisation intentions as a condition of release of samples for research. These samples are almost invariably released in de-identified form.

and institutions should '... develop policies and mechanisms to identify and manage all types of institutional, IRB and investigator conflicts of interest. In particular, all relevant conflicts of interest should be disclosed to participants'.[85] The disclosure of conflict of interest[86] to participants is tending to become the norm in other countries[87] and International Statements.[88]

The mingling of public and private interest in research in the new era of commercialization requires increased accountability and regulation in the systems of ethical review. Detecting and avoiding conflicts of interest by ensuring that full disclosures of interest are made is important for maintaining public trust. Public trust was the focus when the United Kingdom Parliamentary Select Committee on Science and Technology discussed the crisis of trust in society's attitudes towards science[89] and noted particular concerns about challenges to scientific independence because:

> the concept of independence has become problematic, particularly because of the increasing commercialization of the research. In our view, scientists must robustly protect and vindicate their independence. Sponsorships and affiliations must be openly declared, [and] ... research output is submitted to peer review and published in the academic literature.[90]

Public trust requires assurances that the system of independent ethics review is, in fact, independent.[91]

Multi-centre Research and Data-linkage

Medical research and clinical trials have frequently been conducted, not at an institutional level, but on a multi-centre scale. The need for a system of centralised ethics review is one of the issues frequently raised in the literature on ethics review. A lack of centralised ethical approval for multi-centre research has been a frequent

---

85 NBAC Report at Recommendation 3.8.

86 Nicol D., Otlowski M. and Chalmers, D., *loc cit.*

87 These include: UK Medical Research Council, *Human Tissue and Biological Samples for Use in Research. Interim Operational and Ethical Guidelines Issues by the Medical Research Council* (1999); Canadian *Tri-Council Policy Statement, Ethical Conduct for Research Involving Humans* (1998); USA 'Federal Policy for the Protection of Human Subjects' (45 CFR 46) and National Bioethics Advisory Commission, *Research Involving Human Biological Materials: Ethical Issues and Policy Guidance* (1999).

88 For example, HUGO, *Statement on the Principled Conduct of Genetics Research* (1996); HUGO Ethics Committee, *Statement on DNA Sampling: Control and Access* (1998); HUGO Ethics Committee, *Statement on Benefit Sharing* (2000); HUGO, *Statement on Patenting of DNA Sequences* (2000).

89 United Kingdom Parliament, House of Lords Select Committee on Science and Technology 2000 *Third Report: Science and Society*, summary at: http://www.publications.parliament.uk/pa/Idi999000/Idselect/Idsctech/38/3801.htm.

90 *Ibid.*, 50, paras 13-14.

91 Chalmers, D. and Nicol, D., *loc cit.*

cause for researcher complaint about delays, inconsistencies and inefficiencies. Ethical approval for multi-centre research often involves collaborations and partnerships between public and private commercial organisations. Establishing procedures to facilitate such research without compromising proper ethical safeguards is a challenge for review systems. In the UK multi-centre research ethics committees have been introduced to accommodate the 'need to extend research so as to include a number of departments'.[92] Similarly, in New Zealand the Health and Disability Ethics Committees (HDECs) are organized at a regional level and can provide a regional approval as well as reducing 'the potential for conflicts of interest [within an institution]'.[93] In Australia, there is no central approval avenue but the National Statement set up two procedures for handling multi-centre research. First, an ethics committee can adopt the reasons and ethical decisions of other committees, or secondly, institutions may agree to nominate the primary, ethical and scientific assessment process which is subject to the approval of another participating institution's research ethics review committee.

Developments in human genetics have increased the level of multi-centre research aiming to develop research platforms, diagnostic tests or new therapies. The sequencing of the DNA of the human genome was published in 2001[94] and was achieved with the convergence of two separate lines of research, one was 'human genetics, the study of patterns of inheritance ... and the other was molecular biology, which studies the stuff of which genes are made: DNA'.[95] Banked human tissue and databases of health information are now providing rich sources for gene and disease identification studies beyond their traditional and established uses for clinical studies and diagnostic pathology.

The use of these databases has evolved and expanded over recent years and, with data-linkage, they provide many different research purposes. Developments in bio-informatics are facilitating the linkage of information on different database with individual health records and with research and quality assurance projects. Data-linkage is enabling researchers and health care professionals to conduct research, in a manner inconceivable as little as a decade ago. Researchers have been promoting data-linkage for population health research and epidemiological studies to enable not only national but international collaborations. It has been claimed, for example, that had effective data-linkage and multicentre ethical approval been in place, the high incidence of coronary attacks suffered by and poor monitoring of users of the drug, Vioxx, could have been detected a number of years before disparate reports were brought together to establish the serious adverse effects of this arthritis drug. In

92 Mason, McCall Smith and Laurie, G.T., *op cit* (6th ed) at para 19.15, pp. 576-577. See also Fitzgerald, M. and Phillips, P. 'A five nation Comparative Study of Centralised and Non-Centralised Ethics Review', available at: http://www.ethicsproject.com.

93 See Dawson, J. and Peart, N. *op cit*, p. 51.

94 *Science: Special Issue* (2001) Vol 291, 1145-1344 and *Nature: Special Issue* (2001), Vol 409, 745-964.

95 Sulston, J. and Ferry, G., *The Common Thread A Story of Science, Politics, Ethics, and the Human Genome*, London, Transworld.

Australia, the National Statement addresses research on human tissue,[96] but there are currently no specific guidelines on genetic databanks. There have been major efforts to develop a harmonised approach to ethics and privacy of data linkage to enable health department, hospital, research institute and doctors' records to be linked with a number of other specialist databases.[97] Clearly, data linkage arouses concerns about individual privacy and the ethical motivation and conduct of such work. Where tissue or information is provided de-identified (with the donor codes retained and only accessible by an independent intermediary body), there are fewer privacy concerns.[98] In many countries, the privacy legislation is not uniform and the fractured and dislocated ethical review system, based within institutions, places a significant barrier to the responsible development of data linkage systems. In Australia, privacy protection was extended by the National Privacy Principles (NPPs) to the private sector in 2001[99] and now covers private sector hospitals and pathology services. However, this legislation does not cover state agencies such as universities and most hospitals that are established under state acts. This is a major gap in the regulatory regime for the protection for individuals.

The ALRC/AHEC Report mentioned genetic databases,[100] but its recommendations essentially signal further work in this area. There is a general view that the current regulation of human genetic research databases is inadequate and requires reform. The Report recognises the use of genetic databases, both in the private and public sectors, and recommends that the NRMRC provide ethical guidance on the establishment, governance and operation of human genetic research databases, including the registration of these databases on the public register. The Report also recommended the use of a gene trustee system to protect the privacy of samples and information stored in databases. Correctly, the Report recognises the privacy concerns involved with such databases that can hold large amounts of genetic samples and information. An issue of particular relevance to the operation of human genetic research databases is the extent to which researchers obtain consent for unspecified future research. The Report also recognises the potential for complaint and public criticism from the inappropriate use of or access to genetic samples involving a *waiver* of individual consent. The Report recommends that, until the review of the National Statement, research ethics committees should report annually on any research project involving a waiver of individual consent.[101] The Report also

---

96 *National Statement on Ethical Conduct in Research Involving Humans*, 1999 Principles 15.1-15.9 on Human Tissue.

97 See, for example, the initiative of Professor Fiona Stanley, with the Australian Research Alliance for Children and Youth, available at: http://www.aracy.org.au/datanetwork_privacywkshp.htm.

98 For example, the Australia Red Cross Blood Service may release blood samples to researchers for research but holds the identifying codes as an *intermediary* between researcher and donor.

99 See Privacy (Private Sector) Amendment Act 2001 (Cth).

100 Recs 18-1 to 18-3.

101 *Ibid.*, Rec 15-1.

recommended that other collections of tissue be regulated and recommended that the Australian Health Ministers' Advisory Council, in consultation with state and territory Attorney-General's Departments and police services, the Human Genetics Commission of Australia and the NHMRC, develop nationally consistent rules governing the collection, use, storage and disclosure of genetic information held in other tissue collections, including samples in pathology labs.[102]

Conclusion

The dominant theme in research ethics, whether in health and medicine or social science, remains the appropriate balance between the values of scientific freedom and the protection of the essential dignity of the individual research participant, particularly the vulnerable participant. This theme has become a sharper with the major shift of national research efforts towards greater commercial private sector involvement in the research environment. In this regard, public trust is a precondition to the success of health research. In Australia, the government has acknowledged this and made a formal commitment to safeguard health and the environment in promotion of its biotechnology strategy.

The leitmotifs in research ethics are the content and enforceability of codes of research ethics and the future of the institutionally based research ethics review committee in globalised multi-centre projects. The ALRC/AHEC Report *Essentially Yours: A Report into the Protection of Genetic Information in Australia*[103] contains recommendations that are also moving in the direction of stricter regulatory framework for research ethical guidelines and for research ethics committees. The ALRC/AHEC recommendations are in harmony with the stricter regulatory framework implemented non-human research. In these areas, the Australian Parliament has introduced a statutory licensing scheme for GMOs[104] and animal research ethics committees are creatures of statute.[105] Similarly, the controversial area of human embryo and stem cell research[106] is governed by a statutory licensing scheme. The ALRC/AHEC Report favours increased regulation and questions whether Australia's, approximately 220 research ethics committees can continue with their voluntary membership and without mandatory compliance with the National Statement or formal accreditation.

102 Rec 19-1.

103 *Supra cit.*

104 Gene Technology Act 2000 (Cth).

105 Established under state and territory Animal Welfare Acts.

106 Research involving Human Embryos Act 2002 (Cth).

Chapter 7

Ethical and Policy Issues Related to Medical Error and Patient Safety

Gerard Magill

Introduction

In the United States the debate on medical error has created a great deal of heat from the perspective of ethics. Whether discourse on its concomitant topic of patient safety can generate effective light for policy and practice is very much an open question. Certainly, the public's interest in medical error and patient safety has generated considerable attention on the need for continuous quality improvement in healthcare. By reviewing these neuralgic issues in US healthcare, this chapter hopes to shed light on an increasingly urgent problem for healthcare globally. This analysis is presented as a modest tribute to the extraordinary insight that Ken Mason has provided for so many years on the interface between ethics and policy in an abundance of health related controversies.[1]

Increasing Awareness about Medical Errors in US Healthcare

At the turn of the millennium, the US Institute of Medicine (IOM) published a routine report on an issue that generated a revolution among the public and scholars alike. The controversy centered around the claim that between 44,000 and 98,000 patients die each year in US healthcare as a result of medical error. Many of those patients may have been very sick upon admission to the hospitals, but they were expected to leave alive; they were not dying. Yet they left hospital dead as a result of medical error. Based on the higher estimate in the report, the sensational way of reporting the data was to say the figures were the equivalent of a 747 jet going down every day killing all its passengers. Not surprisingly, the media had a feeding frenzy, raising an all too obvious jibe: hospital beds should post a warning that medical care can

1 This chapter was developed (with copyright permission) from teaching materials in a 12-hour online ethics education program on Patient Safety for health professionals. The international online program was developed in partnership between DIA Learning and the Center for Health Care Ethics at Saint Louis University. See: www.dialearning.com.

seriously damage your health! Bearing such dramatic news, the IOM report carried a rather soothing title, *To Err is Human: Building a Safer Health System*.[2]

However, the IOM report did not fall from the sky. It was the result of nearly a decade of scholarly studies. In 1991, a landmark study was published, known as the Harvard Medical Practice Study,[3] reporting data on medical error from 1984; many other studies followed, such as on the prevention of medical errors, on the need for systems analysis, and on the liability of organisations for patient safety.[4] The result of these studies on medical errors in the 1990s focused attention on the issues of who should be accountable for avoiding medical errors and who should be responsible for promoting patient safety.[5]

In 1998, the IOM formed the 'Quality of Health Care in America Committee' to review an emerging problem – the extent of medical error in US healthcare. In 2000, the IOM issued its report extrapolating from results of the Harvard Medical Practice Study and from a study in Colorado and Utah in the early 1990s,[6] to identify the estimated high number of patient deaths in US healthcare each year as a result of medical error. Naturally, such astounding figures were disputed.[7] But in July 2004 'Health Grades Inc.' (a Colorado consulting firm) suggested that the numbers of US deaths from medical error could be more than twice as high as projected by the 2000 IOM report.[8] Whatever the numbers, most accept that the IOM figures at least indicate a very serious problem for medical care and public health alike. By the time the IOM issued its report, there was an increasing recognition of the need to shift the onus of responsibility away from individual professionals and to highlight systems and processes upon which professionals rely for the clinical care of patients. The IOM report wanted to invigorate a national agenda to reduce errors in healthcare

2 Institute of Medicine, Committee on Quality of Health Care in America, *To Err is Human: Building a Safer Health System*, Washington, DC, National Academy Press, 2000.

3 For discussion, see website: http://qhc.bmjjournals.com/cgi/content full/13/2/151; for more information, also see website: http://content.nejm.org/cgi/content/abstract/324/6/370?ijkey=a85a080887f97a7ea7857919df709dcl6be6fl5e&keytype2=tf_ipsecsha.

4 Brennan, T.A. *et al.*, 'Incidence of Adverse Events and Negligence in Hospitalized Patients: Results of the Harvard Medical Practice Study', *New England Journal of Medicine*, 324 (1991): 370-376; Leape, L.L. *et al.*, 'Preventing Medical Injury', *Qual. Rev. Bull*, 19 (1993): 144-149; Leape, L.L. *et al.*, 'Systems analysis of adverse drug events', *JAMA*, 274 (1995): 35-43; Noble, A.A and Brennan, T.A., 'Managing care in the era of Systems-Think: organizational liability and patient safety', *Journal of Law, Medicine, & Ethics*, 29 (2001): 290-304.

5 See, Leape, L.L., 'Error in Medicine', *JAMA*, 272 (1994): 1851-1857; Leape, L.L. *et al.*, 'Promoting Patient Safety by Preventing Medical Error', *JAMA*, 280 (1998): 1444-1447. For data on systems that reduce medical error, see: www.leapfroggroup.org.

6 Thomas, E.J. *et al.*, 'Incidence and Types of Adverse Events and Negligent Care in Utah and Colorado', *Medical Care*, 38 (2000): 261-271.

7 McDonald, C.J. *et al.*, 'Deaths Due to Medical Errors are Exaggerated in Institute of Medicine Report', *JAMA*, 284 (2000): 93-95.

8 Health Grades Quality Study, *Patient Safety in American Hospitals*, Colorado, Health Grades Inc, 2004.

and to improve patient safety. It certainly precipitated quite a firestorm as it sought to engage ethics with policy and practice.[9]

The IOM followed up on its report with another two important studies. The original report in 2000, *To Err is Human*, emphasised the need to focus upon systems as the main cause of medical error. In 2001, the IOM published a related report, *Crossing the Quality Chasm*.[10] This report focused upon the lack of coordination in healthcare that prevents the provision of many medical interventions already recognised and established as benefiting patients. That is, the report addressed the environment of healthcare delivery to highlight the problem of medical error. This report criticised weak systems in the quality and delivery of care because they can increase the probability of error.[11] The study urged a reconfiguration of healthcare delivery in a manner that would enhance patient safety. Then, in 2002 the IOM issued another follow-up report, *Leadership by Example*.[12] This report focused upon the need for urgent improvement in the nation's healthcare safety and quality of care, emphasising quality enhancement processes for about one-third of Americans in six different government programs: Medicare (40 million), Medicaid (42.3 million), the State Children's Health Insurance Program (4.6 million), the Department of Defense (8.4 million), the Veterans Health Administration program (4 million) and the Indian Health Services program (1.4 million). The report took the opportunity of dealing with federally funded government programmes in healthcare as an obvious starting point in the national agenda for promoting patient safety. That is, the report exhorted the government in its federal programmes to establish better quality standards in reporting requirements for clinical data and in standards for purchasing to reward and foster higher levels of quality. Moreover, the report encouraged the development of updated delivery models in healthcare and the expansion of applied health services research to support quality enhancement.

In addition to the follow-up IOM reports, there was an upsurge in landmark studies and publications on medical error and patient safety. For example, in 2000, the National Coalition on Health Care and the Institute for Healthcare Improvement published a study on reducing medical error and improving patient safety, praising the

---

9 See Brennan, T.A., 'The *IOM* Report on Medical Error – Could it Do Harm?', *New England Journal of Medicine*, 342 (2000): 1123-1125; Sharp, V.A., 'Promoting Patient Safety: An Ethical Basis for Policy Deliberation', *Hastings Center Report*, 33:5 (2003): S3-S18.

10 Institute of Medicine, Committee on Quality of Health Care in America, *Crossing the Quality Chasm: A New Health System for the 21st Century*, Washington, DC, National Academy Press, 2001.

11 For a commentary on the first two IOM reports, see, McNeil, B.J., 'Shattuck Lecture – Hidden Barriers to Improvement in the Quality of Care', *New England Journal of Medicine*, 345:22 (2001): 1612-1620.

12 Institute of Medicine, Committee on Enhancing Federal Healthcare Quality Programs, *Leadership by Example: Coordinating Government Roles in Improving Health Care Quality*, Washington, DC: National Academy Press, 2002.

original IOM report.[13] Also in 2000, the American Hospital Association published an important study on adopting a systems approach to improve patient safety.[14] Another example is a study in 2002, in the *Archives of Internal Medicine*, reporting that drug errors occurred daily in one out of five doses in a typical 300-bed hospital.[15] The study focused on the problems arising from administering errors after a physician had properly prescribed for the patient. The data was all the more shocking in so far as the study focused on properly prescribed medications; it did not deal with errors linked with the wrong prescription of a drug by a physician or the wrong filling of a prescription in the pharmacy.

In 2002, the *New England Journal of Medicine* began a series of essays on patient safety.[16] One of these essays emphasised the differing views of physicians and the public on medical error, especially with regard to the disclosure of errors.[17] In the survey, 831 physicians and 1207 members of the public responded, and 35 per cent of the physicians and 42 per cent of the public reported errors in either their own care or a family member's care. Yet 86 per cent of the physicians held the view that medical errors in hospitals should remain confidential; not surprisingly, 62 per cent of the public claimed that information on such errors should be released. The understandable concern of physicians to retain confidentiality seems to have been inspired by a desire to enhance openness among colleagues and a preference to minimise public humiliation and lawsuits which might follow if errors were released. The IOM reports suggest that only remedying the underlying systems (for example, improving quality standards in clinical data reporting requirements) will effectively accomplish the goals of enhancing professional openness and diminishing professional shame for medical errors. A subsequent editorial in the *New York Times* excoriated the physicians in this report for their retrograde attitudes – the editorial emphasised that reform would occur only if the medical profession supported changes that expert groups had identified to reduce harm caused by medical errors.[18] Another

13 National Coalition on Health Care and the Institute for Healthcare Improvement, *Reducing Medical Errors and Improving Patient Safety*, Washington, DC, National Coalition on Health Care, 2000, 1-31, see esp. p. 3.

14 Spath, P.L. (ed), *Error Reduction in Health Care: A Systems Approach to Improving Patient Safety*, Washington, DC, AHA Press, 2000.

15 See, Barker, K.N. *et al.*, 'Medication Errors Observed in 36 Health Care Facilities', *Archives of Internal Medicine*, 162:16 (2002): 1897-1903; also see Haga, S.B and Burke, W., 'Using Pharmacogenetics to Improve Drug Safety and Efficacy', *JAMA*, 291:23 (2004): 2869-2871.

16 For example, see Leape, L.L. and Epstein, A.M., 'A Series on Patient Safety', *New England Journal of Medicine*, 347:16 (2002): 1272-74; Berwick, D.M., editorial, 'Errors Today and Errors Tomorrow', *New England Journal of Medicine*, 348: 25 (2003): 2570-2572.

17 Blendon, R.J. *et al.*, 'Views of Practicing Physicians and the Public on Medical Errors', *New England Journal of Medicine*, 347:24 (2002): 1933-1940.

18 Editorial, 'Errors That Kill Medical Patients', *New York Times*, December 18, 2002: A32.

essay in the *New England Journal of Medicine* made a related point, explaining that as a profession, physicians tend to be averse to conflict and oriented more to individual autonomy than to organisational effectiveness.[19] The resistant attitudes of clinicians and hospitals toward disclosure of medical error present a significant hurdle for patient safety advocates to traverse.[20]

In addition, national agencies published materials for their constituents to adopt more effective measures in reducing medical error and enhancing patient safety. For example, the Joint Commission on Accreditation of Healthcare Organisations (JACHO), a widely used voluntary organisation for accrediting US hospitals, published helpful manuals on issues related to patient safety and root cause analysis.[21] And the Agency for Healthcare Research and Quality updated indicators for patient safety to enable healthcare organisations to track problems.[22]

In sum, from the early 1990s there was a growing awareness of the problem of medical error in US healthcare. The national debate that followed the IOM report in 2000 led to significant developments in the quest to decrease and prevent medical errors and to enhance patient safety through continuous quality improvement in US healthcare, including the safety of human subjects in clinical research trials.[23] Also, there have been high-profile, landmark cases of medical or research error leading to death that elicited a great deal of ethics and policy review, such as the death of Jesica

---

19 Lee, T.H., 'A Broader Concept of Medical Errors', *New England Journal of Medicine*, 347:24 (2002): 1965-1967, at p. 1966.

20 For example, Gallagher, T.H. *et al.*, 'Patients' and Physicians Attitudes Regarding Disclosure of Medical Errors', *JAMA*, 289:8 (2003): 1001-1007; Lamb, R.M. *et al.*, 'Hospital Disclosure Practices: Results of a National Survey', *Health Affairs* 22:2 (2003): 73-83; Mello, M.M. *et al.*, 'The Leapfrog Standards: ready to Jump from Marketplace to Courtroom', *Health Affairs*, 22:2 (2003): 46-59.

21 Joint Commission on Accreditation of Healthcare Organizations, *Root Cause Analysis in Health Care* (2nd ed), Oakbrook Terrace, Illinois, Joint Commission Resources, 2003, and Joint Commission on Accreditation of Healthcare Organizations, *Patient Safety: Essentials for Health Care* (2nd ed), Oakbrook Terrace, Illinois, Joint Commission Resources, 2004.

22 Agency for Healthcare Research and Quality, *Patient Safety Indicators* (Version 2.1), Rockville, Maryland, March 2004.

23 Steinbrook, R., 'Trial Design and Patient Safety in Studies of Acute Respiratory Disease Syndrome', *New England Journal of Medicine*, 348:14 (2003): 1393-1401; Steinbrook, R., 'Trial Design and Patient Safety – The Debate Continues', *New England Journal of Medicine*, 349:7 (2003): 629-630; Meaney, M.E., 'Error Reduction, Patient Safety and Institutional Ethics Committees', *Journal of Law, Medicine & Ethics*, 32 (2004): 358-364; Capron, A.M., 'When Experiments go Wrong: the U.S. Perspective', *Journal of Clinical Ethics*, 15:1 (2004): 22-29.

Santillan after a transplant,[24] and the death of Jesse Gelsinger in a research protocol – the first US gene therapy death.[25]

In light of these developments, this chapter considers the controversial and complicated issues underlying medical error in order to identify appropriate principles and practical measures that can enhance patient safety in healthcare, especially considering the relevant ethical and policy implications. Certainly, the basic tenet of the above developments was the emphatic focus upon systems and processes rather than upon blaming individual professionals as the primary cause of medical error. This focus highlighted the role of systems failures rather than individual carelessness as the pervasive cause of medical errors. To clarify why this basic tenet has become so indispensable, this chapter analyses the major topics around which the current debate revolves on medical error and patient safety: describing different types of medical errors; identifying the tension between professional sanctions and patient safety as contrasting models to reduce medical error; explaining the importance of root cause analysis; and considering how to foster a culture of safety in healthcare.

Describing Different Types of Medical Errors

The theory of errors in the work of James Reason had a substantive influence on the IOM report in 2000, as summarised below.[26] The IOM report welcomed Reason's approach, highlighting the role of systems in accidents and explaining that a system can be understood as a set of interdependent elements that interact to achieve a common aim. It is worth noting that in healthcare a system can refer to many different entities, such as an integrated delivery system, a multi-hospital system and a system with many partners over a wide geographical area. Also, a system can refer to a smaller unit such as an operating room or an obstetrical unit. Specifically, the IOM report adopted Reason's theory to clarify different types of error.[27] There is a crucial distinction between mistakes and slips or lapses. First, a slip or lapse occurs when the action is not what was originally intended – that constitutes an error of execution. This does not mean that a slip or lapse is minor or unimportant – patients can die from them too. Second, in a mistake the action happens as planned but does not accomplish its intended outcome because the original, intended action

24 See, for example, Resnick, D., 'The Jesica Santillan Tragedy: Lessons Learned', *Hastings Center Report*, 33:4 (2003): 12-20; Camarow, A., 'Jesica's Story: One Mistake didn't Kill Her – the Organ Donor System was Fatally Flawed', *US News & World Report* (July 28-August 4, 2003): 51-54.

25 See Magill, G., 'Science, Ethics and Policy', in Magill, G. (ed), *Genetics and Ethics: An Interdisciplinary Study*, Saint Louis, Missouri, Saint Louis University Press, 2004, 253-283, at pp. 259-260.

26 The Institute of Medicine, *To Err Is Human*, 1-16; Reason J.T., *Human Error*, Cambridge, Cambridge University Press, 1990; and Reason J.T., *Managing the Risk of Organizational Accidents*, Aldershot, Ashgate, 1997.

27 Institute of Medicine, *To Err Is Human*, 'Why Do Errors Happen?', pp. 49-68.

was mistaken or wrong – that constitutes an error of planning. Hence, in a mistake or error the intention is not adequate and a failure of planning is involved. Also, the IOM report adopted the important distinction Reason drew between latent errors and active errors, a distinction that has become influential in healthcare analyses.[28] Active errors occur with frontline operators and their effects are felt more or less immediately. Latent errors typically are removed from the operator's control, such as by poor design. It is latent error that presents the greatest threat to safety in a complex system. However, typical responses to errors tend to dwell on active errors in so far as they focus upon the individuals responsible. But the failure of systems has a more important role in errors insofar as these errors tend to be linked with latent failures. So, identifying and fixing latent failures contributes more substantively to creating safer systems. In other words, for the IOM report, adopting Reason's scholarship, safety typically results from the interacting components of a system. That approach diminishes confidence in aligning safety with an individual professional, or healthcare department, or even in a medical device.[29]

The IOM adopted working definitions of safety and error as follows: it defined patient safety as freedom from accidental injury – this constitutes the primary safety goal from the patient's perspective; and it defined medical error as the failure of a planned action to be completed as intended or the use of a wrong plan to achieve an aim. However, not all errors result in harm to the patient. Hence, errors that cause patient injury are referred to as preventable adverse events.[30] For example, some estimate that as many as one-third of adverse drug events among outpatients are preventable or ameliorable.[31] In other words, an adverse event is an injury resulting from a medical intervention; it is not due to the original condition of the patient.

The IOM report explained that medical errors can occur at any stage of care, including diagnosis, treatment and preventive care.[32] Diagnostic errors can occur when there is a mistake or delay in clinical diagnosis, or when there is a failure to provide relevant or indicated tests, or when there is a failure to act on the results of

---

28 On latent and active errors, see Volpp, K.G.M. and Grande, D., 'Residents' Suggestions for Reducing Errors in Teaching Hospitals', *New England Journal of Medicine*, 348:9 (2003): 851-855.

29 See Feigal, D., *et al.*, 'Ensuring Safe and Effective Medical Devices', *New England Journal of Medicine*, 348:3 (2003): 191-192.

30 For discussion of adverse events, see, Vincent, C., 'Patient Safety, Understanding and Responding to Adverse Events', *New England Journal of Medicine*, 348:11 (2003): 1051-1056; also see Vincent, C. (ed), *Clinical Risk Management: Enhancing Patient Safety*, London, British Medical Journal, 2001.

31 Ghandi, T.K. *et al.*, 'Adverse Drug Events in Ambulatory Care', *New England Journal of Medicine*, 348:16 (2003): 1556-1564; Tierney, W.M., 'Adverse Outpatient Drug Events – A Problem and an Opportunity', *New England Journal of Medicine*, 348:16 (2003): 1587-1589; Gallagher, T.H., 'Medical Errors in the Outpatient Setting: Ethics in Practice', *Journal of Clinical Ethics*, 13:4 (2002): 291-300.

32 Institute of Medicine, *To Err Is Human*, 'Errors in Health Care: A Leading Cause of Death and Injury', pp. 26-48.

monitoring or testing, or when there is a use of outmoded tests. Treatment errors can occur in administering a procedure or in a surgical intervention, or in avoidable delay in treatment, or in the dose or method of using a drug, or in inappropriate care for a disease. Preventative errors can occur when there is inadequate monitoring or follow-up or by not providing prophylactic treatment. Also, there can be many other forms of medical error such as can be caused by communication failure or equipment malfunction, or resulting from fatigue among clinicians, or due to infection control, arising from using information technology, and management mistakes etc.[33] Moreover, medication errors can occur in the processes of prescribing, dispensing, administering, monitoring and system and management control.[34]

In sum, by describing the many different types of medical error, the IOM report established a context for understanding the need to focus upon systems rather than individuals in order to deliver safe care. Safety is not merely preventing individuals from making mistakes; above all, safety involves an approach that seeks solutions in a broader systems context.

Professional Sanctions and Patient Safety Models to Reduce Medical Error

The IOM report recognised that a typical initial reaction to medical errors is to assign blame to the individual who may have been responsible. But assigning blame to an individual does not change the systems causing the error. To improve patient safety, a systems approach is required to address the conditions that contribute to the errors. The basic problem of medical errors should not be blamed on individual healthcare professionals, but rather on deficient or inappropriate systems that need to be improved. In other words, effective safety improvements require a systems approach rather than focusing on individuals. This debate on emphasising individuals versus systems is connected to the debate on professional sanctions versus patient safety as contrasting models to reduce medical error. Many prominent scholars emphasise the need to focus on systems to remedy the problem of medical error, thereby shifting primary responsibility from a so-called professional sanctions model to a patient safety model in order to reduce medical error.[35]

---

33 For example, Gaba, D.M. and Howard, S.K., 'Patient Safety: Fatigue Among Clinicians and the Safety of Patients', *New England Journal of Medicine*, 347:16 (2002): 1249-1255; Bates, D.W. and Gawande, A.A., 'Improving Safety with Information Technology', *New England Journal of Medicine*, 348:25 (2003): 2526-2534; Hofmann, P.B., 'Management Mistakes in Healthcare', *Cambridge Quarterly of Healthcare Ethics* 12:2 (2003): 210-202.

34 See, for example, Clerk, P.A., 'Medication Errors in Family Practice, in Hospitals and After Discharge from the Hospital: An Ethical Analysis', *Journal of Law, Medicine & Ethics* 32 (2004): 349-357.

35 Lundberg, G.D. and Stacey, J., *Severed Trust: Why American Medicine Hasn't Been Fixed*, New York, Basic Books, 2001; see Bovbjerg, R.R. *et al.*, 'Paths to Reducing Medical Injury', *Journal of Law, Medicine & Ethics*, 29 (2001): 369-80. The argument here is a development of a previously published online essay by this author (with copyright permission),

A professional sanctions model tends to punish individuals for their medical errors in order to prevent future recurrence. At first glance the model has plausibility, but its failure is widely recognised. This model can be linked with the surge of lawsuits for medical malpractice – there is a strong tension between the patient safety movement and the malpractice system in US healthcare.[36] Yet, despite hefty penalties and personal shame, the extent of medical errors has not abated. This model blames the individual professional for carelessness or incompetence, focusing upon who is responsible rather than ascertaining what caused the problem. The vibrant malpractice system in US healthcare suggests the failure of this model insofar as the goal of deterring future medical mistakes appears so unsuccessful. Certainly, the resistance to open reporting of medical error is a serious problem for quality care,[37] and a malpractice environment can deter open reporting by professionals because of the concomitant climate of fear and shame. Of course, tort law through compensation of victims can clarify the need for improvements in patient safety.[38] Unfortunately, the professional sanctions model, so evident in malpractice claims, does not appear to have much impact in reducing medical errors.

A patient safety model tends to promise greater success in the reduction of medical errors – if this model could become the norm in the litigious culture of US healthcare. This model addresses medical error by seeking changes in the systems and processes of care that support the practices causing individuals to make medical mistakes. So, there is a shift from fixing blame upon individual professionals to fixing problems via root cause analysis of *what* happened. By clarifying what happened, systemic safeguards can be implemented to prevent recurrence. This model can foster quality improvement and can encourage reporting of error to address system glitches that lead to such error (of course, the debate on quality of care is much larger than patient safety, and continues expansively).[39]

Some analogies can help understand the advantages of the patient safety model. An obvious analogy occurs in road safety – when a specific site is associated with several car accidents, safety rails are built to prevent future crashes.

Magill, G., 'Medical Error and Patient Safety', *Health Care Ethics USA*, 10:2 (2002): 4-8, see: http://chce.slu.edu/hceusa.html.

36 Studdart, D.M. *et al.*, 'Medical Malpractice', *New England Journal of Medicine*, 350:3 (2004): 283-292, at 287; Sage, W.M., 'Medical Liability and Patient Safety', *Health Affairs*, 22:4 (2003): 26-36.

37 Leape, L.L., 'Patient Safety: Reporting of Adverse Events', *New England Journal of Medicine*, 347 (2002); 1633-1638; also see Cohen, J.R., 'Future Research on Disclosure of Medical Errors', *Annals of Internal Medicine*, 141:6 (2004): 481; Mazor, K.M. *et al.*, 'Communicating with Patients about Medical Errors: a Review of the Literature', *Archives of Internal Medicine*, 164:15 (2004): 1690-1697.

38 See Weeks, E.B. *et al.*, 'Tort Claims Analysis in the VHA for Quality Improvement', *Journal of Law, Medicine & Ethics*, 29 (2001): 335-45.

39 For example, Steinberg, E.P., editorial, 'Improving the Quality of Care', *New England Journal of Medicine* 348:26 (2003): 2681-2683.

An even stronger analogy is that of airline safety. As early as the 1950s, safety centres for military aviation began to focus on human factors. Likewise, drawing upon military aviation experience, civilian aviation adopted more comprehensive approaches to safety. So, civilian aviation began to implement accident investigations, incident reporting and research for continuous quality improvement. As a result, the Federal Aviation Administration (FAA) assumed regulatory oversight with the responsibility for ensuring flight safety. It became the task of an independent federal agency, the National Transportation Safety Board (NTSB), to conduct accident investigations, making recommendations to the FAA for regulatory action. At the heart of its success is the process of confidential incident reporting that is conducted through the 'National Aeronautics and Space Administration' (NASA) 'Safety Reporting System' (ASRS).[40] As a result, after civilian airlines were freed from regulatory reprisals for reporting pilot error and near misses, pilot co-operation soared. The extensive, confidential reporting and subsequent remedies in the airline industry resulted in much improved safety for passengers. A similar system in healthcare is needed to encourage self reporting of medical error (and near misses) with confidentiality assurances. Such an approach is likely to encourage proper cause analysis, system implementation of preventative measures and appropriate compensation for victims.

Another analogy is occupational health. The Occupational Safety and Health Act of 1970 created the Occupational Safety and Health Administration (OSHA) and its research arm, the National Institute for Occupational Safety and Health (NIOSH). The purpose of OSHA is to encourage the reduction of workplace hazards and to implement new or existing safety and health programs by undertaking the following: providing research in occupational health and safety; maintaining record-keeping systems; developing training programs and enforcing mandatory standards for job safety and health.

The analogies of road safety, the aviation industry and occupational health provide valuable lessons for safety in healthcare. There needs to be an increased awareness of safety concerns and the need to improve performance. Patient safety strategies need to include a focus on appropriate organisational and national leadership, development of a relevant knowledge base, and dissemination of knowledge in a timely manner throughout the industry. Aviation and occupational health have dedicated government agencies with regulatory responsibility for safety that is separate from the agencies responsible for research. The research entities can generate reports that are useful to the regulatory authorities as they set standards. Also, aviation and occupational health recognised the need to expand the knowledge base on safety as well as to establish dissemination processes for this new knowledge, and substantial resources were provided to support these initiatives in aviation and occupational health. Adequate resources were indispensable for steady improvement over time. In other words, safety improvements were not the result of a one-time effort; rather, results occurred

40 The Institute of Medicine, *To Err Is Human*, 'Building Leadership and Knowledge for Patient Safety', at pp. 69-85.

through an ongoing commitment of resources and leadership. A similarly cohesive effort is needed to improve patient safety in healthcare. For example, data safety and monitoring boards present especially tricky ethical challenges in healthcare in order to balance scientific validity with protecting individuals as patients in medical care and human subjects in research trials.[41]

The lessons from other industries, such as aviation or occupational health, tend to suggest that a proactive and preventive patient safety model may have more success than a reactive and punitive professional sanctions model in decreasing medical errors. The problem with the professional sanctions model is that it tends to be very reactive by blaming individuals for medical error. In this mindset, medical mistakes tend to be hidden from families and patients to minimise the threat of litigation, and risk management tends to concentrate on reducing pecuniary penalties rather than reducing risks to the patient of future error. These are not the paving stones for ethical practice in healthcare. Of course, as long as human frailty exists, there are likely to be medical mistakes that result from malice or malpractice, deserving of appropriate lawsuits and penalties. If the malpractice lobby needs consoling when faced with a new vision for patient safety, perhaps it will be satisfied with restricting tort law to injuries associated with intentional or reckless behavior. But a patient safety model can establish a systems approach for reporting medical errors in a proactive environment that implements processes to prevent future mistakes.

In sum, US healthcare can benefit by turning down the heat of malpractice litigation to turn up the light of systems oriented remedies. Healthcare has successfully developed sophisticated management audits to maximise margin and profitability. By investing similar energies and resources into safety audits, healthcare can develop proactive safeguards and processes for patient safety. However, such safeguards and processes will require an indispensable approach in all cases: undertaking a root cause analysis of any medical error that occurs.

Promoting Patient Safety by Root Cause Analysis of Medical Error

In 2003, the Joint Commission on Accreditation of Healthcare Organisations (JCAHO) published an important manual on root cause analysis, as described below.[42] The purpose was to assist healthcare organisations in the reduction of medical error and the enhancement of patient safety by highlighting the prevention of system failures.

Root cause analysis is a process to identify the causal factors that underlie what is referred to as a sentinel event, defined as an unexpected occurrence (or risk) involving death or serious injury. Adopting a systems approach rather than focusing

41 Slutsky, A.S. and Lavery, J.V., 'Data Safety and Monitoring Boards', *New England Journal of Medicine*, 350:11 (2004): 1143-1147.

42 Joint Commission on Accreditation of Healthcare Organizations, *Root Cause Analysis in Health Care*. The analysis in this section of the essay presents a critical appraisal of the explanation and recommendations in this healthcare manual.

upon individuals, a root cause analysis focuses primarily on processes rather than upon personal performance. Hence, a successful root cause analysis does not assign blame, but enables a team to understand the causes or potential causes of medical error and the changes that are likely to prevent their recurrence.

Healthcare organisations can adopt different steps to implement a root cause analysis when medical errors occur. One step involves assigning a team to assess the sentinel event or the potential of one when such circumstances occur. Organising such teams requires leadership to foster environments conducive both to root cause analysis and subsequent safety improvements. Specifically, staff should be assured of the objectivity of any improvement that occurs, such as the identification and reduction of risks instead of any assignment of blame to individuals. And leaders should empower such teams to make recommendations for change, providing resources and ensuring appropriate structures and processes.

Another step in root cause analysis is to study the problem comprehensively. Defining the problem requires an accurate description of what (nearly) happened. Criteria for a well-defined problem include stating what is wrong and focusing on the actual outcome: timely intervention is crucial. The team should consider how information that is gathered will be recorded. Legal counsel can offer guidance with regard to the protection of information from legal discovery through its inclusion in peer review and other means. And the ethics committee can offer guidance about patient confidentiality and information gathered in the process of the root cause analysis. Documentary evidence in a root cause analysis should gather all relevant materials both in paper format and electronic format.

Identifying root causes requires clarifying the systemic underpinning of a problem, including the following: specifying the relevant risk reduction strategies; formulating, evaluating and designing an action plan for improvements; ensuring acceptability of the action plan; implementing the improvement plan; developing measures of effectiveness and ensuring their success; and effectively communicating the results.

In sum, by undertaking a root cause analysis of medical error, healthcare organisations are more likely to adopt a proactive systems/processes approach, rather than a reactive blame-the-individual approach. In doing so, organisations are far better positioned to foster a culture of safety in healthcare.

Fostering a Culture of Safety in Healthcare

It is very important for scholarly debate on reducing medical error and enhancing patient safety to provide practical suggestions for healthcare practitioners. Hence, it can be helpful at the end of a discussion on this topic to provide both a set of principles and specific guidelines to foster a culture of safety in healthcare. These principles and guidelines are drawn from the important contributions of the IOM and JCAHO as very influential bodies in this area.

The IOM emphasised the need for system and process changes to promote a culture of safety in healthcare. To guide these changes, the IOM identified a set of principles that should be applied to large healthcare systems, individual hospitals, and small group practices. The set of principles is described as follows: to provide leadership; to respect human limits in the design process; to promote effective team functioning; to anticipate the unexpected and to create a learning environment.[43]

First, the role of leadership is indispensable for establishing a culture of safety. Effective leadership for patient safety includes the following: making patient safety a priority corporate objective; making patient safety the responsibility of everyone, such as by endorsing non-punitive solutions; making clear assignments for safety oversight; providing resources for error analysis and systems redesign; and developing mechanisms for identifying and dealing with unsafe practitioners, even though the new focus of safety is upon faulty systems.

Second, it is crucial to understand and respect human limits in the design process, such as by: designing jobs for safety, including being attentive to work hours and loads, staffing ratios, sources of distraction, fatigue or sleep deprivation; avoiding reliance on memory, such as by adopting the use of protocols and checklists whenever appropriate; using constraints and forcing functions to guide users to the next action or decision and to structure critical tasks to avoid errors; avoiding reliance on vigilance (because attention spans are limited), simplifying key processes (to minimise problem solving and thereby reduce the likelihood of error), and standardising work processes (enabling newcomers to use devices safely).

Third, safe healthcare requires effective team functioning, which involves not only training in teams the individuals who are expected to work in teams (people tend to make fewer errors when they work in teams), but also including patients in both the design of safety and the process of care.

Fourth, anticipating the unexpected can foster a culture of safety, including the following: adopting a proactive approach by examining processes of care for threats to safety and redesigning them before accidents occur, such as via the automation of tasks that are repetitive, time consuming, and error prone; designing for recovery, such as by making errors visible when possible, making it easy to reverse operations and making it difficult to perform non-reversible operations; and improving access to accurate and timely information at the point of care.

Finally, a culture of safety requires the creation of a learning environment that includes the following: using simulations whenever possible, such as for training, for problem solving and for crisis management; encouraging reporting of errors and hazardous conditions, such as by fostering a culture that shares authority, that collaborates in problem solving and that ensures there are no reprisals for reporting errors; and developing a working culture in which communication flows freely. In an effective learning environment there should be appropriate feedback from errors that occur, such as via reporting of events, understanding what occurred and why it occurred, developing and implementing recommendations for improvements, and tracking changes for subsequent assessment of their effectiveness.

---

43 The Institute of Medicine, *To Err Is Human*, 'Creating Safety Systems in Health Care Organizations', 155-201, at pp. 166-197.

In a complementary study to foster a culture of safety, the Joint Commission on Accreditation of Healthcare Organisations (JCAHO) published the 2nd edition of its manual on patient safety. This 2004 manual presents practical guidelines to foster a culture of safety; the manual describes JCAHO's initiative to continuously improve the safety and quality of care, as described below.[44]

First, JCAHO requires accredited healthcare organisations to integrate patient safety standards into their existing processes and structures. To assist healthcare organisations in this undertaking, JCAHO continues to develop national patient safety goals. JCAHO requires compliance from all accredited organisations that provide care relevant to its stated goals and associated requirements and encourages organisations to consider the goals and requirements comprehensively within the organisation's context of care and services. Hence, every goal and requirement may not apply to each organisation.

Second, JCAHO expects organisations to enforce its sentinel event policy via the following steps: complete a thorough and credible root cause analysis; implement specific improvements to reduce risk; and monitor the improvements for effectiveness. To assist, JCAHO issues its *Sentinel Event Alert*,[45] a periodic newsletter that identifies types of sentinel events, their common causes, and preventive measures.

Third, a culture of safety requires a shift toward an environment that can identify both actual and potential risks in order to prevent or minimise the number and severity of adverse outcomes. The role of leadership responsibility to build such an environment is crucial. Organisations should promote safety through systems enhancement and applied process redesign (in contrast to the previous focus upon punitive actions and retraining or counselling).

Fourth, fostering a culture of safety in healthcare requires the development of a written plan for a patient safety programme. Such a safety plan ought to include a programme for identifying and assessing risks, emphasising how processes or designs can fail and how they can be made safer, and focusing on the cause of error and not on who commits errors. Proactive risk assessment should be applied to all existing processes as well as to the design of new processes. And high-risk care processes are good starting places for risk assessment strategies. Such an approach can dramatically reduce the risk of error and ensure the successful performance of processes. In sum, when healthcare organisations implement proactive risk assessments they can prevent errors as well as near misses and they can protect their patients from harm.

The Joint Commission on Accreditation of Healthcare Organisations (JCAHO) provides many learning opportunities and publications to foster a culture of

---

44 Joint Commission on Accreditation of Healthcare Organizations, *Patient Safety: Essentials for Health Care*, 'Patient Safety: The JCAHO Initiative', at pp. 7-26; for a perceptive commentary on JCAHO's original safety standards, see, LeGros, N. and Pinkall, J.D., 'The JCAHO Patient Safety Standards and the Disclosure of Unanticipated Outcomes', *Journal of Health Law*, 35:2 (2002): 189-210.

45 See http://www.jcaho.org/about+us/news+letters/sentinel+event+alert.

patient safety in healthcare organisations. JCAHO annually publishes its *Hospital Accreditation Standards*, and the 2005 edition continues to give prominence both to implementing its policy on sentinel events and its national patient safety goals.[46] JCAHO also keeps its member organisations updated on medical error and patient safety issues via other publications, such as *Perspectives* (the official Joint Commission newsletter), *The Source* (a publication to disseminate Joint Commission compliance strategies) and *Quality Improvement Online* (providing advice on improving performance and ensuring patient safety).[47] For example, JCAHO celebrated the tenth anniversary of its Sentinel Event Policy in the May 2005 issue of *Perspectives*, and also announced its new international Center for Patient Safety and its new website in the April and June 2005 issues of *Perspectives*.[48]

The set of principles in the IOM report and the practical guidance in JCAHO's accreditation documents provide substantive leadership to foster a culture of safety in US healthcare. Since the 1990s there has been a dramatic increase in the awareness of medical error in the United States. The ensuing debate about how to effectively reduce the many different types of medical error continues to flare. However, it does appear that the basic stand-off between adopting a professional sanctions model and a patient safety model to reduce medical error has tilted in a clear direction. That is, there does appear to be an emerging consensus against focusing reactively upon individuals to blame and punish them for their mistakes (the professional sanctions model) in order to emphasise the proactive approach of undertaking root cause analyses to remedy systems and processes in order to prevent future harms from recurring in healthcare (the patient safety model). In other words, fostering a culture of safety in healthcare entails an approach that seeks solutions to medical error in a broader systems context.

Conclusion

A systems approach to medical error shifts from fixing blame upon individual professionals to fixing problems via root cause analysis of *what* happened, rather than focusing upon *who* was responsible. Of course, ascertaining both *who* was responsible and *what* occurred are indispensable components in a sound approach to patient safety; and how to establish the proper balance with these related elements will continue to be debated. Because of the focus upon a systems approach for over a

---

46 Joint Commission on Accreditation of Healthcare Organizations, *Hospital Accreditation Standards, 2005*, Oakbrook, Illinois: Joint Commission Resources, 2005; see 'Sentinel Events' (SE 1-14) and National Patient Safety Goals' (NPSG 1-6).

47 For *Quality Improvement Online*, see: http:www.jcrinc.com/qionline.

48 'The Joint Commission's Sentinel Event Policy: Ten Years of Improving the Quality and Safety of Health Care', *Perspectives*, 25:5 (2005): 1-2; 'Announcing the New Joint Commission International Center for Patient Safety', *Perspectives*, 25:4 (2005): 1-2; 'Joint Commission International Center for Patient Safety Offers New Web Site', *Perspectives*, 25:6 (2005): 1-2 (http://www.jcipatientsafety.org).

decade in US healthcare, there have been dramatic developments to reduce medical error and to enhance patient safety.

Notwithstanding the substantive progress in patient safety that has occurred in US healthcare, astounding problems remain. For example, infections (such as from staph bacteria) continue to rage through hospitals because of poor hygiene, with an estimated one patient out of 20 being infected during a hospital stay. A *New York Times* editorial suggests that the current annual death rate from patient infection in US healthcare could be as high as the combined deaths from AIDS, breast cancer and road accidents.[49] Clearly, there remains an urgent need to model healthcare on success stories in patient safety, perhaps especially when such successes evidently impact on the proverbial bottom line that is such a strong driver of US healthcare. For example, the escalating costs associated with paying medical malpractice insurance led anesthesiologists to make systems improvements to reduce deaths from medical error. Ever since the mid-1980s, anesthesia-related patient deaths have been reduced from one death per 5,000 cases to one death per 200,000-300,000 cases. As a result, the 30,000 anesthesiologists in the US have moved from being considered one of the riskiest groups to insure, to now paying some of the smallest malpractice insurance premiums in the nation.[50] Sometimes, even the renowned bottom line in US healthcare can yield good ethics practices in developing systems approaches for patient safety.

49 McCaughey, B., 'Coming Clean', *The New York Times*, June 6, 2005: A23.

50 Hallinan, J.T., 'Once seen as risky, one group of doctors changes its ways', *The Wall Street Journal*, June 1, 2005: A1, A9; also see Burke, J.P., 'Infection Control – A Problem for Patient Safety', *New England Journal of Medicine*, (2003): 651-656.

Chapter 8

Autonomy and Its Limits: What Place for the Public Good?[1]

Veronica English, Rebecca Mussell, Julian Sheather and Ann Sommerville

Autonomy: Perceptions and Realities

The importance given to the language of personal choice and autonomy in healthcare has grown considerably in the last 50 years. Autonomy – the capacity to make reasoned decisions and act on them[2] – is often conflated with notions of patients' rights and societal drives to extend consumer choice. All of these centre on self-determination and the empowerment of individuals. Respect for personal autonomy is often perceived as being sovereign among the ethical principles governing medical practice. This implies that individual self-determination is inevitably the key feature in resolving ethical dilemmas and other moral conflicts. Some legal judgments contribute to this perception of the primacy of autonomy, implying that society has obligations to meet the individual's requirements, almost regardless of the consequences for the general public good. This was seen as the implication of the initial stage of the *Burke* case,[3] in which a patient with a degenerative illness sought to oblige doctors to fulfill his demands for certain future procedures. He claimed that guidance from the General Medical Council was unlawful and breached his human rights in permitting doctors rather than the patient to decide on treatment. The judge of first instance agreed, despite commentators warning that this would skew medical practice towards the wasteful provision of futile interventions to the detriment of other patients.[4] The media hailed it as a triumph for patient autonomy and patient rights. Although the judgment was subsequently overturned,[5] its initial message chimed well with the pervasive use of the language of rights in the media

1 The views expressed in this chapter are the views of the authors and should not be attributed to the British Medical Association.

2 Boyd, K.M., Higgs, R. and Pinching, A.J. (eds), *The New Dictionary of Medical Ethics*, London, BMJ Publishing Group, 1997.

3 *R (Burke) v. the General Medical Council and others* (2004) 79 BMLR 126.

4 Gillon, R., 'Why the GMC is right to appeal over life prolonging treatment', *BMJ*, 2004; 329:810-811.

5 *R (Burke) v. General Medical Council (Official Solicitor and others intervening)* [2005] EWCA Civ 1003.

and with government claims to promote patient choice. Such media coverage can disguise the fact that public health and the needs of others also play a large – but often a less openly articulated – part in public health policies.

This chapter questions the reality of a societal perception, arguably fostered by the media, that individual wishes and choices are the key foundation stone of all healthcare decisions. (In our definition of media here, we include such things as television dramas and documentaries which contribute to a public perception that medicine, combined with pharmaceutical advances, is capable of delivering almost everything individuals desire, short of immortality.) While not rejecting the general importance of autonomy as a value, we argue that it can be over-played to the detriment of other important moral values such as altruism and concern for others. We consider some specific areas where an emphasis on autonomy seems unhelpful. A superficial preoccupation with the language of autonomy can even be counter-productive in achieving what individuals would want. Underpinning our case is the argument that – contrary to current public expectation – autonomy should be overtly limited in some areas in the interests of respecting other values. How limits might be set should be a matter of public consultation. Although resources should be a part of such discussion, they are not our main focus here. Our aim is not to argue that patients should renounce their claims to Viagra or cosmetic surgery in favour of more resources going into fertility treatment or care of the elderly. Rather, the argument is for all members of society to accept some degree of control in some healthcare choices where a voluntary limitation would have little or no detrimental impact on their own wellbeing but would significantly benefit the collective. The idea of restricting personal autonomy is unfashionable but not new. Both law and ethical reasoning have always sought to achieve justifiable balances between competing imperatives in particular circumstances. Nevertheless, this is not the impression conveyed in debate on high-profile emotive cases, where appeals to notions of the public good can be drowned out by those centring on individuals' rights.

In reality, patients cannot require that they be given everything they want. Not only are their requests for particular treatments unenforceable, their rights to refuse – which appear more robust in law – are also limited. Even treatment refusal at the end of life, which might appear the epitome of an individual's claim to non-interference, is subject to caveats. Good practice decrees, for example, that a terminally ill patient should not be able to decline some measures such as 'basic care' and hygiene or refuse all pain relief by means of an advance directive.[6] These provisions are based on the assumption that it is bad for society as a whole to tolerate the negative effects of individuals' choices in respect of unrelieved pain or neglect.

Even in situations where autonomy is the determining factor, we consider that more recognition needs to be given to the fact that there are occasions where decision making has to be supported or rescued via interventions that may even override the stated wishes or desires of the patient. Furthermore, autonomy clearly does

6 British Medical Association, *Medical Ethics Today: The BMA's Handbook of Ethics and Law* (2nd ed), London, BMA, 2004, p. 115.

not spring fully armed into the inner lives of human beings. It has to be nurtured and some individuals grow more slowly than others towards self-government, as is reflected in the law's refusal to categorise competence in young people by age alone. Even where there is no obvious evidence of patients' impaired competence, doctors may be obliged to guess whether the individual's stated intention represents a true wish or some temporary aberration. A patient who refuses emergency care or leaves a suicide note declining resuscitation raises questions about whether the decision is an autonomous choice or a confused cry for help. Equally, capacity can decline, disappear or be subject to various impediments. In a society which places personal autonomy above other values, any form of mental illness leaves sufferers at a considerable disadvantage. If they are not to remain marginalised, the case must be made for other values to be engaged.

Notions of Society's Interests and of a Social Contract

The principles underpinning public policies draw their validity from the perceived benefits they convey and the perceived harms they seek to prevent. In the case of autonomy the harm to which it is opposed is tyranny. In healthcare, the principle of autonomy seeks to protect the individual from the tyranny of being subject to unsought-for interventions imposed by the state or by paternalistic professionals. In some cases, however, doctors' justification for intervening may be an assumption that they can assess and promote the individual's best interests more accurately or effectively than the individual himself. In others, the reason for intervening may be based on arguments about societal interests.

Although a respect for autonomy can guard against forms of tyranny, justifications for a measured restriction or limitation of autonomy can be found in social contract theory. Frequently cited as an explanatory model of political legitimacy, at the heart of the social contract lies the notion that certain freedoms are contractually sacrificed in order that others may be guaranteed. An individual's moral or political responsibilities flow from the nature of the contract, and the rights or freedoms of the individual are counterbalanced by corresponding duties. This model can be usefully applied to the public provision of healthcare. It can be argued that individuals' rights to access free healthcare should be balanced by corresponding duties: to permit the use of information that might benefit others, for example. Arguably, however, too great an emphasis on the concept of personal autonomy in healthcare means that patients do not see themselves as having any moral duties (apart perhaps from paying taxes to fund the health service) but only rights. Greater focus on the common good would inevitably give everyone in society some duties. Correspondingly, some freedoms would be limited – uncomfortable and unappealing as that seems in a libertarian society. Nevertheless, there would also be some valuable potential benefits for all, as is shown by the following examples.

Abandoning an Individualistic Model of Information Governance

One facet of autonomy is individuals' claim to control the uses of their own health information. Patient confidentiality is also an established ethical tenet of medical practice, going back to Hippocratic times. Genetic technology provides challenges to traditional ideas of confidentiality and views of autonomy in several ways. A focus on autonomy in healthcare emphasises individual rights and independence in decision making but genetic studies highlight people's interconnectedness. Such studies prove that the interests of one family member cannot be isolated from those of others. Although it would be rare in any branch of healthcare for decisions only to affect the decision-maker and be entirely devoid of repercussions for others, decisions relating to genetics very obviously have wider implications. The fact of shared DNA means that one person's susceptibility to a genetic disorder indicates that blood relatives risk developing that condition. Known carriers of genetic disorders are aware that their knowledge is not only relevant to their own reproductive decisions but also to those of their siblings. Nor is the impact of genetic information restricted to blood relatives. Partners of people affected by genetic conditions also have a direct interest in factors potentially affecting their future children. Thus, genetic information undermines the concept of health decisions being solely personal matters.

The right of individuals to knowledge – in this case by accessing genetic testing – may also reveal to them, by implication, the health status of another family member, challenging the latter's rights to genetic privacy and to ignorance. Although it may be questioned whether there is an absolute 'right' not to know information about oneself, it is widely accepted that the decision about whether or not to access potentially psychologically damaging information is a personal one. People opposed to pre-symptomatic testing, however, can scarcely remain ignorant of their own health status if faced by a positive test by their offspring or identical twin. Is the harm of some people being exposed to unwanted information sufficient to deny their close relatives the option of seeking information important to them? Where a decision has such serious implications for another person, appeals to autonomy are unhelpful since to promote the autonomy of one person inevitably denies it to another.

Knowledge and the ability to make informed choices are often seen as essential components of the valid exercise of autonomy. Many people grow up with the knowledge of familial risks of a genetic disorder. Others do not. People adopted at birth, for example, are unlikely to be aware of their genetic heritage and the importance of conditions such as Huntington's disease. Would respect for autonomy require them to be traced and told of a known risk in their birth family? It is only by having this information, after all, that they can make informed decisions about whether to have children. Clearly, this is too narrow an interpretation of what autonomy means since it is also about choice. The very fact of being given such information reduces the choices available. It removes the option to remain ignorant or to plan unburdened by genetic knowledge. Such cases present real difficulties. It is impossible to ascertain whether people want such information without telling them that information exists that they might want to know.

This tension between the apparently legitimate but contradictory rights of different people lead some to suggest that aspects of communitarianism – with its emphasis on responsibilities of individuals as well as rights – provides a better model than pure autonomy for approaching genetics.[7] The moral underpinning of these responsibilities stems from our special interconnectedness with others – either as a result of shared DNA or because of an intention to enter into a contract with that other person – for example a contract of marriage or agreement to have children. What is particularly significant about these relationships is the extreme degree to which the decisions of one person directly affect the interests of another, combined with their shared history and social interaction. This notion of duties, however, represents a significant shift in moral focus. Clearly articulated rules about helping others are conspicuous by their absence in our society which generally allows, if not encourages, individuals' right to make selfish choices. With the exception of those who have professional duties of care, society imposes no obligations on people to support their relatives (with the exception of their children). Nor is there a general duty to benefit others. Courts, for example, do not require compulsory kidney or bone marrow donation from unwilling but close matching relatives. Nevertheless, the fact that society does not *impose* such duties does not mean that individuals lack such moral responsibilities. In practice, most people acknowledge the moral significance of blood and relationship ties and are willing to share information. What we are arguing for, therefore, is that this decent and humane response which most people automatically show should receive more emphasis as the cultural norm of our society instead of the current expectation that individual autonomy (and by implication selfish choices) should always prevail.

Nevertheless, we are not arguing in favour of going to the opposite extreme. Although a different model of confidentiality is needed to reflect the shared nature of genetic information, a balance is still essential. Some argue that an individual's genetic information 'should not be regarded as personal to that individual, but as the common property of other people who may share those genes, and who need the information in order to find out their own genetic constitution'.[8] The notion that patient confidentiality applies to a whole family rather than an individual is also problematic. Just as a focus on autonomy alone is unbalanced, so is indiscriminate routine sharing, implying incorrectly that all genetic information has significant importance for everyone sharing a genetic signature. Current rules permit patient confidentiality to be breached where failure to disclose information would cause serious harm to another person[9] but this is inadequate in terms of genetic information.

---

7 English, V. and Sommerville, A., 'Genetic privacy: orthodoxy or oxymoron?', *J Med Ethics*, 1999; 25:144-50.

8 Royal College of Physicians, *Ethical Issues in Clinical Genetics*, London, RCP, 1991, para 4.10.

9 General Medical Council, *Confidentiality: Protecting and Providing Information*, London, GMC, 2004, para 27.

Only in very extreme cases is the effect of non-disclosure of genetic information a serious harm. More accurately, it is a failure to provide a benefit to another person.

The Inconvenience of Prioritising Personal Autonomy

Just as genetics require us to re-think the notion of confidentiality, other social and technological developments can also highlight some of the disadvantages in failing to use health data effectively and the benefits of sharing some kinds of personal health information for the common good. A framework has long existed for a certain amount of routine data sharing in the public interest. A common example is the reporting of notifiable diseases. It has also long been clear that, for any individual patient, the right of confidentiality is not an absolute one but rather must be generally balanced by the public interest. Sometimes, however, it is unclear how the public interest should be defined. Thus, over time the ethical principle of confidentiality or privacy has been interpreted in various ways but has always been qualified by some awareness of the societal benefit derived from the use of individuals' data.

Clearly, individuals' health data can be extremely useful for purposes that benefit the whole of society, such as medical research, audit of the quality of services and of their outcomes, risk management planning and the training of future health professionals. In medical research, for example, the use of patient data has contributed to the success of major medical breakthroughs. These included uncovering the hazards of smoking, prevention of coronary disease with lipid lowering and eradication of smallpox.[10] Many of these data were used on an anonymised basis and arguably therefore did not breach confidentiality nor did they need specific patients' consent for data sharing to occur. Ideally, however, patients should have been aware of the uses of anonymised data to benefit the health system and other people. What has always been problematic is that when identifiable retrospective records are involved and consent is desirable, there is rarely an easy way to trace and consult large numbers of individuals. It is likely that, if asked, some patients would refuse to allow the use of their data unless – as in the case of genetic data – they could see benefits for either themselves or their families. The notion of benefiting other vaguely defined patients or the health service generally through the use of personal health information may not be a priority for some people in the absence of a better defined social contract. They might choose to opt out of any information sharing even though there would be no detriment to themselves apart from having their already less than absolute control over their health information further diminished. At the very least, therefore, seeking consent for every use of data in any form would be very inconvenient and at most it could cripple research, hinder planning and make impossible the monitoring of the quality of care provided. Arguably, what is needed is a clear societal agreement that

10 The Wellcome Trust, *Public Health Services: Challenges and Opportunities Report of the Public Health Sciences Working Group Convened by the Wellcome Trust*, London, The Wellcome Trust, 2004, p. 5.

certain kinds of data – preferably anonymised and aggregated – can legitimately be used for some specified purposes that benefit all.

How much would such an agreement change things? Often, in the past, patients were simply not asked and a tacit assumption was made that both anonymised and patient-identifiable data could be used as part of the unarticulated social contract. Perhaps this was partly due to the perception that health information has never entirely been considered as the property of patients but rather partly belonging to those who measure, examine, diagnose, transcribe and record the data. It is also seen as partly the property of those providing the health services in which the data emerge and ultimately as the property of the Secretary of State for Health who provides the materials for recording and storing information. So is it fair to say that NHS data belongs to the State? If so, using it for the benefit of all is clearly desirable. Increasing societal emphasis on autonomy, data protection and privacy, however, has changed this assumption in relation to identifiable data. A more clearly articulated social agreement would at least have the benefit of raising public awareness about how anonymised information, and in limited circumstances identifiable information, continues to be used. The question still arises, however, as to whether there is a point at which public benefits, such as those outlined above, outweigh individuals' rights to control health information collected as part of the State's provision of care?

Another question raised here is whether it is practically possible in modern society to try to insist on maintaining a very high degree of medical confidentiality as we currently understand it. In a technological age, data management in all spheres has undergone rapid change. Although in the past, doctors generally held and controlled their own patients' health information, this is less the reality today. Not only do doctors increasingly work in multi-disciplinary teams which include a range of health professionals, social workers and possibly others such as patient advocates, chaplains and other spiritual advisers, but, over time, the balance of control over information has gradually but inexorably shifted away from doctors. Those working in the NHS increasingly find that various forms of identifiable patient information are required for all manner of purposes supplementary to the treatment of patients, such as GPs' post-payment verification and detection of prescription fraud. The degree to which patients are currently aware of such uses of their information is questionable.

In recent years, some legislative changes were aimed at giving patients more control of their own information and so also lessened the medical profession's ability to determine how it was used. The Data Protection Act 1998, for example, and the various access to records legislation echoed initiatives in other spheres to enhance patient autonomy. Patients could now theoretically choose to whom they were willing to release their health information. At the same time, however, doctors found themselves increasingly besieged by insurers, employers, housing agencies, benefits officers and others requesting access to patients' records. If patients needed insurance, a job, a medical report for state benefits or for housing purposes, they were obliged to provide their written 'consent'. Arguably, therefore, giving patients more control of their medical records had the effect of also increasing the pressures on them to agree to a plethora of applicants having access. So much so that some doctors lobbied unsuccessfully to make it illegal for insurers to require a patient's own GP to provide an insurance report, rather than an independent medical examiner who would not have access to the accumulated confidential background but would judge the patient's health solely on the evidence available through examination. Traditionally, doctors' professional ethics required them to preserve confidentiality even after the patient's death. The access to health records legislation, however, allows legal rights of access to deceased patients' records to any person with a claim arising from the death, so increasing further the numbers of applications for retrospective access by relatives and insurers. The public inquiry into the case of Harold Shipman[11] sought to give relatives further rights of access to information about the deceased person's health history. Privacy, as an expression of autonomy, only holds for the living. Nevertheless, doctors generally oppose the notion that there should be open access to deceased patients' records, not least because this would seriously inhibit the frankness of discussion if patients knew that relatives would later see the record of such conversations. Again a measured balance is needed so that information about deceased people is only disclosed on a 'need to know basis' or to gain some identifiable benefits for society, rather than on simple curiosity.

Although privacy as the primary expression of patient autonomy is generally valued in theory, it is interesting to note how different aspects of privacy appear to attract different levels of public scrutiny in practice. For example, there has been a large amount of scrutiny of how patients' private information is charted and shared within the health service in medical records, but the same level of scrutiny is not given to the lack of privacy afforded to patients in a hospital setting. Here private acts and conversations take place behind wafer thin curtains, in accident and emergency departments or crowded wards, sometimes within ear-shot of visitors. At the same time, however, there have been almost Kafkaesque attempts to protect patients' identity in hospital. Take for example, the case of patients' name boards being removed from their hospital beds in the name of 'patient privacy' in 2004. Respect for autonomy might suggest that patients should have been consulted about the removal of their names, but they were not. A study found that 96 per cent of patients were in favour of retaining name boards. They did not perceive the fact of having their identity revealed in this way as an infringement of their privacy.[12] Healthcare professionals argued that the removal of name boards made locating specific patients difficult and it was potentially dangerous in leading to confusion in medication or treatment. Any aspect of confidentiality needs to be balanced in terms of not inhibiting the healthcare system functioning in an effective and safe way for everyone.

11 The Shipman Inquiry. Full details on the Inquiry can be accessed at: www.the-shipman-inquiry.org.uk/home.asp (accessed 1 August 2005).

12 Gudena, R., Luwemba, S., Williams, A. and Jenkinson, L.R., 'Data protection gone too far: questionnaire survey of patients' and vistors' views about having their names displayed in hospital', *BMJ*, 2004; 328:1491.

The potential to make use of individuals' health information may take on a new dimension with the current proposal to develop independent, but at the same time compatible, national integrated healthcare record systems in all four nations – England,[13] Northern Ireland,[14] Scotland[15] and Wales.[16] At the time of writing, it is hard to predict the final destination of these four initiatives given the political journey they will have to take, but they raise further questions about who controls data. Essentially the proposals are for individuals to have one summary medical record which those who are delivering direct clinical care to the patient can access whenever, and from wherever, that care is being administered; with due respect to confidentiality. The four nations are not alone in proposing such systems Australia is also looking to develop a similar system.[17] The potential societal benefits and 'public good' in the development of such systems, although recognised, are often presented as incidental benefits of the system. For example, extraction of anonymous and aggregate data from the national database for research, public health and health service planning purposes.

With these proposed changes, autonomy still remains the priority – at least in theory. Each of the four national systems is trumpeted as providing benefits to individual patients. Their claimed *raison d'être* is that they will provide better and safer delivery of individual patient care and give patients enhanced access to and control of their information. Autonomy certainly appears to be bolstered by the concept of patients being empowered to seal off certain parts of their records from some care providers and add their own comments on, for example, their future wishes in case of being overtaken by mental incapacity. These anticipated benefits, however, remain to be proven and the system itself obviously needs to be workable in practice. Current designs take into account confidentiality and data protection standards but the project has raised questions about how far such standards are practically deliverable in such large systems. Also, for such systems to be successful, a critical mass of individuals needs to be engaged and have their health records on the system, both for use directly for the clinical care of individuals and for wider secondary care uses. If such systems are the answer to future data management in large health services and offer so many potential societal and individual benefits, how does one ensure that there is sufficient critical mass for them to be viable? Arguably the most effective way of balancing autonomy and the public good in this respect would be to encourage patients to accept their broader social responsibilities,

---

13 Details on the English initiative can be accessed on the *Connecting for Health* website at: www.connectingforhealth.nhs.uk/ (accessed 1 August 2005).

14 Department of Health, Social Services and Public Safety, *Information & Communications Technology Strategy*, Belfast, DHSSPSNI, 2005.

15 NHS Scotland, *National eHealth/IM&T Strategy*, Edinburgh, NHS Scotland, 2004.

16 NHS Wales, *Informing Healthcare: Single integrated electronic health record technical proof of concept*, Cardiff, NHS Wales, 2005.

17 More information about the Australian initiative can be accessed on the Australian Government's Health*Connect* website at: www.healthconnect.gov.au/about/index.htm (accessed 1 August 2005).

participation thereby becoming a more explicit part of the social contract for those using the health service. Nevertheless, in advance of the systems being rolled out, the public needs to be involved in making decisions about how much control individuals need in this sphere.

Guessing Preferences and Sacrificing the Needs of Others

Cadaveric organ donation is another area of public policy where autonomy appears to be viewed as sacrosanct. This was demonstrated in debates in Parliament on cadaveric organ donation in 2004. The notion of consent as the 'golden thread' weaving through the Human Tissue Bill was a constant theme of Ministerial statements.[18] Yet, cadaveric organ donation challenges autonomy in two fundamental ways. First, how can autonomy be a meaningful concept for a deceased person? An appeal may be made to the notion of respect for the past autonomy and former wishes of the individual but it is hard to see how this be achieved when, in most cases, no relevant wishes were expressed. Ironically, in relation to the Human Tissue Act the Government appears to have been so afraid of being accused of not respecting autonomy that it chose the option that, on closer examination, seems least likely to respect the individual's previous wishes.

Coming as it did in the wake of intense media coverage of the organ retention scandal, where children's organs and body parts were retained following postmortem examination without parental agreement, it was inevitable that the new Human Tissue Act[19] would focus heavily on consent. Out of respect for autonomy (and perhaps also fears of a public or media backlash if any other option were followed), the Act, and its codes of practice, strongly emphasise the need to comply with the former wishes of the individual where these are known. Self determination, however, requires a 'self' and 'autonomy' is an oxymoron when applied to the dead. Arguably, dead people cannot be harmed and, if notions of the public good were more high profile, healthcare decisions would focus on lives that could be saved or transformed by donation of an organ. In practice, however, there are good reasons why individuals' wishes are still considered relevant. Although most people accept that the dead cannot be harmed, some people undeniably gain peace of mind during their lifetime from the expectation that their remains will be treated in accordance with their former wishes. The fact that the public exhibition of human cadavers in incongruous poses still has the power to shock[20] reflects a deep-seated notion that corpses continue to have some moral significance and are not simply objects. Proper account also needs to be taken of the sensitivities of relatives for whom the cadaver represents a loved one.

---

18 Dr Stephen Ladyman, *House of Commons Hansard. Standing Committee G*, Tuesday 27 January 2004, Col 66.

19 Human Tissue Act 2004.

20 Details about *Bodyworlds: The Anatomical Exhibition of Real Human Bodies* can be accessed at: www.bodyworlds.com/en/pages/home.asp (accessed 1 August 2005).

Therefore to reassure the living and console relatives, where individuals leave clear instructions about what should happen after their death, those should be followed. It is clear, however, that most people leave no instructions. In such cases, the Human Tissue Acts of 1961 and 2004, and the draft legislation for Scotland,[21] all give relatives responsibility for decision making. Thus although the UK is deemed to have an opt-in system, it is not usually donors themselves who choose. Relatives guess what the individual's wishes would have been and many opt for the default position, which is to refuse to donate. Recent research shows that between 40-48 per cent of relatives refused consent for donation.[22] In some cases, relatives knew that the individual opposed donation, but when these are removed from the calculation, the refusal rate was still 36 per cent. Given that all population surveys show significant support for cadaveric donation – up to 90 per cent in some[23] – the logical conclusion must be that many relatives guess incorrectly in refusing to allow it. This throws doubts on whether the current system can be considered respectful of the former wishes of the deceased in any meaningful sense. Arguably, given clear evidence of public support, it is more appropriate for society to assume that people are willing to help others – where there is no harm to themselves – unless they express a view to the contrary.

The conundrum here is that the current system is effectively one of 'presumed objection' despite the fact that the majority of the population do not object. Although superficially based on concepts of autonomy, statistically the default position is more likely to accurately reflect individuals' former wishes if it presumes them to have been part of the 90 per cent who support donation, rather than the 10 per cent who oppose it. Arguably, therefore, a presumption in favour of donation is more respectful of the deceased person's intention. In some models of presumed consent, such as that espoused by the British Medical Association, relatives' views are still taken into account and any such system would need to be accompanied by effective mechanisms to ensure that all sections of the public were properly informed and could register any objections easily.

The Human Tissue Act 2004 seeks to respect autonomy by emphasising the prior wishes of deceased patients where these are known. Its credentials fail in respect of those who have expressed no choice. It not only fails those who would have been willing to donate but sadly also fails to reflect any notion of the wider public good. This means that the needs of patients desperately awaiting a transplant are unnecessarily sacrificed.

---

21 Human Tissue (Scotland) Bill 2005.

22 UK Transplant, *Potential Donor Audit. 21-Month Summary Report, 1 April 2003 – 31 December 2004*. The report can be accessed at: www.uktransplant.org.uk/ukt/statistics/potential_donor_audit/potential_donor_audit.jsp (accessed 1 August 2005).

23 See for example: UK Transplant, *Barriers to Joining the NHS Organ Donor Register. Qualitative and Quantitative Research Carried Out on Behalf of UK Transplant 2002/03*, Bristol, UK Transplant, 2005

How Focus on Autonomy Disadvantages Some Patients

Our argument so far has been that an apparent societal preference for personal autonomy contributes little to the creation of a culture that recognises individuals' responsibilities for others, even though the illusion of personal control may be comforting for some. There is one category of patient, however, that seriously question the primacy given to personal autonomy: those who suffer from mental health problems. In practice, an emphasis on autonomy marginalises them since they are often excluded from full autonomy, even when they retain decision-making capacity. In some other areas of healthcare, we have argued for slightly less focus on autonomy and more on other values to create a better moral balance. In this section, we argue that a societal preoccupation with autonomy in effect excludes and disadvantages some patients, whereas a more balanced mix of values could be more inclusive. This is an important consideration in a society where one in three people suffer some form of mental health problem over their lifetime and the demographics of an ageing population mean a growing number of elderly people suffer some form of age-related mental impairment.[24] Arguably as well, the concept of mental illness itself challenges the procedural primacy of autonomy, stressing the interdependence of human agency.

In mental health care, ideas of autonomy become blurred. It is the one area of medicine in which treatment refusals by competent adults can be legally overridden. In physical medicine, an individual's ability to make choices is presumed and patients can make risky or life-threatening choices to refuse medical interventions. In mental health care, however, compulsory treatment of patients who retain decision-making capacity is permitted if they are deemed to pose a risk to themselves or to others. A common example is that of an intelligent anorexic who, while retaining decision-making capacity, persistently refuses food. Although there may be some scope for argument about capacity here, mental health legislation permits treatment in the face of a competent refusal.

The imbalance implicit in this lack of recognition of autonomy in mental health care has been challenged. During the consultation process in 2005 leading up to the development of new mental health legislation for England and Wales, the majority of professional and user groups argued that mental health legislation was discriminatory against the mentally ill.[25] They pointed out that people suffering from a physical illness could make self-harming decisions by refusing life-prolonging treatment, for example, while competent mentally ill patients could not. In the latter case, people who reject treatment are treated compulsorily. In response, the government argued that autonomy in this sphere must give way to other interests, particularly the public interest and notions of beneficence.[26] In fact, the draft legislation actively limits the

24 World Health Organization, *Investing in Mental Health*, Geneva, WHO, 2003, p. 8.

25 Joint Committee on the Draft Mental Health Bill, *Draft Mental Health Bill. Vol 1*, London, The Stationery Office, 2005, pp. 25-6.

26 Department of Health, *Government Response to the Report of the Joint Committee on the Draft Mental Health Bill 2004*, London, Department of Health, 2005, p. 4.

autonomy of mentally disordered individuals in a number of striking ways.[27] Where the relevant criteria are met, it would permit, for example, the use of compulsory powers even where there is no beneficial treatment available. Unlike its sister legislation in Scotland,[28] it makes no reference to decision-making capacity, and takes away powers that existed under the 1983 Mental Health Act, for certain groups of mentally disordered individuals to consent to treatment. If a patient presents a risk to others, and the conditions for compulsion are met, then compulsory powers must be engaged.[29]

Partly underpinning the use of compulsion is society's unwillingness to live with the small risk presented by the violent mentally disordered. High profile media coverage of very exceptional random attacks by patients has shaped public opinion in this area. An example was the killing of Jonathan Zito by Christopher Clunis[30] while he was suffering from schizophrenia. Clearly, it must be acknowledged that mental health care is an area of medical practice where the harms of defending autonomy can be highly visible. A classical ethical dilemma in psychiatry relates to the extent to which the choices of self-harming individuals who retain capacity should be respected. If individual autonomy is given the highest value then it follows that, where patients retain capacity, their choices should prevail. Yet the costs of defending autonomy can be severe, particularly where the results of apparently autonomous choices are a descent into mental disorder to an extent that subsequently requires intervention. Doctors sometimes receive information, for example, about patients whose mental health is rapidly deteriorating, who retain decision-making capacity but do not meet the criteria for compulsory treatment. Where such patients refuse to access treatment informally, doctors feel torn between the need to respect apparently autonomous decisions and the desire for more paternalistic interventions to pre-empt what may be an inevitable crisis. We are not arguing, however, that autonomy should necessarily be seen as the key factor in mental health care as it appears to be in most other areas of healthcare but rather that a better model of balanced values should be promoted and made equally applicable to all areas of care.

As yet, it is unclear how a more comprehensive balance of ethical principles could be achieved in mental health care but, in our view, this represents a fertile area for further debate.

---

27 Draft Mental Health Bill 2004.

28 Mental Health (Care and Treatment) (Scotland) Act 2003.

29 At the time of writing, the final version of the Mental Health Bill had not been published. This is taken from the Government's stated intention in its response to the report of the Joint Committee. See note 24.

30 See, for example – Anon, 'Health case for compulsory medication "overstated"', BBC Online, 15 June 1999. Available at: news.bbc.co.uk/1/hi/health/369092.stm (accessed 1 August 2005).

Conclusion

Clearly, it would be foolish to suggest that autonomy is unimportant. That is not our argument. Rather we contend that it can be over-played as a value and that there are situations in which other values need to come to the fore. We have sought to identify some areas where it would be useful to have a different balance and public discussion about some limits on autonomy, defined by a social contract. In genetics, for example, the notion of a truly autonomous decision meets its biggest challenge. The individualistic model that is usually applied to healthcare does not fit well with the shared data that are derived from genetic testing and knowledge. Here, especially, the concept of autonomy needs to encompass a recognition of the moral duties owed to other people. What is perhaps more contentious is the suggestion that unarticulated moral duties lie under the surface in other areas of healthcare, such as the broader sharing of health data for research, planning and administration. We think that a clearly articulated agreement of what can and cannot be disclosed should be made available to all patients so that they are at least aware of societal expectations. In terms of cadaveric organ donation where the individual's wishes are not known, we consider that a focus on the language of autonomy in new legislation is unlikely to promote what the individual deceased person would have wished in the majority of cases. As a general point, we consider that it would be more realistic for the practicalities of healthcare if more attention in all these areas were given to the notion of all patients' responsibilities for promoting the general good. In one area of healthcare, however, it seems that autonomy is side-lined as mental health patients are deemed not to have rights to exercise self determination even if they have mental capacity. Perhaps this group of patients would be the main beneficiaries if our societal culture had a less stark notion of autonomy and promoted a more inclusive and balanced set of healthcare principles.

Chapter 9

The Autonomy of Others: Reflections on the Rise and Rise of Patient Choice in Contemporary Medical Law

Graeme Laurie

Introduction

To understand Ken Mason's contribution to the discipline of medical law it is important to appreciate not only the impact of his training in medicine and the influence of his faith,[1] but also his unwavering commitment to others. His dedication to his students at times knows no bounds; his sense of professional duty – medical and academic – is profound. If ever there was a team player it is Ken Mason. He is a self-confessed 'communitarian' for whom, then, the rise and rise of the role of patient choice in the development of medical law over the course of its relatively short life[2] is something of an anathema.

I feel confident in saying this not only because of my decade-long relationship of working closely with him, but also because of the wealth of publications he has produced which stand as a testament to his views. Central among these is his seminal work with Sandy McCall Smith, *Law and Medical Ethics*, which was first published in 1983 and which went into its seventh edition in 2006; it will henceforth be known as *Mason and McCall Smith's Law and Medical Ethics*. The partnership of Mason and McCall Smith has represented a unique voice in medical law and has never doggedly adhered to the mantra of 'patient autonomy'. Rather, they have sought balance in responding to the – often overwhelming – range of issues which has washed up on their desks demanding attention. At times, that search for a balance

1 'It is important that authors in this field show their colours and I think it only fair to readers to say that I am a practising Roman Catholic; but this does not mean that I can have no individual conscience. In any case, what I am trying to speak of is the ethical practice of medicine, not the application of religious precept': Mason, J.K., *Human Life and Medical Practice*, Edinburgh, Edinburgh University Press, 1988, p.vii.

2 When did medical law begin? Consider the work of the influential figures of Ian Kennedy, Andrew Grubb and Sheila McLean in the 1970s and 1980s, and in whose company we must also include Alexander McCall Smith and Ken Mason himself; but other such figures, including Margaret Brazier and Derek Morgan, have pointed to the as-yet largely unexplored historical jurisprudence in various quarters of the medico-legal world.

has been between private and public interests – where, for example, should we place limits on patient autonomy in defence of broader community interests (whether these be about public health, allocation of resources or the sort of society in which we want to live)? At other junctures the tension to be resolved has been between private interests – what, for example, of the autonomy of the patient *face-à-face* the autonomy of others, such as her parents, relatives or, even, her doctor?

This chapter explores Ken Mason's contributions to medical law by focussing on his writings and other musings in and around notions of personal autonomy. It takes its structure from an event that was held in Edinburgh in 1998 to contemplate 'The Future of Medical Law and Ethics' and at which he delivered the keynote address. In looking forward to where we were going he also looked back to where we had been: his family crest is of a dog marching along and looking over his shoulder and the motto is *Respiciens Surgo* or 'Looking Backwards, I Go Forward'. This chapter involves both a retrospective on cases which Mason has considered to be of crucial importance in the development of medical law, as well as a horizon-gazing exercise for the future, which draws on my own work with him concerning the relative importance and impact of concepts of patient autonomy. I should stress, however, that what follows is a very personal interpretation of what my colleague and friend has had to say.

'The Five Most Significant Decisions in the United Kingdom Over the Past 30 Years'

You can learn a lot from reading the preface of books. The preface to the fifth edition of *Law and Medical Ethics* reads:

> One of us recently delivered a paper in which an attempt was made to choose, and justify the choice of, five most significant decisions in the United Kingdom over the past 30 years. The fact that the choice of *Re B*,[3] *Gillick v Norfolk and Wisbech Area Health Authority*,[4] *Re MB (adult: medical treatment)*,[5] *A-G's Reference (No. 3 of 1994)*[6] and *R v Cox*[7] would be unlikely to be that of any other interested observer goes simply to illustrate the enormous diversity of this academic field.

The paper referred to is Ken Mason's keynote address at the conference 'The Future of Medical Law and Ethics' held in the School of Law at the University of Edinburgh on 31 October 1998. This paper has never been published, but is tantalising in giving us a modicum of insight into his choice of these five cases over the many thousands of others that make up the discipline of medical law.

---

3 [1981] 1 WLR 1421, [1990] 3 All ER 927.

4 [1986] AC 112, [1985] 2 All ER 402, HL.

5 [1997] 2 FCR 541, (1997) 38 BMLR 175, CA.

6 [1998] AC 245, [1997] 3 All ER 936, HL.

7 (1992) 12 BMLR 38.

Re B

It is perhaps ironic to begin a discussion of autonomy with a case which is ostensibly about the best interests of a person who – to all extents and purposes – has *no autonomy*. Much of the value of the case, however, lies in the question, *whose autonomy* is at stake: a perennial issue for Mason.

Re B concerned a child with Down's Syndrome who was also suffering from an intestinal obstruction that would prove fatal but for surgical intervention which, in the event, would be a relatively straightforward procedure. Notwithstanding, the parents felt that it would be unkind to subject their daughter to such an intervention and that it would be best for her not to have the operation; the consequence would be the death of the child within a matter of days. She was made a ward of court in the face of the parents' refusal and moved to another hospital for the operation, but the surgeon charged with carrying it out refused to do so:

> I decided ... to respect the wishes of the parents and not to perform the operation, a decision which would, I believe (after 20 years in the medical profession), be taken by the great majority of surgeons faced with a similar situation.[8]

While other surgeons were found who were prepared to operate, the climate of the time shows that there was genuine ambivalence among the medical profession as to whether and how far parental choice should be respected.[9] The importance of the case lies in the fact that it established for the first time the parameters of the *autonomy of parents* faced with life and death decisions concerning their children. For Mason, however, the case also represents a watershed moment in establishing how the British courts would reconcile tensions between autonomous choices (albeit in the name of another) and the principle of respect for sanctity of life. In his 1988 work, *Human Life and Medical Practice*, for example, he asks poignantly: 'Can we honestly say that parents can and should decide that their child must die when there is no evidence that this is its preferred option?'[10]

This, in fact, also engages a further important perspective that Mason has long supported; namely, the incorporation of the perspective of the incapacitated person into the decision-making process in respect of their care. He has argued in various places for the adoption of an *objective* substituted judgement test as a preferred, more honest, approach to the best interests test which prevails in the United Kingdom.[11]

---

8 *Re B, supra cit* [1981] WLR at p. 1423; [1990] All ER at p. 928.

9 From the leading medical literature of the time we have this: '... in the absence of a clear code to which society adheres there is no justification for usurping parents' rights', see Editorial Comment, 'The Right to Live and the Right to Die', (1981) 283 *British Medical Journal*, 569.

10 *Human Life and Medical Practice*, *op cit.*, at p. 65.

11 See, for example, Mason, J.K., 'Master of the Balancers: Non-voluntary Therapy under the Mantle of Lord Donaldson', [1993] *Juridical Review*, 115-132. In particular, see the rulings of Lord Donaldson in *Re J (a minor)(wardship: medical treatment)* [1990] 2 All ER

Unlike the normal operation of a substituted judgment test which seeks to take the *actual* prior views of a person into account – and so is of no utility if no such prior wishes exist (as in the case of neonates and the life-long incapax) – Mason's construct of an *objective* test asks what would this person want if they could express views on their circumstances, objectively assessed. In a further interesting twist, however, Mason sees this not only as promoting a less paternalistic version of patient autonomy but also as permitting a wider range of extraneous interests to enter the fray, for example, those of relatives, carers or even the state.[12] It is disingenuous to apply a best interests test which, it is claimed, considers all such other interests to be irrelevant, yet which also ignores the realities of medical practice and the fact of overlapping and inter-connected interests.[13] Best interests also deprives the incapax of the opportunity to be altruistic or selfless – which in itself is an interest, and one which we do recognise in other contexts, for example, when involving incapacitated persons in research.[14]

But even this conception of substituted judgment has its limits, as Mason acknowledges, and *Re B* is, indeed, a prime example of this. The court had no evidence whatsoever to determine the future quality of life of the child and as Lord Templeman said:

> [t]he evidence in this case only goes to show that if the operation takes place and is successful then the child may live the normal span of a mongoloid child with the handicaps and defects and life of a mongol child, and it is not for this court to say that life of that description ought to be extinguished.[15]

There is a fundamental distinction to be drawn between physical and mental defects; while we, as potential proxy decision makers, might be able to say how tolerable life might be having to live with physical pain and suffering, none of us who is privileged enough to be free of mental affliction knows what it is like to be a person with Down's Syndrome.[16] Faced with such uncertainty the Court of Appeal in *Re B*

930, (1992) 6 BMLR 25 and *Re J (a minor)(medical treatment)* [1992] 4 All ER 614, [1993] Fam 15.

12 We explore this further in Mason, J.K. and Laurie, G.T., *Mason and McCall Smith's Law and Medical Ethics* (7th ed), Oxford, Oxford University Press, 2006, paras 16.130-16.138.

13 Although see *Re T (a minor)(wardship: medical treatment)* [1997] 1 WLR 242, [1997] 1 All ER 906 in which the court did take into account the impact of requiring a child to undergo a liver transplant on the parents and their ability (and willingness) to care for that child subsequently. Here 'parental autonomy' – in the sense of determining the interest of the family unit and including the child's best interests – was upheld.

14 See, for example, provisions in both the Mental Capacity Act 2005 and the Adults with Incapacity (Scotland) Act 2000 which permit incapacitated persons to take part in research subject to stringent safeguards.

15 *Re B, supra cit*, per Templeman LJ [1981] WLR at p. 1424; [1990] All ER at p. 929.

16 See further Mason, J.K., *Medico-legal Aspects of Reproduction and Parenthood*, Aldershot, Gower Publishing Group, 1990, at p. 262.

preferred to respect the sanctity of the life of the child; in doing so, however, it also raised the possibility of touchstone parameters for future decisions in respect of life and death decisions surrounding the (non)-provision of medical treatment, namely, quality of life and intolerability. As Templeman LJ said:

> There may be cases ... of severe proved damage where the future is so certain and where the life of the child is so bound to be full of pain and suffering that the court might be driven to a different conclusion.[17]

The notion of intolerability and Mason's view of substituted judgment will be returned to presently. For now, it is sufficient to note that Mason's view of substituted judgment is not one that has (yet) been accepted by the British courts.[18] *Re B* proceeded on the basis of an application of the best interests test. It was an *ex tempore* judgment and as such extends to only a few pages; much of its impact therefore was left to be felt in the wake of the subsequent jurisprudence.[19] Notwithstanding, the judgment was clearly the gateway to a new era which positioned the notion of a patient's best interests – essentially a paternalistic stance – at the centre of disputes over the care of incapacitated patients.[20]

While this means that, in the main, the autonomy of the patient is either entirely excluded or resigned to a residual role, the autonomy of others is nonetheless further engaged; *viz*, who will decide those best interests? The subsequent jurisprudence reveals a very strong reluctance on the part of the courts to interfere with clinical autonomy when it comes to assessments as to the futility of beginning or continuing treatment. Indeed, the courts have been loath to require practitioners to administer treatment against their better clinical judgment.[21] Matters may be different when the dynamics of a dispute are reversed; that is, when clinical judgment is *in favour* of care and the carers of the patient disagree.[22] Certainly, the courts have clarified that the best interests test refers to best overall interests and not merely best medical interests.[23] The advent of the Human Rights Act 1998 has done little to change the

---

17 [1990] 3 All ER 927 at p. 929, [1981] 1 WLR 1421 at p. 1424.

18 But see Lord Donaldson in the *Re J* cases, *supra cit.*, and our commentary in *Mason and McCall Smith's Law and Medical Ethics*, *op cit.*, paras 16.35-16.37, where he comes very close to applying a substituted judgment test.

19 We discuss this in *Mason and McCall Smith's Law and Medical Ethics*, *op cit.*, chapter 16.

20 The general principles were laid down in Guardianship of Minors Act 1971, s 1. See, now, Children Act 1989, s 1.

21 See the *Re J* cases, *supra cit*. Compare the first instance ruling in *R (on the application of Burke) v. General Medical Council* [2005] 2 WLR 431, [2004] 3 FCR 579 and our associated commentary: Mason, J.K. and Laurie, G.T., 'Personal Autonomy and the Right to Treatment: A Note on *R (on the application of Burke) v. General Medical Council*', (2005) 9 *Edinburgh Law Review*, 123-132. But see now the reversal of the decision by Court of Appeal on 28 July 2005, available at [2005] EWCA 1003.

22 *Re T*, *supra cit.*

23 *Id.*

established orthodoxy; indeed, in the case of *Re Wyatt (a child) (medical treatment: parents' consent)* it was said that: '... in this case at least the Convention now adds nothing to domestic law'.[24] Although it has been confirmed that disputes over child care and treatment should be referred to the courts because of the need to respect the child's human rights,[25] it has also been confirmed, both domestically[26] and by the European Court of Human Rights itself,[27] that an application of the best interests test by the medical profession on grounds of futility and which leads to the death of the child *can* be perfectly compatible with the Articles of the European Convention on Human Rights.

It seems, then, that the largely paternalistic approach of the best interests test remains ensconced in our law. It deserves such a label for two good reasons: (1) the essential framing of the construct places more focus on third party assessments of interests than on the autonomy of the patient, and (2) because it admits a significant role to the most paternalistic of all professions; a role which is no longer determinative but remains hugely influential. For those for whom *paternalism* remains a very dirty word, then, we might ask if matters could be balanced differently. It is here that we return to Mason's construct of the substituted judgment test. While he acknowledges that in most cases the outcome will be the same whether we apply best interests or substituted judgment, a recent example shows both the development of the law in this field and a perfect illustration of where Mason's model might make a real difference.

W Healthcare NHS Trust v. H and Another[28] involved a patient who had been suffering from multiple sclerosis for 30 years, the last five of which involved artificial feeding and hydration and 24-hour care. She was barely conscious or sentient and when her feeding tube became displaced the question arose of whether it should be replaced. The first important point to note about the Court of Appeal decision is its reliance on the neonate ruling of *Re J*.[29] Mason and I have long maintained that a continuum exists between withholding and withdrawal dilemmas from the beginning of life onwards, and this is the first explicit judicial acknowledgement of this as far as I know. It means, therefore, not only that best interests must apply in these cases, but also that *intolerability* becomes a watch-word as Lord Templeman suggested in *Re B*. Importantly, it meant that the court could not rely on the strong

24 *Re Wyatt (a child) (medical treatment: parents' consent)* [2004] Fam Law 866, para 25.

25 *Glass v. United Kingdom* [2004] 1 FLR 1019, (2004) 77 BMLR 120.

26 *A NHS Trust v. D* [2000] 2 FLR 677, (2000) 55 BMLR 19 (although it should be noted *en passant* that the facts of the case occurred at a time before the Human Rights Act 1998 was in force).

27 *Glass, supra cit.* While the decision went against the United Kingdom in this case, this was primarily because the dispute had not been taken to court; the provisions of Article 8(2) ECHR could not, therefore, be relied upon. Notwithstanding, the ECHR confirmed the acceptability of applying a best interests test.

28 [2004] EWCA Civ 1324, [2005] 1 WLR 834.

29 *Re J* [1990], *supra cit.*

evidence from the family, who were opposing reinsertion of the feeding tube, that their relative would not want to be kept alive in such a state. From the best interests/ intolerability perspective, however, Brooke LJ had this to say, bearing in mind that the patient was not wholly insensate:

> The Court cannot in effect sanction the death by starvation of a patient who is not in a PVS state other than with their clear and informed consent or where their condition is so intolerable as to be beyond doubt ... I cannot say that life-prolonging treatment ... would provide no benefit ... death by this route would ... be even less dignified than the death which she will more probably face at some time in the more distant future.[30]

Mason's subjective judgment approach would elide this outcome, whether on a subjective *or* an objective basis, and may well pay more respect to the patient's residual autonomy as a result. Importantly, however, it would permit the views of the family to be taken into account in at least two senses: that they were saying that this woman would not want to be kept alive, and that this woman would doubtless not want to put her relatives through this experience.

Mason's choice of *Re B* as a seminal case has stood the test of time. It is one of those cases which has found application far beyond its original remit and which has triggered a whole new set of ethical and legal dilemmas. One such other case is Mason's second choice, *Gillick v. Norfolk and Wisbech Area Health Authority*, and these are precisely the reasons why he chose it.

Gillick v. Norfolk and Wisbech Area Health Authority

Gillick arose from the publication of a seemingly innocuous Department of Health memorandum of guidance authorising healthcare professionals to discuss family planning with minors without the explicit consent of their parents, albeit in restricted circumstances. Crucially, however, this extended to the provision of advice on contraception and even contraceptives themselves. Simply,[31] Mrs Gillick sought to have the instruction declared unlawful; the trial judge and Court of Appeal adopted polar opposite views, with the Court of Appeal favouring the 'rights and duties' of parents. In the final analysis, and as Mason has frequently pointed out, more judges agreed with Mrs Gillick than disagreed with her, but the ultimate judgment fell to the House of Lords, and there the majority – 3:2 – disagreed with the appellant.

The seminal nature of *Gillick* stems from its attempt to respond to the realities and vagaries of human development – a complex process that is not amenable to the so-often-crude responses of law. As Lord Scarman stated:

---

30 *Ibid.*, para 22. More recently, the Court of Appeal has stated that while intolerability is not the test of best interests (R (On the application of Burke) v General Medical Council, supra cit, para 63), it can serve as a 'valuable guide in the search for best interests' *(Re Wyatt (a child) (medical treatment: continuation of order)* (2006) 86 BMLR 173, para 76.

31 While other issues were engaged, such as the potential criminal liability of the healthcare professional, here we only consider the autonomy-related aspects of the case.

> If the law should impose upon the process of growing up fixed limits where nature knew only a continuous process, the price would be artificiality and a lack of realism in an area where the law must be sensitive to human development and social change.[32]

The law, of course, does exactly this by setting an arbitrary threshold for maturity based on numerical age and wholly divorced from subjective capabilities. The House of Lords in *Gillick* sought to establish a mechanism whereby more responsiveness to a child's particular circumstances could be shown; it did so not through the parents, however, but through the medical profession, as expressed in the oft-quoted speech of Lord Fraser:

> [T]he doctor will, in my opinion, be justified in proceeding without the parents' consent or even knowledge provided he is satisfied on the following matters: (1) that the girl (although under 16 years of age) will understand his advice; (2) that he cannot persuade her to inform her parents or to allow him to inform the parents that she is seeking contraceptive advice; (3) that she is very likely to begin or to continue having sexual intercourse with or without contraceptive treatment; (4) that unless she receives contraceptive advice or treatment her physical or mental health or both are likely to suffer; (5) that her best interests require him to give her contraceptive advice, treatment or both without the parental consent. [33]

The House of Lords made it abundantly clear that this was not *carte blanche* to the profession to ride rough-shod over the (residual) rights and responsibilities of parents, and this remains embodied in professional guidance to this day.[34] The obvious question in the immediate aftermath of *Gillick* was 'what, precisely, are these (residual) rights and responsibilities?'. This was not, however, the primary preoccupation of most, whose attention, rather, turned to what the *Gillick* ruling meant for the autonomy of the child. Barely pausing for breath, the courts assumed that the precedent was not confined to its particular circumstances of contraception (and confidentiality[35]) but that it extended to the entire field of consent to medical treatment:[36] 'the term *Gillick-competent* is now part of medico-legal lore'.[37] Both issues – that of parental rights and that of child autonomy – converged in the cases

---

32 [1985] 3 All ER 402 at p. 421.

33 *Ibid.*, at p. 413.

34 General Medical Council, *Confidentiality: Protecting and Providing Information* (2004) para 28. See also General Medical Council, *Seeking Patients' Consent: The Ethical Considerations* (1998) para 23.

35 We discuss this in *Mason and McCall Smith's Law and Medical Ethics*, *op cit.*, paras 8.43-8.44.

36 See, for example, *Re P (a minor)* [1986] 1 FLR 272, 80 LGR 301 (court agreed that a schoolgirl aged 15 should be allowed to have an abortion against the wishes of her parents. Butler-Sloss J said: 'I am satisfied she wants this abortion; she understands the implications of it').

37 See, *Mason and McCall Smith's Law and Medical Ethics*, *op cit.*, para 10.27. This is a classic Mason aphorism.

of *Re R*[38] and *Re W*.[39] Each concerned minors of doubtful capacity, not for their immaturity *per se*, but because of mental disorders leading to questions about their ability to decide for themselves. In *Re R* a 15-year-old girl displayed disturbing behaviour for which medication was required, yet she purported to refuse it during her more lucid periods. *Re W* concerned a 16-year-old minor[40] suffering from anorexia nervosa who refused all care and endangered her life in doing so. In both cases the respective courts overrode the children's refusal on the basis of best interests: a court has, through its wardship jurisdiction, the power to overlook any consent or refusal by a child if it is in her or his best interests to do so. As for the residual nature of any parental rights, the courts confirmed that the change that had been brought about by *Gillick* was to remove any right to determine that a mature minor should be treated; there remained, however, a right to consent on the child's behalf, even in the face of the child's objection, provided, once again, that her or his best interests would be served.[41]

So where did this leave the autonomy of mature minors? On one view we might see *Re R* and *Re W* as aberrant cases, distinguishable from *Gillick*, because they concerned children of doubtful capacity and in such cases the general principle of best interests simply applies.[42] But this could not really hold water since there is no suggestion in the rulings that the 'right' of a parent or a court to consent is in any way dependent on the child's incapacity; it exists irrespective of mental capacity and, rather, by dint of immaturity *per se*. This was clearly confirmed in *Re L (medical treatment: Gillick competence)*,[43] which concerned a critically ill 14-year-old girl who professed the Jehovah's Witness faith and refused any treatment involving blood transfusions; treatment which was necessary to save her life. The dispute came to court which ordered treatment against the child's refusal. Despite her maturity, she was adjudged not to be *Gillick*-competent on the basis that she had formed her views within the confines of her community and had not benefited from broader experience, and that she had not been informed of the likely horrific nature of her death, albeit that she understood that she would die as a direct consequence of her refusal.[44] Importantly, however, the court stated obiter that in the circumstances of her case treatment would have been ordered *even if* she had been Gillick-competent. So

---

38 *Re R (a minor)(wardship: medical treatment)* [1992] Fam 11, (1991) 7 BMLR 147.

39 *Re W (a minor) (medical treatment)* [1992] 4 All ER 627, (1992) 9 BMLR 22. For a comparable Australian case, see *DoCS v. Y* [1999] NSWSC 644.

40 The statutory aspects of this under s 8 of the Family Reform Act 1969 are discussed in *Mason and McCall Smith's Law and Medical Ethics*, *op cit.*, paras 10.48-10.51.

41 On the interesting concept of 'family autonomy', protected by the Irish Constitution. see, *North Western Health Board v. W (H)* [2001] IESC 70. For commentary see Laurie, G.T., 'Better to Hesitate at the Threshold of Compulsion: PKU Testing and the Concept of Family Autonomy in Eire', (2002) 28 *Journal of Medical Ethics*, 136-138.

42 See, in fact, *Re R*, *supra cit.*

43 [1998] 2 FLR 810. [1998] 2 FLR 810, [1999] 2 FCR 524, [1998] Fam Law 591.

44 See too *Re E* where it was said of a 15-year-old '*Gillick*-competent' boy who was refusing blood transfusion: 'I respect this boy's profession of faith, but I cannot discount at

the matter seems fairly unequivocal: recognition of a minor's developing autonomy is conditional on treatment decisions being in her or his best interests – as the House of Lords intended – and the concern of their Lordships not to ride rough-shod over residual parental rights remains a core part of the law.

At the risk of continuing the Fox and Hounds metaphor too far, it is nevertheless apt to recall that Ian Kennedy famously said of *Re R* that it was 'driving a coach and horses through *Gillick*'.[45] And in *Re W* we also have Balcolme LJ acknowledging that '[i]n logic there can be no difference between an ability to consent to treatment and an ability to refuse treatment'.[46] But logic is not the only issue, nor is autonomy the only value at stake. Mason has long argued in defence of a more protectionist stance towards the mature minor, particularly where decisions can have serious ramifications such as ongoing suffering or death. But is this a sustainable and defensible position? After years of long drawn-out debate – the subject is one of our favourite 'fights' in classes that we teach together – I rather think that it is; moreover, I think that there are parallels yet to be drawn with the law's attitude towards the adult incompetent that may assist Mason's case.

Mason's starting premise is that truly autonomous choices require not only information but a level of understanding and appreciation of the consequences of each decision. As he has argued:

> … while consent involves acceptance of an experienced view, refusal rejects that experience – and does so from a position of limited understanding. Furthermore, a refusal of medical treatment may close down the options – and this may be regretted later in that the chance to consent has now passed. The implications of refusal may, therefore, be more serious and, on these grounds refusal of treatment may require greater understanding than does acceptance. A level of comprehension sufficient to justify refusal of treatment certainly includes one to accept treatment but the reverse does not hold; the two conditions cannot be regarded as being on a par.[47]

An answer to this is to provide more and better information to facilitate understanding. This, surely, is the criticism to be levelled at the decision in *Re L*. In this sense, the mature minor's position is not that different from the adult incapax who is also held to a higher standard. As *Re C (adult: refusal of medical treatment)*[48] made very clear, a patient of dubious capacity must demonstrate *actual understanding* of the nature and consequences of their decision. Mere *capacity to understand* is not enough as it is for the capax adult, but then, the mature minor and the incapax adult do not

---

least the possibility that he may in later years suffer some diminution in his convictions', per Ward J: *Re E (a minor)* [1993] 1 FLR 386, 394.

45 Kennedy, I., 'Consent to Treatment: The Capable Person', in Dyer, C. (ed), *Doctors, Patients and the Law*, Oxford, Blackwell, 1992, chapter 3.

46 *Re W (a minor) (medical treatment)* [1992] 4 All ER 627, at p. 643.

47 *Mason and McCall Smith's Law and Medical Ethics*, *op cit.*, para 10.52.

48 [1994] 1 All ER 819, [1994] 1 WLR 290.

fall into that category. Nor was the ruling in *Gillick* ever designed to catapult the minor into that category – this comes later when the crude numerical threshold is crossed. Only at that point do all of the attendant consequences of adulthood follow, one of which is the *presumption of capacity*. In this sense, then, the adult incapax is in a diametrically opposite position to the mature minor for whom the default is a *presumption of incapacity*. Mason's argument is not that we should not seek to respect the emerging autonomy of children, but rather that we owe them continuing obligations to protect them from decisions that are manifestly bad for them. How do we know that they are bad? Because the parents or the carers or the courts tell us so. Such an overtly paternalistic view does not devalue autonomy as a relevant criterion but it does seek a more sophisticated accommodation of the values and interests at stake: when autonomy and welfare stand in direct opposition it is by no means clear that autonomy should be the trump card.[49]

In the same way that an incompetent adult is not incompetent in respect of all decisions because the presumption is one *of competence*, the corollary holds that a competent child is not necessarily competent in respect of all decisions because the presumption is one *of incompetence*. But in all cases where incompetence is in issue – either as a presumption or as a fact – the same welfare principles apply if we perceive the patient to be in harm's way. To an extent, however, the framing of the debate in terms of *Gillick*-competence is misleading because this language admits of the possibility that the presumption of incompetence can be rebutted and, for the child, that competence to decide can be demonstrated; the implication from this being that competent decisions – however bad – should be respected. But this is only a part of the considerations required under Lord Fraser's test. No amount of evidence about capacity to decide autonomously can elide the responsibility also to consider whether such a decision is nonetheless in the child's own best interests. Thus, as *Re L* demonstrates, it is entirely possible to acknowledge that a state of competence has been reached and still to decide that manifestly bad decisions will not be respected. It is one of the few areas of medical law concerning 'choice' where autonomy does not have the last say. By the same token, it should not be thought that an autonomy perspective and a best interests perspective are necessarily mutually exclusive. The decisions in this field are replete with references to the need to accommodate the mature minor's views as far as possible. Nor should it be thought that a best interest perspective necessarily means that a refusal of medical care is necessarily an unacceptable option. The case of *Re T*[50] demonstrates judicial sensitivity to the

---

49 *In the Matter of X* [2002] JRC 202 the court respected the refusal of a 16-year-old woman to authorise transfer of tissue from her aborted foetus to the police to determine paternity for the purposes of possible prosecution of a man for unlawful sexual intercourse. This was so despite affidavits from the parents consenting to the procedure. Nonetheless, the court reiterated that its inherent jurisdiction meant that the refusal could be overridden in the child's best interests; in the instance case, however, the court was not convinced that those interests would be served by dismissing the refusal.

50 *Re T (a minor) (wardship: medical treatment)* [1997] 1 WLR 242, [1997] 1 All ER 906.

position of parents who did not want to put their child through painful surgical procedures even although there was overwhelming medical support for intervention and even although the refusal will meant that the child would die. All of this was justified in the child's own best interests.

Those who criticise the rulings typified by *Re R* and *Re W* seek to treat mature minor autonomy in the same crude sense that the law of majority does – once you reach an all-important threshold (be it age or *Gillick*-competence) then the presumption shifts and you are free to take all the bad decisions you want irrespective of their consequences. But being in a state of autonomy is not an all-or-nothing affair nor is it an irreversible state (unlike majority). There may be many times in life when we as adults do not have capacity to take our own decisions; not in an organic disease-related sense, but perhaps because of a lack of information or understanding or guidance from others. The presumption of capacity, however, masks this reality in all but the most clear-cut of cases which usually *are* disease-related. No one is there to protect us from ourselves. In the context of the child, however, where there is a presumption of incapacity and where there is a continuing obligation to protect his or her welfare, such an all-or-nothing attitude to autonomous decisionmaking can be seen as tantamount to abandonment of the patient. While we may find this acceptable in the case of the competent adult, there are too many doubts and unresolved issues to justify the bringing forward of the 'clear-line approach' to maturity and autonomy. There is no such clear line.

Re MB (adult: medical treatment) and A-G's Reference (No. 3 of 1994)

Perhaps the best (or worst?) examples of clear-line thinking in medical law relate to the so-called maternal/foetal conflict and to the question of the legal status of the foetus. These neatly come together in Mason's choice of *Re MB (adult: medical treatment)* and *A-G's Reference (No. 3 of 1994)* in his list of seminal cases and it makes sense, therefore, that they be considered together. The choice of these cases reflects the very strong interest, and influence, that Ken Mason has had in academic discourse on reproductive matters throughout the course of his 'third' career.[51]

Re MB confirmed that the ruling from the earlier decision in *Re T (adult: refusal of medical treatment)*[52] – that an adult patient of sound mind has an absolute right to consent to or to refuse medical treatment – applies equally to the pregnant woman even if her decisions might result in the death of her unborn child. Some doubts about the extension of the 'absolute autonomy' principle to the pregnant woman carrying a viable foetus had been expressed in *Re T* itself,[53] and the distinction was

51 Prior to his position as an Honorary Fellow in the School of Law, Ken Mason was Regius Professor of Forensic Medicine in the University of Edinburgh and prior to that had a very distinguished career as a pathologist in the Royal Air Force.

52 [1992] 4 All ER 649, (1992) 9 BMLR 46.

53 [1992] 4 All ER 649 at pp. 652-653, (1992) 9 BMLR 46 at p. 50.

applied in a handful of extremely contentious cases,[54] but the Court of Appeal was categorical in *Re MB*; at least as to principle. In practice, however, the position has almost always been different and there is precious little evidence of cases in which a pregnant woman's refusal has been accepted. The common scenario in the disputed cases, including *Re MB*,[55] is to impose a finding of incompetence thereby allowing the patient to be treated in her own best interests – the classic default position. For example, in *Bolton Hospitals NHS Trust v. O*[56] the court wholeheartedly endorsed the *Re MB* principle but still found a woman with post traumatic stress temporarily incompetent due to panic induced by flash-backs. Furthermore, the assumption has always been that it is self-evidently in the woman's best interests for the child to be born. Only in *St George's Healthcare NHS Trust v. S, R v. Collins, ex p S* [57] did the Court of Appeal condemn an involuntary caesarean section which had been carried out under the authority of the mental health legislation. This was a trespass on an otherwise competent woman.

For Mason, the tenor of these precedents typifies the bluntness of the law as a tool for social change or for regulating ethical practice. His insights from the medical perspective are strongly cognisant of the challenges faced by medical staff and of the dilemma of being responsible, simultaneously, for two lives. The categorical 'principled' stand of the law which so clearly favours one of those lives does not alleviate the ethical dilemma, even if it makes the position on potential legal liability abundantly clear. It is no wonder that the law is ambivalent in practice, because the practical realities are far more complex than dogged adherence to the principle of the law would suggest. Yet it is questionable whether the law can ever be more responsive to the doctor's dilemma of 'two lives/one choice' in light of the clear preference for, and privileging of, the principle of respect for personal autonomy over other values such as, for example, the principle of sanctity of life. But even if the debate were to be re-framed along autonomy lines – for example, the autonomy of the woman v. the (future) autonomy of the future person – it is still clear that any such conflict could not be resolved '... on autonomy grounds alone'.[58] And all of

---

54 See *Re S (adult: refusal of medical treatment)* [1992] 4 All ER 671, (1992) 9 BMLR 69 which was decided only two and a half months after *Re T*. See too, *Norfolk and Norwich Healthcare (NHS) Trust v. W* [1996] 2 FLR 613, (1996) 34 BMLR 16, *Rochdale Healthcare (NHS) Trust v. C* [1997] 1 FCR 274. and *Tameside and Glossop Acute Services Trust v. CH (a patient)* [1996] 1 FLR 762, (1996) 31 BMLR 93. For analysis see Grubb, A., 'Commentary', (1996) 4 *Medical Law Review*, 193-198. The consequence in each case was the imposition of a caesarean section against the women's express wishes.

55 The woman in *Re MB* suffered from a phobia of needles which led her to refuse a caesarean operation while all the time stating that she wanted her baby. She was declared incompetent as a result; in the event, however, she consented to the procedure.

56 [2003] 1 FLR 824, [2003] Fam Law 319.

57 See [1999] Fam 26, (1998) 44 BMLR 194.

58 I borrow this expression from Ngwena, C. and Chadwick, R., 'Genetic Diagnostic Information and the Duty of Confidentiality: Ethics and Law', 1 *Medical Law International*, 73-95.

this ignores the fact that the two parties to the conflict are not of equal standing, at least in the eyes of the law. Indeed, it was a concern with the particular legal status of the foetus that led Mason to add *Attorney-General's Reference (No. 3 of 1994)*[59] to his list.

Attorney-General's Reference (No. 3 of 1994) is the first of two criminal cases among Mason's top five. Its significance here lies in the ongoing unwillingness of the law – or perhaps more accurately, the courts – to grasp the nettle on the definitive status of the foetus in law. While this is perhaps more understandable in the context of cases which involve a potential conflict between the interests or rights of the mother and those of her foetus (should we ever choose to recognise them), this was not a problem in the instant case. As Mason has commented: 'we are here concerned, not with foetal/maternal conflict, but, rather, with the protection of the foetal/maternal symbiosis'.[60]

Attorney-General's Reference (No. 3 of 1994) was concerned with the relatively straightforward question of whether it would be competent to charge a person with murder for the death of a foetus from injuries sustained *in utero*. The case involved a man who had stabbed his pregnant girlfriend and, in doing so, inadvertently also stabbed the foetus. The woman went into premature labour and the child was born alive, but died 120 days later. The man was charged with the murder of the foetus. In yet another example of clear-line thinking, it is now common ground that an unborn child has interests protected by law in a number of areas,[61] but that none of these crystallises as a 'right' until the child is born alive, and in some cases, survives a requisite period of time.[62] Accordingly, there has never been a recognised crime of foeticide.[63] The refusal to recognise the foetus as a bearer of rights *in se* stems back to the seventeenth century,[64] and *Attorney General's Reference* presented as a perfect opportunity to revisit the rule. In the end, however, the House of Lords did no such thing. Instead, they further obscured the status of the foetus by leaving it in a form of legal limbo-land as neither a 'person' nor a 'thing' but a 'unique organism' which is not merely a part of its mother but which also had no distinct legal personality. Of this ruling Mason has had this to say:

---

59 [1998] 1 Cr App R 91.

60 Mason, J.K., 'A Lords' Eye View of Fetal Status', (1999) 3 *Edinburgh Law Review*, 246-250, at p. 250.

61 For example, in tort, for negligently caused harm both under the Congenital Disabilities (Civil Liability) Act 1976, and at common law (*Burton v. Islington Health Authority, De Martell v. Merton and Sutton Health Authority* [1992] 3 All ER 833 and *Hamilton v. Fife Health Board* 1993 SC 369).

62 The Congenital Disabilities (Civil Liability) Act 1976 requires the child to live 48 hours before it can seek compensation under the Act for negligently inflicted injury in utero.

63 Mason distinguishes *foeticide* from the offence of child destruction under the Infant Life Preservation Act 1929 on the basis that, '[c]riminal abortion involves the procuring of a woman's miscarriage which only results in feticide consequentially', see 'A Lords' Eye View of Fetal Status', *supra cit*, footnote 9.

64 Sir Edward Coke, *Institutes of the Law of England*, Pt III, Chap 7, at p. 50.

> Could it not be that modern genetics, physiology, applied psychology and the rest must now cast serious doubt on the concept that the fetus has no distinct human personality? I suggest that the serious conceptual disagreements between the Court of Appeal and the House of Lords evidence in the *Attorney-General's Reference* under discussion indicate that the time has come for a thorough review of fetal status – at least from the point of view of the criminal law. It seems wholly illogical that there should be an offence of neonatal murder but not of feticide, and that it is safer by far, in both civil and criminal jurisdictions, to kill a fetus rather than to injure it.[65]

One wonders how much logic has to do with it. As was pointed out above in the context of the protection of mature minors, logic is not all that is at issue. Although the absence of maternal/foetal conflict in this case offered an opportunity to establish a precedent that would not necessarily lead to (impossibly) difficult choices as between parties, it must have been at the forefront of their Lordships' minds whether – in these circumstances – any shift from the threshold of 'birth' as the trigger for rights would inevitably lead to similar debates being rehearsed in the maternal/foetal context. I have considered elsewhere the long-standing ambivalence of the courts to take on board arguments about foetal 'human rights',[66] and Mason has commented more recently on the same phenomenon.[67] This may be an area where maintaining clear-line thinking – even if the thinking itself is far from clear – is the only acceptable judicial policy.

R v. Cox

The above comment on reluctance to recognise any form of foetal rights for fear of losing control of the field, is, essentially, a point about slippery slopes, and nowhere are such concerns more prevalent than in the field of euthanasia. Mason's final choice of a criminal prosecution of a doctor for the deliberate taking of a patient's life is apt, in bringing together the three main branches of medical law – medicine, law and ethics – in a particularly acute form where the ultimate respect that might be paid to a patient's autonomy – respect for their choice to die – potentially conflicts with the 'autonomy' of the medical profession in respecting its primary guiding principle: First do no harm.

It will be recalled that Dr Cox, a consultant rheumatologist, was convicted of attempted murder after administering potassium chloride – which is entirely toxic to the human organism and has no therapeutic application – to his patient, Mrs

65 Mason, 'A Lords' Eye View of Fetal Status', *loc cit.*, at p. 249.

66 For consideration of whether a human rights analysis might strengthen the legal position of the foetus, see Laurie, G.T., 'Medical Law and Human Rights: Passing the Parcel Back to the Profession?', in Boyle, A. *et al.* (eds), *Human Rights and Scots Law: Comparative Perspectives on the Incorporation of the ECHR*, Oxford, Hart Publishing, 2002, pp. 245-274.

67 Mason, J.K., 'What's In a Name? – The Vagaries of *Vo v. France*', (2005) 17 *Child and Family Law Quarterly*, 97-112.

Lillian Boyes, on her repeated request to be helped to die to release her from the excruciating pain of her rheumatoid arthritis.[68] Dr Cox was convicted because the jury had no real choice. The usual devices that are employed on behalf of the medical profession to avoid the charge of euthanistic practices were not available to Dr Cox. Mrs Boyes was not terminally ill and there was therefore no medical intervention keeping her alive that could be withdrawn. The agent administered to her had no analgesic effect, so it could not be argued that the 'real' intention was to relieve pain, and that death only came as an attendant consequence. Indeed, the facts pointed to the conclusion that death *was* the primary intention. And finally, since the criminal law universally treats motive as irrelevant, the jury was left with the crude question: did Dr Cox intend to kill his patient?[69] To which the answer was an unqualified 'yes'. The law in the United Kingdom is currently too intransigent or inflexible to accommodate subtle, but crucial, distinctions between cases which *do* depend on motive.[70] As Mason has said: '... Dr Cox was certainly not a murderer as the word is commonly interpreted'.[71]

So should the law in this field be changed, and what would inform our answer to this question one way or the other? It is illuminating within the field of medical law in the United Kingdom to contrast the views of Mason with those of Emily Jackson,[72] because they each come to the discipline from very different perspectives.[73] In the present context, for example, Jackson has recently argued that the continuing prohibition on active euthanasia at the explicit request of a patient runs entirely contrary to the autonomy ethos that has gripped the discipline in recent years. In particular, Jackson is extremely skeptical of the standard position of the medical profession that the mantra 'First do no harm' justifies a blanket ban on physician-assisted or accomplished death.[74]

Mason has himself pointed to the obvious answer to involving physicians in active euthanasia, namely; using specialists in the care of the terminally ill.[75] But his concerns are far more deep-rooted and, as one would imagine, are not resolved by an appeal to autonomy alone. First, he is acutely sensitive to the position of responsible

---

68 *R v. Cox* (1992) 12 BMLR 38.

69 *R v. Cox* (1992) 12 BMLR 38 at p. 39.

70 Contrast this with the position in Switzerland where the legality of an act to assist another in dying is all about motive. So long as the assistance is provided is a selfless act – that is it is not for a selfish motive – then no criminal liability will flow from a successful assisted suicide. For commentary, See Guillod, O. and Schmidt, A., 'Assisted Suicide under Swiss Law', 12(1) (2005) *European Journal of Health Law*, 25-38

71 *Mason and McCall Smith's Law and Medical Ethics, op cit.*, para 17.28.

72 Professor of Medical Law at Queen Mary College, University of London.

73 Compare, for example, Mason, J.K., *Medico-Legal Aspects of Reproduction and Parenthood*, Second Edition, Aldershot, Dartmouth, 1998 and Jackson, E., *Regulating Reproduction*, Oxford, Hart Publishing, 2001.

74 Jackson, E., 'Whose Death Is It Anyway? Euthanasia and the Medical Profession', (2004) *Current Legal Problems*, 415-442.

75 Mason, J.K., 'Death and Dying: One Step at a Time?', in McLean, S.A.M. (ed), *Death, Dying and the Law*, Aldershot, Dartmouth, 1996, 161-178.

medical staff who are asked to comply with requests to die when '[s]tandard medical teaching remains that we should never willingly and deliberately shorten life'.[76] This may be anachronistic for Jackson, but Mason's perspective nevertheless accurately reflects the attitude of much of the profession whose professional autonomy is at stake within any legally sanctioned euthanasia regime.[77] This brings us to another of Mason's concerns; *viz*, the necessity of a conscience clause in any such framework. Recent legislative proposals in the House of Lords have reflected this, and the second of two Bills proposed by Lord Joffe included not only a conscience clause but also an associated obligation for anyone purporting to rely on the clause to refer the patient to a colleague who is prepared to adhere to the patient's request.[78] It is interesting to speculate what Mason's response would be to the recommendations from the House of Lords Select Committee set up to consider the Bill. In one respect, the Committee took a broad team-based approach to the issue of conscience, acknowledging that:

> Conscientious objections could however arise not only from doctors but also from other health care professionals, including nurses and pharmacists ... [and that any new Bill] ... should seek to address such situations as that in which, for example, a nurse with conscientious objections is asked by a patient to raise with a doctor on his or her behalf a request for assisted suicide or voluntary euthanasia.[79]

I imagine that this would be entirely in keeping with Mason's own perspective.[80] But the Select Committee also recommended that the obligation to refer the patient should be removed because, '[an] ... obligation to refer a requesting patient to a

---

76 See *Mason and McCall Smith's Law and Medical Ethics*, *op cit.*, para 17.105 and quote from the medical correspondent of *The Times* in note 196 associated with this paragraph.

77 Evidence led to the House of Lords Select Committee on Assisted the Assisted Dying for the Terminally Ill Bill suggested that '... the Bill, if it were to become law, might well be unworkable because of the conscientious objections of many of those who would be called upon to put it into practice', see House of Lords Select Committee on Assisted the Assisted Dying for the Terminally Ill Bill, Assisted Dying for the Terminally Ill Bill – First Report, HL 86-I, 2005, para 113. The Report continues: 'We did not, it has to be said, receive indications from the authorities in other countries where legislation of this nature has been enacted that significant problems had been encountered in regard to conscientious objection by large numbers of doctors and nurses, though it is perhaps necessary to bear in mind that the composition of the medical and nursing professions in this country is rather different from that in, for example, Holland, where over 90 per cent of doctors are of Dutch origin', *ibid.*, para 114.

78 Two Bills were proposed in 2003 and 2004 respectively; the latter being the Assisted Dying for the Terminally Ill Bill. A House of Lords Select Committee reported on the matter in April 2005 (Select Committee on the *Assisted Dying for the Terminally Ill Bill, Assisted Dying for the Terminally Ill Bill – First Report* (2005)) and recommended that a new Bill be introduced. The *Assisted Dying for the Terminally Ill Bill* appeared in November 2005 and was due for its second reading at the time of going to press (May 2006).

79 Select Committee Report, *supra cit.*, para 262.

80 See, for example, in the context of abortion, Mason's comments on *R v. Salford Health Authority, ex parte Janaway* [1998] 2 WLR 442, CA; *sub nom Janaway v. Salford Area Health*

colleague could nonetheless be regarded as an infringement of conscience'.[81] I suspect that this would jar with Mason as coming close to patient abandonment in a time of need. However much he might disagree with the request, he would probably consider it part of a professional's ongoing commitment to the patient to facilitate their autonomous choices where the law is set up to see those choices through. The limit here would be on *professional autonomy*.

Perhaps contrary to what one might expect from Mason's medical training and religious faith, he is not entirely against assisting people to die; rather, his contribution to the debate has focused on the lack of clarity in what we mean by 'euthanasia' (only some forms of which he will endorse); it has drawn attention to the hypocrisy of the law in adhering to non-distinctions such as the act/omission distinction; and it has called for a more honest approach to what the medical professions are asked to do when the direct result of their actions is the death of their patients. All of this distils to the question of how acceptable forms of euthanasia may be brought within the fold of legally acceptable practice. Of course, what is 'acceptable' is highly subjective, but for Mason this is found in two sets of circumstances: the patient in Persistent (or Permanent) Vegetative State (PVS) and Physician-Assisted Suicide (PAS). Mason stops short, however, of endorsing active euthanasia in circumstances such as those in which Dr Cox found himself, largely on the grounds of concerns about slippery slopes, informed by the experiences of the Netherlands.[82] Indeed, he endorses an experiential and incremental approach to the legalisation of euthanistic practices.[83]

It is at this point that Mason and I part company. I am not convinced that any slippery slopes that might be deduced from the practice of euthanasia in one (or more) countries (and this itself is a disputed matter) necessarily prevents us from adopting a principled approach to euthanasia – an approach which *is* a logical extension of the principle of respect for personal autonomy. Nor do I see the impact on patient autonomy of disrespecting requests for assistance in dying as comparable to the impact on professional autonomy of respecting such requests. The disparity is simply too great not to prefer the former over the latter. But, then, this chapter is not about me.

The role of legislation in this field is integral to Mason's approach. We have argued elsewhere in the context of the PVS patient that to rely on the fallacy of

---

Authority [1989] AC 537, HL in *Medico-legal Aspects of Reproduction and Parenthood, op cit.*, at pp. 127-129.

81 Select Committee Report, *supra cit.*, para 32. Clause 7(3) of the 2005/6 Bill reads: "No person shall be under any duty to raise the option of assisted dying with a patient, to refer a patient to any other source for obtaining information or advice pertaining to assistance to die, or to refer a patient to any other person for assistance to die under the provisions of this Act."

82 See, *Mason and McCall Smith's Law and Medical Ethics, op cit.*, paras 17.16-17.23 and paras 17.120-17.124.

83 Mason, J.K. and Mulligan, D., 'Euthanasia by Stages', (1996) 347 *The Lancet*, 810-811.

'futility' to justify the withdrawal or withholding of artificial feeding and hydration from such a patient is fundamentally dishonest in that it obscures the reality that we have taken a quality of life decision that this person should die. No amount of semantics can avoid this, yet the continued reliance on this reasoning leaves the courts with only one option: to authorise the starvation of patients to death. This cannot now be changed save through statute and we have advocated that this should be so.[84] In the context of Physician-Assisted Suicide, Mason has proposed a number of reforming measures,[85] including this simple amendment to the Suicide Act 1961:

> The provisions of s 2(1) shall not apply to a registered medical practitioner who, given the existence of a competent directive, is providing assistance to a patient who is suffering from a progressive and irremediable condition and who is prevented, or will be prevented, by physical disability from ending his or her own life without assistance.

In the final analysis, however, and as is stated above, Mason would not go so far as to condone, let alone legalise, what Dr Cox did for Lillian Boyes. In fact, his concerns may be summed up best if I rephrase this slightly: He would not condone nor legalise what Dr Cox did *to* Lillian Boyes. And, this, perhaps, is where the heart of the concern lies – the prospect of the medical professional taking on the mantle of the Bringer of Death is too much for a medical man whose conscience, and whose commitment to others, cannot allow autonomy arguments to triumph – however logical they may be.

---

84 See Mason, J.K. and Laurie, G.T., 'The Management of the Persistent Vegetative State in the British Isles', [1996] *Juridical Review*, 263-283, and for problems with the current statutory provisions, see Laurie, G.T. and Mason, J.K., 'Negative Treatment of Vulnerable Patients: Euthanasia by any Other Name?', [2000] *Juridical Review*, 159-178.

85 See, for example, 'Euthanasia by Stages', *supra cit.*, and Myers, D.W. and Mason, J.K., 'Physician Assisted Suicide: A Second View from Mid-Atlantic', (1999) 28 *Anglo-American Law Review*, 265-286.

Chapter 10

Conceptualising Privacy in Relation to Medical Research Values

Deryck Beyleveld

Introduction

Many medical researchers are hostile towards laws that protect privacy, For example, in November 2000 the *Health Service Journal* reported on a campaign by cancer epidemiologists led by Professor Peto (henceforth, 'the Peto campaign'), that called for all medical research to be exempted from the UK Data Protection Act 1998 and for the common law on confidentiality to be relaxed.[1] In particular, the epidemiologists claimed that the need to obtain consent was impracticable and led to poor research results, which meant that more people were dying than need be the case.

This campaign suggests a particular conception of the relationship between protection of privacy (and other fundamental rights and freedoms implicated in data protection/the protection of confidentiality) and the values that guide (or should guide) medical research, which I will designate 'the conflict model' of the relationship between privacy and medical research values, coupled with a 'narrow' conception of the right to privacy, according to which the only legitimate privacy interest that persons have in the use made of sensitive personal data relating to them is in protection of their personal identities. Such a 'narrow' conception of privacy, which implies that the right to privacy is not engaged in the use of personal data once it has been rendered anonymous, has received some support from the Court of Appeal of England and Wales.[2] However, I shall argue that the jurisprudence surrounding Article 8.1 of the European Convention on Human Rights (ECHR) consistently propounds a broad conception of this right, according to which it protects a very wide range of interests. Indeed, under this 'broad' conception, any use made of sensitive personal data engages Article 8.1 of the ECHR unless explicit consent has been given by the person to whom it relates. Without this consent, *any* use made of sensitive personal data will be a breach of Article 8 ECHR, *unless* a justification for

---

1 'Cancer Experts Call for Action on GMC's Confidentiality Rules', 2 November 2000 *Health Service Journal*, 4.

2 *R v. Department of Health, Ex Parte Source Informatics Ltd.* [1999] 4 All ER 185 in the High Court, [2000] 1 All ER 786 in the Court of Appeal of England and Wales. See note 3.

this is available under Article 8.2 ECHR. Given the place of the ECHR in relation to UK domestic law, to EC law, and the relationship between EC law and UK domestic law, legally, the broad conception must be adopted.

I will also argue that the broad conception of privacy implies a complex set of relationships between privacy and medical research values, in which these values, while certainly capable of coming into conflict, can also systematically support each other, which suggests a different model, which I will call the 'co-operative model'. I will argue that this conception is also implied by standard public interest reasons (ignored by the Court of Appeal in *Source Informatics*[3]) for considering data relating to a person's health given to health professionals to be confidential. In addition, there are good ethical reasons for preferring the co-operative model.

Finally, I will make some suggestions as to how conflicts between privacy and medical research values (which can still arise within the co-operative model) are to be assessed.

Narrow Conception: The Source Informatics Case

In *R v. Department of Health Ex Parte Source Informatics Ltd.*,[4] Source Informatics Ltd., a database company seeking to obtain information about GPs prescribing habits from pharmacists, which it hoped to sell to pharmaceutical companies for the purposes of direct marketing of GPs, applied for declaratory relief against advice given to pharmacists and GPs by the Department of Health in a letter to Health Authorities. The letter advised that GPs and pharmacists who participated in such schemes without the consent of patients would be acting in breach of confidence even if the information was disclosed to database companies like Source Informatics Ltd. in anonymous form, because patients give the information for their treatment not for the purposes of these schemes. In the High Court, Latham J declared the Department of Health's advice to be lawful. However, this judgment was overturned on appeal (in which the General Medical Council, the Medical Research Council, the Association of British Pharmaceutical Industries and the National Pharmaceutical Association all intervened on the side of Source Informatics Ltd.). The Court of Appeal's reasoning (Simon Brown LJ giving the leading judgment, which was supported without comment by Aldous LJ and Schiemann LJ) was essentially that the basis of the duty of confidence in the use of information given by patients to health professionals for their treatment lies in equity, with the consequence that the scope of the duty rests on nothing more and nothing less than whether there can be further use or disclosure of the data without unfair treatment of the patient.

3 *Supra cit.*

4 *R v. Department of Health, Ex Parte Source Informatics Ltd, supra cit.* For full commentaries see Beyleveld, D. and Histed, E., 'Anonymisation is not Exoneration', 4 (1999) *Medical Law International*, 69-80 and Beyleveld, D. and Histed, E., 'Betrayal of Confidence in the Court of Appeal', 4 (2000) *Medical Law International*, 277-311.

According the Court, unfair treatment is treatment contrary to the legitimate interests of the patient, and in:

> a case like the present which involves personal confidences ... [t]he concern of the law ... is to protect the confider's personal privacy. That and that alone is the right at issue in this case.[5]

In relation to this, the Court held that concealment of the confider's personal identity in any further disclosures or uses of the confided information is sufficient to secure protection of the confider's personal privacy.[6] Thus, since pharmacists were only handing over anonymised (indeed, aggregated) data, '[t]he patient's privacy will have been safeguarded, not invaded. The pharmacists' duty of confidence will not have been breached'.[7]

While the Court did not go quite so far as to declare that once personal information is rendered anonymous it can, under no circumstances whatsoever, continue to attract a duty of confidence,[8] the Court nonetheless adopted a very narrow conception of privacy. In particular, the Court rejected the idea that the use of the information without the consent of the patient necessarily involves a breach of confidence, because a breach of confidence is not, in essence, use of information contrary to the purposes for which it was confided; the test is rather whether or not further use satisfies the confidant's 'own conscience, no more and no less'.[9] On this, it matters only what a reasonable confidant may do. Thus, the Court is required to ask:

> [O]n the facts of this case: would a reasonable pharmacist's conscience be troubled by the proposed use to be made of the patients' prescriptions? Would he think that by entering Source's scheme he was breaking his customers' confidence, making unconscientious use of the information they provide?[10]

And the Court gave clear indication that not only would it not consider unconsented use to be unfair (and by the same token, a breach of privacy/confidentiality), but that it would even be prepared to countenance use against the patient's explicit objection, for in the Court's view, there is a need to find a solution to:

> [s]uch problems as the well-recognised reluctance of certain people to accept the views of those in authority as to just what is or is not good for them, and, let us postulate, the occasional patient who expressly purports to refuse permission for his prescription form to be used for any purpose save only the dispensing of the prescribed drug.[11]

---

5 [2000] 1 All ER 786, at p. 797.
6 *Id.*
7 *Id.*
8 *Ibid.*, at p. 792.
9 *Ibid.*, at p. 796.
10 *Id.*
11 *Ibid.*, at p. 800.

While the case concerned confidentiality, not data protection, it should be noted that the Court was drawn to declare that processing of the information by the GPs and pharmacists would not fall under the Data Protection Directive[12] because Recital 26 thereof states that the principles of data protection shall not apply to data rendered anonymous in such a way that the data subject is no longer identifiable directly or indirectly by anyone. When it was argued on behalf of the Department of Health that the Directive, by specifying anything done 'upon' personal data as processing of it, including deletion and destruction of it, renders anonymisation of it a process performed upon personal data,[13] to which (according the Recital 26) the principles of protection must apply, the Court held that this only has a bearing on cases where erasure 'could impair the patient's own health requirements'.[14] Bearing in mind that Article 1.1 of the Directive has it that the object of the Directive is to protect fundamental rights and freedoms, in particular, privacy, in the processing of personal data, this is questionable unless a very narrow conception of privacy is employed.

Broad Conception: Jurisprudence of the ECHR

A different conception of privacy is to be found in the jurisprudence of the European Court of Human Rights and the (now defunct) Commission on Human Rights of the Council of Europe.

According to Professor Jacques Velu, the right to respect for private life under Article 8.1 of the European Convention on Human Rights protects the individual against:

1. attacks on his physical or mental integrity or his moral or intellectual freedom;
2. attacks on his honour and reputation and similar torts;
3. the use of his name, identity or likeness;
4. being spied upon, watched or harassed;
5. the disclosure of information protected by the duty of professional secrecy.[15]

Similar statements are routinely made by the European Court of Human Rights in its judgments.[16]

So broad is the conception of this jurisprudence that, as L.G. Loucaides has rightly concluded, case law under the European Convention on Human Rights:

---

12 Directive 95/46/EC.

13 See Article 2(c).

14 [2000] 1 All ER 786, at p. 799.

15 'The European Convention on Human Rights and the Right to Respect for Private Life, the Home and Communications', in Robertson, A.H. (ed), *Privacy and Human Rights*, Manchester, Manchester University Press, 1973, 12-128, at p. 92.

16 See, e.g., *P.G. and J.H. v. the United Kingdom* (44787/98 [2001] ECHR 546 (25 September 2001), para 56 and the further references given there.

> has expounded and upheld the protection of privacy to such a degree that, for all practical purposes, the right of privacy has become a functional equivalent of a right of personality, potentially embracing all those constituent parts of the personality of the individual that are not expressly safeguarded by the European Convention.[17]

Furthermore, that this jurisprudence is contrary to the 'narrow' conception has been explicitly recognised by the Commission of the Council of Europe, according to which, while:

> [f]or numerous Anglo-Saxon and French authors the right to respect for 'private life' is ... the right to live as far as one wishes, protected from publicity ... the right to respect for private life does not end there [but includes also the right to] ... the development and fulfilment of one's own personality.[18]

From this it should come as no surprise that, according to the European Court of Human Rights, failure to obtain explicit consent for the use of sensitive personal information automatically engages Article 8.1 of the ECHR (hence the right to private life, and privacy), meaning that any unconsented use of such information is a violation of the right to privacy, *unless* justified within the terms of Article 8.2.[19]

The Narrow Conception and the Conflict Model of the Relationship

The conflict model of the relationship between privacy and medical research values is characterised by the idea that privacy conflicts with medical research and does not in any way support it. However, this idea can lead to two opposed views because neither the relative value to be attached to medical research values and privacy, nor a specific view of what values medical research seeks to protect, are part of the conflict model *per se*. However, those medical researchers who see privacy as essentially a hindrance to medical research to be removed are apt to claim (or at least strongly imply) that the values that medical research seeks to promote are exclusively values like human health and human life. If so, it is reasonably inferred that the values that medical research seeks to promote are always more important than privacy. Ergo, if there is any conflict between privacy and medical research, then privacy must give way. At the extreme, particularly if the narrow conception of privacy is coupled with the conflict model, this can result in the view that patients have a duty to engage in medical research to the extent that their consent is not required unless the research itself is life threatening or involves serious risk of physical harm. On the other hand,

17 'Personality and Privacy Under the European Convention on Human Rights', *British Yearbook of International Law*, LXI, 1990, 175-197, at p. 196.

18 Application No. 6825/74 DR5, 87.

19 See, e.g., the European Court of Human Rights in, e.g., *Z. v. Finland* [1997] ECHR 10 (25 February 1997), paras 96-97, *M.S. v. Sweden* (1997) 28 EHRR 313, para 34 (in relation to medical data) and in *Peck v. the United Kingdom* [2003] ECHR 44 (28 January 2003), paras 78-80 (in relation to other sensitive personal data).

opposed to this, if the conflict model is coupled with the broad conception of privacy that sees it as a personality right, it can be held that the right to privacy is, in effect, the right to autonomy, even the right to dignity, in which case (because human dignity is often thought of as the basis of human rights),[20] this can yield the view that medical research can never be undertaken without consent.[21] However, because the conflict model is normally associated with the narrow concept of privacy and, as I will argue in the next section, there are tensions, even a contradiction between the conflict model and any conception of privacy that is at least as broad as that operated by the European Court of Human Rights, I will not consider this coupling further.

When the narrow conception of privacy is coupled with the conflict model, there are at least two other variables that are capable of influencing the effect of this coupling on the importance to be attached to privacy in any conflict with medical research values. The first of these is the view taken of the basis of the values at stake. The second, which might not be entirely independent of the first, is the view taken of the kind of exercise that must be performed to assess the weight that the conflicting values have. In relation to the first of these, those who adopt the narrow conception-conflict model coupling frequently (though not necessarily) tend to regard the right to privacy as grounded in the value to be given to a person's personal wishes (as a personal interest), whereas they tend to see the values of medical research to be grounded in the public interest (what is good for people in general). In relation to the second of these, they tend to see the balance to be assessed in a utilitarian manner, which is to say by the idea that the overarching value to be served is the promotion of the wishes/the good of the greatest possible number. This combination inevitably has the consequence that restrictions on privacy (serving to promote the general good) are to be broadly defined, whereas privacy restrictions on medical research (serving only individual interests) are to be narrowly defined. This has the further effect that the onus is on those whose privacy is threatened by medical research to establish their case, should the possibility that they might have a case be recognised at all.

The Broad Conception and the Co-operative Model of the Relationship

The central idea that guides a co-operative model of the relationship between privacy and medical research interests is that while the two sets of values are capable of coming into conflict, they are also capable of supporting each other. Essentially, the idea is that protecting privacy can facilitate medical research interests and, conversely, medical research can enhance privacy interests.

---

20 See the opening of the Preamble to the Universal Declaration of Human Rights proclaimed by the General Assembly of the United Nations on 10 December 1948, which Declaration the European Convention on Human Rights aims to give partial effect to.

21 Such a broad view of the right to privacy must not be confused with the broad conception operated by the European Court of Human Rights. The right to privacy under Article 8 ECHR cannot be a right to autonomy as such and certainly not the right to human dignity as the basis of human rights. Were this the case, the ECHR could not provide derogations from privacy in its Article 8.2, which it does.

The idea that protecting privacy can support medical research is not novel. For example, it has long been recognised that one of the reasons for the law to protect privacy[22] and confidentiality[23] is that it is in the public interest to do so. That those who become ill seek proper medical treatment is in the public interest, because for them not to do so means that the risk that they might pass diseases on to others is increased, and they are more likely to be absent from work, both of which are contrary to the public interest. It is also in the public interest that patients are candid with the information they provide to those who are to treat them. Inadequate or false information will, at the very least, not facilitate adequate treatment. However, if they are to seek treatment and be candid with their doctors, patients must trust them to respect their privacy and confidences (to the extent of not making any unconsented use of the information that the patients would find objectionable, as well as not disclosing information in a way that might embarrass or harm them).

While this thinking is most familiar in the context of medical treatment, it may, however, also be applied to medical research. This is for at least two reasons. First, medical researchers are very often clinicians, so to facilitate trust in clinicians is to facilitate trust in medical researchers (and conversely, to damage trust in clinicians is to damage trust in medical researchers and *vice versa*). Secondly, even when medical researchers are not clinicians, the information they disclose in medical research is equally sensitive and, by the same reasoning applicable to information disclosed for medical treatment, must be handled with respect for privacy and confidentiality.

In relation to this, it should be noted that supporting privacy in medical research does not merely make it more likely that persons will agree to be subjects in medical research. Trust in medical researchers makes it very much more likely that the information gained will be accurate and reliable, which is essential for research to meets its objectives.

Another way in which protecting privacy might support medical research is suggested by the thinking behind the EC Data Protection Directive. As I have already mentioned, the aim of Directive 95/46/EC is to protect fundamental rights and freedoms, in particular privacy in the processing of personal data. However, as Recitals 7 and 8 of the Directive make clear, at least part of the thinking behind this is that such protection is necessary for it to be possible for there to be transfer of data across the European Union. This is because Member States, being party to the European Convention on Human Rights and other international human rights instruments, are committed to protection of fundamental rights and freedoms, and many of them have this protection enshrined in their constitutions. Thus, if personal data does not receive the necessary rights protection, Member States will not permit personal data to be transferred to countries that do not provide the necessary protection needed for the internal market in personal data to be possible. However, given such a context and given the need for multi-national medical trials if such

22 See, e.g., the European Court of Human Rights in *Z v. Finland* (22009/93) [1997] ECHR 10 (25 February 1997), para 85.

23 See, e.g., *W v. Egdell* [1990] Ch 359, at p. 419 and p. 422.

research is to be most effective, protection of privacy, etc., is necessary for such medical research.

The idea that medical research can support privacy is, perhaps, less obvious. However, this idea is inherently plausible under the broad conception of privacy. Under this conception, the values that privacy protects include rights to bodily integrity and rights to control over persons' personal lives. Medical research, by, at least in principle, facilitating alternative and better treatments and a better quality of life for those who become ill or simply age, has the potential to give people more control over their lives by providing them with more and better therapeutic options.

One of the consequences of a broad conception of privacy is that privacy does not merely protect one value, but several. So, not only is privacy capable of conflicting with other non-privacy interests, but some privacy interests are capable of conflicting with each other. Furthermore, such a conflict need not be interpersonal, it can also be intrapersonal. Bearing in mind that medical researchers, patients and research subjects are not inherently different populations, all have interests in medical research and privacy. Consequently, the complex interactions that exist between privacy and medical research mean that conflicts between privacy and medical research values may often be best described as conflicts between difference privacy values or as between different medical research values.

Justifying the Co-operative Model

If the broad conception of privacy outlined implies a co-operative model, then justifying this conception will justify this co-operative model. Since this conception is that of the European Court of Human Rights, this can be done by justifying following this Court's jurisprudence. In the UK, at least, a strong case can be made for this from a legal point of view.

First, Section 3 of the Human Rights Act 1998 requires all legislation and indeed, all common law (see s 6) to be interpreted so as to be consistent with the rights granted by, *inter alia*, Articles 2-12 and 14 of the ECHR, unless prevented from doing so by primary legislation, if it is at all possible to do so. Regarding this latter proviso, the UK Courts have been prepared to strain interpretative licence to the limit to avoid declarations of incompatibility with the ECHR.[24] Furthermore, s 2.1(a) of the Act requires the UK courts to take favourable account of the views of the European Court of Human Rights.[25] While this is weaker than a requirement to comply with the views of the Strasbourg Court, not to do so is an open invitation for litigation at the Court, with the almost inevitable result that judgment will be against the UK. While the UK Government has recently made noises about ignoring such judgments, such action has not yet been taken.

---

24 See, e.g., *R v. A* [2001] 3 WLR 1546 and *R v. Lambert* [2001] 3 WLR 206.

25 The *Source Informatics* judgment was delivered shortly before the Human Rights Act 1998 came into force.

Secondly, the use of personal health data in all research falls within the scope of Directive 95/46/EC on data protection, and clinical trials on medicinal products for human use fall within the scope of Directives 2001/20/EC ('Clinical Trials Directive') and Directive 2005/28/EC ('Good Clinical Practice Directive') (both of which require Directive 95/46/EC to be observed). Article 6(2)EU requires the EU to respect the rights guaranteed by the ECHR as general principles of EC law (and Article 288 of the EC Treaty requires the European Court of Justice (ECJ) to apply general principles common to the Member States, which has led the ECJ to go so far as to declare that any EC legislation that does not comply with such principles is null and void).[26] Of course, the EU is not as such party to the ECHR and the European Court of Human Rights is not a court of the EU, so its judgments can only have persuasive, not legally binding, effect. However, for the ECJ to rule contrary to such judgments is to invite constitutional crisis in the Member States because of the doctrine of supremacy of EC law and the fact that many Member States are bound by their constitutions to respect the views of the European Court of Human Rights.

Apart from strictly legal reasons to adopt the broad conception/the co-operative model, there are also ethical reasons. The co-operative model of the relationship between privacy and medical research values sits naturally with a co-operative model of the relationship between medical researchers and medical subjects. In this latter model, research subjects must be viewed as partners in a communal enterprise in which there is mutual (and not merely reciprocal) respect for the rights and fundamental interests of all parties. In effect, researchers must view research subjects not as information crops to be harvested for the common good or their own purposes, but as partners whose purposes are to be respected as though they were the researcher's own. In Kantian terms, research subjects are to be treated as ends in themselves, with their consent *always* being required for invasions of their rights unless it is necessary to override this for the more important rights of others. But, crucially, researchers must not merely not interfere with the rights of research subjects, but must positively assist them to enjoy these rights. This is especially important where research subjects are concerned, and even more so when they are patients. This is because patients and research participants are in a vulnerable position in relation to unconsented use of their personal data – for example, they might not know of various uses at all; even when they do, the damage might already have been done; and, in such cases, their opportunities for redress will be slim (they are not usually in a good position, due to lack of resources or knowledge, to complain, let alone take legal action, and must further risk conflict with those upon whom they rely for their treatment when they are ill or weak). Consequently, unless the research culture is regulated (and better still guided) by the goal of respecting research subjects as ends in themselves, the rights and interests of research subjects will be endemically threatened by medical research.

Finally, there are pragmatic reasons for adopting the broad conception/co-operative model. A research culture that is based first and foremost on consent encourages trust

---

26 See, e.g., *The Second Nold Case (Case-4/73)* [1974] E.C.R. 507.

and enables data to be kept in a form that is of most use for research, as it can be richer, is more likely to be accurate and can be corrected. It also, generally, carries the fewest legal risks and is likely to be associated with the best clinical outcomes.[27] Such reasons, of course, are those that lie behind the idea that protection of privacy is in the public interest[28] and, indeed, in the public interest in medical research.

The Co-operative Model and Assessing Conflicts of Interest

Even within the co-operative model conflicts of interest are possible. The right to privacy is not absolute, and can be overridden by other values. This is expressly recognised by Article 8.2 of the ECHR, according to which no public authority[29] may interfere with the right granted by Article 8.1:

> except such as is in accordance with the law and is necessary in a democratic society in the interests of national security, public safety or the economic well-being of the country, for the prevention of disorder or crime, for the protection of health or morals, or for the protection of the rights and freedoms of others.

This provides the general framework for considering conflicts between privacy and research values. As Article 8.2 has consistently been applied, research values can only be permitted (by public authorities, including, most particularly, the State) to override the right to privacy if to do so is necessary for the protection of one of the values expressly stated in Article 8.2, the derogation is proportionate (i.e., no greater than necessary), and the derogation is provided for by law. In principle, subject to these conditions, to the extent that medical research can be held to be for the protection of the rights and freedoms of others/be for the protection of health, derogation is available for this purpose. However, it should not be thought that this

27 See Beyleveld, D. and Brownsword, R., 'Ethics Committees: Public Interest, Private Interest, and the Ethics of Partnership'. in Lebeer, G. (ed), *Ethical Function in Hospital Ethics Committees*, Amsterdam, IOS Press, 2002, 135-149.

28 It is worth noting that the Court of Appeal, unlike the High Court, in *Source Informatics*, ignored this consideration altogether.

29 While the ECHR is directly enforceable only against public authorities at the European Court of Human Rights (i.e., is only vertically effective), it does not follow that the rights granted by the ECHR are not rights held against individuals (i.e., not horizontally applicable). The idea that the right of Article 8.1 may be derogated from for the rights of others implies that the rights of the ECHR are held against individuals (i.e., that they are horizontally applicable). So, it is arguable that effect can only be given to them domestically if they are horizontally effective in domestic law (see, further, Beyleveld, D. and Pattinson, S., 'Horizontal Applicability and Horizontal Effect', October (2002) *Law Quarterly Review*, 623-644). However, even if this is controversial, the ECHR will, in any event, be horizontally effective in domestic law when used to interpret domestic law that provides actions against individuals.

provides the opening for a *carte blanche* exemption for research from the need to protect privacy.

In the first case, this is because it is questionable to what extent medical research may be said to be for the protection of health or represent a right or fundamental freedom of others. The basic reason for this is that privacy (like all the human rights and freedoms of the ECHR) is a fundamental value, and it is in the nature of fundamental values that they can only be set aside to protect other (indeed, more important) fundamental values. It might be objected to this that, in that case, reference to anything other than the rights and freedoms of others is the only purpose necessary. However, this does not actually follow. It is surely the case that the other purposes mentioned are all things that are necessary to protect very important rights and freedoms of others: breakdowns in public safety, health, national security, etc. can (indeed, often do) all threaten life and the necessary means to these (such as adequate food, clothing, shelter, etc.). With this in mind, I suggest that specific reference to the rights and freedoms of others is reference to case specific conflicts between rights, whereas the other derogatory purposes are purposes that, in a standing way, are rights threatening. Thus, the first problem for a *carte blanche* exemption for medical research is that its purposes might not be purposes that constitute the protection of a human right or that are expressions of a fundamental freedom.

But there is also another problem. This is that the condition of proportionality is not merely applicable to the degree of rights violation. It also involves the idea that the overriding purpose must be more important than the value to be overridden in case of conflict. This raises the question of how to assess the relative value of different rights and fundamental freedoms in the ECHR. While it is arguable that the rights protected by those Articles of the ECHR that are subject to very restricted derogation outweigh those (mainly Articles 8, 9, 10, 11 and 12) that are subject to wide derogatory provision, this does not help with conflicts between the right of an individual of Article 8 and the rights of others of Articles 8, 9, 10, 11 and 12), and it still leaves the rights that are more important without a clear rationale for ordering.

However, it is surely irrational to grant a right to something yet not to grant a right to the necessary means to enjoy this right. So, if there are conditions that are necessary for the exercise or having of all rights, then a right must be granted to these no matter what rights are granted. Since, in principle, rights could be granted to any actions, such conditions must be necessary for all actions. I suggest, therefore, that the difference between a fundamental right and freedom and other rights and freedoms is that the latter are things the absence of which is detrimental to the having of any rights or their exercise (and, hence, detrimental to any actions).

Alan Gewirth calls such conditions 'generic features of action'.[30] These are ordered in two ways. First, things that are needful to even attempt to act (interference hinders an ability to act at all) ('basic needs': such as life, mental equilibrium, the general ability to exercise choices, and the necessary means to these, such as food,

30 Gewirth, A., *Reason and Morality*, Chicago, University of Chicago Press, 1978, pp. 48-63.

clothing and shelter) are distinguished from things needful for general chances of success in achieving purposes through one's actions (subdivided into things needful to maintain abilities to act – 'non-subtractive needs', such as accurate information; and things that generically enhance one's abilities to act – 'additive needs', such as further education). Second, within and between these categories, importance is to be assessed by the degree to which the generic features are needful for action and successful action (in relation to which Gewirth suggests that the psychological theory of Maslow[31] might be helpful).

Gewirth makes much larger claims for this scheme of rights: *viz.*, that agents deny that they are agents if they fail to recognise and act according to it. However, while I believe that Gewirth is right about this,[32] it is not necessary to accept this to see the use (even the necessity) of deploying such a scheme given a recognition of human rights).[33]

From this perspective, the Peto campaign[34] is based on mistaken or misguided thinking on a number of counts. First, the campaign seeks a *carte blanche* exemption for medical research. This ignores the fact that privacy is a human right and that not all medical research purposes engage human rights and fundamental freedoms: it is too broad a church for that. Since this is so, there can be no avoiding the need to make purpose by purpose assessments of the *possibility* of an exemption.

Second, even if a fundamental value is engaged by the research, it must be necessary to override privacy. In other words, the research goals must *require* privacy to be overridden. However, provided that consent is obtained, there is no conflict; the research may be carried out without interference with the right to privacy. On this front, the Peto campaign claimed that consent was impracticable. However, while this might be the case where data has been collected in the past without consent, it is difficult to see how this can be the case when data is being collected prospectively. It is often said that more harm is caused by putting clinicians to the inconvenience of getting consent than by not obtaining consent. However, this judgment is usually made from the perspective of ignoring the public interest reasons for protecting privacy and is not often accompanied by any consideration of how consent might be obtained without placing too great a burden on clinicians. Additionally, the Peto campaign claimed that it is necessary to obtain data from 100 per cent of the population for epidemiological studies on cancer, so the fact that some patients or research subjects might refuse consent damages the research irremediably. This is, however, extremely dubious if generalised to all medical research. Indeed, if the claim is sound it would argue for all medical research to be carried out without

31 Maslow, A.F., *Motivation and Personality*, New York, Harper and Brothers, 1954, pp. 80ff.

32 See Beyleveld, D., *The Dialectical Necessity of Morality*, Chicago, University of Chicago Press, 1991.

33 For further elaboration, see Beyleveld, D. and Brownsword, R., *Human Dignity in Bioethics and Biolaw*, Oxford, Oxford University Press 2001, pp. 79-86.

34 See note 1, *supra.*

consent. It is also very dubious in relation to cancer epidemiology since the idea of a 100 per cent sample can only really mean 100 per cent of the human race. The fact of the matter is that research results can be of varying degrees of value: they are not either perfect or of no value at all, and degrees of compromise are necessary and possible to get the optimal balance of protection. Any other way of thinking ignores that breaches of privacy must be proportionate.

Of course, the Peto campaign will have been bolstered by the decision of the Court of Appeal of England and Wales in *Source Informatics*. However, the Court's idea that privacy is not engaged unless breach of privacy would cause specific extrinsic harms (which would render processing of the information unfair) simply does not accord with the view of the European Court of Human Rights that the right to privacy is always engaged by the use of health data without explicit consent. It is clear that one of the motivations behind the Court's judgment was to do away with case by case judgments of whether or not confidentiality (and by the same token, privacy) may be overridden in the public interest (or by countervailing values).[35] However, the Court seemed to be oblivious of the fact that it was merely replacing the need for case by case assessment of this by case by case assessments of fairness. But, most seriously, the Court's thinking simply does not conform with the thinking required by recognition of the fact that privacy is a human right and the jurisprudence of the European Court of Human Rights on this matter.

Conclusion

Prima facie, the idea that privacy in medical research protects merely against disclosure of sensitive or confidential personal information and the extrinsic harms that this can cause is attractive to medical researchers, because it suggests that protecting against such disclosures is all that is necessary for such information to be used in research. However, I have argued that such a position is not legally tenable, because the interfaces between UK domestic law, EC law and the European Convention on Human Rights, require a broad concept of privacy to be deployed. While this is likely to prompt many researchers to call for the law to be changed, it should now be clear that this is short-sighted. There are both ethical and pragmatic reasons for adopting a broad conception of privacy. These are not merely negative (e.g, appreciation that consent fosters an atmosphere of trust which is necessary for medical research to flourish), they are also positive (e.g., a consent culture actively encourages a willingness for people to engage in medical research and improves the quality of results). Wholehearted adoption of the broad conception, however, requires the deployment of a co-operative model rather than a conflict model of the relationship between privacy values and medical research values.

35 [2000] 1 All ER 796, at p. 800.

Chapter 11

Human 'Guinea Pigs': Why Patients Participate in Clinical Trials

Pamela R. Ferguson

Introduction

A clinical trial has been defined as:

> any investigation in human subjects … intended –
> (a) to discover or verify the clinical, pharmacological or other pharmacodynamic effects of … medicinal products,
> (b) to identify any adverse reactions …
> (c) to study absorption, distribution, metabolism and excretion of … such products,
> with the object of ascertaining the safety or efficacy of those products.[1]

A recent editorial in the British Medical Journal reported a survey by Harris Interactive Inc., which explored the attitudes of the American public to clinical trials.[2] More than half of those surveyed considered patients who participate in such trials to be akin to 'guinea pigs'.[3] Other studies have explored the attitudes of lay people towards hypothetical trials, but it is suspected that their views may differ markedly from those who have actually taken part in a trial.[4] This chapter describes a study in the UK in which the author explored the motivations of patients involved in clinical trials.[5] The

1 Reg. 2 of the Medicines for Human Use (Clinical Trials) Regulations 2004 (2004 No. 1031).

2 Sackett, D.L., 'Participants in research', (2005) *BMJ*, 330: 1164.

3 In response to the statement that 'people who participate in clinical trials are like guinea pigs' 14 per cent 'strongly agreed' and 37 per cent 'somewhat agreed'. The results of the Harris Interactive survey are available at: http://www.harrisinteractive.com/news/allnewsbydate.asp?NewsID=812.

4 Schain W., 'Barriers to clinical trials: Part II: knowledge and attitudes of potential participants', (1994) *Cancer*, 74 (suppl): 2666-71, at p. 2667. See also Featherstone, K., Donovan, J.L., 'Random allocation or allocation at random? Patients' perspectives of participation in a randomised controlled trial', (1998) *BMJ*, 317:1177-80 where it is suggested that interpretation of many studies on patients' motivations is difficult 'because of their reliance on general issues or hypothetical trials, which do not have direct relevance to actual participation in real trials'.

5 The study was based in Tayside, Scotland.

study also investigated medical researchers' perceptions of patients' motivations. The chapter reports both the patients' and researchers' views, and the findings from the two groups are compared, in an attempt to explore whether researchers have an accurate awareness of why patients take part. The views of patients in the UK study are also compared to those expressed by patients in the Harris Interactive survey to see whether there are different incentives in the United States.

The UK study found that, while the desire to secure the best treatment for themselves was a motivation which was frequently given by patients, the wish to benefit other patients was expressed more often. The desire to assist their doctors was relevant to a lesser extent. The medical researchers attributed a number of different motives to patients, with altruism towards other patients being regarded as particularly relevant. Similar motivations exist for patients in the USA, but financial incentives seem to be stronger there.

Hans Jonas has argued that:

> [The patient's] physical state, psychic preoccupation, dependent relation to the doctor, the submissive attitude induced by treatment – everything connected with his condition and situation makes the sick person inherently less of a sovereign person than the healthy one ... In fact, all the factors that make the patient, as a category, particularly accessible and welcome for experimentation at the same time compromise the quality of the responding affirmation that must morally redeem the making use of them.[6]

It is the patients' freely given, informed consent which renders their participation morally acceptable.[7] Examination of patients' motivations is important since inappropriate reasons for participation, such as guilt or fear of the consequences of refusal, cast doubts on the authenticity of this consent.

Study Design

Researchers

For the UK study, the author obtained from a Local Research Ethics Committee (LREC) the names of all Principal Investigators who had submitted clinical trial proposals during a five month period. A 'snowball sampling' technique was adopted whereby interviewees were asked to suggest the names of colleagues who might be suitable for interview. Semi-structured interviews were employed, since they tend

6 Jonas, H., 'Philosophical reflections on experimenting with human subjects', in T. Beauchamp and L. Walters (eds), *Contemporary Issues in Bioethics* (3rd ed), Belmont, Wadsworth, 1989, at p. 438.

7 See also Schafer, A., 'Although there may be no question of force, fraud, or deceit, the circumstances surrounding serious illness may be thought to constitute a kind of duress. Illness frequently makes a patient more-than-normally dependent upon and eager to please his doctor.' Schafer, A., 'Experimentation with human subjects: a critique of the views of Hans Jonas', 1983 *Journal of Medical Ethics*, 9: 76-79, at p. 78.

to yield a higher response rate than mail questionnaires and allow the interviewer to probe behind answers in a way which is not possible in a questionnaire. It was made clear that any publication of results would not reveal the specific details of any research, nor the identity of those interviewed. All respondents were interviewed personally by the author at their place of work.

Patients

Researchers whose trials were ongoing were asked for permission to interview their patients. The author was aware of the type of trials being conducted and it was felt that a direct approach to patients would not generally be appropriate. To respect patient confidentiality, it was agreed with the LREC that researchers would inform the author of the times of their patients' next appointments. The author attended the GP surgery or out-patient clinic at those times, and the researchers or nursing staff asked the patients whether they were willing to be interviewed. This allowed them to refuse to participate without their identities being revealed to the author.

Patients were advised that the author was an academic researcher rather than a medical professional; that their answers would not be communicated to their doctors; and that any publication of results would not reveal their identities. It was explained that they were under no obligation to participate in the interview. No questions were asked about their medical conditions or histories. This preliminary information was approved by the LREC. The questions to be put to patients were discussed with a medical researcher with a wealth of experience in drug studies, scrutinised by the Ethics Committee and piloted with eight patients.[8] The questions were slightly modified in light of comments from the Ethics Committee and pilot group. An additional question was added in light of the responses given by researchers during their interviews.[9]

Data for the Harris Interactive survey was derived from online interviews, conducted during a period of 11 days.[10] The website which reports the survey results does not comment on the ethical aspects of acquiring the data. The UK study required approval from a LREC because participants were recruited in their capacity as NHS patients. The American survey approached members of the public rather than patients as such, hence may have avoided the need for ethical approval.

8 Patients in the pilot group were invited to comment on the clarity of the questions and on the range of available responses. This checked for ambiguity and any other difficulties in answering.

9 See the section on 'free drugs', below. The LREC was informed of all changes.

10 This survey used the term 'clinical research study' rather than 'clinical trial' because 'the word "trial" has sometimes inhibited participation'. See note 3, *supra*.

Data Collection

Data from the UK study were entered on to SPSS and statistical methods used to explore the relationships between the variables.[11] Most of the data will not be described in this chapter, which is devoted solely to a discussion of patients' motivations for participation.[12]

Researchers

Semi-structured interviews were conducted with 78 researchers, 65 per cent of whom were male. The majority were hospital doctors (68 per cent) and the remainder were GPs (8 per cent), nurses (23 per cent) and research co-ordinators (1 per cent). Their clinical trial experience included Phase II and Phase III trials of unlicensed drugs, involving small numbers of patients, and Phase IV trials in which thousands of patients were involved on a nation-wide basis.

Patients

Of the 104 patients interviewed for the UK study, 54 per cent were female. Basic demographic details are given in Table 11.1. To determine the extent to which they were 'repeat players', patients were asked whether they had been involved in any other drug trial within the preceding five years. As Table 11.1 shows, for the vast majority of patients this was their first involvement in a clinical trial.

The Harris Interactive survey involved 5,822 people but only 656 of them had taken part in a clinical trial. No demographic information is available about interviewees. Since this chapter is concerned with the views of patient participants, rather than those of the public more generally, the comparisons drawn with the Harris Interactive survey are confined to data from the latter group.

Motivations for Participating

Six potential motivations were suggested to patients in the UK study. They were asked to say whether each was 'highly relevant', 'relevant to some extent' or

11 The author is grateful to Drs Morag Smith and Suzanne Zeedyk, Department of Psychology, University of Dundee, for their assistance with this.

12 See, however, Ferguson, P.R., 'Legal and ethical aspects of clinical trials: the views of researchers', (2003) *Medical Law Review*, 11:1, 48-66; Ferguson, P.R., 'Information giving in clinical trials: the views of medical researchers', (2003) *Bioethics*, 101-111; Ferguson, P.R., 'Selecting participants when testing new drugs: the implications of age and gender discrimination', (2002) *Medico-Legal Journal*, 70:3, 130-134; Ferguson, P.R., 'Patients' perceptions of information provided in clinical trials', (2002) *Journal of Medical Ethics*, 28:1, 45-48; Ferguson, P.R., 'Do researchers feel a LREC hinders research?', (2001) *Bulletin of Medical Ethics*, 17-19; Ferguson, P.R., 'Patients' experiences and views of clinical trials', (2001) *Medicine and Law*, 20:1, 143-152.

'not at all relevant' as a reason for agreeing to take part in a clinical trial. In the event, it proved necessary to add a further category to accommodate patients who felt unable to respond to questions about their motivations. The motivations and patient responses are given in Table 11.2. Table 11.3 shows the five motivations which were suggested to researchers. They were asked to assess each according to the same criteria as above (i.e., 'highly relevant', 'relevant to some extent', etc.) The potential motivation of avoiding prescription fees was not put to researchers, as will be explained below. Table 11.4 shows the 14 potential motivations suggested to respondents in the Harris Interactive survey, and Table 11.5 compares the relevant data from the survey with that from the UK study. In Table 11.5 the per centages given for the UK study have been collated to include both 'relevant' and 'highly relevant' ratings.

Securing the Best Medication

Patients' views One obvious reason why patients might agree to take part is the belief that this gives them a chance to try a new and promising therapy. For patients with incurable illnesses, participation might provide access to the only potential treatment and one might expect this to be a prime motivation for some. As Table 11.2 shows, 74 per cent of patients in the UK study rated this as a relevant factor, with 51 per cent of these considering it 'highly relevant'. Several patients stated that participation was indeed their only chance of a cure. This is illustrated by the comment from a patient involved in testing a highly experimental combination of drugs for a seriously debilitating condition:

> The drug costs £6,000 a time ... I'd not get it otherwise.[13]

There was, however, recognition by many patients that they might not, in fact, receive the test medication. This is typified by the patient who stated that while his 'main reason' for taking part was 'self-interest', he accepted that:

> Since there is a placebo element, I may not personally benefit.[14]

Researchers' views 76 per cent of researchers in the UK study felt that the belief that the test drug was the best treatment was a 'relevant' or 'highly relevant' factor for patients (see Table 11.3). Others were quick to point out that patients should not be motivated by this since they may be getting the standard therapy or even a placebo, rather than the test drug. According to one experienced researcher:

> While we make it clear to them that the drug study might not help them specifically, many patients will have the expectation that it will do so. Not all drugs can be continued with

13 Patient No. 73.
14 Patient No. 43.

> after the trial, even if it's working well for the patient. One must be careful not to overplay the possible benefits for that patient.[15]

Others had no such misgivings:

> The belief that the new drug is the best treatment is a highly relevant motivator in some studies for the patient, and the doctor can be influenced by this, too and can't help but communicate this.[16]

Helping Other Patients

The UK Royal College of Physicians has acknowledged that:

> [I]n much research in patients there is no likelihood of benefit to the individual patient. In this case a desire to help others who may have the disease, or mankind, is the major motive.[17]

Patients' views As Table 11.2 shows, 83 per cent of patients in the UK study rated the desire to benefit people who might develop a similar illness in the future as relevant to their decision to take part. In similar vein, Alderson found that 92 per cent of women involved in a research project for the treatment of breast cancer gave 'to help other people' as a motive for participating.[18] In the author's study, a number of patients with chronic, debilitating conditions cited this as a reason, but it was also seen as highly relevant by patients who were not in that position:

> I felt that I was lucky because my [illness] was not as bad as other people, so I wanted to help other people.[19]

Some trials offer no realistic possibility of benefit to participants; hence their motives are purely altruistic. This is illustrated by comments such as:

> I know it won't help me in the least but it might help someone coming on after me not to go through what I went through.[20]

The spirit of altruism is also reflected in the comment that:

---

15 Researcher No. 43.

16 Researcher No. 44.

17 Royal College of Physicians, *Research Involving Patients*, London, RCP, 1990 at para 7.75.

18 Alderson, P., 'Equipoise as a means of managing uncertainty: personal, communal and proxy', (1996) *Journal of Medical Ethics*, 22:135-139, at p. 138. Fifty women were interviewed.

19 Patient No. 52.

20 Patient No. 87.

> [Participating] might not do anything for me but I may one day be a grandmother and it may help my grandchild.[21]

As Table 11.4 shows, taking part in order to help others with their condition was a factor for only 45 per cent of patients in the Harris Interactive survey. However, 56 per cent did cite 'to advance medicine/science' as a reason for participating. This desire to assist medical progress was also expressed by patients in the UK survey:

> Somebody's got to do it. [My illness] is incurable, so what is there to lose as long as something useful comes out of it. Someone's got to do it otherwise there wouldn't be any cures for anything, would there?[22]

> Someone should do it. I'd been asked to do it and would have felt refusal would have been churlish. It's a way of contributing something rather than just taking all the time.[23]

> [I want to help] to improve medical science. I don't mind being the guinea pig.[24]

Researchers' views Table 11.3 shows that altruism towards other patients was felt by almost 90 per cent of researchers to be a 'relevant' or 'highly relevant' reason for their patients' decision to take part:

> They want to stop other people from suffering in the way that they have been suffering.[25]

Some researchers had heard patients expressing such sentiments:

> Patients will say 'well, even if I'm on a placebo, I'm helping someone else'.[26]

> Patients say: 'I realise that drugs have to be tested and that I benefit today because others tested them in the past'.[27]

Another admitted:

> We emphasised in the information sheets that by participating the patient would be helping other, future patients.[28]

As one might expect, researchers' responses were dependent to some extent on the type of illnesses to which their trials related. Some felt that helping others was particularly relevant for patients where those others could be family members:

---

21 Patient No. 78.
22 Patient No. 89.
23 Patient No. 74.
24 Patient No. 31.
25 Researcher No. 73.
26 Researcher No. 52.
27 Researcher No. 44.
28 Researcher No. 49.

> This [motivation] is especially so when we are looking at preventative measures for a patient's siblings.[29]

> Helping future sufferers is especially important in [certain] studies, since [the illness] runs in the family, and in [other] studies there is a genetic element.[30]

Certain types of patients were felt to be more altruistic than others:

> Older patients are keen to help … future patients ... [31]

> This is quite an important motivation for older people, but not in younger ones.[32]

Only 4 per cent of researchers felt that helping others was not at all relevant:

> Most ... are mostly self-motivated – they want to help themselves ... [33]

Helping the Doctor

According to the Royal College of Physicians:

> Undoubtedly, patients who like their doctors and have confidence in them are inclined to agree to proposals to take part in research. The reasons are probably multiple and complex. For example patients may feel gratitude for attention received, or hope to secure extra attention in future; they may simply wish to please their doctor ... [34]

Patients' views While helping the doctor was a less important motivator than helping other patients or securing the best treatment for themselves, it was 'relevant to some extent' for 44 per cent of the UK study sample and 'highly relevant' for a further 18 per cent (Table 11.2). This factor was not suggested to participants in the Harris Interactive survey (see Table 11.4). This may perhaps reflect the fact that medical interactions in the US are contractual arrangements; healthcare professionals may be regarded as providing a service akin to that of a lawyer or accountant. In contrast to this, comments from the UK participants illustrate the sense of gratitude some patients have to their doctors and/or the NHS:

> The department has done a lot for me ... giving something back ... I was only too willing to do so.[35]

---

29 Researcher No. 77.
30 Researcher No. 28.
31 Researcher No. 40.
32 Researcher No. 16.
33 Researcher No. 69.
34 See note 17, *supra*, at p. 27, para 7.78.
35 Patient No. 101.

He'd [the patient's GP] been so good to me and I [felt] I could oblige him.[36]

Researchers' views Patients' desire to help their doctors was considered to be a 'relevant' or 'highly relevant' motivation by 75 per cent of researchers (Table 11.3). Comments here included:

> I tell them it's not for me, as such, but wanting to help the doctor is bound to have some impact.[37]

> Some patients have a rapport with the doctor. People who agree to take part have a different relationship with their doctor than those who won't take part.[38]

> This depends on the doctor/patient relationship. Sometimes you know before you even ask them that they will participate. Our patients [suffer from a chronic condition] and you get to know them quite well and over a number of years.[39]

> Some have an identification with the healthcare system – they want to put something back into a system when they have got something out of it.[40]

A nurse in a GP clinic stated:

> Loyalty to their doctor is important, especially older patients ...[41]

That patients might agree out of a sense of obligation was viewed as potentially problematic by some researchers:

> This is still an issue – we have a close working relationship with patients ... They may feel slightly duty-bound to the doctor.[42]

> This is an ethical issue because of the kind of relationship you have with patients. They'll almost do anything for you, so you must respect that trust they have when it comes to studies, especially commercial studies.[43]

> Some [patients] find it difficult to say no – they want to help the doctor out. You can tell that they are less than enthusiastic about it.[44]

Some researchers had taken steps to try to ensure that patients did not act out of misplaced loyalty:

---

36 Patient No. 93.
37 Researcher No. 75.
38 Researcher No. 58.
39 Researcher No. 44.
40 Researcher No. 43.
41 Researcher No. 16.
42 Researcher No. 71.
43 Researcher No. 76.
44 Researcher No. 44.

> Some patients have been on two or three trials – they are keen to do it for the doctor. [The doctor] writes to them first or gets me [a nurse] to phone them, so that it is easier for them to say no.[45]

> ... the doctors do not generally get involved until after the patients have agreed to take part in the study, so the patients don't feel intimidated into agreeing to take part.[46]

More Health Checks or Tests

Patients' views As Table 11.2 shows, only 32 per cent of patients in the UK study felt that being seen more frequently by a doctor or having additional tests was of any relevance to them. For 25 per cent of patients this motivation was not applicable, since they had received a one-off treatment and were not given any more health checks than they would otherwise have received. A further 42 per cent rated this factor as 'not at all relevant', reflecting the fact that many did not appreciate prior to taking part that participation would have the added benefit of more health checks. However, one of those who rated this as a relevant reason added:

> Getting regular check ups was the main thing. If I'd not taken part I probably would not have seen the doctor again. This way, I'm seen every three months.[47]

One patient gave the impression that his doctor had used the prospect of more frequent appointments as an incentive:

> This didn't occur to me [as a reason for taking part], but the doctor pointed it out ... My doctor more or less said that I'd be getting better taken care of.[48]

Several patients stated that, although not a reason for taking part, they now realised that this was an added benefit. Three had found the extra check-ups to be particularly beneficial to their general health. One of these commented:

> They discovered one or two minor things [which were wrong with me] that I didn't know about.[49]

Another explained:

> If I hadn't said yes [to the trial] I wouldn't be here today, because they discovered an illness, lung cancer, that I didn't know I had.[50]

---

45 Researcher No. 16.
46 Researcher No. 27.
47 Patient No. 49.
48 Patient No. 8.
49 Patient No. 90.
50 Patient No. 103.

The motivation of more health checks was not a factor which was suggested in the Harris Interactive survey (see Table 11.4). This is surprising, since it has been suggested that:

> Survey researchers [in the US] have found that the majority of [patients] view ... participation as a way to gain access to superior medical care.[51]

Researchers' views This was rated as relevant for their patients by 61 per cent of researchers (Table 11.3). Comments included:

> There is a perception that the care is better in centres that are involved in trials ... The centres doing trials tend to be at the cutting edge. [Patients] feel they'll get better over all care.[52]

> They do have a perception that their care and their condition will be managed better.[53]

Some researchers admitted that this perception was not mistaken, and that patients involved in a trial did, in fact, get more health checks, or at least a better service.

> They get a ... test on the trial, which they wouldn't otherwise get, and they get a [second procedure] much quicker if they are on the trial.[54]

> Being in a study gives them a definite time to come – no hanging about in out-patients for a long time.[55]

> If patients have been on other studies in the past, then they are aware that they get super-duper health care. If you phone us with a side effect, you get dealt with right away – some have actually said this.[56]

Many saw no problem with this, and one researcher had used it to promote his trial. The Royal College of Physicians has, however, cautioned against this:

> Although participation in research may sometimes bring benefits, such as those which may result from unusually detailed and careful supervision, improved care should not be offered as an inducement to participate.[57]

---

51 Levine, R.J., 'Ethics of clinical trials: Do they help the patient?', (1993) *Cancer*, 72: 9, 2805-10, at p. 2808.

52 Researcher No. 47.

53 Researcher No. 76.

54 Researcher No. 16

55 Researcher No. 4.

56 Researcher No. 34.

57 See note 17, *supra*, at p. 27, para 7.77.

More than a third of researchers felt that the prospect of more tests would not be regarded by patients as a motivation; more hospital appointments might be a *dis*incentive:

> The motivator of wanting more health checks is less important in [the sort of trials which we do], since the patients are seen very frequently anyway. Some of them are not interested if more visits and tests are involved – they feel they spend enough time in the hospital.[58]

> The patients are attending hospital enough already, and are being seen by their GPs.[59]

> They are not motivated by this. The downside to a study is that they have to come [to the hospital] more often.[60]

Others pointed out that patients are not generally aware of this additional benefit, when being invited to take part in a clinical trial:

> It is true that they get more health checks, but they don't know that when they agree to take part.[61]

> There is more of an awareness of this among doctors than patients.[62]

One doctor felt that this perception raised concerns about the scientific validity of drug studies:

> We should offer the same level of treatment – whether a patient is in a trial or not should not be an issue, but it is. If there is a perception among patients that care is better in a trial and that is accurate, then the science is biased.[63]

Whether these perceptions of more health checks and better care are accurate or not, does this translate to a better treatment outcome? According to Ian Chalmers:

> Patients receiving treatment as participants in [randomised controlled] trials seem to fare better than apparently comparable patients receiving the same treatments outside trials.[64]

One UK study compared the clinical outcomes of trial participants with those of patients who had been eligible for these trials, but who had not been recruited.[65]

---

58 Researcher No. 44.

59 Researcher No. 70.

60 Researcher No. 77.

61 Researcher No. 76.

62 Researcher No. 53.

63 Researcher No. 53.

64 Chalmers, I., 'What do I want from health research and researchers when I am a patient?', 1995 *BMJ*, 310: 1315-18, at p. 1316.

65 Braunholtz, D.A., Edwards, S.J.L. and Lilford, R.A., 'Are randomised clinical trials good for us (in the short term)? Evidence for a "trials effect"', (2001) *J. Clin. Epid.*, 54: 217-24, cited in Sackett, *loc cit.*

The researchers found that 'while the evidence is not conclusive, it is more likely that clinical trials have a positive rather than a negative effect on the outcome of patients'.[66]

Looking for a Better Therapy

One reason for agreeing to participate in a clinical trial may be dissatisfaction with the level of pain relief or symptom control offered by current therapy.

Patients' views There has been an increase in the proliferation of 'me-too' drugs which may offer little therapeutic advance over existing formulations, but whose side effects have not yet been established. Research Ethics Committees are rightly concerned that patients are not given a new drug where the only reason for the change is that their doctor is being paid by a pharmaceutical company to recruit patients for a trial. It may be of comfort to Ethics Committees to note that in the 13 trials looked at in the UK study this did not appear to be happening; as Table 11.2 shows, for most patients (63 per cent) participation was offered to them at the start of their treatment regime. For other patients, particularly those with certain debilitating, incurable conditions, there was no alternative therapy available. Only 22 per cent of patients in the UK study regarded this as relevant.

As can be seen from Table 11.5, the proportion of patients in the Harris Interactive survey who felt that this was a relevant factor was twice as high (at 44 per cent) as in the UK study.[67] Other American studies have found that between 52 per cent and 75 per cent of patients take part in clinical trials in the expectation of improved medication. These findings from the US may reflect the absence of a comprehensive National Health Service in that country: patients with no or insufficient insurance may find that taking part in a trial is the only means of securing appropriate medicine.[68]

Researchers' views The search for a better treatment was felt by 67 per cent of researchers to be a 'highly relevant' or 'relevant' reason (Table 11.3):

> Patients are dissatisfied with the control of their existing condition and are looking for improvement. There is a feeling that 'new' must mean 'better'.[69]

> They want to feel better, healthier, fitter. We're often trying to improve the efficacy of what they're already on.[70]

66 'Patients who participated in the trials fared better in nine of … 11 studies, and in six the difference in outcomes was big enough to reach significance. The other two studies found no evidence of any effect of being in a trial …' Sackett, *loc cit.*

67 That is, 44 per cent of patients in the Harris Interactive survey and 22 per cent in the UK study – see also Tables 11.2 and 11.4.

68 See Levine, *loc cit.*

69 Researcher No. 57.

70 Researcher No. 77.

Free Drugs

Patients do not generally have to pay for medication which they receive as part of a clinical trial. It did not initially occur to the author that the prospect of free drugs might influence a patient's decision hence the eight patients in the pilot study were not asked about this. However, interviews with medical researchers revealed that some felt that this might be a motivation for patients, and that rising prescription costs might make this increasingly important:

> We say 'we'll give you the drug for nothing if you agree to take part in the study'. It is provided by the pharmaceutical company, so the patient saves on prescription costs.[71]

This potential incentive was put to the remaining 96 patients. For 81 per cent of patients this could not be a motivating factor, since either they were exempt from prescriptions charges[72] or they had received the medication as a hospital in-patient. Only 2 per cent of patients rated this as relevant; they were concerned that they might be paying for a placebo (Table 11.2). In contrast, 77 per cent of participants in the Harris Interactive survey cited financial motivations, with 27 per cent agreeing that obtaining 'free medication' was a factor, and a further 50 per cent giving 'to earn extra money' as a potential inducement to participation (see Table 11.4, points 5 and 9).

Other Reasons

Patients and researchers in the UK study were invited to suggest any other reasons which might have acted as a motivation.

Patients' views For some patients there was a sense of doing something to help themselves. This was described by one as 'the psychological side of it'.

> While I'm in the [trial], I'm not just sitting waiting for a wheelchair. You're helping yourself, you're still trying. I told them in advance, if you've any studies, I'll take part.[73]

Some said that they had participated to find out more about their illness.[74] One patient stressed the 'relationship side' and the 'social interaction' of coming regularly to the same clinic. Some seemed to feel that they ought to participate since they were available and able to do so. This applied in particular to retired people and those on invalidity benefit who were aware that it was easier for them to attend the hospital or GP surgery than for people who were in employment. Comments here included:

---

71 Researcher No. 13.

72 E.g. – retired, unemployed, on disability benefit, diabetic.

73 Patient No. 77.

74 In the Harris Interactive survey, 'to obtain education about my treatment/improving my health' was given as a motivation by 39 per cent of patients (see Table 11.4).

> I had the time for the visits, and I thought it would be interesting.[75]

> I'm sitting at home doing nothing and they've got to have people like me to find something. You've got to help.[76]

Others seem to have agreed to take part simply because they were asked. They do not seem to have given the matter a great deal of consideration:

> The doctor just said 'do you want to try something new?' I said 'why not?'[77]

> I wouldn't volunteer for anything but it came my way and I didn't think of a reason to say 'no'.[78]

It is disappointing to note that a small number felt that they had little option:

> I felt I was conned, when I think about it now. I was having ... problems and went to see the consultant ... He said to come back in six months time. When I came back I saw a different doctor who said 'would you like to see [Dr A]?' ... I agreed, and next thing I was talking to [Dr B] and I was signed up for the [trial].[79]

The 12 per cent of patients who felt 'unable to comment' on their motivations for agreeing to participate were all involved in the same trial. They had been told about the trial and asked to consent to take part when in great pain. Several felt that they had little alternative:

> I was in such pain – I said 'do anything you want'.[80]

> [Because I was in pain] I'd have said 'yes' to anything, then.[81]

This raises the issue of whether these patients were able to give truly informed consent, in the circumstances.[82]

Researchers' views One nurse suggested that where the patients have a great deal of faith in the doctor's ability, they give little thought to taking part in a study:

---

75 Patient No. 9.
76 Patient No. 80.
77 Patient No. 39.
78 Patient No. 46.
79 Patient No. 71.
80 Patient No. 14.
81 Patient No. 15.
82 This issue is not addressed in this chapter, but see Ferguson, P.R., 'Testing a drug during labour: the experiences of women who participated in a clinical trial', (2000) *Journal of Reproductive and Infant Psychology*, 18:2, 117-131.

> Patients say: 'If the doctor thinks it's good for me, I'll take it'. They have tremendous confidence in the advice she [the doctor] gives. She thinks this is for their own good, and they have tremendous faith in her.[83]

Similarly:

> In [certain] studies, older patients tend to do as doctors suggest. They are happy to do it and that's usually the end of it – they are given the [consent] forms, but they don't read [them].[84]

Some researchers suggested that many patients simply like being part of a study:

> A lot of people are really quite interested ... They feel they're quite important, once they've seen the extra attention, then at the end of the study they'll say 'what can I do next?' Some enjoy it. If they are older and not employed it becomes almost a hobby for them, to do clinical trials. They are very useful – they learn the ropes and make very compliant patients. They'll fill in the diary cards and bring back empty packaging. They almost become professionals.[85]
>
> Being part of a study means that patients must follow their treatment regime rigorously, hence it encourages greater compliance, and some of them find the discipline of this to be a benefit.[86]

That patients might be motivated by feelings of self-importance was mentioned by 5 per cent of researchers:

> People do like to be involved in scientific studies – they like to tell their friends they are in a study – they feel increasingly important in their eyes – they are proud to be in a study.[87]
>
> Patients might think that they are special – being in the study might make them feel important.[88]
>
> Regular patients with long term consequences feel special because they've been asked to take part.[89]
>
> Some patients do like the feeling of being at the cutting edge of medical practice – a feeling that they themselves are making a contribution. It's a feeling of self-importance, but I don't think that's an unreasonable feeling.[90]

---

83 Researcher No. 1.
84 Researcher No. 28.
85 Researcher No. 72.
86 Researcher No. 38.
87 Researcher No. 34.
88 Researcher No. 55.
89 Researcher No. 62.
90 Researcher No. 71.

Conclusions

The reasons why patients agree to participate in clinical trials are varied and complex. There is evidence that some patients find it difficult to decline to take part in such trials,[91] and a report by the British Medical Association concluded that patients can be 'left feeling guilty or uncaring if they refuse'.[92] The Royal College of Physicians has suggested that the desire to help themselves is 'probably the commonest reason'.[93] The author's study found that, although this was given by patients as a reason for participation, the desire to help other people was more often expressed. It may, of course, be the case that patients wish to appear more altruistic than they really are. Helping their doctors was also said by patients to be relevant, but less so. Financial incentives were of little importance. The professionals who conduct clinical drug trials ascribed a range of motives to patients, with the desire to help other patients being regarded as relevant by the highest percentage of researchers. The survey by Harris Interactive suggests that many of the same motivations operate in the USA, but it is noteworthy that financial incentives, whether in terms of obtaining free medication, or actual payment for taking part in a clinical trial, seem to be much stronger than in the UK.

---

91 Hewlett, S.E., 'Is consent to participate in research voluntary?', 1996 *Arthritis Care Research*, 9:5, 400-4 at p. 402. See also 'Research', Chapter 8 of *Medical Ethics Today: Its Practice and Philosophy*, London, BMA Publishing Group, 1993, 195-229 at p. 208: '... patients may submissively agree because they wish to please the medical team, to appear co-operative and to be "good patients" or because they have not initially understood fully their options, including the option to say "no".'

92 *Id.*

93 *Op cit.*, at para 7.75.

Table 11.1 UK Study: Demographic Characteristics of the Patients

Age Group	(%)
18-25 yrs	10
26-45 yrs	26
46-65 yrs	41
66+ yrs	23
Employment Status	
Employed (full/part time, self-employed)	30
Unemployed	5
Retired	38
Student	1
In Receipt of Disability Payments	13
Housewives	14
Prior Involvement in a Clinical Trial	(%)
1 or 2 studies	11
3 or 4 studies	3
No prior involvement	87

Figures show percentage of sample falling into each subgroup.
(Percentages in all tables are to nearest 1%)

Table 11.2 UK Study: Patients' Motivations for Taking Part in a Clinical Trial

Motivating Factor	Highly Relevant	Relevant to Some Extent	Not at All Relevant	Not Applicable	Unable to Comment
To what extent did you agree to take part in this trial	(%)	(%)	(%)	(%)	(%)
1. To secure the best medication for your condition?	51	23	27	0	12
2. In the hope that by doing so you would benefit people who might develop your illness or condition in the future?	60	23	18	0	12
3. In the belief that in doing so you would be helping your doctor?	18	44	39	0	12
4. In the belief that you would get more health checks in the trial than you would otherwise be given?	14	18	42	25	12
5. Because you were looking for an improvement on your current therapy?	15	7	15	63	12
6. Because you would get the trial drug without having to pay a prescription fee?	0	2	17	81	12

Table 11.3 UK Study: Researchers' Views of Patients' Motivations

Motivating Factor	Highly Relevant	Relevant to Some Extent	Not at All Relevant	Not Applicable	Unable to Comment	Other
To what extent do you believe that patients agreed to take part in your study:	(%)	(%)	(%)	(%)	(%)	(%)
1. In the belief that the test drug is the best treatment/ medication for them?	35	41	22	0	1	1
2. To help others who may develop their illness or condition in the future?	54	36	4	0	3	4
3. To help their doctor?	15	60	19	0	1	4
4. So that they can have more health checks?	24	37	35	0	1	3
5. To see if the test drug will be an improvement on their existing therapy?	40	27	18	14	1	0

Table 11.4 Harris Interactive Survey

Patients' Reasons for Participation	(%)
1. To advance medicine/science.	56
2. To help others with the condition.	45
3. To obtain better treatment for [my] condition.	44
4. To obtain free medication.	27
5. There were no other treatment options available.	7
6. The information I read, saw, or had heard about the study influenced me.	41
7. To obtain education about treatment/improving my health.	39
8. I was curious about the specifics of the study.	32
9. To earn extra money.	50
10. My doctor recommended the study.	21
11. Family/Friend recommended the study.	13
12. I have a life-threatening illness.	7
13. There are no reasons in particular.	1
14. Other.	11

Table 11.5 UK/US Patients Comparison

Motivation	Relevance: UK study (%)	Relevance: US survey (%)
1. To secure the best treatment	74	—
2. To benefit other patients	83	45
3. Looking for an improvement on current therapy	22	44
4. To obtain free medication	2	27
5. To earn extra money	—	50
6. To assist my doctor	62	—

Chapter 12

Human(s) (as) Medicine(s)[1]

Margot Brazier

Introduction

Not long ago, when Professor Mason and I were both a little younger, medicines caused little moral concern. Medicine tended to come in a brown, opaque bottle – any 'yuck factor' was found in the taste. The nastier the taste, the better the medicine, or so our mothers assured us. In the twenty-first century, medicines are more complex products. Pharmaceutical companies manufacture an ever growing range of essentially chemical drugs with the power to do much more good than the simpler preparations of the mid-twentieth century. Enhanced therapeutic effect brings with it greater risk of harm, and consequent, albeit usually unsuccessful, litigation.[2] What I want to contemplate in this essay is not the regulation of 'traditional' medicines, but the diverse means by which we ourselves may be used as medicine; the notion of humans as medicines.[3]

Biological materials harvested from human sources offer a promise of 'cure' for disease in many different contexts. I suggest just a few examples. Blood products have been utilised now for nearly a century.[4] *In vitro* fertilisation (IVF), and the host of reproductive technologies which IVF gave birth to, bring hope to the infertile.[5] Pre-implantation genetic diagnosis (PGD) allows parents to avoid the birth of a child with some devastating genetic disease. PGD, when linked with Human Leukocyte

---

1 I would like to thank Alastair Campbell and Rodney Brazier for their helpful comments on an earlier draft of this chapter.

2 See generally Ferguson, P.R., *Drug Injuries and the Pursuit of Compensation*, London, Sweet & Maxwell, 1996; Teff, H. and Munro, C., *Thalidomide: The Legal Aftermath*, London, Saxon House, 1976.

3 I shall not address, in any detail, questions of product liability and bodily products. See Mason, J.K., McCall Smith, R.A. and Laurie, G.T., *Law and Medical Ethics* (7th ed), Oxford, Oxford University Press, 2006, at pp. 339-344.

4 Systematic 'safe' transfusions date from the early 1900s although blood products had been experimented with much earlier; see Machin, S.J., 'Contaminated Blood', (2004) 72 *Medico-Legal Journal*, 77-87.

5 On the legal and ethical issues generated by the reproductive technologies generally see Lee, R. and Morgan, D., *Human Fertilisation and Embryology: Regulating the Reproductive Revolution*, London, Blackstone, 2001; Jackson, E., *Regulating Reproduction: Law, Technology and Autonomy*, Oxford, Hart, 2001.

Antigen Tissue Typing (HLA), allows the creation of so-called saviour siblings, enabling one child to be created to become the source of survival for another.[6] Organ transplants save lives.[7] Stem cell therapies may one day let us manufacture new tissue and organs in the laboratory.[8] Organ retention enables scientists to increase their understanding of disease and save more lives.[9] Yet each and every one of these life saving therapies has caused controversy and sometimes outrage.

The nature of these controversies often appears very different and context specific. Opponents of embryo research and stem cell therapies rage against the destruction of unborn human beings.[10] Concern about saviour siblings focuses on the use of one child as a means to an end. Few people object to organ transplants *per se*, but the question of payments for organs provokes immense dispute, and the debate on explicit or presumed consent for cadaver organs continues unabated.[11] Organ retention generated an almost unprecedented public outcry centred on what many families saw as 'theft' of their relative's (and thus their) bodily material.[12]

This apparent diversity in the kinds of controversy, and the underlying scientific and medical advances, has meant that for the most part each ethical conundrum is examined separately. What, it may be asked, links the furore about saviour siblings with the anger of families involved in the organ retention scandals? I want to suggest, tentatively, that there is a link. It is a profound and continuing unease within society about how we use 'human material'.[13] How do we reconcile the beneficial uses of

---

6 See *R (on the application of Quintavalle) v. Human Fertilisation and Embryology Authority* [2005] 2 All E.R. 555, HL. The ethics of PGD and HLA are discussed most elegantly in Sheldon, S. and Wilkinson, S., 'Hashmi and Whitaker: An Unjustifiable and Misguided Decision', (2004) 12 *Med. L. Rev.*, 137-163.

7 See Price, D., *Legal and Ethical Aspects of Organ Transplantation*, Cambridge, CUP, 2000.

8 See Halliday, S., 'A Comparative Approach to the Regulation of Human Embryonic Stem Cell Research in Europe', (2004) 12 *Med. L. Rev.*, 40-69; Brownsword, R., 'Regulating Human Genetics: New Dilemmas for a New Millennium', (2004) 12 *Med. L. Rev.*, 14-39.

9 See Price, D., 'From Cosmos and Damien to Van Velzen: The Human Tissue Saga Continues', (2003) 11 *Med. L. Rev.*, 1-47.

10 The attempt by Enoch Powell MP to ban embryo research altogether was tellingly entitled the Unborn Children (Protection) Bill; see Brahams, D., 'Human Embryo Research and the Law', (1987) 137 *N.L.J.*, 290-293.

11 See the discussion in Liddell, K. and Hall, A., 'Beyond Bristol and Alder Hey: The Future Regulation of Human Tissue', (2005) 13 *Med. L. Rev.*, 170-223.

12 See *inter alia* the Bristol Inquiry Interim Report *Removal and Retention of Human Material* (2000); *The Royal Liverpool Children's Inquiry Report* (the Redfern Report), London, The Stationery Office, 2001. *The Isaacs Report – The Investigation of Events that Followed the Death of Cyril Mark Isaacs* (DOH 2003); Scottish Executive *Final Report of the Independent Review on the Retention of Organs at Post Mortem* (2001); *Report of the Human Organ Inquiry* (Northern Ireland, 2002).

13 The very language used to debate these ethical conundrums can of itself fuel controversy. In the context of organ retention the Bristol Interim Inquiry Report, *supra cit.*, recommended the use of the apparently neutral term 'human material' to include both

bodily material (and bodies themselves) with essential respect for ourselves and our human family? How do we distinguish 'ourselves' from our physical bodies?

This is in no sense a new question. The relationship of 'self' and 'body' has been debated since classical times.[14] Dualism or monism has generated thousands of scholarly works. David Price[15] has skilfully drawn together the threads of those debates in the context of organ transplantation. I argue that our inability to agree how we distinguish ourselves from our component parts crucially impairs our ability to meet the challenges offered by the notion of humans *being*, not just taking, medicine. In this chapter, I merely scratch the surface of this vexed question. I use only limited examples and constraints of space prevent me from exploring the literature in all its rich extent. My interest in the ethical debate about human tissue was ignited long ago. As has been so often the case, it was Professor Ken Mason who prompted that interest. I have not always agreed with him, but I have always found it difficult to justify any disagreement!

A 'Miracle Cure' – Called Sam

I begin with that favourite tool of philosopher friends – the thought-experiment. Imagine that in 2010 a baby boy is born in Manchester. His parents name him Sam. Sam grows and thrives until, at the age of about three, he contracts meningitis. His recovery is swift, so swift that it is unlikely that the prescribed antibiotics had time to take effect. Tests reveal an amazing result. Sam carries within him cells that can fight off most diseases and his organs and tissue have a capacity for regeneration, unless catastrophically injured. Scientists believe (with justification) that Sam could be used to understand and cure most human diseases unrelated to the aging process. The question is, how far can they go?

Few would, I suspect, dissent from the view that with his parents' consent, doctors could take blood and tissue samples from Sam. And could they take stem cells to manufacture cell lines? As long as any risk or distress to Sam was minimal, moral objections to minor intrusive procedures would be subdued. Legally the position is more dubious; are any of these procedures in Sam's best interests?[16] But what if his parents say no – you may not so much as touch our boy again? Or his parents offer conditional consent. You may 'experiment' on our Sam, but you must first pay us £500,000 and give us a 20 per cent royalty on any therapies developed from

---

organs and tissue. A number of families reacted with fury – their child or relative was not just *material*. See further (below) at 189.

14 See, for example, Campbell, A.V., 'Why the Body Matters: Reflections on John Harris's Account of Organ Procurement', in Holm, S. and Takala, T. (eds), *A Life of Value*, Rodopi, 2005.

15 *Op cit.*, at pp. 8-10, 32-36, 64-65.

16 On the limits to parental powers to authorise procedures relating to young children in England and Wales, see Brazier, M., *Medicine, Patients and Law* (3rd ed), Penguin, 2003, at pp. 355-58. It might well be argued that such procedures are not 'against Sam's interests'.

Sam's cells.[17] These altered scenarios introduce some of the underlying themes of real debates about bodily material. Must an absolute *veto* on a procedure which will do untold good and little if any harm be respected? Given the good that could ensue, why should Sam's parents not be paid? We may consider it bad taste, but, parents make money out of exceptionally beautiful children starring in advertisements. Why should Sam's parents not profit from their 'miracle' son?

Let us make the scenario darker. In order to profit fully from our miracle boy, doctors need access to every organ in his body, to every speck of his tissue. To put it brutally, to find out Sam's amazing biological secrets and share them more widely, we need to kill Sam. His parents (a little reluctantly) agree. Would even the most observant and strict utilitarian consider that Sam's murder was justifiable despite the much greater good which could accrue to the much greater number? The instinctive reply might be that even the most extreme utilitarian could not justify human sacrifice, however great the good to others. Yet as Calabresi notes, in other contexts we conscript bodies. Young men and women are conscripted to military service and sent to near certain death.[18]

But what if Sam was killed in a road accident, his skull crushed in an instant? Even Sam's miraculous properties cannot save him. His dead body contains the secrets of his 'miracle medicine'. His parents refuse consent to any form of intrusion on their son's dead body beyond what is required for the coroner's autopsy. Here, there are those who will argue that parental objections should carry much less weight than the imperatives of science and the potential good to humanity.[19]

Or let us hypothesise that Sam's miracle cells are identified long before Sam is born. His parents undergo IVF with PGD to avoid genetic disease. Eight embryos are successfully fertilised. Three carry the affected gene and will be discarded. Four are normal and healthy. One is the miracle embryo which, or who,[20] will, if implanted, grow into Sam. His parents consent to donate this miracle (Sam) embryo to science. Many (though not all) would applaud their altruism. For those who praise Sam's parents, the essence of the matter is that the embryo in the Petrie dish is not Sam. Similarly, those who would conscript the three-year-old Sam's dead body to the service of science would argue that the corpse is no longer Sam. At the centre of perplexity about proper uses of bodily material lies discomfort about what makes us special – what makes us, us. And when we are agreed that we and other fellow humans are special, what consequences follow?

---

17 Consider the case of the woman who made millions of dollars selling blood in the USA because of the rarity of her blood group; see Calabresi, G., 'Do We Own Our Bodies?', in Dickens, B.M. (ed), *Medicine and the Law*, Aldershot, Dartmouth, 1993, 1-17, at p. 14.

18 Ibid., at p. 7.

19 See Harris, J. 'Law and regulation of retained organs: the ethical issues', (2002) 22 *LS*, 527-550.

20 Whether we say embryo *which* or embryo *who* immediately signals how we perceive that entity, whether or not *it* or *he* is in any sense *Sam*.

Conscripting the Dead?

A fundamental cause of the controversy surrounding organ retention was the chasm of misunderstanding between so many families and many clinicians.[21] The clinicians perceived the body of the deceased as biological material of potential use in the advancement of medicine. The person who had inhabited the body was gone. It was wasteful not to make use of what was left behind. The parent of a dead child, the widow of a murdered husband, still saw their child or husband. The Bristol Inquiry Interim Report encapsulated the dilemma:[22]

> For the parents of a recently deceased child, human material, certainly substantial specimens such as organs or parts of organs, and even smaller parts are still thought of as an integral part of the child's body, *and, thus, are still the child.* For the pathologists and clinicians, the material is regarded as a specimen or an object. *It is dehumanised* (my emphases).

So returning to Sam, even after his tragic death in the road accident, his parents may still regard him as their beloved child, not a laboratory tool. If Sam's family are orthodox Jews or Muslims, their faith may mandate the burial of his body intact. Belief in bodily resurrection and/or that bodies as much as souls are gifts from God renders the dead body as much worthy of respect as the living breathing organism.[23]

'Bunkum' is how some will respond to religious arguments about dead bodies. Superstition and 'irrational' illusions cannot be allowed to impede medical progress and waste salvageable lives.[24] Others may reflect surprise that such a furore about the use of dead bodies should erupt in an era when religious practice is in decline. Dissection of the dead is an age-old controversy. Burke and Hare were the bogey men of their day, a day when most of those who feared the body-snatchers literally believed in bodily resurrection. Ruth Richardson[25] has admirably dissected the historical debate on uses of whole bodies. The criminals and paupers who ran the risk of dissection feared that the State sought to deny them immortal life as well. At the end of the twentieth century, only a minority of people believed literally in bodily resurrection. Belief in the survival of the immortal, immaterial soul is on the wane. I suspect that many of the families who inquired about organ retention did not do so from a faith-based perspective. We may ask whether the wane of orthodox religious belief paradoxically confer a greater weight to bodily remains? If there is

21 See Morrison, D., 'A Holistic Approach to Clinical and Research Decision-Making: Lessons from the UK Organ-Retention Scandals', (2005) 13 *Med. L. Rev.*, 45-79.

22 Bristol Interim Inquiry Report, *supra cit.*, at para 33. See also, Price *op cit.*, at pp. 32-36.

23 See Brazier, M., 'Retained Organs: Ethics and Humanity', (2002) 22 *LS*, 550-569 .

24 See Harris, *op cit.*, at p. 548.

25 See R. Richardson, *Death, Dissection and the Destitute* (2nd ed), Chicago Press, 2000.

no real hope of an afterlife, does the body acquire a greater, not lesser significance? His mortal remains are literally all that is left of Sam.

Many of those who attended meetings of the Retained Organs Commission, which was established *inter alia* to oversee the return of identifiable body parts in the wake of the organ retention scandals in England, said that, had they been asked to consent to retention of body parts from their deceased relatives and could be assured that those parts would be beneficially and respectfully used, they would have agreed.[26] They had no immutable objection to the use of their relative's body to do good. Some families had even offered to donate organs for transplantation. What does this tell us about how the families regarded the body of their relative? Are willingness to donate organs, yet fury that organs were taken without permission, reconcilable viewpoints? A lack of understanding about organ retention undoubtedly played a part. To quote the Bristol Inquiry Report again:

> The fact that parents and the public were unaware that human material was routinely taken and used for a variety of purposes and large collections existed around the country was unacknowledged or ignored.[27]

Cadaver transplantation is better understood. The grieving parent asked to donate a dead child's heart can make an immediate connection between his pain and another's joy. If Sam's parents are asked to donate his heart for transplant, it may be easier to see this as a gift from their Sam to another couple's child. They know what will happen. A part of their child lives on. Asked to donate Sam to medical research, several spectres haunt the mortuary. Will Sam be used to good ends? Will others profit from him? Might he (without his parents' knowledge) be cloned? Suspicion is, however, not entirely absent from the transplantation scenario. In the early years of transplantation, fears were voiced that surgeons, eager for organs, were not too fussy about whether the donor was truly dead. Even today, doubts are occasionally expressed about the reliability of criteria for brain stem death.[28] The problems of identity continue, vividly illustrated by controversy about the possibility of face transplants. If a child is given Sam's face, does he become Sam?[29]

In a vigorous attack on what he perceives as the irrational fuss about organ retention, John Harris[30] notes a paradox. The Church that places such value on respect for the dead retains (almost certainly without informed consent) the relics of 'assorted saints'. How can you justify prohibiting retention of Sam's 'miracle corpse' but allow display of relics that 'work miracles'? I doubt you can, but you can perhaps understand a difference. The relic of St Cecilia remains that saint. She is not

26 See *Remembering the Past, Looking to the Future*, The Final Report of the Retained Organs Commission, London, DOH, 2004, at para 1.9.

27 At para 32.

28 The relevant literature is cogently analysed in Price, *op cit.*, at pp. 40-72.

29 See Hartman, R.S., 'Face Values: Challenges of Transplant Technology', (2005) 31 *American Journal of Law and Medicine*, 7-47.

30 Harris, *op cit.*, at p. 529.

robbed of her identity, but rather gains a kind of immortality amongst us mortals. Organs, and even whole bodies of infants, stored in laboratories, are reduced to things, cut off from the families who nurtured the children they once were.

'Medicine' from the Living?

The impact of bereavement and loss inevitably makes debates about the uses of post mortem tissue poignant and complex. Use of bodily materials taken from the living should be a more straightforward issue. Alas it is not.

Blood transfusions are routine. The use of blood as medicine dates from early in the twentieth century. The greatest practical problems remain to encourage a sufficient number of people to become donors and ensure an uncontaminated supply of blood.[31] Moral controversy seems muted at first sight.[32] Jehovah's Witnesses refuse transfusions as sinful for Witnesses. They do not seek to ban the practice for those outside their faith. Note, however, one of the grounds on which the Jehovah's Witnesses prohibit transfusion.[33]

> Simply be firmly resolved not to eat the blood, because the blood is the soul ...[34]

Blood is prohibited for it is seen as the essence of the person. The Lord will not permit the donation of the soul. However, Jehovah's Witnesses are a small minority group. For the overwhelming majority allowing blood transfusions is not a societal problem.[35]

The risk and discomfort are negligible, the benefit is great. Donating a kidney, or a lobe of your lung, or a segment of your liver, however, demands more courage and a higher pain threshold. In the early years of organ transplantation, doubts were expressed about the legality of live donation. Could you consent to bodily mutilation of no physical benefit to yourself?[36] The legality of such live donation is now well settled.[37] Altruistic donation of an organ is normally commended. But live donation remains hedged about with legal obstacles. Should I propose to donate my kidney to my dying brother, my wish will be likely to be granted and applauded. Should I

---

31 See Machin, *loc cit.*

32 Though note the Papal ban on blood transfusions in 1678; see Machin, *loc cit.*

33 A number of additional verses of the Bible are also cited as prohibiting the use of blood products.

34 Deuteronomy 12:23-25.

35 That is to say the principle is applauded but too few donors still put principle into practice.

36 See Dworkin, G., 'The Law Relating to Organ Transplantation in England', (1970) 33 *M.L.R.*, 353-377, at p. 362.

37 Law Commission Consultation Paper No. 139, *Consent in the Criminal Law*, London, H.M.S.O., 1999, at para 8.32. See also Price, *op cit.*, at pp. 225-229.

offer a kidney to a stranger, my altruism may be regarded with suspicion. Should I advertise my kidney for sale, I will fall foul of UK law.[38]

It is this ban on the sale of organs that has excited the most overt moral controversy surrounding live organ donation. The nature of this controversy appears on the surface to be radically different from concerns about posthumous organ retention and transplantation. In the latter instance the alleged 'evil' rests in fears that organs will be taken without any sort of appropriate consent or authorisation. The 'donor' is in truth a conscript. The live 'donor' seeking to sell an organ is by contrast a willing vendor. She actively seeks transfer of her kidney. All sorts of practical arguments bedevil debates on markets in organs. Many rightly centre on how such a market could effectively ensure that the vendor is in truth willing and informed. Let us assume a regulated market which offered adequate protection to vendors and purchasers is possible;[39] do any remaining objections to organ sales hold good? Powerful voices say no:

> The weakness of the familiar arguments suggests that they are attempts to justify the deep feelings of repugnance which are the real driving force of the prohibition and feelings of repugnance among the rich and healthy, no matter how strongly felt, cannot justify removing the only hope of the destitute and dying.[40]

Mason and Laurie agree, with some apparent reluctance, asking:

> Is it impossible that a commercial *donor* could make his decision in a reasoned manner and on his own *altruistic* grounds? ... It is at least arguable that, in closing the door on the use of an *inessential* part of one's body for gain, Parliament is striking at the individual publican's autonomy in favour of the corporate Pharisee's inner virtues (my emphases).[41]

Consider this limited claim. The commercial donor is said to act on altruistic grounds – 'his own altruistic grounds'? Why retain the language of donation? And if we jettison the language of donation in favour of sale, why should a sale be altruistically motivated? Imagine I inherit my mother's wedding ring, an object of great sentimental value to myself, my brother and her granddaughters. I choose neither to bury it with her nor to retain the ring as a family keepsake. I put it up for sale, seeking the highest price. There is no altruism in my conduct. Most readers will consider my conduct somewhat shabby. No-one, however, will, I think, regard my conduct as so unethical that it should be illegal. If the sale of human biological material is morally legitimate, why do its proponents still cling to any notion of altruism?

---

38 Sales of organs for transplantation were first criminalised by the Human Organs Transplant Act 1989. That prohibition is continued by s. 32 of the Human Tissue Act 2004. A similar prohibition is contained in s 17 of the Human Tissue (Scotland) Bill 2005

39 See Harris, J. and Erin, C., 'An Ethically Defensible Market in Organs', (2002) 325 *BMJ*, 114-115.

40 Radcliffe-Richards, J., Daar, A.S., Guttman R.D. *et al.*, 'The Case for Allowing Kidney Sales', (1998) 351 *Lancet*, 1950-1952.

41 Mason and Laurie, *op cit.*, at p. 490.

Professor Mason and his co-authors speak carefully of 'an inessential part of one's body'. They exclude non-regenerative organs – some sort of commercial sacrifice. The living vendor still has plenty to sell besides her kidney. Blood, bone marrow, skin, gametes, lobes of lung and segments of liver could all be put to profitable use by a human 'pharmacy'. A free market allowing purchasers to fix prices would render such a venture profitable. Few voices advocate such a 'career'[42] as well suited to someone physically healthy, but less able to profit from their brain than professors of medical law or ethics. Yet society does not cavil at certain sorts of bodily sales. Selling hair is accepted as ethically uncontroversial and legal.[43] Is this because we overtly shed our hair?[44] Hair is an adornment more closely related to our clothing than ourselves. We mould our hairstyle to the latest whim. However, in relation to more intimate parts of our body, the influence of Titmuss's gift relationship endures.[45] Many of his practical arguments no longer hold good. Prohibition of payments for blood failed to guarantee the safety of blood products.[46] Supply falls far short of demand. Nonetheless we cling to some notion of donation.

Selling Our Dead?

In considering commodification of organs, debate more usually focuses on living vendors. What of cadaver sales? I might wish to enhance my daughter's inheritance by issuing advance directions authorising the sale of my organs. Or she, as the sole beneficiary of my estate, and finding it sorely lacking in substance, might seek to auction off my corpse. Why should she not? Of course, she cannot do so in England at present,[47] and every lawyer reading this essay will now be clamouring to remind me there is no property in the body.[48] The ethical and social question remains, if human biological material is just that, *material*, why do advocates of markets remain so squeamish? Why is a stronger case not made for cadaver organ sales?

Mason and his co-authors do not duck this issue. They say tentatively that they '... find payment for the organs of the dead far less easy to justify than payment to

---

42 Though note the tale of the 'commercial human bloodbank' related by Calabresi; see Calabresi *op cit.* at p. 10.

43 Hair and nail clippings are expressly excluded from the otherwise broad remit of the Human Tissue Act 2004; see s 53 (2) (b).

44 In fact our skin and blood cells alter as rapidly but we do not observe the process.

45 Titmuss, R.M., *The Gift Relationship: From Human Blood to Social Policy*, London, Allen and Unwin, 1971. See also Price, *op cit.*, at pp. 367-418.

46 See Farrell, A., 'The Emergence of EU Governance in Public Health: the Case of Blood Policy and Regulation', in Steften, M. (ed), *Health Governance in Europe: Issues, Challenges and Theories*, London, Routledge, 1995, 134-151.

47 Strictly speaking only sales of organs for transplantation are illegal, the government backed down from its original proposal to ban all payments for human tissue; see Human Tissue Act 2004, s 32.

48 See, for example, Mason, J.K. and Laurie, G.T., 'Consent or property: Dealing with the body and its parts in the shadow of Bristol and Alder Hey', (2001) 64 *M.L.R.*, 710-729.

the living donor'.[49] Mason and Laurie go on to say that if a commercial market in cadaver organs succeeded in saving lives '... reward for donation of cadaver organs appears in a less scandalous light than it did at first sight'.[50] Why is a market in cadaver organs harder to justify? Why is it more 'scandalous' for his parents to sell dead Sam's miraculous tissue, than for an adult Sam himself to make such a sale? Advocates of markets, who argue powerfully markets do not degrade, remain concerned about the risks to, and exploitation of, vulnerable living donors.[51] Rationally should we prefer markets in cadaver organs to markets dependent on living vendors? Do we remain uncomfortable because the notion of profit and bereavement sit so uncomfortably together?[52]

Of Embryos and Unborn Babes

If we return again to the miracle cure, called Sam, part of the objection to the several 'good' uses to which he and his body might be put rests on the perceived wrongfulness of using Sam as a means to an end. At three, Sam is on anyone's account a person.[53] He is recognisable as one of us – a fellow human of intrinsic value. Having been Sam, he remains even after death, still Sam. But what if 'Sam' never was? His miraculous properties are discovered at the blastocyst stage. His 'parents' consent to scientists taking and developing the embryo for research purposes and developing cell lines from that embryo. Its miraculous qualities will then be utilised in the service of medicine. Who could object?

Opponents of embryo research contend that from the point of fertilisation a new, and usually unique, human being comes into existence. Sam's life begins at fertilisation – the embryo is Sam even if he never receives a name.[54] Embryo 'Sam' deserves equal protection to infant Sam. The battle against embryo research *per se* was hard fought and lost in 1990 with the legitimisation of embryo research in the Human Fertilisation and Embryology Act 1990. It could not have been won without outlawing IVF too. If the embryo must be protected from destruction then either no surplus embryos must be created, or all must be preserved. If alleviating infertility is sufficient justification for destroying some embryos, research to improve human

49 Mason and Laurie *op cit.*, at p. 504.

50 *Ibid.*

51 See, for example, Duxbury, N., 'Do Markets Degrade?', (1996) 59 *M.L.R.*, 331-348.

52 'Slippery slopes' also slither into the equation. If it is acceptable for my daughter to sell my organs for transplant, why should she not also offer me to Professor Gunther Von Hagens if he will offer a better price to include me in his [in]famous exhibition of plastinated bodies *Bodyworlds*?

53 See Harris, J., *The Value of Life*, London, Routledge, 1985, at pp. 12-18.

54 See Holland, A., 'A Fortnight of My Life is Missing: A Discussion of the Status of the Pre-embryo', (1990) 7 *J. Appl. Philosophy*, 25-37.

health is arguably a better justification.[55] The 1990 Act adopted the uneasy Warnock compromise. The embryo up to 14 days or the development of the primitive streak '... ought to have *special* status'.[56]

Such a mealy mouthed compromise was forcefully rejected by Mason as long ago as 1988.[57] He said:

> Either the *in vitro* embryo of Homo sapiens is a human being with rights that are absolute in themselves, and which only become comparative when they are in conflict with those of human beings in a more developed state,[58] or it is an artefact to be regarded in the same light as any other biological product of the laboratory.

So what, if anything, does 'special status' entail?[59] The ambivalent status of 'special' embryos is well illustrated by the media outrage about 'orphan embryos' in 1996. The 1990 Act provided that frozen embryos could be preserved for five years. At the end of that original five year period, unused embryos should be 'allowed to perish'.[60] In 1996, the five year term for embryos initially stored under the Act came to an end. Clinics were often no longer in contact with the gamete donors. The media had a field day expressing outrage at the destruction of thousands of 'orphan embryos'.[61] The government responded by providing that under certain conditions the storage period could be extended from five to ten years.[62] What was the fuss about? If the imperilled embryos should be regarded as orphaned children, first, they should not have been created 'doomed to die' and, second, given they were created, arrangements should have been made for their speedy pre-natal adoption. If the stored embryos were merely useful biological material, they should have been put to good use, either in research, or offered to infertile couples to 'cure' their infertility. Such use of the 'orphan embryos' however, offended the principles governing gamete donation. Where no contact could be established with the parents, or rather gamete donors, no 'effective consent' could be obtained to donate the embryos for research or pre-natal

---

55 See Brazier, M., 'The challenge for Parliament: a critique of the White Paper on Human Fertilisation and Embryology', in Dyson, A. and Harris, J. (eds), *Experiments on Embryos*, London, Routledge, 1989, 127-141.

56 Report of the Committee of Inquiry into Human Fertilisation and Embryology, Cmnd 9314/1984, para 11.17.

57 Mason, J.K., *Human Life and Medical Practice*, Edinburgh University Press, 1988, at p. 94.

58 See Brazier, M., 'Embryos' "Rights": Abortion and Research', in Freeman, M.D.A. (ed), *Medicine, Ethics and Law*, London, Stevens, 1988.

59 See generally Lee and Morgan *op cit.* at pp. 56-101.

60 See s 14 (5) (c), of the Human Fertilisation and Embryology Act 1990. See also Lee and Morgan, *op cit.*, at p. 121.

61 See, for example, *The Independent*, 2 August 1996 'Day of national shame'.

62 See the Human Fertilisation and Embryology (Statutory Storage Period for Embryos) Regulations 1996 (SI 196 No 375).

adoption. Yet if embryos are children, parental interests give way to their welfare. And if embryos are mere materials, why ascribe such rights to their donors?[63]

Continuing confusion about how society regards embryos is illustrated starkly by the 'saviour sibling' scenario. Parents with a sick child dying of a genetic disease now have the opportunity to create another child whose umbilical cord could contain stem cells offering a cure to his brother or sister. Embryos are created by IVF, and PGD is used to screen the embryos to screen out embryos also affected by that disease. To create a 'saviour sibling', tissue typing (Human Antigen Tissue Typing – HLA) is then used to find a compatible match to the sick child.

'Pro-life' groups challenged the legality of PGD with HLA in the much publicised case of *R (on the application of Quintavalle) v. HFEA.*[64] Zain Hashmi suffered from *beta thallasaemia*, a genetic disease. Without a bone marrow transplant he would die within a few years. Having failed to find a compatible donor within their existing family, Zain's parents sought PGD and HLA. The Human Fertilisation and Embryology Authority gave the clinic treating the Hashmis permission to go ahead. Josephine Quintavalle, on behalf of a pressure group dedicated to protecting human embryos, challenged the decision. The trial judge found in her favour. The Court of Appeal reversed his decision[65] and the House of Lords ultimately endorsed the legality of PGD with HLA to create a possible 'cure' for Zain.[66] The HFEA's decision in relation to Zain Hashmi contrasted sharply with their original decision in the case of Charlie Whitaker. Charlie suffered from Diamond Blackfan Anamia (DBA). Stem cells from a tissue matched sibling offered Charlie a 25 per cent chance of recovery. DBA is not thought to be a genetic disease. When Charlie's parents asked the HFEA to allow PGD and HLA to create a saviour sibling for Charlie they were told no. The sibling to be created was not himself at risk of DBA. PGD on potential baby Hashmi was justified to avoid baby Hashmi being born with BT. Potential baby Whitaker faced no such risk. S/he would be purely a means to an end.

The distinction made between Zain Hashmi and Charlie Whitaker was vigorously attacked[67] – so vigorously that the HFEA ultimately changed its mind.[68] The Whitakers successfully sought treatment abroad. The stem cell transplant appears to have worked and Charlie looks set for recovery. Once again the question arises, what was the fuss about? If embryos can be used and manipulated to alleviate infertility, or to research the causes of congenital disease, or develop procedures such as PGD, how can the chance to cure a sick child be any less of a justification?

It is argued that the wrongfulness of creating 'saviour siblings' lies not in what is done to the embryo, but what might ensue for the saviour child. S/he will not be

---

63 See Brazier, M., 'Regulating the Reproductive Business?', (1999) 7 *Med. L. Rev.*, 166-193.

64 [2003] 2 All E.R. 105.

65 [2003] 3 All E.R. 257, CA.

66 [2005] 2 All E.R. 555, HL.

67 See Sheldon and Wilkinson *loc cit.*

68 See *The Times*, 22 July 2004.

valued for him/herself. Fears are voiced that if the transplant of cells from the copy fails, parents will try again with more intrusive and risky procedures.[69] The infant will be subjected to a bone marrow transplant. The child will be conscripted as a kidney donor. S/he will be no more than a repository of spare parts. Yet the creation of saviour siblings changes little. If a sick child *happens* to have a born sibling who is a suitable tissue match, no eyebrows are raised when his parents authorise a bone marrow transplant from their healthy to their dying child.[70] Should any parent go the further step of attempting to use a healthy child as a kidney donor, doctors are unlikely to act on their request. The 'saviour sibling' once born is protected in just the same way as his 'accidental' sister. Objections to 'saviour siblings' must either derive from an absolute objection to the use of embryos, or some more profound discomfort about the deliberate use of humans as medicine.

Embryos and Propagation

The victory by those supporting embryo research, won in 1990, resulted in a period of peace on that particular battlefield. Controversy about the reproductive technologies focused more on emerging developments in fertility treatment, such as the fierce disputes about post menopausal motherhood and PGD. The truce was not to last. The advent of cell nuclear replacement (CNR) '... invigorated the opposition of those who have a principled objection to any form of embryo research'.[71] Dolly, the 'miracle sheep', earned her place in human history in leading the way to mammalian, and potentially, human cloning. CNR involves the insertion of the nucleus of an adult cell (taken from A) into an emptied egg cell. The egg cell is then subjected to an electrical impulse and (with luck) begins to divide and develop into an embryo. The 'embryo' is then implanted into a surrogate and a child could be born, a replica of the donor of the nucleus (A). Given the ability to clone a growing range of mammals, it seems likely that human reproductive cloning would be feasible. The cost would, however, be prohibitive for most of us. Moreover, the risk to the women bearing the clones and the clones themselves remains huge. The 'wastage' is immense. There is little support currently to allow reproductive cloning.[72] What the United Kingdom government has permitted is therapeutic cloning, more usually now referred to as stem cell therapy.[73]

---

69 For a dramatic fictional account of such a scenario see Picoult, J., *My Sister's Keeper*, London, Hodder and Stoughton, 2005.

70 See Brazier, M., *op cit.*, at pp. 422-24.

71 Mason and Laurie, *op cit.*, at p. 707.

72 Though see Harris, J., *Clones, Genes and Immortality*, Oxford, OUP, 1998; and note Mason and Laurie who say possibly presciently: 'We suspect that the days of the outright prohibition of reproductive cloning are numbered' (*op cit.*, at p. 252).

73 See The Human Fertilisation and Embryology (Research Purposes) Regulations 2001. And see HFEA/HGAC *Cloning Issues in Reproduction, Science and Medicine* (1998); *Expert group of the CMO Stem Cell Research, Medical Progress and Responsibility*, 2000.

Once an embryo is created by CNR, stem cells can be collected from that embryo. Embryonic stem cells retain their pluripotency. Thus, those cells can then be cultured to grow into diverse kinds of tissue, perhaps ultimately into whole organs. Tissue so derived from the original donor of the nucleus (i.e. from A) will be an exact match for her. So in the not too distant future, were I to succumb to a disease such as Parkinson's, stem cell therapy could utilise my bodily material to create stem cells that are a tailor-made medicine for me. Put in that way, the process sounds no more controversial than an autologous blood transfusion. And who would object should I arrange to have my own blood collected for use in planned surgery?

The objection centres on that crucial stage in the process whereby an embryo is created which could, if successfully implanted in a woman, develop into a baby. Opponents of embryo research argue that that embryo, an embryo created by propagation rather than fertilisation, is morally undistinguishable from the embryo resulting from the fusion of egg and sperm. But no new genetic entity is created. The embryo created by CNR from my nucleus is as much Margot as the cells currently in my body? Is it, as Mason argued in 1988, any more than a 'laboratory artefact'?[74] For Mason it is implantation that alters the nature of the embryo granting it the 'capacity for meaningful development'.[75] Mason does not distinguish between the embryo created by fertilisation or propagation. All are no more, but no less, than cultures of human tissue.[76] Why does Mason so forcefully promote the significance of implantation? Pragmatism plays a role,[77] albeit in my judgment a minor role. Mason relies rather on a degree of intuition and his emphasis on 'attachment'.[78] It is the creation of the physical bond between mother and child that introduces the implanted embryo to the human race.[79]

I did not agree with Mason in 1988. I am not sure if I do so now. However, the advent of CNR, rather than strengthening my personal opposition to embryo research, has caused me to doubt the validity of that opposition when research can advance human medicine.[80] The crucial importance of Mason's stance on embryos and implantation is this. He emphasises and seeks to illustrate how we may give rational form to our sense of when we recognise biological material composed of human DNA as 'one of us' not just 'a by-product of us'.

---

74 *Op cit.*

75 Mason and Laurie, *op cit.*, at p. 99; Mason *op cit.*, at 76-78, 94-99.

76 Mason and Laurie, *op cit.*, at p. 99.

77 Mason, *op cit.*, at p. 99.

78 *Ibid.*, at pp. 75-78, 96-105.

79 See Bateman-Novaes, S. and Salem, T., 'Embedding the Embryo', in Harris, J. and Holm, S. (eds), *The Future of Reproduction*, Oxford, OUP, 1998, 101-126.

80 See Brazier, *op cit.*

The Tyranny of Language

I have struggled with language. Language bedevils the debates addressed in this chapter and the literature on medical ethics and law more generally. Language can be used to bemuse the audience. Call an embryo a 'pre-embryo' and you seek to put a further distance between that entity and any perception of a baby.[81] Speak about 'rewarding donors' and your case for selling organs sounds much more worthy than applauding selling off body parts.

Deliberately manipulating language is not the only problem. Words themselves have multiple meanings. Normally, we applaud altruism. We laud sacrifice. The soldier who sacrifices his life to save his comrade is a hero. In the context of medicine, society is ambivalent about sacrifice. David Price[82] notes this ambivalence in relation to living organ donors. He quotes Elliot's account of 'our divided intuitions' making 'self sacrifice ... a double-edged sword'.[83]

The same ambiguity is found in our response to 'saviour siblings'. The term saviour connotes good purposes. We hail the saviour, and those of us who profess Christianity worship our Saviour, who sacrificed Himself. So when we contemplate the use of science to create a saviour sibling, we see the child as both saviour and possible sacrifice. Sacrifice makes us uncomfortable.

As society struggles with substance and language while humans become ever richer sources of medicine, is there any solution to the dilemma? 'Solutions' lie at the extremes. Proponents of personhood have no difficulty distinguishing the person, Sam, from the biological materials that can readily be used in medicine's service. The orthodox Roman Catholic would have no difficulties either, but would reach diametrically opposite conclusions about the status of the embryo 'Sam'. The devout Muslim would know where s/he should draw the line. All those lines are drawn at different places.

Is society asking the wrong question? Should we cease to struggle so hard to distinguish between 'human material' and 'human family'? We readily accept the services of other humans in delivering medicine, in tending and caring for us in sickness. We accept, indeed expect, a degree of 'sacrifice' from them. Doctors and nurses run risks of infection. The nurse who clocked off as soon as his shift ended, leaving a naked patient in pain or discomfort half way through her bed-bath, would be seen as a thoroughly bad nurse. Most of us lack the intellect and/or the dedication to become health professionals. Should we learn to celebrate the evidence that within our bodies, and those of our children, born and unborn, lie 'medicines' of benefit to ourselves and to others? Giving blood, donating a kidney, giving a surplus embryo is

81 See Lee and Morgan, *op cit.*, at p. 64. See also, Laing, J.A. and Oderberg, D.S., 'Artificial Reproduction, The 'Welfare Principle' and the Common Good', (2005) 13 *Med. L. Rev.* (forthcoming).

82 *Op cit.*, at pp. 251-3.

83 Elliott, C., 'Doing Harm: Living Organ Donors, Clinical Research and The Tenth Man', (1995) 21 *Journal of Medical Ethics*, 91-96, at pp. 91-2.

not simply dealing in a *thing*. Even the smallest scrap of bodily material is at least a representation of a person (or a family).

Mason argued long ago that it '... would be unreal not to admit that human biological material has a special position'.[84] If we could accept his claim, we might find a way to construct a less polarised debate about bodily material. There would still be a host of questions, old and new. I have not touched on the vexed question of the human genome. My concerns about others having access to my bodily material today may centre more on the knowledge that material gives them. I have not entered into the new debates surrounding artificial gametes.[85] All such debates will take us nowhere unless we first think more clearly about ourselves as 'medicines'. Acknowledging that bodily material at the least represents the people we are, or have been, or may become, does not mean society should restrict the use of such material. Rather, to the contrary, it requires us to consider what we owe others. The adult who passed by while a child drowned might in England escape legal censure. However, she behaves unethically; she merits moral censure. So we must all consider much more carefully when we owe a duty to rescue others, not by jumping in the pool to save the child, but by making available parts of ourselves to save others.

84 See Mason, *op cit.*, at p. 98.

85 See Newson, A. and Smajdor, A.C., 'Artificial Gametes: New Paths to Parenthood', (2005) 31 *JME*, 184-186.

Chapter 13

The Ethical Challenges of Biobanks: Safeguarding Altruism and Trust

Alastair V. Campbell

Introduction

The current rapid emergence of large biobanks – major collections of biological, genetic, environmental and health data – has raised some fascinating issues at the nexus of medical law and medical ethics. Since the controversies surrounding the Icelandic Health Sector Database (HSD), set up at the end of the last decade,[1] there has been a growing awareness that such projects raise a novel set of ethical and legal issues, most obviously in relation to the nature of the consent gained, but also across a whole range of other social and moral concerns. In this chapter I want to focus on what I regard as the two central ethical features of collections of this kind: their dependence on both altruism and trust from those who donate their samples and health data, and the corresponding duties which rest on the creators and custodians of biobanks to honour these commitments from the donors.

I accept that biobanks could be created (or may currently exist) which do not rest on these ethical foundations. For example, commercial enterprises such as pharmaceutical companies or biotechnology firms may (at least in some countries) purchase samples and data in order to enhance their research into profitable innovations.[2] However, my focus is on those major collections which seek to facilitate the study of the health of whole populations, in order to develop more effective means of diagnosis, therapy, health promotion and disease prevention.[3] In Europe the main examples are the Icelandic project referred to above, the Estonian Gene

1 For a good survey of the proposals and the controversy see Árnason, V., 'Coding and consent: moral challenges of the database project in Iceland', *Bioethics*, 2004, 18; 1:27-49; Nomper, A., *Open Consent – A New Form of Informed Consent for Population Genetic Databases*, Estonia, Tartu University, 2005 (Doctoral Dissertation). The Icelandic project entailed creating a population-wide database and linking this to both a genealogical register and to genetic and other information gained from blood samples.

2 Hansson, S.O., 'The ethics of biobanks', *Cambridge Quarterly of Healthcare Ethics*, 2004; 13: 320. He notes that in the USA 'biorepositories' have become big business.

3 The question of how biobanks are to be defined is itself a complex one. Nomper, *loc cit.*, suggests the useful term, 'Population Genetic Database', to describe this type of major project.

Bank Project and the UK Biobank. Although these three projects differ in some important respects, they all seek to study the health of whole populations (in the UK by a structured sample of 500,000 adults in the age range 40 to 69), to provide a rich data source for a wide range of prospective studies, and to offer the possibility of linkages between different types of health, biological and genetic data. Such major enterprises are mainly looking to the health of future generations, and are – or ought to be – of major interest and concern to the populations in which they are based.

The specific characteristics of these three projects will not be discussed; rather this chapter will consider in general terms the key ethical questions they raise. These questions are: the nature of the consent required from those enrolled in the project; their ongoing relationship with the project, particularly in relation to feedback of results; the control of access to data held by the project; and the influence of the participants and the population as a whole on the uses of the resource. The first section of this chapter will discuss each of these issues in turn; in the second section I shall focus on the broader themes of altruism and trust, which emerge from the discussion of these key issues.

Biobanks: The Key Ethical Issues

The Vexed Question of Consent

More ethical ink has been spilt on this question than on any other of the concerns voiced about the establishment of biobanks. It was one of the major sources of controversy in Iceland, since the Act which established the HSD did not require specific consent from the individuals whose data were being stored, although, after much debate, an opting out provision was provided. But even when explicit individual consent is required (as is the case with the UK Biobank and the Estonian project), the question remains as to the nature of the consent. The whole rationale of the biobank enterprise means that those enrolling cannot be told precisely what uses will be made of the resource in the future. Since the data gathering will last several years and the resource itself will continue to grow and to be available for use for at least two or three decades, the aims of the project must necessarily be described in very broad terms. It is clearly impossible to know at the outset the range of possible research uses. Thus, the consent being gained is quite different from the standard consent to participation in health research, when a full description has to be given of a specific research proposal, with a justification for the use of tissue or data, as well as a statement of the likely outcomes of the research.

This unusual feature of biobanks has led to many attempts to define variants of the standard form of consent, enshrined in the Declaration of Helsinki and numerous other international documents. Nomper describes an amazing range of newly coined terms: open-ended consent, blanket consent, generic consent, general consent, generalised consent, advance consent and broad consent.[4] Nomper himself favours the term 'open consent', which he defines as '... a research subject's affirmative agreement to participate in a population genetic database and in research projects that use tissue and data from that database'.[5] He argues that, provided participants are made fully aware of all of the provisions for protection of the data, for control of its use and for decisions about appropriate uses in line with the broad description of the purposes of the resource, then their consent can be seen to be fully informed and valid.

However, a number of writers do not regard this form of open consent as ethically acceptable. Some would insist that participants be re-contacted to consent to every new use (or at least to be able to request such re-contact). Others argue that this type of open consent cannot ever be valid, and so recommend different terms like 'authorisation'[6] or 'general permission'.[7] A modified position has been suggested by Kaye.[8] She wants a distinction to be made between the initial consent to have one's sample and data included in the biobank and subsequent consent regarding the uses of the resource. The former she describes as 'broad consent', which, she agrees is all that is possible when the resource is being set up. However, she does not regard this as a sufficient safeguard of individual rights, arguing that:

> ... this broad consent cannot also apply to all other research conducted on the population collection. Once the researchers and the type of research is known there is a moral obligation to give this information to individuals and to allow them to make a decision as to whether their information should be used for such purposes.[9]

In view of practical difficulties in her proposal, given the huge number of people involved in population databases, she accepts that opting out of specific projects rather than opting in would be necessary. However, she also would make it a requirement that every individual be re-contacted every five years so that they can renew their broad consent to the use of the database. Kaye argues that this is necessary because of the complex and sensitive nature of the data being collected over time.

Every proposal of this kind adds to the already very high cost of setting up and maintaining a comprehensive biobank. (The initial budget for the UK Biobank was between £50 and £60 million and for the Estonian project $US150 million.) While cost alone can never be a decisive factor in determining ethical norms, additional consent requirements that will require extra resource need to be backed up with a

4 Nomper, *loc cit.*, at p. 93.

5 *Loc cit.*, at p. 90.

6 Arnason, *loc.cit.*, at p. 44.

7 Greely, H.T., 'Breaking the Stalemate', *Wake Forest Law Review*, 1999, 34: 737-766.

8 Kaye, J., 'Abandoning informed consent: the case of genetic research in population collections', in Tutton, R. and Corrigan, O. (eds), *Genetic Databases: Socio-ethical Issues in the Collection and Use of DNA*, London, Routledge, 2004, 117-138.

9 *Ibid.*, at p. 131.

cogent ethical justification. Kaye's main argument appears to be that people simply cannot know what they are letting themselves in for when the initial consent is given. She also suggests that there are possible harms entailed in signing up for this kind of large data gathering exercise. (For example, people may withhold sensitive information when consulting their doctor if they know that that information will be transferred (albeit anonymised) to a database to which unknown third parties have access.[10])

In response to such concerns, we need to look more carefully at the nature of the consent given by competent individuals, when this entails agreement to participation in a general project, the full details of which cannot yet be specified. Here, Onora O'Neill's description of consent appears to be the most useful:

> Genuine consent is not a matter of overwhelming patients with information. The quest for perfect specificity is doomed to fail, since descriptions can be expanded endlessly, and there is no limit to a process of seeking more specific consent. It is not, however, difficult to give patients control over the amount of information they choose to receive ... Patients who know they have access to *extendable information* and that they have *rescindable consent* have in effect a *veto* over what is done.[11]

The attraction of this approach to the concept of consent is that it emphasises what is arguably the central ethical feature of the activity – control by the person consenting. The Kaye model appears somewhat paternalistic, demanding that the initial inadequacy (as she sees it) of the consent given be corrected by subsequent requirements on participants to consider each project with a view to opting out and to re-affirm their consent at regular intervals. O'Neill, on the other hand, leaves the control to the participants – respecting more their autonomy, one might say. They can seek more information, once available, should they wish it, and, on the basis of this additional information (or for any other reason), they can rescind their consent.

In this context, some research into the consent gained for blood samples for a Swedish biobank is illuminating. Hoeyer studied a group of people in an area of Sweden, who, while attending a clinic for a regular health check, were asked for consent to taking extra blood to be included in a commercial research biobank.[12] On the basis of participant observation and subsequent interviews with 29 patients, Hoeyer concludes that consent for the inclusion of a blood sample in the biobank depended minimally on the information provided about it. By far the most important factors were the patients' trust in the clinic staff and their sense that this was a worthwhile project:

---

10 *Ibid.*, at p. 130.

11 O'Neill, O., 'Some limits of informed consent', *Journal of Medical Ethics*, 2003; 29: 6.

12 Hoeyer, K., '"Science is really needed – that's all I know": informed consent and the non-verbal practices of collecting blood for genetic research in Northern Sweden', *New Genetics and Society*, 22; 3: 239.

> Trust in the nurse and faith in biomedical research are part of the moral domain of the clinic, and it might be that this confidence excludes questioning. Even when a nurse insists on telling the patient about the biobank, she is often interrupted by the patient eager to get on with the examination saying, 'Yeah, yeah, it's fine, just great. We really need research!'.[13]

Such a cavalier attitude to informed consent may be shocking to ethical purists, but it does suggest that the way people make decisions in these circumstances relates much more to their overall values and their trust in those seeking consent, than to any philosophical account of adequate information as the basis of valid consent. People can chose to trust, and, provided the structures are in place to ensure that that trust is not betrayed, it is not clear why they should not make that choice. This is especially true when there is no clear evidence of risk of harm to them, should they consent. However, this means that the ethical concern should shift from the question of information to that of the context for obtaining consent and the motivations of those who enrol in the project.

What's in It for Me?

The Swedish Biobank, referred to above, gained its participants from a clinic setting, in which there were obvious advantages to the people attending, because they were getting a full health check. Hooking the collection of research samples onto existing healthcare activities is a quite common way of building up resources of this kind. Clearly, as we have already seen, people are likely to consent to the additional sample because of their trust in and gratitude towards the clinic and clinic staff. However, creating a major resource like UK Biobank is an entirely different proposition. This project requires a comprehensive range of information from a stratified sample of the population within a given age range. Thus it depends on the recruitment of volunteers through letters of invitation to attend assessment centres, where the tests and measurements are carried out, samples obtained and questionnaires on health and lifestyle are completed. In addition the volunteers are asked to consent to full access to their health records, past and future, with the guarantee that their anonymity will be fully protected.

Why would anyone consent to this major personal involvement with the project? One possible motivation might be to obtain a free health check, but this is clearly ruled out by the Ethics and Governance Framework (EGF), which defines all of the ethical requirements of the Biobank.[14] As the EGF points out, the purpose of collecting the data is to set up a resource for future studies of health and illness. It would be misleading to suggest that an assessment centre, whose purpose is solely to create a research resource, can provide the individual with a full and accurate interpretation of their health status. There may be an *indirect* benefit to participants, since they will be provided with the basic findings (such as blood pressure, body

13 *Ibid.*, at p. 239.

14 Available at: http://www.ukbiobank.ac.uk/ethics/efg.php.

mass index and other basic measurements) and these will (with their permission) also be sent to their General Practitioner. But later in the life of the resource, no feedback at all will be provided, since the findings will all be in an aggregate form, with no release of individual data.[15] Thus the creation of a biobank must not be confused with a healthcare service, such as a health check, being offered to the individual participants.

Why, then, would anyone – clearly informed of this lack of personal relevance – enrol in a biobank? The answer has to lie in some understanding of a communal commitment, similar to that which supports the British NHS and universal healthcare schemes in other European countries. Here again the research conducted by Hoeyer is illuminating. His respondents, coming from a country which has a strong history of universal healthcare, saw a connection between medical research and their own commitment to helping others:

> *Informant*: Why you can contribute to this sort of thing, you know, it's because you can feel that you can assist with something. If it's good for humanity, it's good for me too. Those are the sorts of things I think about when contributing to research.[16]

The motivation may thus be an altruistic one for participants in biobanks – or some combination of self-interest and altruism, as suggested in the above quotation. If persuaded by the worth of the project, its capacity to make a real difference to health prospects in the future, people may willingly surrender their time and risk some loss of privacy, in order to be part of the endeavour. However, this places a major onus on those who oversee biobanks of this type to ensure that that altruistic commitment is respected and honoured in the way the bank operates. (This point will be returned to later.)

Is there Risk of Harm?

Nomper has identified three possible types of harm to participants in biobanks – physical, psychological and informational.[17] The only physical risk relates to taking a blood sample, and consent procedures for this are well established. Psychological risks may be of two kinds: unwanted information (for example, findings that affect family members who have not themselves participated in the biobank) and research uses, which offend the moral views of some participants (examples could be research related to abortion or research involving animal experimentation). These psychological risks can, to some extent, be dealt with by flagging them up in

15 There will be a provision for communication of initial seriously abnormal findings, for example, indicators of diabetes or of advanced cancer, but this will be only exceptional, and recruitment materials will not mention it, since it could give the false impression that no communication from Biobank meant a 'clean bill of health'. There is, in any case, no guarantee that the relevant tests would be carried out on the samples.

16 O'Neill, *loc cit.*, at p. 235.

17 Nomper, *loc cit.*, pp. 39ff.

information about possible uses of the resource or possible findings from subsequent research, allowing potential participants to decide that they prefer not to incur such risks and refusing to enrol. An alternative might be the option of selective opting out recommended by Kaye (see above).

Nomper sees the third type of risk – informational – to be the most significant. This risk relates to uses of the information derived from the resource and from access to the resource, which could be directly or indirectly detrimental to the participant. In a recent article Hansson has explored this third risk in some detail.[18] He describes it as the risk of 'violation of personal integrity', which can occur simply through a failure to safeguard the identity of individual participants, or more subtly through adverse effects of subsequent research on the group of which they are a member. The former risk is minimised by a rigorous system of data protection, including highly restricted access to the key to the codes employed to protect data. (However, as I discuss shortly, biobanks may be forced to break the code.) The more subtle risk is one where the subsequent research may suggest a link between an ethnic or other identifiable social group and a specific disease. If this disease is itself stigmatising – for example, a sexually transmitted infection or a psychiatric illness – then harm may be done to individuals in that group, possibly including discrimination against them in work or home situations.

It is very hard to estimate the probability of complex risks of this sort, especially when the range of uses of the resource cannot be predicted at the outset. Moreover, such risks are not specific to biobanks – they remain possibilities in all of those types of health research which seek correlations between health prospects and social or ethnic groups. The remedy for such dangers seems to lie not in the enrolment process, since it would be most unfortunate if fears of this unquantifiable risk led to inadequate representation of some ethnic groups. Rather, the solution lies, as Hansson argues, in social and political measures to prevent discriminatory practices. In addition, it should be the responsibility of the guardians of the resource to ensure that all research based on it is well designed and responsible and that results are not falsely presented or sensationalised.

There is a widespread view that the risks to participants in biobanks are minimal, and that measures exist to control virtually all of them. Certainly, many of them must be regarded as speculative at this stage. Moreover, as Hansson points out, too restrictive an approach to biobank uses can act *against* participants' interests, since they are also potential beneficiaries of the outcomes of the research.[19] However, there remains one example of access to the resource by third parties which could clearly be damaging to some individual participants. This is court authorised access for criminal or forensic purposes by the police. There have already been examples of this. For example, in the UK Scottish police seized materials from a study of

18 Hansson, M.G., 'Building on relationships of trust in biobank research', *Journal of Medical Ethics*, 2005; 31: 415-418.

19 *Ibid.*, at p. 416. See also Hansson, *loc cit.*, in which the dual role of 'donor' and 'beneficiary' is pointed out.

HIV, leading to the conviction of an individual for culpable and reckless conduct and a five-year prison term.[20] In Sweden, a research biobank was used by the police to identify the killer of the foreign minister, Anna Lindh.[21] Some countries may legislate against the forensic use of health databases, but, in the UK at least, this seems unlikely. Surveys of opinion on this have consistently shown a large majority in favour of such access.[22] The stated policy of UK Biobank is to contest any such requests, but there is, of course, no guarantee that the courts will refuse a request. This, then, is the clearest risk to participants, and one which must be clearly stated in any information material at enrolment. However, this risk must be put in the context of a secure guardianship of the resource against any other access by third parties, other than for genuine research purposes and in a manner in which the anonymity of the participant is fully protected.

A Community Resource?

The last ethical question relates to the custodianship and use of such biobank resources. Much of the controversy surrounding the Icelandic project arose from the decision of the government to put the creation of the Health Sector Database out to tender. The result was that a genetic research company, deCode Genetics Inc, was given an exclusive licence to operate the database for 12 years.[23] A similar situation occurred in Estonia. Originally the project was to be a mixture of public and private finance, setting up a non-profit foundation under state control. However, the foundation then granted exclusive rights to a private company, Egeen, to commercialise information contained in the database in return for substantial private financing. Subsequently this agreement was terminated, and the project now relies on grants and research funds if it is to continue. Public trust in the project has declined considerably as a result of these changes.[24] The UK Biobank, on the other hand, was set up with a mixture of government research funding (the Medical Research Council, the Department of Health and the Scottish Executive) and health charity funding (the Wellcome Trust). The legal custodian of the bank is UK Biobank Ltd., a charitable company limited by guarantee. Biobank will charge fees for access to the resource, but no exclusive rights will be granted to any users.

These differences between the biobanks are significant since, despite public controls in Iceland and Estonia, only the UK has made an unambiguous division between the biobank project and private enterprises in biotechnology. However, this is only a first step in the process of ensuring public benefit. Critical questions will arise when decisions of access to the resource are made, since it is possible that the

---

20 Williams G. and Schroeder, D., 'Human biobanking: altruism, benefit and consent', *New Genetics and Society*, 2004, 23; 1, p. 94.

21 Hansson, *loc cit.*, at p. 322.

22 See Nomper, *loc cit.*, at p. 45.

23 Arnason, *loc cit.*, at p. 28.

24 Nomper, *loc cit.*, pp. 34ff.

main users of the resource could be private companies with a very narrow research agenda. Since biobanks have to charge access fees to meet the ongoing costs of such a major enterprise, it is possible that the big financial players could dominate the scene. Williams and Schroeder make this point strongly:

> ... attention must be devoted to the specific duties of custodians and public sponsors, and to the specific institutional arrangements that will ensure those duties are fulfilled. Only those measures can ensure that samples are used for public good and for publicly endorsed ends. Given the predominance of commercial interests, and the often haphazard nature of coordination of researchers' efforts, the grave danger exists that sample collections will be selectively exploited – worse still, exploited on terms set by commercial partners.[25]

There is also the question of the role of donors to the bank in influencing decisions about use. Kaye argues for a specific role for participants in decisions about the uses to which their samples and data are put, suggesting that representatives of the participant group should be both on the management committee of the resource and on bodies deciding research priorities.[26] Another perspective is offered by Chadwick and Berg.[27] Arguing on the basis of our duties to benefit others, they believe that refusal to take part in studies unless they are of direct benefit to oneself could be overridden (morally at least) by the principles of solidarity and equity. Thus they would argue that humanitarian imperatives for equitable benefit of society should be the guiding principles in the use of genetic and other data. This view gives no special role to participants in deciding research priorities.

Whatever the final mechanisms for deciding priority uses of the resource, and whatever principles are regarded as overriding in making such decisions, one thing is clear: any biobank which enrols people on the basis of enhancing the public good in the health sphere has to have open, independent and accountable mechanisms to ensure that the promise to participants is honoured. It was noted earlier that the primary motivation for enrolment in a project that offers no personal financial or health benefit, must be commitment to the health of future generations. Thus participants see the biobank as a community resource (perhaps on the analogy of a blood bank). To fail to use the resource for community benefit would be a betrayal of that trust.

Safeguarding Altruism and Trust

In this final section, I will briefly consider the broader issues of altruism and trust, which were raised by the specific ethical dilemmas in biobanking. We must begin by stressing the degree of commitment of those who respond positively to a request to enrol in a project of this nature. Not only do they agree to a set of physical

25 Williams and Schroder, *loc cit.*, at p. 100.

26 Kaye, *loc cit.*, at p. 133.

27 Chadwick, R. and Berg, K., 'Solidarity and equity: new ethical frameworks for genetic databases', *Nature Reviews Genetics*, 2001; 2: 318-321.

measurements, to the donation of samples (e.g. of blood and urine) and to answering what could be seen as an intrusive questionnaire about their health and lifestyle, they also grant full access to their health records, past and future, up to and beyond their death, unless they withdraw from the project.[28] Such a major and long-term commitment must depend both on a strong motivation to assist in the project and a high level of trust in the organisation carrying it out. How then can we ensure that such altruism and trust are safeguarded? I will suggest the following measures: genuine participation and partnership; independent scrutiny; public openness and accountability.

Participation and Partnership

The research community is slowly beginning to change the language of involvement in research by patients and the general public. Research 'subjects' have become research 'participants', and some genuine attempts have been made to involve consumer groups in determining relevant research projects. For biobanks, especially those dependent on volunteers from the community at large, such a change, not only of language but also of attitude, is vital. Individuals may choose to make their only involvement with a biobank the initial visit, when samples and data are obtained and access is granted to health records. But the project will have truly succeeded when a majority of those enrolled become active and interested participants in the evolving resource, especially when it begins to attract research proposals. This may be relatively easy for smaller, more focussed projects: for example, the Avon Longitudinal Study of Parents and Children (ALSPAC) has maintained a very high enthusiasm through its 'Children of the Nineties' activities and information. However, for a national database involving many thousands of people, this is a major challenge.

It is important to note the ethical dimension of such endeavours. It is not part of the protection of individual rights, but rather the support and re-enforcement of the altruism, which motivated the participants in the first place. Thus Kaye's proposals, described above, for giving an opt-out option for each project and for including participant representatives in the project management, do not meet this ethical concern. Indeed they could be seen as undercutting it, by suggesting that individual donors have ongoing rights to exercise control over uses of the resource. Normally, donation carries with it a willing surrender of individual control of the donation: for example, donors of blood or kidneys have no right to determine the recipients of their donation. The requirement, then, is not to try to create some form of participant control, since this would in any case be contrary to the stated aim of the project which is to enhance the health of all, not just of the participants. However, the participants' awareness of how the project is developing and their input into how it might meet

---

28 I am describing the main features of the UK Biobank protocol. Not all biobanks seek such a comprehensive range of information.

its aims would be invaluable. Partnership of this kind will require sophisticated and effective ongoing communication with participants at very regular intervals.

Independent Oversight

I described earlier the potential risks of involvement in biobanks, the greatest of which was informational. Minimising such risks is one way of safeguarding the trust reposed in the bank by the participants. In addition, the open consent entailed in enrolment requires a guardian of the donated samples and data, to ensure that the stated purposes of the bank are in fact being consistently followed throughout the life of the project, which could potentially last for three decades or more. The prime responsibility for safeguarding the trust, data and samples invested in the bank must be the governing body of the bank itself. They have entered into an agreement in relation to data security, proper stewardship of the resource and granting of access in accordance only with the purposes of the collection. Thus they are bound both morally and legally to proper governance and appropriate use of the resource. However, additional independent oversight seems a necessary part of this safeguarding of trust. This can ensure both that participants know from an independent source how the bank is operating, and that the bank itself can resist any external pressures (for example, commercial) to dilute the requirements for ethical governance.

Most biobanks have some kind of ethics oversight body, though this may not necessarily be one which deals only with that project. The UK Biobank appears to have the most extensive arrangements of this kind. Its own protocol, and all research proposals which it considers, have to be approved by a NHS Research Ethics Committee, but in addition it is bound to act in accordance with a detailed Ethics and Governance Framework, and it is monitored by an independent Ethics and Governance Council (EGC), appointed by the funders of the project.[29] An important aspect of the monitoring by the EGC is that it has full access to all activities of the Biobank and it reports its findings regularly to the public. Since public confidence and trust are essential to the success of any biobanking project, this public reporting constitutes a powerful sanction. The tasks of the EGC include issuing guidance on the details of materials produced for the enrolment process, assessing criteria for feedback of results, and considering proposals for ongoing contact with participants, including exploring the desirability and feasibility of providing an opt out for individuals from specific research proposals. In addition, however, the monitoring body has to be fully involved in decisions about access to the resource, since these entail ethical as well as scientific questions. Biobanks which enlist people on the promise of a resource to improve the health of future generations cannot escape from the difficult task of deciding where the priorities should lie in health research in order to give preference to those most likely to bring genuine improvements in public health. Thus the independent monitoring body has a major role to play in

29 For details of the Council see: http://www.egcukbiobank.org.uk/. I am currently Chairman of the Council.

helping to establish criteria for prioritising access (especially to the depletable parts of the resource) and in ensuring their implementation.

Openness and Accountability

As noted above, regular reports by an independent oversight body can help provide accountability of biobanks to the public whose data and samples they hold. But Biobanks are such massive enterprises that questions of accountability go beyond the issues which an oversight body may debate. This is partly because of the scope of potential health applications of the data as genetic factors become ever more fully understood and as the interplay of genetic with lifestyle and environmental factors becomes mapped in ever more fine detail. In addition, the revolution in electronic data handling holds huge potential for both benign and less than benign applications. The existence and potential of a large-scale biobank cannot be treated in isolation from broader questions of the delicate balance between personal privacy and public good. In Europe, while biobanks are being developed relatively slowly, there are rapid expansions in forensic DNA databases, with quite different criteria for control and use. For these reasons, large-scale population genetic databases must not be allowed to develop without full public debate and accountability to the public at large and specifically to parliament. There is no question that the motivations of all parties, from the funders, through the scientists involved, to those who volunteer their data, are entirely beneficent. But constant public accountability and full public scrutiny will be essential in case such altruism becomes translated into social solidarity, and solidarity in turn becomes the imposition of measures for the 'public good', including national security. These may prove to be unjustified concerns, but it will be worth being sure that the safeguards are in place to prevent a future generation turning these rich databases into instruments for social control or private profit. For, as T.S. Eliot put it:

> The last temptation is the greatest treason:
> To do the right deed for the wrong reason.[30]

Acknowledgement

I wish to thank Adrienne Hunt, Secretary of the Ethics and Governance Council of UK Biobank, for invaluable research assistance in preparation of this chapter.

30 Eliot, T.S., *Murder in the Cathedral*, Act I.

Chapter 14

Law Reform, Clinical Research and Adults without Mental Capacity – Much Needed Clarification or a Recipe for Further Uncertainty?

Jean McHale

Introduction

Since the decision of the House of Lords in *Re F* in 1990 the legality of the inclusion of adults lacking mental capacity in clinical research in England and Wales has been riven with uncertainty.[1] However, over the last few years this situation has begun to change and recent developments are set to impact considerably in this area; notably the EU Clinical Trials Directive and the consequent Medicines for Human Use (Clinical Trials) Regulations 2004,[2] the Human Tissue Act 2004 and most recently the Mental Capacity Act 2005. While some clarification of the existing legal position is obviously to be welcomed, is it the case that these changes will necessarily be for the better? This chapter seeks to explore the extent to which the recent reform agenda will result in a real improvement in the regulation of clinical research involving adults without mental capacity in England and Wales, and asks whether, on the other hand, it is the case that we are left with a recipe for future uncertainty?

Adults – Clinical Research and Re F

The drive to regulate clinical research practices over the last few decades is of course rooted in Nuremberg. Over the last half century there has been a plethora of international, European and professional practice guidelines concerning research

1 *Re F* [1990] 2 AC 1.

2 Directive 2001/20/EC on the approximation of the laws, regulations and administrative provisions of the Member States relating to the implementation of good clinical practice in the conduct of clinical trials on medicinal products for human use OJ 2001 L 121/34; Medicines for Human Use (Clinical Trials) Regulations 2004 SI 1031.

activity.[3] Notable steps along the way include the Declaration of Helsinki,[4] the Council of Europe Convention on Human Rights and Biomedicine and the additional protocol on medical research.[5] However despite the growth in guidelines regarding research governance and the establishment of research ethics committees to approve such projects in the context of the NHS,[6] the legal regulation of research in England and Wales has been notable for the absence of any comprehensive statutory framework.[7] Instead the legality of research projects has been largely ascertainable by reference to analogous common law principles. This was of particular concern in relation to the inclusion of adults without mental capacity into clinical trials.

For many years the basis on which adults who lacked mental capacity could be given treatment had remained the source of uncertainty. In 1990 the position was clarified by the House of Lords in the case of *Re F*.[8] Here, their Lordships confirmed that there was no residual *parens patriae* jurisdiction which applied in the context of adults who lacked capacity. No-one had the power to act as a proxy decision maker on behalf of an adult without mental capacity; so for example, the practice of getting the signature of relatives to consent to surgical procedures had no legal validity. Nonetheless, that did not mean that it was impossible to treat such patients. Rather it was the case that treatment could be given after an assessment had been made by the health professionals caring for that patient that the treatment was in the patient's best interests – under the doctrine of necessity. Best interests was to be ascertained by reference to the *Bolam*[9] test – i.e. a professionally based assessment of what was in the interests of the patient.

This approach was not uncontroversial. It can be argued that what constitutes the 'best interests' of an individual is not something which could, nor indeed necessarily should, be considered in isolation from other factors than those which were purely

3 See generally Plomer, A., *The Law and Ethics of Medical Research: International Bioethics and Human Rights*, London, Cavendish Publishing, 2005.

4 Adopted by the 18th World Medical Assembly, Helsinki, Finland, 1964.

5 Additional Protocol to the Convention on Human Rights and Biomedicine on Biomedical Research, adopted by the Committee of Ministers 30th June 2004.

6 See further McHale, J.V., 'Clinical Research', in Grubb, A. (ed), *Principles of Medical Law* (2nd ed), Oxford, OUP, 2004, 855-856.

7 On the legal regulation of clinical research in England and Wales see generally Mason, J.K., McCall Smith, R.A. and Laurie, G.T., *Law and Medical Ethics* (6th ed), London, Butterworths, 2002, chapters 19 and 20; Grubb, A., *Kennedy and Grubb Medical Law* (3rd ed), London: Butterworths, 2000, chapter 14; McLean, S., 'Regulating Research and Experimentation: A View from the UK', (2004) 32 *Journal of Law Medicine and Ethics*, 602; Montgomery, J., *Health Care Law* (2nd ed), Oxford, OUP, chapter 14; Fox, M., 'Clinical Research and Patients: the Legal Perspective', in Tingle, J. and Cribb, A. (eds), *Nursing Law and Ethics* (2nd ed), Oxford, Blackwell Scientific, 2002. See further regarding the interface with the ethical debate, Foster, C., *The Ethics of Medical Research on Humans*, Cambridge, CUP, 2001.

8 *Re F* [1990] 2 AC 1.

9 *Bolam v. Friern Hospital Management Committee* [1957] 2 All E.R. 118.

medical, such as the interests of family care-givers.[10] Subsequently judicial responses have shown heightened awareness of the complexity and interface with social care issues. The courts have indicated that they are prepared to scrutinise the evidence advanced by a body of medical practice[11] and go beyond a purely 'medically based' assessment, to encompass a broader-based test taking into account a wider range of factors.[12]

The decision of the House of Lords in *Re F* concerned medical treatment – the sterilisation decision of a woman who lacked mental capacity – but the extent to which adults lacking capacity could be included in clinical research remained uncertain. If the research could be seen as therapeutic then it was arguable that this could be regarded as justifiable because it was in an individual's 'best interests'. It was notable that in *Simms v. Simms and an NHS Trust* in 2002, the Court of Appeal approved administration of experimental therapy upon two patients with Creutzfeldt Jakob Disease (CJD).[13] However questions still remained as to how the interests of research participants who lacked mental capacity could be effectively safeguarded. In particular, problems could be seen to be associated with the use of the professional practice based 'best interests' test, and the fact that the ultimate decision maker would be the healthcare professional who may have some personal interest in the research process.

Following *Re F*, particular difficulties also concerned procedures which were non-therapeutic in nature. As the Law Commission commented in its 1995 'Mental Incapacity' Report:[14]

> Non-therapeutic research, on the other hand, does not claim to offer any direct or immediate benefit to the participant. Such procedures may well be scientifically and ethically acceptable to those who are qualified to decide such matters. If, however, the participant lacks capacity to consent to his or her participation, and the procedure cannot be justified under the doctrine of necessity, then any person who touches or restrains that participant is committing an unlawful battery. The simple fact is that the researcher is making no claim to be acting in the best interests of that individual person and does not therefore come within the rules of law set out in *Re F*. It was made abundantly clear

---

10 See further Grubb, A., 'Treatment decisions: Keeping it in the family', in Grubb, A. (ed), *Choices and Decisions in Health Care*, Chichester, Wiley, 1993.

11 *Bolitho v. City of Hackney HA* [1998] AC 232.

12 See e.g. *Re SL* [2000] 3 WLR 1288.

13 [2003] Fam 83 and see Harrington J., 'Deciding Best Interest: Medical Progress, Clinical Judgment and the "Good Family"', (2003) 3 *Web Journal of Current Legal Issues*.

14 Law Commission, *Mental Incapacity* (Law Com No 231), London, HMSO (1995), para 6.29. For a general overview of the report see Wilson, P., 'The Law Commission's Report on Mental Incapacity: Medically Vulnerable Adults or Politically Vulnerable Law?', [1996] 4 *Med L Rev*, 227. The English Law Commission's report can also be usefully contrasted with the approach in Scotland, see Mason, McCall Smith and Laurie note 7, *supra*, at para 10.37 and the Adults with Incapacity (Scotland) Act 2000.

to us on consultation, however, that non-therapeutic research projects of this nature are regularly taking place.[15]

It thus appears that the consequence of the decision in *Re F* was that non-therapeutic research undertaken involving adults without capacity in England and Wales in the years which followed the House of Lords decision was likely to be unlawful.[16] Despite this, however, it did not stop such research being undertaken, and indeed it appeared that the legality of non-therapeutic research appeared to be misunderstood by some researchers.[17]

The Law Commission Mental Incapacity Report

Given this legal uncertainty for potential research participants, families, carers and researchers alike the inclusion of medical research in the Law Commission's 1995 'Mental Incapacity' Report was to be welcomed. The 1995 Report was a broad document setting out the structure for comprehensive legislation concerning adults lacking mental capacity. Determining whether an adult possessed capacity was, as at common law, to be a decision relative test and if an adult lacked capacity then decisions were to be undertaken on the basis that they were in their best interests.[18] (The test was 'best interests' and the alternative approach of 'substituted judgement' was rejected.)

The Law Commission considered the inclusion of adults without mental capacity in relation to both therapeutic and non-therapeutic research. It suggested that the decision as to whether to include an adult who lacked capacity in therapeutic research was something which could be left to the broad general authority to act reasonably which the Law Commission proposed in their report.[19] The person exercising this authority would be required to act in the best interests of the adult lacking mental capacity. This may seem on its face legitimate given that what is envisaged is research to benefit the research subject. But closer examination illustrates that it may

15 The Law Commission further commented that 'We were told of a research project into the organic manifestations of Alzheimer's disease which involves the administration of radioactive isotopes to sufferers, followed by extensive testing of blood and bodily functions. Another project was said to involve the examination of written patients' records, although they are unable to consent to this examination. In some cases relatives are asked to "consent" to what is proposed, and do so. It appears that some funding bodies and Ethics Committees stipulate for consent by a relative where the research participant cannot consent. As a matter of law, such "consent" is meaningless'.

16 Although contrast the thoughtful examination of an alternative approach in Lewis, P., 'Procedures that are against the medical interests of incompetent adults', (2002) 22 *Oxford Journal of Legal Studies,* 575, at p. 578.

17 *Ibid.*, at para 6.29.

18 *Ibid.* Part II – the common law test of capacity was set out in *Re C* [1994] 1 All ER 839 and refined in subsequent cases notably *Re MB* [1997] 2 FLR 426.

19 *Ibid.*, at para 6.28.

be somewhat more problematic. Deciding what amounts to a 'therapeutic' procedure is very much a task for the person assessing it. Moreover, it cannot be assumed that a proposed new procedure or treatment will necessarily prove to be in an individual's best interests; certain 'extra-ordinary' or 'heroic' procedures may indeed prove ethically highly controversial.

In relation to non-therapeutic research, the Law Commission recognised that adults lacking capacity are a potentially vulnerable group and that the inclusion of such adults in clinical research necessitated the introduction of appropriate safeguards. Its response was to state that:

> We recommend that research which is unlikely to benefit a participant, or whose benefit is likely to be long delayed, should be lawful in relation to a person without capacity to consent if (1) the research is into an incapacitating condition with which the participant is or may be affected and (2) certain statutory procedures are complied with.[20]

A two-stage process of statutory safeguards was proposed. First, the Law Commission recommended the establishment of a new body – a Mental Incapacity Research Committee.[21] It was envisaged that this body would operate alongside and 'supplement' existing NHS research ethics committees. The Law Commission recommended that non-therapeutic research would only be lawful where this had been approved by the Committee.[22] The Committee could approve research where it was satisfied that:

> (1) that it is desirable to provide knowledge of the causes or treatment of, or of the care of people affected by, the incapacitating condition with which any participant is or may be affected,
> (2) that the object of the research cannot be effectively achieved without the participation of persons who are or may be without capacity to consent and
> (3) that the research will not expose a participant to more than negligible risk, will not be unduly invasive or restrictive of a participant and will not unduly interfere with a participant's freedom of action or privacy.[23]

In addition, although the Committee would be concerned with the general approval of such trials the Law Commission recommended that there should be additional safeguards for the individual participant. After the research protocol had been approved, researchers would then need to assess whether an individual had capacity to make a decision him/herself whether to be involved in a clinical trial.[24] Where the adult lacked capacity the Law Commission was of the view that there needed to be an independent 'check' on their involvement in the research:[25]

20 Draft Bill, clause 11(1).
21 Draft Bill, clause 11(2).
22 See note 14, *supra*, at para 6.34.
23 *Ibid.*, clause 11(3).
24 See note 14, *supra*, at para 6.36.
25 *Ibid.*, para 6.37.

> We recommend that, in addition to the approval of the Mental Incapacity Research Committee, non-therapeutic research in relation to a person without capacity should require either:
> (1) court approval,
> (2) the consent of an attorney or manager,
> (3) a certificate from a doctor not involved in the research that the participation of the person is appropriate, or
> (4) the designation of the research not involving direct contact.[26]

The fourth criterion may be seen as somewhat problematic. The Law Commission suggested that this category may involve observation or photography and they suggested that while ethical issues may be involved these could be referred to a standard research ethics committee.[27] It can be argued that, although observational research does not involve direct contact it may cause some harm/distress to the particular participant and thus should be subject to some individual form of approval process.

When assessing whether an adult without mental capacity should be included in research, the Law Commission recommended that this decision should be made in accordance with the factors set out in the 'best interests' checklist which they included in their draft Bill.[28] This was a much broader approach than that initially taken by the House of Lords in *Re F*. Factors to be taken into account included any ascertainable past and present wishes and feelings of the individual and factors which they would consider if able to do so, and the views of other people whom it was appropriate and practicable to consult.[29] The Law Commission also recommended that where an individual refused to participate then they should not be included in the research, nor should they be included if they had made an 'effective advance refusal to participate'.[30] The Law Commission's proposals represented a structured approach to the problem of the legality of including adults without capacity in clinical research. However these recommendations were not taken forward by the Government. In its consultation document *Who Decides?* in 1997, although announcing the intention to enact some of the recommendations of the Law Commission, the Government was not convinced that there was a need for an additional mental incapacity research committee.[31] The Law Commission's proposals were not taken forward in *Making Decisions* in 1999.[32] Somewhat, surprisingly when the Draft Mental Incapacity Bill was published in 2003 there was no separate reference to research whatsoever.

---

26 Draft Bill, clause 11(1)(c) and (4).
27 See note 14, *supra* at para 6.36.
28 *Ibid.*, at para 6.38
29 *Ibid.*, at para 6.28.
30 *Ibid.*, at para 6.39.
31 Lord Chancellor's Department, *Who Decides*, London, LCD, 1997, para 5.41.
32 Lord Chancellor's Department, *Making Decisions*, London, LCD, 1999.

The Recent Reforms and Reform Proposals

The Clinical Trials Directive

The change to the regulation of clinical research concerning adults lacking capacity did not initially flow from the recommendations proposed by the Law Commission; instead the catalyst was the European Union in the form of the Clinical Trials Directive.[33] This Directive regulates the conduct of clinical trials on medicinal products, i.e., drug trials.[34] It requires that such trials be formally approved by research ethics committees, thus providing for the first time in English law a legal requirement for such research to be approved by research ethics committee.[35] In addition, the Directive and consequent regulations set out time limits for the consideration of applications[36] and also criteria for research ethics committees to consider when reviewing trial protocols.[37] The research ethics committee is required to weigh up any foreseeable risks and inconveniences against any anticipated benefit. Fundamentally trials must be conducted in accordance with 'good clinical practice'.[38] The Directive was implemented into English law by the Medicines for Human Use (Clinical Trials) Regulations 2004.[39] The implementation of this Directive has not been uncontroversial – in many respects the scientific community appeared caught off-guard and the Directive itself has been viewed as highly problematic.[40]

33 Directive 2001/20/EC on the approximation of the laws, regulations and administrative provisions of the Member States relating to the implementation of good clinical practice in the conduct of clinical trials on medicinal products for human use OJ 2001 L 121/34. See further, Hervey, T.K. and McHale, J.V., *Health Law and the European Union*, Cambridge, CUP, 2004, chapter 7, Baeyens, J., 'Implementation of the Clinical Trials Directive: Pitfalls and Benefits', (2002) 9 *European Journal of Health Law*, 31.

34 As defined in Directive 65/65/EEC OJ 1965 L 369/65. Medicinal products are 'any substance or combination of substances presented for preventing disease in human beings or animals' and 'any substance ... which may be administered to human beings or animals with a view to making a medical diagnosis or to restoring, correcting or modifying physiological functions in human beings or in animals'.

35 Directive 2001/20/EC Article 6 and Article 9(1).

36 Directive 2001/20/EC, Article 9(4).

37 Directive 2001/20/EC, Article 6.

38 Directive 2001/20/EC, Article 1(2), defined as a 'set of internationally recognised ethical and scientific quality requirements which must be observed for designing, conducting, recording and reporting clinical trials that involve the participation of human subjects. Compliance with this good practice provides assurance that the rights, safety and well-being of trial subjects are protected and that the results of the clinical trial are credible'.

39 2004 SI 1031.

40 Watson , R., 'EU legislation threatens clinical trials', (2003) 326 *BMJ*, 1348; Watson, R., 'Research Bodies lobby EU governments over trials legislation', (2003) *BMJ*, 1136. Watson, R., 'Scientists beg EU to repeal new rules for clinical trials', (2004) 328 *BMJ*, 187.

Approval of Trials Concerning Adults Lacking Mental Capacity

Specific reference is made in the Directive to adults who lack mental capacity.[41] Article 5 of the Directive requires that the design of the trial shall minimise pain, discomfort, fear and any other foreseeable risk relating to the disease or developmental stage.[42] Article 5(e) provides that, trials can only be undertaken where:

> the research is essential to validate data obtained in a clinical trial on persons able to give informed consent or by other research methods and relates directly to a life-threatening or debilitating clinical condition from which the incapacitated adult concerned suffers.

Furthermore the Directive – and consequent regulations – goes on to provide that the research shall be approved only where:

> (i) there are grounds for expecting that administering the medicinal product to be tested will produce a benefit to the patient outweighing the risks or produce no risk at all.[43]

In addition the Directive also requiring that there should be reference to an ethics committee specialised in such issues or that appropriate advice on 'clinical, ethical and psychosocial' questions in relation to the disease or the particular patient population[44] should be obtained. The Directive provides that ultimately 'the interests of the patient always prevail over those of science and society'.[45]

Consent and the Legal Representative

First, it is notable that consent to the inclusion of the adult without capacity in the trial may be given by a third party. This is sanctioned under Article 3(2) of the Directive which provides that consent may be given in the case of a person who lacks capacity by their 'legal representative'. Who exactly the 'legal representative' should be is something on which the Directive is silent and is left to individual member states to determine.[46] The Medicines for Human Use (Clinical Trials) Regulations which implements the Directive into English law now provide for consent to be given by a legal representative.[47] This is either to be:

> (i) a person, other than a person involved in the conduct of the trial, who:

---

41 Directive 2001/20/EC, Article 5.

42 Directive 2001/20/EC, Article 5(f) and see note 41, *supra*, schedule 1 part 5 paras 10 and 11.

43 Directive 2001/20/EC, Article 5(i) and see note 41, *supra*, schedule 1 part 5 para 9.

44 Directive 2001/20/EC, Article 5(g).

45 Directive 2001/20/EC, Article 5(h) and see note 41, *supra*, schedule 1 part 5 para 15.

46 Directive 2001/20/EC, Recital 5.

47 Medicines for Human Use (Clinical Trials) Regulations (2004) schedule 1 part 1 paras 2(a)(b).

(aa) by virtue of their relationship with that adult or that minor, is suitable to act as their legal representative for the purposes of that trial and
(bb) is available to act and willing to so act for those purposes, or
(ii) if there is no such person, a person, other than a person connected with the conduct of the clinical trial, who is:
(aa) the doctor primarily responsible for the medical treatment provided to that adult, or
(bb) a person nominated by the relevant health care provider ...

Thus for the first time in English law there was specific provision for a proxy decision maker regarding a health-related issue.[48] This is a notable difference from *Re F*, and presented the prospect of an anomaly facing research ethics committees. While under the Directive consent would be required from a legal representative, in contrast at common law the individual lacking mental capacity could potentially be included in a research project where it was deemed to be in their best interests under the doctrine of necessity but with no requirement to consult or to appoint a specific third party decision maker. The potential confusion for researchers, research participants and research ethics committees alike was clear. Moreover there is another fundamental issue – the extent to which reference of this decision to a third party to give consent is at all appropriate. Whilst some individuals would be perfectly happy for their spouse or daughter to give consent on their behalf should they suffer from a degenerative mental disorder others might take a very different view and this goes against the approach taken in English law since *Re F*.

Further uncertainties surround the ascertainment of the person who can act as legal representative. While the regulations provide for permission to be sought from the professional decision makers where a person is not able to act 'by virtue of their relationship',[49] it appears that there still may be uncertainty surrounding the extent to which such decision makers may consent for more than one person. Earlier draft guidance envisaged the prospect of 'block-booking' of consent.[50] So, for example, in the case of nursing home residents the suggestion that a 'professional' legal representative could give consent in relation to the inclusion of several patients in relation to the same trial gives rise to considerable concern.[51]

The Directive states that that the consent given by the legal representative must 'represent the subject's presumed will'.[52] The consent can be revoked at any time and this must be without any consequent detriment to the subject. Even although

48 Although this was swiftly followed by provision for appointment for a 'nominated representative' under the Human Tissue Act 2004 and provision for lasting powers of attorney under s 9 of the Mental Capacity Act 2005.

49 See note 46, *supra*, schedule 1 Part 5.

50 See discussion in McHale, note 5, *supra*, at p. 885 and *Draft Guidance on Consent by a Legal Representative on Behalf of a Person Not Able to Consent under the Medicines for Human Use Clinical Trials) Regulations*, London, DOH, March 2003.

51 See further, McHale, note 5, *supra*.

52 Directive 2001/20/EC Article 5(a), and see note 47, *supra*, schedule 1 part 5, para 12.

the adult may not have capacity to give consent, the Directive still provides for the individual to receive information according to their 'capacity for understanding regarding the trial, risks and the benefits'.[53] Where an adult – who is capable of forming an opinion – assesses the information and then wishes to refuse to be involved, then the investigator should take this into account, although interestingly objection does not necessarily preclude involvement.

The impact of the Directive and the consequent enacting regulations is that the approval processes for trials involving adults lacking capacity concerning medicinal products are formalised. The role of research ethics committees is incorporated in law, as is the role of the proxy decision maker. This structures the decision making process and requires that the researcher must formally justify the inclusion of adults lacking mental capacity in trials involving medicinal products. Research ethics committees who consider such trials are now required to have members with requisite expertise in relation to health and social care issues concerning adults lacking mental capacity. However, the enactment of the Directive gave rise to an anomaly – namely, while the role of research ethics committees is clarified in relation to one specific area of research activity, the uncertain common law position regarding research concerning adults without mental capacity remained. Moreover there is the possibility of family members or carers being bypassed by the decision being given to another person to act as 'legal representative'.

Research and Emergency Medicine

In addition, subsequent to the enactment of the Regulations some problems were identified regarding the conduct of research in emergency medicine. A major international cardiac trial studying cardiac arrest, the TROCIA trial, illustrated that it is impossible to guarantee that consent from a legal representative be obtained in such emergency situations and as a consequence, the Government indicated that a consultation exercise would be undertaken regarding amendment to the regulations.[54] This is currently being undertaken by the Medicines and Healthcare products Regulatory Agency.[55] The recent consultation document states that the current requirement to consult the legal representative may result in making certain forms of research in emergency medicine impossible or extremely difficult to undertake. The document rejects the suggestion of obtaining consent from paramedics as this was unlikely to be compliant with the Directive as paramedics may not be regarded as having sufficient independence from the decision being made.[56] It is thus proposed

53 Directive 2001/20/EC Article 5(b), and see note 47, *supra*, schedule 1 part 5, para 13.

54 Secretary of State for Health: *Written Ministerial Statement on Medicines for Human Use (Clinical Trials) Regulations 2004*, 18th January 2005.

55 Medicines and Healthcare Products Regulatory Agency, *Consultation on Amendment to the Medicines for Human Use (Clinical Trials) Regulations 2004*, SI 2004/1031, MLX 326, 1 August 2005.

56 *Ibid.*, para 7.

that in such situations it should be possible to undertake research where consent had not been given by a legal representative in a situation in which the research protocol had received independent ethics committee approval and that in addition retrospective consent should be obtained as soon as possible and no later than 24 hours after participation has begun.[57] Although this proposal goes beyond what is explicitly sanctioned under the Directive the consultation document states that it would be 'within the spirit of the Directive'.[58] However this interpretation may yet prove controversial and, if adopted, may result in legal challenge in the future.

The Mental Capacity Act 2005

The second reform measure which relates to clinical research is the Mental Capacity Act 2005. As noted above, despite the Law Commission's recommendations, the original draft Mental Incapacity Bill published in 2003 did not include specific reference to clinical research. However, the Joint Select Committee scrutinising the Bill considered this issue.[59] Evidence to the Committee supported the enactment of specific statutory provisions governing the research process. The Royal College of Psychiatrists, for example, noted that if the current situation was retained the development of trials and treatments for persons with Alzheimer's Disease would be problematic.[60] They were concerned that, in the absence of statutory regulation, the opportunity for abuse with research being undertaken where it was not in the patient's best interests was much greater, and stated that:

> the inclusion of statutory provisions governing such research would enable the ethical requirements that must underpin research involving people with incapacity to be clearly enshrined in statute.[61]

The Joint Select Committee recommended that the Bill should set out key provisions as in the Declaration of Helsinki. These included recommendations that there should be a review of such research by an independent ethics committee, that where the adult has capacity to consent his/her decision should be respected and that care should be taken to ensure consent was freely given. In addition, they recommended that the inclusion of adults without capacity should only take place where it was not possible to undertake research on adults who did possess mental capacity and where the research has the prospect of direct benefit to the adult lacking capacity.

---

57 *Ibid.*, para 10 and 12.

58 *Ibid.*, para 9. It is also suggested in the consultation document that it would be in accordance with the guidelines operated by the International Conference on Harmonisation, *Note for Guidance on Good Clinical Practice*, CPMP/ICH/135/95.

59 Joint Select Committee on the Draft Mental Capacity Bill First report, Session 2002-03 HL Paper 189-I HC 1083-I, see chapter 15.

60 *Ibid.*, at para 279.

61 *Ibid.*, at para 284.

Furthermore any discomfort or risk should be minimal.[62] The Joint Committee also proposed that the Code of Practice should set out specific issues which research ethics committees should be obliged to consider in relation to any research which involved persons who lack mental capacity.[63] In their response to the Bill, the Government recognised the need to safeguard the interests of vulnerable adults in the research context, but at the same time noted that without such research treatment/prevention of certain illnesses in relation to this group might be inhibited. They stated that their key concern was 'whether satisfactory safeguards could be introduced to achieve the benefits, whilst limiting the risks'.[64]

When the revised Mental Capacity Bill was introduced into the Commons, new provisions had been included governing research and these now form part of the legislation. Section 30(1) of the 2005 Act now makes it unlawful to undertake 'intrusive' research on a person who lacks capacity unless it is part of a research project approved by an 'appropriate body' in accordance with section 31 and with safeguards set out in sections 32 and 33. Section 30 provides that:

> (2) Research is intrusive if it is of a kind that would be unlawful if it was carried out –
> (a) on or in relation to a person who had capacity to consent to it, but
> (b) without his consent.

The legislation provides that an 'appropriate body' will be a person/committee/other body specified in regulations.[65] The Explanatory Notes to the Act state that this is likely to be a research ethics committee. However, this left uncertain as to what form the research ethics committee would take. Would this be a specialist form of research ethics committee as per the Law Commission proposals or would it instead be a task entrusted to local research ethics committees? Despite the lack of clarity in the Explanatory Notes, some light is shed on this in the Draft Mental Capacity Act Code of Practice which assumes that this does refer to a local research ethics committee.[66]

It should be noted that the Act expressly excludes those trials which are regulated under the Clinical Trials Regulations.[67] In addition, the Act does not extend to include human material or information. This is because according to the Explanatory Notes these are/will be regulated under the Human Tissue Act 2004 and data protection legislation.[68] The Act will also operate alongside existing research governance

62 *Ibid.*, at para 289.

63 *Ibid.*, at para 291.

64 Department for Constitutional Affairs, *The Government's Response to the Scrutiny Committee's Report on the Draft Mental Incapacity Bill*, February 2004, para 16.

65 S 30(4).

66 Mental Capacity Bill: Draft Code of Practice, September 2004.

67 S 30(3).

68 The Explanatory Notes make reference to the 'Data Protection Act 1984' an obvious typographical error given that this legislation was supplanted by the Data Protection Act 1998.

frameworks.[69] Thus Draft Mental Capacity Act code of practice states that principal investigators are required to comply with the existing provisions of the research governance guidelines.[70]

Requirements for Approval of Research Under the 1995 Act

Section 31 of the 1995 Act sets out the basis on which the 'appropriate body' will approve a 'research project'. It relates to both therapeutic and non-therapeutic research:

> (2) The research must be connected with –
> (a) an impairing condition affecting P, or
> (b) its treatment

The section defines an 'impairing condition' as one:

> which is (or may be) is attributable to, or which causes or contributes to (or which may cause or contribute to), the impairment of, or disturbance in the functioning of, the mind or brain.[71]

The principle of ensuring that wherever possible research is undertake on adults with mental capacity is enshrined in section 31(4) which provides that:

> (4) There must be reasonable grounds for believing that the research of comparable effectiveness cannot be carried out if the project has been confined to, or relate only to, persons who have capacity to consent to taking part in it.

In addition subsection 5 goes on to provide that:

> (5) The research must –
> (a) have the potential to benefit P without imposing on P a burden that is disproportionate to the potential benefit to P, or
> (b) be intended to provide knowledge of the causes or treatment of, or of the care of persons affected by, the same or a similar condition.

In relation to non-therapeutic research, subsection 31(6) goes on to provide that

> (6) If the research falls within paragraph (b) of subsection (5) but not within paragraph (a), there must be reasonable grounds for believing –
> (a) that the risk to P from taking part in the project is likely to be negligible, and
> (b) that anything done to, or in relation to, P will not –
> (i) interfere with P's freedom of action or privacy in a significant way, or

---

69 See further, Department of Health, *Research Governance Framework for Health and Social Care* (2nd ed), London, DOH (2005).

70 Draft Mental Capacity Act Code of Practice, London, DeCaf (2004), para 12.14.

71 S 32(3).

(ii) be unduly invasive or restrictive.

This resolves the uncertainty for those wanting to undertake non-therapeutic research on adults lacking mental capacity following *Re F* in 1990. Much will depend upon how the issue of 'negligible risk' is interpreted. A further point is that, given the definition of 'intrusive' research, observational research may still be unregulated as a result of the Act.

The Role of the Carer

While the provisions of the Clinical Trials Directive require that consent is to be given by the 'legal representative', in contrast the Mental Capacity Act 2005 requires that third parties – namely carers – may be *consulted.* However in contrast to the position under the Directive and implementing regulations, the ultimate decision will not lie with them but rather with the healthcare professional – they are consultees rather than decision makers.

Section 32 makes it a requirement that, if a researcher is undertaking an approved research project, s/he must take reasonable steps to identify someone who is engaged in caring for the person without mental capacity or is interested in their welfare, other than in their 'professional capacity or for remuneration', and who is prepared to be consulted under this section.[72] It should be noted that the legislation also explicitly states that the fact that someone is a donee of a lasting power of attorney under the Act[73] does not preclude them from being the person consulted under this section.[74] This provides a further check or balance. Section 32(3), goes on to provide that, if the researcher is unable to identify such a person, then, in accordance with guidance issued by the appropriate authority must nominate someone who is prepared to be consulted but does not have a connection with the research project.

Section 32 requires the researcher to provide the person being consulted with information regarding the project and ask their advice regarding the inclusion of the adult without capacity in the research process as well as their opinion as to what the adult's views would have been regarding inclusion in the project if s/he had had capacity to make the decision her/himself.[75]

The Act envisages that the role of the carer in the research process will not only operate at the point at which the initial decision is made whether to include a person in the trial, but will be ongoing. So for example states that the researcher must withdraw the adult lacking capacity from the research project, if in the opinion of the person being consulted the adult's wishes/feelings would be likely to lead him/her to decline to take part in the project or to withdraw from it.[76] However it should be noted that the researcher may decline to follow this advice where this

72 S 32(2).

73 This is a new power introduced by the Mental Capacity Act 2005.

74 S 32(7).

75 S 32(4).

76 S 32(5).

relates to treatment which is being given as part of the project and the researcher has reasonable grounds for believing that to discontinue it would amount to a significant risk to their health.[77]

The 'Emergency' Situation

The requirement to consult carers is not absolute and it may be overridden. Section 32 subsections (8) and (9) make special provision for emergency situations. They provide that where treatment is to be provided or is being provided as a matter of urgency and the researcher is of the view in relation to the nature of the research and the circumstances of this case it is necessary to go ahead with the research as a matter of urgency, and it is not reasonable to consult, then the researcher may include the adult without capacity in the research. The section provides that the researcher must obtain the agreement of a registered medical practitioner not involved in the organisation or conduct of the research or alternatively may proceed as long as he acts in 'accordance with a procedure approved by the appropriate body at the time when the research project was approved under section 31'.[78] It is envisaged that the 'appropriate body' is the research ethics committee. The only caveat is that the researcher may not continue to rely on that subsection where the emergency has passed.[79]

This subsection highlights the tensions which arise in the context of research in emergency medicine and the boundaries of legitimacy in proceeding with inclusion with research in such a case. The implication of this section (which pre-dates the proposed reforms of the Medicines for Human Use Regulations discussed earlier) is that there will be situations in which the only effective check/balance on the inclusion of an individual in a particular project will be that of the initial approval given by the research ethics committee. This is where it is particularly critical that any research ethics committee examines such proposals with sufficient care.

Additional Safeguards

Some additional safeguards in relation to the conduct of research involving adults lacking mental capacity are included under section 33 of the Act. Research must not be continued if the participant objects, e.g., by showing resistance or where this would be contrary to an advance decision/statement which is still of continuing validity.[80] In addition the participant must be withdrawn from the research if the criteria for inclusion set out in section 31(2)-(6) discussed above are no longer relevant.[81] However the section excludes treatment which has been given as part of

77 S 32(6).
78 S 32(9).
79 S 32(10).
80 S 33 (2).
81 S 32(5).

the project where there are reasonable grounds for believing that to discontinue that treatment would result in significant risk to his health.[82] Section 34 also states that further provision is to be made in regulations to prescribe in detail the circumstances in which a person, who initially possesses capacity at the commencement of research but then loses capacity, may still have continued involvement in the research project.

The Mental Capacity Act 2005 went much further than could have been envisaged following the initial response of the government to the Law Commission's Mental Incapacity Report. Clarification of the legal position in this uncertain area is much to be welcomed but the ensuing legislation gives rise to its own complexities – we return to this issue in the concluding section below.

Human Tissue Act 2004

A further dimension to this area has arisen as a result of the regulation of human material under the Human Tissue Act 2004. The Act is a wide ranging piece of legislation introduced following the organ retention scandals and the subsequent Bristol and Royal Liverpool Children's Hospital Inquiry reports.[83] The Act contemplates a range of uses of human tissue for research and treatment purposes. It is predicated upon the concept of consent regarding the use of such material, although there are exceptions such as in relation to anonymised material used for therapeutic purposes where sanctioned by a research ethics committee.[84] Use of human material is to be subject to the regulation of a new body, the Human Tissue Authority,[85] which will have powers regarding licensing, and is charged with the production of Codes of Practice.[86] Space precludes any detailed examination of the Act.[87] However a few brief points are worthy of note.

Originally there was no specific reference to the use of material from adults who lack capacity in the Human Tissue Bill and this was only inserted during the passage of the legislation.[88] The issue of what happens in relation to the use of material from living persons where they lack capacity to give consent to the use of their material for therapeutic or for non-therapeutic purposes is governed by section 6 of the Act, which leaves the detail concerning use of material in such a situation to subsequent

82 S 33(6).

83 *Report of the Inquiry into the Royal Liverpool Children's Hospital* (Alder Hey) (2001) http://www.rclinquiry.org.uk. Bristol Inquiry Interim Report, *Removal and Retention of Human Material* (2000) http://www.bristol-inquiry.org.uk.

84 S 1(7),(8),(9),(10).

85 S 13-6.

86 S 16-29.

87 See generally on the legislation Liddell, K. and Hall, A., 'Beyond Bristol and Alder Hey; the future regulation of human tissue', [2005] 13(2) *Medical Law Review*, 170; McHale, J., 'The Human Tissue Act 2005: Innovative Legislation, Fundamentally Flawed or Missed Opportunity?', [2005] 26 *Liverpool Law Review*, 169.

88 See Liddell and Hall, note 87, *supra*, at pp. 193-194.

regulations. Draft regulations were issued for consultation in summer 2005.[89] Where there has been no prior decision made while they possessed capacity the use of human material from adults lacking capacity is legitimated in three main situations. First, where it is use and storage has been undertaken for a 'qualifying purpose'[90] and in the best interests of the person lacking capacity; second, where it is for the purpose of a trial authorised under the Clinical Trials Regulations – in which case the research is subject to the provisions set out in those regulations. Third, 'any other research' is permitted where approved by a research ethics committee who expressly approved the storage and use for these purposes.[91] The draft regulations provide that research should be approved here only where it:

> is in connection with disorders, or the functioning of the human body and there are reasonable grounds for believing that research of comparable effectiveness:
>
> (a) cannot be carried out in circumstances such that the person carrying it out is not in possession, and not likely to come into possession, of information from which the person from whose body the relevant material has come can be identified, or
> (b) cannot be carried out if the research has to be confined to, or relate only to, persons who have capacity to consent to taking part in it.[92]

The draft regulations make similar provision for the non-consensual analysis of DNA from adults who lack mental capacity.

Thus again save where the research concerns clinical trial concerning medicinal products and where it is directly related to the best interests of the person in question authorisation of the research will be subject to the oversight of the local research ethics committee. Here also use of the material will depend upon anonymisation of information concerning the person from whom the material has been removed. The use of anonymisation as a means of legitimising use of material is something which has arisen in the debates regarding the Human Tissue Act – again space precludes further consideration of the issue of the extent to which anonymisation provides a solution or is something which may give rise to further ethical dilemmas.[93]

Conclusions: Welcome Reform or a Recipe for Future Uncertainty?

In the years which followed *Re F*, the involvement of adults without capacity in clinical research has been riven with uncertainty. While research involving adults without capacity was undertaken, the legal status of many research studies remained

89 *Consultation on Regulations to Be Made under the Human Tissue Act 2004*, London, Department of Health (July 2005). Human Tissue Act 2004 (Persons who lack capacity to consent) Regulations 2005 (draft).

90 Part 1 of Schedule 1 of the Human Tissue Act 2004.

91 *Ibid.*, para 2(3).

92 *Ibid.*, para 3(3).

93 See further, e.g., McHale, J., note 87, *supra*.

questionable. Given this, any attempt to clarify this position is surely to be welcomed in the interests of researchers and participants alike.

Nonetheless, while the varying strands of reform in the form of the Clinical Trials Directive and consequent regulations, the Mental Capacity Act and the Human Tissue Act have provided some clarification, the parallel operation of different approval procedures in relation to research processes by researchers and research ethics committees alike will clearly be complex. This leads to concerns that there may be resultant confusion in the future. So, for example, when considering the consent aspect of the trial process, trials regarding medicinal products will have third party decision makers in the person of the legal representative (though not if the current consultation proposals are supported in the context of emergency medicine) – whereas research under the Mental Capacity Act 2005 will simply be subject to *consultation* with carers, or in the case of tissue presumably in some situations in the case of a 'qualifying purpose' simply where it is deemed to be in the best interests of the adult lacking capacity.

As noted throughout this chapter, in determining the legitimacy of the inclusion of adults lacking capacity an important role is to be played by research ethics committees. The new legislative provisions increase their role and indeed legal responsibilities. The complexity of the system which has been created necessitates that particular care is used to ensure that such trial approval processes operate effectively. There is a trend towards increasing central regulation of research ethics committees through for example, the establishment of the UK ethics committee authority[94] and it is vital that, in the absence of a single specialist committee reviewing such issues as was envisaged by the Law Commission, clear central guidance on this complex area is produced and disseminated. A further note of caution here is that there is the risk that reliance upon local scrutiny leads to the prospect of divergent approaches nationally in the future. This is something which warrants effective monitoring at national level.

In addition to the dissemination of effective central guidance and direction, there also needs to be practical support for research ethics committees as their role further develops. It is vital to ensure that local research committees have adequate resources and training to undertake their work effectively. The role of research ethics committees has come under recent scrutiny by an Ad Hoc Advisory Group.[95] Space precludes any effective examination of the recommendations of the group which include radical proposals – such as a movement towards a professional membership for research ethics committees – but it is to be hoped that the Group's report presents an opportunity for a wide-ranging debate of the role of research ethics committees.

94 See note 46, *supra*, part 2, para 5.

95 See Report of the Ad Hoc Advisory Group on the Operation of NHS Research Ethics Committees, London, Department of Health, 2005 and commentary by Angus Dawson in Dawson, A., 'The Ad Hoc Advisory Group's proposals for research ethics committees: a mixture of the timid, the revolutionary and the bizarre', [2005] 31 *Journal of Medical Ethics*, 435.

We have come a long way since the position pre *Re F* in the discourse of healthcare law and adults who lack capacity have gained increasing visibility. A decade after the Law Commission Mental Incapacity report was published, we finally have a raft of legislation and new guidance being made available which can potentially provide enhanced safeguards for adults without capacity in the clinical research process. However, a note of caution should be sounded. Critically, the legislative reforms present themselves very much as reactive – in response, for example, to the Clinical Trials Directive or almost as an afterthought, as in the Mental Capacity Act 2005 and the Human Tissue Act 2004. It is to be regretted that the Law Commission's recommendation for a specialist mental incapacity research committee was not adopted. In its absence, it is critical that local research ethics committees maintain effective scrutiny and independence in reviewing and monitoring such research and have the necessary Governmental support to undertake their role. Otherwise there is a real risk that, ten years on the reforms of 2004-2005 will be viewed not as much needed clarification but as a recipe for fundamental uncertainty.

Chapter 15

Continuing Conundrums in Competency

John Devereux

Introduction

It is inevitable, in a chapter entitled 'continuing conundrums in ...' that what follows is likely to raise more questions than it answers. This chapter will explore ongoing difficulties in the definition of competency. It takes as its starting point some apparently agreed ideas about competency. The chapter then proceeds to discuss how those ideas may be less clear than might first appear, and aims to uncover those matters which are obscured by the 'broad brush' approach the law takes to defining competency.

Competency – The Poor Cousin?

In very many senses, competency has been viewed as 'the poor cousin' in medico-legal discourse. While active debate raged about the appropriate standard by which to judge whether a doctor was or was not negligent,[1] isolating a clearer meaning of the term 'competency' to consent to medical treatment was relegated to the back-burner. As the definition of a doctor's duty of care became clearer, attention has diverted to the question of whether a particular patient is or is not competent to authorise treatment.

Competency – The Agreed Facts

It is generally agreed that competency performs two functions. The first, an ethical function, is to operate as a guide to doctors as to whether the bioethical principle

1 The trend is particularly prominent in Australia. Originally Australia adhered to the *Bolam* standard (a practitioner-centred standard) of medical negligence. Then, in *Rogers v. Whitaker* (1992) 175 CLR 479, the High Court adopted a different standard in respect of failing to advise of material risks. In *Naxaxis v. Western General Hospital* (1999) 197 CLR 269, the High Court signaled continuing developments away from the professional centred standard, this time in respect of diagnosis and treatment. The advent of the Civil Liability Acts in Australia has largely restored the *Bolam* standard in respect of diagnosis and treatment.

of autonomy or beneficence will be paramount.[2] A competent patient is one whose decisions about medical treatment need to be respected – and thus respect for autonomy is dominant. A patient who is not competent, is not exercising autonomous choice, and thus need not have his/her autonomy respected. In such circumstances, subject to the existence of a statutory scheme which prescribes otherwise, the doctor may prescribe treatment which is perceived to be in that patient's best interest (beneficence).

At a legal level, competency is one of the determining factors as to whether a patient may give a valid consent to treatment. A valid consent to treatment is a defence to a battery action. Battery protects the physical inviolability of a patient. It ensures that a patient is only administered treatment to which he or she has given consent. It pays no heed to whether the treatment is in the best interests or will benefit the patient. It simply asks the question – did this patient consent to this procedure?

The law defines the elements of consent in such a way that competency is a pre-requisite to its exercise. So, a valid consent has three components:[3]

- volition
- information
- competency

A patient who is forced to have a procedure has not given consent.[4] A patient agrees to treatment without having had a minimal level of information provided to give him or her the possibility of choice, has not given consent.[5] Nor has a patient who lacks capacity to consent (competency), given a valid consent.[6]

Competency – The Uncertainties

The Nature of Treatment

At the most basic level, competency determinations are still riddled with uncertainty.

One means of defining competency proceeds from the basis that its meaning may be inferred from the surrounding elements of a valid consent. Thus, competency has been viewed as an ability to process information about the nature of the treatment,

2 I have described this function elsewhere as a 'gatekeeper' function. See generally Devereux, J.A., 'Competency to Consent to Treatment: An Introduction', in Freckelton. I. and Petersen. K., *Controversies in Health Law*, Sydney, The Federation Press, 1999.

3 Jones, M., *Medical Negligence*, London, Sweet and Maxwell, 1991, at p. 200.

4 *Freeman v. The Home Office (no.2)* [1984] 1 QB 524; *Beausoleil v. Sisters of Charity* (1964) 53 DLR (2d) 65.

5 *Chatterton v. Gerson* [1981] QB 432.

6 *Secretary Department of Health and Community Services v. JWB and SMB* (1992) 175 CLR 218.

the information being provided by the medical practitioner. This definition draws upon the information element of consent. Put simply, competency is an ability to understand the nature of the treatment which is proposed.[7]

What type of information is relevant, however? Need a patient understand all the risks and side effects of a treatment? Or is something lesser sufficient?

Nature as Encompassing Only the Level of Physical Intervention The simplest formulation of what amounts to the nature of the treatment sees descriptions of the physical intrusions the practitioner is to perform as the nature of the treatment, all else being secondary. Thus it has been said that a patient need not 'understand the precise physiological processes involved' in medical treatment before he/she may be said to understand the nature of the treatment.[8] It has been suggested to be consistent with the general nature of a battery action that the consent 'is to the plaintiff's conduct rather than to its consequences'.[9] This principle would explain the finding of the Court in the criminal battery case of *R v. Clarence*.[10] In that case a man had sexual intercourse with his wife, when he knew he was infected with gonorrhea. His wife was unaware of that her husband had a sexually transmitted disease. When she contracted the disease, she brought an action in battery against him alleging that her consent was not real as, at the time she consented, she was not aware of the fact that she could contract a disease from her husband. The Court dismissed the action on the basis that knowledge of the consequences of the act was not relevant to the nature of the touching. Accordingly, Mrs Clarence's consent to connection with her husband was real.

It would be easy to dismiss Clarence's case as a criminal law – not a tortious – case. *Clarence* has, however, formed the basis of the law also in tortious cases – most notably the Irish case of *Hegarty v. Shine*.[11]

There are two reasons a court today may not, however, apply Clarence's case in a medical context. It has been pointed out that the Court in Clarence's case consisted of Victorian judges who were predisposed to support the social climate of the time that husbands were the dominant partners in marriage. It followed that it was no business of the courts to create a criminal offence arising out of the exercise of a husband's conjugal rights.[12] The House of Lords abandonment of the view that sexual

---

7 *Re C (Refusal of Medical Treatment)* [1994] 1 FLR 31.

8 *R v. Mental Health Act Commission ex parte X* (1991) 9 BMLR 77, at p. 87, per Stuart-Smith LJ.

9 Keeton, D.P., Dobbs, D.B., Keeton, R.E. and Owen, D.G., *Prosser and Keeton on the Law of Torts* (5th ed), West Publishing Co, St Paul, at p. 118. See also *R v. Raabe* [1985] 1 Qd R 115, at p. 124, per Derrington J., followed in *Lergesner v. Carroll* [1991] 1 Qd R 206 at p. 219 per Cooper J. and Kniepp J., at p. 206.

10 (1889) 22 QBD 23.

11 (1878) 14 Cox CC 145.

12 Grubb, A. and Pearl, D.S., 'HIV Testing and the Law', in *Blood Testing, Aids and DNA Profiling: Law and Policy*, Family Law Series, Jordan and Sons Ltd, Bristol, 1990, at p. 9.

intercourse is a husband's right[13] may cause some re-assessment of the reasoning of the Judges in *Clarence*.

Moreover, if the Judges had held that Mrs Clarence needed to know that her husband had a venereal disease in order validly to consent to having sexual intercourse with her husband, it would seem that Mrs Clarence could not lawfully have consented to sexual intercourse at all. This follows from the principle that no person can consent to serious harm upon him/her self.[14]

The principle in Clarence's case can be seen applied in a medical context – most notably in *Chatterton v. Gerson.*[15] In that case a female patient sued her surgeon following an intrathecal block which had been performed upon her. The block was designed to aid in her relief from pain associated with a post operative scar. Instead, the block succeeded in making the pain much worse. She sued in both battery and negligence.

The English High Court held that once a patient is informed in broad terms of the nature of a procedure, and gives her consent; that consent is real and no action will lie in battery. Knowledge of risks, they suggested, sounds in negligence rather than in battery. A similar view has been expressed by the High Court of Australia.[16]

Although the definition appears clear enough, uncertainties persist. What, precisely, is the nature of a treatment? At its most minimal level, it would appear to include information about the type of physical intrusion involved in the procedure. For example, cutting, breaking or applying pressure. But is it right to suggest that no side effect or risk, however serious, can alter the nature of the treatment?

Nature as Encompassing the Beneficial or Deleterious Aspects of Treatment In medical cases there are two situations in which the law may be prepared to hold that the treatment is of a different nature, despite being of the same physical scope as that to which consent was given.[17] It has been suggested that a court would distinguish between a procedure which was of benefit to a patient and one that was not. A similar distinction between the nature of therapeutic and non-therapeutic procedures is suggested by Somerville.[18]

The distinction between treatments which are for the benefit of patients and those that are not is apparently of ancient origin. Thus, in the nineteenth-century English case of *R v. Rosinski*[19] a man held himself out as being able to cure disorders. He was approached by a girl who wished to be cured of fits. Rosinski took off her clothes and rubbed her with some liquid from a bottle. This was done not to cure the girl, but

13 *R v. R* [1992] 1 AC 599.

14 *R v. Brown* [1993] 2 WLR 556.

15 *Supra cit.*

16 *Rogers v. Whitaker* (1992) 175 CLR 479.

17 Skegg, P.D.G., 'Informed Consent to Medical Procedures', (1975) 15 (2) *Medicine Science and the Law*, 124-132, at pp. 125-126.

18 Somerville, M.A., 'Structuring the Issues in Informed Consent', (1981) *McGill Law Journal*, 740-808.

19 (1824) 1 Lew CC 11, 1 Mood CC 19.

for Rosinski's 'own lewd gratification'.[20] The Court held that the girl did not consent to the procedure.

The view that the nature of the treatment is dependent upon whether the treatment is beneficial for the patient or not is not without controversy. There are two cases from Canada, and one from Australia, which emphasise the difference in approach.

In *R v. Bolduc and Bird*,[21] Bolduc was a medical practitioner who was treating Mrs Osborne for an erosion of the cervic uteri. On one occasion when Mrs Osborne presented herself for treatment, Bolduc attended with a man attired in a white coat who was wearing a stethosocope. Bolduc introduced the other man as an intern who had no experience of the sort of the procedure Bolduc was about to perform. He asked whether Mrs Osborne had any objection to the intern being present during the examination. She replied that she did not mind.

In fact, the intern was a musician friend of Bolduc with no medical training. Dr Bolduc conducted a careful examination of Mrs Osborne's vaginal region, subsequently inserting a speculum in order to examine her more thoroughly. Bird (the musician friend) stood some 12 to 18 inches away and did not touch Mrs Osborne. A charge of indecent assault was brought against Dr Bolduc. At first instance, he was convicted.

On appeal before the British Columbia Court of Appeal, all Judges held that the nature and quality of the act that Mrs Osborne had consented to was substantially different from that which she had done to her. Lord JA held that the nature and quality of the act to which the patient consented was her doctor examining her in the presence of an intern, not in front of a person who, aided by the doctor's deception, was present solely for his own gratification.[22] Maclean JA held that the patient's consent was obtained by false and fraudulent representations as to the nature of the act. The nature of this fraud was that the nature of the act was for medical treatment, whereas in fact it was partly for treatment and partly to satisfy the curiosity of a masquerader.[23] Macfarlane JA held that 'the thing done was not a thing to which the patient consented at all'.[24]

The Supreme Court of Canada held:

> ... the conduct of the doctor was unethical and reprehensible but that the consent of the patient was not obtained by false and fraudulent representations as to the nature and quality of the act to be performed by the doctor. The fraud was as to the friend being a medical intern. His presence as distinct from some overt act by him was not an assault.[25]

The Supreme Court went on to note that if Bird had performed an overt act, then he would have been guilty of an assault. From this, Somerville concludes that

20 *Id.*

21 [1967] SCR 677.

22 [1967] 61 DLR (2d) 494, at p. 495.

23 *Ibid.*, at p. 496.

24 *Ibid.*, at p. 497.

25 [1967] SCR 677, at p. 679.

fraud as to the possession of a medical qualifications may alter the nature of what is occurring.[26] This may be supportable but it is submitted that what matters more is the question of the whether the interference is treatment or simply interference, rather than being a question of qualifications *per se* (i.e., whether the interference is good for the patient or not). By contrast, with the majority decision of the Supreme Court Spence J (dissenting) said the patient had consented to being touched by the doctor in the presence of a doctor and not a mere layman and that this was central to the offence.[27]

In *R v. Maurantonia*,[28] the accused falsely held himself out to be a medical practitioner. He admitted that the complainants had only consented to being intimately examined and treated because they believed he was a medical practitioner. In submitting that Maurantonia was not guilty of indecent assaults, his counsel argued that fraud as to the nature of his qualifications was fraud in the inducement, but not fraud in the factum. Accordingly, the fraud was not as to the nature of the act. The majority of the court held that there had been fraud as to the nature of the act. Thus it was noted that the words nature and quality:

> Should not be so narrowly construed as to include not only the physical actions but rather must be interpreted to encompass those concomitant circumstances which give meaning to the particular physical activity in question.[29]

The Judge continued that:

> It was only to a medical examination or medical treatment, including the reasonable intimate physical contact necessary thereto, that each complainant consented. If that to which they were subjected was not in fact of the nature of a bona fide medical examination or treatment then it was something entirely different to which they consented.[30]

The fact that the defendant held himself out as a medical practitioner was thought not to be the inducement for the complainant submitting to physical interference; rather the inducing representation was that the defendant was to carry out a medical examination on her.

Bolduc and Maurantonia were considered in *R v. Mobilio*.[31] In this case, a radiographer carried out internal examinations upon women without any clinical need and apparently for his own gratification. In overturning Mobilio's conviction for rape,[32] the Court of Criminal Appeal held that the patient's consent to the procedure

26 *Supra*, note 18 at p. 743-745.

27 *Ibid.*, at p. 684.

28 [1968] 1 OR 145.

29 *Ibid.*, at p. 153, per Hartt J.

30 *Id.*

31 [1991] VR 339. See generally Morgan, J., 'Rape in Medical Treatment: The Patient as Victim', (1991) 18 (2) *Melbourne University Law Review*, 403-427.

32 Using the statutory definition of rape in s 2A(b) of the Crimes Act 1958 (Vic) as including penetration of the vagina, by any object, without consent.

was not vitiated where the person carrying out the examination lacked a medical purpose for so doing. This decision has now been overturned by statute.[33]

Nature of the Treatment as Encompassing the Experimental Nature of the Treatment
In circumstances where the person administering medical treatment is not medically qualified, it would seem that legitimate concern may be raised as to whether the patient understands the nature of the treatment,[34] simply because in those circumstances it may not be *medical* treatment. What, though, is the position of the medically qualified practitioner who administers treatment which is experimental – that is, he is not sure to what extent the treatment can be said to be beneficial and he has not explained to his patient, nor does his patient understand the uncertainty?

This question came up for consideration in the Canadian decision of *Coughlan v. Kuntz*.[35]

In that case the plaintiff was involved in a motor vehicle accident and sustained an injury to his left shoulder. He was referred to the defendant, an orthopaedic surgeon, who made an initial diagnosis of painful arc syndrome. The defendant requested that x-rays be carried out to check for other injury. The x-rays revealed there had been a narrowing of the fifth and sixth cervical disk space. The defendant recommended an anterior cervical discectomy and 'an instant interbody fusion'. The latter was a procedure which had been developed by the defendant, and involved the insertion of a plastic spacer between the vertebrae. Prior to the plaintiff's consultation with the defendant, the defendant was notified that the College of Physicians and Surgeons was concerned about the defendant's use of this untested technique and had asked him to undertake a voluntary moratorium on the procedure. The defendant had refused.

The defendant suggested to the plaintiff that he check with the Workers Compensation Board to see whether they would fund the procedure. The Board declined to fund the operation, but the defendant nonetheless obtained the consent of the plaintiff and performed the procedure.

A few weeks after the surgery, the artificial spacer slipped forward and jutted into the plaintiff's oesophagus. This proved to be both physically irritating and mentally distressing. The plaintiff experienced continuing problems with his left shoulder. He required two further operations (performed by different surgeons) and the removal of the disk spacer. He commenced actions in negligence and battery. It was held that, in not informing the patient of the experimental nature of the surgery, the plaintiff could not 'understand and appreciate the nature of the procedure'.[36]

---

33 Section 3 Crimes (Sexual Offences) Act 1991 (Vic) introduced what is now s 36 of the Crimes Act 1958 (Vic) which provides: Consent to conduct which could otherwise constitute rape or indecent assault is of no effect if it was obtained by a false representation that the conduct was for medical or hygienic purposes.

34 Jones, *op cit.*, at p. 206.

35 [1990] 2 WWR 737.

36 *Ibid.*, at p. 748. It is true that the trial Judge, in coming to the conclusion endorsed by the Court of Appeal also mentioned the facts that the defendant had not made mention of the

A similar finding was made in the English case of *R v. Mental Health Act Commission ex parte X.*[37] That case considered the relevance of the experimental aspect of a treatment to that treatment's nature. The Court had to deal with a situation where, unlike in *Coughlan*, the doctor did not hide the experimental aspect of the procedure; indeed, he was quite frank about it. The applicant, X, was a compulsive paedophile. He contacted a psychiatrist with experience of treating sex offenders. The psychiatrist prescribed some sexual suppressant drugs, though they were of minimal effect at the recommended levels. The psychiatrist then prescribed Goserilin, a drug used in the treatment of prostate cancer, which reduced testosterone to castration levels. The psychiatrist contacted the Mental Health Act Commission to enquire whether the drug came within the ambit of the procedures prescribed by regulation 16(1) of the Mental Health (Hospital Guardianship and Consent to Treatment) Regulations,[38] as requiring not only the consent of the patient, but also a second opinion.[39] The Commission decided the treatment did require a second opinion and X applied for judicial review of this finding.

In holding that the drug was not of a type which required a second opinion and could therefore be consented to by X, provided that X understood the nature of the treatment, Stuart-Smith LJ noted:

> … in this case, where the treatment was not routinely used for control of sexual urges and was not sold for this purpose, it was important that the applicant should realize that the use on him was a novel one and the full implications with use on young men had not been studied, since trials had only been involved with animals and older men … it is perfectly clear that the applicant knew this.[40]

The experimental aspect of a proposed treatment may also be relevant if a distinction as to the nature of treatments can be drawn between procedures which are inherently dangerous, and those which are not.

Nature as Encompassing Safe or Dangerous Aspects of the Treatment Is there a distinction in terms of the nature of a treatment between a safe procedure, and an unsafe one? It is apparent that drawing this distinction highlights the question of the consequences of the treatment. While the view has often been expressed that consequences are irrelevant to whether a person has consented, it seems there are exceptions to this rule.[41]

---

other types of treatment which were available, that the workers compensation board felt the operation was unnecessary and that the defendant had not outlined the potential risks of the surgery; see *Coughlan v. Kuntz* (1987) 17 BCLR (2d) 365, at pp. 391-392. These other matters may be viewed as proof of the experimental nature of the surgery.

37 (1991) 9 BMLR 77.

38 S.I. 1983 No. 893.

39 Mental Health Act 1983 (Imp), s 57.

40 *Ibid.*, at p. 86.

41 Garrett, T.M., Baillie, H.W. and Garrett, R.M., *Health Care Ethics: Principles and Problems*, Prentice Hall, Englewood Cliffs, New Jersey, p. 30: 'in the context of health

In actions for battery, courts have distinguished between a valid and invalid consent on the basis of the consequences flowing from the touching concerned. Thus a distinction has been drawn between touching an ordinary, as opposed to a heated, coin.[42] In *Nash v. Sheen*,[43] a hairdresser applied a dye (referred to as a 'tone rinse') to her client's hair. The client had wanted only a perm. Despite the difference being one as to consequences rather than touching, the Court found the hairdresser liable in battery. In *Burrell v. Harmer*,[44] a tattooist was approached by two boys who wished to have tattoos on their arms. He did so, and their arms subsequently became inflamed. The Court upheld a conviction for battery on the ground that the boys had not consented to a touching of the type that had taken place. It seems not to have been at issue that the boys knew the type of physical touching involved in applying a tattoo.

In *Mobilio*, the Court of Criminal Appeal held that, in order to consent to what would otherwise amount to rape, the woman needs to understand more than what is proposed in the physical act of penetration. The Court held also that the woman needs 'some further perception of what is about to take place'.[45] In referring specifically to the question of the amount of knowledge required of a person to give consent to a complex surgical procedure, the Court noted that, although a complete knowledge of 'all that is involved' was not needed, 'some knowledge of [the procedure's] possible or probable immediate effects of future consequences', was.[46]

English decisions, too, confirm, at least in some cases, the inapplicability of the simple physical intrusion view of the nature of a procedure. In *Potts v. North West Regional Health Authority*,[47] the plaintiff agreed to be vaccinated against rubella. Unknown to her, the syringe with which she was injected also contained the contraceptive drug Depo-Provera. The defendants were held liable in battery. Again, it was not simply a matter of a different level of physical intrusion being involved. Both drugs were administered using the same physical means. While Mrs Potts had agreed to be vaccinated against rubella, she did not anticipate, nor did she wish for, the side-effects of bleeding, loss of libido and depression which were inherent in the administration of Depo-Provera.

The *Potts* case raises real questions about the idea that the patient needs to understand only the level of the physical intrusion, if the patient is to be said to understand the nature of the treatment.

How may the above cases be reconciled with the general view that consequences do not form part of consent to what otherwise would be a battery? It has been

---

care ethics, we mean by competence the ability to make choices based on an understanding of the relevant consequences of that choice on oneself and others'. See also Skegg, *loc cit.*, at p. 17.

42 Anon., noted in (1926) 70 *Sol J*, 334.

43 *The Times*, 13 March 1953.

44 (1996) 116 *New Law Journal*, 1658.

45 See Morgan, *loc cit.*, at p. 350.

46 *Id.*

47 *The Guardian*, 23 July 1983.

suggested that 'policy considerations rightly loom large in any decision as to whether the procedure performed was the same as the one consented to'.[48]

Nature as Including Essential or Significant Risks of Treatment It is tempting to try to describe some collateral (that is not part of the nature of the procedure) features as being part of the risks of the treatment:

> The nature and purposes of the procedure does not necessarily require any reference to undesirable side-effects. Informing a patient of these side-effects does not help describe, yet alone define, what is being done by the doctor.[49]

It is clear that a practitioner who fails to disclose risks that a reasonable practitioner would have divulged may be liable to a finding of negligence. In these circumstances, it would seem groundless to base liability for failure to disclose of risks in battery as well. As noted above, modern authority supports a clear distinction between the nature of the treatment and its risks.

The principle derived from *Chatterton v. Gerson*[50] glosses over a basic difficulty. Is it not possible that some risks or consequences of a treatment could be so serious that, without them, the whole nature of the treatment changes?[51] Suppose, for example, that a patient is advised to have a tonsillectomy. He may believe that he is consenting to a procedure that is routine, minor and safe. If, however, in this particular patient's case, the procedure was complex and dangerous and the practitioner knew this would be the case, it could be said that the patient had not consented to the operation. He had consented to a minor, safe operation – what he got was a dangerous, complex one.[52] A more extreme example is outlined in one commentary,[53] which describes a hypothetical situation in which a patient consults a medical practitioner complaining of listlessness. The practitioner prescribes heroin for the patient saying that it will make him feel better. If the idea of risks being irrelevant to the nature of the treatment is followed, then the patient has consented, notwithstanding the possibility of adverse reactions to the drug and the possibility of addiction. The heroin will make him feel better.

However, what he consented to was of a different order of seriousness than what he received. He likely thought he was receiving a mild stimulant or tonic and in the circumstances that would be the reasonable expectation. Heroin is something different altogether. In a fairly clear way, the physician went beyond that to which there was consent even though the descriptions match if we ignore risks or the general

48 Skegg, *loc cit.*, at p. 126; Grubb and Pearl, *loc cit.*, at p. 6.

49 Grubb and Pearl, *loc cit.*, at p. 8.

50 *Supra cit.*

51 Skegg, *loc cit.*, at p. 126, Tan, K.F., 'Failure of Medical Advice: Trespass or Negligence?', (1987) 7 *LS*, 149-168, at p. 155.

52 Gochnauer, M. and Fleming, D.J., 'Comments on Cases', (1981) 15 *UBCLR*, 475-497, at pp. 487-488.

53 *Id.*

order of seriousness of the treatment. There was consent to a range of mild, routine drugs not consent to a dangerous therapeutically unusual drug. And this is true even though heroin may in fact be 'something to make him feel better'. A necessary part of the treatment is the general magnitude of its seriousness.[54]

This idea that the risks and levels of seriousness of the treatment are relevant to determining the nature of the treatment can be seen in the decision of the Court of Appeal in *Re T*.[55] T was a 20-year-old woman who had been brought up by her mother. T's mother was a devout Jehovah's witness and although T never became a member of the sect, she was brought up in accordance with the sect's tenets. Following a car accident, T was admitted to hospital. She went into labour, and her doctors decided to deliver her baby by way of a caesarian section. T indicated her objection to having a blood transfusion and asked whether there were alternatives. She was told by her doctor that blood transfusions were often not necessary and that there were alternatives to blood transfusions even if the situation arose where she would need a transfusion. T signed a refusal of consent form without reading it or having its contents explained to her.

T's condition deteriorated to such an extent that a blood transfusion was clinically indicated to save her life. T's boyfriend and father brought an application seeking a declaration that such a blood transfusion would not be unlawful. At first instance, Ward J granted the application.

In dismissing the appeal, the Court of Appeal held, *inter alia*, that there was a difference between T's refusal of treatment when she thought that other alternative treatments were available (that is her refusal in circumstances where such refusal would be non life-threatening) and refusal of a blood transfusion where it would result in T's death.[56] The consequences of a failure to treat were different in the two circumstances. This difference in consequences changed the nature of the treatment. T had refused treatment on the basis that it was a non-life threatening decision. As the nature of the treatment had changed, a new consent or refusal to consent was required. However, as T was by then in a critical condition on a ventilator and was incompetent to give or refuse consent, her doctors could treat her in accordance with what they perceived to be in her best interests.

The idea that some risks may be part of the nature of the treatment has been supported by some authority in other Commonwealth jurisdictions. In *Kelly v. Hazlett*,[57] the plaintiff had a deformity in her right elbow as a result of rheumatoid arthritis. Her elbow was stiff and she experienced numbness in her hand. She consulted the defendant, an orthopaedic surgeon. He told her he could relieve her numbness by a procedure called an ulnar nerve transplant. He said he could also relieve the deformity in her elbow by an osteotomy. As the latter procedure would

54 *Ibid.*, at p. 488.

55 [1993] Fam 95.

56 *Ibid.*, per Lord Donaldson MR at p. 114; per Butler-Sloss LJ, at p. 120; per Staughton LJ, at pp. 121-122.

57 (1976) 15 OR (2d) 290.

involve breaking her arm and placing the arm in a sling, inducing a long period of inactivity, he recommended against it. Mrs Kelly decided to proceed only with the nerve transplant. Subsequently, she decided to undergo the osteotomy which was also performed by the surgeon. The defendant surgeon did not tell the plaintiff of the risk of additional stiffness following the osteotomy. The risk materialised and the plaintiff sued for battery and negligence. Mordern J upheld the plaintiff's claim for negligence. In the course of his judgment he commented upon the relationship of risks to the nature of the treatment. He said:

> In some cases it may be difficult to distinguish and separate out the matter of consequences or collateral risks from the basic character and nature of the operation or procedure to be performed. The more probable the risk, the more it could be said to be an integral feature of the nature and character of the operation.[58]

The most stunning example of where a serious risk may be considered to be part of the nature of the treatment is *D v. S.*[59] In that case the plaintiff had a breast reduction operation. She was concerned that the operation might cause scarring, but her medical practitioner assured her that scarring was unlikely and that, should she experience any, it would be superficial and would fade. After the operation, however, the plaintiff's breasts were badly and permanently scarred. In addition, her nipples were relocated unevenly. She suffered both pain and embarrassment. In upholding her actions for both negligence and battery, the court held that the plaintiff's consent to the operation was not a valid consent because the medical practitioner had not told her about the risks of the operation. Similar attention to the risk of treatment can be seen in the case of *F v. R.* [60]

The same distinction between safe and unsafe procedures might also be raised where a procedure is experimental and, therefore, because the procedure is new, nothing could be safely asserted about the possibility of the procedure being dangerous or safe.[61]

Part of the problem is, of course, that 'one man's meat is another man's poison'. The same treatment may be used for different purposes. Sometimes whether something is part of the essential nature of the treatment – as opposed to a risk or side effect of the treatment – is dependent upon the purpose for which that treatment is used. Take, for example, the oral contraceptive pill. The oral contraceptive pill is provided free of charge in the UK, provided that it is prescribed for contraceptive reasons. The pill may also be used to regulate hormonal fluxes or for the treatment

---

58 *Ibid.*, at p. 313. The Supreme Court of Canada in *Reibl v. Hughes* (1977) 114 DLR (3d) 1, at p. 11 admittedly suggested differently.

59 (1981) 93 LS (SA) JS 405. See also *Informed Decisions About Medical Procedures*, A Joint Report of the Law Reform Commission of Victoria (Report No. 24), The Australian Law Reform Commission (Report No. 50) and the New South Wales Law Reform Commission (Report No. 62) June 1989, at p. 33.

60 (1982) 29 SASR 437; (1983) 34 SASR 189.

61 *Coughlin v. Kuntz, supra cit.*

of acne. What, then is the nature of the oral contraceptive pill? What parts of the treatment amount to side effects?

Uncertainties – Understanding

It will be appreciated that, even utilising the definition of competency as understanding the nature of the treatment, it is not sufficient that a patient have explained to him or her, information about the nature of the treatment. He or she must also *understand* that information before he or she may be regarded as competent.

Three Senses of Understanding[62] The term 'understand' is deceptively simple. At the risk of entering a circular argument, we all think we understand what understanding means.

Schwartz and Roth note:

> The courts tend to use the words 'inform' and 'understand' interchangeably, reflecting a simplistic assumption that understanding is the natural and expected consequence of adequately informing an individual.[63]

Psychology and philosophy give us little guidance as to the meaning of understanding.[64] The focus in psychology has been upon how people understand through cognitive and neuropsychological processes. Psychology offers writings on the structure of memory and understanding, discourse interpretation and the effect of stress on learning abilities.[65] Philosophical concepts focus upon ideas, perceptions and processes of knowing, rather than analysing understanding.[66]

A linguistic analysis may assist. Linguistically, we refer to understanding in three senses. The first, 'understanding how', describes that a person is in possession of practical skills which he or she can apply to the situation. Thus 'I understand how to drive'. The second sense may be described as 'understanding that'. This means a person can make sense of information with which he or she is provided, and believes it to be true. So, a person might say 'I understand that you are a lawyer'. Understanding might also encompass 'understanding what'. This differs from 'understanding that',

---

62 See generally Devereux, *loc cit.*

63 Schwartz, H.I. and Roth, L.H., 'Informed Consent and Competency in Psychiatric Practice', in Tasman, A., Hales, R.E. and Frances, A.J. (eds), *Review of Psychiatry*, Vol. 8, American Psychiatric Press, Washington, DC, 1989, 409-431, at p. 417.

64 Faden, R. and Beauchamp, T., *A History and Theory of Informed Consent*, New York, Oxford University Press, 1986, at p. 249.

65 See for example, Sternberg, R.J. and Powell, J.S., 'Comprehending Verbal Comprehension', (1983) 38 *American Psychologist*, 878-893; Harris, R.J. and Monaco, G.E., 'Psychology of Pragmatic Implication: Information Processing Between the Lines', (1978) 107 *Journal of Experimental Psychology*, 1-22. See generally Flores D'Arcais, G.B. and Jarvelle, R.J. (eds), *The Process of Language Understanding*, New York, John Wiley and Sons, 1983.

66 Faden and Beauchamp, *op cit.*, at p. 249.

in as much as a person to whom information is provided need not understand the truth of what is asserted. So if a person was told in alarmed terms that Australia was being invaded by Martians, when he or she failed to respond, the questioner might say 'don't you understand what I am saying?' The response might well be, 'I understand what you are saying' (i.e., I can make sense of what you have told me) – 'I just don't believe it to be true'.

Which sense (or senses) of understanding are relevant to a consent scenario? Faden and Beauchamp suggest that:

> The typical pattern of understanding in informed consent settings is for patients or subjects to come to understand that they must consent or refuse a particular proposal by understanding what is communicated in an informational exchange with a professional.[67]

It is suggested here that this analysis is flawed. No objection is taken to the first part of the analysis, but the second part suggests that the patient need not believe the truth of the information imparted to him by a practitioner. If this is so, surely it cannot be said that he appreciates the information he has been told?

Suppose, for example, a practitioner told a patient that a proposed operation was for the purpose of relieving the pain associated with his sinusitis. The patient understands what relief of pain from sinusitis is about (that is, he understands what he is told) but believes that the doctor is lying (that is, he does not believe the truth of the information with which he has been provided). He does not believe the operation is for the purpose of relieving the pain associated with his sinusitis. In fact, he believes it will do nothing to affect the pain he is suffering. He wrongly believes that the practitioner is placing some sort of tracking device in his nose so that the practitioner will know the patient's movements. The patient's knowledge would satisfy Faden and Beauchamp's definition of understanding what is imparted – but would we really say such a consent was real?

The relevant sense of understanding, it has been argued elsewhere,[68] is 'understanding that'. In other words, a patient need not only make sense of what he or she is told – but also be able to apply it to his or her situation.

Understanding That – and a Little Bit More (Communicating a Choice) The idea of understanding in a competency sense being 'understanding that' has some support from case law. In *Re C (Refusal of Medical Treatment)*[69] a 68-year-old man suffering from paranoid schizophrenia refused a leg amputation. Thorpe J noted:

> I consider helpful Dr E's analysis of the decision making process into three stages: first, comprehending and retaining treatment information, secondly believing it and thirdly weighing it in the balance to arrive at a choice.[70]

67 Faden and Beauchamp, *op cit.*, at p. 250.

68 *Supra*, note 2.

69 *Supra*, note 7.

70 *Supra cit.*, at p. 36.

The Law Commission of England and Wales' test of competency is broadly similar:

A person should be regarded as lacking capacity if suffering from a mental disability and unable to make a decision because:

(a) he or she is unable to understand or retain the information relevant to the decision, including information about the reasonably foreseeable consequences of deciding one way or the other or failing to make the decisions; or
(b) he or she is unable to make a decision based on that information.[71]

With respect to the Law Commission, a further element is probably required – that of being able to communicate a choice. The Law Commission's definition fails to account for the patient who, while having decision making processes intact, is unable to communicate that decision to others. An example might be a patient suffering from Guillain-Barre syndrome, or certain types of autism. Such a patient may be able to understand treatment information, and weigh it in the balance but, absent an ability to communicate the choice, is incompetent. This additional capacity is reflected in the definition of 'an inability to make a decision' in the Mental Capacity Act 2005[72] and the Adults with Incapacity (Scotland) Act 2000.

Of course, the addition of such a requirement opens up other uncertainties. Parker and Cartwright argue that:

> if more needs to be done to promote the autonomy of physically disabled citizens, then the notion of capacity should take account not just of purely cognitive capacity, but also of executive control functions such as physical voluntariness and specific difficulties such as aphasia ...[73]

The authors note the existence of a difficult 'half way house':

> where structural brain damage or injury results in the severance of connections between emotional effect and the various intellectual functions such as attention, memory reasoning and inference.[74]

The difficulty with a patient suffering from such an injury would be, of course, that the patient would *appear* to have competency because they might demonstrate understanding but, 'subsequent action can be haphazard, apparently due to the failure

71 The Law Commission of England and Wales, *Mentally Incapacitated Adults and Decision Making*, London, 1995.

72 Mental Capacity Act 2005 (Imp.) s 3.

73 Parker, M. and Cartwright, C., 'Mental Capacity in Medical Practice and Advance Care Planning: Clinical, Ethical and Legal Issues', in Collier, B; Coyne, C. and Sullivan, K., *Mental Capacity: Powers of Attorney and Advance Health Directives*, Sydney, Federation Press, 2005, 56-92, at p. 64.

74 *Ibid.*, at p. 65.

to attach to mentally represented situations the appropriate emotional preference, or any emotional affect at all'.[75]

The patient in a 'half way house', it is suggested, may not be competent due to a failure in cognitive processing which meant he or she was not truly applying the information to his or her situation. Such a finding may appear a stretch of the 'understanding that' concept. It is possible that the 'understanding that' concept may need additional elements to take into account patients in a 'half way house'.

It should be noted that the adoption of the 'understanding that' principle in respect of competency is by no means universal. Parker and Cartwright, after acknowledging that 'comprehension, retention and weighing information all presuppose that the information provided is believed'[76] caution against an uncritical assumption of the 'understanding that' principle. They argue that a clear point of distinction is established according to the reasons the information in believed:

> If it is thought that a patient's disbelief is caused by a mental condition, the law will recognise this as interfering with capacity, whereas if it derives from a stable but different view of the world from the medical interpretation, it will not.[77]

Moreover, Parker and Cartwright see no difference between the 'understanding how' test of competency and 'understanding that':

> … there is no inconsistency between the definition of competence as simply the ability to perform a task and the cognitive account … since it is cognitive abilities which underpin the specific task of medical decision making.[78]

With respect, the same could be said for any 'understanding how' criteria. Understanding how to drive a pushbike is a combination of physical attributes (having legs) and underlying cognitive abilities. It is suggested, with respect, that a cognitive 'understanding that' approach to competency is a more appropriate test, focused as it is on cognitive abilities.

Understanding the Nature of a Procedure – Necessary but Not Sufficient It is suggested that the idea of understanding in broad terms the nature of a procedure is in some sense a necessary but not sufficient definition of understanding. True, a patient must understand the nature of a procedure – but there is more detail required.

The notion of understanding the nature of treatment in the medical consent context encompasses three processes. The first may be referred to as being aware. A patient who is completely sense deprived is unaware and thus incompetent. Not being able to receive information as to the treatment, he or she cannot process that

75 *Id.*

76 *Id.*

77 *Ibid.*, at p. 69.

78 *Id.*

information. A patient must have at least one other sense in order to be able to receive the information.

The second process is referred to as appreciation.[79] This involves two skills – first, an understanding that the information provided by one's doctor is not hypothetical or theoretical knowledge. The second prerequisite is an understanding that the information applies to the present treatment options facing the patient. Drawing on the linguistic analysis above, appreciation is the same as 'understanding that'. Examples of the appreciation principle are found in three cases. In *Khan v. St Thomas Psychiatric Hospital et al.; Advocacy Resource Centre for the Handicapped, Amicus Curae*,[80] a woman suffering from paranoid schizophrenia was found to be incompetent. Although she understood what paranoid schizophrenia was and could understand the proposed medication and its side effects, the Court noted she did not believe she was ill. Similarly, in *Norfolk and Norwich Health Care (NHS) Trust v. W*,[81] a patient arrived at a hospital in an advanced state of labour. She denied that she was pregnant. In these circumstances a Court had little trouble establishing that she was not competent. An example from an American context is the Supreme Court decision in *Zinermon v. Burch*.[82] There, a patient who volunteered for hospitalisation and thought he was entering heaven was found to be incompetent.

Finally, the patient needs to understand that he or she must either consent to treatment or refuse consent to that treatment. In respect of this latter type of understanding, it is clear that the extent of the understanding need not be great. The patient need neither have a lawyerly appreciation of a battery action, nor need s/he have a detailed knowledge of human anatomy. It is sufficient if s/he understands s/he is granting a medical practitioner permission to do something s/he would not otherwise have permission to do.

Understanding – The Relevance of Perseverance? Kerridge, Lowe and McPhee have as part of their definition of competency, the capacity 'to persevere with the choice until the decision is acted upon'.[83] This author regards such an inclusion as curious. If it were applicable, it would place a premium on the persistent, belligerent patient over the shy, timid or easily persuaded to the contrary patient. There is little doubt that a patient whose consent is obtained by threats, fraud, the administration of drugs or other pressure has not given a valid consent. But this is surely the province of another element of a valid consent – the requirement of volition – rather than that of competency?

79 Hoffman, B.F., 'Assessing Competency to Consent to Treatment', (1980) 25 *Canadian Journal of Psychiatry*, 354-362.

80 (1992) 87 DLR (4th) 289.

81 [1996] 2 FLR 613.

82 110 S.Ct 975 (1990).

83 Kerridge, I., Lowe, M. and McPhee, J., *Ethics and Law for the Health Professions*, Katoomba, Social Science Press, 1988, at p. 162.

An alternative reading of the criterion is possible. Perhaps what is envisaged is the patient who has understood the information, applied it to his or her situation, and then evidenced a choice but, having done so; within a few minutes, though still correctly understanding and applying the information to his/her own circumstances, comes up with a different choice. If this is what is envisaged, the criterion places a premium on the definite patient over the cautious or unsure patient. Again, this seems to be beyond the scope of a proper determination of competence.

Understanding – Ability to Understand or Actual Understanding? In the literature on competency, there has occasionally been debate as to whether, in order to be competent, a patient needs to demonstrate actual understanding of the treatment information or merely an ability to understand treatment information.[84]

There is a real difference between understanding actual information with which one is presented, and, having categorised that information of being of a certain magnitude of complexity, demonstrating an ability to understand information of a similar complexity. The latter, referred to as possessing an ability to understand, is an indirect assessment of understanding. Its usefulness is demonstrated in the case of a patient, who, paralysed with fear when presented with his/her diagnosis and thus unable to open his/her mind to the particular information with which he/she is presented, can be regarded as competent because, although not understanding what he or she is told about his/her own condition, s/he is cognitively sophisticated enough to understand information of equivalent complexity.

Thus, suppose we have decided that the complexity of information about an angioplasty is the same as solving a quadratic equation. Suppose then that a particular patient is told that she needs, due to an underlying medical condition, to undergo an angioplasty. She is so shocked by the news she is unable to process the information. In shock she refuses to deal with the situation. Presented with three quadratic equations and asked to solve them, she does so flawlessly. On the ability to understand idea of competency, she is competent. On a definition of competency which requires actual understanding of the treatment information, she is not.

Kennedy and Grubb warn against using the actual understanding test, on the grounds that it could lead to an attribution of incompetence on the basis that a patient was supplied with insufficient information.[85] The advantage of using the ability to understand criterion is that the focus is on that which is 'within' the patient. Again, with respect, the learned authors confuse two of the criteria for a valid consent. In order for a patient to give a valid consent, he or she must be provided with sufficient information by the medical practitioner. Absent sufficient information, no valid

84 It seems likely that the focus on the difference between actual understanding and ability to understand derives from Roth, L., Meisel, A. and Lidz, C.W., 'Tests of Competency to Consent to Treatment', (1977) 134 *American Journal of Psychiatry*, 279-284.

85 Kennedy, I. and Grubb, A., *Medical Law: Text with Materials*, London, Butterworths, 1994, at p. 107.

consent can be given. To borrow a phrase from computer programming parlance 'junk in equals junk out'.

Biegler and Stewart argue that the standard used in Australia is actual understanding, since it is endorsed by various scholars on competence, but that use of this standard mandates adequate disclosure as a prerequisite for a finding of incompetence.[86] It is suggested that Biegler and Stewart's view is the better view. The problem with using the ability to understand test is that it does not easily accord with the understanding that view of competence. If a patient is so paralysed by fear that he or she is unable to turn his or her mind to their own situation, it is hard to establish that s/he understands information and applies to his/her own circumstances.

Conclusion

In the 1980s it was noted in respect of the assessment of patient competence that '... ad hoc decisions on the basis of unarticulated criteria were the norm'.[87] Much has been achieved since then.

At the same time, it is clear that glib statements that a patient must understand in broad terms the nature of a procedure, are inadequate in detail. Further thought needs to be devoted to the production of a detailed account of competency – and how to assess that capacity.

86 Biegler, P. and Stewart, C., 'Assessing Competence to Refuse Medical Treatment', (2001) 174 *Medical Journal of Australia*, 523-525.

87 Lidz, C.W., Meisel, A., Holden, J.L., Marx, J.H. and Munetz, M.R., 'Informed Consent and the Structure of Medical Care', in *Making Health Care Decisions*, The Presidents Commission for the Study of Ethical Problems in Medicine and Biomedical and Behavioral Research, Washington, DC, 1982 Vol. 2, 317, at p. 362. Similar confusion in respect of competence determination was noted in the 1990s by Alderson, P., 'In the Genes or in the Stars? Children's Competence to Consent to Treatment', (1992) 18 *Journal of Medical Ethics*, 119-124 , at p. 120.

Chapter 16

Chester v. Afshar: Sayonara, Sub Silentio, *Sidaway*?

David Meyers

The Facts

Carole Chester suffered from chronic low back pain.[1] Conservative treatment over a span of years was unproductive. An MRI scan showed bulging lumbar discs. She was referred to Dr Fari Afshar, a consultant neurosurgeon, for evaluation. Miss Chester's referring doctor advised Dr Afshar that she was anxious to avoid surgery if possible. Following examination Dr Afshar recommended disc-removal surgery. Three days later the surgery was performed and resulted in significant nerve damage and partial lower extremity paralysis.

There was a dispute in the evidence as to what warnings and explanations Dr Afshar gave to Miss Chester concerning the surgery. The trial judge accepted the patient's version of the conversation. She testified she had heard a lot of 'horror stories' about surgery and wished to know the risks it entailed, but that the doctor failed to inform her of them. One of those risks was an approximately 1-2 per cent chance of resulting nerve damage and/or paralysis. She did not mention paralysis nor did he. The doctor's reply to the risk inquiry of Miss Chester was characterised as 'a throw away line'.[2] The doctor answered the inquiry by stating that he 'had not crippled anyone yet'.[3]

Miss Chester further testified that had she been informed of the risk of nerve damage and paralysis that eventuated, she would not have gone forward with the surgery when she did, but rather would have first sought at least two further opinions on the need for surgery before undergoing it. The evidence showed that Miss Chester's condition resulted from contusion of a spinal nerve root, the cauda equina. Dr Afshar had never before or since had the same outcome in a long and distinguished career.

The doctor testified at trial that he had explained the small risk of cauda equina nerve root injury to Miss Chester and that he 'thought' he had told her of the risks

1 *Chester v. Afshar* [2004] 4 All E.R. 587 (hereafter '*Chester*').

2 At para 44.

3 *Id.*

of sensory disturbance or even paralysis resulting therefrom. However, he failed to persuade the trial judge that he had done so.

By the time of trial, six years post surgery, Miss Chester's disabilities had improved, but evidence on their extent was not presented. Rather, trial on the damages portion of her case was adjourned pending resolution of Dr Afshar's appeal of the court's liability determination.

The Decision at First Instance

Having accepted Miss Chester's evidence, the trial judge concluded that Dr Afshar had breached his duty of reasonable care by failing to disclose to his patient the 1-2 per cent risk of serious neurological injury from the recommended surgery; that the risk had eventuated despite the doctor's competent, non-negligent performance of the surgery; that a proper risk warning would have dissuaded Miss Chester from undergoing surgery when she did; and that, therefore, sufficient causation between breach of duty and injury had been established for her to recover damages.[4]

Dr Afshar appealed the finding that the injury was caused by his inadequate disclosure of surgical risks. The Court of Appeal dismissed this appeal.[5]

Setting the Stage for the House of Lords: Why was There a Duty to Disclose the Risk?

The Trial Court: Three Plausible Bases for Imposing the Duty

The trial court found Dr Afshar had a legal duty to inform his patient of the 1-2 per cent risk of serious neurological damage inherent in the spinal surgery he proposed. What does not emerge from the opinion in the House of Lords is *why* the doctor had such a duty. Nearly 20 years before, in their seminal, if muddied, opinion in *Sidaway*,[6] the Lords had found that a doctor had no legal duty to inform his patient of an almost identical risk: a 1-2 per cent risk of spinal cord injury, including paralysis. Why was this case different? Several possibilities present themselves. The undisclosed testimony of all of the medical experts may have concurred that, under the circumstances, no reasonable neurosurgeon would have failed to disclose the risk of spinal injury that eventuated, thereby triggering liability under the traditional rubric of the *Bolam* test.[7]

Alternatively, the parties to the dispute may have agreed that disclosure of the risk was warranted under the circumstances. The Court of Appeal noted that it was

4 The finding on causation is beyond the scope of this chapter.

5 [2002] EWCA Civ. 724, [2003] QB 356.

6 *Sidaway v. Bethlem Royal Hosp. Governors* [1985] A.C. 891, 1 All E.R. 643 (hereafter '*Sidaway*').

7 *Bolam v. Friern Hosp. Mgt. Committee* [1957] 1 W.L.R. 582 (hereafter '*Bolam*').

'common ground' during the trial that the defendant, in accordance with good medical practice, should have warned Miss Chester of the risk of spinal injury, including paralysis.[8] Dr Afshar's counsel was perhaps confident that the non-disclosure could not be said to have caused Miss Chester's injury, since the evidence did not foreclose the possibility that she would have decided, after further consultation, to undergo the same surgery, carrying the same magnitude of inherent risk, regardless of who may have performed it.[9] Most plausibly, the obligation to disclose was found, not because of the likelihood of the risk of neurological harm, but rather because of the specific inquiry about surgical risks made by Miss Chester which the doctor was duty-bound under established precedent, including *Sidaway*, to answer 'truthfully' and 'fully', but did not.[10]

The Court of Appeal: Good Professional Practice Sets the Standard for Answering the Patient's Risk Inquiries

The trial judge had found that the doctor led the patient to understand that there were no surgical risks of spinal damage, including paralysis. He found that this inadequate disclosure constituted negligence under *Bolam.*[11] The Court of Appeal upheld these findings. In doing so it quoted the trial judge's summary of Miss Chester's evidence, including this key exchange:

> I said I had heard a lot of horror stories about surgery and I wanted to know about the risks. The reply I got from Mr Afshar was: 'Well, I have never crippled anybody yet'. It was a throwaway line. He did add: 'Of course, you could be my first'.[12]

The trial judge had concluded that the doctor's response was not legally adequate. He relied upon the conclusions of Lords Bridge and Templeman in *Sidaway* that had Mrs Sidaway asked questions about the risks of surgery, she should have been informed of the 1-2 per cent risk of spinal injury. The trial judge found, in this respect, that the law relevant to the doctor's duty to warn of surgical risks was 'not controversial':[13] when a patient questions her doctor about the risks of the surgery proposed, the doctor must answer 'both truthfully and as fully as the questioner requires'.[14] Where the patient asks for more information about the surgery than the doctor has felt necessary to disclose, that information should be provided so that the

---

8 [2003] QB 356, 367, para15.

9 The opinion was principally concerned with this issue of legal causation, but it is beyond the scope of this chapter.

10 *Sidaway*, at p. 898 (Lord Bridge), at p. 902 (Lord Templeman).

11 [2003] QB 356, 368, paras 17-18. The Court of Appeal denied permission to appeal against the judge's factual findings on the doctor's failure to disclose the risks of surgery to Miss Chester.

12 [2003] QB 356, 360, para 6.

13 [2003] QB 356, 366, para 14.

14 *Ibid.*; *Sidaway*, at p. 898 (Lord Bridge).

patient may reach a 'balanced judgment in deciding whether or not to submit to the operation'.[15]

These *Sidaway* dicta would seem to impose a disclosure obligation on the doctor independent of, and supplemental to, his or her *Bolam* responsibilities to explain the risks posed by surgery that other reasonable physicians would normally disclose. However, in concluding its discussion, the Court of Appeal reiterated that doctors have the duty to inform their patients of the risks attendant to the proposed treatment *and* to answer questions put to them as to that treatment and its risks, 'such answers to be judged in the context of good professional practice'.[16] Thus, the Court of Appeal applied the *Bolam* standard of reasonable professional care both to the doctor's duty affirmatively to disclose risks and to answer questions about risks put by the patient. In this latter respect, its decision flew in the face of the dicta of Lords Bridge and Templeman in *Sidaway*. The Court of Appeal offered no explanation to temper this rather surprising conclusion, other than to say that 'good professional practice ... has tended to a greater degree of frankness over the years, with more respect being given to patient autonomy'.[17]

Pearce v. United Bristol Healthcare NHS Trust:[18] A Challenge Waiting to be Answered

In reaffirming that *Sidaway*, and *Bolam* before it, controlled the doctor's information disclosure duty to his or her patient, the Court of Appeal in *Chester* ignored Lord Woolf's groundbreaking opinion in *Pearce*. No attempt was made to challenge or distinguish its reasoning, despite its 'elephant in the room' legal presence.

In *Pearce*, the patient asserted that her doctor had negligently failed to disclose the small (0.2 per cent) risk of stillbirth from a recommended delay in inducing labor and delivery. The risk eventuated, but the doctor was found not to have been negligent in not disclosing it, given its likelihood and the patient's already distressed condition. In the course of affirming the trial judge, Lord Woolf embarked on what some have suggested was a 'creative'[19] analysis of the opinions in *Bolam, Sidaway* and *Bolitho*.[20] He then concluded that a synthesis of these decisions led to what was clearly a new standard of information disclosure. He characterised it in the following language:

> In a case where it is being alleged that a plaintiff has been deprived of the opportunity to make a proper decision as to what course he or she should take in relation to treatment, it seems to me to be the law, as indicated in the cases to which I have just referred, that if

15 *Ibid.*; *Sidaway*, at p. 902 (Lord Templeman).

16 [2003] QB 356, 379, para 47.

17 *Id.*

18 [1999] PIQR P.53, (1999) 48 B.M.L.R. 118 (CA) (hereafter '*Pearce*').

19 Grubb, A., 'Commentary', 1999 *Med. L. Rev.*, 63.

20 *Bolitho v. City and Hackney Health Authority* [1998] AC 232.

> there is a significant risk which would affect the judgment of a reasonable patient, then in the normal course it is the responsibility of a doctor to inform the patient of that significant risk, if the information is needed so that the patient can determine for him or herself as to what course he or she should adopt.[21]

This was a remarkably bold departure from established English precedent. *Pearce* did not change the traditional rule that breach of duty is determined by what a 'reasonable doctor' would have done in the circumstances. What it did, however, was obligate the 'reasonable doctor' to disclose to his or her patient that risk information which a reasonable patient would consider significant in making up his or her mind, not what other, reasonable, doctors might conclude the patient should be told.[22]

Lord Woolf recognised that it was not possible to talk in 'precise percentages' when seeking to define what is a 'significant risk'. Rather, the doctor was compelled to 'take into account all relevant considerations'.[23] Those included the patient's ability to comprehend the risk information to be imparted by the doctor, as well as the patient's physical and emotional state at the time.

Sidaway Recast

While the confusing mix of speeches in *Sidaway* invited their creative synthesis by Lord Woolf in support of his opinion, it can be said nonetheless that *Pearce* essentially adopted Lord Scarman's minority speech in *Sidaway*.[24] Lord Scarman had concluded that *Bolam* provided a satisfactory standard for judging the adequacy of diagnosis and treatment, but not for risk information disclosure to the patient:

> In my view the question whether or not the omission to warn constitutes a breach of the doctor's duty of care towards his patient is to be determined not exclusively by reference to the current state of responsible and competent professional opinion and practice at the time, though both are, of course, relevant considerations, but by the court's view as to whether the doctor in advising his patient gave the consideration which the law requires him to give to the right of the patient to make up her own mind in the light of the relevant information whether or not she will accept the treatment which he proposes.[25]

While Lord Scarman's views failed to convince his colleagues in *Sidaway*, there was language in the speeches of Lords Bridge and Templeman that Lord Woolf could point to for support. Lord Bridge qualified the application of *Bolam* to disclosure cases,

21 [1999] PIQR 53, at p. 59.

22 Grubb, *loc cit.*

23 [1999] PIQR 53, at p. 59.

24 [1985] A.C. 871, at pp. 876, 881-90 (the doctor has a duty to warn his or her patient of the material risks of treatment, the test of materiality being 'whether in the circumstances of the particular case the court is satisfied that a reasonable person in the patient's position would be likely to attach significance to the risk'. *Id.*, at p. 889).

25 *Ibid.*, at p. 876.

concluding that the trial court could find in certain circumstances that 'disclosure of a particular risk was so obviously necessary to an informed choice on the part of the patient that no reasonably prudent medical man would fail to make it'.[26] In such situations, illustrated by the 10 per cent risk of stroke in the Canadian case of *Reibl v. Hughes*,[27] disclosure would be required out of respect for the patient's 'right of decision'.[28] There was to be carved out from the protective mantle of *Bolam* disclosure of treatment risks that were 'substantial' and 'grave'. Lord Bridge thus recognised that the patient was 'entitled to decide for himself whether or not he will submit to a particular course of treatment',[29] after first being informed of risks that were both substantial – not remote – and grave – not inconsequential.

Lord Templeman also pointed out in *Sidaway* that risk disclosure was called for when it was necessary for the patient to consider it before reaching a 'balanced judgment' whether or not to submit to the treatment (surgery).[30] That could be the case, depending upon the 'nature or magnitude' of the risk,[31] or if it was one peculiar or 'special' to the patient.[32] Again referring to *Reibl v. Hughes* to illustrate his point, he concluded that the patient there should have been informed of the 4 per cent risk of death and of the 10 per cent risk of paralysis posed by the surgery, 'in order to be able to form a balanced judgment in deciding whether or not to submit to the operation'.[33] Yet he too offered no clear standard by which to judge future cases.

Though without question imposing a definite restriction on the unimpeded reliance upon *Bolam* in disclosure cases, these tantalising qualifications failed to chart its extent or the standard by which to determine its application. After *Sidaway*, UK jurisprudence and doctors were left adrift. Doctors, in general, could disclose or not disclose treatment risks based upon the practices of their peers. However, certain 'significant' risks had to be disclosed. For example, a 4 per cent risk of death was to be disclosed, as was a 10 per cent risk of paralysis, but, a 2 per cent risk of paralysis need not be disclosed.[34] What of a 5 per cent risk of paralysis? If the risk was 'substantial' and 'grave', or 'special' to the patient, it was to be disclosed, regardless of professional opinion to the contrary. However, no meaningful criteria were given by which to define those exceptions beyond the two examples cited from *Reibl*.

---

26 *Ibid.*, at p. 900 (Lord Keith concurred with Lord Bridge).

27 (1980) 114 DLR (3d) 1.

28 [1985] A.C. at 900.

29 *Ibid.*, at p. 897.

30 *Ibid.*, at p. 902.

31 *Id.*

32 *Ibid.*, at p. 903.

33 *Id.*

34 All the medical experts in *Sidaway*, including the plaintiff's, testified that non-disclosure under the circumstances was accepted as proper by a responsible body of neurosurgical opinion and neither the trial nor the appeal Judges suggested overriding that opinion should be entertained.

In *Bolitho*,[35] though not a disclosure case, some further articulation of the qualification of *Bolam* wrought by *Sidaway* was offered. The court had the power, it was held, to reject expert medical evidence where it concluded that it was not reasonable or responsible opinion. Such evidence, to be accepted by the court, had to be capable of 'withstanding logical analysis'.[36] The court was the ultimate arbiter of whether the practice of 'reasonable' physicians was adequate to set the standard of care in the circumstances of the case before the court. If the court did not retain this authority, then it abdicated to the profession the power to determine the standard of care by which to judge its own practices and whether or not it had been breached in the particular case at hand: a rather clear case of putting the fox in the hen house!

Bolitho was a further chink in the armour of *Bolam*. However, it did little to resolve the uncertainty left in the wake of *Sidaway*. It was left for *Pearce*[37] to jump-start that process.

Post-Pearce and Pre-House of Lords

Until the arrival of *Pearce*, few doubted that the doctor's duty to disclose risk information was to be judged by the same *Bolam*, reasonable practice standard applicable to her or his duty to diagnose and treat. While *Sidaway* and *Bolitho* had imposed the vague limits of logic and responsibility upon the profession, no one doubted the continuing viability of the professional standard by which to judge negligence alleged in such cases.[38] For example, as Lord Caplan stated in *Moyes*,[39]

> I can read nothing in the majority view in *Sidaway* which suggests that the extent and quality of warning to be given by a doctor to his patient should not in the last resort be governed by medical criteria.

Pearce implicitly recognised the confusion in the *Sidaway* speeches and perhaps saw that as exhibiting a lack of resolve, or a discomfiture with the result, by the majority. Lord Woolf quite boldly seized upon the language 'qualifying' *Bolam* found in both *Sidaway* and *Bolitho* in reaching his judgment.

When *Chester* came to the Court of Appeal four years after *Pearce*, no published decision had rejected or accepted *Pearce* as correctly stating the law. The silence was becoming deafening. Yet, despite the obvious significance of *Pearce,* and its rather apparent departure from a strict reading of earlier precedent, the Court of Appeal in *Chester* choose to ignore it. In doing so, and in reaching a contrary legal conclusion on the standard by which to judge the doctor's duty of disclosure, the

---

35 [1998] A.C. 232, [1997] 3 WLR 1151.

36 3 WLR 1151, at p. 1160 (Lord Browne-Wilkinson).

37 *Pearce v. United Bristol Healthcare Trust* (1999) 48 BMLR 118

38 For an interesting comment, see Mason, K. and Brodie, D., '*Bolam, Bolam – Wherefore Art Thou Bolam?*', Vol. 9 *Edinburgh Law Review*, 298–306 (May 2005).

39 *Moyes v. Lothian Health Board* 1990 SLT 444, 449.

Court of Appeal in *Chester* set the stage for the House of Lords. Now there was good reason for the Lords to opine not only on the question of legal causation expressly raised, but also presented to them was the opportunity, if they chose to accept it, to clarify the standard of information disclosure to be applied to the physician. The Lords took advantage of that opportunity.

The Decision in the House of Lords

Why did the Lords feel Compelled to Consider the Scope of the Doctor's Duty to Disclose?

The central question on appeal to the Lords was one of causation: since Miss Chester had not ruled out proceeding with the same surgery, which carried the same risks, had she been informed of the risks of spinal injury and paralysis, how could the doctor's failure to disclose these risks be said to have legally caused the injury that eventuated? Yet the Lords felt compelled to first address the scope of the duty to disclose before deciding the issue of legal causation. Lord Hope justified this on the basis that damages are only awarded in negligence actions if the claimant's loss falls within the scope of the defendant's duty of care.[40] Therefore, it was first necessary to delineate the scope of Dr Afshar's duty to warn Miss Chester of the risks of surgery before it could be ascertained if the breach of that duty caused her ensuing injuries. One must wonder, however, how essential this was and whether the Lords rather saw *Chester* as presenting them with the opportunity to clarify what duty of information disclosure was to be applied in such cases. Was *Pearce* to be accepted, or rejected or *Sidaway* reaffirmed?

What Was the Basis of the Doctor's Duty to Warn of Risks?

Although the Lords split 3–2 on the central question of causation, there was little disagreement on the scope and importance of the doctor's duty to disclose the risk of spinal injury, including paralysis, to Miss Chester. Lord Bingham, in dissent, said Dr. Afshar was duty bound to warn of this 'small but unavoidable risk' and that 'the existence of such a duty is not in doubt'.[41] Lord Hoffman, also in dissent, recognised failing to warn the patient of risk 'was an affront to her personality and leaves her feeling aggrieved'.[42] Lord Steyn said the patient had a 'prima facie right to be informed by a surgeon of a small, but well established, risk of serious injury'.[43] Lord Walker said that the doctor's duty to warn was closely connected to the need for the patient's consent and provided the foundation for it.[44] Finally, Lord Hope said it was without dispute that the patient had a right to be warned of the known, small

40 Para 51.

41 Para 5.

42 Para 33.

43 Para 16.

44 Para 93.

risk of paralysis.[45] The duty to warn the patient was so that she could make up her own mind whether or not to consent to the surgery proposed.[46]

What Precedent did the Lords Rely Upon to Determine the Scope of the Duty to Warn?

On first reading of *Chester*, one is immediately likely to ask; why was a similar risk of similar spinal harm a legal obligation of the surgeon to disclose in *Chester*, but not in *Sidaway*? The basic difference of course was that Ms Chester asked and Mrs Sidaway did not! The Lords could have unequivocally answered this question and reconciled both decisions by pointing out, as did the trial judge, that the doctor had violated his duty as established in *Sidaway*, to answer the patient's risk inquiries 'truthfully' and as 'fully' as she required to be properly informed.[47] However, the Lords did not choose to do that.

The Acceptance of Pearce *and the Marginalising of* Sidaway

Lord Steyn's speech is the clearest in its acceptance of a new standard for risk disclosure. First, as do Lords Walker[48] and Hope[49] later in the decision, he makes clear that the rights of the patient to information allowing an informed decision and the duty of the doctor to provide that information are correlative.[50] Whether a patient has made an informed choice is dependent upon, and goes hand in glove with, what information she has been given upon which to base that choice. In perhaps the most critical passage in the decision, he concludes:

> How a surgeon's duty to warn a patient of a serious risk of injury fits into the tort of negligence was explained by Lord Woolf, MR, with the agreement of Roch and Mummery LJJ, in *Pearce v. United Bristol Healthcare NHS Trust* [1999] PIQR P53. After reviewing a trilogy of decisions in *Bolam*, *Sidaway* and *Bolitho* [citations omitted], Lord Woolf observed, at Page 59: 'In a case where it is being alleged that a plaintiff has been deprived of the opportunity to make a proper decision as to what course he or she should take in relation to treatment, it seems to me to be the law, as indicated in the cases to which I have just referred, that if there is a significant risk which would affect the judgment of a reasonable patient, then in the normal course it is the responsibility of a doctor to inform the patient of that significant risk, if the information is needed so that the patient can determine for him or herself as to what course he or she should adopt.'[51]

---

45 Para 48.

46 Para 55.

47 See [2003] QB 356, 366, paras 14-15.

48 [2004] 4 All E.R. 587, para 93 ('The [doctor's] advice is the foundation of the [patient's] consent').

49 *Ibid.*, para 55 (the right and the duty 'go hand in hand').

50 *Ibid.*, para 14.

51 *Ibid.*, para 15.

With little more than a single sentence, it seems Lord Steyn approved *Pearce* as stating the relevant legal standard.[52] In so doing, he changed the doctor's duty of disclosure in Britain from one largely based upon professional standards of practice, on *Bolam* and *Hunter v. Hanley*,[53] to one largely based upon the needs of the reasonable patient.

With no fanfare, no apology and no soul searching of any kind, *Pearce*, which essentially marginalized *Sidaway*, the heretofore leading case in the field, was accepted by Lords Steyn, Hope and Walker as the law. This seems as remarkable as was Lord Woolf's earlier holding in *Pearce*. In both instances there was no suggestion that *Bolam* and *Sidaway* presented any obstacle to adoption of this new standard of disclosure. Rather, the implication in both opinions is that the emergence of the 'reasonable patient' standard of disclosure is a natural outgrowth of *Bolam*, *Sidaway* and *Bolitho*. Although the speeches in *Sidaway* did seem to give something to everyone, there is no doubting that *Pearce* and now *Chester* have dramatically changed the inquiry in medical disclosure cases from what physicians reasonably think the patient should be told to what reasonable patients in the circumstances would want to be told.

Lord Steyn offered several justifications for his conclusion. First, 'medical paternalism no longer rules and a patient has a prima facie right to be informed by a surgeon of a small, but well established, risk of serious injury as a result of surgery'.[54] Second, the patient's right to be warned appropriately is 'an important right which should be given effective protection whenever possible'.[55] Third, requiring the surgeon to obtain the patient's 'informed consent'[56] makes the occurrence of a risk that is unacceptable to the patient less likely because if the patient is properly informed he or she is less likely to give consent to the treatment posing that risk.[57] In addition, it 'ensures that due respect is given to the autonomy and dignity of each patient'.[58] Finally, had the patient been warned of the small, but serious risk of paralysis, the actual injury the patient wished to avoid would not have occurred when it did.[59]

Lord Steyn found no need to discuss or distinguish *Bolam* or *Sidaway* from the facts of *Chester*. The only reference to either case is his notation that Lord Woolf had reviewed them before adopting the holding in *Pearce*.[60] Lord Hope, to the contrary, spends considerable time characterizing the holding in *Sidaway* and its significance

52 With the express approval of Lords Hope and Walker, *Ibid.*, paras 89, 90.

53 (1955) S.C. 200, (1955) S.L.T. 213.

54 *Chester* [2004] 4 All E.R. 587, para 16.

55 Para 17.

56 Para 18.

57 *Id.*

58 *Id.*

59 Para 19.

60 Para 15.

to *Chester.*[61] He suggests that the majority in *Sidaway* recognised the 'logical force' of the reasonable patient disclosure standard represented by the American decision in *Canterbury v. Spence*,[62] but rejected it in favor of the *Bolam* reasonable physician standard. However, he goes on to emphasise that all the speeches in *Sidaway* recognised the 'fundamental importance of the patient's right to decide for herself whether to submit to proposed treatment'. He then points out that the more difficult it is for a patient to prove breach of duty in the disclosure context, the less likely it is that the law of informed consent can be said to protect patient autonomy.[63] If that is a worthwhile goal of the law, then the bar for the patient to cross to prove breach of duty should not be set too high. Surely this suggests a preference for the reasonable patient standard of *Canterbury*. For, after all, the reasonable doctor standard, before the gloss added by *Sidaway* and *Bolitho*, allowed the doctors to place the bar as high as they wished. Lord Hope concludes by suggesting the need for a 'more substantive "right" to truly informed consent for patients'.[64]

Lord Hope's comments on the doctor's disclosure duty leave us with some uncertainty as to where he stands on *Sidaway*'s continuing viability. He seems to be saying that the reasonable patient standard is the preferable standard by which to promote and protect patient autonomy, that all the Judges in *Sidaway* recognised its 'logical force', and that it provides the means to ensure that the patient's consent to, or refusal of, proposed treatment will be informed. These suppositions seem corroborated by Lord Hope's express approval of Lord Steyn's and Lord Walker's speeches.[65] In effect it can be suggested that his speech lets down *Sidaway* gently; not rejecting it outright, but rather pointing out its emphasis on the patient, not the physician, as the ultimate treatment decisionmaker. Even Lord Walker distances himself from *Sidaway* by pointing out that the importance of patient autonomy has been 'more and more widely recognised' in the 20 years since *Sidaway*.[66] It appears that little has been left of *Sidaway* by the analyses of Lords Steyn, Hope and Walker in *Chester*. *Chester* has effectively marginalised *Sidaway*'s application of *Bolam* in the disclosure context. *Pearce*, on the other hand, comes away intact, unscathed and expressly approved.

It is perhaps worth recalling here that in the first reported case applying the *Bolam* standard to a disclosure case, the court was careful to link the doctor's professional duty to the patient's right to come to an 'informed decision' whether or not to consent to the treatment proposed.[67] It was this linkage and tension between the doctor's duty of reasonable care and the patient's right to exercise a truly informed consent that eventually required the courts to choose which value was the most fundamental.

61 Paras 51-9.

62 (1972 DC) 464 F.2d 772; *Chester*, at para 53.

63 *Chester*, para 57.

64 Para 58.

65 Para 89.

66 Para 92.

67 *Chatterton v. Gerson* [1981] 1 All E.R. 257, [1981] Q.B. 432, at pp. 441-2.

Chester, both in its acceptance of *Pearce* and in the majority speeches, seems to have resolved any doubts that it is the patient's right to be properly informed that must predominate over accepted standards of medical practice that do not assure that result. Medical evidence will continue to play a vital role in such cases, defining the severity and likelihood of the risks posed by treatment. This medical evidence will undoubtedly determine the 'significance' of the risks posed in most cases. However, the medical evaluation of the risks posed no longer dictates whether disclosure must be made to the patient. Rather, the doctor must 'take into account all the relevant considerations', including the patient's mental capacity and her physical and emotional condition, and disclose the risk information that a reasonable patient under the circumstances would consider significant, would want to be told to reach an informed decision on treatment.[68] Patients make decisions based upon what they think is important, on weighing risks and benefits, which does not necessarily comport with what physicians, who administer the treatment but do not personally assume the risks, will think is important or even determinative. The result is that it will ultimately be for the factfinder – judge or jury – to determine if a reasonable person would attach significance to particular medical information in coming to an informed decision whether or not to consent to that treatment and therefore whether it should have been disclosed.

In reaching their decision in *Chester*, the Lords came to a conclusion remarkably similar to noteworthy precedent in other parts of the common law world.

The Influence of Other Common Law Decisions: Australia, Canada and the US

The US: Canterbury v. Spence[69]

The groundbreaking decision of the US Court of Appeals for the District of Columbia in *Canterbury* was the precedent which occupied much of the time of Lord Bridge for the majority and Lord Scarman in dissent in *Sidaway*. Like Ms Sidaway and Ms Chester after him, Mr Canterbury underwent spinal surgery without being informed of the 1 per cent risk of paralysis inherent in the procedure. Like Ms Sidaway, Mr Canterbury did not inquire about the risks posed. Like Ms Chester, Mr Canterbury's mother did inquire if the surgery was serious and Dr Spence replied, 'not anymore than any other operation'.[70] The claimant in fact sustained partial paralysis and sued for negligent failure to disclose risk. In language strikingly similar to that in *Pearce* and *Chester, Canterbury* concluded, '[a]dequate disclosure and informed consent are, of course, two sides of the same coin – the former a *sine qua non* of the latter'.[71]

68 *Pearce* [1999] PIQR, at p. 53, at p. 59.
69 *Canterbury v. Spence* (1972 D.C. App.) 464 F.2d 727.
70 464 F.2d, at p. 777.
71 464 F.2d, at p. 780.

In rejecting the 'reasonable physician' standard, *Canterbury* concluded that 'respect for the patient's right of self-determination ... demands a standard set by law for physicians rather than one which physicians may or may not impose upon themselves'.[72] The patient had to be provided with sufficient information to enable him or her to make an informed or intelligent choice. That in turn meant that information 'material' or 'significant' to such a choice was to be disclosed.[73] An objective standard for judging materiality was adopted, whereby a risk was deemed material and to be disclosed:

> when a reasonable person, in what the physician knows or [reasonably] should know to be the patient's position, would be likely to attach significance to the risk or cluster of risks in deciding whether or not to forego the proposed therapy.[74]

Factors to be considered in evaluating risk were the inherent and potential hazards of the procedure, the alternatives to it, the incidence of injury and the degree of harm threatened.[75] In *Canterbury* whether the small but serious risk of paralysis should have been disclosed was open to reasonable debate. Therefore, it was for the trier of fact to decide whether on all the evidence it was material information that should have been disclosed.[76]

Canada: Reibl v. Hughes[77]

The decision of the Supreme Court of Canada in *Reibl* figured prominently in *Sidaway* as well. Lord Bridge saw the 10 per cent risk of stroke from surgery acknowledged in *Reibl* as a 'substantial risk of grave adverse consequences' that the court was entitled to assume no reasonably prudent doctor would fail to disclose.[78] Lord Templeman felt similarly, concluding that to reach a 'balanced judgment' about the treatment proposed it was incumbent on a surgeon, as in *Reibl*, to disclose both a 4 per cent risk of death and a 10 per cent risk of stroke the proposed operation posed.[79]

Reibl, like *Canterbury* before it, concluded that the doctor was under a duty to disclose the material risks of proposed surgery to his patient. Materiality was a question of fact for the jury. It was not a question that could be decided on the basis

---

72 464 F.2d, at p. 784.

73 464 F.2d, at pp. 786-7.

74 464 F.2d, at p. 787, citing Waltz and Scheuneman, 'Informed Consent to Therapy', 64 *N.W.U.L.*, Rev. 628, at p. 640.

75 *Id.*

76 For a similar decision reached by the California Supreme Court, see *Cobbs v. Grant* (1972 Cal.) 8 Cal.3d 229, at p. 245 ('the patient's right of self-decision is the measure of the physician's duty to reveal').

77 *Reibl v. Hughes* [1980] 2 S.C.R. 880, 114 D.L.R. (3d) 1.

78 *Sidaway* [1985] A.C. 871, 900.

79 *Ibid.*, at p. 903.

of expert medical evidence alone.[80] This was because the duty was imposed so that the 'patient's right to know what risks are involved' could be protected.[81] Only in this way could the patient's right to decide for herself or himself whether to consent to the proposed treatment be safeguarded. Medical evidence was, of course, relevant to show the magnitude of the risk based upon its likelihood or frequency and its gravity.

The Canadian Supreme Court, in a companion case to *Reibl, Hopp v. Lepp*,[82] further refined its holdings. The doctor must answer specific questions put by the patient, disclose the nature of the procedure, its gravity, any material risks it posed and any special or unusual risks it posed. Mere possibilities of risk which ordinarily would not be material to the patient's decision and therefore need not be disclosed became material risks to be disclosed if their occurrence would cause serious consequences such as stroke, paralysis or death.

Australia: Rogers v. Whittaker[83]

Things were quiet in the Commonwealth for a time after *Sidaway*. Then came the decision of the High Court of Australia in *Rogers*. It was a significant decision, not only because it was handed down by Australia's well-regarded High Court, but also because, unlike *Canterbury* and *Reibl*, it was decided after *Sidaway*, evaluated the suitability of the modified *Bolam* disclosure standard adopted by *Sidaway* and rejected it.

Ms Whittaker underwent eye surgery in the hope of regaining sight in her right eye. After surgery the right eye was unimproved, inflammation developed in her left eye and she lost all sight in it as well. She sued Dr Rogers for negligence and the trial judge found in her favour, concluding that the surgery was performed without negligence, but that the doctor had improperly failed to disclose the risk that eventuated. Though the risk was small, as in *Chester* to come, the patient had expressed a desire to know the risks of and complications after surgery, including any risks to her 'good' eye.[84] The Court of Appeal dismissed the doctor's appeal and special leave was granted to appeal to the High Court.

The appellant argued that since the evidence disclosed that a reasonable and responsible body of medical practitioners would not have disclosed the small risk of total blindness that eventuated, *Bolam* and *Sidaway* compelled a judgment of non-liability.[85] However, the High Court noted that earlier, lower court decisions had discarded the *Bolam* principle where the failure of the doctor to adequately

---

80 [1980] 2 S.C.R. 880, at p. 895; 114 D.L.R. (3d), at p. 13.

81 *Id.*

82 [1980] 13 C.C.L.T. 66 (S.C.C.).

83 *Rogers v. Whittaker* [1992] 175 C.L.R. 479, 109 A.L.R. 625.

84 175 C.L.R., at pp. 482, 491. The occurrence rate was only slightly greater than 1 in 14,000 (less than .001 per cent).

85 There was also evidence from equally responsible practitioners that they would have disclosed the risk to the patient, 175 C.L.R., at p. 484.

disclose risk was at issue. Rather, they had adopted the principle that it was for the court to determine the appropriate standard of care, taking into account the medical practice, but giving 'paramount consideration' to the patient's right to make up his or her own mind.[86] The *Rogers* court felt that the qualification of *Bolam* brought about by *Sidaway* was inadequate and only protected the patient and gave her a claim if she asked the right questions, but not where a reasonable patient would, in the circumstances, have wanted the risk information that the physician failed to disclose.

Whether a patient had been given all the relevant information so as to allow a meaningful choice to be made regarding whether to undergo treatment was not to be decided by medical practice, because it was not 'a question the answer to which depends upon medical standards or medical practices'.[87] The question was whether the doctor had warned the patient of the material risks inherent in the treatment proposed. The majority[88] concluded:

> a risk is material if, in the circumstances of the particular case, a reasonable person in the patient's position, if warned of the risk, would be likely to attach significance to it or if the medical practitioner is or should reasonably be aware that the particular patient, if warned of the risk, would be likely to attach significance to it.[89]

In so holding, the High Court imposed upon the doctor both an objective disclosure obligation – where a reasonable patient would consider the information material – and a subjective disclosure obligation – where the doctor actually knows, or reasonably should know, that his or her particular patient would consider the information material in making the treatment decision. The disclosure rule announced in *Pearce* and approved in *Chester* talked only in terms of the former situation, the 'reasonable patient', but explicit in *Chester* is that the doctor should have known his particular patient would have considered the small but serious risk of paralysis posed by the surgery to be material information. If the doctor must disclose what the hypothetical reasonable patient would want to know, then how can he or she not have the concomitant obligation to disclose what the doctor should reasonably know his or her patient would want to know? Surely these are two sides of the same coin.

Rogers was not mentioned in *Pearce* or *Chester*, but it is hard not to characterise it as another elephant in the closet. The Court had quite clearly elected not to follow *Bolam* and *Sidaway*, but rather to prefer Lord Scarman's dissent in *Sidaway*. It set the stage for both *Pearce* and *Chester*.[90] It seems unlikely that it was not in the minds of the Law Lords in *Chester*.

---

86 175 C.L.R., at pp. 487-8; see also, *F. v. R.* (1983) 33 S.A.S.R. 189, 193-4 (So. Aust. Supreme Ct.).

87 175 C.L.R., at pp. 489-90.

88 Mason, CJ, Brennan, Dawson, Toohey and McHugh JJ.

89 *Ibid.*, at p. 490.

90 See also *Rosenberg v. Percival* [2001] 205 C.L.R. 434, 439. *Chester* did acknowledge, of course, its heavy reliance on *Chappel v. Hart* (1998) 195 C.L.R. 232, in regards to the

Conclusion

Chester is heralded principally as a case extending the rules for establishing causation. Certainly the Law Lords saw it as the 'central question' raised.[91] However, it may be that *Chester* will prove to be more noteworthy for defining the scope of the doctor's duty to warn his or her patient of the risks inherent or special in the treatment being proposed. By adopting the standard for disclosure set out in *Pearce*, the majority in *Chester* have changed the British law of medical negligence in a material way. No longer can the reasonable doctor standard of *Bolam*, as applied in the disclosure of risk context by *Sidaway*, be said to be the law.[92] Rather, the UK position seems now essentially indistinguishable from that of Canada and Australia.[93] The reasonable patient standard seems to have been accepted. Surely there is no real difference between requiring disclosure of a treatment risk that 'a reasonable person in the patient's position, if warned of the risk, would be likely to attach significance to'[94] and disclosing a 'significant risk which would affect the judgment of a reasonable patient ... if the information is needed so that the patient can determine ... what course he or she should adopt'.[95] Both standards are driven by what the reasonable patient would want to be told, not by what the reasonable physician might decide to tell the patient.

Sidaway and *Bolam* have been effectively relegated to the rear of the field. They will continue to govern the identification of treatment risks of which a prudent physician should be aware, including their likelihood, frequency and severity. After *Chester* they no longer control what the patient should be told. Still, in many cases the old *Bolam-Sidaway* standard and the new *Pearce-Chester* standard will be the same: the practice of reasonable doctors will be to tell reasonable patients what they would want to be told. However, in those cases where the trier of fact concludes that the patient reasonably would have wanted and was therefore entitled to be told more, but was not, out of respect for her right of 'autonomy and dignity',[96] liability for negligent non-disclosure will follow and *Bolam-Sidaway* will provide the doctor with no refuge.

The result is unlikely to be earth shaking. The medical negligence plaintiff still faces significant hurdles in all but the most clear-cut cases of liability, damage and causation. It can be hoped and expected, however, that patients will be better informed, feel more involved in their treatment decisions, and that physicians will

---

fundamental causation question before the House of Lords.

91 *Chester v. Afshar, supra cit.*, paras 1 (Lord Bingham), 11-13, 24 (Lord Steyn), 28-9 (Lord Hoffman), 40, 51 (Lord Hope) and 90-1 (Lord Walker).

92 See Mason and Brodie, *supra cit.* ('The conclusion is forced that the professional standard of disclosure of risk has now been displaced by a test based on patients' rights – *Bolam* has left the medical jurisprudential arena', at p. 302.)

93 See *Grubb, supra cit.*, at p. 63.

94 See note 88, *supra*.

95 See note 51, *supra*.

96 *Chester v. Afshar, supra cit.*, para 24.

of necessity be more connected to the reasonable hopes and fears of their patients. It is to be hoped that the result will be better, more individualised, more satisfying medicine for both patient and physician.

Chapter 17

'Informed Consent' to Medical Treatment and the Impotence of Tort

Emily Jackson

Introduction

JK Mason has undoubtedly been responsible, along with a handful of other innovative academics, for the development of medical law as an academic subject in its own right, and not simply as a branch of tort law. In my view, this development has been welcome for a number of reasons. Partly, of course, it is because the field of medical law extends far beyond the narrow bounds of tort law, into subjects as diverse as end of life decision making and the regulation of stem cell research. In addition, however, I think that tort law itself sits increasingly uneasily with the reality of medical practice. The government has recently acknowledged this by announcing its intention to introduce legislation which will abandon, at least in part, the clinical negligence system.[1] But, as will become apparent, I believe that tort law's failings extend beyond the well-rehearsed defects of the 'blame-culture' which results from negligence's adversarial response to adverse events.[2]

The purpose of this chapter is to criticise tort law's approach to what is often referred to as the doctrine of 'informed consent'. Informed consent is commonly used as a shorthand for two distinct duties: the duty to obtain the patient's consent before treatment, and the duty to ensure that the patient has been properly informed about its risks and benefits.[3] In the UK, the duty to obtain a patient's consent is protected by the tort of battery, while the duty to ensure that a patient has been given enough information (whatever that might mean) is part of the doctor's ordinary duty of care, meaning that a failure to offer sufficient information might ground an action in negligence. My intention in this chapter is to argue that neither of these two causes of action is capable of capturing all of the interests which are at stake when patients are deprived of information that may be necessary before they can reach an informed decision about whether to consent to a proposed course of treatment. In fact, both

1 NHS Redress Bill 2005.

2 Department of Health Expert Group, *An Organisation with a Memory* (2000); Bristol Royal Infirmary Inquiry, *Learning from Bristol: The Report of the Public Inquiry into Children's Heart Surgery at the Bristol Royal Infirmary*, 1984-1995 (HMSO 2001) Cm 5207.

3 Skegg, P.D.G., 'English Medical Law and "Informed Consent": An Antipodean Assessment and Alternative', *Medical Law Review*, vol. 7 (1999) 135-65, at p. 138.

suffer from such significant defects that I will advocate abandoning tort law as the mechanism through which a patient's interest in the provision of information is protected.

While the competent adult patient's right to make decisions about her medical treatment is robustly protected by English law, the patient's interest in access to sufficient information with which to make these medical decisions has received much less protection. In the first section of this chapter, I criticise the courts' approach to cases in which patients have claimed that they were not provided with enough information before consenting to a particular procedure. As is well documented, there is little prospect of a patient bringing a successful action in either battery or negligence for inadequate disclosure of information. The judiciary has been hostile to the use of the tort of battery in all but the most exceptional circumstances, and a claimant alleging negligent disclosure faces two significant obstacles: first, the courts' definition of the relevant standard of care makes it extremely difficult to establish that a doctor's nondisclosure was negligent, and second, proving causation is, as I explain below, virtually impossible.

Yet unlike many commentators, I do not believe that the solution is to tinker with the tort of negligence in order to make it more 'patient-orientated'. Abandoning the *Bolam*[4] test in favour of the so-called 'prudent patient' test for the standard of care might be a step in the right direction, but it would leave intact some of the more fundamental reasons why negligence is not the answer here. Even if the courts were to adopt a subjective test for both the standard of care and causation, the tort of negligence would remain an inadequate tool with which to protect patients' interests in access to relevant information.

In the second half of this chapter, I expand upon this claim, arguing that we should remember *why* it is important to give patients information. Patients need information in order to make informed choices about their care, *not* in order to protect themselves against medical accidents. Yet the tort of negligence – bizarrely in my view – effectively provides inadequately informed patients who can jump through the hurdles of proving breach and causation with strict liability for medical mishaps, but cannot offer a remedy for the real wrong suffered by a patient who was deprived of material information before embarking upon medical treatment. I conclude that tort law has proved to be largely irrelevant in determining what information doctors should provide to their patients.

The Failings of Tort

Battery

Trespass to the person can be both a tort (battery) and a crime (assault). A patient's consent to medical treatment will only absolve the medical practitioner from liability

4 *Bolam v. Friern Hospital Management Committee* [1957] WLR 582.

in battery for unlawful touching if the consent is 'real': the patient must know what she is consenting to. If the patient consented to a procedure which is wholly different from that which was in fact performed, there was no real consent, and the doctor will have committed the tort of battery, and the crime of assault. An example cited by Bristow J in *Chatterton v. Gerson*[5] was a case from the 1940s in which a boy was admitted to hospital in Salford for a tonsillectomy, but, due to an administrative error, he was circumcised instead. According to Bristow J, the appropriate cause of action here would have been battery.

Trespass to the person can also be a criminal offence. In *R v. Tabassum*,[6] T – who had no medical qualifications at all – was convicted of indecent assault after he persuaded the three complainants to consent to him showing them how to carry out a breast self-examination. Each complainant said they had only consented because they thought T had medical qualifications or relevant training. The Court of Appeal upheld his conviction on the grounds that 'there was no true consent'.

But while these sorts of extreme examples of non-consensual touching are relatively straightforward, the problem lies in working out when information about a proposed treatment is so fundamental that, without it, consent must be regarded as ineffective. For example, could the non-disclosure of information about the risks or side effects of treatment ever vitiate the patient's consent?

The advantage of an action in battery is that it is not necessary to establish that any physical harm has been caused by the doctor's inadequate disclosure. As we see below, causation represents an almost insuperable obstacle to most claimants' actions in negligence because of the need to prove that proper disclosure would have prompted the patient to reject the proposed course of treatment. Instead, a successful action in battery will lead to compensation for the dignitary harm of being treated without consent. This more accurately protects the patient's interest in self-determination, because it is the violation of the patient's right to make an informed choice which is being compensated, rather than the materialisation – through nobody's fault – of some remote risk. Patients who are inadequately informed about an alternative treatment option will only be able to recover in negligence if the treatment that they received goes wrong and they suffer physical injury as a result. Yet arguably, a patient's right to make an informed choice may have been compromised regardless of whether she also happens to have suffered physical injury.

Despite appearing to go more precisely to the infringement of patient autonomy involved in depriving patients of material information, judges have tended to confine the use of battery to the extremely rare case in which the patient was not told about the nature of the treatment she received. Provided that the patient was informed 'in broad terms' about the proposed treatment and agreed to it, her consent will be effective and no action in battery will lie. In part, this judicial hostility to the use of battery in medical cases flows from the assumption that battery involves *deliberately* inflicted injury. A doctor who fails to tell a patient about a small inherent risk posed

5 [1981] QB 432.

6 [2000] 2 Cr App Rep 328 (CA).

by a proposed course of treatment does not intend to injure her. And because a battery will often also be an assault, judges have been reluctant to criminalise by association a doctor's well-meaning but misguided decision to withhold information from a patient.[7]

But even if judges could be persuaded to carve out an expanded role for the tort of battery, there are other reasons why battery would continue to protect a patient's interest in being provided with relevant information before making a decision about her medical treatment inadequately. An action in battery is possible only if there has been some sort of physical contact between doctor and patient. But while medical treatment does commonly involve touching, this is not always the case. The prescription of drugs, for example, does not involve any physical contact, and so the tort of battery could not offer a remedy to a patient who was inadequately informed about a medicine's side effects. Similarly, a patient who is not told about the availability of a more appropriate therapeutic option, and who opts for no treatment at all rather than take up the doctor's unacceptable suggested option, has not been touched, and again could have no action in battery.

Negligence

There are three stages to an action in negligence. First, the defendant must owe the claimant a duty of care of the scope contended for, second he must breach that duty, and third, the breach must have caused the claimant's damage. The first requirement is easily satisfied in non-disclosure cases. It is axiomatic that doctors owe a duty of care to their patients, and it is clear that providing information is one aspect of the doctor's duty towards her patients. In relation to non-disclosure cases, it is the requirement to establish that the doctor's duty has been breached, and the need to prove causation which cause difficulties. Let us examine both stages in turn.

The Standard of Care

A doctor will only be found to have breached her duty if she has fallen below the standard of care which patients are entitled to expect. But how is that standard defined? In the context of non-disclosure, there are generally thought to be two contrasting possibilities: the 'reasonable doctor' test, and the 'prudent patient' test. The 'reasonable doctor' test is effectively the *Bolam* test, and its clearest expression in relation to information disclosure comes from Lord Diplock's judgement in *Sidaway v. Governors of the Bethlem Royal Hospital and the Maudsley Hospital*,[8] a case in which the House of Lords rejected Mrs Sidaway's claim that her doctor's failure to warn her about an operation's small risk of damage to her spinal column had been negligent. Lord Diplock thought that the *Bolam* test applied to all aspects of

7 Robertson, G., 'Informed Consent to Medical Treatment', 97 *Law Quarterly Review*, (1981) 102-26, at p. 123.

8 [1985] 2 WLR 480.

a doctor's duty of care, and saw no reason to treat advice differently from diagnosis and treatment: the doctor's disclosure should therefore be judged by its conformity with responsible medical practice.

The 'prudent patient' test, which has gained favour in some states in the US, and in Canada, Australia and New Zealand, instead suggests that doctors should be under a duty to disclose risks which are material to the reasonable patient. Probably its most famous formulation is taken from the 1972 US case *Canterbury v. Spence*:[9]

> In broad outline, we agree that '[a] risk is thus material when a reasonable person, in what the physician knows or should know to be the patient's position, would be likely to attach significance to the risk or cluster of risks in deciding whether or not to forego the proposed therapy'.

The clearest advocate of the 'prudent patient' test in the UK was Lord Scarman in *Sidaway*. He argued that the doctor's duty of disclosure arose from the patient's 'basic human right' to make her own medical decisions, and was persuaded that the common law should follow the example set in cases from Canada and the US, and adopt a 'prudent patient' test: the doctor's duty should be to disclose that which a reasonable, prudent person in this patient's position would want to know, subject only to the 'therapeutic privilege'[10] (see below).

English law, like the majority judgements in *Sidaway*, almost certainly falls somewhere between these two extreme positions. In *Sidaway* Lord Bridge (with whom Lord Keith agreed) adopted a modified *Bolam* test. Disclosure, he argued, was '*primarily* a matter of clinical judgment' (my emphasis),[11] but this did not mean that the profession was entirely free to set its own standards of disclosure. Rather, in certain circumstances the judge might conclude that a risk ought to have been disclosed even if there was a body of responsible medical opinion which would not have warned the patient about it. The sort of risk he had in mind was 'an operation involving a substantial risk of grave adverse consequences', and the example he gave was a 10 per cent risk of a stroke.[12] Lord Templeman also advocated a modified *Bolam* test. There is, he argued, 'no doubt that a doctor ought to draw the attention of a patient to a danger which may be special in kind or magnitude or special to the patient'.[13] When a risk is 'special', the *Bolam* test is not necessarily determinative,

---

9 464 F.2d 772 (DC Cir. 1972) at 787. See also the leading Australian case, *Rogers v. Whitaker* (1992) 175 CLR 479, at p. 483, in which a risk was defined as material if 'in the circumstances of the particular case, a reasonable person in the patient's position, if warned of the risk, would be likely to attach significance to it or if the medical practitioner is, or should reasonably be aware that the particular patient, if warned of the risk, would be likely to attach significance to it'.

10 [1985] 2 WLR 480, at pp. 493 and 495.

11 *Id.*, at p. 505.

12 *Id.*

13 *Id.*, at p. 507.

and a judge might decide that a doctor's nondisclosure was negligent despite evidence that she had conformed with responsible medical practice.

Subsequently, in *Pearce v. United Bristol Healthcare NHS Trusts*, Lord Woolf MR held that there should be disclosure of 'a significant risk which would affect the judgement of the reasonable patient',[14] and this was quoted with approval by Lord Steyn in *Chester v. Afshar.*[15] While this might appear to be more patient-centred than the 'reasonable doctor' test, the critical question is how the courts will determine whether a risk is 'significant', or 'special' or 'substantial'. In *Pearce*, Lord Woolf MR had to decide whether the doctors should have disclosed a 0.1-0.2 per cent risk of stillbirth, and he said that 'the doctors called on behalf of the defendants did not regard that risk as significant, nor do I'.[16] Thus he appeared to rely upon *clinical* judgement of whether the risk was 'significant', and not on Tina Pearce's own assessment of whether the risk was sufficiently material that it would have affected her decision to accept medical advice and proceed to a natural birth.

In practice then, English law applies a test which lies somewhere between the 'reasonable doctor' and the 'prudent patient' test. Many would argue that moving further towards the 'prudent patient' test would better protect patients' interests in information disclosure. However, my argument here will be that *neither* test is capable of adequately protecting patients' interests in being properly informed about their medical treatment. In the next sections, I evaluate their pros and cons, and conclude that both are seriously defective.

The 'Reasonable Doctor' Test

The advantage of a 'reasonable doctor' test for the standard of disclosure is its comparative ease of application. Should a doctor be sued in negligence, expert witnesses can – as in other malpractice actions – offer evidence as to whether other doctors would have acted in the same way if faced with a similar patient. In contrast, if the test is instead what *this* patient would want to know, doctors will be forced to guess what might matter to this patient. It is increasingly rare for doctors – particularly those carrying out specialist treatments such as surgery – to have had any contact at all with the patient prior to their admittance to hospital. Without knowing anything about the patient's values and goals, the doctor has no way of determining which pieces of information matter to her. In order to avoid liability, the doctor may therefore be tempted to give the patient more information than she could possibly digest, thereby reducing rather than enhancing her ability to make an informed choice.

The 'reasonable doctor' test does, however, suffer from a number of disadvantages. First, and most importantly, it does not protect the patient's right to self-determination. The central problem with employing a professional standard test in order to

14 (1998) 48 BMLR 118, at p. 124.

15 [2004] UKHL 41, [2004] 3 WLR 927.

16 (1998) 48 BMLR 118, at p. 124.

determine what information patients need in order to make informed choices about their medical treatment is that, unlike diagnosis and treatment, this is not a question which requires clinical expertise. On the contrary, if the patient has the right to decide whether to consent to a proposed treatment, she can only exercise meaningful choice over this decision if she has sufficient information to allow her to weigh up its advantages and disadvantages, in the light of her own priorities. Medical progress has expanded the range of available treatment options, and there is also always the possibility of declining treatment altogether. Most treatments will have side effects, the acceptability of which can be judged only from the patient's own perspective. Cancer of the throat, for example, can be treated by surgery or by radiation. Surgery is more effective, but will deprive the patient of normal speech. Only the patient herself can determine whether the higher chance of prolonging life outweighs the reduction in the quality of her life. As Harvey Teff has explained:

> The relative importance which patients attach, for example, to quality as against length of life, and to physical integrity or appearance as against diminution of pain, may reflect personal values, circumstances and priorities of which the surgeon, in particular, is initially unaware and may never become sufficiently apprised.[17]

Second, there may be a tension between English law's robust defence of a patient's right to refuse medical treatment 'for rational reasons, for irrational reasons or for no reasons at all',[18] and its much more paternalistic approach to the provision of information. A patient's right to make her own decision about whether to consent to a particular procedure is rigorously protected by the judiciary, and yet the information which may be necessary in order to take full advantage of this right to self-determination can be withheld with relative impunity.

Third, the reasonable doctor test inevitably emphasises the question of what the doctor actually said: would other doctors have given the same advice to patients in these circumstances? But if the purpose of giving information to patients is to ensure informed decision making, the question should instead be: does the patient have an adequate *understanding* of the relative advantages and disadvantages of treatment. Simply offering patients a standardised information sheet may absolve a doctor of negligence, but it is by no means an ideal way to promote meaningful patient choice.

Fourth, the emphasis on consent implies a paternalistic model of medical decision making in which a doctor offers the patient one treatment option, which can then be accepted or declined. There is rarely only one possible course of action, and so framing the issue in this way already implicitly accepts that the doctor should have the power to determine which treatment is appropriate, with the patient's participation limited to agreeing with the doctor, or rejecting treatment altogether.

---

17 Teff, H., 'Consent to Medical Procedures: Paternalism, Self-Determination or Therapeutic Alliance', (1985) 101 *Law Quarterly Review*, 432-53.

18 See, for example, *Re MB (An Adult: Medical Treatment)* [1997] 2 FLR 426 and *Re T* [1993] Fam 95.

Choice, on the other hand, is a much more patient-centred concept which might involve much greater emphasis upon the various alternative courses of action open to the patient.

Fifth, the 'reasonable doctor' test offers little prospective guidance for doctors faced with the question: 'what am I legally required to disclose to this patient?' The rather cryptic and unhelpful answer to this question must be that a doctor should tell the patient that which no reasonably prudent doctor would fail to disclose, as determined retrospectively by a court. Sixth, even if a customary standard for the provision of information could be said to exist, it might be wholly inadequate and would be perpetuated by a 'reasonable doctor' standard of disclosure. Finally, the 'reasonable doctor' test largely ignores the role of other health care professionals who are not medical practitioners. Nurses, for example, may have more time to spend discussing treatment options, and might be better at communicating with patients than doctors.

The 'Prudent Patient' Test

The 'prudent patient' test would appear to offer better protection of patients' interests in information disclosure, since what doctors should disclose is judged from the perspective of the reasonable patient, rather than the reasonable doctor. It places doctors under a duty to work out what most patients would want to know, rather than what their other colleagues might do, and this certainly looks like a more patient-centred approach to information disclosure.

But the 'prudent patient' test is not without disadvantages. First, how are doctors supposed to know in advance what the abstract hypothetical reasonable patient would want to know? Since the standard of care in a particular case could only be conclusively determined *retrospectively* by the courts, the doctor will have to second guess a future court's assessment of what a reasonable patient would consider material. Since there are very few cases in this area, and even fewer readily accessible legal judgements, doctors facing a decision about how much information to provide to a particular patient will gain little practical assistance from consulting the law. Instead, they are likely to seek guidance from *other doctors* as to what patients generally want to know. It is easy to see how in practice this test could become indistinguishable from a 'reasonable doctor' test.

Second, this problem is exacerbated, as I explain later, by the application of an objective 'reasonable patient' test for causation. If the claimant must prove, not that she herself would have refused treatment if she had been properly informed, but rather that the reasonable patient would not have consented to the treatment in question, the right to act according to one's own preferences and priorities is not protected at all.

It is certainly instructive that the practical application of the 'prudent patient' test in other countries has not transformed patients' access to effective remedies for inadequate disclosure of information. In Gerald Robertson's study of 'informed consent' litigation in Canada in the ten years following the adoption of the prudent patient test in *Reibl v. Hughes*,[19] only 11 per cent of malpractice claims were based upon the failure to obtain informed consent.[20] The informed consent claim was dismissed in 82 per cent of cases (compared with patients' success rates of 56 per cent in ordinary malpractice actions).[21] Of those patients who did manage to prove that the doctor had breached his duty of disclosure, 56 per cent failed to establish causation.[22]

It could also be argued that there is a tension between the so-called 'therapeutic privilege', which is subjectively assessed, and an objective approach to the standard of care. In all the jurisdictions which have adopted the 'prudent patient' test, it has been subject to an exception, known as the therapeutic privilege, whereby the doctor's duty to provide her patient with material information is suspended if, in the doctor's judgement, the information would be likely to cause *this* patient harm, such as severe distress or anxiety. Why should doctors be entitled to take into account the patient's special sensibilities when deciding *not* to tell her about a particular risk, while her individual and perhaps idiosyncratic preferences do not determine whether the doctor should positively disclose information?

More importantly, it could be argued that the reasonable patient test also fails to protect patient self-determination. Individual patients' interests in information will vary dramatically. People have different priorities, beliefs and family histories, all of which will affect the relative importance they attach to the risks and benefits of medical treatment. Giving all patients the information that the abstract reasonable patient in their position would require might be preferable to the *Bolam* standard of disclosure, but it will result in some patients being provided with information that they do not want, while others will have been deprived of facts about the proposed treatment that are of vital importance to them. As Alexander Capron has persuasively argued, the:

> patient owes no one a duty to decide prudently or to require for his decision only the facts that an ordinary person would want. The [prudent patient] rule would bar recovery by a patient whose idiosyncratic decisionmaking takes him outside the realm of the 'reasonably prudent person'. This is equivalent to a defence of contributory negligence, which has no place in an action for failure to obtain informed consent.[23]

A subjective standard of disclosure might appear more precisely to fulfil the autonomy-based justification for obtaining informed consent. It acknowledges that people have highly variable informational needs, and imposes a duty upon doctors to tailor their disclosures according to the individual patient's own priorities and

19 [1980] 2 SCR 880.

20 Robertson, G., 'Informed Consent to Medical Treatment', 97 *Law Quarterly Review*, (1981) 102-26.

21 *Id.*

22 *Id.*

23 Capron, A.M., 'Informed Consent in Catastrophic Disease Research and Treatment', (1974) 123 *University of Pennsylvannia Law Review*, 340-438, at p. 410.

concerns. In practice, however, a subjective standard would prove almost impossible to enforce. Doctors cannot be expected to know enough about their patients' characters and beliefs to predict accurately what factors will be material to their decision making. Given the time constraints under which health care professionals must operate, eliciting all of a patient's relevant values, background characteristics and goals would be an impossible task. Instead, patients must rely on their doctors to make judgments about what factors are likely to be important to them. And of course, in making this assessment, doctors will inevitably rely upon evidence of what other doctors generally do in such circumstances, and what patients generally appear to want to know.

This is not to say that the subjective standard should be completely dismissed as an impractical moral ideal. Although it would seem harsh to find a doctor liable for nondisclosure where there was no reason to believe that an apparently trivial fact was of particular importance to this patient, it might nevertheless be valuable for doctors to at least attempt to discover the individual patient's subjective priorities by means of questioning.

Causation

For a successful action in negligence, the claimant must not only prove the existence of a duty of care and its breach, but also that damage or loss has been caused by the defendant's breach of duty. Thus a doctor's failure to disclose material information will only be actionable in negligence if it caused the claimant to suffer some injury or loss. Even if a subjective patient-orientated standard of care were to be adopted, in my view the need to prove a causal link between inadequate disclosure and actionable damage fatally undermines the capacity of the tort of negligence to accommodate the real harm suffered by patients who have been given insufficient information prior to medical treatment. Before I flesh out this claim in more detail, let me first explain how difficult it is for patients to prove that a doctor's inadequate disclosure caused their loss.

Applying the ordinary 'but for' test to disclosure cases means that we should ask whether, but for the doctor's failure to disclose this information to this patient, the patient would have suffered this particular injury. So we need to know whether the injury would still have occurred if the patient had been properly informed. Causation will therefore be established if the patient can prove that proper disclosure would have caused her to decline the treatment which has resulted in injury. But of course, this question is almost impossible to answer. Not only is it a speculative inquiry about what the patient might have done in different circumstances, but also the patient now has the benefit of hindsight. She knows that a particular remote risk *has* materialised. From her perspective, the 1 per cent risk of an adverse outcome has ceased to be a remote hypothetical possibility, and has become a 100 per cent certainty. It is therefore possible that a patient's assertion of what she would have done had she known about the risk will be coloured by her knowledge that she has the misfortune of falling within the 1 per cent of patients who suffer a particular adverse side effect.

This problem has resulted in some modifications to the 'but for' test which are arguably inconsistent with the ordinary principles of tort law. The 'but for' test requires us to ask whether *this patient* would have rejected a treatment proposal if she had been properly informed. If *she* would have had the treatment anyway, the doctor's breach of duty did not cause her loss. On the other hand, if *she* would have refused treatment, and hence avoided the risk which has now materialised, causation is established. Causation is therefore normally judged subjectively – we ask whether this claimant would still have suffered the loss even if the defendant had not been negligent. But a reluctance to rely too heavily on the patient's own testimony in disclosure cases has led some to argue for an objective test for causation, or at least for objective considerations to carry more weight than they do normally.

A hybrid objective/subjective test was adopted in *Smith v. Barking, Havering and Brentwood HA.*[24] Hutchison J suggested that an objective test should be used to 'test' the truth of the patient's assertion that she would not have consented if she had been told about a particular risk. If a reasonable patient would have agreed to the proposed treatment even if she had been told about the particular risk, then the onus would be on the patient to produce some evidence to back up her claim that she would have declined the treatment:

> the assertion from the witness box, made after the adverse outcome is known, in a wholly artificial situation and in the knowledge that the outcome of the case depends upon the assertion being maintained, does not carry great weight unless there are extraneous or additional factors to substantiate it.[25]

But how might a patient prove the truth of what is by definition a hypothetical assertion? While a patient with unusual religious beliefs might be able to demonstrate that she would have acted differently, it will usually be difficult for a claimant to produce evidence to support her claim. And it is at least arguable that the introduction of a rebuttable presumption that the claimant's evidence as to causation is false is inconsistent with basic principles of justice. Furthermore, adopting an objective test for establishing causation will enable the doctor to rely on evidence that patients in general very seldom refuse to consent to the procedure in question. This sort of solid, empirical evidence contrasts sharply with the claimant's easily discredited *post hoc* assertion that they would not have consented if they had been properly informed.

A further problem with adopting an objective approach to causation is that it confuses the question of the *credibility* of the claimant's evidence with its objective reasonableness. A patient is under no duty to make decisions which are consistent with those of an ordinarily prudent patient. On the contrary, as Butler-Sloss LJ explained in *Re MB (An Adult: Medical Treatment)*:[26]

24 (1988) reported [1994] 5 Med LR 285.

25 *Ibid.*, at p. 289.

26 [1997] 2 FLR 426, at 432.

> A mentally competent patient has an absolute right to refuse to consent to medical treatment for any reason, rational or irrational, or for no reason at all, even where that decision may lead to his or her own death.

Testing a claimant's evidence against what a hypothetical reasonable person in her situation would have done significantly undermines her right to make foolish or idiosyncratic choices about her medical care. The credibility of evidence from a patient with peculiar priorities should be assessed in the ordinary way – does the judge believe her account? – rather than against a standard of objective reasonableness.

But even if a subjective test for causation were to be adopted, for a number of reasons the requirement that the claimant prove that the doctor's inadequate disclosure *caused* their injury represents an insurmountable barrier to the capacity of the tort of negligence to offer appropriate remedies to inadequately informed patients.

First, the principal purpose of the requirement that doctors should give their patients adequate information is to protect the patient from making uninformed choices about their medical care, *not to prevent physical injury.* If the purpose of giving patients information is to facilitate informed decision making, then any failure to disclose material information will have interfered with her ability to make an autonomous choice, regardless of whether she happens to have *also* suffered physical injury as a result. Yet this free-standing interest in the capacity to make an informed choice cannot be protected by the tort of negligence.

Second, a successful claim in negligence for failure to disclose a material risk is in practice synonymous with strict liability for adverse events. Doctors who exercised all due care and skill in the performance of an operation can be found liable for the consequences of an accident which they could have done nothing to prevent because their pre-operation disclosures were inadequate. Perhaps it would be more appropriate for the doctor to be liable for the interference with her patient's ability to reach an informed choice – and we would of course have to think about how to quantify this sort of dignitary injury – but not for the unfortunate but blameless medical mishap.[27]

Third, because the claimant must prove that the inadequate disclosure caused an injury, cases only come before the courts where the patient has not been informed about the risk of an adverse outcome *which has then materialised.* Adequate information is not, however, confined to the disclosure of risks. In order to exercise meaningful choice, it is important that patients are told about alternatives to the proposed treatment, including the option of no treatment at all. A patient might want to know if their doctor stands to benefit financially from their decision to opt for a particular course of treatment. Patients might also feel that they should be told who will carry out the procedure. But because the failure to give these other types of

---

27 Cane, P., 'A Warning about Causation', (1999) 115 *Law Quarterly Review*, 21-7, at p. 23.

information will tend not to result in physical injury, equally important aspects of informed choice are marginalised.

Fourth, because inadequate disclosure of remote risks will seldom result in any physical injury at all, it will invariably be immune from potential liability in negligence. But even in cases where a risk has materialised, as I explained above, it is so inherently unlikely that a patient will succeed in proving that inadequate disclosure caused their injury that doctors will hardly ever be held to account for a failure to tell their patients about the risks associated with treatment.

Finally, 'cause' appears to have acquired a rather special meaning in failure to warn cases. The injury has been caused by an unfortunate and inherently unlikely combination of circumstances, and not by anything the doctor did. The doctor instead *created the situation* in which a particular extraordinary sequence of events could occur. The question of whether a doctor should be liable for a failure to disclose a risk is more accurately stated as whether she should be liable for creating the situation in which an accidental injury might or (more likely) might not occur.

Conclusion

In this chapter it has been argued that tort law seldom provides an effective solution for patients who believe that they have not been properly informed by their doctors. The reforms to the negligence system to be effected by the NHS Redress Bill are unlikely to make any difference at all to this situation because patients will only be eligible for a remedy if they are able to prove that they have suffered damage as a result of poor medical treatment, and as we have seen, the law does not recognise being inadequately informed as actionable damage.

The chief problem with tort law's response to information disclosure is that it points to a significant gap in the law's protection of patient autonomy. It may be true that competent adult patients have an almost absolute right to refuse unwanted treatment. But we have to remember that their ability to take advantage of this right may depend critically upon having sufficient understanding of the relative merits and disadvantages of the available treatments. Yet as we have seen, whether or not patients will get this information still generally lies within the doctor's discretion.

The focus of this chapter has been the largely impotent role tort law plays in the protection of patients' interests in information disclosure. But does this matter? It might be argued that because the guidance doctors receive from the Royal Colleges, the Department of Health, the BMA and the GMC stresses the importance of giving patients sufficient information, the fact that this is not backed up by remedies in tort law is of comparatively little importance. The GMC guidelines, for example, state that:

> When providing information you must do your best to find out about patients' individual needs and priorities. For example, patients' beliefs, culture, occupation or other factors may have a bearing on the information they need in order to reach a decision. You should not make assumptions about patients' views, but discuss these matters with them, and

> ask them whether they have any concerns about the treatment or the risks it may involve. You should provide patients with appropriate information, which should include an explanation of any risks to which they may attach particular significance. Ask patients whether they have understood the information and whether they would like more before making a decision.[28]

Doctors wanting to know what they should disclose to patients will usually consult professional guidance, rather than the law reports, and so, in practice, the inadequacies of tort law may have little practical impact upon the provision of information to patients. Nevertheless, while in practice most doctors do attempt to find out what each individual patient wants to know, and try to provide this information in an accessible and straightforward way, this is certainly not because of the 'deterrent' effect of tort law. On the contrary, it is *despite* the complete absence of any effective deterrent to inadequate disclosure in the law of tort. Law students are usually told that tort law serves two principal functions: compensation and deterrence. In relation to information disclosure, it serves neither. As a result, I think there is an increasing need to think seriously about abandoning the pretence that tort law offers any protection at all to patients' interests in access to information about their medical treatment.

---

28 General Medical Council, *Seeking Patients' Consent: The Ethical Considerations*, GMC, 1998, para 5.

Chapter 18

Mark Anthony or Macbeth: Some Problems Concerning the Dead and the Incompetent when it Comes to Consent

John Harris[1]

Introduction

Consent is one of the oldest of old chestnuts in bioethics and many will be amazed to think that there is any mileage left in it. However, the fact that it is such an old chestnut has led to the most staggering complacency about the assured role that consent in general and fully informed consent in particular plays in many contexts. This chapter seeks to challenge that complacency.

In making this challenge I have drawn on work done on consent over the last ten years and tried to present it in what I hope is a coherent account of problems with traditional conceptions of consent and received views of its role in medical decision making at all stages of life. I have chosen these themes for my contribution to this book because I was inspired to think again about consent by Ken Mason. From 1996-1999 I chaired a working party on 'Values and Attitudes on Ageing' for the charity Age Concern as part of their initiative 'The Millennium Papers'.[2] Ken Mason was a member of this working party and his presence, wit and sage contributions made the whole experience a great pleasure for me and for all the other members of the working party. He kept us all up to the mark with his characteristic blend of profound scholarship and humour, deployed in a light-hearted but pithy style and always precisely on target. I remember him remarking that it was the presence of someone as old as himself in our group that gave it any semblance of credibility. Whether or not this was true, it was certainly his presence that made the working party work. Early in our deliberations Ken Mason made a remark about the problems of appreciating whether or

---

1 Copyright John Harris 2005. In this chapter I draw on my 'Law and regulation of retained organs: The ethical issues', in *Legal Studies*, 2002, Vol. 22, No 4. 527-549 and my 'Consent and end of life decisions', in *The Journal of Medi*, Vol. 29, No. 1, 10-16.

2 The Millennium Papers: 'Values and Attitudes in an Ageing Society', Age Concern England, London.

not consent had actually been given and received in many cases concerning the elderly. This prompted me to think again about the entire problem of autonomy and consent, a problem that I had, like many others in bioethics, largely 'taken for granted' in the sense of simply assuming that the main problems were well established and broadly understood. Stimulated by his question, I came to see that this was far from the case. I believe that everyone involved in bioethics in the United Kingdom will agree that bioethics is a discipline characterised by goodwill, co-operation and immense mutual respect. Ken Mason is the epitome of all these virtues and his towering presence in this community, virtually from the start of the 'modern era', has helped to make this such a great discipline in which to work and play.

The role of consent in many contemporary contexts is highly problematic although this fact is seldom recognised. Indeed, as I have just indicated, it was Ken Mason who made me see just how problematic an issue consent is. I am thinking particularly of the way consent has been appealed to in the debate concerning posthumous organ and tissue retention and use and in debates concerning the ethics of genetic testing or profiling of embryos, children at birth or indeed at any time before they can consent to what happens to them, as well as in all cases of problematic capacity to consent.

I will look first at consent for the retention or use of organs and tissue after death and then at the issue of consent on behalf of children for genetic testing or profiling. In this later case much of what I have to say will apply to anything at all done to, for or on behalf of children by adults.

Organ and Tissue Retention and Use

Why have so many people thought that consent is a requirement in the case of posthumous retention, storage or use of organs, tissue or other body parts or products? Perhaps they are assuming that, as in other areas of medicine, consent is required by acceptance of the principle of autonomy or by the principle of 'respect for persons'; however as we shall now see this cannot be the case. For even where the deceased herself has made a competent direction prior to death as to the disposal of tissue and organs posthumously, such a 'consent' is not like the other paradigm cases of consent in medical contexts.

Although both ethics and law recognise that persons may have enduring interests that survive death, posthumous interests are not necessarily like those interests that consent traditionally protects. The principal function of consent is either to protect – indeed facilitate – autonomy or to protect bodily integrity from acts that, without consent, constitute a violation. Autonomy involves the capacity to make choices; it involves acts of the will. The dead have no capacities, they have no will, no preferences, wants nor desires. The dead cannot therefore be autonomous and so *a fortiori* cannot have their autonomy violated. Equally the dead cannot have their bodily integrity violated, for violation consists not simply in a breach of bodily integrity but in a breach of bodily integrity that is not consented to.

'Offences' against the dead do not involve violations of their autonomy.[3] Indeed, as been established in English law at least, the human body neither owns itself (contra many theories of self-ownership concerning the bodies of the living[4]) nor is it usually owned by others, unless those others have 'mixed their labour' with the corpse or parts of it, thereby enhancing its value or utility.

Posthumous Rights

What about the rights of the dead? It is doubtful whether there is any such thing as a posthumous right. There are two main theories of rights: choice theory and interest theory. Choice theory sees rights as securing 'the protection and promotion of autonomy or liberty' and interest theory sees rights as serving to further individual well being or welfare.[5] Clearly on choice theory there are no such things as posthumous rights, because the dead are not autonomous and so their rights cannot be analysed in terms of choices. Even according to interest theory, posthumous rights are doubtful because, arguably, the dead have no welfare interests left to be served, and such interests as they might be said to retain have to be strong enough to impose a duty on others. Joseph Raz for example suggests that an individual is capable of possessing rights 'if and only if ... his well-being is of ultimate importance'.[6] Clearly, the dead have no wellbeing for the simple and sufficient reason that they have no 'being' at all – they are not beings, but ex-beings or former beings. They were once beings whose wellbeing had ultimate value, but no more![7]

Shakespeare gave eloquent expression to both sides of the coin. Mark Anthony, in *Julius Caesar*, certainly talks as if the dead can be wronged: 'I rather choose / to wrong the dead, to wrong myself and you / Than I will wrong such honourable men'.[8] But in *Macbeth* Shakespeare takes a harder line: Macbeth himself, talking of the murder of Duncan whom he has 'sent to peace' says: 'Duncan is in his grave; /After life's fitful

---

3 There is some legal support for this, See *People v. Kelly* and *People v. Sellars California Supreme Court* cited in Cook and James, see Cook, D.S. and James, D.S., 'Necrophilia: Case report and consideration of legal aspects', 5 *Medical Law International*, 2002, 199-204.

4 A locus classicus is Cohen, G.A., *Self-Ownership, Freedom, and Equality*, Cambridge, Cambridge University Press, 1995, at p. 68. This originally appeared in Cohen's 'Self-ownership, world-ownership, and equality', in Lucash, F. (ed), *Justice And Equality Here And Now*, Ithaca, NY, Cornell University Press, 1986, at p. 109. See also Steiner, H., *An Essay on Rights*, Oxford, Blackwell, 1994.

5 On rights theories generally see Sumner, L.W., *The Moral Foundation Of Rights*, Oxford, Clarendon Press, 1987, and Waldron, J., *The Right to Private Property*, Oxford, Clarendon Press, 1988, chapter 3. Steiner, H., *An Essay on Rights*, Oxford, Blackwell, 1994, Dworkin, R., *Taking Rights Seriously*, London, Duckworth, 1977, and Dworkin, R., *Life's Dominion*, London, Harper Collins, at pp. 210-216.

6 Raz, J., *The Morality of Freedom*, Oxford, Clarendon Press, 1986, at p. 166.

7 See Raz, *id.* A related conception in terms of welfare rather than wellbeing is offered by Sumner, L.W., *The Moral Foundation Of Rights*, *op cit.*, at p. 47.

8 William Shakespeare, *Julius Caesar*, Act III, Scene II.

fever he sleeps well; / Not steel, nor poison, / Malice domestic, foreign levy, nothing / Can touch him further.'[9] However although the dead, on Anthony's view, can be wronged, on the normal distinction between harming and wronging they probably cannot be harmed. Harming involves damage to the body or the mind whereas 'wronging' involves the violation of rights or of morally protected interests.[10]

Persisting or 'Critical' Interests

There is a real sense in which individuals may have some interests that survive their death and hence there are some senses in which an individual's interests are still in play *post mortem*. For example, if I have an interest during my life that my children are provided for after my death, and I seek to secure that interest by executing a will, it remains true that if the provisions of that will are not respected my interests have been harmed, although of course neither will I be aware of that fact, nor will it affect my wellbeing in any way.[11] Interestingly for our present argument, at English common law we cannot determine by will what will happen to our bodies after death, but an exception to this common law rule was introduced by The Human Tissue Act 1961[12] (as amended[13]) which makes an exception in the case of disposition for therapeutic purposes. If anything can be read into this exception it is perhaps the idea that therapeutic dispositions have a moral and perhaps social priority that overrides other considerations.[14]

While such interests deserve some respect, they are, I would submit, relatively weak[15] when compared with the interests of living persons who exist to be harmed in person by the neglect of those interests. The issue of whether or not persisting interests of the dead should be respected is not different in principle from the question of whether their wishes as to the disposal of other parts of their estate should be respected. The appropriate principle should be that their wishes when alive as to post mortem affairs should be respected subject to reasonable demands of public interest. This is not because we respect the autonomy of the dead, but because living people want a mechanism for disposing of their assets after death and recognise that, if their wishes are to be carried out, reciprocity is required. They must implement the now extinguished wishes of the dead in order to have confidence that their own wishes will be implemented once they are no longer capable of wishing anything. This is

9 William Shakespeare, *Macbeth*, Act III, Scene II.

10 On this distinction see Feinberg, J., *Harm to Others*, New York, Oxford University Press, 1984, at p. 102. See also Harris, J., *Wonderwoman and Superman*, Oxford, OUP, 1992, at pp. 84ff.

11 See, for example, Dworkin, R., *Life's Dominion, op cit.*, at pp. 210-216 and Harris, J., *Wonderwoman and Superman, op cit.*, at p.100ff.

12 Section 1(1).

13 Human Tissue Act 2004; see also the Human Tissue (Scotland) Bill 2005.

14 Although this is I must confess a rankly partisan reading!

15 *Wonderwoman and Superman, supra cit.*, at pp. 100-101.

of course the case with wills and other testamentary dispositions (the public interest is after all respected in the payment of death duties – taxes which are usually very much against both the wishes of those anticipating death and contrary to interests of the dead).[16] We should remember that the public interest serves principally the interests of existing and future individuals. Research and therapeutic use of archived samples of deceased citizens might be regarded as analogous to taxing their estate to raise revenue.[17] The point is, of course, that the requirement to respect such interests is much weaker than the obligation to respect the rights of existing persons to bodily integrity or freedom from physical violation.[18]

Now consider autonomy. We do clearly have autonomous preferences about what happens to our bodies after death. In so far as these are not complied with, our autonomous wishes have been frustrated, but whether it follows that our autonomy has been violated is another matter. I wish that certain things had not happened to me while I was a child. At the time I was not autonomous and had formed no views about them. Did those things frustrate my autonomy because I now wish that they had not been done? Equally with things I now wish won't happen after I lose my autonomy. In neither case does it follow from the fact that someone has autonomous wishes about something that happens when they are not autonomous, either in the past or the future, that those things violate their autonomy, although they are of course contrary to their wishes as held at a particular point in time.

This raises an interesting question about why we should respect the advance directives of individuals who have ceased to be persons. Respecting advance directives can have nothing to do with the respect due to autonomy, although most commentators have assumed that it does.[19] Where individuals who were once autonomous have permanently lost autonomy, it is the responsibility of those who care for them or who have care of them to act in their best interests. Knowing what the subject would have wanted is a powerful 'steer' as to what their interests are and hence as to how to act in their best interests. However, some individuals may not have any interests that can be protected. Suppose Tony Bland, the patient left in permanent vegetative state (PVS) following the Hillsborough disaster,[20] had left an advance directive to the effect that he wanted to be kept alive at all costs; would the House of Lords have done wrong to have given permission for the withholding of life sustaining measures? In English law it is not permissible to kill even those who

16 Of course it might be argued that taxes serve the interests of all because of the uses to which they are put.

17 There is I believe a lesson to be learned here for the case of cadaver organ donation which I raised in my *The Value of Life*, London, Routledge and Kegan Paul, 1985, at pp. 219-223.

18 On this point see Harris, J., 'Ethical genetic research', in *Jurimetrics: The Journal of Law, Science, and Policy*, Fall 1999 issue, Vol. 40, no. 1, 77-93.

19 A related argument in the context of personal identity has been employed by Buchanan, A., 'Advance Directives and the Personal Identity Problem', in Harris, J. (ed), *Bioethics*, Oxford, OUP, 2001, 131-157. And also Dworkin, *Life's Dominion, op cit.*, at pp. 180 ff.

20 *Airedale NHS Trust v. Bland* [1993] 1 All ER 821 (HL).

want to die and statements of a disinclination to have life shortened do not add to the legal duties we have to preserve life. Equally, while patients may refuse treatment in virtue of their common law entitlement to be protected from unlawful assaults they may not direct doctors or others to perform any particular treatments (although they may of course request them). Lord Mustill in the *Bland* case noted that:

> The distressing point, which must not be shirked, is that the proposed conduct is not in the best interests of Anthony Bland for he has no best interests of any kind.[21]

While Lord Mustill is perhaps slightly overstating the case, his main point is surely powerful and that is because of another feature of morality that we need to reflect upon.

Person-affecting Restrictions on Moral Duties

It is tempting to think of those sorts of interests have been termed 'critical' or 'persisting' as contrasted with so called 'experiential' interests – interests that we are aware of and aware of being either served or not served by what happens. Ronald Dworkin highlights this particular contrast, defining experiential interests as things we have an interest in because we like the experience of doing them. Critical interests on the other hand are those 'interests that it does make ... life genuinely better to satisfy'.[22] Most of our critical interests concern interests we have while alive but some, as we have noted, survive our deaths. Things that happen after our death can be critical interests of ours just because, whether they happen or not, may contribute to whether our lives have gone well as a whole. To persevere with the example already used, if my children are provided for after my death this will make my life more successful overall than if this were not the case; that is why what happens to them is one of my critical interests whether or not I am there to experience their fate one way or the other. However, there is another distinction that has some importance and that is whether or not particular interests are 'person-affecting' in the sense that their satisfaction or frustration would be good or bad for the person whose interests they are. It is widely accepted in contemporary ethics that 'the part of morality concerned with human wellbeing should be explained entirely in terms of what would be good or bad for those people whom our acts affect'.[23] So, although what happens to my children, or my body after my death, can involve my critical interests in the sense that it contributes both to the success or failure of my life as a whole and to whether or not it has achieved the meaning with which I had hoped to endow it, such things

21 *Ibid.*, at p. 894.

22 Dworkin, *Life's Dominion, op cit.*, at pp. 201ff.

23 Parfit, D., following Narveson, J. defines the person-affecting restriction thus: 'This part of morality, the part concerned with human wellbeing, should be explained entirely in terms of what would be good or bad for those people whom our acts affect'. See *Reasons and Persons*, Oxford, Clarendon Press, 1984, at p. 394.

are not person-affecting – they are not good or bad for me, they do not affect my wellbeing, because 'I' no longer exist. I am simply not there to be affected one way or the other. In short, though in a sense my *interests* persist, *'I'* do not.

Some, but not all, critical interests will be person-affecting – all experiential interests will – but person-affecting is what counts when we are principally concerned with human wellbeing, or with personal rights or interests. Posthumous interests are never person-affecting nor are posthumous frustrations of autonomous choices.

We must, I believe, think of the preferences of subjects about what happens to them after death as not 'self-regarding' preferences but 'other-regarding' preferences; that is, preferences the value of which must necessarily be balanced against the interests of others and hence cannot have the status of rights – interests that can trump those of others. The self, the subject of the preferences no longer exists. Ronald Dworkin called such preferences 'external' to distinguish them from 'personal' preferences.[24] Dworkin suggests that external preferences should count for nothing when set against personal preferences, that only such an approach is compatible with the equal consideration of preferences because, on the assumption that each person is equal (before morality and before the law each counts for one and none for more than one), then only person-affecting preferences reflect this conception of equality which is at the basis of our entitlement to have our preferences respected at all.[25]

I attempted to articulate more precisely why persisting interests were, of necessity, less significant than person-affecting interests some time ago in *Wonderwoman and Superman*.[26]

> It is I admit, hard work imagining why one should separate harming someone's interests and harming that someone. But the point of doing so is perhaps this: if we damage the environment irreparably today, this will harm the interests of future generations but it will not harm individuals as yet undifferentiated until they come into being. It harms their interests now and them only when they exist. Similarly the interests of actual people persist after their deaths. When they are alive you can harm (or benefit of course) both the individual and her interests. Once she is dead only her interests remain to be harmed.
>
> This is why the damage to the persisting interests of the dead must be set against the damage to the persisting interests of the living, damage which, in the case of the living, also affects the persons whose interests they are. This double damage will for all practical purposes always give the edge to the interests of the living.[27]

---

24 See Dworkin, R., *Taking Rights Seriously*, Duckworth, *op cit.*, at pp. 234 ff.

25 Dworkin's interests in his discussion of this distinction are rather far from ours and a full discussion would take us too deeply into the theory of equality.

26 Oxford, Oxford University Press, 1992, chapter 5, at pp. 100-101.

27 While the life of a person then is affected by frustration of interests the dead are not affected 'in person' by this. Note that it is not a question of experiential versus critical interests but person affecting versus persisting interests. Person-affecting considerations affect living persons whether or not they experience them in the sense of being aware of them. I am affected in person for example by malicious gossip; it is person-affecting even if I remain unaware of it.

One conclusion is that the primacy that has hitherto been very widely accorded to both advance directives of the subject and to the wishes of parents and other relatives of the deceased with respect to posthumous organ and tissue retrieval or retention, lacks the justification that has usually been assumed to underpin its central role. That is not to say, of course, that consent here has no justification, but it does show that an altogether different justification is required.

Since the dead subject has ceased to be the subject of person-affecting morality, since she has neither autonomy rights nor interests to protect and only some rather attenuated persisting or critical interests if any, her wishes do not have the primacy that rights and person-affecting interests can claim in moral argument. They cannot function, in Dworkin's famous terminology, as 'trumps' in moral and legal argument.[28] Equally the wishes of parents or next of kin lack their normal central role. Next of kin or 'guardians' are called upon to make decisions for the incompetent only on the assumption that these represent safeguards of best interests or sometimes (I believe erroneously),[29] as interpretations of the wishes of the incompetent individual. Here again the wishes of next of kin, guardians or other relatives as to what happens to their deceased relation cannot have the primacy that they have traditionally been accorded, in that they represent neither the expression of the rights nor the person-affecting interests of the deceased. They cannot function as 'trumps' in moral argument.

Person-affecting Posthumous Interests

There is a sense in which what happens to my body after death is person-affecting; it is just that it is not me who is the affected person. They are person-affecting in the sense that they affect the persons who will benefit, for example, from research using my body or its parts, and indeed the persons who are distressed by the tissue being collected, retained or used.

Having expressed scepticism as to the existence of most posthumous rights or interests we must now turn to the issue of whose rights or interests may be relevant to the question of posthumous retention or use of tissue and organs. And here the issue of consent may now be seen as highly problematic because, as we have noted, the usual basis of respecting the consent of the subject is absent and the consents of others play a role very far removed from the usual one in which consents are requested and given for medical procedures.

28 Dworkin, *Taking Rights Seriously*, *op cit.*

29 See for example Harris, J., 'The Welfare of the Child', in *Health Care Analysis*, 2000, 1-8 and Harris, J., 'Consent and end of life decisions', in *The Journal of Medical Ethics* (in press).

Particular Consents

It is well established and almost universally agreed now in medical ethics that the subject himself or herself is entitled to give or withhold consent to all medical or scientific procedures and that such procedures cannot, except *in extremis*, proceed without consent and we have already noted the basis for the primacy of consent in this context. Where the individual is not competent to give consent, procedures must only be carried out in the best interests of the subject and consent is sometimes given by parents or guardians but only on the presumption that they are the most obvious and reliable protectors of the best interests of the subject. They do not have the right to give consent merely because they stand in a particular relationship to the subject but because the fact that they stand in that relationship creates a presumption that they are appropriate guardians of the best interests of the subject. Where that presumption is defeated they have no further standing. Here law and ethics are, I believe, at one. This holds true for all procedures on living, that is existing, beings. However once a human individual has died it is arguable that they have no further moral rights or interests in that they can no longer be harmed or benefited. We have already noted Lord Mustill's firm statement on this matter and also the fact that while, Mustill notwithstanding, it is possible as we have already noticed to attribute some persisting interests to the dead, these are necessarily somewhat attenuated or weakened interests because they are not person-affecting in any sense with respect to the subject of those interests.

If it could be argued that the interests of a deceased, whether a child or an adult, are harmed by the donation or retention of tissue or organs then an interest might arise. In the absence of such an argument, there seems to be no legitimate interest that could be asserted by friends or relatives.

If the organs or tissue were to be used for some immoral purpose, or if their removal or retention constituted some immoral act, for example gross indecency, or if the process by which they were removed was immoral or indecent in some way, the rights or interests not only of friends or relatives but indeed of any citizen might be engaged. But if they are retained for important and realistic scientific purposes, or as part of the human tissue archive, the nature of any legitimate ethical role for friends or relatives must be sought elsewhere.

Secondly, if the relatives or friends are themselves adversely affected by the retention or use of the tissue then their legitimate interests might again be engaged. For example all tissue contains DNA from which the complete genome of the tissue provider can be obtained. The information is also information about family members and these family members might have legitimate concerns about their own genetic privacy and the use to which such genetic information might be put. This point could be very important as it is becoming widely accepted that where genetic information on individuals is stored the information should be suitably anonymised and securely held.

They also might have religious or culturally based beliefs about the disposal of the dead which might be engaged. Finally they might simply want very much that all the remains of their child are buried with the body, perhaps because it seems to them simply fitting or appropriate. In this case, their powerful feelings deserve respect, but so might the powerful feelings of others who want the organs of the dead to be available for science or for life saving or other therapeutic purposes because this forms part of *their* deeply held beliefs and values.

Ultimately, this conflict of interests or of values will be resolved by considerations of which interests or values carry most moral weight – for example whether the interests served by one set of values are more significant or vital that those of the other. This might happen if one set of values protected an interest in life itself (actually involved saving a life), whereas the counterpoised interest protected some less significant or less urgent value, for example, a sense of what is appropriate or 'fitting'. Or, the resolution of such differences might turn on a fairly full description of what society would be like if one set of values rather than the other prevailed. For example, if the bereaved could not bury the dead in their own way they might choose to reject the obligation to do so at all and the burden and expense of this might fall on society.

Suppose we grant that the removal of organs and tissue serves some beneficial altruistic or important purpose? Suppose, for example, that organs are removed posthumously for transplantation and that tissue is removed for storage and investigation for public health reasons or in the pursuit of therapeutic research. Grant that these uses are altruistic and beneficial to other individuals (those whose lives may be saved by organ donation or those whose diseases may find cures through scientific research) and two things become clear. The first is that it could not be in the deceased's interests to frustrate the course of science or to make more probable the deaths of other people.[30] Thus if any presumptions are to be made about what the deceased would have wished it is surely more reasonable to suppose that, if the purposes for which the tissue or organs are retained or used are beneficial and altruistic, the deceased, if they wished anything, would have wished to act beneficially and altruistically towards others. So if any presumption is made in the absence of an advance directive or a clear autonomous expression of will, it should not be that the deceased would have wished to frustrate altruistic or beneficial purposes – it should rather be a presumption in favour of their good character that they would have wished to promote such purposes.

This 'constraint' on what might be presumed to have been the wishes of the deceased in the absence of evidence to the contrary should surely operate on presumptions made by relatives and friends as well as on those that might be made by public bodies or the courts.

30 See for example Harris, J., 'Scientific Research is a Moral Duty', *The Journal of Medical Ethics*, Vol. 31, No. 4, April 2005, 242-248.

Consent on Behalf of Children

A UK Government White Paper recently proposed that genetic profiling might be carried out at birth and that the genetic information might be stored for future use.[31] The possible advantages of taking a sample at birth are that it would be convenient to collect, there are precedents for sampling at birth (Guthrie tests) and that the linkage of such data to an individual's medical record might also in time confer a clinical advantage as gene and environment interactions become better understood. The data generated from these samples could also, with appropriate consent, allow large scale prospective research into the combined effects of genetic and environmental factors on disease risk. It is sometimes suggested that profiling at birth carries additional profound ethical implications, because the individual concerned is unable to give personal consent. As a result it is sometimes asked whether genetic profiling of babies is appropriate at all, and whether the discussion should focus instead on whether the profiling or analysis of the sample, although taken at birth, should await the attainment of the age of majority.

The Consent of the Incompetent

If we consider the issue of the role consent plays in decisions about what happens to the incompetent, of whom children are a sub-class, we may be able to see more clearly what the ethical issues here really are.

Children are a sub-class of the incompetent only, of course, in so far as they actually are incompetent or rather are not competent to make authentic (autonomous, if you like) decisions. I will not discuss further now the vexed problem of the competence of children. Suffice it to note that there is nothing essentially incompetent about children – we have to decide for each decision whether or not it can be competently made. Let us turn now to the suggestion that the inability to make a competent consent (or refusal) in any way limits what adults with 'care and control' of children may do on their behalf.

The suggestion that it might be wrong to do something to or for children because they are not in a position to consent is simply absurd. If decisions could not be made for children, unless and until they could consent to those decisions themselves, they would never grow up not to be children. Indeed they would not live long at all. All sorts of decisions are routinely made for children. Their parents (usually) or guardians or those charged with their care (hopefully) dress them, feed them, talk to them, play with them, hug and kiss and cuddle them, sleep with them, eat with them, travel with them, educate them. Less unproblematically, they indoctrinate them in religion and other prejudices, expose them to dangers such as carrying them on bicycles, in cars, on aeroplanes, cross busy roads with them and sometimes let them cross busy roads or play at the edge of busy roads by themselves, take them to McDonald's, buy them, or let them eat, or prepare for them, or let them prepare,

31 *Our Inheritance, Our Future*, Cm 5791, London, HMSO, 2003.

all sorts of unsuitable foods rich in cholesterol, sugar, salt, unhealthy fats, etc. Some of these are part of every child's upbringing. How did we allow this state of affairs to occur?

In medical contexts where the consent of a patient cannot be obtained because that patient is a child or otherwise supposedly incompetent someone else consents of their behalf. This is called 'presumed consent' or 'substituted judgement' or 'proxy consent'.

I suggest however that the reason why it is right to do what 'presumed consent' or 'substituted judgement' or 'proxy consent' seems to suggest in these cases, is simply because treating the patient in the proposed ways is in his best interests and to fail to treat him would be to deliberately harm him. It is the principle that we should do no harm that justifies treating the patient in particular ways.

The justification for treatment is not that the patient consented, nor that she would have, nor that it is safe to presume that she would have, nor that she will consent when he regains consciousness or when, on ceasing to be a child she becomes competent, but simply that it is the right thing to do, and it is right precisely *because* it is in her or his best interests.

That it is the 'best interests' test that is operative is shown by the fact that we do not presume consent to things that are not in the patient's best interests, even where it is clear that he would have consented. We do not usually mutilate patients who have expressed strong desire for mutilating operations for example. We do not, except where we believe it to be in the patients' best interests, amputate healthy limbs of patients suffering from Body Dysmorphic Disorder.[32]

If we do not give beneficial treatment to patients who have refused, say by advance directive, we perhaps do not do so because we believe this would constitute an assault and a violation of their will. But it is not a violation of someone's will, nor is it an assault, to give a treatment they have not refused, the withholding of which would constitute an injury.

The reason it is not a violation is not because they have consented in some notional or fictional sense, but because it is the right thing to do. And if we seek the reason why it is the right thing to do the answer is that to fail, or omit, to do it would injure the patient. It is the infliction of that injury, by act or omission,[33] that would constitute the violation or assault.

So where, in medical contexts, we act in the best interests of patients who cannot consent, we do so, I suggest, because we rightly believe we should not harm those in our care and not because some irrelevant person or the law has constructed a consent.

---

32 Indeed doctors at Falkirk and District Royal Infirmary were recently much criticised for so doing: http://news.bbc.co.uk/hi/english/uk/scotland/newsid_625000/625680.stm.

33 I argued against the relevance of the moral distinction between acts and omissions in *Violence and Responsibility*, London, Routledge & Kegan Paul,1980 This irrelevance has recently and belatedly been recognised by the highest court in the United Kingdom. See Lord Mustill's judgement in *Airedale NHS Trust v. Bland,* [1993] 1 All ER. 821 (H.L).

So much for medical contexts. If we consider again the case of profiling babies at birth, or for that matter all the other decisions that parents and others make for or on behalf of children, we can see that the best interests test is not really helpful either. This is because, whereas it is in the best interests of children that they are fed, clothed, educated and many other things by competent individuals whether adult or not, this does not justify any particular decision. Indeed of all the ways in which a particular parent may, let us say, choose to feed, clothe, talk to, travel with a particular child it is unlikely that any would pass the *best* interests test and many would scarcely count as in the child's interests at all.

So, our question then must be: what justifies the imposition of a 'best interests' criterion – as for example in the case of a decision to consent on a child's behalf to an appendectomy, or to dental care, or to take a child in a baby seat on a bicycle, or to McDonald's for lunch, or to the clinic for an MMR vaccine? The latter is of course added to the list because, whereas MMR vaccination is in the public interest, because of herd immunity and the 'free-rider' effect, it is unlikely to be in the interests of any particular child to be subjected to even the remote risk involved in MMR in a context where most children are being vaccinated. The answer seems to be 'nothing'. In other words there really is no feature of decision making on behalf of children which justifies or rather requires the imposition of a 'best interests' test rather than of simply a requirement that the decision taken on behalf of children must not be grossly against their interest or manifestly dangerous. Here the standards of danger must be pretty high or bicycle rides and fatty foods would be permanently off the menu.

The bottom line seems to be that if we are to permit parents or guardians care and control – in short, if family life is to be protected – huge latitude must be allowed to parents in decision making on behalf of children. There seems to me no reason why that latitude should be denied in the case of genetic testing or profiling at birth or in childhood. Add to this the powerful reasons on both sides of the argument to add to the lack of clarity and the safe side must surely remain with parental discretion.

An important argument made in relation to a child's 'right' not to know[34] concerns the removal of the possibility of the child making his/her own decision whether to undergo medical treatment at a future time. In the context of genetic testing, it been said, for example, that:

> Testing during childhood removes the individual's future autonomy and confidentiality, and may cause damage to their self-esteem and future interpersonal relationships.[35]

Any supposed 'right' of children to make up their own minds about having such a test when they are older, must, however, be balanced against claims that the failure to test deprives children of the 'right' to grow up in an atmosphere of openness and

---

34 These ideas are further elaborated in Harris, J. and Keywood, K., 'Ignorance Information and Autonomy', in *Theoretical Medicine and Bioethics*, 415-436.

35 See Clarke, A. and Flinter, F., 'The genetic testing of children: A clinical perspective', in Marteau, T. and Richards, M. (eds), *The Troubled Helix*, Cambridge, CUP, 1996.

understanding of their situation and a 'right' or interest not to form unrealistic hopes and plans about the future. These might include the right to make informed plans and decisions about, for example, rational education prospects (how long a period of preparation for a career would be rational?), rational career prospects, rational marriage plans and rational timing of children.

This is not to say that it is obviously in a child's interests to be tested. Indeed, there may be situations when testing is manifestly contrary to a child's best interests. The point to be made, however, is that such interests cannot be determined solely by reference to a child's autonomy interests.[36] Such cases raise real questions about where the balance of a child's best interests lie and consideration must be given to factors other than autonomy that may determine whether a child's medical/genetic status is to be known.

One clear conclusion here is that there is no sense in which a decision not to test children, even for late onset conditions, protects their autonomy whereas a decision to test violates it. Again autonomy walks both sides of this street and any such decisions must be based on a calculation of the best interests of the child and on whether or not there are sufficiently powerful and clear grounds to override the parents' presumptive claim to be the guardian of such interests.

If decisions must be taken on behalf of children, the presumption must surely be that health screening is primarily a matter for parents. This and most societies operate rightly with the view that unless and until it can be shown that the presumption that parents are the best guardians of their children's interests must be overturned in order to protect children from serious harm, decisions about most things concerning children should remain with parents.[37]

It is true that to raise a child in the knowledge that he or she will develop a dreaded familial disease, may cause additional harm but there is no reason to assume that this must be so. Unless there is strong reason to suppose that serious harm will result, which I doubt, the principle of non-maleficence cannot be invoked. The psychological impacts, for example, of being informed of a familial disease, are contested.[38] Furthermore, it should be noted that even where the principle of non-maleficence is appropriately invoked, that is where disclosing information about the

---

36 In the recent case of *Re C (HIV test)* [1999] 2 FLR 1004, it is noteworthy that the High Court did not consider as part of its determination of baby C's best interests; the child's autonomy interests. Compelling C's parents to have the child tested for HIV undoubtedly removes the possibility of C deciding at a later date whether to have the test or not, an argument which C's mother put to the court and which was regarded as a 'hopeless programme for the baby's protection'.

37 There are also arguments, which assert and defend a right or entitlement to reproductive liberty to the same effect. See Harris, J., 'Genes, Clones and Human Rights', in Burley, J.C. (ed), *The Genetic Revolution and Human Rights: The Amnesty Lectures 1998*, Oxford, OUP, 1999, 61-95. See also Robertson, J., *Children of Choice*, Princeton, New Jersey, Princeton University Press, 1994.

38 Laurie, G.T., 'In defence of ignorance: Genetic information and the right not to know', *European Journal of Health Law*, 6 (1999), 119-132, at p. 122.

child's health status is likely to do more harm than good, it is always a further and separate ethical question as to whether disclosing information the results of which may not be in the child's overall interests is wrongful. Many people believe that bringing children up in a religion, for example, is strongly against the child's interests, but it does not follow that this practice must be prevented. It would be difficult to defend a diet of so called 'junk food' or of pulp fiction or of the tabloid press, or of game shows, 'soaps' and reality television. We tend to forget how much of what happens to children as a result of parental choice, or at least of parental 'consent' or acquiescence, is scarcely describable as either in the child's best interests or indeed even in the child's interests at all. We should be cautious about moving from plausible judgments about the interests of the incompetent to drastic conclusions as to what may or may not be permitted. This caution has bccn singularly lacking in the literature invoking child welfare and we should all be reluctant to consent to being controlled by those who believe the enforcement of morality is a first duty rather than, perhaps, a last resort.

Consent then is a conscious, deliberate, autonomous act. The dead, the un-dead (those yet to be born) and the incompetent are necessarily incapable of consenting to anything. What we do to and for them is then either a matter of their rights or interests. We have noted that they have no rights and only attenuated interests. Nothing of the force (persuasive, logical or rhetorical) that would be enough to give third parties an entitlement to consent of their behalf. Why then so many people have thought that the concept of consent, or the extensive literature of informed consent, can in any way illuminate the problem of what do to, for or about these three important groups of vulnerable individuals is, and remains, a mystery.

Chapter 19

No More 'Shock, Horror'? The Declining Significance of 'Sudden Shock' and the 'Horrifying Event' in Psychiatric Injury Claims

Harvey Teff

Introduction

A familiar refrain of the law on negligently caused psychiatric harm is that more attention should be paid to advances in medicine.[1] Yet, in an area notorious for its incoherence and elaborate restrictions on liability,[2] there remains a marked lack of fit between law and scientific progress. The legal construct of 'pure' psychiatric harm defies understanding of the physical processes associated with mental activity, and legal principles pay scant attention to the causes of psychiatric illness. This mismatch is not an inevitable consequence of outdated precedent, as several of the 'rules' are far from doctrinally secure. Even the key requirement of a 'recognisable psychiatric illness' as the liability threshold rests on very slender authority.[3] In recent years, added confusion has been caused by the problematic division of claimants into 'primary' and 'secondary' victims,[4] the latter having to overcome a number of largely arbitrary legal hurdles. Prominent among them is the need to prove that their psychiatric illness was induced by the 'sudden shock' of a 'horrifying event'.[5]

---

1 E.g., *McLoughlin v. O'Brian* [1983] 1 AC 410, at p. 443, per Lord Bridge; *Page v. Smith* [1996] AC 155, at p. 188, per Lord Lloyd, and *White v. Chief Constable of South Yorkshire* [1999] 2 AC 455, at p. 492, per Lord Steyn.

2 A 'patchwork quilt of distinctions which are difficult to justify', *White*, *supra cit.*, at p. 500, per Lord Steyn.

3 '... [N]o deliberative consideration seems to have accompanied the use of the expression. It can be traced to a statement by Lord Denning in *Hinz v. Berry* ... Subsequent courts have adopted the phrase and embedded it in the law', *van Soest v. Residual Health Management Unit* [2000] 1 NZLR 179, at p. 204, per Thomas J. Lord Denning may simply have repeated the term used in evidence by the psychiatrist describing the claimant's condition.

4 See pp 310-12, *infra*.

5 *Alcock v. Chief Constable of South Yorkshire* [1992] 1 AC 310, at p. 401.

The term 'nervous shock', first used in forensic medicine in the mid-nineteenth century and promptly adopted by the legal profession,[6] was standard usage for many years in describing the action for psychiatric harm. Increasingly condemned as unscientific, by the 1930s it had no place in medicine. A confusing, somewhat patronising, label, 'nervous shock' unhelpfully blurred the distinction between the nature of the condition described and its cause.[7] In the late twentieth century, the courts, too, began distancing themselves from it, though it lingers on in some of the judgments.[8] Whereas several jurisdictions have abandoned the requirement that psychiatric injury be shock-induced, in England, as in Scotland, it survives,[9] if diluted in various pockets of case law. How much longer can this obstacle to liability endure, and what would be the impact of its demise?

Primary and Secondary Victims

First, we need to address the primary/secondary divide, now central to whether or not a duty of care exists. For primary victims, a narrowly defined category, it is unclear whether a *shock-induced* injury is ever required.[10] For the potentially much larger category of secondary victims, this requirement was conclusively established in *Alcock v. Chief Constable of South Yorkshire*, where the primary/secondary distinction was first mooted, by Lord Oliver. He classified primary victims as 'involved participants' in an accident, according only secondary status to passive, unwilling witnesses of injury to others.[11] In *Alcock*, the unsuccessful claimants were relatives and close friends of spectators who had died or were injured in the Hillsborough football disaster. They were characterised as secondary victims, because they either saw what was happening from a distance at the ground, or on live or recorded television: they were not 'involved participants'. A narrower conception of primary victims was to emerge from the House of Lords decision in *Page v. Smith*,[12] where Lord Lloyd said of the claimant that he was 'a participant ... directly

---

6 Pugh, C. and Trimble, M.R., 'Psychiatric Injury after Hillsborough', (1993) 163 *British Journal of Psychiatry*, 425-429, at p. 425.

7 See *Campbelltown City Council v. Mackay* (1989) 15 NSWLR 501, at p. 503.

8 E.g., 'There is nothing disreputable about a claim for damages based on psychiatric injury, commonly *and with slightly disparaging overtones* characterised by lawyers as damages for "nervous shock"': *Young v. Charles Church* (1998) 39 BMLR 146, CA, at p. 163, per Hutchison LJ. Emphasis added.

9 E.g., it no longer applies in Australia and South Africa. Scottish law on liability for psychiatric harm is broadly similar to that in England. See L Com, *Liability for Psychiatric Illness*, Consultation Paper No 137 Appendix, pp. 94-5; Sc L Com, *Damages for Psychiatric Injury*, Discussion Paper No 120.

10 In *Sion v. Hampstead Health Authority*, the Court of Appeal said that it was not: [1994] 5 Med L R 170, at p. 173, per Staughton LJ and at p. 176, per Peter Gibson LJ, and see Howarth, D., in Grubb, A. (ed), *The Law of Tort*, London, Butterworths, 2001, at 12.176.

11 *Alcock, supra cit.*, at p. 407.

12 *Page, supra cit.* (minor traffic accident).

involved in the accident, and well within the range of foreseeable *physical* injury. He was the primary victim'.[13] On one view, the allusion to physical imperilment was essentially descriptive, highlighting physical involvement as a *sufficient* rather than a *necessary* attribute of primary status. However, *Page* was also open to the narrower interpretation that physical endangerment[14] was a *prerequisite* of primary status and, importantly, was so construed by the majority of the House in *White v. Chief Constable of South Yorkshire Police*,[15] when they rejected the claims of several traumatised, on-duty police officers at Hillsborough.

Clearly, establishing primary status is a major advantage for claimants. It enables them to recover for any *personal* injury (physical or psychiatric) foreseeably caused by the defendant's negligence. That they were not physically injured, or that their psychiatric illness was not foreseeable, does not matter. They are essentially to be treated like any 'ordinary' personal injury claimants. By contrast, 'secondary' victims are treated much less favourably. First, they must prove that, in the circumstances, psychiatric illness would have been reasonably foreseeable in persons of 'normal fortitude'. In addition, they have to overcome several other obstacles, a legacy of earlier case law. These include the need for close ties with an immediate victim and closeness in time and space to a directly perceived accident (or its immediate aftermath) which has induced psychiatric illness by shock. In Lord Ackner's words, '"[s]hock", in the context of this cause of action, involves the sudden appreciation by sight or sound of a horrifying event, which violently agitates the mind'.[16]

The above references to an 'event' and perception of an 'accident' immediately suggest a particular kind of occurrence, namely, a physical happening or incident of some description, usually in the form of the rail or road crashes which largely shaped the early law, but also encompassing mass disasters at particular venues. Even in these paradigmatic settings, the primary/secondary divide has proved to be a distinct embarrassment, its application often proving a source of contention. For example, in the Court of Appeal judgment concerning the police at Hillsborough, Rose LJ saw the claimants as primary victims (directly involved); Judge LJ saw them as secondary victims, (physically unendangered) and Henry LJ said: 'I am not sure that the labelling of each plaintiff as a primary or secondary victim really matters!'[17] Shortly afterwards, the House of Lords reversed *Frost*, holding that physical endangerment was essential for primary status. A few months later, in *W v. Essex HA*,[18] Lord Slynn described the question of classification as 'not ... finally closed'. It was, he said, 'a concept still to be developed in different factual circumstances'.[19] In *W*, the parent-

13 *Ibid.*, at p. 184. Emphasis added.

14 Or a reasonable belief that one was physically endangered: *McFarlane v. E.E. Caledonia Ltd.* [1994] 2 All ER 1, CA.

15 [1999] 2 AC 455.

16 *Alcock*, *supra cit.*

17 *Frost v. Chief Constable of South Yorkshire Police* [1997] 3 WLR 1194, CA, at p. 1213.

18 *W v. Essex County Council* [2001] 2 AC 592.

19 *Ibid.*, at p. 601.

claimants fostered a child who, the Local Authority negligently assured them, had no known or suspected history of child abuse, but who subsequently abused their own children. The parents sued the Authority for psychiatric illness stemming from guilt feelings about being unwitting agents of the abuse. Lord Slynn found that they might be entitled to primary victim status,[20] though there was no suggestion that *they* had been physically endangered. As regards any claim to secondary status, it is hard to see how they could have satisfied the proximity requirements as to time and space and, most importantly for our purposes, their psychiatric harm was not caused by sudden shock. In short, *W* was not a standard 'accident' case.

Insistence that claimants cannot recover unless they satisfy the criteria for primary or secondary status disregards the fact that, in numerous settings, those criteria have little or no meaningful purchase.[21] A raft of recent cases has highlighted the problem, several judges expressing their distaste at having to acquiesce.[22] In some instances of 'non-accident' litigation, there is often no one who fits the narrow *Page* formula for primary victims, and no secondary victim.[23] For example, when psychiatric illness is induced by occupational stress, there is commonly a single victim, who has not been exposed to physical danger and whose condition has not been caused by a discrete event or sudden shock. Similarly, when harm to the psyche is caused by negligent exposure to a prolonged distressing process,[24] disturbing misinformation,[25] the gradual onset of fear as to what might happen in the future,[26] or the negligent provision of services,[27] there is no accident scene or 'zone of danger', and often little or nothing to engage the special control mechanisms. As conventionally understood, there is no 'horrifying event' inducing 'sudden shock'.

---

20 *Ibid. W* was a striking out application.

21 See Hilson, C., 'Nervous Shock and the Categorisation of Victims', (1998) 6 *Tort L Rev*, 37-55, at p 55, and 'Liability for Psychiatric Injury: Primary and Secondary Victims Revisited', (2002) 18 *PN*, 167-176, at p. 176.

22 E.g., 'Whether we like it or not, we are constrained [to apply the control mechanisms]': *Galli-Atkinson v. Seghal* [2003] Lloyd's Rep Med 285, CA, at p. 290 [23], per Latham LJ. *Cf A B v. Leeds Teaching NHS Trust & Cardiff and Vale NHS Trust* [2005] Lloyd's Rep Med 1, at p. 32 [197].

23 E.g., *Farrell v. Avon* [2001] Lloyd's Rep Med 458, and *Walters v. North Glamorgan NHS Trust* [2002] Lloyd's Rep Med 227. See further, Case, P., 'Curiouser and Curiouser: Psychiatric Damage Caused by Negligent Misinformation', (2002) 18 *PN*, 248-259, at p. 248.

24 E.g., *Sion, supra cit.*

25 See note 23, *supra.*

26 E.g., *CJD Disease Litigation: Group B Plaintiffs v. Medical Research Council* [2000] Lloyd's Rep Med 161.

27 *McLoughlin v. Jones* [2002] 2 WLR 1279, CA.

Shock and the Secondary Victim

Why should secondary victims have to prove 'shock'? More precisely, why must they prove that their psychiatric condition stems from an immediate emotional reaction to a stressor prompted by physical presence at a specific incident? Neither presence at an incident nor immediacy of reaction is a necessary trigger for psychiatric illness, and 'sudden shock' is often a poor predictor of it. Acute emotional responses are normally transient and of little, if any, medical or legal consequence by comparison with delayed, prolonged or cumulative emotional impact. Empirical evidence has demonstrated that it is the duration and severity of a distress reaction that typically induces psychiatric illness, especially, but not exclusively, when the illness takes the form of depression.[28] Responding to the English Law Commission on the issue, the Royal College of Psychiatrists' Mental Health Law Group was scathing:

> For psychiatrists the 'shock-induced' requirement causes serious problems. The term is vague, has no psychiatric meaning and is emotively misleading. The requirement should be abandoned. Psychiatric evidence should require demonstration, or not, of a psychiatric disorder distinct from a normal mental reaction and, if present, its relationship with the index event. This is usually possible. The requirement to fit the evidence around the concept of whether or not the disorder is 'shock-induced' has no scientific or clinical merit. It is simply playing with words.[29]

Yet the law remains captivated by an image of immediate reaction to a directly perceived 'shocking event'. Words like 'horror', 'fright' and 'terror' have long been part of the common currency in claims for mental harm.[30] Sometimes the judicial phraseology has amounted to little more than colourful intensifiers, occasionally invoked to ludicrous effect, as in Lord Denning's notorious contrast between the 'terrifying descent' of the lorry in *Hambrook v. Stokes* and the 'slow backing of the taxicab' in *King v. Phillips*.[31] It is all about 'being there', in the 'zone of danger', instinctively reacting to a traumatic stimulus. When there is a reluctant concession to presence at the aftermath, it must be the 'immediate' aftermath. Only a couple of hours' leeway is allowed and, again, the horror of the scene which confronts the claimant looms large.[32] This preoccupation with instant fright at a horrifying event epitomises the fatal flaw of nearly all of the special controls imposed on secondary claimants – attaching undue causal significance to what are often no more than circumstantial details.

---

28 Tennant, C., 'Liability for Psychiatric Injury: An Evidence-based Approach', (2002) 76 *Australian Law Journal*, 73-79, at p. 73.

29 Law Com Report, *Liability for Psychiatric Illness* (1998), para 5.29 (2).

30 See, e.g., the note 'Terror as a Cause of Action', (1919) 63 *SJ*, 239, and the note 'Damages for Fright', (1957) 101 *SJ*, 275.

31 *Hambrook v. Stokes* [1925] 1 KB 141, and *King v. Phillips* [1953] 1 QB 429, at p. 442, respectively.

32 *McLoughlin v. O'Brian, supra cit.*

Even as a *legal* requirement, 'shock' is high on the list of doctrinally fragile concepts. There is no clear indication that, prior to *Alcock*, the instant display of emotional shock had ever been a prerequisite of liability in English law.[33] This development can be traced to Brennan J's assertion, in the leading Australian case of *Jaensch v. Coffey*, that there had to be a 'sudden sensory perception … that … affronts or insults the plaintiff's mind',[34] which appears to have prompted Lord Ackner's graphic depiction in *Alcock*, though he cited no authority for it.[35] It is true that, in *Alcock*, Lord Oliver described 'sudden and unexpected shock' as one of the 'common features' of all of the previous English authorities on secondary claims,[36] but this leaves open the question whether 'suddenness' had been a requirement or a mere contingency. In the first half of the twentieth century, many judges would doubtless have assumed that serious mental conditions normally resulted from momentary fright or terror – a 'shock to the system'.[37] Yet, in a number of pre-*Alcock* decisions, the onset of psychiatric illness is more plausibly explained by gradual, cumulative assaults on the nervous system.[38]

If the terminology of 'shock, horror' in the earlier cases largely reflected popular contemporary misperceptions, it was also partly explicable by a different, if related, concern – the perceived need for evidential purposes of a shattering event, with patently visible effects. Initially, this was a major concern because plaintiffs were not allowed to provide direct testimony as to their condition,[39] and sophisticated techniques for determining both cause and authenticity were lacking. More broadly, the adversarial process has always been most effective in handling self-contained, one-off incidents. The causes of mental harm following an instantaneous rail or car crash are often more readily established than, say, the more complex relationship between caring over time for a negligently injured close relative and gradually emerging depression. Here, too, the problems are essentially evidential, rather than conceptual, such as the potential contribution of a claimant's life events to the onset of their psychiatric condition.

---

33 'Whilst the requirement for "shock" to induce the psychiatric illness was not explicit in English case law until the *Alcock* case, it has been applied since that decision with some rigour by the Court of Appeal'. *Tan v. East London and City Health Authority* [1999] Lloyd's Rep Med 389, at *p.* 395. See further, Teff, H., 'The Requirement of "Sudden Shock" in Liability for Negligently Inflicted Psychiatric Damage', (1996) 4 *Tort L Rev*, 44-61.

34 *Jaensch v. Coffey* (1984) 155 CLR 549, at p. 567.

35 *North Glamorgan NHS Trust v. Walters* [2003] Lloyd's Rep Med 49, per Ward LJ, at pp. 55-6 [25].

36 *Alcock, supra cit.*, at p. 411.

37 See *Rhodes v. CNR* (1990) 75 DLR (4th) 248, at p. 280, per Southin JA.

38 E.g., *McLoughlin v. O'Brian, supra cit.*, and *Chadwick v. British Railways Board* [1967] 1 WLR 912, decided on the basis that it was 'the horror of the whole experience which caused the [claimant's] reaction' (over some 12 hours).

39 Earengay, W., 'The Legal Consequences of Shock', reprinted in (1992) 60 *Medico-Legal Journal*, 83-109, at p. 85 (first appearing in Vol 1, of *Medico-Legal and Criminological Review* (1933) 14-30.

Lord Ackner's Conception of Shock

Where there is no incident or spectacle to be perceived or experienced, there is no natural means of applying the shock requirement in what the courts regard as its most authoritative form, as stipulated by Lord Ackner:

> "Shock", in the context of this cause of action, involves the sudden appreciation by sight or sound of a horrifying event, which violently agitates the mind. It has yet to include psychiatric illness caused by the accumulation over a period of time of more gradual assaults on the nervous system.[40]

The immediate impression conveyed by this formulation is of some dramatic occurrence, eliciting an instant reaction – an arresting, if stereotypical, image of psychiatric harm and its assumed triggers. Before examining its various threads, a few preliminary observations should be made. First, strictly speaking, Lord Ackner's characterisation of shock was only *obiter*, as none of the claimants in *Alcock* was found to be a secondary victim in any event. Secondly, it was one of several propositions on the then prevailing liability criteria for psychiatric harm, all prefaced by the words, '[w]hatever may be the pattern of the future development of the law in relation to this cause of action …'.[41] The force of the qualification that the law 'has yet' to include more gradual, cumulative assaults on the nervous system is unclear. Though he possibly intended it as a plain factual statement, Lord Ackner may have been counselling against such a development, anticipating it, or both.

The Event

Insofar as the 'event' in the earlier cases was considered as a virtually instantaneous occurrence, so, too, was its perception. However, if a broader view is taken of what constitutes an event, Lord Ackner's wording may allow for more flexibility than appears at first sight. In *McLoughlin*, Lord Wilberforce described an Australian decision as 'based soundly' on 'direct perception of some of the events which go to make up the accident as an entire event [including] the immediate aftermath'.[42] In the recent decision of *Walters*, Ward LJ invoked this interpretation to construe a series of incidents over a 36 hour period in a hospital as the 'entire event'. 'One looks', he said, 'to the totality of the circumstances which bring the claimant into proximity … to the accident'.[43] He also said that what the claimant is *told* may be relevant. Whereas it has long been the law that 'merely being informed of, or reading, or

40 *Alcock, supra cit.*, at p. 401.

41 *Ibid.*, at p. 400. And see *North Glamorgan NHS Trust v. Walters, supra cit.*, at p. 60, *per* Clarke LJ.

42 *McLoughlin v. O'Brian, supra cit.*, at p. 422, in reference to *Benson v. Lee* [1972] VR 879, 880.

43 *Walters, supra cit.*, at p. 55 [23]. *Cf Tredget, supra cit.*, (48 hours), and *Chadwick, supra cit.*

hearing about the accident' does not ground liability, '[i]nformation given *as the events unfold before one's eyes* is part of the circumstances of the case to which the court is entitled to have regard'.[44]

If a series of 'mini-events' or a single elongated process, together with oral communications along the way, can be construed as the 'entire event', does not the phrase '*sudden* appreciation of a *horrifying* event' part company with its more natural meaning? Admittedly, it has been held that the issue is not whether the defendant's conduct was 'shocking' in the sense of the claimant witnessing a sudden and violent incident; it is rather the *unexpected* nature of what the claimant sees or experiences that counts.[45] But it remains artificial to describe claimants who have reacted to a series of events in a process, as in the hospital cases,[46] as having 'suddenly' been 'horrified'.

Suddenness

It is clear that, for Lord Ackner, 'suddenness' was a key ingredient of liability, as evidenced by his explicit contrast with gradual assaults. After *Alcock*, it was routinely required in standard 'accident' cases and, initially, when denying claims involving a prolonged 'process'.[47] Nonetheless, only a year or so after *Alcock*, a more pragmatic approach began to emerge as regards negligence in the hospital setting,[48] and, over the last decade or so, the courts have come close to abandoning the shock requirement where there are long drawn-out medical processes.[49] There have also been signs of a similar shift in respect of other professional services,[50] and occasionally even in mainstream 'accident' cases.[51]

It is significant that several judges have begun to use more neutral, less emotive, terminology. By the mid-1990s, in *Page v. Smith*, we find Hoffman LJ referring to 'damage caused by mental trauma',[52] and Henry LJ, in *Frost*, also preferring 'trauma' to 'shock', stressing that 'what matters is not the label on the trigger for psychiatric damage, but the fact and foreseeability of psychiatric damage, by whatever process'.[53]

44 *Walters, ibid.*, at *p.* 58 [35]. Emphasis added.

45 *Sion, supra cit.*, at p. 176, *per* Peter Gibson LJ. In *Jaensch, supra cit.*, at p. 567, Brennan J referred to the plaintiff's perception of a 'phenomenon', which would not necessarily connote an event.

46 See pp. 310-12, *infra*.

47 See *Sion, supra cit.*, and *Taylorson v. Shieldness Produce Ltd* [1994] PIQR 329.

48 *Tredget, supra cit.*

49 E.g.,*Walters, supra cit.* and *Froggatt v. Chesterfield and North Derbyshire Royal Hospital NHS Trust* [2002] All ER (D) 218. *Aliter, Tan v. East London and City Health Authority* [1999] Lloyd's Rep Med 389. See further, pp. *infra*.

50 *McLoughlin v. Jones, supra cit.*

51 E.g., *Galli-Atkinson, supra cit.*

52 *Page v. Smith* [1994] 4 All ER 522, CA, at pp. 549-50.

53 *Frost, supra cit.*, at p. 1208.

Horror, Violently Agitating the Mind

Though the main focus of the shock requirement has been on 'suddenness', the issue of whether the circumstances are sufficiently 'horrifying' has also proved capable of limiting the scope of 'secondary' claims.[54] Of the Law Lords in *Alcock*, Lord Ackner alone referred to the need for a 'horrifying' event.[55] We have already noted the limited significance of instant horror and fright as reliable indicators of various forms of psychiatric illness.[56] It may well be that the contemporary prominence and graphic media portrayals of post traumatic stress disorder (PTSD) have served to muddy the waters in this respect. When PTSD is thought of as almost synonymous with psychiatric harm, it is easy to assume that all such harm entails exposure to an event which is both 'sudden' and 'horrifying', such as to precipitate the 'violent agitation' associated with 'flashbacks' as a characteristic symptom of PTSD.[57] In one relatively recent case, the only substantive judgment in the Court of Appeal referred to 'negligently caused psychiatric injury or nervous shock, now more commonly referred to as post traumatic stress disorder'.[58] It is precisely this kind of equation that invites dubious, often invidious, judicial exploration of how macabre the scene must be to justify recovery, speculating on whether the immediate traumatic stressor was truly 'horrifying' or *merely* very distressing – as if this distinction were the key to ensuing psychiatric damage.

Claims Resulting from Medical Negligence

The shortcomings of the liability rules for psychiatric harm have been exposed with particular clarity in a spate of recent claims arising from medical negligence. In the fraught environment of the hospital, the natural anxieties of patients and people intimately connected with them are often heightened by inadequate information or mixed messages. In this setting, the case for restricting 'secondary' claims for want of 'sufficient proximity' looks distinctly thin. There is commonly a nexus between the hospital and those closest to the patient, whose 'presence', when not actually known about as a fact, is readily foreseeable, even if they seldom directly perceive a shocking event. The traumatic experience of a long drawn-out vigil, with intermittent crises and hopes raised only to be dashed, or an extended process of dawning realisation culminating in the trauma of attendance at the mortuary, normally

54 See *Ward v. Leeds Teaching Hospitals NHS Trust* [2004] Lloyd's Rep Med 530, pp. 312-13, *infra*.

55 Though, in the Court of Appeal, Nolan LJ said that 'the expression "nervous shock," as used in the decided cases, connotes a reaction to an immediate and horrifying impact', *Alcock* [1991] 3 WLR, 1057, CA, at p. 1095.

56 See p. 305 *supra*.

57 See Tennant, *supra cit.*, at p. 77.

58 *Chief Constable of West Yorkshire v. Schofield* [1998] 43 BMLR 28, at p. 33, *per* Hutchinson LJ.

provide ample evidence of '*causal* proximity'.[59] Yet under *Alcock*, whatever the surrounding circumstances, secondary claims would appear to require a specific traumatic incident.

Taylor v. Somerset Health Authority[60] was a case in point. Mr Taylor's fatal heart attack at work, months after the negligent diagnosis and treatment which had caused it, was the culmination of a deteriorating heart condition. His wife, informed that he had been taken ill, went straight to the hospital where a doctor told her that he had died. A few minutes later, she went to the mortuary, mainly to settle her disbelief. Her claim for psychiatric injury was dismissed for want of any 'event' to which the 'immediate aftermath' principle could be applied. Even if the death could have been so construed, her illness did not result from exposure to an 'external traumatic event, in the nature of an accident or violent happening'.[61] For good measure, we are told that, in the mortuary, the dead body 'bore no marks or signs to her of the sort that would have conjured up for her the circumstances of his fatal attack'.[62] The insistence on instant reaction to a discrete, traumatic event was unsurprising, coming so soon after *Alcock*. It was reinforced by the Court of Appeal, in *Sion*, where due to an allegedly negligent hospital diagnosis, the claimant's son deteriorated, fell into a coma and died.[63] His father's claim for psychiatric illness, following an 18-hour-a-day vigil for 14 days, which included a series of traumatising events, was struck out. There was, said Staughton LJ, 'no trace in [the medical] report of "shock" *as defined by Lord Ackner* …'. Rather, it was 'a process continuing for some time, from first arrival at the hospital to the appreciation of medical negligence after the inquest'.[64]

It is true that, by this time, hints of a more flexible approach were evident, most notably in *Tredget and Tredget v. Bexley Health Authority*.[65] *Tredget* involved a claim by parents for psychiatric illness, when, due to medical negligence, a prolonged, difficult labour and traumatic delivery had culminated in their child's death. According to White J, '[a]lthough lasting for over 48 hours from the onset of labour to the death, this effectively was one event'.[66] However, as late as 1999, we find a striking example of more restrictive analysis in *Tan v. East London and City Health Authority*,[67] despite overwhelming evidence of the claimant's foreseeable presence. Mr Tan's wife had been admitted to hospital for an elective caesarean. Before this could take place, he received a telephone call from the consultant informing him of the baby's death, which, it was later conceded, resulted from negligence. Mr Tan went to the hospital immediately, arriving an hour and a half later, and for nearly two

59 See *Jaensch v. Coffey*, *supra cit.*, at p. 607, per Deane J.

60 (1993) 4 Med LR 34.

61 *Ibid.*, at p. 37. But see note 45, *supra*, and related text.

62 *Id.*

63 See note 10, *supra*.

64 *Ibid.*, at p. 174. Emphasis added.

65 See note 10, *supra*.

66 *Ibid.*, at p. 184.

67 [1999] Lloyd's Rep Med 389.

hours he comforted his distressed and 'obviously extremely shocked' wife. There was then a caesarean delivery (just under four hours after the death). Mr Tan briefly held the dead child, kept vigil overnight and saw her being placed in a metal box. In dismissing his claim for psychiatric illness, the court held that the death *in utero*, or its immediate aftermath, constituted the accident or event at which he needed to have been present. He was not present at the death, and the phone call did not constitute direct perception. The death, stillbirth, overnight vigil and removal of the baby were not construed as all one event such as to satisfy the aftermath test. Though death in the womb and stillbirth are two events that are 'inextricably linked', the stillbirth was unrelated to the actual *circumstances*, as distinct from the *fact*, of the death. Furthermore, the *Alcock* 'shock' requirement was deemed not to have been met, for several reasons: the foreknowledge, planning and timing of the stillbirth (just under four hours after the death not satisfying the immediate aftermath test); the ordinary way in which the operation was conducted, and the appearance of the baby, looking normal as if asleep.

The last few years have seen a pronounced decline in the 'sudden shock' requirement in the hospital setting. In *North Glamorgan NHS Trust v. Walters*,[68] the hospital failed to diagnose acute hepatitis in a 10-month-old baby, whose epileptic fit, witnessed by his mother, was more serious than the staff had indicated. Told later that his severe brain damage ruled out any quality of life, she agreed to the withdrawal of life support, and he died in her arms, some 36 hours after the seizure. She suffered a pathological grief reaction from witnessing, experiencing and participating in these events, and the Court of Appeal endorsed the finding that the 36-hour period could be construed as 'one horrifying event'.[69] Because each traumatic event had an instant impact, the need for 'sudden' appreciation was deemed satisfied but, significantly, Clarke LJ intimated that even if the decision had involved an incremental step advancing the frontiers of liability, he would have taken it.[70] Similarly, in *Froggatt v. Chesterfield and North Derbyshire Royal Hospital NHS Trust*,[71] where a woman had been negligently misdiagnosed with cancer, her husband's first sight of her body after a mastectomy was treated as sudden appreciation of a horrifying, shocking event – not something 'expected'.[72] This was so, despite his advance knowledge of the operation and the inevitable delay before he saw her, suggesting a conception of the 'immediate aftermath' that goes well beyond what was envisaged in *McLoughlin v. O'Brian* and *Alcock*.[73] It is also of interest that, in apparent disregard of the direct

68 See note 35, *supra*.

69 '[A] seamless tale with an obvious beginning and an equally obvious end': *ibid.*, at p. 58 [34], per Ward LJ.

70 *Ibid.*, at *p.* 60 [51].

71 [2002] All ER (D) 218.

72 *Cf Sion, supra cit.*, *per* Peter Gibson LJ, at p. 174.

73 See Jones, M., *Medical Negligence* (2nd ed), London, Sweet & Maxwell, 2003, p. 147, para 2-129. In the Personal Injury Bar Association Annual Lecture (2004), 'Liability for Psychiatric Injury', Lord Phillips referred to *Froggatt*, as evidence of the 'considerable elasticity' of the aftermath concept.

perception requirement, Mr Froggatt's 10-year-old son recovered from the shock of *overhearing* a telephone conversation in which his mother had referred to her 'cancer'. These more liberal interpretations, in the hospital context, of the sudden event, immediate aftermath and unaided perception are beginning to have a broader resonance. In a mainstream road accident case, decided a few months after *Walters*, Latham LJ drew on the decision to assert that a sudden event did not require a 'frozen moment in time'; rather, he said, 'both an event and its aftermath could be made up of a number of components'.[74]

This is not to say that the potential for restrictive analysis in the medical context, as elsewhere, is entirely a thing of the past, as is illustrated by the recent case of *Ward v. Leeds Teaching Hospitals NHS Trust*.[75] In *Ward*, the claimant's 22-year-old daughter was admitted to hospital for the extraction of wisdom teeth. Due to the defendant's negligence, she failed to regain consciousness after the surgery and was pronounced dead some 48 hours later. Mrs Ward claimed for psychiatric injury in the form of PTSD, on the basis of various events surrounding the death. These included initially having seen her daughter in the recovery room; then in the intensive care unit; after the ventilator was switched off, and finally at the mortuary. However, the court accepted the defence expert's analysis that a severe and prolonged bereavement reaction was the overwhelming cause of her condition and that there was no 'shocking event of a particularly horrific nature'[76] to justify a diagnosis of PTSD.

Ward is of interest primarily for its observations on shock-induced injury or, more specifically, the 'horror' component of the requirement. Adopting Lord Ackner's definition, the judge observed that death of a loved one in hospital was not:

> an event outside the range of human experience, unless also accompanied by circumstances which were wholly exceptional in some way so as to shock or horrify. Mrs Ward's own descriptions of these incidents did not strike me as shocking at the time in that sense, although undoubtedly they were distressing. To describe an event as shocking in common parlance is to use an epithet so devalued that it can embrace a very wide range of circumstances. But the sense in which it is used in the diagnostic criteria for PTSD must carry more than that colloquial meaning.[77]

In *Walters*, it was said of the claimant that '[h]er hopes were lifted then they were dashed and finally destroyed when … she was advised to terminate treatment on the life-support machine'.[78] The events which caused her pathological grief reaction 'must have been *chilling moments*, truly shocking events … distressing in the extreme'.[79] Mrs Ward, too, had her hopes lifted and dashed. When present in the

74 *Galli-Atkinson v. Seghal, supra cit.*, at p. 290, para 25. Cf *Walters, supra cit.*, at p. 55 [23], *per* Ward LJ.

75 [2004] Lloyd's Rep Med 530.

76 *Ibid.*, at p. 535, [21].

77 *Id.*

78 *North Glamorgan NHS Trust v. Walters, supra cit.*, at p. 58 [36], *per* Ward LJ.

79 *Ibid.*, at pp. 58-9 [36]. Emphasis added.

recovery room, 'she still thought she would be taking her daughter home'.[80] She, too, experienced some traumatic, even perhaps 'chilling' moments, as when, before she had internalised the possibility of her daughter dying, she was told in the ICU to keep talking to her, because the hearing was the last thing to go,[81] or when she saw her in the mortuary with some blood in her ears and some bruising around her neck.

None of this is to take issue with the finding in *Ward*, where *Walters* was plausibly distinguished as based on agreed psychiatric evidence. *Ward* was pleaded as a case of PTSD, for which the evidence seemed slim. In a sense, pleading PTSD ups the stakes by requiring a particularly severe stressor;[82] the real indictment is the law's undue preoccupation with horror as a determinant of liability for psychiatric harm. In so far as it is conceded that shock need no longer be 'sudden', the case for it being 'horrifying', in a narrow sense, would seem to evaporate too. Yet the courts remain committed to a strong sense of 'horror' – an image of someone shuddering with terror. If Lord Ackner's comment that the law had yet to include gradual assaults on the nervous system was meant as a portent of things to come, it would indeed have been ironic since, at the outset of his speech, he noted that liability for the cause of action had 'greatly expanded ... largely ... due to a better understanding of mental illness and its relation to shock'.[83] As Professor Sims observed in his medical report for the police officers in *Frost*:

> In fiction, and perhaps in a layman's view of shock as a psychological event, the individual experiences a grossly untoward event or situation with one or more sensory modalities but almost always vision and is instantaneously 'shocked' or traumatised. In practice this almost never occurs and it is in the nature of psychological trauma that exposure for several hours results in much more severe long-term symptoms than the instantaneous exposure to shock and then the removal of the aversive stimulus.[84]

Concluding Remarks

In one respect, of course, there is no mystery about the endurance of the pronounced divergence between law and science in regard to psychiatric harm. It is largely driven by a fear of proliferating claims if the special controls were to be replaced by a straightforward test of reasonable foreseeability. A dominant theme of the leading cases, this fear is often expressed in quite extravagant terms. In *Alcock*, for example, Lord Oliver conjured up the spectre of 'virtually limitless liability'.[85] In *Page*, Lord Lloyd said that, without the controls, 'a negligent defendant might find himself

80 *Ward, supra cit.*, at p. 532 [10].

81 *Ibid.*, 533 [11], another instance of third party communication contributing to the total experience of someone present and directly perceiving events? *Cf Walters, supra*, note 44, and related text.

82 See Horne's commentary on *Ward*, note 75 *supra*, at p. 536.

83 *Alcock, supra cit.*, at p. 399.

84 *Frost, supra cit.*, at p. 1207.

85 See note 83, *supra*, at p. 417.

being made liable to all the world'.[86] A restrictive definition of primary victims, and stiff hurdles for the potentially more numerous secondary ones, were apparently seen as necessary to avert a ceaseless avalanche of claims. Yet no hard data has been provided to substantiate the nightmare vision. It is by no means universally accepted by the English judiciary,[87] still less by those Commonwealth jurisdictions which do not subscribe to the primary/secondary divide and the special control mechanisms.[88] As regards traumatised long term carers, for example, there are various extra-legal considerations that make claims about limitless liability sound rather overblown. So, too, dire warnings of the courts being inundated with trivial claims have a somewhat hollow ring, certainly as long as the 'recognisable psychiatric illness' threshold is retained.

The 'shock, horror' conception of psychiatric harm ('violently agitating the mind') has had an enduring hold on the popular imagination, which has been mirrored in the legal setting.[89] If significantly diminished of late in the case law, it still has undue capacity to determine legal outcomes. It was precisely in regard to Lord Ackner's characterisation of shock, in *Alcock*, that Henry LJ indicated his preference for the term 'trauma', as more aptly conveying that 'the length of the exposure and the circumstances of the exposure ... caused the psychiatric illnesses'.[90] Though the shock requirement may loom large in the cases, it is only one facet of the fundamental problem, namely, the abdication of principle which has created the 'patchwork quilt', with all its attendant casuistry. In the same passage, Henry LJ stressed the primacy of foreseeability of psychiatric damage over the 'label on the trigger'.[91] Calling off the search for principle is not a laudable response. Nor was it seen as adequate in the Australian High Court's path-breaking decision in *Tame v. New South Wales*, where the 'sudden shock' requirement was roundly rejected and, in effect, a reasonable foreseeability regime established.[92] Abandonment of the shock requirement would be an important symbolic, as well as practical, step towards the more progressive understanding of psychiatric harm that the House of Lords has rhetorically asserted in recent years.

In *White*, Lord Steyn said that '[c]ourts of law must act on the best medical insight of the day'.[93] At root, the legal framework for psychiatric injury perpetuates

---

86 *Page*, *supra cit.*, at p. 189.

87 In *White* itself, Lord Hoffmann, though emphatically dismissing the actions, distanced himself from knee-jerk resort to the floodgates argument, as lacking empirical evidence: *White*, *supra cit.*, at p. 510.

88 See *Tame v. New South Wales; Annetts v. Australian Stations Pty Ltd* (2002) 76 *ALJR*, 1348 (Australia); *Barnard v. Santam Bpk* 1999 (1) SA 202 (South Africa). See also, Thomas J (diss.) in *van Soest v. Residual Health Management Unit* [2000] 1 NZLR 179.

89 See Mendelson, D., *The Interfaces of Medicine and Law*, Aldershot, Dartmouth/Ashgate, 1998.

90 *Frost*, *supra cit.*, at p. 1208, citing Professor Sims's report.

91 *Id.*

92 See note 88, *supra*.

93 *White*, *supra cit.*, at p. 492.

a gross mismatch of law and medicine, which ill serves meritorious claimants and undermines the law's own reputation. What is required to repair the damage is resolute commitment to harmonising the law and medical understanding – in short, the kind of insight and commitment that have been such abiding features of Ken Mason's medico-legal scholarship.

Chapter 20

Is There a Right Not to Procreate?[1]

Elaine E. Sutherland

Introduction

At first glance, the question posed by this chapter may seem largely academic. As a practical matter, a person who does not wish to procreate has the fail-safe options of either remaining celibate or engaging only in same-sex relations in order to avoid procreation. Aside the usual, but nonetheless tragic, case of a rape victim who became pregnant as a result of her attack, the decision not to procreate seems to be within every individual's control. However, there is ample case law to demonstrate that it is not as simple as that, not least because it is common for heterosexuals to want an active sex life without any children resulting. While contraception offers something of an answer, it can fail, as can the more radical option of sterilisation. In addition, individuals who once wanted to have a child together may change their minds for any number of reasons, often because their relationship has broken down. In short, numerous examples present themselves where an individual's freedom not to procreate is at issue.

Using some examples of individuals who have made a choice not to procreate, this chapter will explore the extent to which that choice is respected and protected by the legal systems in the UK and the US. It will assess whose interests and rights prevail, and why this should be so, before concluding with an attempt to answer the question posed at the outset – 'Is there a right not to procreate?'.

The Right to Procreate

Before we explore the right *not to* procreate, it is worth making a brief mention of its corollary, the right *to* procreate.[2] That there is a right to procreate is so well established as to be almost axiomatic. There is support for it in numerous international human

---

1 I would like to thank Professor Emeritus J. Kenyon Mason for his most helpful comments on an earlier draft of this chapter, albeit each of us wondered what the etiquette was, given the nature of this book. The usual disclaimer applies and responsibility for the chapter remains mine alone.

2 In a sense, talk of a 'right to procreate' is somewhat misleading, since what is being protected is the right to attempt to do so, unfettered by external interference from the state.

rights instruments[3] and a good example can be found in the Universal Declaration of Human Rights, which provides:

> Men and women of full age, without any limitation due to race, nationality or religion, have the right to marry and to found a family.[4]

As far as domestic law in the UK is concerned, Article 12 of the European Convention on Human Rights is of particular relevance.[5] It provides:

> Men and women of marriageable age have the right to marry and to found a family, according to the national laws governing the exercise of this right.[6]

While the rights articulated in Article 12 are subject to national laws governing their exercise, this should not be read as permitting the state to make any regulation it chooses. The, now defunct, European Commission, and the European Court have consistently taken the view that regulation must not be such as to rob the right of all content.[7] Nonetheless, the margin of appreciation allowed to states gives them some latitude in assessing how to balance community and individual interests due to 'their direct and continuous contact with the vital forces of their countries'.[8] As a result, while respect for the right to procreate does not necessarily mean that all people are

3 See, for example, the American Declaration of the Rights and Duties of Man, O.A.S. res. XXX (1948), Article VI; the International Covenant on Civil and Political Rights, 999 U.N.T.S. 171 (1966), Articles 2(1) and 23 (1); and the American Convention on Human Rights, O.A.S. Treaty Series No. 36 (1969), Article 17(2).

4 G.A. res. 217 A(III), U.N. Doc. A/810 (1948), Article 16(1). Article 16 continues: '(2) Marriage shall be entered into only with the free and full consent of the intending spouses. (3) The family is the natural and fundamental group unit of society and is entitled to protection by society and the State'.

5 The substantive content of the European Convention was incorporated into domestic law by the Human Rights Act 1998.

6 European Convention of Human Rights and Fundamental Freedoms, E.T.S. No.5 (1950), as amended by E.T.S. No. 155, Article 12.

7 *Belgian Linguistic Case*, (1968) E.H.R.R. 252, at para 5 (regulation 'must never injure the substance of the right'); *Golder v. United Kingdom*, 1975 (1975) 1 E.H.R.R. 524, para 38 ('regulation must never injure the substance of the right [in this case, to education] nor conflict with other rights enshrined in the Convention'); *Hammer v. United Kingdom* (1982) 4 E.H.R.R. 139, para 63 ('any restriction or regulation of the exercise of that right must not be such as to injure its substance'); *Rees v. UK* (1987) 9 E.H.R.R. 56, para 50 (regulation 'must not restrict or reduce the right in such a way or to such an extent that the very essence of the right is impaired').

8 *Handyside v. United Kingdom* (1976) 1 E.H.R.R. 737, para 48.

entitled to be accommodated in all circumstances,[9] it does place a heavy burden on the state to justify its failure to respect an individual's right to procreate.[10]

For our present purpose, the real significance of recognising a right to procreate lies in the extent to which a 'right to' carries with it a 'right not to', since the latter may be as important to a given individual as the former. Certainly, the European Court has acknowledged that 'some of the guaranteed Convention rights have been interpreted as conferring *rights not to* do that which is the antithesis of what there is an express right to do',[11] and the Court went on to give the examples of the right *not* to express thoughts (Article 9), the right *not* to join an association (Article 11), and the right *not* to marry (Article 12).[12] However, it was at pains to point out that not all Convention rights carry similar antithetical rights when it concluded that the right to life, under Article 2, does not bring with it any corresponding right to die.[13] Clearly, then, the trick is to establish into which category a particular right falls.

In the US, the development of procreative freedom has, from the outset, acknowledged the notion of a right not to procreate. It was from the Constitutional

9 See, for example, *Briody v. St. Helens and Knowsley Area Health Authority*, [2002] Q.B. 856. There, a young woman who had a sub-total hysterectomy (she retained her ovaries) following complications during the birth of her second child was awarded substantial damages. However, the court was not prepared to award damages to cover the cost of using a surrogate to enable her to have another child. Addressing the issue of procreative freedom under Article 12, Mrs. Justice Hale observed, at para 26, 'While everyone has the right to try to have their own children by natural means, no-one has the right to be provided with a child.' This decision has to be read in the light of *R (on the application of Burke) v. General Medical Council*, [2005] EWCA Civ. 1003.

10 The procreative freedom of prisoners is a good example of a disputed area and one which has been resolved differently in the UK and the US: see Sutherland, E.E., 'Procreative Freedom and Convicted Criminals in the United States and the United Kingdom: Is Child Welfare Becoming the New Eugenics?', 82 *Oregon Law Review*, 1033 (2003). The rights of single women and female same-sex couples to access to assisted reproductive technology has proved controversial in the UK: see Sutherland, E.E., '"Man Not Included": Single Women, Female Couples and Procreative Freedom', (2003) 15 *Child and Family Law Quarterly*, 155.

11 See *Pretty v. United Kingdom* (2002) 35 E.H.R.R. 1, para 6 (emphasis in the original). Domestic courts have taken this idea on board: see, for example, *Torbay Borough Council v. News Group Newspapers* [2004] EWCA 2927, at para 36: 'Article 8 embraces both the right to maintain one's privacy and, if that is what one prefers, not merely the right to waive that privacy but also the right to share what would otherwise be private with others or indeed, with the world at large. So the right to communicate one's story to one's fellow beings is protected not merely by article 10 but also by article 8'.

12 *Pretty v. United Kingdom, supra cit.*, at para 6.

13 *Id.* There was found to be no breach of Article 2 in refusing to guarantee immunity from prosecution to the husband of a terminally ill woman who wanted, and needed, his help to commit suicide.

right to privacy,[14] in the sense of freedom from governmental interference, that Justice Douglas was able to discern guaranteed 'zones of privacy', formed by penumbras and emanations from the rights guarantees by the Bill of Rights.[15] One such penumbra enabled the Court to strike down a statutory provision criminalising the use of contraceptives by married couples.[16] It was this notion of personal privacy that led to the landmark decision in *Roe v. Wade*,[17] where a woman's right to choose abortion was upheld, albeit subject certain state interests.[18] The importance of procreative freedom and its protection through the right to privacy is best summed up in the oft-quoted words of Justice Brennan:

> If the right of privacy means anything, it is the right of the individual, married or single, to be free from unwarranted governmental intrusion into matters so fundamentally affecting a person as the decision whether to bear or beget a child.[19]

Thus, the right not to procreate is clearly centre stage in the US, albeit, as we shall see, the actual availability of the means to ensure effect is given to the right is far less secure.

Non-procreation Within Marriage

Procreation and child-rearing are often seen as two of the functions of marriage and, for some, they are its *raison d'être*.[20] Those who take this absolute position on the centrality of children to marriage find themselves in a somewhat awkward position, since the logical conclusion of their view must be that the marriages of couples who have chosen to remain child-free or cannot have children, are invalid. That is simply not the position of developed legal systems. If the spouses are content with the absence of children, then the legal system, quite rightly, does not interfere.

---

14 While the word 'privacy' does not appear in the Constitution at all, the concept recurs throughout the Bill of Rights. See, the First Amendment (right of association), the Third Amendment (prohibition on quartering soldiers without consent), the Fourth Amendment (security from unreasonable searches and seizures), the Fifth Amendment (protection from self-incrimination), and the Ninth Amendment (enumeration of rights does not deny others).

15 *Griswold v. Connecticut*, 381 U.S. 479 (1965), at p. 484.

16 *Griswold v. Connecticut, supra cit.* This right of privacy was extended to unmarried persons in *Eisenstadt v. Baird*, 405 U.S. 438 (1972).

17 410 U.S. 113 (1973).

18 For a brief discussion of abortion in the US, see p. 323, below.

19 *Eisenstadt v. Baird*, 405 U.S. 438 (1972), at p. 453.

20 This is a central argument of the minority of academic writers who support the Marriage Movement, in the US, and those opposed to same-sex marriage. See, for example, Spaht, K.S. 'Revolution and Counter-Revolution: The Future of Marriage in the Law', 49 *Loyola Law Review*, 1, at p. 4 (2003) ('Lack of child centeredness in American culture affects an understanding of the purpose of marriage, that being the procreation and acculturation if children').

What of the situation where one spouse wants to have children and the other spouse refuses to reproduce? Certainly, the legal systems in the UK respect the choice not to procreate in so far as it will not order a spouse to do so. However, it is interesting to note that these same legal systems have long accepted a reasonable expectation of at least attempting to procreate as part of the marriage package. Under the fault model of divorce, courts have recognised that denying a spouse the opportunity to have children might amount to cruelty or, to use more modern terminology, unreasonable behaviour.[21] Similarly, where one spouse precludes the possibility of procreation through surgery, the other spouse could, most probably, secure a divorce.[22] As we shall see, while a husband cannot prevent his wife from having an abortion,[23] if she does so in the face of his opposition, he may well obtain a divorce on the basis of her action. While financial provision on divorce generally no longer penalises 'bad' behaviour, the fact that a person can be divorced, against his or her will, is arguably a penalty since a variety of rights, including the right to live in a family home owned by the other spouse, the right to future support, and the right to pensions and other benefits, often cease on divorce. Thus, while courts have not been prepared to require a spouse to participate in the procreative process, the fact that the non-procreating spouse may suffer penalties suggests, at least at first sight, less than full respect for his or her choice. However, when one considers that the state is simply refereeing a dispute between individuals who are making incompatible choices, and is freeing the spouse who does want to procreate to go off and find a new partner, it becomes apparent that the legal system's position is one of respecting the position of both parties.

A point worth noting about much of the UK case law here is that it is rather old and, thus, has not been subject to analysis under the European Convention on Human Rights. Whether the Convention would make any difference is questionable. Certainly, the non-procreating spouse might found on the privacy right guaranteed by Article 8. However, it will be remembered that Article 8 rights are subject to lawful and necessary state interference on a number of grounds, including the rights and freedoms of others. Arguably, then, interference, in terms of permitting divorce,

---

21 In England, it has been accepted that 'for a man deliberately and without good reason permanently to deny a wife with a normally developed maternal instinct a fair opportunity of having even a single child is of itself cruelty when injury to her health results'; *Knott v. Knott* [1955] p. 249, per Sachs J, at p. 256. There does not appear to be any Scottish case law on this point but it is reasonable to expect that this would be the interpretation applied to the Divorce (Scotland) Act 1976, s 1(2)(b). See Sutherland, E.E., *op cit.*, para 11.8.

22 In *Bravery v. Bravery* [1954] 1W.L.R. 1169, p. 1173, Lord Hodson expressed the view that, 'As between husband and wife for a man to submit himself to [a sterilisation operation] without good medical reason ... would, no doubt, unless his wife were a consenting party, be a grave offence to her which could without difficulty be shown to be a cruel act, if it were found to have injured her health or to have caused reasonable apprehension of such injury.' In the event, the wife had consented in that case. Again, there is a dearth of Scottish case law on this point, but see Sutherland, E.E., *op cit.*, para 11.8.

23 Abortion is discussed at p. 322, below.

can be justified as respecting the other spouse's Article 12 right to found a family, by freeing him or her up to go on to form a relationship with a new partner.

In the US, the position is more varied. Certainly, courts will not order an unwilling spouse to procreate.[24] However, in states where fault grounds apply, courts have taken a more mixed view on the question of whether refusal to have children justifies the granting of a divorce, and desertion, rather than cruelty, is normally the applicable ground if a divorce is granted.[25] The increase in the number of US states making no-fault divorce available probably explains the dearth of recent case law on this point.

Abortion

Much has been written on the subject of abortion, which is fortunate, since constraints of space necessitate that it be given a relatively brief treatment here. The passing of the Abortion Act 1967 marked the widespread availability of legal abortions in the UK.[26] While the woman's choice to seek a termination triggers the process, she must satisfy two registered medical practitioners that she qualifies under one of the four conditions provided in the Act,[27] and certain other restrictions apply.[28] Thus, the legal

---

24 See the discussion of disputes over frozen embryos, discussed at p. 330, below for a possible exception (if it is an exception) to this.

25 *Kreyling v. Kreyling*, 23 A.2d 800 (N.J., 1942) (divorce for desertion granted); *Kirk v. Kirk*, 120 A.2d 854 (N.J. Super. 1956) (divorce for desertion refused, but largely due to the relevant statute requiring the desertion to continue for two years prior to raising the action); *Zagarow v. Zagarow*, 105 Misc.2d 1054 (N.Y. 1980) (husband refused divorce for either constructive cruelty or constructive abandonment).

26 Prior to the passing of the Act, while procuring or performing an abortion was illegal, it was a defence to show that the abortion was necessary to save the life of the pregnant woman or to protect her physical or mental health. In England and Wales, see, *R v. Bourne*, [1939] 1 K.B. 687. In Scotland, see G.H. Gordon, *The Criminal Law of Scotland* (3rd ed) Edinburgh, W. Green, 2001, paras 28.01-28.04.

27 The conditions, provided in s 1(1) of the 1967 Act, as amended, are: (1) that continuation of the pregnancy would involve greater risk to the physical or mental health of the woman or any existing children in her family than would a termination; (2) That the termination is necessary to prevent 'grave permanent injury to physical or mental health of pregnant woman'; (3) That continuation of the pregnancy would involve risk to life of the pregnant woman greater than termination; or (4) That there is substantial risk that if the child were born alive it would suffer from such physical or mental abnormalities as to be seriously handicapped.

28 For example, the first of the conditions discussed above is subject to a 24-week time limit: 1967 Act, s 1(1) and there are mounting calls for this time limit to be reduced to 20 weeks: Templeton, S-K., 'Abortion clinics back cut to a 20-week limit', *The Sunday Times*, April 3, 2005, at p. 5 (reporting that Lord Steel, who, as David Steel MP, had been instrumental in getting the 1967 Act through Parliament, supported the reduction, as did Marie Stopes International, the largest provider of abortion services in the UK after the NHS, albeit MSI also proposed abortion on demand up to 12 weeks, with the approval of a single doctor

system's respect for a woman's choice not to procreate is not absolute. In practice, there is little doubt that articulate, well-educated women have little difficulty in securing terminations at will and at state expense, while their poorer, less well-educated sisters have a harder time. This is a facet of the general accessibility to healthcare options rather than any law or policy on abortion itself. Where a woman can pay for the procedure herself it is widely believed that abortion on demand is very much the order of the day.

So much for the woman's position *vis à vis* the state, but what if the potential father is opposed to her having the termination? It is now thoroughly well established that the decision to seek a termination lies with the pregnant woman and the potential father, whether a husband or a non-marital partner, has no standing to prevent her carrying out her decision.[29] To date, this approach has withstood challenge under the European Convention on Human Rights.[30] As was the case with the decision not to procreate within marriage, a woman who chooses to have a termination in the face of her husband's opposition could expect him to be successful if he sought a divorce on the basis of her behaviour and, again, she might suffer adverse economic consequences as a result.

To describe the history of abortion, in the US, as a 'battleground' is no overstatement. Since the landmark decision in *Roe v. Wade*,[31] in 1973, a veritable war has waged between the anti-abortionists and the pro-choice lobby, with frequent forays to the US Supreme Court.[32] Doctors who perform abortions have been

---

being required between 13 and 20 weeks). In addition, in all cases, the termination must be performed by a registered medical practitioner and in a National Health Service hospital or place approved by the Secretary of State: 1967 Act, s 1(1).

29 In England and Wales, see, *Paton v. Trustees of BPAS*, [1979] Q.B. 276 and *C v. S*, [1987] 1 All E.R. A similar view was taken in Canada: *Tremblay v. Daigle*, (1989) 62 D.L.R. (4th) 634. The only Scottish authority on this issue is *Kelly v. Kelly*, (1997) S.L.T. 896 where a separated husband was unsuccessful in seeking an interim interdict to prevent his wife having a termination and decided not to take the case further and seek full interdict. In *Kelly*, the pursuer, very wisely in the light of the case law from other jurisdictions, did not found on his position *qua* husband. Instead, he sought interim interdict as the potential guardian of the potential child who, if born alive, would have an action in respect of ante-natal injury. The court rejected this ingenious argument.

30 In *Paton v. United Kingdom*, (1980) 3 E.H.R.R. 408, at para 26, the European Commission took the view that, in so far as a husband is given no right to prevent his wife having a termination, this interference with his right to respect for family life, under Article 8(1), is justified under Article 8(2) as being necessary to protect the rights of another person (the wife). Mr. Paton's contention that the Abortion Act 1967 violated the rights of the foetus, under Article 2, was found to be manifestly ill-founded and his claims under Articles 5, 6 and 9 were found to be irrelevant.

31 410 U.S. 113 (1973).

32 See, for example, *Planned Parenthood of Central Missouri v. Danforth*, 428 U.S. 52 (1976) (spousal and parental consent to abortion struck down); *Carey v. Population Services International*, 431 US 678 (1977) (supply of contraceptives to minors upheld and spousal notification of intention to have an abortion struck down); *Maher v. Roe*, 432 U.S. 464 (1977)

murdered by anti-abortionists, abortion clinics have been bombed, and patients attending the clinics have been harassed.[33] The issue is a political hot potato and, since compromise is not a realistic option, no end to the dispute is in sight, resulting in the ever-present spectre of the Supreme Court narrowing the grounds on which abortion need be made available in the states.

Subsequent case law[34] has modified the trimester approach taken in *Roe v. Wade*[35] and the position can now be summarised thus: (1) prior to foetal viability, the state cannot place a substantial obstacle in the way of a woman seeking a termination; (2) after viability, the state had a substantial interest in potential life and can take measures to inform her of the options, with the purpose of persuading her to continue her pregnancy, provided the measures taken do not place an undue burden on her choice; (3) the state may pass regulations to promote the health and safety of the woman seeking an abortions, again, subject to the undue burden test; (4) after viability, the state may regulate or prevent abortions due to its interest in human life, except where the preservations of the life and health of the pregnant woman is implicated.

In the light of the vociferous debate, it is interesting that potential fathers in the US fare no better than they do in the UK. Even the earlier cases were hostile

(no obligation on the state to provide for abortions); *Harris v. McRae*, 448 U.S. 297 (1980) (prohibition on the use of federal funds for abortions upheld); *H.L. v. Matheson*, 450 U.S. 398 (1981) (parental notification of abortion in respect of immature minor upheld); *Webster v. Reproductive Services*, 492 U.S. 490 (1989) (prohibition on the use of state facilities for abortions upheld); *Madsen v. Women's Health Center, Inc.*, 512 U.S. 753 (1994) (right to unobstructed access to abortion clinics upheld; inroads on trimester approach and husband notification struck down).

33 See *Scheidler v. National Organisation of Women (NOW)*, 537 U.S. 393 (2003) and the earlier stages of that case.

34 See, in particular, *Planned Parenthood of South East Pennsylvania v. Casey*, 505 U.S. 833 (1992) and *Sternberg v. Carhart*, 530 U.S. 914 (2000). At the time of writing, all eyes are on South Dakota where the legislature introduced a near-total ban on abortion. A challenge to the leigslation may reach the US Supreme Court.

35 The trimester approach, as originally provided for in *Roe v. Wade*, divided the pregnancy into three stages or 'trimesters'. During the first trimester, the abortion decision was between the woman and her physician and the state had no role. During the second trimester, the state could regulate abortion in ways 'reasonably related to maternal health'. During the third trimester (understood to be after viability), the state could regulate and even proscribe abortion, except where it was necessary 'to preserve the life or health' of the pregnant woman. One problem with the trimester approach is that, as medicine develops, foetal viability is occurring earlier.

to husbands[36] or other male partners[37] seeking to prevent a woman from having an abortion. Having already decided that a statute, requiring a woman to obtain her husband's consent prior to having a termination was unconstitutional,[38] the US Supreme Court has gone on to strike down a similar state statute requiring a woman to notify him of her intention to do so.[39]

The Unintentional Father

To what extent does the legal system protect a man who claims to have had parenthood foisted upon him in circumstances where he was entitled to believe this would not be the result? The most common example here is of a man who is led to believe, by the woman with whom he is involved, that she is either sterile or is taking effective contraceptive measures. He proceeds with intercourse in the belief that pregnancy will not occur, only to discover that he was misled as to the facts and is now a father. Usually, such men have raised the circumstances of the child's conception in the attempt to avoid having to support the child financially. In both the UK[40] and the US[41] they have been unsuccessful, usually on the basis that financial support is for the benefit of the child and the mother's conduct, in misleading the father, is irrelevant. Clearly, any right to non-procreation the father had is being trumped by the child's rights and interests in being supported and, possibly, the state's interest in placing the primary obligation to support the child on someone other than the taxpayer.

In a number of cases in the US, the aggrieved father has taken a different tack in responding to unintended paternity. Rather than defend the action for child support, these men have raised actions against the child's mother, based on breach

---

36 *John Doe v. Jane Doe*, 314 N.E.2d 128 (Mass. 1974); *Poe v. Gerstein*, 517 F.2d (Ct. App. 5th Cir. 1975) (striking down as unconstitutional Florida statute requiring husband's written consent). More recently, see, *Rhode Island Medical Society v. Whitehouse*, 66 F.Supp.2d 288 (1999).

37 *Rothenberg v. Doe*, 374 A.2d 57 (N.J. Super. 1977); *Doe v. Smith*, 486 U.S. 1308 (1988).

38 *Planned Parenthood of Central Missouri v. Danforth*, 428 U.S. 52 (1976).

39 *Planned Parenthood of South East Pennsylvania v. Casey*, *supra cit.*

40 UK case law on the issue is not plentiful but see, *Bell v. McCurdie*, 1981 SC 64, for an example of the approach of the Scottish courts. In considering whether to permit a variation from the maintenance calculation for child support purposes, the Secretary of State is directed not to consider the fact that the child was unplanned by one or both parents: Child Support (Variations) Regulations 2000, SI 2001/156, reg 21(2).

41 There is a very substantial body of case law on this point in the US. See, for example: *Murphy v. Meyers*, 650 N.W. 2d 752 (Minn., 1997); *Welzenback v. Powers*, 660 A. 2d 1133 (N.H., 1995); *Linda D v. Fritz C*, 687 P. 2d 223 (Wash., 1983); *Erwin L.D. v. Myla Jean L.*, 847 S.W. 2d 45 (Ark., 1993); *Beard v. Skipper*, 451 N.W. 2d 614 (Mich., 1990); *Hughes v. Hutt*, 455 A. 2d 623 (Pa., 1983); *In re L. Pamela P. v. Frank S.*, 449 N.E.2d 713 (N.Y., 1983).

of contract, tort, or the like.[42] The actions to date have been unsuccessful and it is worth exploring a recent example to see why this has been the case. In *Wallis v. Smith*,[43] prior to sexual intercourse, the couple discussed birth control and agreed that the defendant would take birth control pills since the plaintiff had made clear that he did not wish to become a father. The defendant abided by the agreement for some time but changed her mind and, without telling the plaintiff, stopped taking the pills. Intercourse continued and she duly became pregnant and gave birth to a healthy baby girl. The plaintiff sued the defender for fraud (Smith's deception of him regarding contraception), breach of contract (the agreement that Smith would take the pills), conversion (use of Wallis' genetic material without his consent) and *prima facie* tort. Realising that the plaintiff was simply seeking to offset his child support liability by another route,[44] the majority of the New Mexico Court of Appeals affirmed the lower court's decision and dismissed his claims on public policy grounds and, in particular, the clear policy articulated by the legislature that parents should support their children. In short, the majority was not prepared to allow him to achieve by the back door what he could not by the front. In a specially concurring judgment (agreeing with the result, but for different reasons), Alarid J founded his rejection of Wallis' claim primarily on fundamental privacy interests: that is, he took the view that existing causes of action should only be extended to intimate interpersonal behaviour where there was some compelling consideration – a consideration he found to be lacking in this case.[45]

To date, aggrieved fathers in the UK (and their lawyers) have not shown themselves to be as imaginative as their US counterparts, but the acquisition of such ingenuity is probably only a matter of time. How might courts across the UK approach such an action based on fraud, breach of contract, delict or tort? In all likelihood, they will react every bit as unsympathetically to fathers as have the US courts. Again the child's rights and interests, as well as the interests of taxpayers, would probably trump any rights fathers might have in respect of non-procreation. What of the European Convention on Human Rights? A claim based on the father's Article 8(1) privacy rights would be likely to fail when account is taken of the qualification on these rights expressed in Article 8(2), which permits lawful and necessary interference with these rights on a number of grounds, including the economic wellbeing of the country and the rights and freedoms of others. Again, while Article 12 might be used by a father to claim infringement of his right to procreative freedom, proportionality would apply to permit the state to interfere with the right to protect the countervailing interest of the child.

42 See, for example: *Hendon v. Sorrell*, 1999 WL 5630 (Tenn. Ct. App., 1999); *Moorman v. Walker*, 773 P. 2d 887 (Wash., 1989); *Douglas R. v. Suzanne M.*, 127 Misc. 2d 745 (N.Y., 1985); *Stephen K. v. Loni L.*, 105 Cal. App. 3d 640 (1980).

43 22 P. 3d 682 (N.M., 2001), cert. denied April 19, 2001.

44 'Although Wallis insists that he is not attempting to circumvent his child support obligations, we cannot agree. It is self-evident that he seeks to recover for the very financial loss caused him by the statutory obligation to pay child support', per Bosson J, at p. 684.

45 *Ibid.*, at p. 688.

The Unintentional Mother

What of the woman who has parenthood foisted upon her through deception?[46] Should she have any recourse against the man who has deceived her, independent of any claim for support on behalf of her child? A good example of this can be found in *C.A.M. v. R.A.W.*,[47] where the plaintiff alleged that the defendant had claimed to have had a vasectomy. He had not and, after having unprotected sex with him, the plaintiff became pregnant and duly gave birth to a healthy child. The Superior Court of New Jersey affirmed the lower court's dismissal of her action for damages based on a variety of tort claims. It took the view that, as a matter of public policy, courts should not seek to regulate intimate personal relations and, indeed, that judicial enquiry into this sphere might involve 'impermissible State interference with the privacy of these individuals'.[48] It noted that the right to privacy does not insulate all sexual conduct from judicial scrutiny.[49] However it approved the distinction[50] between tort actions relating to intimate relationships where there was no child involved and, thus 'no potential for harming innocent children'[51] and cases, like the one before it, where there was a child. The view was expressed that 'to allow one parent to sue the other over the wrongful birth of their child ... could seldom, if ever, result in benefit to the child'.[52] Somewhat surprisingly (at least to a UK reader), the court indicated that, had the case proceeded, it might have been prepared to consider the plaintiff's failure to mitigate her loss by opting for abortion or, possibly, adoption.[53]

46 A pregnancy resulting from rape would provide another example of interference with the woman's right to choose not to procreate and it should be noted that her claim in tort or delict for the rape itself would separate to any claim regarding the pregnancy.

47 237 N.J. Super. 532 (1990).

48 *Ibid.*, at p. 537. The court found support for its position in *Perry v. Atkinson*, 195 Cal. App. 3d 14 (1987), where a woman who had terminated a pregnancy due to the false promise by the man involved that he would impregnate her again the following year was unsuccessful in her tort action.

49 See, for example: *Barbara A. v. John G.*, 145 Cal. App. 3d 369 (1983) (cause of action accepted where a woman suffered injuries from an ectopic pregnancy, having become pregnant after relying on the man misrepresentation that he was infertile); *Kathleen K. v. Robert B.*, 150 Cal.App. 3d 992 (Cal., 1984) (action by woman who had contracted genital herpes from her partner).

50 The distinction had been made in an earlier case, *Richard P. v. Gerald B.*, 202 Cal. App. 3d 249 (Cal., 1988), where a husband, who had been led to believe he was the father of his wife's children, raised an action in tort for intentional infliction of emotional against the man who was their father.

51 *Supra*, note 47, at p. 541.

52 *Id.*

53 *Ibid.*, at pp. 543-544. The court made clear that it would not necessarily have upheld such an argument and other courts in the US have been unsympathetic to any suggestion that parents should be forced to mitigate damages by means of abortion or adoption or that failure to do so should offset their claim; *In re University of Arizona v. Superior Court*, 667 P. 2d 1294 (Ariz. 1983).

How might a UK court approach an action of this kind? A woman would, at least arguably, have a claim for both her own pain and suffering, occasioned by the pregnancy and birth, and for the costs of raising the child or, at least, those costs which the child's father was not already meeting through child support. Given that even the House of Lords in *McFarlane v. Tayside Health Board*[54] accepted that the health board was liable for the former claim where it was negligent, it seems reasonable that the wrongdoer, in the context of intentional infliction of harm, should be every bit as liable as the wrongdoer, in the context of negligence. The latter claim, the cost of raising the child, was, of course, rejected in *McFarlane*, but, again, that was in the context of negligence. It can be argued that, where the wrongdoing was intentional, there is no case for limiting damages on the basis of what is 'just and reasonable' or on the basis of assumed risk. It is unlikely that a UK court would feel compelled to refrain from involving itself in intimate personal relations on the basis of privacy. Privacy, in the European context, is a very different animal to privacy under the US Constitution.[55] The argument that claims should be denied because it is detrimental to a child to know that he or she was unplanned has been rejected in the UK.[56] While a father might claim that any award of damages would infringe his Article 12 right to procreate, the exercise of a right by means of fraud is unlikely to receive a sympathetic hearing in the courts. Thus, the unintentional mother might fare rather better in the UK courts than have her sisters in the US.

Wrongful Conception or Wrongful Pregnancy

As Professor Mason has rightly pointed out, the terminology in this area is not without its problems.[57] What we are addressing here is the possibility of recovering damages for negligence where sterilisations have failed. At one time in the UK, it was a fairly settled law that, where a person sought to avoid procreation by having such an operation and, either the operation itself was performed negligently, or the hospital authorities were negligent in claiming that the operation had been successful,

---

54 2002 S.L.T. 154. The case is discussed at p. 329, below.

55 For example, in *Troxel v. Granville*, 530 U.S. 57 (2000), the Supreme Court struck down a Washington state statute which permitted any person with an interest to apply to the court for visitation (contact) with a child, in part, because it violated the privacy rights of a fit parent to determine with whom his or her child spent time. The statute in question is very similar to the parallel provisions in the Children (Scotland) Act 1995 and it is extremely unlikely that a privacy argument, based on Article 8 of the European Convention would be successful here.

56 *McFarlane v. Tayside Health Board*, 1998 SLT 307, per Lord Justice Clerk Cullen at pp.212-313 where he notes this as one of the policy considerations advanced before concluding, 'I am not persuaded that there is any overriding consideration of public policy which the awarding of damages to the pursuer would contravene'. See also the Australian case, *Cattanach v. Melchior*, [2003] H.C.A. 38.

57 Mason, J.K., 'Wrongful Pregnancy, Wrongful Birth and Wrongful Terminology', (2002) 6 *Edinburgh Law Review*, 46.

damages could be recovered for the pregnant woman's pain and suffering and loss of wages and for the cost of raising the resulting child.[58] That remains the position in the US today.[59]

In the UK, the decision of the House of Lords in *McFarlane v. Tayside Health Board*[60] brought an end to this eminently sensible approach. It is difficult to extract a clear *ratio* from their Lordships' speeches, but recovery for the cost of raising the child was denied on the basis that it is pure economic loss and, as such, could only be upheld where it would be 'fair, just and reasonable' or where the defender had assumed responsibility for the pursuer's economic interest.[61] In addition, some reliance was placed on the notion of distributive justice.[62] In any event, despite indications of distaste for the position taken by the House of Lords in *McFarlane*,[63] their Lordships took the opportunity to reaffirm their position in *Rees v. Darlington Memorial Hospital NHS Trust*[64] and, indeed, to make clear that it extended to cases where the patient had sought to avoid pregnancy due to her own disability.

For our present purpose, it is worth noting that their Lordships did not give explicit endorsement to the 'joys and blessings' argument, used by Lord Gill in the

---

58 See, for example, *Emeh v. Kensington Area Health Authority*, [1985] 1 QB 1012; *Thake v. Morris*, [1986] 1 QB 644; and *Anderson v. Forth Valley Health Board*, 1998 SLT 588. As a result of what was thought to be established law, settlements were reached in a number of cases. See, for example, *Pollock v. Lanarkshire Health Board*, (1987) and *Lindsay v. Greater Glasgow Health Board*, (1990), discussed in Mason, J.K.. and Laurie, G.T.,*Mason and McCall Smith's Law and Medical Ethics* (7th ed), London, Butterworths, 2006, para 6.19.

59 For an early case, see *Sherlock v. Stillwater Clinic*, 260 N.W.2d 169 (1977). For a recent example, see *Rose v. Garza*, 2004 WL 2940882 (Ohio App., Dec. 20, 2004).

60 2002 SLT 154. Their Lordships upheld Ms McFarlane's claim in respect of her pain and suffering and other costs associated with the pregnancy.

61 In this respect, the decision reflects the evolving law of tort/delict in the UK: see *Caparo Industries plc v. Dickman*, [1990] 2 AC 605. It can be argued, of course, that the claim here was not for pure economic loss at all.

62 As developed in *Frost v. Chief Constable of South Yorkshire*, [1999] 2 AC 455. Lord Steyn, in a phrase which is already coming back to haunt the courts, referred to 'the commuter on the Underground' and his or her perception of what would be fair.

63 Some indication of the lack of enthusiasm for the decision of the House of Lords in *McFarlane* can be seen by the willingness of the Court of Appeal, in England, to distinguish the instant case from it. See, *Parkinson v. St. James and Seacroft University Hospital NHS Trust*, [2001] 3 All ER 97 (negligent sterilisation, recovery allowed for additional costs associated with child's disability but not for ordinary costs of raising the child) and *Rees v. Darlington Memorial Hospital NHS Trust*, [2002] 2 All E.R. 177 (negligent sterilisation, recovery allowed for additional cost of raising the child associated with the mother's disability), overruled at [2003] 3 All E.R. 987, discussed briefly below. In Scotland, see the dissenting judgment of Lord Morison in *McLelland v. Greater Glasgow Health Board*, 2001 S.L.T. 446, at p. 457. See also the decision from the High Court of Australia in *Cattanach v. Melchior*, [2003] H.C.A. 38, discussed at J.K. Mason, 'From Dundee to Darlington: An End to the *McFarlane* Line?' (2004) *J.R.* 365.

64 [2003] 3 All E.R. 987.

Outer House to deny recovery in *McFarlane*.[65] According to that line of thinking, the joys associated with the birth of a healthy child always outweigh the disadvantages, a view rejected, very firmly, by the Inner House when it considered the case.[66] If one accepts the view that a child is always an unequivocal joy and blessing, then it is more difficult to advance the case that there is, or should be, a right not to procreate, aside perhaps from cases where the pregnant woman's life was at stake. Then again, one is under no obligation to accept a blessing.

Frozen Embryos

Perhaps the paradigm for testing any right not to procreate lies in what have come to be known as the 'frozen embryo' cases. These cases arise where a couple has created embryos, but then find themselves in dispute over the use of the embryos. The most common scenario presenting in the cases is of a married couple who arrange for embryos to be created using their gametes, the intention being that, at a later stage, at least some of the embryos will be implanted in the wife and she will give birth to their children. Before this happens, the couple's relationship deteriorates and they decide to divorce. The wife still wants to use the embryos but the husband no longer wants to have children with his soon-to-be ex-wife and wishes the embryos destroyed. Who should prevail? Should the legal system support the wife's right to procreate or the husband's right not to do so? As the case law demonstrates, there are variations on this scenario and an almost infinite number of variables, which can be built into it.[67] Regardless of the variables, what is clear is that the procreative freedom of one individual is on a collision course with that of another. Respecting one person's right will involve denying that of the other but, then, that is the sort of dilemma the law is designed to resolve.

In the UK, the Human Fertilisation and Embryology Act 1990, as amended, provides the *régime* for the operation of assisted reproductive technology. The Act created the Human Fertilisation and Embryology Authority (HFEA), which, in turn, has produced a Code of Practice to supplement the Act.[68] The 1990 Act requires gamete contributors to give written consent to the future storage and use of embryos

---

65 *McFarlane v. Tayside Health Board*, 2000 S.C. (H.L.) 1.

66 *McFarlane v. Tayside Health Board*, 1998 S.L.T. 307, at pp. 312, 316 and 318. That view had already been rejected in *Anderson v. Forth Valley Health Board*, 1998 S.L.T. 588, at p. 605.

67 For example, the woman may wish the embryos destroyed, while the man wishes to use them with a new partner or a surrogate. Neither partner may wish to use them, but one might want them donated to a third party while the other prefers destruction. The position might be complicated further where only one of the partners donated gametes towards the embryos' creation, with the remaining gametes being provided by a third party. A further possibility is that the embryos were created wholly from third party gametes.

68 The most recent edition of the Code of Practice (6th, 2004) came into force in March 2004 and can be found at: http://www.hfea.gov.uk.

and is backed up by a statutory maximum period of storage.[69] It was thought that this would avoid the kind of problem outlined in the example above. In particular, it was hoped that the plethora of litigation between separated or divorced couples over the use of their embryos in the US would not arise the UK. Any such hopes proved to be illusory when, in 2003, two women in England sought to prevent their former partners from destroying frozen embryos created when the couples were together.[70] The court took the view that the legislation was quite clear and unambiguous in giving each partner the right to withdraw consent before the embryos had been 'used'. Addressing the human rights dimension, it noted that, and that this position was not contrary to the women's Article 8 rights to private and family life, since their former partners too had an equal and counter-balancing right to private and family life which had to be accommodated under Article 8(2). In only one of the cases did the woman appeal against the decision. While she was unsuccessful,[71] at the time of writing, she is seeking to take her case to the European Court of Human Rights.[72]

In the US, there is no national regulation and there are sound constitutional reasons why that is so.[73] Certainly, there is the Uniform Parentage Act 2002,[74] but it has not been widely adopted.[75] In the context of frozen embryo disputes, the result has been a plethora of litigation with courts working their way through a variety of models for resolving the disputes. While that is fascinating for academics, such uncertainty is

---

69 Human Fertilisation and Embryology Act 1990, Sched 3.

70 *Evans v. Amicus Healthcare Ltd; Hadley v. Midland Fertility Services Ltd.*, [2003] 4 All E.R. 903. Ms Evans had created the embryos along with her former fiancé, prior to her having her ovaries removed in the course of treatment for cancer. Ms Hadley had created the embryos with her ex-husband. A further dispute arose in 2003, in Scotland, when embryos were destroyed on the instruction of an ex-husband without the ex-wife, who had not contributed any genetic material to the embryos, being informed. The HFEA Code of Practice (6th ed, 2004), para 8.11, which post-dates the dispute, now provides that a woman in this position would be informed of the intention to destroy stored embryos. This would not give her any right, however, to prevent the destruction of the embryos.

71 *Evans v. Amicus Healthcare Ltd.*, [2004] 3 All E.R. 1025.

72 In only one of the cases did the woman appeal against the decision. She was unsuccessful in both the UK domestic courts [footnote 71: *Evans v Amicus Healthcare Ltd* [2004] 3 All E.R. 1025] and before the European Court of Human Rights [footnote 72: *Evans v United Kingdom*, Application No 6339/05, discussed at 'Embryo has no right to life', *The Times*, March 17, 2006.]

73 See, Annas, G.J., 'The Regulation of Human Reproduction in the US', in Sanford, N., Katz, J., Eekelaar, J. and Maclean, M., *Cross Currents: Family Law and Policy in the United States and England*, Oxford University Press, 2000, at p. 145, where Annas laments the lack of national regulation and attributes it to historic, economic and political factors. While Annas argues for federal regulation of the interstate commercial aspects of assisted reproduction, so many of the issues arising from ART relate to family law that a comprehensive national system of regulation is most unlikely.

74 For the text of the Act, see: http://www.law.upenn.edu/bll/ulc/upa/final2002.htm.

75 For the states which have adopted at least parts of the Act and in what form, see: http://www.nccusl.org/Update/ActSearchResults.aspx.

arguably undesirable for the parties involved and for the legal system. While clinics often seek to avoid litigation by ensuring that the couple sign a contract to determine what will happen to the embryos in the event of a dispute, this solution has proved to be no more of a guarantee against litigation than has the 1990 Act in the UK.[76]

Courts in the US have employed a number of analytical approaches, using concepts of contract, property and custody, in resolving disputes over frozen embryos. A sense of the variety of approaches can be gleaned from *Davis v. Davis*,[77] not least because it proceeded through the various levels of the court system in Tennessee, with different courts applying different analytical models. The embryos in question had been produced from the couple's gametes but the couple had divorced before they could be used. The former wife wanted to use some of the embryos in order to have a child, while the former husband wanted them destroyed. The trial court took a 'right to life' approach, treating the embryos as human beings, and determined the case as if it were a custody (residence) dispute. Perhaps inevitably, it found that the best interests of the embryos would be served by an award of custody to the woman who wished them to be implanted.[78] That approach was rejected, on appeal, with the appellate court treating the dispute as one over marital property, and awarding 'joint control' of the property to the former spouses.[79] Of course, this approach did not get the couple any further in resolving their dispute over whether the embryos could be implanted. The Tennessee Supreme Court sought to steer a middle course between these approaches and avoided referring to the embryos as either 'lives' or 'property'. Instead, it viewed them as having a 'special significance', greater than inanimate objects, but less than people. It devised a six-step test for determining what should happen to the embryos[80] and concluded that, in this case, the interests of the former husband in not procreating outweighed his former wife's interests in using the embryos. Ms Davis was unsuccessful in her attempt to take the case to the US Supreme Court[81] and, thus, the matter remains one which will be resolved on a

---

76 In *AZ v. BZ* 725 N.E.2d 1051 (Mass, 2000), for example, the couple has executed written agreements on seven different occasions, but litigated their dispute nonetheless.

77 1989 Tenn App LEXIS 641 (Tenn. Cir. Ct. 21 September 1989); 1990 WL 130807 (Tenn. App. 13 September 1990); 842 S.W.2d 588 (Tenn. Sup. Ct. 1992).

78 1989 Tenn App LEXIS 641 (Tenn Cir. Ct. 21 September 1989).

79 1990 WL 130807 (Tenn. App, 13 September 1990).

80 842 S.W.2d 588 (Tenn. Sup. Ct. 1992), at p. 604. Briefly, the steps are as follows. (1) The court must consider the wishes of the interested parties including the gametes providers above any other authority like the health care organisation or clinic. (2) If the gametes providers cannot agree, the court should enforce any prior contractual agreement between them. (3) The court must balance the interests of the parties in use and non-use of the embryos. (4) The party who wished the embryos destroyed should prevail unless the other party had no other way of having a child. (5) The court should consider the argument of the party who wanted the embryo implanted either in herself or in a willing third party. (6) If the couple were in dispute over whether or not to donate the embryos to a third party, the party opposed to donation should prevail.

81 Cert denied 61 U.S. 3437.

state-by-state basis. Ultimately, then, the Tennessee Supreme Court in *Davis* came out in favour of the party who was exerting his right not to procreate. A similar approach has been followed in a number of other states.[82]

Conclusion: Is There a Right Not to Procreate?

As we saw at the outset, everyone has the freedom not to procreate through either remaining celibate or engaging only in same-sex relationships. However, these are not realistic options for many individuals. Thus, legal systems have been confronted with the issue of the choice not to procreate in a whole variety of circumstances. To what extent do the legal systems in the UK and the US respect and support this choice to the extent that there can be said to be 'a right not to procreate'?

Even within marriage, an environment which legal systems have traditionally viewed as related to procreation, an individual's choice not to procreate is respected. Granted, refusal to have children often opens the door to divorce, where the spouses disagree over the decision, but that is to say no more than that choices have consequences. Indeed, if the rights of the both spouses are to be respected, then making divorce available in these circumstances seems the only option available to a legal system.[83] Where the dispute between the parties involves the future use or destruction of embryos, the right not to procreate is supported on both sides of the Atlantic, with courts being unwilling to foist parenthood on the partner who does not want it.

In the context of abortion, the legal systems considered here do slightly less well in terms of respecting the decision not to procreate. While the availability of legal abortion, at all, is a step towards that end, the fact that the state places restrictions thereon, well in excess of those required to preserve the health or life of the women involved, is a serious qualification on respecting the choice not to procreate. Even here, however, the legal systems are in no doubt over prioritising the rights of private individuals, with the woman's choice not to procreate trumping that of the potential father.

What of the 'unintentional parent'? As far as unintentional fathers are concerned, the right of the child to be supported takes priority over any regard for the father's

---

82 *AZ v. BZ*, 725 N.E.2d 1051 (Mass, 2000); *Kass v. Kass*, 663 N.Y.S.2d 581 (Sup. Ct. N.Y. App. Div., 1997), affirmed, 696 N.E.2d 174 (N.Y. Ct. App., 1998); *JM v. BM*, 783 A.2d 707 (N.J., 2001); *Litowitz v. Litowitz*, 48 P.3d 261 (Wash., 2002). For a different approach, see the decision of the Supreme Court of Israel in *Nachmani v. Nachmani*, 50(4) P.D. 661, discussed by Schuz, R., 'Israel: The right to parenthood: surrogacy and frozen embryos', in Bainham, A. (ed), *International Survey of Family Law, 1996*, Bristol, Family Law/Jordans, 1998.

83 As we have seen, no-fault divorce enables the parties to resolve the matter for themselves without the courts having to address the issue of procreative freedom at all. Arguably, this is a better solution, since it permits those most intimately involved in the issue to deal with the matter themselves.

original choice not to procreate. It can be argued that this is simply a matter of prioritising the rights of an innocent third party over those of those of the individual who took a risk. That might be a justification where the parents were using contraception, but it is hardly a satisfactory explanation of the legal system's stance where the father believed the child's mother to be sterile and, thus, did not think he was taking any risk at all. In that situation, the legal system may be doing nothing more than giving effect to a policy decision of the legislature to make parents, rather than the taxpayer, liable to support children. The unintentional mother has fared little better than the unintentional father in terms of her choice not to procreate gaining legal recognition. Again, there is some prioritising of the rights of the child over the parent's rights, in so far as courts in the US have based their decisions on the undesirability of a child knowing he or she was unplanned. However, it is notions of privacy that have been much more influential in the decisions. Whether courts in the UK would take a similar approach remains to be seen and, certainly, there is scope for them taking a different tack.

In short, legal systems have shown themselves most willing to respect the right not to procreate when refereeing the interests of private individuals. It is tempting to say that, once the rights of a third party enter the picture, respect for the choice not to procreate takes second place, and the courts' lack of sympathy for the rights of the unintentional father is, perhaps, the best example here. Acknowledging the rights of a 'third party', the potential child, might also explain the legal systems' rather ambivalent approach to respecting the choice not to procreate in the context of abortion.[84] This analysis might even be stretched to the case of wrongful pregnancy. In the US, the aggrieved parents are given full redress against the private entity – the doctor or the hospital. In the UK, the state itself has an interest, since liability will attach to what is, usually, a public entity – the NHS doctor or the hospital trust. All of this suggests that there is, indeed, a right not to procreate. That the legal systems in the UK and the US sometimes place restrictions on this right is clear, but there is nothing unusual in this approach to rights. It can be concluded, then, that the right not to procreate, like its counterpart, the right to procreate, is not absolute.

84 That the courts, in the US, and the legislature, in the UK, have not applied this thinking, by analogy, to the frozen embryo cases creates an anomalous situation which, sadly, must be left for exploration another day.

Chapter 21

Conscientious Objection: A Shield or a Sword?

Bernard M. Dickens

Introduction

Under the inspiration of human rights values, many individuals, institutions and governments recognise the need for legal protection of religious freedom. The Universal Declaration of Human Rights, adopted by the United Nations in 1948, provides in Article 18 that 'Everyone has the right to freedom of thought, conscience and religion; this right includes freedom to manifest his religion or belief in teaching, practice, worship and observance'. These words are substantially repeated in Article 18(1) of the International Covenant on Civil and Political Rights. Article 18(3) recognises the constraints, however:

> Freedom to manifest one's religion or beliefs may be subject only to such limitations as are prescribed by law and are necessary to protect public safety, order, health or morals or the fundamental rights and freedoms of others.

Human rights values similarly provide that individuals should not suffer discrimination on grounds of their religious or other convictions, but these values tolerate religious institutions which follow practices that disqualify individuals from holding religious office or rank on grounds, for instance, of sex, marital status or age.

Respect for the human right of religious conviction, while fundamental to human liberty and dignity, is accordingly not absolute. Balances must be struck between individuals' rights to manifest their religious faith and convictions, and others' rights to health, liberty and equal rights of conscience. The limitation that neither individuals nor institutions may compel others' obedience to the individuals' or institutions' vision of conscientious conduct is recognised by both legal and religious authorities. For instance, Pope John Paul II stated in 1991 that it was necessary 'that each individual's conscience be respected by everyone else; people must not attempt to impose their own 'truth' on others'.[1]

John Paul II spoke consistently with Article 18(3) of the International Covenant on Civil and Political Rights in observing that:

---

1 John Paul II Address 'If You Want Peace, Respect the Conscience of Every Person', Vatican City 1991 Message for the 24th World Day of Peace 1991, para 4.

> freedom of conscience does not confer a right to indiscriminate recourse to conscientious objection. When an asserted freedom turns into license or becomes an excuse for limiting the rights of others, the State is obliged to protect, also by legal means, the inalienable rights of its citizens against such abuses.[2]

The boundary between legitimate conscientious objection and an indiscriminate appeal to conscience in violation of law and of others' rights is not always easy to determine. Defiance of mandatory laws, such as on military conscription, or on laws against obstructing passage on public highways or footpaths during political protests, is often described as 'civil disobedience'. This may be legally punished, for instance by direction of objectors into non-combat roles under military law or by fine or usually brief imprisonment, for instance of protest leaders. Conscientious objection tends to involve refusal to participate in lawful acts, rather than participation in unlawful acts, but conscientious objection was invoked for instance by physicians in South Africa who treated patients in violation of the apartheid laws that were intended to enforce racial segregation.

Reproductive Health

Physicians' recourse to conscientious objection more commonly takes the form of their refusal, on grounds of their religious convictions, to participate in abortion and sterilisation procedures, and sometimes to prescribe contraceptive products or to supply or fit contraceptive devices. Since the 1980s, some have similarly objected to participation in medically assisted reproduction through such techniques as *in vitro* fertilisation (IVF), which often involve the planned and even legally required wastage of human embryos. At the other end of the life cycle, some object to administering treatments that are expected to result in death, such as withdrawal of artificial life supports.

In recent years, however, as restrictive laws on sterilisation and particularly abortion have become progressively liberalised,[3] there has been increasingly widespread reliance on rights of conscientious objection, not simply to excuse physicians and related health service providers from direct participation in lawful medical procedures they find offensive, but to obstruct and prevent the access of patients – overwhelmingly women patients – to lawful procedures they want.

The 1973 decision of the United States Supreme Court, in *Roe v. Wade*,[4] which decriminalised first and second and some third trimester abortion, triggered legislation in many American states that protected healthcare professionals who objected to participation in abortion procedures on religious grounds. The development of present concern is apparent not only in the United States, however,

---

2 *Ibid.*, para 24.

3 Dickens, B.M. and Cook, R.J., 'Human Rights Dynamics of Abortion Law Reform', 25 *Human Rights Quarterly*, (2003), 1-59.

4 *Roe v. Wade*, 410 U.S. 113 (U.S. Supreme Court, 1973).

but also elsewhere, particularly where the Roman Catholic Church is influential, such as in Central and South America. The goal of this development is to resist and frustrate implementation of the concept of 'reproductive health', that has been developed over the last decade. The concept was pioneered in 1987 at the World Health Organisation, and acquired international status and widespread endorsement in 1994 and 1995 at the International Conference on Population and Development (the Cairo conference) and the International Conference on Women (the Beijing conference) respectively. The concept, which was bitterly resisted by the Holy See at Cairo and Beijing, includes that people 'have the capability to reproduce and the freedom to decide if, when and how often to do so'.[5] This implies 'the right of men and women to be informed and to have access to safe, effective, affordable and acceptable methods of family planning of their choice, as well as other methods of their choice for regulation of fertility which are not against the law'.[6] Nonetheless, international momentum has been generated aggressively to frustrate women's access to safe medical procedures for termination of pregnancy. In Southern Italy, for instance, lawful abortion is often unavailable because few, if any, physicians in this area will respond to requests that they undertake the procedure.[7]

Resistance Through Conscience

As restrictive laws against abortion, sterilisation and contraception have been relaxed and liberalised in the second half of the last century, particularly under governments that are democratically accountable, and societies have progressively required access to these procedures in legality, dignity and safety, religious institutions and personnel doctrinally opposed to related services have mounted resistance. Building on physicians' and nurses' long-recognised rights of conscientious objection, they work to expand these rights to actions quite remote from participation in clinical procedures, to an increasing range of healthcare and health facility personnel, and to institutions themselves such as hospitals, clinics and public- and private-sector health service insurance providers. Legislation has been enacted in many of the United States, for instance, to provide comprehensive legal immunity from liability for professional negligence and failures both to obtain patients' informed consent to their management, and failure to refer patients who request services that healthcare providers oppose on grounds of conscience to non-objecting service providers. These legal immunities, which are often described in the US as 'refusal clauses' (after a clause to allow refusal of abortion services that was buried in a 1,600 page federal

---

5 United Nations, 'Population and Development, i', Programme of Action Adopted at the International Conference on Population and Development, Cairo, 5-13 September 1994 (New York: UN, ST/ESA/SER. A/149, 1994), para 7.2.

6 *Id.*

7 United Nations, 'Report of the Committee on the Elimination of Discrimination Against Women', 17th Sess. Doc. A/52/38/Rev. O.1.353, at p. 360 (12 August 1997).

spending bill), favour health service providers' claims of conscience over the needs of their dependent patients.[8]

A model of a conscientious objection law that fairly balances interests of patients and healthcare providers is found in the UK, where the Abortion Act 1967 provides in section 4 that:

> (1) Subject to subsection (2) of this section, no person shall be under any duty, whether by contract or by any statutory or other legal requirement, to participate in any treatment authorised by this Act to which he has a conscientious objection:
> Provided that in any legal proceedings the burden of proof of conscientious objection shall rest on the person claiming to rely on it.
> (2) Nothing in subsection (1) ... shall affect any duty to participate in treatment which is necessary to save the life or to prevent grave permanent injury to the physical or mental health of the pregnant woman.
> (3) In any proceedings before a court in Scotland, a statement on oath by any person to the effect that he has a conscientious objection ... shall be sufficient evidence for the purpose of discharging the burden of proof imposed upon him by subsection (1) of this section.

In the English case of *Barr v. Matthews*,[9] involving a general practitioner's duty under the Act, the judge observed that 'once a termination of pregnancy is recognised as an option, the doctor invoking the conscientious objection clause should refer the patient to a colleague at once'.[10] The courts have also interpreted exemption from the duty 'to participate in any treatment' very narrowly, to 'exclude from its ambit all healthcare professionals and other staff who are not directly taking part ... in the patient's treatment'.[11] Referral for a colleague's decision is not 'participation' in any treatment decided upon. Patients' interests are further protected in that the right of objection does not apply to peripheral actors. For instance, it excludes nurses involved in patients' general care and ancillary staff who deliver meals or change bed sheets, and physicians' secretarial staff who prepare referral correspondence.[12] The 1967 Act protects nurses' rights of objection to direct participation in abortion procedures, and protects those who participate in prostaglandin-based procedures, in which nurses manage expulsion of uterine contents under physicians' authority, and with their back-up support if required.[13]

---

8 Sonfield, A., 'New Refusal Clauses Shatter Balance Between Provider "Conscience", Patient Needs', *The Guttmacher Report on Public Policy*, August 2004, 1-3.

9 *Barr v. Matthews* (1999), 52 BMLR 217 (Queen's Bench Division).

10 *Ibid.*, at p. 227.

11 Grubb, A. (ed.), *Principles of Medical Law* (2nd ed), Oxford, Oxford University Press, 2004, at p. 770.

12 *Janaway v. Salford Health Authority*, [1989] A.C. 537; [1988] 3 All E.R. 1079 (House of Lords)

13 *Royal College of Nursing v. Department of Health and Social Security*, [1981] A.C. 800 (House of Lords).

The Expansion of 'Conscience'

In contrast to balanced laws are several enacted or under consideration in US states, such as the Mississippi Health Care Rights of Conscience Act, which took effect in July 2004. The Act originated in the particular context of abortion, but was later extended to govern all healthcare services, defined in section 2(a) as:

> any phase of patient medical care, treatment or procedure, including, but not limited to, the following: patient referral, counseling, therapy, testing, diagnosis or prognosis, research, instruction, prescribing, dispensing or administering any device, drug, or medication, surgery or any other care or treatment rendered by health care providers or health care institutions.

The Act protects from involvement in such procedures all health service providers, including any:

> physician, physician's assistant, nurse, nurse's aide, medical assistant, hospital employee, clinic employee, nursing home employee, pharmacist, pharmacy employee, researcher, medical or nursing school faculty student or employee, counselor, social worker or any professional, paraprofessional, or any other person who furnishes, or assists in the furnishing of, a health care procedure.[14]

Healthcare institutions and healthcare payers are defined in comparably comprehensive terms, and are accorded a conscience, meaning 'the religious, moral or ethical principles held by a health care provider, the health care institution or health care payer',[15] as determined by reference to an institution's or payer's 'existing or proposed religious, moral or ethical guidelines, mission statement, constitution, bylaws, articles of incorporation, regulations or other relevant documents'.[16]

Against this definitional background, section 3 provides:

> (1) *Rights of Conscience*. A health care provider has the right not to participate, and no health care provider shall be required to participate in a health care service that violates his or her conscience ...
>
> (2) *Immunity from Liability*. No health care provider shall be civilly, criminally, or administratively liable for declining to participate in a health care service that violates his or her conscience ...

This provision would apparently afford immunity for refusing to terminate a life-endangering pregnancy, including an ectopic pregnancy, resulting in a woman's death. Perhaps the most significant aspect of the right and immunity of conscience, however, is in subsection (3), which provides comprehensive legal protection

14 s .2(b).
15 s. 2(h).
16 *Id.*

for persons, institutions and insurance agencies that invoke conscience, by an antidiscrimination provision:

> (3) *Discrimination.* It shall be unlawful for any person, healthcare provider, healthcare institution, public or private institution, public official, or any board which certifies competency in medical specialties to discriminate against any healthcare provider in any manner based on his or her declining to participate in a healthcare service that violates his or her conscience. For purposes of this act, discrimination includes, but is not limited to: termination, transfer, refusal of staff privileges, refusal of board certification, adverse administrative action, demotion, loss of career specialty, reassignment to a different shift, reduction of wages or benefits, refusal to award any grant, contract, or other program, refusal to provide residency training opportunities, or any other penalty, disciplinary or retaliatory action.

Comparable provisions in sections 4 and 5 address the rights, immunities and protection against discrimination of healthcare institutions and of healthcare payers respectively. Civil remedies for violations under the Act are by injunction and/or punitive damages set by section 6(2), at 'threefold the actual damages, including pain and suffering sustained [to be not less than $5,000 and] ... costs of the action and reasonable attorney's fees', which US courts do not customarily award. Accordingly, every effort and legal strategy have been employed to protect individuals, healthcare institutions and healthcare payers whose religious, moral or ethical principles oppose any particular healthcare service. No similar protections against discrimination or other violations of civil rights are afforded patients, healthcare providers and institutions or other agencies whose religious, moral or ethical principles support provision of prompt, safe healthcare services, including abortion, contraception, emergency contraception and sterilisation.

At least 23 states in the US have enacted or are considering legislation such as that enacted in Mississippi,[17] to extend refusal clauses to cover the full range of reproductive health services. With the introduction of medication abortion, by prescription of the so-called 'abortion pill' (RU 486), similar efforts have been made to ensure that pharmacists and pharmacies enjoy the same protection of conscience. Further, disregard of legally endorsed medical data showing that emergency contraception is not abortifacient[18] has allowed objection to abortion to be extended to emergency contraception, meaning post-coital contraception undertaken within 72 hours of unprotected intercourse.

Under such comprehensive refusal clauses, hospital workers may refuse to clean instruments used in abortion or sterilisation procedures, and nurses may refuse not only to provide care during procedures, but also to provide pre-surgical preparation

---

17 Davy, M. and Belluck, P., 'Pharmacies Balk on After-Sex Pill and Widen Fight', *The New York Times*, 19 April, 2005, pp. 1, 16; Charo, R.A, 'The Celestial Fire of Conscience – Refusing to Deliver Medical Care', 352 *New England J. Medicine*, (2005) 2471-2473.

18 *R. (on the Application of Smeaton on behalf of SPUC) v. Secretary of State for Health*, [2002] EWHC 610 (Admin); (2002) 66 BMLR 59 (Munby J).

and post-surgical care, possibly extending to all hospital workers' refusal to deliver meals and provide hygienic care to patients admitted for opposed procedures. Pharmacists may similarly refuse to dispense or fill prescriptions for contraceptive products. An instance is recorded in Wisconsin in 2002 in which a pharmacist not only refused to fill a prescription for a contraceptive drug but also refused to refer the patient to other pharmacists and to return the physician's prescription form to the patient,[19] which constitutes theft. Ambulance attendants have refused to take women for elective abortions, police officers have refused to protect abortion clinics against aggressive picketers, and, for instance, secretaries have refused to type physicians' abortion referral letters. In an English case, the highest court upheld a secretary's dismissal for such refusal,[20] since typing was too remote from participation in a medical procedure, but could not have done if the secretary's comprehensive immunity was legislated, as in Mississippi.

From a Shield to a Sword?

Legislation of broad refusal or conscientious objection laws regarding reproductive health services turns the historical tolerance of religious freedom and diversity, which served as a shield to protect religious conviction and accommodation of difference, into a sword to compel compliance with religious beliefs by those who do not share them. Religious institutions historically have served a noble mission in many countries to provide healthcare for the needy. However, refusal clauses pervert this commitment, since their purpose is to afford legal justification for the denial of care. The healthcare services intended to be denied with impunity are primarily those sought by women, reflecting how casually exclusively male or male-dominated religious and political institutions can constrain women's healthcare choices. The movement towards expansive conscientious objection immunity is not casual, however, but deliberate. It gained momentum in response to recognition of rights to reproductive health as part of women's self-determination and empowerment. Reproductive health rights were established at the Cairo and Beijing conferences. They were strenuously opposed at both conferences by the Holy See, which exploited its spurious claim to statehood by heavy representation and sought to buttress its resistance by collaboration with reactionary Islamic countries.

An emerging international strategy is apparent in the Draft Treaty between the Slovak Republic and the Holy See on the Right to Exercise the Objection of Conscience.[21]

Because the Roman Catholic Church, through the Holy See, enjoys the historical privilege among the world's religious denominations to possess status as an international entity analogous to a state, the agreement will be presented to the

19 Sonfield A., *loc cit.*, at p. 1.

20 *Janaway*, *supra cit.*

21 Basic Treaty ratified by the National Council of the Slovak Republic on 4 December 2000, Official Law Collection, No. 329/2001.

country and beyond as an international human rights treaty, as opposed to a mere national agreement. Under the Slovak Republic's Constitution, international treaties can supersede domestic laws, with the potential to affect the processes of democratic government. The purpose of the Treaty is to protect the 'free and unlimited' exercise of conscientious objection by state officials, based on Catholic doctrines of faith in any area regulated by law. Accordingly, delivery of several state services, including healthcare, education and provision of legal services, would be conditional on compliance with Roman Catholic teaching. The Treaty provides that, if requested, an authority of the Holy See will interpret the teaching of faith and morals of the Catholic church.

The effect of this Treaty, if implemented, would probably be to limit state provision of the full range of reproductive health services, including contraception, emergency contraception, sterilisation and abortion, although the treaty requires that 'the exercise of the conscientious objection cannot threaten human life'.[22] In particular, because Catholic doctrine on complicity makes it as illicit to facilitate a wrong as to commit it, the treaty would probably permit objection not only to performance of certain reproductive health procedures but also referral of patients to non-objecting practitioners.

Such refusal could constitute a breach, for which the state is responsible, of international human rights treaties. For instance, the Slovak Republic has ratified the International Convention on the Elimination of All Forms of Discrimination Against Women (The Women's Convention), Article 12(1) of which requires states 'to ensure, on a basis of equality of men and women, access to healthcare services, including those related to family planning'. A cynical reading of this provision may be that denial of family planning services to both sexes is non-discriminatory, but human rights Treaties are to be construed and applied to expand rather than to deny rights. Article 31(1) of the Vienna Convention on the Law of Treaties provides that a treaty shall be interpreted 'in good faith ... in the light of its object and purpose', which in this case is to protect and extend rights. Article 7 of the Women's Convention defines discrimination as including denial of human rights in effect as well as on purpose, and denial of family planning services affects women's lives, health and rights significantly more than those of men.

The European Court of Human Rights has applied Article 9 of the European Convention for the Protection of Human Rights and Fundamental Freedoms[23] to limit public acts of conscience. Article 9(1) protects everyone's 'right to freedom of thought, conscience and religion', and to 'manifest his religion or belief, in ... practice and observance'. Article 9(2) provides that:

> Freedom to manifest one's religion or beliefs shall be subject only to such limitations as are prescribed by law and are necessary in a democratic society in the interests of public

22 Article 6.2.

23 Signed through the Council of Europe in Rome on 4 November 1950. European Treaty Series No. 5.

> safety, for the protection of public order, health or morals, or for the protection of the rights and freedoms of others.

In *Pichon and Sajous v. France*[24] the Court dismissed an appeal under Article 9 brought by joint owners of a pharmacy that was the only reasonably accessible pharmacy in their area, who were convicted of breach of the Consumer Code for refusal to provide medically prescribed contraceptive products. The Court ruled that:

> [A]s long as the sale of contraceptives is legal and occurs on medical prescription nowhere other than in a pharmacy, the applicants cannot give precedence to their religious beliefs and impose them on others as justification for their refusal to sell such products, since they can manifest those beliefs in many ways outside the professional sphere.[25]

This ruling upheld the conviction imposed by the Bordeaux Court of Appeal, which had noted that the defendants' pharmacy was the only one in their town, and supported the view that those who object to direct provision of, or participation in, reproductive health services may in principle satisfy their legal responsibilities if they refer applicants to reasonably accessible alternative providers. The religious concept of complicity is as wide-ranging as religious authorities choose to make it, but where laws may permit one person to compromise or prejudice another's rights, the laws are to be interpreted narrowly. For instance, in Britain, lawful objection 'to participate in any treatment' under section 4(1) of the Abortion Act 1967 would not include objection to referral of a patient to another physician, since the referral would occur before any treatment was initiated or prepared.[26] Accordingly, a balanced legal and ethical requirement would be that those who invoke their own conscience to refuse participation in reproductive health services show equal respect for patients' consciences by referring them, in good faith, to sources of such services that do not conscientiously object to provide them. This requirement would preserve rights of conscientious objection as a legitimate shield of religious belief, but not permit its conversion into a sword to compel non-believers' compliance.

Referral: The Challenge to Professionalism

An initial challenge to professional associations is whether those who enjoy the legally protected monopoly to practice their professions are free to discard the knowledge they publicly profess to have mastered and to employ, and instead to apply their personal religious convictions or belief systems. Physicians are licensed to practice, and attract patients, on the basis of their mastery of medical science, not on grounds of their religious or other non-scientific beliefs. A case in point is whether physicians and, for instance, pharmacists, can proclaim, contrary to the scientific understanding

24 *Pichon and Sajous v. France* (2001) App. No. 49853/99 (Eur.Ct. H. Rights).

25 Grubb, *op cit.*, at p. 771.

26 Carefully reviewed in the *Smeaton* case, *supra cit.*

of their professions,[27] that emergency contraception is abortifacient, and refuse to offer it on that ground. A minimum ethical requirement of medical professionals who encourage patients to entrust their care to them but who refuse to provide abortion, contraception and related services because of their personal conscience, is that they refer their patients to providers who do not refuse such services. The ethical duty can be recognised by professional associations even when a duty is not so clearly recognised by laws, and even when a duty is removed by laws.

In light of the origin and inspiration of laws that give effect to modern comprehensive refusal clauses, such as enacted in Mississippi, there can be little doubt that their intention is to afford everyone – including those only indirectly associated with a patient's purpose to have abortion, sterilisation or contraception – full protection against legal liability for obstructing, frustrating or preventing that purpose. The protection, however, is only against legal liability. Many professions assess their members' ethical conduct even when members do not violate the law. An obvious instance is when physicians have sexual relations with patients who freely consent. Employment of legal power is not necessarily ethical. Professionals legally entitled to object to participation in procedures on grounds of conscience may be bound by the ethics of their profession to refer their patients or clients to other appropriate professionals who do not object. Physicians who set limits to the self-sacrifice historically associated with their calling cannot ethically sacrifice their patients by preventing access to care to whose provision they object. They remain bound by the ethical duty of referral.

The broad scope of conscientious objection or refusal clauses presents a challenge to health service professionalism. Refusal clauses authorise but do not mandate claims to the right of conscientious objection. Professionals who invoke this claim in principle may be ethically bound by their professional associations, for instance, to provide services when they are medically necessary to preserve patients' physical or mental health, and to refer patients in good faith when asserting their rights of non-participation. Professional associations may properly declare this ethical duty, even if legislation restricts professional disciplinary enforcement. That is, the medical, nursing, pharmacy and related professional associations may declare that they find the legislation to offend professional ethics, and state their expectation that professionals will not avail themselves of its full breadth to refuse referral.

National and leading international ethical principles require appropriate referral. For instance, the 2005 Medical Ethics Manual of the World Medical Association (WMA) recognises that a physician may have legitimate grounds to withdraw from a patient's treatment, but then requires that 'the physician should help the patient find another suitable physician'.[28] This is consistent with the WMA variant of the Hippocratic Oath, the Declaration of Geneva, by which the graduate admitted to practice pledges that 'I will practise my profession with conscience and dignity; The

27 Also reviewed in the *Smeaton* case, *supra cit.*

28 World Medical Association, Medical Ethics Manual, Ferney-Voltaire, France, WMA, 2005, at p. 40.

health of my patient will be my first consideration'. The World Health Organisation describes 'health' as a state of physical, mental and social wellbeing,[29] so that physicians' prevention of their patients' achieving their reproductive health goals compromises patients' health. The WMA Declaration on the Rights of the Patient states that 'The patient has the right to self-determination ... The patient has the right to the information necessary to make his/her decisions'.[30] Accordingly, the deliberate withholding of information about a patient's option of abortion, sterilisation, or, for instance, emergency contraception, and of information about an alternative provider of a service a patient requests but that the physician refuses to provide on grounds of conscience, even when legally protected by a refusal clause, remains medical professional misconduct.

Can the Sword be Double-edged?

Religious conviction is not the only ground on which conscience can be based. The Mississippi legislation defines 'conscience' to cover 'religious, moral or ethical principles'. Some notable expressions of conscience, such as that of South African physicians and hospitals who treated injured people in defiance of the pre-1991 apartheid racial segregation laws, were based on ethical and political rather than religious conscience. A more recent example involves Italian IVF practitioners who refuse to transfer grossly abnormal embryos into their patients, although Italy's restrictive assisted reproduction legislation of February 2004 requires that no more than three embryos be created at a time and that every embryo created *in vitro* be transferred to the uterus simultaneously. The requirement to transfer all embryos explains the rise of abortion from 17.1 per cent to 23.1 per cent after IVF treatment in Italy.[31] Refusal to transfer invokes the ethical and professional principle to 'Do No Harm' (non-maleficence).

Protection of conscience should be pluralistic, since it is contradictory and even hypocritical, to urge protection of one's own conscience while denying or suppressing the conscience of others. However, where religious fundamentalism prevails, as seen on such issues as abortion and contraception, different conscience may be opposed and outlawed. This opposition may itself violate religious teaching, for instance in the Roman Catholic tradition. In January 1991, Pope John Paul II observed that:

> Intolerance can also result from the recurring temptation to fundamentalism, which easily leads to serious abuses, such as the radical suppression of all public manifestations of diversity.[32]

---

29 World Health Organisation, Preamble to the Constitution of the WHO.

30 World Medical Association, *Declaration of Lisbon on the Rights of the Patient 1981*, as amended 1992, para 3a, 3b.

31 Progress Educational Trust, London, 311 *BioNews*, week 30/5/2005-5/6/2005, p. 2.

32 Note 1, *supra*, at para 15.

Accordingly, hospitals that refuse to allow abortion procedures, and whose staff characterise emergency contraception as abortion, should tolerate physicians of a different conscientious conviction to prescribe emergency contraception, for instance to victims of sexual assault and contraceptive failure, in order to reduce the risk of unplanned pregnancy and the dilemma of (perhaps unsafe) abortion. Similarly, the use and distribution of condoms should be tolerated where spread of sexually transmitted infections and HIV/AIDS is prevalent, especially among vulnerable populations, even though condoms were developed for contraceptive purposes. In this spirit, Cardinal Georges Cottier, theologian of the pontifical household and a senior Vatican official, has declared condom use 'legitimate' where use can save lives in the poorest parts of Africa and Asia.[33]

When a woman's life is endangered by continuation of her pregnancy, termination of the pregnancy to preserve her life is not only frequently legally required[34] but also spiritually tolerable. Religious teachings recognise the philosophical principle of double effect, by which a valid primary motivation for action does not create moral responsibility for a known, unintended, but unavoidable secondary effect.[35] Accordingly, termination of life-endangering pregnancy is not characterised as abortion, and surgical removal of cancerous testicles, which results in sterility, is not characterised as sterilisation. However, religious application of the double effect principle may not accommodate every application of the philosophical principle, particularly where, as under the Slovak Republic's draft treaty with the Holy See, religious authorities may interpret the legal scope of conscientious objection. A hospital that refuses to allow abortion in principle may have to determine whether it can permit such a procedure when it is assessed to fall outside the scope of religious acceptance when a physician conscientiously believes it necessary to save a woman's life.

A further confounding factor arises when the risk perceived to a woman's life from her pregnancy is not from physical hazards, but from suicide. Pregnancy by rape, or where pregnancy outside marriage or across ethnic boundaries is socially punished, may induce a suicidal response. In religious assessments where both abortion and suicide are mortal sins, undertaking abortion to avoid suicide may not satisfy the requirements of double effect, and may indeed be an aggravating factor since abortion, unlike suicide, will implicate the physician as well as the woman. Abortion to forestall the risk of familial 'honour killing' may be seen more sympathetically. In either case, however, physicians may claim tolerance of restrictive institutions when they feel conscientiously compelled to terminate pregnancies that present risks of suicidal or homicidal responses, or that women could survive but only at serious hazard to their physical or mental health. Similar tolerance may be claimed

---

33 World in Brief, 'Vatican Official Supports Condom Use in AIDS Fight' *The Globe and Mail*, Toronto, 1 February 2005, p. 6.

34 See the UK Abortion Act 1967, s. 4(2), *supra.*

35 Boyle J.M., 'Toward understanding the principle of double effect', 90 *Ethics* (1980), 527-538.

for those who conscientiously undertake to sterilise requesting women (or perhaps their consenting husbands) when further pregnancies would be life-endangering, or to provide them with contraceptive care.

The most comprehensive refusal clauses, such as that legislated in Mississippi's Health Care Rights of Conscience Act, would not directly protect these expressions of conscience, since their purpose and scope is to defend non-provision of services that offend religious conscience, not their provision. Mississippi's Act protects only the right not to participate,[36] and affords a healthcare provider with immunity only 'for declining to participate in a healthcare service that violates his or her conscience'.[37] To provide services in institutions committed to exclude them might fall under the jurisdiction's general law on civil disobedience, which would not necessarily reflect the generous accommodation of conscience provided by refusal clauses. Nevertheless, in light of countries' international commitments under human rights treaties and agreements to provide women with reproductive health services, such as arose from the Cairo and Beijing conferences, courts might interpret laws to protect conscientious provision of such services in the same way as laws protect conscientious objection. Finding reinforcement in anti-discrimination laws, and respect for professional ethics, courts might apply the protection provisions of religious, moral and ethical conscience to cover delivery as well as denial of reproductive health services.

Provisions as expansive as Mississippi has enacted might operate to negate other anti-abortion laws on pre-abortion counselling. Legislation in Kentucky, for instance, requires abortion providers to purchase and distribute government-sponsored pamphlets on foetal development, designed to persuade women not to proceed to termination.[38] Since delivery of information is an abortion-related service, providers might be immune from observing this law, on the ground that it risks causing patients distress, and providers are conscientiously, morally or ethically opposed to creating that risk of harm.

Conclusion

The ethical principle that people be respected as the individuals they are requires that their profound religious, moral and ethical beliefs be afforded generous accommodation and protection. Expressions of individuals' sincere convictions should be tolerated and facilitated as far as reasonably possible, and healthcare providers should not be required to take actions in direct opposition to what they consider right. Because others are equally entitled to respect for their own convictions, however, not every conscientious conviction can be fully accommodated. For instance, the ethical principle of double effect, which justifies acts to save life or seriously endangered health, does not necessarily compel such acts. The duty to

36 s 3(1).

37 s 3(2).

38 Kentucky Revised Statutes, ch. 311, 725 (2004).

save life and health is imposed by legal principles and medical professional ethics, because it creates a fair balance between competing rights of healthcare providers and those in need of care.

Religious teachings that it is as essential to avoid complicity in another's sin as to avoid committing sin oneself may go further than legal and ethical principles can accommodate. For instance, in several countries in which publicly funded healthcare systems provide or subsidise abortion services, individuals opposed to abortion have declined to pay a portion of their public taxes, claiming that even indirect payment for abortion constitutes complicity in sin. Highest courts have rejected claims to conscientious objection to payment of such taxes, and have upheld fines and imprisonment.[39] Similarly, a large-chain pharmacy company in Texas lawfully dismissed three pharmacists who, citing their religious or moral objections, denied emergency contraceptive pills to a rape victim.[40]

Refusal not only to perform abortion or related procedures but also to refer patients to other practitioners accessible to patients who do not object is ethically unacceptable, because it denies patients the information and care to which they are entitled. This is the basis on which, in February 2005, the American Bar Association House of Delegates resolved:

> That the American Bar Association opposes governmental actions and policies that interfere with patients' abilities to receive from their healthcare providers, including healthcare professionals and entities, in a timely manner: (a) all of the relevant and medically accurate information necessary for fully informed healthcare decision-making, and (b) information with respect to their access to medically appropriate care, as defined by the applicable medical standard of care, whether or not the provider chooses to offer such care.[41]

This resolution does not require any health service provider to endorse or offer any particular service, but it does require timely care or referral, and that information, for instance on emergency contraception, be based on medically accurate information rather than on religious belief.

The willingness of some politicians and healthcare professionals to follow religious and comparable authorities that urge them to invoke conscience to deny or obstruct patients' access to medically appropriate care raises the issue of whether 'conscientious objection' is actually conscientious, or a manifestation only of obedience to authority. Religious leaders can appear as authority figures, and the historic study by the social psychologist Stanley Milgram, in his 1974 book

39 See the Canadian case of Joseph Borowski, shown in *Ministry of Justice v. Borowski* (1981), 130 DLR (3d) 588, at p. 600, item 5c.

40 Zwillich, T., 'US pharmacies vow to withhold emergency contraception', 365 *The Lancet*, (2005) 1677-1678.

41 American Bar Association House of Delegates, Resolution 104, adopted 14 February 2005.

Obedience to Authority: An Experimental View,[42] showed how ordinary individuals might be induced to commit atrocities and cruelty against others when directed by an authority figure.

In a review of a biography of the author of the 1974 study,[43] a prominent medical ethicist observed that 'Milgram's work taught us something profoundly revealing about human nature: how prone we are to obey the commands of an authority even where they conflict with our expressed desires or moral principles'.[44] If religious, political or other authorities intolerant of conscientious preferences different from their own succumb to 'the recurring temptation to fundamentalism, which easily leads to serious abuses',[45] they may act cruelly, such as by denying rape victims emergency contraception, or refusing to inform parents about availability of vaccine for their children developed with use of tissue from aborted foetuses.[46] Under the oppression of such fundamentalism, the challenge of protecting patients' rights to reproductive and other healthcare against healthcare providers' and others' abuses of conscientious objection laws will be profound.[47]

---

42 New York: Harper and Row, 1974.

43 Blass T., *The Man Who Shocked the World: The Life and Legacy of Stanley Milgram*, New York, Basic Books, 2004.

44 Cassell, E.J., '"Consent or Obedience" Power and Authority in Medicine', 352 *New England J. Medicine*, (2005) 328-332, at p. 328.

45 Pope John Paul II, *supra*, note 1, at para 15.

46 Charo, *loc cit.*

47 See for instance Austria, C.S.R., 'The Church, the State and Women's Bodies in the Context of Religious Fundamentalism in the Philippines', 12 *Reproductive Health Matters*, (2004) 96-103.

Chapter 22

Classifying Abortion as a Health Matter: The Case for De-criminalising Abortion Laws in Australia

Kerry Petersen

Introduction

Regulating human reproduction is a complex task in a liberal democracy as it brings politics into the personal domain of moral and ethical values. The history of abortion over the last two centuries illustrates that prohibitive laws are unworkable because they ignore pluralism and generate illegal practices. Throughout the twentieth century, the medicalisation of abortion reduced the high incidence of maternal morbidity and mortality caused by illegal abortions. It also subjugated abortion to medical control without decriminalising abortion or expressly recognising a right to reproductive choice, without any real public debate. This was a partial solution to the imminent problem of the 'unenforceable law' and resulted in women having access to safe and affordable abortions even though the state criminal statutes were retained in their original form. Increasingly, the medicalisation of abortion was endorsed by the courts and through reform legislation. During the latter half of the twentieth century, the women's movement challenged the medical model because it vested control over decision making in the medical profession rather than in the pregnant women; and right wing religious groups opposed abortion prioritising the rights of the foetus over unwillingly pregnant women.[1]

In Australia, as in Britain, no court or parliament has expressly given women a right to abortion, even though it is subsidised by the state and widely available.[2] The High Court of Australia went so far as to recognise the link between human reproductive rights and the right to personal inviolability in *Secretary, Department of Health and Community Services v. JWB and SMB* (Marion's case),[3] but the High Court also made it clear that there is no right to reproduce and we must therefore

1 Luker, K., *Abortion and the Politics of Motherhood*, Berkeley, University of California Press, 1984, ch.3.

2 Rankin M.J., 'Contemporary Australian Abortion Law: The Description of a Crime and the Negation of a Woman's Right to Abortion', (2001) 27 *Mon Law Rev*, 229-252.

3 (1992) 175 CLR 218.

conclude that the common law in Australia does not support a right *not* to reproduce. However, the fundamental human right to personal inviolability which exists in the common law provides a foundation for reproductive freedoms and liberties and the courts in Australia and Britain recognise that personhood commences upon the live birth of a baby.

This fusion of politics and personal values is complicated by the degrees of opinion which range from extreme to moderate, on both sides of a broad spectrum.[4] At one extreme of the spectrum, some oppose abortion in all circumstances and at the other extreme, some support the woman's right to make a reproductive choice throughout the entire pregnancy. The first group argues that the life of the foetus commences at conception and advocates total prohibition of abortion. The second group regards the autonomy of the pregnant woman as absolute for the whole of the pregnancy and supports de-criminalisation. In this ideological battle the foetus is pitted against the woman, and although these two opposing positions are coherent, establishing a legal framework reflecting either of them would be politically impossible.

The pattern of regulation in Australia reflects a middle ground position which balances the competing claims of the foetus and the pregnant woman and imposes a range of conditions on abortion practice. This form of regulation generally involves legal cut-off points based on the reason for the abortion and the period of gestation. Where to draw the line and how to agree upon appropriate reasons are contentious matters. Although laws which reflect the middle ground are politically pragmatic and require ideological compromises on all sides, there is no evidence that illegal abortion is a social problem in contemporary Australia. This solution to the unenforceable law particularly offends those at the both ends of the spectrum and thus results in a continuous undercurrent of political discontent and moral conflict.

The fundamental right to personal autonomy has dominated the health law discourse over the past few decades and has generally trumped medical paternalism and beneficence in the courts. However, women's autonomy in abortion decisions is severely curtailed and subject to a medical assessment in most Australian jurisdictions. Officially, the reasons for abortion are commonly described (or disguised) as social/psychiatric even though most women seek an abortion for the simple reason that they want to end an unwanted pregnancy. Medical practitioners have a right to refuse to be involved in abortion practice if they have a conscientious objection and this is re-enforced in the Australian Capital Territory, the Northern Territory South Australia, Tasmania and Western Australia where statutes permit a health professional to refuse to participate in abortion treatment.[5] By contrast, the unwillingly pregnant women has no rights.

---

4 Dworkin, R., *Life's Dominion: An Argument about Abortion and Euthanasia*, London, Harper Collins, 1993, ch. 2.

5 Medical Practitioners Act 1930 (ACT) s 55E; Criminal Code Act 1983 (NY) s 174 (2); Criminal Law Consolidated Act 1935 (SA) s 82A (5); Criminal Code Act 1924 (Tas) s 164 (7); Health Act 1911 (WA) s 334 (2); AMA Position Statement Reproductive Health and Reproductive Technology 1998, *Termination of Pregnancy*, 1-3 at p. 2.

This chapter examines the regulation of abortion in contemporary Australia and it is shown that, although abortion is treated predominantly as a health matter, it is singled out from other health matters. It is argued that this legal solution acts to contain the issue of abortion and serves the health interests of women. However, it also reduces the scope for a debate on reproductive freedom and the interests of the foetus, as well as the incentive to re-evaluate and develop social policies which could reduce the incidence of abortion.

Abortion in Australia: Social Context

Opinion polls are often regarded as imprecise and confusing. However, they have consistently shown that there is little public support for introducing restrictive laws.[6] A recent survey of Australia general practitioners found that 84 per cent believe that all women should have access to termination services and 74 per cent classify them selves as broadly pro-choice.[7] Statements made by medical professional bodies also support these trends. The Australian Medical Association (AMA) respects the rights of doctors to hold different views regarding termination of pregnancy, and where the law permits termination, requires doctors to maintain appropriate standards of healthcare.[8] The Royal Australian and New Zealand College of Obstetricians and Gynaecologists (RANZCOG) has published a 'College Statement' stating that:

> [The] RANZCOG recognises termination of pregnancy as an important health issue, which affects around one third of women during their lifetime. The College is committed to improving the health and well being of all women and to the advancement of knowledge of the health effects of unplanned pregnancy and pregnancy termination on a woman's health. The College acknowledges that people may have strong personal beliefs about termination.[9]

The available information about the incidence of the *national* abortion rate is not reliable because of the lack of data available in Australia. However, statistics have been collected in South Australia (from 1970), the Northern Territory (from 1974) and Western Australia (from 1998) and Chan and Sage have based the following

6 Wilson, S. and Gibson, R., *Australian Survey of Social Attitudes, Version A*, The Australian National University: ACSPRI Centre for Social Research, 2003; Bean, C., Gow, D. and McAllister, I., 'Australian Election Study 2001. User's Guide for the Machine-readable Date File. SSDA Study No.1048', p. 27. Available at: ssda.anu.edu.au/codebooks/aes2001/d1048cbk.rtf, accessed on 21/7/05; Roy Morgan Poll 1998: http://www.roymorgan.com/news/polls/1998/3058/, accessed on 21/07/05.

7 *General Practitioners: Attitudes to Abortion* (2004) This research was commissioned by Marie Stopes International, see: http://www.mariestopes.com.au, accessed on 20/04/05.

8 AMA Position Statement Reproductive Health and Reproductive Technology (1998) *Termination of Pregnancy*, 1-3 at p. 2.

9 RANZCOG, College Statement, *Termination of Pregnancy*, (2005) 1-3.

estimates on an extrapolation of South Australia data with a few adjustments.[10] The overwhelming majority of abortions referred to in the Tables below take place at 12-14 weeks' gestation. The first table (Table 22.1), labelled 'Estimated abortion numbers, rates and proportions, Australia 1985-2003' shows that the estimated Australian abortion rate increased from 17.9 per 1000 women aged between 15-44 years in 1985 to a peak of 21.9/1000 in 1995, then declined to 19.7/1000 in 2003 (estimated number of abortions, 84,460). The next table (Table 22.2), labelled 'Abortion rates and abortion proportions in some developed countries, for most recent years available', shows that when compared to nine other developed countries, Australia has the third highest rate after the United States and New Zealand and is followed by Sweden. Overall, these statistics suggests that abortion is practised widely in Australia as it is in other developed countries.

Models of Regulation

The Australian Constitution give the states and territories power over criminal and health matters, and – like many other areas where states and territories have jurisdiction – abortion laws are not uniform. In most jurisdictions, abortion practice functions in the shadow of the criminal law and doctors are granted a quasi-judicial role (for which they are not necessarily qualified), while women are denied the right to make their own reproductive decisions. The ACT is the only jurisdiction where the criminal laws have been repealed and doctors are not appointed as legal gatekeepers.

Until fairly recently the *Common Law Model* and the *Reform Legislation Model* were the two main models of abortion regulation in Australia. The *Health Model* is a relatively new addition and the repeal of criminal laws in the ACT represents an important shift in the way abortion is perceived in the public forum.

The Common Law Model[11]

In Victoria, New South Wales and Queensland, the courts rather than the parliaments have liberalised the original criminal statutes by the application of the common law defence of necessity. Lawful abortions can be performed on 'maternal health

---

10 Chan, A. and Sage, L.C., 'Estimating Australia's Abortion Rates 1985-2003', (2005) 182 (9) *Medical Journal Australia*, 447-452; see also Pratt, A., Biggs, A. and Buckmaster, L., 'How Many Abortions Are There in Australia? A discussion of abortion statistics, their limitations, and options for improved statistical collections', *Research Brief*, Canberra, Department of Parliamentary Services, Parliament of Australia, 14 February 2005, No. 9, 2004-05.

11 Crimes Act 1958 (Vic) ss 10, 65-66; Crimes Act 1900 (NSW) ss 82-83; Criminal Code Act 1899 (Qld) ss 224- 226, 282.

Table 22.1 Estimated Abortion Numbers, Rates and Proportions, Australia 1985–2003

Calendar year	From Medicare claims* by private patients (A)	From hospital morbidity statistics† for public patients (B)‡	Estimate 1 of TNA (A + B)	Estimate 2 of TNA, adjusted for over-estimation of SA numbers only	Estimate 3 of TNA, adjusted for over-estimation§ and underestimation	Abortion rate per 1000 women aged 15-44 (based on Estimate 3)	Abortion proportion per 100 live births** and abortions
1985	56 371	(10 183)	66 554	66 384	65 240	17.9	20.9
1986	59 876	(10 816)	70 692	70 522	69 296	18.6	22.2
1987	60 271	(10 887)	71 158	70 988	69 752	18.3	22.2
1988	62 420	(11 275)	73 695	73 525	72 240	18.5	22.7
1989	66 414	(11 997)	78 411	78 258	76 862	19.3	23.5
1990	69 223	(12 504)	81 727	81 576	80 113	19.9	23.4
1991	70 361	(12 710)	83 071	82 842	81 430	20.0	24.0
1992	73 448	(13 267)	86 715	86 400	85 003	20.8	24.3
1993	74 395	12 470††	86 865	86 542	85 153	20.8	24.7
1994	76 691	13 044	89 735	89 388	87 965	21.5	25.3
1995	77 218	14 783	92 001	91 606	90 182	21.9	25.9
1996	77 375	13 494	90 869	90 490	89 076	21.5	25.9
1997	75 569	13 691	89 260	88 874	87 497	21.0	25.6
1998	75 183	13 429	88 612	88 213	86 862	20.8	25.4
1999	73 392	14 068	87 460	87 014	85 731	20.4	25.1
2000	74 888	13 795	88 683	88 205	86 931	20.6	25.4
2001	76 332	13 753	90 085	89 607	88 306	20.8	25.9
2002	75 282	13 013	88 295	87 817	86 552	20.3	25.5
2003	72 967	13 195	86 162	85 684	84 460	19.7	‡‡

SA = South Australian. TNA = total number of abortions. * Medicare Benefits Schedule item 35643. †Principal diagnosis codes for medical abortion 635.00-635.92 (ICD-9-CM) or O04.0-O04.9 (ICD-10-AM). ‡Figures in parentheses are estimates based on the average (15.3%) that hospital statistics comprised of total abortions for the period 1994–2002. §Overestimation proportions applied nationally for Medicare and hospital morbidity statistics were estimated from SA data. Underestimation proportion was estimated from studies of NSW and Victorian private-abortion-clinic patients. ** Sources for numbers of live births: Australian Bureau of Statistics (1985–1993), Australian Institute of Health and Welfare National Perinatal Statistics Unit (1994–2002). ††Jan–Jun 1993 statistics may not be exact but have been included, as the pattern was similar to 1994. ‡‡2003 Australian live birth numbers not yet available.

Table 22.2 Abortion Rates and Abortion Proportions in Some Developed Countries, for Most Recent Years Available*

Country	Abortion rate per 1000 women aged 15-44 years	Abortion proportion per 100 live births and abortions
Germany	7.7	15.2
The Netherlands	8.7	12.7
Finland	10.9	16.4
Norway	14.8	19.6
Canada	15.4 (2000)	24.2 (2001)
England and Wales	16.1	22.8
Sweden	19.6	25.8
Australia	19.7 (2003, estimated)	25.5 (2002, estimated)
New Zealand	21.0 (2003)	24.8 (2003)
United States	21.3 (2000)	24.5 (2000)

* Figures are for 2002 except where otherwise specified.

grounds'. In the pivotal Victorian case of *R v. Davidson,*[12] Menhennitt J ruled that an abortion would be lawful if a doctor honestly believed on reasonable grounds, when the abortion was being performed, that it was necessary to preserve the woman's life or physical or mental health and was proportionate to the danger to be averted. The grounds in New South Wales were extended in *R v. Wald* (1971)[13] to expressly include economic and social grounds. Furthermore, even though the defence of necessity does not generally apply to the Queensland Criminal Code, in *R v. Bayliss and Cullen,*[14] McGuire J took this step because the 'history of the development of certain branches of the law shows that there are times when logic has to be sacrificed on the altar of expediency'.[15] Women and doctors remain legally vulnerable in these jurisdictions and doctors are advised to obtain a second opinion before performing an abortion to demonstrate good faith.[16] The criminal onus of proof which requires

12 *R v. Davidson,* [1969] VR 667 has been upheld in other jurisdictions in the following cases: *R v. Wald,* (1971) 3 NSW DCR 25; *K v. T,* [1983] Qd R 396; *R v. Bayliss and Cullen,* (1986) 9 Qld Lawyer Reps 8; *CES v. Superclinics Australia Pty Ltd.* (Supreme Court of NSW, 18 April 1994 Newman J unreported); *CES v. Superclincs Australia Pty Ltd.*, (1995) 38 NSWLR 47 (CA).

13 (1971) 3 NSW DCR 25.

14 (1986) 9 Qld Lawyer Reps 8.

15 *Ibid.*, at p. 33.

16 De Crespigny, L. and Savulescu, J., 'Abortion: Time to Clarify Australia's Confusing Laws', (2004) 181 (4) *Medical Journal Australia*, 201-203.

the Crown to prove beyond reasonable doubt that the accused did not act in good faith is a difficult obstacle for the prosecution. These prosecutions are rare.

The Reform Legislation Model[17]

In South Australia, the Northern Territory and Tasmania, the parliaments rather than the courts have liberalised and clarified the original criminal abortion laws by passing reform legislation which did not challenge medical control or acknowledge reproductive rights. Criminal statutes are retained and amended. However, medical practitioners may perform lawful therapeutic abortions as long as they act in good faith and comply with specified conditions. These reform laws permit abortions on 'maternal health grounds'. Tasmania and the Northern Territory, unlike South Australia, do not include a specific social or fetal disability ground. However, the legislation is broad enough for a doctor to provide a lawful abortion in these circumstances as long as good faith can be demonstrated. The Northern Territory statute has stricter gestation limits than the other two states and lawful abortions may be performed between 14 and 23 weeks only when immediately necessary to prevent grave injury to the woman's physical and mental health. Even though abortion laws have been clarified in these jurisdictions to provide for lawful abortion, two medical opinions are still required. Furthermore, abortions must be performed by specialists in obstetrics or gynaecology in the Northern Territory and Tasmania even though abortion is not a technically demanding procedure.

The Health Model[18]

In Western Australia and the Australian Capital Territory, the parliaments rather then the courts introduced changes to the law. An abortion is lawful in Western Australia if it is performed by a registered medial practitioner in good faith with reasonable care and skill and is justified under section 333 of Health Act 1911.[19] The justification requirement is satisfied if the woman gives an informed consent or for health or social reasons. In spite of these reforms two medical opinions are still required. After 20 weeks' gestation, an abortion will only be lawful if two doctors from a panel of six, agree that the pregnant woman or the foetus has a severe medical condition justifying abortion, and the abortion is performed in an approved hospital, In the ACT the woman can request an abortion in the same way as she can request other health procedures. A woman's access to abortion in these jurisdictions is not conditional upon her reasons for wanting to terminate her pregnancy and women can no longer be prosecuted in either jurisdiction. Only registered medical practitioners

17 Criminal Law Consolidated Act (SA) 1935, ss 81, 82, 82A; Criminal Code Act 1983 (NT), ss 172 – 174; Criminal Code Act 1924 (Tas), ss 134,135, 164, 165.

18 Criminal Code Act 1913 (WA), ss 199, 259; Health Act 1911 ss 334, 259; Medical Practitioners Act 1930, ss 55A–42.

19 Criminal Code Act 1913 (WA), s 199(1)(2).

can perform lawful abortions in Western Australia but, unlike their counterparts in the ACT, they can still be prosecuted if they fail to act lawfully. In the ACT abortion is a health matter and medical practitioners are regulated by the Medical Practitioners Act 1930. The requirement that abortions must be performed in specified hospitals is the only condition which distinguishes abortion from other health matters.

Child Destruction Laws[20]

The separate offence of child destruction still applies in most Australian jurisdictions and is treated as a more serious matter than early term abortions. New South Wales is the only state which does not have child destruction legislation and the ACT, which no longer criminalises early abortion, has child destruction legislation. This offence prohibits the intentional killing of an unborn child who is 'capable of being born alive' unless the act or omission is done in good faith to preserve the life of the mother. It covers the gap between abortion and the crime of homicide which only applies to live beings. In Queensland, Western Australian and the Northern Territory, the offence must take place around the time of delivery. In the ACT the provision is very broad and refers to an 'act or omission occurring in relation to a childbirth'.[21] In Victoria, South Australia and Tasmania, the time frame is very broad and it could come down to 24 weeks' gestation if there was medical evidence that the child would have been capable of breathing independently or with the aid of a ventilator.[22] There is no judicial precedent on the meaning of the term unlawfully in this context and a court could hold that the Menhennitt ruling applies to the offence of child destruction as well as abortion, if it found that the doctor honestly believed on reasonable grounds that the procedure was necessary to preserve the mother's life or physical or mental health. Doctors are faced with difficult decisions in these cases as their duty to act in the best interests of a patient can expose both to legal proceedings.[23]

Late term abortions have become more central to the debate with the focus on foetal viability, advances in neonatal medicine and medical procedures, even though

---

20 Crimes Act 1900 (ACT), s 42; Criminal Code Act 1899 (Qld), s 313; Criminal Code Act 1983 (NT), s 170; Criminal Code Act 1924 (Tas), s 165; Criminal Code Act 1913 (WA), s 290; Crimes Act 1958 (Vic), s 10; Criminal Law Consolidation Act 1935 (SA), s 82A (7-8).

21 Crimes Act 1900 (ACT), s 42.

22 In *C v. S*, [1987] All ER 1230, it was held that a foetus at 18 to 21 weeks is not 'capable of being born alive under the Infant Life (Preservation) Act 1929 (Eng) because it could not breathe naturally or unnaturally'. In *Rance v. Mid-Downs Health Authority*, [1991] 1 All ER 801801 it was held that a foetus of 26 to 27 weeks' gestation was 'capable of being born alive' if born alive and able to breathe on its own.

23 Skene, L. and Niselle, P., 'Late Termination of Pregnancy: When is it Lawful', (2000) *Medicine Today*, 103; de Crespigny, L. and Savulescu, J., 'Abortion: Time to Clarify Australia's Confusing Laws', (2004) *Medical Journal Australia*, 201.

they remain relatively rare and little information is available.[24] It is reported that in South Australian, less than two per cent of induced abortions took place at or after 20 weeks between 1994 and 2002[25]and in Western Australia, only 0.5 per cent of abortions were carried out at 20 weeks or over and none of these were approved for social and/or psychiatric reasons. Five applications for a post 20-week termination on psychiatric/social ground were denied but it is recognized that the severe psychiatric disorder could satisfy the legal criteria.[26] In the *Report on Late Term Terminations of Pregnancy* the Medical Practitioners Board of Victoria (MPBV) stated that later terminations in Victoria are largely confined to foetal abnormalities and a very few of them are performed for maternal illness. Some of the situations in which later term terminations for pregnancy can be requested include:

- late maternal presentations;
- organisational delays resulting in post 20 week investigation;
- difficulties in interpreting ultrasound abnormalities by staff and the repeat of such tests at a later stage of pregnancy;
- patients have a change of mind regarding prenatal diagnosis;
- abnormalities coincidentally identified during a post 20-week ultrasound examination carried out for other reasons;
- some conditions such as hydrocephaly and some skeletal dysplasias may not be detectable or confirmed until post 20 weeks;
- intra-uterine infection may sometimes be only confirmed post 20 weeks; and
- conditions recognised prior to 20 weeks may subsequently worsen. For examples, renal abnormalities.[27]

---

24 Late-term abortions can be defined as those which take place after 20 weeks' gestation, or after 24 weeks, or those performed after the point at which the foetus could survive outside the mother's womb. See, Pratt, A., Biggs, A. and Buckmaster, L., 'How many abortions are there in Australia? A discussion of abortion statistics, their limitations, and options for improved statistical collections', *Research Brief*, Canberra: Department of Parliamentary Services, Parliament of Australia, 14 February 2005, No.9, 2004 - 05. Fn 38.

25 Pratt, A., Biggs, A. and Buckmaster, L., 'How many abortions are there in Australia? A discussion of abortion statistics, their limitations, and options for improved statistical collections', *Research Brief*, Canberra, Department of Parliamentary Services, Parliament of Australia, 14 February 2005, No.9, 2004-05.

26 Western Australia, *Report to the Minister of Health on the Review of Provisions of the Health Act 1911 and the Criminal Code Relating to Abortion as Introduced by the Acts Amendment (Abortion) Act 1998* (17 June 2002) 5.1. Available at: http://www.telehealth.health.wa.gov.au/publications/documents/ABORTIONREVIEWmaster180602.pdf, accessed on 03/02/05; Department of Health Western Australia, A Maternal and Child Health Unit, Information Collection and Management Induced Abortion in Western Australia 1999-2004 Report of the WA Abortion Notification System (2005) 4.2.

27 MPBV, *Report on Late Term Terminations of Pregnancy* (1998).

Similarly in Britain, the percentage of all abortions performed at 20 weeks or more is small and has remained at between 1 and 1.6 per cent of the total number of terminations for many years. A diagnosis of foetal abnormality is the most common reasons for British women seeking a late-term abortion, but other compelling 'non-medical' reasons for the incidence of late-term abortions suggest:

> The reasons why women have abortions late are ... almost entirely beyond their own control. In most cases – available evidence suggest at least 80 percent – women terminating pregnancies late do not realise they need to request abortion until they are more than three to four months pregnant.[28]

Restricting access further would mean that more women, particularly young ones, would have unwanted babies or they would seek abortions overseas or outside the mainstream hospital system.

Confidentiality

A doctor has a legal and ethical duty to respect confidentiality and patients, including mature minors, have a right to assume that the doctor will not disclosure personal information to a third party without their consent.[29] Nevertheless, there are many exceptions to the duty of confidentiality including an exception on the grounds of the Crown Privilege or public interest immunity which permits confidential information to be disclosed in some circumstances.

The public interest immunity regarding disclosure of health information was very controversial in a recent case where hospital records were sought by the MPBV after a notification was made by the anti-choice National Party Senator Julian McGauran to the MPBV about a late-term abortion performed at the Victorian Royal Women's Hospital (RWH) in 2000. The complaint was based on information obtained from private medical records in a police file which had been given to Senator McGauran by the State Coroner, Graham Johnstone. The police had decided that there was no case to answer.

The case involved an abortion at 32 weeks' gestation which took place at the RWH. The woman, Mrs X, had become hysterical and suicidal after she was told that the foetus was diagnosed with dwarfism and she asked for a termination. The decision to go ahead was made after considerable deliberation by four doctors: an ultrasonologist, an obstetrician, a geneticist and a psychiatrist. Subsequently, the MPBV determined to conduct a preliminary investigation but it was hampered by the lack of medical records as Mrs X, upon legal advice, did not wish to be involved in

---

28 Pro-Choice Forum, *Late Abortion: A Review of the Evidence*, (2004) p. 13, available at: www.prochoiceforum.org.uk, accessed on 25/07/05.

29 *Gillick v. West Norfolk and Wisbech Health Authority*, [1986] AC 112; See MPBV, *Consent for Treatment and Confidentiality in Young People*, http://medicalboardvic.org.au, accessed on 20/07/06.

the investigation and refused to give the MPBV access to her medical records. After considerable legal activity, the Magistrate's Court found that the medical records were not protected by the public interest immunity (Crown privilege) and ordered the RWH to hand them over to the MPBV. The RWH appealed against the Magistrate's decisions to the Supreme Court of Victoria. In the *Royal Women's Hospital v. Medical Practitioners Board of Victoria*,[30] Gillard J upheld the Magistrate's ruling and recognised the competing public interest between the RWH's duty to maintain patient confidentiality and the MPBV's duty to regulate the standards of medical practice, Gillard J held that the public interest in the proper investigation and determination of complaints made against registered medical practitioners outweighed the public interest in protecting the medical records of women patients in public hospitals seeking advice and treatment about reproductive health matters. He refused to accept that the disclosure of the confidential information would deter pregnant women from seeking the health services from the hospital or would adversely interfere with the capacity of the RWH to perform its functions. The appeal by the RWH against this decision was dismissed by the Victorian Court of Appeal.[31] Even although the case has not yet reached the final stage, the events to date reinforce the argument that abortion has become increasingly classified as a health matter and the MPBV has a role in maintaining medical standards. However, the twist here is that most notifications are made to the MPBV by patients, and therefore disclosure of medical records to a third party is usually done with the patient's consent. In this case, the notification was made by Senator McGauran for ideological reasons and the patient refused to give a consent to her medical records being handed over to the MPBV because, *inter alia*, of the possibility of self-incrimination if criminal proceeding were taken against her. Under Gillard J's ruling the woman becomes liable to prosecution if the MPBV is forced to surrender these medical records to the police, as she does not appear to have received the usual indemnity from prosecution that most women are given if they provide evidence on behalf of the Crown in abortion cases. If the criminal abortion laws were repealed this would be a different issue. However, as they are still on the statute books this scenario sets a worrying precedent for the future. It may commence with the more serious offence of child destruction, but the flow-on effect could place *all* women who have pregnancies terminated and their doctors, in danger of being sent to prison.

A doctor also has a legal and ethical duty to respect confidentiality when the patient is a competent minor but the obligation regarding an incompetent child is not clear.[32] The doctor has a particularly important role to play in counselling and advising young people regarding contraception, pregnancy and abortion. Minors

---

30 [2005] VSC 225.

31 *Royal Women's Hospital v. Medical Practitioner's Board of Victoria* [2006] VCSA 85 (20 April 2006).

32 *Gillick v. West Norfolk and Wisbech Health Authority*, [1986] AC 112; See MPBV, *Consent for Treatment and Confidentiality in Young People*, http://medicalboardvic.org.au, accessed on 20/07/05.

need to be informed that they have a right to expect that the doctor will not disclose any information to a third party without their consent. In spite of the criminal 'age of consent' laws, it is lawful for a doctor to assist sexually active children under the age of 16 years as the duty to maintain confidentiality and the duty of care overrides the criminal law in this situation.[33] However, the doctor may be justified in breaching confidence if there is evidence of child abuse, incest or the risk of suicide.[34]

Consent: Adults

As with other medical procedures, the doctor has an ethical and legal duty to obtain a valid consent from a woman before performing an abortion and to respect the duty of confidentiality. Accordingly, the consent must be a voluntary one, the woman must have sufficient capacity to understand the potential risks of having an abortion or continuing with the pregnancy, and she must have sufficient information to enable her to make an informed decision.[35]

Common Law

Most of the recent developments relevant to consent have taken place in negligence law where the leading case of *Rogers v. Whitaker*[36] introduced the term – the duty of disclosure – and ruled that it is part of a doctor's duty of care to inform patients about the material risks of a procedure before they agree to undergo treatment. Failure to disclose this information can amount to a breach of the standard of care. The High Court of Australia deliberately eschewed the term informed consent in *Rogers v. Whitaker* and placed the onus on the doctor to provide information about material risks. A risk is material if a reasonable person in the patient's position, if warned of the risk, would be likely to attach significance to it or if the medical practitioner is or should reasonably be aware that the particular patient if warned of the risk would be likely to attach significance to it.[37] The doctor is responsible for deciding what information is material and must take into account the following factors:

---

33 Petersen, K., 'The Sexual Zone Between Childhood and the Age of Majority: Claims to Sexual Freedoms Versus Protectionist Policies', in Brooks-Gordon, B., Gelsthorpe, L., Johnson, M. and A. Bainham (eds), *Sexuality Repositioned:Diversity and the Law*, Oxford, Hart Publishing, 2004, ch. 16, pp. 351-372.

34 MPBV, *Consent for Treatment and Confidentiality in Young People*, http://medicalboardvic.org.au, accessed on 20/07/05. The law regarding confidentiality and incompetent children is unclear.

35 If a woman is not competent, and no-one has been authorised to make decisions on her behalf, a decision maker will have to be appointed. The relevant guardianship legislation varies from jurisdiction to jurisdiction. See Skene, L., *Law and Medical Practice: Rights, Duties Claims and Defences* (2nd ed), Australia, Butterworths, 2004, ch. 5.

36 (1992) 175 CLR 479.

37 (1992) 175 CLR 479, 490.

- the nature of the matter to be disclosed
- the nature of the proposed treatment
- the desire of the patient for information
- the temperament and health of the patient
- the general surrounding circumstances.[38]

In the case of abortion, the doctor should advise the patient about the technical nature of the procedure for the period of gestation and the physical and psychological risks with respect to both a termination and carrying the pregnancy to term. The detail and extent of the information would be balanced against the doctor's assessment of the patient's needs and circumstances. The doctor could also withhold information under the therapeutic privilege, if he or she honestly believed that information could cause serious harm to the patient. This discussion would be more complex in a later term pregnancy.

The RANZCOG advises that:

> A woman's physical, social, emotional and psychological needs should be taken into account in the course of counselling and decision-making. Pregnancy termination services should be provided in an approved facility, incorporating all appropriate standards for clinical assessment, procedural safety and after-care. The availability of a range of medical and surgical methods of termination is seen as ideal. Pre-and post-termination counselling by appropriately qualified personnel should be routinely available. Confidentiality of all possible identifying information of women undergoing termination of pregnancy is essential.[39]

Statutory Informed Consent

In spite of the existing common law consent requirements and the rejection of the term 'informed consent' by the High Court of Australia, abortion has been singled out from other medical procedures by the inclusion of specific 'informed consent' requirements in the Tasmanian and Western Australian amending statutes. These provisions are mandatory and abortions are unlawful if they are not followed. In Tasmania and Western Australia the doctor must provide the woman with counselling about the medical risks of termination and carrying a pregnancy to term.[40] In Tasmania, the doctor must also refer the woman to counselling about non-medical matters, while in Western Australia, the doctor is only required to inform the woman about non-medical counselling.[41]

38 See *F v. R*, (1983) 33 SASR 189, 192.

39 RANZCOG College Statement, *Termination of Pregnancy*, (2005) 1-3.

40 Criminal Code Act 1924 (Tas), ss 164 (1) (b), 164 (9); Health Act 1911 (WA), s 333 (5) (a) & (b).

41 Criminal Code Act 1924 (Tas), s 164 (9); Health Act 1911 (WA), s 333 (5).

Consent: Children

Children or minors in these circumstances are girls under 18 years. The term 'mature minor' is also used for young people who are close to attaining majority. The doctor must obtain a valid consent from the custodial parent(s), the minor or a legal guardian before proceeding with an abortion. When assessing competence, the doctor should consider whether she understands the potential risks of the proposed abortion and the risks of continuing with the pregnancy, and whether she has enough understanding and intelligence to make the decision and give a valid consent.[42] If there is disagreement between the parents and an incompetent child, an application can be made to the Family Court of Australia and the decision will be based on the Court's assessment of her best interests.[43] Legislation has been passed in New South Wales giving a child of 14 years the right to consent to medical treatment, and also in South Australia where the age is 16 years.[44]

Special consent requirements apply to young women in the Northern Territory and Western Australia. In the Northern Territory, a minor is not able to give a consent until she has reached 16 years.

Western Australia imposes an additional requirement on a dependent minor[45] seeking a termination which is unique in Australia. Either her custodial parent or legal guardian must be informed that an abortion is being considered and given an opportunity to participate in the counselling/consultation with the medical practitioner; or an order must be made by the Children's Court of Western Australia dispensing with this requirement.[46] When the custodial parent or legal guardian participates in the counselling/consultation with the medical practitioner, the dependent minor gives an informed consent irrespective of the views of the custodial parent or legal guardian. The Children's Court cannot grant permission for an abortion or order an abortion. Twenty six applications were made to the Children's Court between 1998

42 *Gillick v. West Norfolk and Wisbech Health Authority*, [1986] AC 112; See MPBV, *Consent for Treatment and Confidentiality in Young People*, http://medicalboardvic.org.au, accessed on 20/07/05.

43 *Secretary, Department of Health and Community Services v. JWB and SMB*, (Marion's case) (1992) 175 CLR 218. There is no reported case on this issue in Australia but in *Re P (a minor)*, [1986] FLR 272 (an English decision which was decided in 1981 but reported in 1986) the court decided that a 15-year-old schoolgirl with a criminal conviction in the care of the local authority should be permitted to have an abortion in spite of her parents' objection. The court found that there were grounds for a lawful abortion, she wanted an abortion and she understood the nature and implications of the procedure.

44 Minors (Property and Contracts) Act 1970 (NSW), s 49 (2); Medical Treatment and Palliative Care Act 1995 (SA), s 6.

45 This refers to a young girl under 16 years who is being supported by a custodial parent or legal guardian. See Health Act 1911 (WA), s 133 (8) (b).

46 Health Act 1911 (WA), s 333 (8-11).

and 2002. All of them were approved for reasons which included fears of violence, retribution, cultural and religious reasons.[47]

Conclusion

As this chapter has shown, there have been a number of important changes to abortion laws over the last decade and the regulatory pattern throughout Australia reflects the lack of public support for passing or enforcing prohibitive laws. In general, women have access to safe abortions and the overwhelming majority are performed before 20 weeks' gestation. Nevertheless availability varies from state to state and also depends on the willingness of doctors to perform abortions.

The parliaments in South Australia, the Northern Territory, Tasmania and Western Australia have taken steps towards de-criminalising abortion by legalising medical abortions. The general trend is towards classifying abortion as a health matter 'with a difference' by appointing doctors as legal gatekeepers and requiring two medical opinions as well as mandatory 'counselling/informed consent' provisions. These conditions are not designed to protect the health interests of women as abortion is not a difficult procedure; the woman can make her own diagnosis and the woman is the best person to decide which course to follow. These conditions are also superfluous to existing common law consent requirements. In sum this approach has the effect of re-enforcing the medical model and interfering with the exercise of reproductive choice. The ACT is the only jurisdiction which has repealed criminal abortion statutes, but abortions are restricted to specified hospitals and subject to hospital policy. Availability is dependent on the attitudes of doctors to abortion and in this respect, abortion is still different from other medical procedures.

In the remaining states of New South Wales, Queensland and Victoria the courts have liberalised the criminal laws by applying the defence of necessity, and although there are no laws which distinguish abortions from other medical procedures, abortion in these states is treated predominantly as a health matter and is under the control of the medical profession. Two medical opinions are generally obtained and special counselling provided to establish good faith in case of prosecution. In practice, free standing or private clinics have been operating in Queensland, New South Wales and Victoria since the 1970s and even though they operate under the stick of the criminal laws, they provide women with the opportunity to obtain safe abortions virtually on request. This political tolerance has acted as a safety valve and reduced moral and political conflict. It also helps to explain why the state parliaments have been reluctant to introduce reform laws which will trigger public debate and conflict.

---

47 Western Australia, Report to the Minister of Health on the Review of Provisions of the Health Act 1911 and the Criminal Code relating to Abortion as Introduced by the Acts Amendment (Abortion) Act 1998 (WA 17 June 2002), pp. 25-27. Available at: http://www.telehealth.health.wa.gov.au/publications/documents/ABORTIONREVIEWmaster180602.pdf, accessed on 03/02/05.

Late-term abortions are regulated in Western Australia and the Northern Territory, by statutory gestation limits and in all jurisdictions, except New South Wales, by child destruction statutes, which prohibit the killing of a viable foetus unless the pregnancy threatens the life of the pregnant woman. Late-term abortions are rare and usually performed after of a diagnosis of foetal abnormality. Until recently, most would have agreed that doctors in New South Wales and Victoria are unlikely to be charged with criminal abortion or child destruction offences given that the last time prosecutions were taken against doctors for abortion or child destruction offences in New South Wales or Victoria was in the 1970s.[48] However, a Sydney doctor has recently been accused of inducing a late-term abortion. She is the first medical practitioner to be charged over a termination in either of these states since 1971.[49]

On the one hand, classifying abortion as a health matter is a positive step because it diffuses conflict, distances the issue from the criminal law and most importantly serves the health interests of women. On the other hand, this legal solution is problematic too. It promotes polarisation and ongoing conflict amongst a minority of people with extreme views and, in the prevailing conservative political environment, reduces the scope for serious debate on reproductive freedom principles and foetal interests. Pro-choice groups focus on women and anti-choice groups focus on the foetus and both sides are locked into extreme positions. As a consequence, there is a continuous undercurrent of political discontent which manifests mainly in the context of late-term abortions, even though there are few of them and the reasons for having them are often beyond the control of the women who seek them. Abortion is represented as the 'problem' and criminal law is presented as the 'solution' with the result that there is insufficient incentive for all sides of abortion politics to look beyond the law.

In a de-regulated environment, minus the shadow of criminal laws, abortion practice could be regulated through state medical boards and ethics committees. This would give more freedom to both sides of abortion politics to acknowledge the unique relationship between the pregnant women and her foetus and also to acknowledge the woman's right to decide whether or not to have and to care for a future child. In Australia, this would involve a thorough overhaul and re-evaluation of social policies such as those concerned with the rights of, and facilities for, disabled people, subsided child care, 'family friendly' workplaces agreements, social and economic support and educational opportunities for single mothers and sex education. Changes to these policies would not eliminate abortion practice, but would give women more choice and may reduce the incidence of abortion. Paradoxically, the conservative governments which are strongly supported by the fundamentalist anti-choice Christian groups generally have social polices which stand in direct opposition to those outlined above.

---

48 Skene, *op cit.*, at pp. 372-373.

49 Jacobsen, G., 'Doctor Charged with Killing Foetus', (2005) August 9, *Sydney Morning Herald*, 1.

Chapter 23

What's Love Got to Do With It? Regulating Reproductive Technologies and Second Hand Emotions

Penelope Beem and Derek Morgan

Introduction

The desire for a child sometimes seems all consuming. IVF and its myriad cousins might seem to offer entitlement to a child; that every woman (we reserve discussion of men)[1] who wants a child deserves a child. Whether the inability to procreate results from nature, career development, lack of attention from the opposite sex, the prospect of a second or later-in-life marriage, or some other social obstacle, there is an emergent notion that IVF will deliver what nature or nurture has not. This desire for a child could appear somewhat like an arranged marriage. The desire seems to be more about completing the status of the person, rather than a relationship: being married or being a mother, rather than having a husband or having a child. One could ask; what has love got to do with it?

The stigma of single parenthood, while still attracting negative attention when associated with poverty and the mean streets, has attained almost heroic status in the leafy, wealthy avenues. Single/career women without partners can now be admired for taking the road to single parenthood via their 'right to reproductive choice', when compared with earlier generations of women who had single parenthood thrust upon them through lack of education, naivety, religious commitment, war or other circumstance.

IVF has been one of the most spectacular technologies of the twentieth century, yet too much still remains unknown about the long-term health implications as the UK Medical Research Council observed in a recent report.[2] Success rates are low and it is expensive technology that is suitable for only a small percentage of infertile

1 That they 'fragment fatherhood' too is powerfully illustrated in Sheldon, S., 'Fragmenting Fatherhood: The Regulation of Reproductive Technologies', (2005) 68(4) *Modern Law Review*, 523-53 and Beem, P., 'Where Does a Man Stand on Issues of Assisted Reproduction, Surrogacy, Artificial Insemination within Lesbian Relationships and Posthumous Conception?', (2004) 18 *Australian Journal of Family Law*, 41-68.

2 MRC *Assisted Reproduction: A Sound, Safe Future*, London, Medical Research Council, 2004.

women and only a few of these can afford them. That society should be confused about the outcomes of IVF services and the type of family and 'designer' babies it facilitates is unsurprising. The progress of medical science and practice is often so swift that it tends to hijack the original issue; the problem is not always the outcome but how to manage the resultant situation. Children will, in most events, flourish in a loving and supportive environment whatever we call that child's family situation; the concern is more about reducing the stigma associated with the more unusual family constructs.[3] Society therefore has to determine whether to manage the outcome of IVF treatment, or its aftermath.

National governments exhibit varied responses depending on the nature and degree of direct clinical involvement or experience, the appetite of government to constrain market regulation,[4] the nature of social mores affected by changes in reproductive practices,[5] and other more nuanced considerations. South Korea,[6] Italy[7] and member states of the EU[8] have recently introduced significant reforms, and the US President's Bioethics Commission report of 2004 may well yet have international ramifications.[9] Here, though we review regulation of, and eligibility and access to,

3 Tobin, J., *The Convention on the Rights of the Child: The Rights and the Best Interests of Children Conceived Through Assisted Reproduction*, Melbourne, Victorian Law Reform Commission, August 2004; McNair, R., *Outcomes for Children Born of A.R.T. in a Diverse Range of Families*, Melbourne, Victorian Law Reform Commission, August 2004.

4 The most comprehensive consideration of a market in reproductive services has been suggested by Posner, R.A., *Sex and Reason*, Cambridge, Mass., Harvard University Press, 1992, at pp. 404-434. The belief that Posner, or any other 'law and economics' analysis, thereby posits an *unregulated* market is examined and corrected by Duxbury, N., 'Do Markets Degrade?', (1996) 59 *Modern Law Review*, 331-53. For a comprehensive account and anylysis of IVF as a business enterprise see Deborah Spar, *The Baby Business*, Cambridge, Mass., Harvard Business School Press, 2006.

5 'Technologies such as IVF and other ARTs inevitably provide normative challenges as they widen the scope of reproductive options and contest the traditional notions of motherhood, pregnancy and childbirth.' Peterson M.M., 'Assisted Reproductive Technologies and Equity of Access Issues', (2005) 31 (5) *Journal of Medical Ethics*, 280-85, at p. 281.

6 South Korea, Bioethics and BioSafety Act 2004.

7 Italy illustrates some of the tensions in recent reform of an unregulated jurisdiction to a tightly regulated, see Law on medically assisted reproduction, February 19th 2004, n. 40 (Gazzetta Ufficiale February 24th 2004, n. 45).

8 EU Directive on Tissues and Cells (Official Journal L 102, 07/04/2004 P. 0048 – 0058).

9 US President's Council on Bioethics report *Reproduction & Responsibility: The Regulation of New Biotechnologies*, Washington, 2004; Chaired by Leon Kass.

IVF services in Australia, New Zealand,[10] Canada,[11] the UK, and Ireland[12] – broadly similar legal jurisdictions.[13]

It has been said that:

> The discipline of comparative law … has the … inestimable value of sharpening our focus on the weight of competing considerations. And it reminds us that the law is part of the world of competing ideas markedly influenced by cultural differences.[14]

The comparative approach brings fresh insights, suggests possible solutions and facilitates identification of new problems.

United Kingdom: The Human Fertilisation and Embryology Act 1990

The HFE Act encourages a 'broadly facilitative' approach;[15] the 'central role' granted to professionals is one of the 'key features' of the Act.[16] The legislation was a mirror of the approach adopted in the Report of the Committee of Inquiry into Human Fertilisation and Embryology (Warnock Report);[17] that is, as 'more of an exercise in pragmatism than an exploration of the philosophy underpinning issues of reproductive choice'.[18] The Human Fertilisation and Embryology Authority, which was established by the 1990 Act, has been both widely admired and subject to external criticism, some of which goes with its very contested territory. The HFE Act 1990 was passed in part to allay public fears about 'new' reproductive technologies. There was a real concern for the children who might be born of the use of these technologies and the effects on the accepted family form. Physical health was not

10 Human Assisted Reproduction (HART) Act 2004.

11 Assented to 29th March, 2004, An Act Respecting Assisted Human Reproduction and Related Research.

12 *Report of The Commission on Assisted Human Reproduction* (Dublin, April 2005) Chaired by Professor Emeritus Dervilla Donnelly, University College Dublin.

13 Canada has a Charter of Fundamental Rights and Freedoms; New Zealand a Bill of Rights; Ireland a State Constitution (Art. 40.3.3 of which may be of particular relevance); the UK has adopted the European Convention on Human Rights in the Human Rights Act 1998, (several articles of which have already led to relevant litigation), while Australia, having no Bill of Rights has strong Commonwealth anti – discrimination legislation (the basis of significant challenges to and reform of State legislative provisions in respect of assisted conception).

14 Lord Steyn in *MacFarlane v. Tayside Health Board* [1999] 4 All ER 961, at p. 976.

15 Jackson E *Regulating Reproduction: Law, Technology and Autonomy*, Oxford, Hart, 2001, at p. 259.

16 Brazier M 'Regulating the Reproduction Business', (1999) 7 *Medical Law Rev*, 166-93, at p. 178.

17 Cmnd 9314/1984.

18 Brazier, *loc cit.*, at p. 173.

the issue, rather the focus was on the children's social or moral welfare; what kind of children were these – 'begotten or made'?[19] Who were they?

It has been 15 years since debates on the HFE Bill and much has changed in the environment surrounding medical practice generally and the delivery of assisted conception services specifically. There are new agencies to supervise aspects of patient health and safety; with specific guidelines on assisted conception, and the centrality of patient autonomy and choice has come to be recognised. Scientists and doctors have become more sensitive to the need to communicate both with individual patients and the wider public. There has been a growing questioning of ethical governance by committees of appointed members where questions of accountability appear to be at one remove. In reproductive medicine there has been a growing understanding of the possibilities – some of them morally controversial – and the limitations – some of them apparently immutable – of the technology. And there have been significant changes in social and legal conventions which have seen the emergence more fully of arguments from a human rights perspective and a more accommodating ethic in relation to choice of family form; access to assisted conception need not be limited to the married heterosexual couple and cannot be justified where it appears to be – or appears to be capable of being – based in discriminatory assumptions rather than uncontroverted evidence. The ability of individuals or couples to gain easy access to unregulated markets in assisted conception services both discloses a global demand for treatment services and, to some degree, questions the utility of regulation.

The two most significant legislative developments in the UK since 1990 have been the Human Fertilisation and Embryology Authority (Disclosure of Donor Information) Regulations 2004, which remove the ability of new donors to remain anonymous once the child has reached 18, and the Human Fertilisation and Embryology (Deceased Fathers) Act 2003 which allows a man to be registered as the father of a child conceived after his death using his sperm or using an embryo created with his sperm before his death, even though done without his written consent. The latter Act was a direct response to the campaigning litigation pursued by Diane Blood since 1997[20] and the former in part a response to the litigation pursued by Joanna Rose in *R v. Secretary of State for Health ex parte Rose*.[21]

Moving from Warnock's caution as to the 'new reproductive technologies' the House of Commons Select Committee on Science and Technology in its 2005 report, *Human Reproductive Technologies and the Law*,[22] concluded that:

> there should be a presumption that individuals should be free to make their own reproductive choices, in the absence of evidence of physical or psychological harm to children born

19 O'Donovan, O., *Begotten or Made?*, Oxford, Clarendon Press, 1984.

20 *R. v. Human Fertilisation and Embryology Authority Ex p. Blood*, [1999] Fam. 151 [1997] 2 W.L.R. 807.

21 *Rose v. Secretary of State for Health and the HFEA*, [2002] EWHC 1593; see also *Mikulic v. Croatia*, [2002] ECHR 27, *Odievre v. France*, [2003] ECHR 86.

22 *Eighth Special Report of Session 2004–05*, HC 491, 24 March 2005

23 *Ibid.*, at para 390.

> as a result of techniques designed to alleviate infertility or of negative impacts on society as a whole … the current regulatory model … should be replaced with a system which devolves clinical decision-making and technical standards down to professionals while at the same time strengthening Parliamentary and ethical oversight.[23]

How have other jurisdictions responded to the 'fear factor' and the 'liberty line'?

Australia

The National Picture

With 6,000 births per year in Australia IVF is now clinically well established, but in a state of regulatory flux. Despite continued calls by the National Health and Medical Research Council (NHMRC) for uniform state legislation for Assisted Reproductive Technologies (ART), so far only Victoria,[24] Western Australia[25] and South Australia[26] have complied. New South Wales has draft legislation but the Bill has been stalled in Cabinet for nearly two years. The other states and territories have no specific ART legislation and providers are regulated through clinical accreditation, under ethical guidelines for ART generated by the National Health and Medical Research Council[27] and the Fertility Society of Australia's (FSA) Code of Practice.[28]

Do you have to need IVF to have access to IVF? If the purpose of treatment programs is to assist in achieving conception, should treatment simply be available to all those who could benefit from the technology? IVF *is* different from other medical treatments or services in that if it is successful, the result is the creation of another life. Furthermore, it is not a treatment without some risk to both the mother and the potential child; potential morbidity and mortality of both mother and child might suggest only clinical need for treatment is good medical practice. However, patients can consent to dangerous or risky medical treatment where they fully understand and accept those risks and individual autonomy is identified as one of the considerations for treatment in the NHRMC guidelines.

Victoria, the stalwart and progenitor of the legislative regime is currently undertaking a comprehensive legal review, enquiring and reporting on the desirability and feasibility of changes to the Infertility Treatment Act 1995 (Vic) to expand eligibility to treatment services. The Victorian Law Reform Commission's

24 Infertility Treatment Act 1995.

25 Human Reproductive Technology Act 1991.

26 Reproductive Technology (Clinical Practices) Act 1988.

27 Australian Health Ethics Committee, *Ethical Guidelines on the Use of Assisted Reproductive Technology in Clinical Practice and Research*, September 2004.

28 Reproductive Technology Accreditation Committee, April 2002.

review[29] has sparked controversy at the federal level, as it threatens the concept of the traditional nuclear family so fervently maintained by conservative governments and religious organisations. In a perhaps not totally unrelated move, the Australian Federal Health Minister has initiated a review to consider the clinical and cost effectiveness of assisted reproductive technologies for the purposes of public funding under the Medicare Benefits Schedule. The review will make recommendations on the clinical appropriateness and effectiveness of ART, societal impacts, and the extent to which ART should be publicly funded, having regard to effectiveness, access and equity.[30] If IVF is to be seen as an established health care service, it may indeed have to be accepted as a service in which the public purse is entitled to triumph over private desire, or even need. All western societies are accustomed to realising that the health spend is not elastic and that hard choices have to be made.

In Australia those states and territories without specific ART legislation are regulated through clinical accreditation, under ethical guidelines generated by the NHMRC[31] and the Fertility Society of Australia's (FSA) Code of Practice.[32] The Reproductive Technology Accreditation Committee (RTAC) must sanction all IVF services and the providers of these must comply with the RTAC code of practice and NHMRC guidelines absent supervening state legislation.

Since 1992 the Australian Health Ethics Committee (AHEC) and NHMRC have issued ART guidelines, and the current 2004 guidelines are premised on the notion that the welfare of people born as a result of ART is paramount,[33] and that the autonomy and the long-term welfare of men and women participants must be respected.[34] The RTAC's Code states that the objective of ART should be the live birth of a single healthy child.[35] Unfortunately, despite this invocation the objective all too often still remains elusive at the end of treatment.

Specific States *Human Reproductive Technology Act 1991 (WA)* The objects of the Human Reproductive Technology Act 1991 (WA) are very broad and not prioritised. Section 4(1) provides, inter alia, that beneficial developments in reproductive

---

29 Victorian Law Reform Commission, *Assisted Reproduction and Adoption: Should the Current Eligibility in Victoria be Changed?*, Consultation Paper, December 2003. There are three Occasional Papers: Tobin, J., *The Convention on the Rights of the Child: The Rights and the Best Interests of Children Conceived Through Assisted Reproduction*, August 2004; McNair, R., *Outcomes for Children Born of A.R.T. in a Diverse Range of Families*, August 2004; Seymour, J. and Magri, S., *A.R.T., Surrogacy and Legal Parentage: A Comparative Legislative Review*, August 2004.

30 Available at: http://www.health.gov.au/internet/ministers/publishing.nsf/Content/health-mediarel-yr2005-ta-abb084.htm.

31 Australian Health Ethics Committee, *Ethical Guidelines on the Use of Assisted Reproductive Technology in Clinical Practice and Research*, September 2004.

32 Reproductive Technology Accreditation Committee, April 2002.

33 Paras 2.5 and 5.1.

34 Paras 2.6 and 5.1.

35 RTAC Code of Practice, para 5.1.

technology should be set against discouragement, and if necessary prohibition, of developments or procedures that are not both 'proper and suitable'; artificial fertilisation procedures may only be carried out for the benefit of persons who, in accordance with the Act, are eligible to be treated; the prospective welfare of the resultant child must be 'properly taken into account' and equity, welfare and general community standards are to be taken into account in the practice of reproductive technology. The Preamble to the 1991 Act is more enlightening:

> … the primary purpose and only justification for the creation of a human embryo in vitro is to assist persons who are unable to conceive children naturally due to medical reasons or whose children are otherwise likely to be affected by a genetic abnormality or a disease …

Reproductive Technology (Clinical Practices) Act 1988 (SA) The South Australian legislation is more precise and succinct; the welfare of the child is of paramount importance and is the fundamental principle in the formulation of the code of ethical practice.[36]

Infertility Treatment Act 1995 (Vic) Section 5 (1) of the Infertility Treatment Act (ITA) 1995 also prioritises the considerations for treatment, and, as with South Australia, the welfare and interests of any person born or to be born as a result of a treatment procedure are paramount. This is followed by the imperative that human life should be preserved and protected, then the interests of the family should be considered, and finally infertile couples should be assisted in fulfilling their desire to have children.

When considering whether to treat a person with a clinical need for that treatment, it is perhaps curious to give priority to the rights or interests of another – in this case, an unborn person. This is not to suggest that the interests of a potential child are unimportant; rather to question whether they should have primacy. It begs the question: what is an acceptable level of parenting?, and the further question of whether it is appropriate in any liberal society for government to make personal decisions on behalf of autonomous citizens.[37] Despite the invidiousness of the determination, South Australia ventures some guidance in making these decisions.[38]

Under states' legislation, access to treatment was originally confined to those within the traditional nuclear family, based on the concept that a child has a right to a

---

36 SA ss 10(2) & (5); Reproductive Technology (Code of Ethical Clinical Practice) Regulations 1995 – Schedule s 13.

37 This argument finds support in Jackson, E., 'Conception and the Relevance of the Welfare Principle', (2002) 65 *Modern Law Review*, 176-203, where she discusses the welfare principle in relation to s 13(5) of the Human Fertilisation and Embryology Act 1990.

38 Reproductive Technology (Code of Ethical Clinical Practice) Regulations 1995. Schedule s 11(c) requires the applicants to provide a statutory declaration confirming that they are not subject to a term of imprisonment, have not been found guilty of a sexual offence involving a child or involving violence, or had a child removed from their care.

mother and a father. Support for this is found variously in Article 7 of the Convention on the Rights of the Child (CRC)[39] and s 60B (2)(a) of the Family Law Act 1975 (Cth); children have a right to know and be cared for by both their parents. The preamble to the CRC also supports a child's interest and government intervention in promoting the family. Yet South Australian[40] and Victorian legislation[41] have been challenged and found to be in breach of s 22 of the Sex Discrimination Act 1984 (Cth),[42] which makes it unlawful to discriminate on the basis of marital status and, constitutionally, federal law prevails.[43] Western Australia has amended its HRT Act to bring it into line with the Acts Amendment Act (Lesbian and Gay Law Reform) Act 2002 (WA), although the remedy for the successful applicants is compensation for unlawful discrimination, not an order for services.

States Without Legislation The remaining states and territories operate ART services outside the constraints of legislation. The Demack Report (Qld, 1984)[44] concluded that 'law and public authorities should not intrude upon the way in which qualified persons practice medicine except so far as this is regarded as necessary in the public interest'.[45] Yet medical practitioners in the unregulated states have not gone unchallenged in their practice. In *JM v. QFG & GK*,[46] a lesbian refused treatment alleged discrimination on the basis of her lawful sexual conduct and that consequently the medical practitioner was in breach of the Anti-Discrimination Act 1991 (Qld) (ADA).[47] The court accepted the practitioner's definition of infertility as the failure to conceive after 12 months of unprotected intercourse rather than the claimant's 'social' infertility, and concluded it was not the fact that she was a lesbian that prevented her from treatment; rather it was her heterosexual inactivity. There was no indirect discrimination as it could be reasonable to select on the basis

---

39 Otlowski, M. and Tsamenyi, B.M., *An Australian Family Law Perspective on the Convention on the Rights of the Child*, Unitas Law Press, Hobart, Tasmania 1992, p. 55.

40 *Pearce v. South Australia Health Commission* (1996) 66 SASR 486.

41 *MW, DD, TA & AB v. Royal Women's Hospital* [1997] HREOC 6; (1997) EOC92-886.

42 Section 22(1) *SDA*.

43 Australian Constitution s 109.

44 *Report of the special committee appointed by the Queensland government to enquire into the laws relating to artificial insemination, in vitro fertilization and other related matters* (1984) (Demack report).

45 Demack report, at p. 50.

46 [1998] QCA 228, on appeal from the Qld Anti-Discrimination Tribunal. The appeal was allowed in *QFG & GK v. JM* [1997] QSC 206. On further appeal to the Queensland Court of Appeal (*JM v. QFG & GK* [1998] QCA 228) that appeal was dismissed. JM applied for special leave to the High Court but leave was refused. The matter was remitted to the Qld Anti-Discrimination Tribunal in *Morgan v. GK* [2001] QADT 10 where it was found there was no indirect discrimination under the Anti-Discrimination Act 1991 (Qld).

47 Section 7(1) *ADA*.

of clinical infertility alone. This does not mean that single or lesbian women will necessarily be refused treatment, but rather they *can* be on the basis of infertility.

All three 'legislation' states require that the person be 'infertile' in order to qualify for treatment, or be at risk of transmitting a genetic defect to a child conceived naturally.[48] Legal opinion for the Infertility Treatment Authority (Vic) observes that women seeking treatment must be 'clinically' infertile.[49] Similarly, the South Australian Council on Reproductive Technology has determined that the SA Act intends treatment to be offered in cases of medical infertility requiring medical practitioner referral stating the incidence of the infertility.[50] Thus a single woman or lesbian could access treatment if they were medically infertile but not if 'socially' infertile, whereas a married woman can access treatment if she is either medically or socially infertile (i.e., if her husband is infertile). This discrimination on the basis of marriage has not yet been challenged.

In the unregulated states there is generally someone willing to provide a market service. Once a person has passed the infertility hoop the question still arises: is treatment in the welfare interests of any potential child? Maternal age might be an issue; there has been concern about older mothers giving birth. The initial concern of maternal and foetal health has been alleviated to some degree by selecting out women with significant health issues and early delivery of the child. Yet while the argument remained that older mothers were socially unacceptable, this has not been flagged as such, in either the ethical guidelines, professional codes of practice or legislation.[51] Exceptionally, WA prescribes that age is not an indicia of infertility.[52] Both the Western Australian Reproductive Council[53] and the South Australian Council on Reproductive Technology[54] have considered the issue of age. The debates followed overseas examples, where a 59-year-old woman gave birth to twins and a 53-year-old woman to triplets. In January 2005, a 66-year-old Romanian woman, Adriana Iliescu, gave birth to a daughter after conceiving with donor gametes and in the UK Patricia Rashbrook announced an IVF pregnancy at the age of 63. Perhaps complacently, this has been generally agreed not to be an issue requiring present legislative intervention.

It is well accepted that there is little chance of women aged 45 years and older becoming pregnant with their own eggs,[55] and currently in Victoria clinics encourage

---

48 SA s 13(3)(b); WA s 23; Vic s 8(3)(a) ITA.

49 Opinion of Griffith, G. QC, at http://www.ita.org.

50 Section 11(b) Reproductive Technology (Code of Ethical Clinical Practice) Regulations 1995.

51 Apart from WA.

52 WA s 23(d) the reason for infertility is not age.

53 Western Australian Reproductive Council, *Age and Assisted Reproduction: Contributions to the Ethical Debate*, 12 April 1994.

54 South Australian Council on Reproductive Technology, *Age and Eligibility Report*, Feb 2000.

55 Monash IVF opened in the early 1970s, and 400 cycles of IVF have been administered to women 45 and older, with only one pregnancy. Jones, K., 'IVF limit for over-45s', *Herald*

women in this age group to use donor eggs if they want treatment. Legislation not only does not prohibit older women becoming pregnant, but medical practice now actually increases the chances of older women conceiving by giving them access to younger donor eggs. RTAC guidelines advocate an age restriction for donor gametes but not restrictions for recipients of donor gametes.

Donor eggs are already a scarce resource, possibly even more so now that the 2004 NHMRC guidelines require that clinics not use donated gametes in reproductive procedures unless the donor has agreed to the release of identifying information.[56] This directive is based on a child's right to knowledge about their genetic parents and siblings, and it may disadvantage older mothers, as when donor eggs are in short supply there is a tendency to allocate them to younger women who potentially have a greater chance of conceiving, or to require the client to find their own egg supply. In the case of the older woman whose friends are of the same vintage, it is possible that the only available donor eggs may be from a family member: her daughter. The South Australian Council on Reproductive Technology recommended a prohibition on familial intergenerational gamete donation,[57] and New Zealand has legislated that specific permission would be required for familial donations.

Ireland

IVF was first practised in Ireland in 1987 and up until 2002 the six clinics offering services looked to the standards set by the UK's HFEA, and to Ethical Guidelines established by the Irish Medical Council, for supervision.[58] Approximately 2000 couples are believed to be treated annually by these clinics, but many Irish couples travel to the UK for treatment. The fifth edition of the Medical Council's *Guide to Ethical Conduct and Behaviour and to Fitness to Practice*[59] recommended that techniques such as IVF be used only after thorough investigation has failed to reveal a treatable cause for infertility. A previous prohibition on the use of donated gametes was relaxed and the freezing of fertilised ova for later use is now clearly sanctioned in the sixth edition of the *Guide* (2004)[60] which provides that:

> Any fertilised ovum must be used for normal implantation and must not be deliberately destroyed. If couples have validly decided they do not wish to make use of their own fertilised ova, the potential for voluntary donation to other recipients may be considered.[61]

Sun, 9 June 2005.

56 NHRMC guidelines 2004 para 6.1.

57 South Australian Council on Reproductive Technology, *Age and Eligibility Report*, Feb 2000. Available at: http://www.dh.sa.gov.au/reproductive-technology/sacrt.asp.

58 This draws from Madden, D., *Medicine, Ethics and the Law*, Dublin, Butterworths, 2002, ch. 4.

59 Dublin, 1998.

60 Para 24.4.

61 Para 24.5.

Against this background the *Report of The Commission on Assisted Human Reproduction*,[62] chaired by Professor Dervilla Donnelly, is all the more remarkable. The specific question on regulation addressed to the Commission was whether legislation was necessary to regulate AHR or whether continued reliance on voluntary regulation by the Medical Council was satisfactory. For a number of reasons, including the welfare of the child, the Commission decided that a new Act of the Oireachtas should be passed to establish a regulatory body to regulate AHR services in Ireland. This body would be charged with issuing licences to service providers, and it would be mandatory for any provider of AHR services to obtain a licence from the statutory body in respect of the provision of any of the clinical and laboratory services specified in the legislation.

The Donnelly Commission recounts its view that the welfare of the child was a major factor in their thinking on the need for statutory regulation. This is mirrored in the recent NZ legislation and contrasts with, for example, the Demack report in Queensland, which observed that the welfare of the child emerged rather late in the day as a major question of concern, as it did in debates in the UK leading to the 1990 Act, and then only after an amendment to restrict the provision of treatment services to married couples had been narrowly defeated in the House of Lords by one vote (60–61).

Donnelly observed that Article 40.3.3 of the Irish Constitution provides constitutional protection for the 'unborn' but that it is not clear whether protection applies from fertilisation or from some subsequent point. It is accepted that clarification can only be sought from the Supreme Court or by way of constitutional referendum, and the further issue of whether a gamete provider has ownership or property rights in respect of his/her gametes has not been tested in an Irish court. Donnelly also examined whether AHR should be available only to married people; attitudes among providers and the public in general, the Commission observed, appear to be 'sharply divided'. After admittedly 'lengthy consideration' the Commission felt that services should be available without discrimination on the grounds of gender, marital status or sexual orientation subject to the best interests of any children that may be born. Legislation on the provision of AHR services should reflect the general principles of the Equal Status Acts 2000-2004 subject to the qualifications set out in section 4.8.[63] These derogations relate to the upper age of patients and to circumstances where the welfare of the child might be at risk. Where there is 'objective evidence' of a risk of harm there should be a 'presumption against treatment'.[64] A more liberal attitude to access is coupled with a requirement to justify refusal of treatment. But access to what?

The Commission recommends that while all necessary steps must be taken in the selection of donors so as to ensure that donated sperm/ova are free from the risk of transmitting disease, and that appropriate counselling should be provided for all

62 Dublin, April 2005.

63 Recommendation 17.

64 Recommendation 18.

donors as a pre-requisite of informed consent, donation should be permitted and appropriate guidelines should be put in place to govern the freezing and storage of gametes and the use of frozen gametes. The recommended regulatory body should also have power:

> to address cases where gametes are abandoned, where the commissioning couple cannot agree on a course of action, where couples separate or where one or both partner(s) dies or becomes incapacitated.[65]

While not unanimous, the Commission avers that appropriate guidelines should be put in place 'to govern the options available for excess frozen embryos', [66] including voluntary donation to other recipients, for research 'or allowing them to perish'. Implicitly, the Commission does not appear to accept Art. 40.3.3 as requiring legal recognition of an embryo from the onset of conception.

Generally, donors should not be allowed to specify conditions for the use of their gametes and the regulatory body is envisaged as having the power to override or at least supersede the wishes of the providers of gametes for treatment services in specified circumstances.[67] Donors should not be paid for donations, and children born through donated gametes should be entitled to know the identity of their genetic parents. Finally, there are specific recommendations that admit of the particular cultural and especially religious sensitivities of a jurisdiction such as Ireland; recommendation 6 provides that 'Service providers should facilitate users who wish to avoid any treatment that might result in the production of "surplus" embryos'.

New Zealand: Human Assisted Reproduction Act 2004 (HART)[68]

Of children born in New Zealand, 1.6 per cent are now conceived through ART. New Zealand funds two cycles of treatment for eligible couples and spends NZ$9.5 million on tertiary fertility services with access determined using a social and diagnostic 'scoring' method to prioritise 'deserving' couples and achieve consistency for national waiting times. Until 2005, funding was restricted to one cycle, but after agreement that 'single embryo transfer' would be introduced (to minimise twin or multiple pregnancy) a second cycle was added. Clinics have voluntarily sought Reproductive Technology Accreditation Committee (RTAC) sanction since its introduction in 1990. In the absence of legislation, NZ clinics have been alone in the IVF community in using only egg and sperm donors prepared to waive anonymity. This is now on a statutory footing, requiring details of the donor's name, gender,

65 Recommendation 4.

66 Recommendation 10.

67 Recommendation 4.

68 For a brief overview of the pre-existing position in New Zealand see Daniels, K., 'Genetics and Artificial Procreation in New Zealand', in Mulders-Klein, M.T., Deech, R. and Vlaardingbroek, P. (eds), *Biomedicine, the Family and Human Rights*, The Hague, Kluwer Law International, 2002, 123-32.

address, date, place, and country of birth, height, eyes and hair colour, ethnicity (if a Maori donor, whanau, hapu iwi affiliations), relevant medical/genetic history and the donor's reasons for donating.[69]

The NZ HART Act 2004 received assent on 21 November 2004. Guided by the National Ethics Committee on Assisted Human Reproduction, the seven operative ART clinics in New Zealand supported the introduction of the Act, particularly the weight given to the paramountcy of the interests of the child. Section 4 sets out guiding principles for the Act. The health and wellbeing of children born of an assisted reproductive procedure 'should be an important consideration in all decisions about that procedure'; human health, safety and dignity of present and future generations should be preserved and promoted; and 'while all persons are affected by assisted reproductive procedures and established procedures, women, more than men, are directly and significantly affected by their application, and the health and wellbeing of women must be protected in the use of these procedures'.[70] This is to be achieved largely through the operation of 'informed choice' and 'informed consent',[71] and by ensuring that donor offspring are made aware of their genetic origins and are able to access information about those origins.[72] As well as ensuring that the needs, values and beliefs of Maori should be considered and treated with respect, different ethical, spiritual and cultural perspectives in society should be recognised.[73] Section 13(1) achieves something that other regulators have long sought; 'No person may give or receive, or agree to give or receive, valuable consideration for the supply of a human embryo or human gamete'.

The two principal aims of the HART Act are to prohibit the performance of assisted conception (other than 'established procedures') and human reproductive research without approval of an ethics committee and to establish a process for people to access information about their genetic origins. The Act, in section 80, provides that the Health and Disability Services (Safety) Act 2001 applies to fertility services (further defined in section 80(2)), so as to attract the New Zealand Human Rights Act 1993, which makes it unlawful to discriminate on the grounds of disability, sexual orientation and family status. The Bill of Rights Act 1990 had already prohibited age and race discrimination.

The HART Act and Orders made under it create a regulatory framework for the performance of assisted reproductive procedures and the conduct of relevant research.[74] The framework outlaws certain procedures, subjects others to ethical review on a case by case basis and provides that certain procedures are to be 'established' procedures, initially determined by Order in Council on the recommendation of the Minister of

69 HART Act 2004 s 47.

70 Section 4(c).

71 Section 4(d).

72 Section 4(e).

73 Section 4(f) and (g).

74 Section 76 gives to the Governor General by Order in Council wide regulation making powers.

Health.[75] Established procedures (which do not require ethical approval[76]) include collection of eggs or sperm for assisted reproductive procedures; IVF; ICSI; GIFT; assisted hatching and blastocyst hatching (both within IVF and ICSI): AI: freezing of eggs, sperm, embryos and ovarian tissue and the use of previously cryopreserved sperm and embryos in treatment, and PGD for specified purposes.[77]

A Ministerial Advisory Committee comprising experts in ART procedures, human reproduction research, ethics, Maori customary values and practice, will advise on the ART-related issues and issuing guidelines on ART procedures and research.[78] Specifically this will include germ-line genetic modification and non-reproductive embryo cloning.[79] Applications to conduct such activities will not be considered until advice has been provided and any guidelines, regulations or restrictions that are considered necessary are in place.[80] The Advisory Committee is also to provide specific information, advice and, if it thinks fit, recommendations on donations of embryos, embryo splitting, gametes derived from deceased persons, requirements for informed consent, selection of embryos using pre-implantation genetic analysis and the import into, or export from, New Zealand of in vitro donated cells or in vitro donated embryos.[81] NECAHR (or a series of ethics committees) will consider individual applications for non-established ART procedures and all research; ethical approval will for the first time become mandatory and committees will only be able to approve applications for activities for which there are guidelines or advice from the Advisory Committee. The use of an established procedure for a new or different purpose will require ethical approval.

Part 2 of the Schedule to the Order in Council of 2005 removes certain procedures from the protection of notification as an 'established procedure', including inter-familial donations, diagnosis of certain familial single-gene or chromosomal disorders, and in defined conditions, diagnosis of non-familial chromosomal disorders (aneuploidy testing) where either the woman is of advanced reproductive age, or she has had recurrent implantation failure or recurrent miscarriage. In each of these cases, approval of an ethics committee must be sought before the treatment is undertaken.

---

75 Human Assisted Reproductive Technology Order 2005 approved by the Governor General on 27 June 2005.

76 Under cl 5, Part 1 of the Schedule of the 2005 Order. Aspects of each of these procedures are more fully defined and explained for the purposes of the 2004 Act in the Order.

77 Note 76 above.

78 Section 35.

79 The advisory committee has the functions assigned to it by s 35(1).

80 HART 2004 s 8.

81 Section 38.

Canada

According to Health Canada,[82] an estimated one in eight Canadian couples experience infertility. The Canadian Assisted Human Reproduction Act (AHR Act) received Royal Assent on 29 March 2004; a number of provisions came into force on 22 April 2004, the remainder coming into force on a day or days to be fixed.[83] The AHR Act 2004 results from a 15-year process initiated with the *Royal Commission on New Reproductive Technologies* (Baird Report). After much fractious argument, seeing the resignation of several Commissioners, Baird's final report *Proceed with Care*[84] was delivered in 1993 and contained some 293 recommendations. Baird recommended the establishment of a regulatory body to govern permissible activities, and a ban on certain others. The Federal Government responded in 1995 by introducing a voluntary moratorium on sex-selection for non-medical reasons; commercial surrogacy agreements; buying and selling of gametes or embryos, egg-sharing; germ-line genetic alteration; ectogenesis; cloning of human embryos; formation of animal-human hybrids; and retrieval of sperm or eggs from cadavers or foetuses for treatment or research.[85] These activities are now prohibited activities under the 2004 Act.[86] The Human Reproductive and Genetic Technologies Bill (Bill C-47) was introduced in 1996 but died when Parliament was dissolved in 1997. The current AHR Act began life in May 2001 as draft AHR legislative proposals and became law in 2004.

The AHR Act has three objectives: (i) prohibiting human cloning, genetic alteration[87] and the commercialisation of human reproduction;[88] (ii) promoting the health and safety of Canadians using ART services and (iii) introducing a licensing system to regulate, and enforce all activities controlled under the Act, including research, through the establishment of the AHR Agency.[89] The Canadian Charter of Rights and Freedoms provides for equality before and under the law,[90] and this is replicated in the defining principles of the AHR Act. The Act provides that people undergoing assisted reproduction procedures must not be discriminated against on the basis of their sexual orientation or marital status. Health Canada believes the Act ensures that Canada now has one of the most comprehensive legislative frameworks in the world; it has had the benefit of reviewing numerous other relevant legislative

82 See http://www.hc-sc.gc.ca/english/lifestyles/reproduction/intro_e.html.

83 Section 78 AHR Act.

84 Royal Commission, *Proceed with Care: Report of the Royal Commission on New Reproductive and Genetic Technologies*, Ottawa, Canada, 1993.

85 Marleau, D., Press Release on the Voluntary Moratorium, 25 July 1995, cited in Haase, J., 'Canada: The Long Road to Regulation', in Blyth, E. and Landau, R. (eds), *Third Party Assisted Conception Across Cultures*, London, Jessica Kingsley Publishers, 2004, 55-72, 58.

86 Sections 5-9 AHR Act.

87 Section 5.

88 Sections 5, 6 and 7.

89 Sections 21-64.

90 Section 15 Canadian Charter of Rights and Freedoms.

instruments, and has replicated much of their structure and content. Yet this is a surprisingly bold claim, given that the implementation of the provisions of the Act are gradual and the regulatory scheme will not be fully implemented until 2007/8; only on 9 May 2005 did the Federal Government identify Vancouver as the AHR Agency's home from January 2006.

The Canadian Act introduces criminal penalties (on indictment or summarily) for contravening the prohibited provisions,[91] and provides similar consequences for contravening any other provision.[92] Prosecution is only with the consent of the Attorney-General of Canada.[93] Other methods of enforcement (in accordance with the regulations) may involve the amendment, suspension or revocation of a licence.[94] Throughout this tortuous history of Canadian AHR legislation there has been consistent concern for particular activities, especially the commercialisation of gametes and embryos, the practice of assisted reproduction itself and whether or not to pursue donor anonymity.

Prior to the coming into force of the AHR Act, payment for sperm was well established and egg-sharing was accepted practice, not least because of the scarcity of egg donors.[95] Egg-sharing is criticised as undermining informed consent – the strong desire for a child may overshadow the implications for donor and recipient.[96] Donor identification may remain elusive and the likelihood of multiple children from individual donors may yet increase. Mirroring UK debate, removal of payment for gametes is regarded as a deterrent to donate and it is feared that removing donor anonymity will compound the grave shortage of donated gametes. Most Canadian clinics rely on sperm banks, often those in the United States,[97] and as payment is permitted there for both sperm and eggs this may undermine the potential impact of the AHR Act's prohibition.

Most Canadians fund their own infertility treatments, and while the Canadian federal government financially assists the provinces and territories with expenditure,[98] the provinces and territories are responsible for managing and delivering their own health services. Although health care in Canada is publicly funded, only the province of Ontario extends this funding to IVF services, and only where there is an incidence of bilateral blockage of the fallopian tubes, which is not the result of surgical sterilisation, and for only three IVF cycles.

The AHR Agency, when established, will maintain a personal health information registry containing 'health reporting information'[99] about participants in assisted

---

91 Section 60.

92 Section 61.

93 Section 63.

94 Sections 41, 42.

95 Section 7(4).

96 Shanner L. and Nisker, J., 'Bioethics for clinicians: 26. Assisted reproductive technologies', (2001) 164 *Canadian Medical Association Journal*, 1589-1594.

97 The AHR Act is silent on the importation of gametes.

98 Canada Health Act 1985.

99 This information is defined to include identifying information, section 3 AHR Act.

reproduction procedures.[100] Currently Canada has no central registry, but the Act maintains donor anonymity unless the donor gives written consent.[101] Donor anonymity is thus preferred over the emergent international consensus that favours the 'identity' interest, and despite the apparent paramountcy of the 'welfare' criterion to guide all decisions in respect of infertility technologies.[102] The Act does provide that any two individuals can apply to the AHR Agency where they have 'reason to believe' that either or both were conceived by assisted reproduction and the Agency will be required to disclose to them whether they are genetically related and, if so, the nature of the relationship.[103] While anyone can make such an application, in practice it will rely, as in other jurisdictions, on people being aware of the origin of their conception; something which often remains unknown. Some parents may assume that if a child is not able to discover their genetic origins, telling them that they are the product of donation may cause more anguish than not knowing.

The Canadian Government considers that any payment relating to any assisted reproduction devalues life, including that of the child. It argues that this is most evident in relation to surrogacy; it is claimed that payment treats children as objects and women's reproductive capacity as economic activity. The AHR Act does not ban surrogacy but prohibits such activity for women under the age of 21,[104] and will eventually subject reimbursement of expenditures to scrutiny under section 12. Sex selection is statutorily forbidden except to prevent, diagnose or treat a sex linked disorder or disease;[105] any other attempts to select a child's gender offends the equal value and status of both sexes. These two provisions seem to underscore the Canadian commitment to the 'dignity' interest in assisted conception, and, in an arguably similar vein, the AHR Act will eventually prohibit posthumous conception without written consent.[106]

So, What *Has* Love Got to Do With It?

Fifteen years ago Bartha Knoppers and Sonia Le Bris identified basic principles either already discernible in approaches to assisted conception or that might be thought desirable in responding to the emergent sciences and practices.[107] These entailed:

---

100 Section 17.

101 Sections 15(4), 18 (2) and (3).

102 Section 2(a).

103 Section 18(4).

104 Section 6(4).

105 Section 5(1)(e).

106 Section 8(2).

107 'Recent Advances in Medically Assisted Conception: Legal, Ethical and Social Issues', (1991) 17 *American Journal of Law & Medicine*, 329-363.

- a respect for human dignity
- security of human genetic material;
- measures to underpin the quality of assisted conception services;
- the inviolability of the human person; and
- inalienability of the human body.

The fundamentals of this 1991 approach are still illuminating.

Don Chalmers has cautioned in respect of regulatory debates that 'there is no doubt that much of the heady and excitable drive to regulation was a result of pressure groups rather than the formulation of good public policy'.[108] This nicely poses the question of what regulatory systems are there *for*. As the US President's Commission on Bioethics observes of what it calls the 'patchwork' but generalised regulatory standards potentially applicable to assisted conception across the United States:

> A first question might be whether such a system of regulation, involving multiple authorities, is well suited to address the concerns [that they had identified]. To the extent that the harms are sufficiently grave and commonly recognised, a uniform system might be preferable to this patchwork one. On the other hand to the extent that the ethical concerns reflect matters of personal morality and autonomy, a system of diverse or decentralised regulation might be preferable. [109]

There are acknowledged advantages of regulation of assisted conception through law; it creates or lends authority to certainty, stability and consensus forming, and there is an important dimension of political and democratic accountability and legitimacy. But it is clear that there is now an emergent debate in assisted conception and in the associated sciences and applications of genetics about *levels* of regulation.[110] Where regulation is primary level, its purpose is to control, confine and channel *ex ante* the particular aspect of the practice that is its target. Where such primary level regulation is successful, such practice operates (by and large) in accordance with the rules laid down by the regulatory order. Where, by contrast, regulation is secondary level, no attempt is made to control, confine, or channel some given aspect of particular practice; regulators have abandoned such *ex ante* primary level intervention. Instead, secondary level regulation operates *ex post*, endeavouring to compensate for, or adjust in response to, the consequences of a genetic practice that cannot be, or has not been, controlled by primary level regulation.

---

108 'Professional Self-Regulation and Guidelines in Assisted Reproduction', in Coady M. and Peterson, K. (eds), 'Regulating Reproductive Technologies', (2002) 9 *Journal of Law & Medicine*, 414-28, at p. 425.

109 *Reproduction and Responsibility: The Regulation of the New Biotechnologies*, Washington DC, 2004, at p. 75.

110 Brownsword, R., 'Regulating Human Genetics: New Dilemmas for a New Millenium', (2004) 12 *Medical Law Review*, 14 -39, at pp. 15-16.

Common themes in recent reports and legislative reviews include the definition of infertility and questions of access to reproductive technologies; the use of human gametes after death and other social and ethical grounds for limiting or reviewing access, such as age, marital or other social status, commercialisation and the extent to which questions of human dignity are raised. Debate seems to be gathering over the most redundant concept originally introduced into the debates on reproductive technology – as a surrogate for express provisions for limiting access to treatment services – the 'welfare of the child' criterion. This general import from family law may have had, marginally, some base meaning, but its substantive content as such has been doubted.[111] In fact it has emerged as a bargaining chip to offset against other considerations on which as the Irish Commission puts it people 'sharply divide'. The 'welfare' criterion is an example of what we call a 'second hand emotion'; seldom is it used as a concept with particular force and scope; more often is it adumbrated as a surrogate for other concerns about access to assisted conception and related services. Over time, this second hand emotion has been steadily challenged by the first principle requirement of respecting identity.[112] 'Welfare' is indeed an example of a social as much as an ethical consideration.[113] Yet it has shown resilience in jurisdictions that otherwise have some sort of constitutional guarantees of access to infertility treatment; the welfare criterion has figured centrally in debates in Canada, New Zealand and Ireland. In the UK it has come to be seen as a focal point for those who criticise the subterranean operation of ethical concerns through the medium of the legislation, and in Australia it is regarded with some similar suspicion; and in both it has been translated into the 'identity' question.

There is an evident consensus that we have moved away from arguing over who may access treatment services to a new concern; where anonymity is established and commercialisation is eradicated, the question will be access to what? If legislatures maintain a line in favour of donor identity (the 'welfare' and 'rights' argument) and against commercialisation (the 'dignity' argument), the ensuing scarcity of resources (donor gametes and embryos) necessary for the continuance and longevity of the well established and profitable assisted reproduction industry will again rely on the ingenuity of medical scientists. In a new age of medical products, such as manufactured and cloned gametes, there will be those legislatures that try to pre-empt perceived disasters, as was the concern in the early days of assisted reproduction technology, and there will be those legislatures that limp behind and deal with the aftermath. There will also be those of us willing, and keen, to contemplate these dilemmas from an ethical and legal perspective. Assisted conception has health,

---

111 For an attempt to give more substance to the concept see Human Fertilisation and Embryology Authority, *Tomorrow's Children: A Consultation on Guidance to Licensed Fertility Clinics on Taking into Account the Welfare of Children to Be Born of Assisted Conception Treatment*, London, HFEA, 2005.

112 For particularly clear expressions of the content of this principle see the ECHR judgments in *Mikulic v. Croatia* [2002] ECHR 27 and *Odievre v. France* [2003] ECHR 86.

113 Jackson, E., 'Conception and the Relevance of the Welfare Principle', (2002) 65 *Modern Law Review*, 176-203.

social, ethical, legal and financial implications perhaps beyond the understanding of reporters, regulators, recipients and reproductive scientists even 20 years ago. What is becoming more clear in each of the states that we have briefly reviewed is that IVF is but the top of the technological iceberg drifting steadily towards the ship of state. A titanic argument about health care costs for ageing populations lies ahead. In this debate, love has very little to do with emotion; debates will focus on the rhetoric of rights and the reason of responsibility, the designs of dignity and the demands of duty.

Chapter 24

Saviour Siblings

Michael Freeman

Introduction

The advent of medically assisted reproduction has had many consequences barely anticipated at the time of the Warnock report[1] and not provided for in the Human Fertilisation and Embryology Act 1990. Cell nucleus replacement is one such example – this is now the subject of legislation[2] – and pre-implantation genetic diagnosis (PGD) and tissue typing (HLA) is another.[3] PGD was first successfully used in 1989 by removing a single cell at the eight-cell stage of embryonic development and testing the sex of the cells, so that a female embryo could be implanted and a sex-linked disorder that occurred only in males avoided.[4] Two years later, the same doctor tested for a genetic mutation that causes cystic fibrosis and enabled a high-risk couple to implant an embryo free of the disease. Today, PGD is used to screen for a handful of genetic diseases, including beta thalassaemia, sickle-cell disease, haemophilia, Tay-Sachs and fragile X syndrome. The procedure is expensive, is not available everywhere, and can be used to target only a small number of conditions.[5] But it is foreseeable that none of these limitations will last long.

How are we to respond to PGD? It has clearly proved controversial in two areas: sex selection,[6] where this is not for therapeutic purposes, and where it is used to

---

1 *Report of the Committee of Inquiry into Human Fertilisation and Embryology*, Cmnd. 9314/1984 (Warnock Report) chapter 12 of which looks at 'Possible Future Developments in Research including "selective breeding"' (para 12.16).

2 Human Reproductive Cloning Act 2001.

3 See Botkin, J.R., 'Ethical Issues and Practical Problems in Preimplantation Genetic Diagnosis', (1998) 26 *Journal of Law, Medicine and Ethics*, 17-28.

4 See HFEA/ACGT Consultation Document, *Pre-Implantation Genetic Diagnosis*, London, 1999, para 10.

5 And see Wells, D. and Sherlock, J.K., 'Strategies for Preimplantation Genetic Diagnosis of Single Gene Disorders by DNA Amplification', (1998) 18 *Prenatal Diagnosis*, 1389-1401. There have been only 500 cases involving PGD since the 1990 Act was passed (see H.C. Science and Technology Committee, *Human Reproductive Technologies and the Law*, 5th Report of Session 2004-05 (March 2005), para.109).

6 The Warnock Report, *supra cit.*, contains an early discussion of this: see paras 9.4-9.12; see also The House of Commons Select Committee, *supra cit.*, at paras 131-142. The

produce a child to save the life of an existing child. The latter is the subject of this chapter. But first a few preliminary points.

As has already been indicated, PGD is not specifically tackled in the 1990 Act. But since it involves the creation and use of embryos, it must be licensed by the Human Fertilisation and Embryology Authority (HFEA) to be lawful.[7] The HFEA has licensed PGD for certain severe or life-threatening disorders at a limited number of clinics.[8] It has also firmly rejected the use of PGD for sex selection for social reasons.[9] Some jurisdictions, for example Victoria, Australia, have specifically banned sex selection, in Victoria's case unless it is necessary for the child to be of a particular sex so as to avoid the risk of transmission of a genetic abnormality or a disease to the child.[10] There is legislation in some US states too, and also (and importantly) in the Indian state of Maharashta.[11] The United Kingdom legislation does not ban sex selection being carried out for social purposes – it was not an issue in 1990. The HFEA does prohibit sperm sorting, although it is difficult to see on what legal basis,[12] and in 2003 it recommended a ban on sex selection.[13] It may be that a new 'reproduction' Act will ban it, although the House of Commons Select Committee can find 'no adequate justification for prohibiting the use of sex selection for family balancing'.[14] Indeed, if and when the European Convention on Human Rights and Biomedicine comes to be ratified, it will have to be outlawed. Article 14 of this states: 'the use of techniques of medically assisted procreation shall not be allowed for the purpose of choosing the future child's sex, except where hereditary sex-related disease is to be avoided'. And this, in my opinion, is right.

The HFEA also allows for PGD is situations where abortion legislation would permit the termination of a pregnancy, that is where there is 'a substantial risk that if the child were born it would suffer from physical and mental abnormalities as

---

Government response is to find no adequate justification for prohibiting the use of sex selection for 'family balancing' Cm 6641/2005, at p. 19.

7 See Human Fertilisation and Embryology Act 1990 s 3(1). The problems the HFEA had with PGD generally were partially attributable to the fact that it 'does not appear on the face of the legislation' per Suzi Leather, Chair of HFEA, quoted in House of Commons Select Committee Report, *supra cit.*, at para 248.

8 This is said to be 'implicit' in the Act.

9 For an example see the Louise and Alan Masterson case, *The Guardian*, 16 October 2000. See also the House of Commons Select Committee report, *supra cit.*, at para 138.

10 Infertility Treatment Act 1995 s 50.

11 Regulation of Pre-Natal Diagnostic Techniques Act 1988.

12 No licensed activity is performed where there is sperm sorting before artificial insemination in a woman receiving treatment together with a man whose sperm underwent this process.

13 See HFEA, *Sex Selection; Options for Regulation*, November 2003.

14 Select Committee Report, *supra cit.*, at para.142.

to be seriously handicapped'.[15] This too must be right[16] and, although he does not discuss PGD, it would have the support of Ronald Dworkin, for whom the wasting of 'natural investment'[17] would be so very much less at pre-implantation stage.

Hesitantly, it has also allowed PGD to be employed to produce a child who would be a good tissue match for a sibling who needed a bone marrow transplant.[18] PGD and HLA had already been used for this purpose in Colorado in the USA in the *Nash* case,[19] and a British couple had taken advantage of the facility there to do the same thing,[20] before HFEA gave the go-ahead to the Hashmis in Leeds in 2001.

In doing so, did HFEA exceed its remit? When PDG was developed it was envisaged that embryos would be selected for their own intrinsic merit and not for their utility to another person. The 1990 Act offers little guidance. A licence can be granted only if the activity is 'necessary or desirable'.[21] This hardly assists since it leaves open the ethical assessment. In addition, there is the welfare provision in s 13(5), which requires account to be 'taken of the welfare of any child who may be born as a result of treatment ... and of any other child who may be affected by the birth'. This is a much-criticised provision,[22] and is unlikely to survive any review[23] of the 1990 Act. But it may be a useful resource in helping the determination of a case like that of the Hashmis. Indeed, it is difficult to think of a better example of where treatment service will impact upon the welfare of an existing child, and do so positively. Ironically, the legislature's concern was that existing children might be harmed by the addition of a new child.[24]

But what of the welfare of the child created to save the life of an existing sibling?

---

15 See Abortion Act 1967 s 1(i)(d).

16 There is a useful discussion of this in Steinbock, B., 'Preimplantation Genetic Diagnosis and Embryo Selection', in Burley, J. and Harris, J. (eds), *A Companion To Genethics*, Oxford, Blackwell, 2002, 175-190, at pp. 175-181.

17 *Life's Dominion*, London, Harper Collins, 1993, at p. 87.

18 Ethics Committee of HFEA, *Ethics Issues in the Location and Selection of Pre-Implantation Embryos to Produce Tissue Donors*, 22 November 2001.

19 See Dobson, R., '"Designer Baby" Cures Sister', (2000) 321 *British Medical Journal*, 1040. Stem cells from Adam Nash's umbilical cord were used to treat his sister Molly, who was suffering from Fanconi Anaemia.

20 See Gottlieb, S., 'US Doctors Say Selection Acceptable for Non-Medical Reasons', (2001) 323 *British Medical Journal*, 828.

21 Schedule 2, para 1(3).

22 For example, Jackson,E.,'Conception and the Irrelevance of the Welfare Principle', (2002) 65 *Modern Law Review*, 176-203. See also her 'Fertility Treatment: Abolish the "Welfare Principle"', *Spiked Online*, 11 June 2003.

23 One is currently (2005) being conducted: see Human Fertilisation and Embryology Authority, *Tomorrow's Children*, London, 2005. See also the criticism by the House of Commons Select Committee, *supra cit.*, at paras 94-107.

24 See s 13(5)'s reference to 'any other child who may be affected by the birth'.

The Hashmi Decisions

A first instance court in England ruled that HFEA was wrong to allow PGD to be used in the *Hashmi* case to select an embryo, which could be tissue-typed to find the best match for an existing child, Zain Hashmi, who has beta thalassaemia major.[25] Maurice Kay J held that the only embryo testing permitted by the legislation is PGD in so far as that is necessary to ensure that the woman can carry the child successfully to full term; that is, embryonic screening to eliminate those genetic defects which might affect the viability of the foetus, and no other.

The Court of Appeal[26] and the House of Lords,[27] correctly in my opinion, disagreed, and as a result have given the green light to an attempt to save Zain Hashmi's life. The Court of Appeal's decision is the more fully argued and I will look at it first. Significantly, one of the judges, Mance LJ, was influenced by the welfare imperative in s 13(5) of the 1990 Act.[28] This, he said, 'points towards a wider concern for the future child and siblings, which is better served if the legislation is read as permitting (the) screening'[29] envisaged in the *Hashmi* case. He had no doubt that 'the language of [s 13(5)] does not exclude positive effects'.[30] Lord Phillips of Worth Matravers MR was persuaded that if the Act permitted the licensing of embryo research activities for the purpose of 'developing methods for detecting the presence of gene or chromosome abnormalities in embryos before implantation',[31] the clear inference was that Parliament approved of PGD to avoid implantation of embryos carrying genetic defects. 'Parliament chose to permit the licensing of research. It makes little sense for Parliament, at the same time, to prohibit reaping the benefit of that research, even under licence'.[32]

The Court of Appeal also had no doubt that genetic analysis for the purpose of tissue typing was 'necessary or desirable for the purpose of providing treatment services'.[33] Lord Phillips of Worth Matravers conceded that his 'initial reaction'[34] was the same as the first instance judge;[35] that is that the phrase suggests 'treatment designed to assist the physical processes from fertilisation to the birth of a child'.[36]

25 *R (on application of Quintavalle) v. Human Fertilisation and Embryology Authority*, [2003] 2 All ER 105.

26 *R (on application of Quintavalle) v. Human Fertilisation and Embryology Authority*, [2003] 3 All ER 257.

27 *R (on application of Quintavalle) v. Human Fertilisation and Embryology Authority*, [2005] 2 All ER 555.

28 He is the only judge in either the House of Lords or Court of Appeal to refer to it.

29 See p. 283.

30 *Ibid.*, at p. 286.

31 See Schedule 3, para 3(2)(e).

32 See p. 269.

33 *Ibid.*, at p. 270.

34 *Id.*

35 *Quintavelle* (2003), *supra cit.*, at p. 111.

36 See p. 270.

But he now saw that 'if the impediment to bearing a child is concern that it may be born with a hereditary defect, treatment which enables women to become pregnant and to bear children in the confidence that they will not be suffering from such defects can properly be described as "for the purpose of assisting women to carry children"'.[37] He concluded that:

> whether the PGD has the purpose of producing a child free from genetic defects, or of producing a child with stem cells matching a sick or dying sibling, the IVF treatment that includes PGD constitutes 'treatment for the purpose of assisting women to bear children'.[38]

Of the three judges in the Court of Appeal, only Mance LJ grasped the nettle of the so-called 'designer baby'.[39] Lord Phillips of Worth Matravers appeared to leave decisions regarding this entirely to the discretion of the HFEA.[40] Mance LJ, on the other hand, saw a clear distinction between 'screening out abnormalities' and 'screening in preferences' (for example, and most immediately,[41] as to sex on social grounds only). 'Preferences', he noted, 'suggests personal indulgence or predilection and the luxury of a real choice', and, of course, the last thing that desperate families like the Hashmis were trying to do was 'indulge themselves'.[42] Mance, LJ, did, however, note that Parliament did not include 'any absolute prohibition in the area of sex selection for "social purposes"'.[43] And he added, the Hashmi request was 'much less obviously problematic'.[44]

The House of Lords agreed.[45] There are only two speeches (Lord Hoffmann and Lord Brown of Eaton-under-Heywood). Lord Brown, rather like Lord Phillips of Worth Matravers in the Court of Appeal, confesses that he was initially attracted by the CORE[46] argument:

> that PGD screening is one thing … tissue typing a completely different concept and impermissible. It is one thing to enable a woman to conceive and bear a child which will itself be free of genetic abnormality, quite another to bear a child specifically selected for the purpose of treating someone else.[47]

---

37 *Id.*

38 *Ibid.*, at p. 271.

39 On designer babies see Mance LJ who discusses the concept at p. 287.

40 See p. 271.

41 The issue has become more urgent with the publication of the House of Commons Select Committee report, *supra cit.*, which despite identifying the objections (see para 134) thought the 'onus should be on those who oppose sex selection for social reasons using PGD to show harm from its use' (para 142).

42 See p. 287.

43 *Ibid.*, at p. 289.

44 *Id.*

45 See *Quintavalle* (2005), *supra cit.*

46 Comment on Reproductive Ethics.

47 See para 51.

But neither he nor Lord Hoffmann did come to this conclusion.

The question, as formulated by Lord Hoffmann, is whether PGD and HLA typing are 'activities which (HFEA) can authorise to be done "in the course" of providing her with IVF treatment'.[48] These activities include 'practices designed to secure that embryos are in a suitable condition to be placed in a woman or to determine whether embryos are suitable for that purpose'.[49] The Act does not say – it could hardly do so since PGD and HLA were unknown when it was passed – that PGD or HLA should constitute treatment services.[50] But they must be activities 'in the course' of such services, that is in the course of providing IVF treatment.

CORE's argument against this interpretation invoked the slippery slope. As summarised by Lord Hoffmann:

> It would enable the authority to authorise a single cell biopsy to test the embryo for whatever characteristics the mother might wish to know: whether the child would be male or female, dark or blonde, perhaps even, in time to come, intelligent or stupid.[51]

In other words, it could lead to 'designer babies'. On CORE's interpretation 'suitable' cannot just mean 'suitable for that particular mother'.[52] For CORE, it was argued that 'suitable' meant 'capable of becoming a healthy child, free of abnormalities'.[53] Thus, it believed – or its counsel so argued – that PGD to establish that an embryo is free from genetic abnormalities is acceptable, but not HLA typing. Of course, what the Hashmis want is not just a healthy child, but one that would meet the needs of Zain.

'Suitable', of course, is context-dependent: 'a suitable hat for Royal Ascot is very different from a suitable hat for the Banbury cattle market'.[54] The Warnock report only addresses the issue of suitability in the context of sex selection, upon which it made no positive recommendation.[55] Importantly, it did not recommend that sex selection on social grounds should be banned, leaving the decision on this to, what became, the HFEA. Lord Hoffmann inferred that:

> the Warnock Committee did not intend that selection of IVF embryos on grounds which went beyond genetic abnormality should be altogether banned.[56]

48 Para 10.

49 Human Fertilisation and Embryology Act 1990 Sch. 2, para 1(3)(d).

50 PGD was foreseen, but HLA was not. And see Lord Hoffmann at para 29.

51 Para 13.

52 *Id.*

53 *Id.*

54 Para 14.

55 It 'should be kept under review'. In fact there was no reconsideration until the HFEA report in 2003, *supra cit.*, and the discussion in the House of Commons Select Committee Report, *supra cit.*, in 2005.

56 Para 19.

The White Paper which examined the Warnock report, prior to the 1990 Act, was adamant that designer babies should not be permitted,[57] as it was with cloning, although neither it nor the legislation which followed anticipated the 'Dolly' technique.[58] However, as Lord Hoffmann acknowledges, there was no proposal to ban 'the testing of embryos to enable the mother to choose to carry a child with characteristics of her choice'.[59] This is not entirely true, for it was clear that she could not choose 'designer'-type characteristics. In the arguments before the Lords everything hinged on the choice of what characteristics were permissible, on the drawing of a line between saviour siblings and designer babies (and 'more sinister eugenic practices'[60]).

In Lord Hoffmann's view these ethical distinctions were left to the HFEA. He thought it inconceivable that the 1990 Act:

> said nothing on the subject ... because Parliament thought it was clearly prohibited by the use of the word 'suitable' or because it wanted to leave the question over for later primary legislation.[61]

It was thus his view that the only reasonable inference is that Parliament intended to leave the matter for the Authority to decide.[62] It could decide to allow sex selection on social grounds, he thought. And once the concept of suitability could be so interpreted:

> it is impossible to say that selection on the grounds of any other characteristics which the mother might desire was positively excluded from the discretion of the authority, however unlikely it might be that the authority would actually allow selection on that ground.[63]

Lord Hoffmann therefore concluded that both PGD and HLA typing could lawfully be authorised by HFEA as 'activities to determine the suitability of the embryo for implantation within the meaning of paragraph 1(1)(d)'.[64]

It is only at the end of his judgment that Lord Hoffmann addresses what many will consider to be the principal ethical question. A concern of CORE's, as formulated by its counsel, is the way HFEA's policy has changed so as to allow the use of bone marrow rather than umbilical cord blood.[65] It may have had little option since,

---

57 *Human Fertilisation and Embryology: A Framework for Legislation*, Cm.259/1987, para 37.

58 It only considered cell nucleus substitution.

59 Para 22.

60 Para 25. A more positive view is Mehlman, M.J., *Wondergenes*, Bloomington, Indiana, Indiana University Press, 2003.

61 Para 29.

62 *Id.*

63 *Id.*

64 Para 35.

65 The HFEA endorsed with amendment a recommendation of its Ethics and Legal Committee to this effect on 21 July 2004.

once an embryo had been implanted and a child conceived, the case goes outside its remit. Nevertheless, there is a real dilemma posed, because the taking of bone marrow, though relatively straightforward and otherwise uncontentious, is invasive. The HFEA itself, in authorising the extension, noted that the threshold for permitting medical procedures to be performed on a child where they were non-therapeutic was higher, and that courts could overrule parental consent where the procedure was not in the child's best interests.

Lord Hoffmann contended himself with saying, '[t]hese reasons appear to be valid'.[66]

He had no doubt that 'medical practitioners' take very seriously the law:

> that any operation upon a child for which there is no clinical reason relating to the child itself must be justified as being for other reasons in the child's best interests.[67]

He added, '[t]he Authority is entitled to assume that a child conceived pursuant to its licence will, after birth, receive the full protection of the law'.[68]

This is a real concern and one insufficiently addressed by the House of Lords. Was the one authority that might conceivably have been relevant (*Re Y*[69]) cited to the Lords? It is not referred to in either of the two judgments. It is, of course, a controversial decision, not least because of the expansive meaning given to a learning disabled adult's best interests, one that would need to be extended further to embrace bone marrow donations by a saviour sibling who clearly would not have the psychological ties which Connell J in *Re Y* found to exist in the unusual family circumstances of that case.[70]

Lord Brown does not address this question, and his judgment broadly mirrors Lord Hoffmann's. But rather than trying to distinguish therapeutic from social embryo selection, he attempts to distinguish the two by jurisdiction. As he puts it, 'whereas … suitability is for the woman, the limits of permissible embryo selection are for the authority'.[71] He assumes that HFEA would not license selection for purely social reasons. If it did, he envisages Parliament intervening or 'in an extreme case' (he does not specify what would be extreme) the court's supervisory jurisdiction being invoked.[72]

In the Hashmi case the intention was for blood to be taken from the baby's umbilical cord, which is rich in stem cells, and infused into the sick child. Zain

---

66 Para 38.

67 *Id.*

68 *Id.*

69 [1997] Fam. 110.

70 The learning disabled young woman would suffer psychologically if her mother's visits decreased as they were likely to do if her sister did not receive bone marrow from her.

71 Para 62.

72 *Id.* On the legality of PGD elsewhere see Shaun Pattison's very helpful table in *Influencing Traits Before Birth*, Aldershot, Ashgate, 2002, Appendix 2. The Committee believes the regulation of pre-implantation testing is highly satisfactory (see para 244).

Hashmi had a hereditary and fatal blood disorder. Other children involved in other similar cases have suffered from rare blood disorders like 'Diamond Blackfan anaemia' from which Charlie Whitaker suffered.[73] A more emotionally fraught scenario, or ethical dilemma, it would difficult to imagine.

The Ethical Questions

I turn now to the ethical questions. I start from the premise that in a liberal society autonomy – in this case reproductive autonomy – is important.[74] The principle of autonomy is clearly enunciated in Mill's *On Liberty*: 'Over himself, over his own body and mind, the individual is sovereign'.[75] It is a cornerstone of medical law (and ethics). As Lord Goff noted in *Re F*, 'we have to bear well in mind the libertarian principle of self-determination'.[76] Autonomy is clearly related to dignity,[77] which is an equally important principle to observe.[78] So unless it harms, or misuses or abuses the new child, I start from the position that parents like the Hashmis (or the Whitakers[79] or Fletchers[80]) should be able to exercise their reproductive autonomy.

It should be stressed – for autonomy can all too easily be seen in individualistic terms – that what these desperate parents want is, what has been called, 'relational autonomy';[81] that is to say the exercise of reproductive decision making made with reference to others. It is not that they want their views to prevail, so much as wanting

---

73 See Hall, C., 'Two Cases Have Similarities and Vital Differences', *The Daily Telegraph*, 3 August 2002.

74 And so obviously no prenatal screening should be carried out without consent. On issues relating to this see Andrews, L., 'Prenatal Screening and the Culture of Motherhood', (1996) 47 *Hastings Law Journal*, 967-1006.

75 First published in 1859.

76 [1990] 2 AC 1, 73.

77 On the relationship see Raz, J., *The Authority of Law*, Oxford, Clarendon Press, 1979, at p. 221. 'Respecting human dignity entails treating humans as persons capable of planning and plotting their future. Thus, respecting people's dignity includes respecting their autonomy, their right to control their future'. But see Gill, R. and Stirrat, G. (2005) 31 *Journal of Medical Ethics*, 127-130, who argue that 'conceptions of individual autonomy cannot provide a sufficient and convincing starting point for ethics within medical practice'. But compare Macklin, R., 'Dignity Is a Useless Concept', (2003) 327 *BMJ*, 1419-1420.

78 And see Brennan J in *Secretary, Department of Health v. JWB and SMB*, (1992) 66 ALJR 300, 317: 'each person has a unique dignity which the law respects and which it will protect'.

79 The Whitaker case is discussed by the House of Commons Select Committee report, *supra cit.*, at paras 246-248).

80 The HFEA Licence Committee granted a licence to HRGC to provide HLA tissue typing for the Fletchers on 6 September 2004.

81 See Nedelsky, J., 'Reconceiving Autonomy: Thoughts and Possibilities', (1989) 1 *Yale Journal of Law and Feminism*, 7-36.

to improve the welfare of one of their children and thus the welfare of the whole family.[82]

We must therefore ask whether this is an exercise of autonomy which harms, misuses or abuses the new child. We must not ignore the dignity of the child-to-be. Will his/her interests be compromised in any way to promote those of the existing sick child?

Is it a valid objection that parents are having a child for the wrong reasons? Those who are against bringing a child into the world to save another child believe the 'saviour sibling' will be treated as a commodity rather than as a person; as a means to cure a sick sibling rather than as an end in him/herself. This argument resounds to echoes of Kant's dictum – quoted invariably out of context and often misunderstood – that you should 'never use people as a means but always treat them as an end'.[83]

However, Kant was not against treating people as a means, but rather was opposed to treating them *solely* or *merely* as a means. Few of us get through life without treating others as a means. Should we stop organ transplants or blood transfusions on the grounds that we are treating the donors as a means to our ends? As Hans Ever commented the creation of a child to save another child 'is morally acceptable if the use as a donor is not the only motive for the parents to have a child: i.e. they intend to love and care for this child to the same extent as they love and care for the affected child and if the planned procedure would be acceptable for an existing donor child'.[84]

This commodity argument also fails to identify and explain what is wrong with creating a child as a 'saviour sibling' when creating a child for other instrumental purposes is allowed. We do not normally investigate the reasons why people decide to have children. We do not condemn those who have a baby to provide a companion for an existing child or even those who do so to save a failing marriage. There may be all sorts of less-than-worthy motives for having a child. Of course, we must not ignore the dignity of the child-to-be. But will his/her interests be compromised in any way to promote those of the existing sick child? If the stem cells used are from the umbilical cord blood, there will not even be physical intrusions upon the baby – there is with a bone marrow donation, but these have been relatively uncontroversial for many years.[85] Whether they will remain uncontroversial where the bone marrow is sought from a 'saviour sibling' is less clear.

82 See Bennett, B., 'Choosing a Child's Future? Reproductive Decision-Making and Preimplantation Genetic Diagnosis', in Gunning, J. and Szoke, H. (eds), *The Regulation of Assisted Reproductive Technology*, Aldershot, Ashgate, 2003, 167-176.

83 Lord Winston is cited by Lord Brown (at para 43) as believing that it commodifies the child-to-be. He is also quoted in BBC News, 13 December 2001.

84 Quoted in Sheldon, S. and Wilkinson, S., 'Hashmi and Whitaker: An Unjustifiable and Misguided Distinction?', (2004) 12 *Medical Law Review*, 137-163, at pp. 146-147. Professor Hans Ever is Chairman of the European Society of Human Reproduction and Embryology.

85 And see C.H. Baron *et al.*, 'Live Organ and Tissue Transplants from Minor Donors in Massachusetts', (1975) 35 *Boston University Law Review*, 159-193, at p. 159.

Provided, as is very likely to be the case, that the new child is wanted and will be loved and nurtured in his/her own right, it is difficult to see how his/her dignity can be thought to be compromised in any way. If there were no intention to bring the child up, the case would look different, albeit little different from a surrogacy arrangement and, though we deprecate these,[86] we do not ban them.[87] Even so, there would remain the argument that it is better to be an adopted child than a non-existent one. However, I would not defend the parents who had a saviour sibling, solely as such, and intended to reject the child once he/she had served the purpose for which he/she was procreated. What would such a child be told about his/her origins? That he/she was indeed a means to someone else's end.

The commodity objection is posed another way as well. It is sometimes said that the more choice parents have as a result of reproductive techniques, the more likely they are to develop 'consumerist' attitudes towards children, which in turn will affect the relationship between parents and children. This may well lead to a value, even a monetary value, being put on children, as, indeed, I have argued elsewhere:[88] perhaps the main objection to surrogacy arrangements is their potentiality to commodify children.[89] However, whether it also leads to children being maltreated or rejected is dubious to say the least. There is no evidence to show that children born as a result of assisted reproduction are more likely to end up as abused children. Psychological research studies have identified that children born through assisted reproduction technology have just as close a loving relationship with parents and just as full a psychological development as children born in the more conventional way.[90] On the commodity argument the jury is out – and I suspect is likely to be unable to return a verdict for a very long time. But intuition suggests there is no basis to the argument. And, of course, the alternative to being a 'saviour sibling' – or a commodity – is non-existence. Is this preferable?

Another argument adduced by those who oppose 'saviour siblings', as was observed in CORE's arguments in the *Hashmi* case, is that by allowing this to happen we will step on to the slippery slope[91] that will end with designer babies[92] – with parents selecting height or hair or eye colour or intelligence.

---

86 See Surrogacy Arrangements Act 1985, which was hurriedly passed to meet a moral panic.

87 Surrogacy agreements are, however, unenforceable and also contrary to public policy.

88 'Is Surrogacy Exploitative?', in McLean, S.A.M. (ed), *Legal Issues in Human Reproduction*, Aldershot, Dartmouth, 1989, 164-184.

89 On which see Radin, M., 'Market – Inalienability', (1986) 100 *Harvard Law Review*, 1849-1937 and *Contested Commodities*, Cambridge, Mass., Harvard University Press, 1996.

90 An interesting discussion is Schultz, K., 'Assisted Reproduction and Parent-Infant Bonding' in Evans, D. (ed) *Creating the Child*, The Hague, Martinus Nijhoff, 1996, 229-238.

91 The concern, more generally, of Francis Fukuyama, *Our Posthuman Future: Consequences of the Biotechnology Revolution*, New York, Farrar, Strauss and Giroux, 2002.

92 On which see Gosden, R., *Designing Babies*, New York, W.H. Freeman, 1999.

There are, of course, different versions of the slippery slope argument.[93] One approach looks to the horrible mess at the bottom of the slippery slope. As Josephine Quintavalle, the initiator of the *Hashmi* challenge, put it: 'the new technique is a dangerous first step towards allowing parents to use embryo testing to choose other characteristics of the baby, such as eye colour and sex'.[94] The second version of the argument emphasises consistency. It suggests that allowing the creation of 'saviour siblings' is not morally different from allowing people to choose babies with designer attributes such as a particular hair or eye colour. Logic dictates that if we reject one – as of course we should – we should reject the other.

There are different ways of challenging the slippery slope argument. The easiest is to question the supposed evilness of the end product, to say in effect 'so, what is wrong with designer babies?'[95] This would be an interesting argument to run, but it is outside the scope of the chapter, and I will not attempt it here. Or, one could argue that there is no moral equivalence between 'saviour siblings' and 'designer babies', so that it is perfectly possible to legitimise the creation of 'saviour siblings', whilst opposing the creation of 'designer babies'. In comparison to the goal of creating a 'saviour sibling', which is to save life, the reasons for seeking to 'design' a baby pale into insignificance. The 'saviour sibling' may eliminate an abnormal characteristic: the designer baby merely filters out what most would regard as a normal characteristic, albeit one to which those parents object. It may be difficult in the hard case to define a genetic defect but that is not so here.

The third objection to the slippery slope argument is that it is possible to allow the creation of 'saviour siblings' without giving the green light to 'designer babies'.

Why? First, because those who object to saviour siblings have given no evidence as to why allowing 'saviour siblings' will lead to the creation of 'designer babies'. Secondly, it is probably easier to create a 'saviour sibling' than a 'designer baby'. To create a 'designer baby' a large number of embryos would be needed as a pool for the selection process. The probability is thus that it would be expensive (itself an argument against it because it would be limited to the rich and to those in rich countries[96]). And, thirdly, because regulation can ensure that selection is restricted to acceptable goals. The HFEA's remit enables it to regulate and to draw distinctions,

93 See Williams, B., 'Which Slopes Are Slippery?', in Lockwood, M., *Moral Dilemmas in Modern Medicine*, Oxford, Oxford University Press, 1987.

94 Quoted in Sheldon, S. and Wilkinson, S., 'Should Selecting Saviour Siblings Be Banned?', (2004) 30 *Journal of Medical Ethics*, 533-537, at p. 534.

95 The natural corollary of today's common emphasis (e.g. Robertson, J., *Children of Choice*, Princeton, N.J. 1994) on reproductive autonomy. But see, further, Stock, G., *Redesigning Humans*, London, Houghton Mifflin, 2002.

96 A point made (in a slightly different context) by Parens, E., 'Justice and the Germline', in Stock, G. and Campbell, J. (eds), *Engineering the Human Germline*, New York, Oxford University Press, 2000, 122-124, at p.123. He points to the 'already obscene gap between those who have and those who don't'. This raises the question of the extent to which these new techniques should become part of social medicine, an issue that NICE had recently to grapple when it recommended IVF on the NHS.

and this role should continue.[97] At present, parents have to apply for a licence from HFEA to go through the procedure of PGD and HLA tissue typing to create a 'saviour sibling', and the procedures are permitted on a case-by-case basis using strict guidelines. The HFEA has ruled that the disease needs to be very serious and life threatening, and in effect that the creation of a 'saviour sibling' must be a last resort: if there is another way of treating the child, this should be used.[98] Also, it did not until recently allow parents who suffer from a genetic disease to create a baby to treat their own disease.[99] I think it was wrong to make this change which is not defensible in the way in which having a child to save a child is. Those who object to the creation of 'saviour siblings' have not demonstrated that this system of regulation is likely to fail, though there may be concerns with the way HFEA exercises its powers. The slippery slope criticism thus lacks any real support, and must be rejected.

The third argument adduced against the creation of 'saviour siblings' focuses on the welfare of the child. Reference has already been made to the way this argument was used constructively by Mance LJ in the Court of Appeal in the *Hashmi* case.[100] For as long as section 13(5) remains part of the law,[101] all treatment services must be guided by a welfare principle. But, of course, this was inserted with one-parent families and lesbian couples in mind,[102] not 'saviour siblings' (or for that matter other new developments like fertility treatment for post-menopausal women[103]). Where 'saviour siblings' are to be created, the treatment proposed involves benefits to another person. Is it for the baby-to-be's welfare to be born to save the life of a person who will become his/her sibling? In so far as life, almost any life, is a good, valuable in itself, it may be said that the issue does not arise. Nevertheless, the HFEA uses the 'welfare' provision in the 1990 Act to make a risk/benefit calculation.[104]

Those who oppose creating a baby to save a child's life point to two possible harms that may be caused to the new baby. These are damage to physical health, and psychological harm.

As far as physical health is concerned, when the baby is born it does not suffer any harm, since the taking of stem cells from the umbilical cord blood is not an

97 Though in the wake of the House of Commons Select Committee report, *supra cit.*, it may not do so.

98 See Chair's letter: CH (04) 05 (4 August 2004). The criteria are set out more fully in the House of Commons Report, *supra cit.*, at Table 14 on p. 112.

99 It has recently changed its policy so as to allow this now.

100 See above, xx.

101 As already indicated, it seems likely that it will be repealed in future legislation.

102 When the Human Fertilisation and Embryology Bill was before Parliament an amendment was proposed (and lost by one vote in the House of Lords) which would have limited fertility treatment to married couples.

103 On which see Fisher, F. and Sommerville, A., 'To Everything There is a Season? Are There Medical Grounds for Refusing Fertility Treatment To Older Women?', in Harris, J. and Holm, S., *The Future of Human Reproduction*, Oxford, Clarendon Press, 1998, 203-220.

104 See House of Commons Report, *supra cit.*, para 247.

invasive procedure. Nothing is done to the baby him/herself. If the creation of 'saviour siblings' were not to be allowed, the invasive procedure of taking cells from an existing child's tissue-matched bone marrow would have to be undertaken (a procedure already used, unsuccessfully, in all the much-publicised cases). As Vivienne Nathanson of the British Medical Association said, commenting on the *Whitaker's* case:

> As doctors we believe that where technology exists that could help a dying or seriously ill child without involving major risks to others, then it can only be right that it is used for this purpose.[105]

Of course, PGD will lead to the destruction of some embryos during the selection process. Those who object to this object also to in vitro fertilisation, embryo research, abortion and probably to contraception.[106] Their arguments have been countered elsewhere,[107] and it would be superfluous to this chapter to examine them here. It would be different were there to be any detrimental effects to the embryos used in the reproductive process. The evidence thus far does not point to any short-term detriments. However, the use of PGD to create 'saviour siblings' is new – the technology of PGD itself is relatively so – and more research is needed before we can rule out any long-term effects. An editorial in *The Lancet* has made much of this point: 'whilst embryo biopsy for PGD does not seem to produce adverse physical effects in the short term … it is too early to exclude the possibility of later effects'.[108] We can say with confidence that a child created to save the life of another will suffer no more physical health deficits than any other child born as a result of selection during pre-implantation genetic diagnosis.

Opponents of the creation of a child to save another also point to, what they consider, the psychological harm that may be inflicted on the new baby. There are two arguments.

The first is that if the child finds out that he/she was not wanted for him/herself but rather for the ulterior purpose of assisting a sibling to live, this may cause psychological harm. But it is just as likely that such a child will feel pride and contentment in the knowledge that he/she is responsible for saving the life of a sibling. By contrast, an existing child who finds out that he/she is unable to act as a tissue donor for a sibling is much more likely to be psychologically damaged. It is also argued, equally unconvincingly, that psychological harm may occur because a 'saviour sibling' may experience a less close or loving relationship with their

---

105 Quoted in Bhattacharya, S., 'Banned "Designer Baby" is Born in UK', *New Scientist*, 14 June 2003.

106 It is extraordinary that we even question the loss of embryo in the saviour sibling process when we allow experimentation on embryos for 14 days and, of course, allow for the destruction of surplus embryos, and permit abortion. See further Hursthouse, R., *Beginning Lives*, Oxford, Open University Press, 1987.

107 For example, in Harris, J., *The Value of Life*, London, Routledge, 1985.

108 Editorial: 'Preimplantation Donor Selection', (2001) 358 *Lancet*, 1195.

parents. This is supposedly explained by the 'fact' that parents will value such a child less because he/she was born only to save another child. Presumably, those who believe this will think this even more likely when the 'saviour sibling' has failed to do this. I think these sorts of arguments fail to understand that these are parents who have demonstrated love, care, devotion and who have acted with the highest motives. They are parents for whom the concept of parental responsibility has true meaning.[109] As excellent parents they are as likely to be aware of these concerns as any critic of the procedure and to be on their guard against it happening. They are compassionate, not heartless, and are ill served by this blunt criticism.

Overall, then, if child welfare is the issue, it would make the case for, and not the case against, the practice of creating a child to save the life of an existing child. It is in the interests of a child to be born to save another child of the family. The HFEA accordingly was right to approve the creation of a child to attempt to save Zain Hashmi, and to do so also for Joshua Fletcher. It gave the latter approval in September 2004 even though Joshua Fletcher suffered from a non-genetic disease (Diamond Blackfan anaemia).[110] It had previously refused permission in a similar case (that of Charlie Whitaker) because, since the disease cannot be screened for, the tissue typing would be carried out solely for the benefit of the existing child and not in order to identify whether the embryos carried a genetic disorder.[111] In the *Fletcher* case, the parents have been allowed to go through HLA tissue typing to ensure the embryo will be a tissue match for Joshua, even though there can be no guarantee that the new baby will be free from the disease. This may be more difficult to justify than the *Hashmi* case but I believe it can be justified. The HFEA will continue to vet and act on a case-by-case basis. It has stated also that the disease needs to be serious and life-threatening before it will give a go-ahead, and that if there are other courses of action open to parents these options must first be explored first.[112]

There are thus many objections adduced to the creation of saviour siblings: the commodity argument, that which fears a slippery slope; and that which emphasises welfare and points to the harm it believes the donor child may suffer. As I have shown, none of these is convincing. Are there any other arguments which could be constructed? I discount the concern that some have with innovation. The precautionary principle has value, but scientific advancement can be stifled by over-caution.[113] Nothing ventured, nothing gained can be expected to be the response of the parent with the very sick child. And even if, as I believe has happened in

109 That is, they behave with responsibility. See, further, Eekelaar, J., 'State of Nature or Nature of the State?', (1991) *Journal of Social Welfare Law*, 37.

110 See the decision of the HFEA Licence Committee, *supra cit.*

111 That the distinction between the *Hashmi* and *Whitaker* cases is wrong is argued by Sheldon, S. and Wilkinson, S., '*Hashmi* and *Whitaker*: An Unjustifiable and Misguided Distinction?', (2004) 12 *Medical Law Review*, 137-163.

112 See Chair's letter, *supra cit.*

113 A critical discussion of which is Furedi, F., 'The Dangers of Safety', (1996) *Living Marxism*, 16-22. The House of Commons Select Committee, *supra cit.*, discusses it at paras 273-276.

he *Hashmi* case, the existing child has not yet been cured,[114] the experiment will not be totally in vain if the lessons learned assist other children in the future.

Just as weak is the argument that parents are seeking to create children as much for their own benefit or, indeed, primarily for their own benefit and to their detriment of their child, existing or to-be. The cynical response to this is to ask why any parents have children. We do not inquire into their motives. But in the case under examination this seems unlikely. These parents are not acting for their own benefit, as, for example, the deaf parents who deliberately want to create a deaf child are doing[115] – and many,[116] though not myself,[117] support their decision. The plausibility of the argument that parents create saviour siblings for their own benefit would be stronger if parents could not go through the process of PGD and HLA tissue typing in order to treat an illness of their own.[118] Until very recently they were not permitted to do so but, as slippery slope opponents of saviour siblings warned, PGD and HLA would be extended to allow for this. I think the HFEA has now erred in permitting parents to do this, but also think it is wrong to use this to argue against saviour siblings.

Finally, there is the argument, heard so often in other contexts, that the process necessarily involves the destruction of embryos, and thus life. To some this is akin to murder. An examination of this argument will take me into well-trodden terrain, and unnecessarily so.[119] This is a weak argument and it has been knocked down many times. Were it to prevail, there would be no abortion, fertility treatment or embryo research. United Kingdom law allows experiments on embryos (and therefore their destruction) for 14 days,[120] and pregnancy terminations in exceptional cases to term.[121] How then can we object to embryo wastage which is incidental to the creation of a 'saviour sibling'?

---

114 See *The Guardian*, 20 April 2004.

115 There is 'an asymmetry between the limitations on opportunity that deafness brings and the goods of membership in the deaf community' per Buchanan, A., *et al.*, *From Chance to Choice: Genetics and Justice*, Cambridge, Cambridge University Press, 2000, at p. 283.

116 For example, Holm, S., in Harris, J. and Holm, S., *The Future of Human Reproduction*, Oxford, Clarendon Press, 1998, 28-47.

117 The case is arguably comparable to deliberately deafening a hearing baby (which would be seen as child abuse by everyone). But see, Hayry, M., 'There is a Difference Between Selecting a Deaf Embryo and Deafening a Hearing Child', (2004) 30 *Journal of Medical Ethics*, 510-512.

118 This is now permitted.

119 A good discussion is Lee, R. and Morgan, D., *Human Fertilisation and Embryology Regulating the Reproductive Revolution*, London, Blackstone Press, 2001, ch. 3.

120 See Human Fertilisation and Embryology Act 1990 s 3(3)(a), (4).

121 See Abortion Act 1967 s 1(b), (c), (d).

Is There a Parental Obligation to Have a Saviour Sibling?

There is another question which is less commonly raised.[122] Do parents like the Hashmis or the Fletchers have an *obligation* to have another child in order to save an existing child? The legal answer is clear. It must be their choice. We should not investigate their reasons for not doing so. They cannot be compelled by doctors to do so, or by a court, any more that they can be compelled to donate blood, tissue or organs to save a child of theirs.[123] It is clear that there is no legal obligation. And, although the concept of a legal obligation has been stretched somewhat by cases such as *Re Y*,[124] I doubt whether the common law is capable of accommodating such an obligation. It might lead to specific performance of sexual intercourse!

But do parents with a sick child who might be cured by a saviour sibling have a *moral* obligation to create a new child? Could we see this as an element of parental responsibility?[125] There have been several investigations as to the basis of parental rights;[126] fewer of the reasons for vesting responsibility in parents. Does the chance to save a child trump reproductive autonomy? How far are parents required to go? Would we say that parents like the Hashmis, if they refused to attempt to create a saviour sibling, were being unreasonable? Would we censure them? Has the *Hashmi* case and its successors created a new standard which others can be expected to follow?[127]

And there are other questions too. Suppose an embryo which is to be a 'saviour sibling' is created: can the mother change her mind and refuse to have it implanted? The ultimate decision must belong to the woman,[128] though we might censure her if

---

122 Savulescu, J., 'Procreative Beneficience: Why We Should Select The Best Children', (2001) 15 *Bioethics*, 413-426 does raise it briefly (at p. 415). Robertson, J.A., *et al.*, 'Conception To Obtain Haematopoietic Stem Cells', (2002) 32 (3) *Hastings Center Report*, 34-40 say the question 'can be put swiftly to rest' and provide a negative conclusion (at p. 36).

123 The analogy is the medically-indicated Caesarean section, on which see Rhoden, N.K., 'The Judge in the Delivery Room: The Emergence of Court-ordered Caesareans', (1986) 74 *California Law Review*, 1951-2030. See also *McFall v. Shimp*, (1978) 10 Pa D & C 90 (CE Comm PS, Pa).

124 [1997] Fam 110. See also *Curran v. Bosze*, (1990) 566 NE 2d 1319 (Illinois Supreme Court).

125 See Children Act 1989 s 3.

126 For example, Hill, J., 'What Does It Mean To Be A "Parent"? The Claims of Biology As The Basis For Parental Rights', (1991) 66 *New York University Law Review*, 353. See also Barton, C. and Douglas, G., *Law and Parenthood*, London, Butterworths, 1995, ch. 2.

127 In Hart's sense (see Hart, H.L.A., *The Concept of Law*, Oxford, 1961).

128 This is also the view of John Harris (see Harris, J. and Holm, S. *The Future of Human Reproduction*, Oxford, Clarendon Press, 1998, 5-37, at p. 33). Of course it is not as simple as this. Why shouldn't the male partner have rights at least at the pre-implantation stage? Suppose he wants PGD and she doesn't. And what of the gamete donor who says you can have my gametes but I object to pre-implantation testing (or I suppose to abortion)? There are many questions which have not been considered, but which would require investigation further in another paper.

she refused. The 'father' presumably would have no rights.[129] Nor can it be argued that doctors have a legal duty to implant the embryo.[130]

And what of the converse case – doctors do not wish to implant the embryo but the woman wants to take the chance? Can she insist? Draper and Chadwick have argued that once women have parted with their gametes and the resulting embryos have been tested, 'it is possible for them to lose control over what happens next', and 'she cannot compel him to implant embryos against his wishes'.[131] But though this may not impugn her bodily integrity, it certainly undermines her reproductive autonomy, and arguably also her dignity. But one would not expect any court to compel a doctor to implant an embryo against his clinical judgment, nor, I suggest, would it have the authority to do so. As ever with medico-ethical questions the questions are endless – and the answers often elusive!

---

129 The abortion analogy may not always work, but I think it must hold here. In relation to abortion see *Paton v. Trustees of British Pregnancy Advisory Service*, [1998] 2 All ER 987.

130 But see the arguments of King, D., 'Preimplantation Genetic Diagnosis and the "New" Genetics', (1999) 25 *Journal of Medical Ethics*, 176-182, at p. 180.

131 'Beware! Preimplantation Genetic Diagnosis May Solve Some Old Problems But It Also Raises New Ones', (1999) 25 *Journal of Medical Ethics*, 114-120, at p. 119.

Chapter 25

Wrongful Life, the Welfare Principle and the Non-Identity Problem: Some Further Complications

Søren Holm

> Law is more than an exercise in logic, and logical analysis, although essential to a system of ordered justice, should not become an instrument of injustice. Whatever logic inheres in permitting parents to recover for the cost of extraordinary medical care incurred by a birth-defective child, but in denying the child's own right to recover those expenses, must yield to the injustice of that result.[1]

Introduction[2]

I should probably start this chapter with a confession. Although I belong to one of the traditional professions, although I love to dissect arguments and to participate in argument myself, and although I have been employed in law schools for the last seven years, I am not a lawyer, but just a humble medical doctor and philosopher. And if being a non-lawyer admits of degrees I am much more of a non-lawyer than Ken Mason, and I cannot even claim anything approaching his huge expertise in medical law. I am, however, interested in some of the same issues that he is interested in, especially concerning reproduction, wrongful life cases and the intricacies of arguments involving the question of when prenatal harm becomes a wrong.[3]

---

1 *Procanik v. Cillo* (1984) 97 N.J. 339, at p. 351.

2 As will be evident my views on the matters discussed in this chapter have been shaped by many years of discussion with John Harris. He will undoubtedly disagree with almost all of this chapter. Previous versions of this chapter have been given at seminars at the University of Manchester and University of Oslo. I thank the participants for their helpful comments. The responsibility for all remaining errors is, as usual, my own.

3 Mason, J.K., 'Wrongful Life: The Problem of Causation', (2004) 6 *Medical Law International*, 149-161; Mason, J.K., 'Discord and Disposal of Embryos', (2004) 8 *Edinburgh Law Review*, 84-93.

Mason, J.K., 'Clones and Cell Nuclear Replacements: A *Quintavalle* Saga', (2003) *Edinburgh Law Review*, 379-387.

Mason, J.K., 'From Dundee to Darlington: An End to the *McFarlane* Line?', (2004) *The Juridical Review*, 365-386.

In this chapter, I will first discuss the issue of prenatal harm in the context of reproductive technologies as a philosophical problem and then go on to explore what implications this analysis may have for the discussions about wrongful life and wrongful birth litigation.

Prenatal Harm and the Welfare of the Child

A recurrent question in discussions about new reproductive technologies as applied to human reproduction is to what extent the welfare of the child who is the result of the process should count in the moral or legal analysis of the situation. In many cases participants in the debate who are sceptical about the use of some reproductive technology put forward arguments of the type: 'The use of the technology is morally problematic because the children produced will have a life that is worse than the lives of other children'. Arguments of this kind are often rather summarily dismissed by reference to Parfit's discussion of the so-called 'non-identity' problem.[4]

Recent examples of such exchanges were occasioned by the possibility of human cloning in the wake of the cloning of Dolly the sheep, but they can be found in discussions of almost all reproductive technologies. A fairly typical example can be found in a paper by Justine Burley and John Harris. They write:

> We begin by outlining what Derek Parfit has called the 'non-identity problem'. As we will demonstrate, this problem, when explored and understood properly, shows that those who object to human cloning on the grounds that it would have compromising effects on a *particular* child's welfare are making an error in reasoning.[5]

In legal writing we can find the same claim made by Emily Jackson who quotes John Robertson's seminal paper on reproductive liberty[6] as the authority for the argument that:

> … if the alternative is non-existence, it will in fact invariably be in the particular future child's best interests to be conceived. It is therefore simply illogical for the HFEA to insist that treatment … should be refused if the centre believes that it would not be in the interests of any resulting child.
>
> This is because, as John Robertson has explained, 'from the child's perspective, the risk-creating activity is welcome, since there is no alternative way for this child to be born'.

Mason, J.K., 'Wrongful Pregnancy, Wrongful Birth and Wrongful Terminology', (2002) *Edinburgh Law Review*, 46-66.

4 Parfit, D., *Reasons and Persons*, Oxford, Oxford University Press, 1984, ch. 16.

5 Burley, J. and Harris, J., 'Human Cloning and Child Welfare', (1999) 25(2) *Journal of Medical Ethics*, 108-113, at p. 108.

6 Robertson, J., 'Embryos, Families and Procreative Liberty: The Legal Structure of the New Reproduction', (1986) 59 *Southern California Law Review*, 939-1041, at p. 987.

> Jackson concludes, therefore, that 'distributing assisted conception services according to whether a child's welfare will be served *by her own conception* is clearly nonsensical'.[7]

But is it really this simple? The first point to realise is that if it is this simple it also follows that we should not be worried about the safety of the reproductive technologies we use, except in so far as the users of them are worried or if they are unsafe for the men and women using them. The physical/medical welfare of the children produced cannot enter into the equation because it is equally true of this kind of welfare that '... the risk-creating activity is welcome, since there is no alternative way for this child to be born'.[8] This conclusion is denied by Jackson who in the introduction to her paper claims that:

> I am not concerned here with the question of whether a particular assisted conception technique is *safe*, when I acknowledge both that doctors have special expertise in evaluating its impact upon future children, and that they are entitled to take this into account when making treatment decisions. If this were the sole purpose of the pre-conception welfare principle, it would be as uncontentious as basing the decision not to prescribe a particular medicine to pregnant women upon evidence of its propensity to cause birth defects.[9]

Unfortunately we get no explanation of what the difference is that makes consideration of one type of welfare 'clearly nonsensical' and consideration of another type of welfare 'uncontentious', and no such explanation could be given, because the non-identity argument is perfectly general.[10] If the welfare of the child does not matter on principle, the medical welfare of the child does not matter either.

This initial problem with the argument makes it *prima facie* interesting to take a closer look at it.

In the following I will do two things. I will analyse what view(s) of personal identity the standard use of the non-identity problem commits the proponents to, and I will show that philosophers who combine acceptance of Parfit's analysis of the non-identity problem with acceptance of the view that what gives full moral status is being a person (and not just being a member of the human species or being a potential person) make themselves vulnerable to certain rather counter-intuitive conclusions. This part of the chapter is thus not aimed at showing that there is any

---

7 Jackson, E., 'Conception and the Irrelevance of the Welfare Principle', (2002) 65(2) *Modern Law Review*, 176-203, at p. 193 (emphasis in original, references in original omitted).

8 We might of course wish to develop a more safe technology, partly because it would be preferred by the parents, partly because it would make the world a better place to be in the long run. But as long as there is no alternative to the unsafe treatment we cannot reject it based on child welfare or prenatal harm considerations, if we accept the Parfitian argument. In general we would only have child welfare reasons for choosing a safer technique if we had a choice between two or more techniques that would lead to the birth of the same children.

9 *Ibid.*, at p. 176 (emphasis in original).

10 See for instance Harris, J., *On Cloning*, London, Routledge, 2004 (especially Chapter 4).

formal inconsistency in the Parfitian analysis of the non-identity problem, but just aimed at showing (1) that it may not have the implications for the ethical analysis of human reproduction that it is believed to have, and (2) that it may lead to even more counter-intuitive conclusions than have hitherto been demonstrated (and it should perhaps here be noted that the non-identity problem plays a crucial role in Parfit's generation of the much discussed 'repugnant conclusion' about population size so it is already involved in some fairly counter-intuitive conclusions).

The Non-identity Problem

The non-identity problem occurs because the following claim seems to be uncontroversial:

> If any particular person had not been conceived within a month of the time when he was in fact conceived, he would in fact never have existed.[11]

If somebody had not been conceived as a result of the union of a specific sperm and a specific egg then he or she would, in fact, have been someone else, and since we can safely assume that if there is more than a month between two possible conceptions these will involve different sperm and egg, the claim made by Parfit is justified. If the conception that would have produced a specific person does not take place this month, he or she will never exist, because any later conception will produce somebody else.

The argument thus assumes that it is a necessary condition for identity of human beings that they are the result of a specific instance of conception (or cloning in the case of clones). It is however important to note that the claim is only outlining a necessary condition for identity, not a sufficient condition. The existence of monozygotic twins shows, for instance, that the condition cannot be a sufficient condition (since they would otherwise have to be numerically identical). This conclusion seems to have wide ranging implications for the moral assessment of human reproductive choices. This is brought out by Burley and Harris:

> To give shape to the non-identity problem we will now consider the following two cases. The first is Parfit's and involves a 14-year-old prospective mother:
> This girl chooses to have a child. Because she is so young, she gives her child a bad start in life. Though this will have bad effects throughout the child's life, his or her life will, predictably, be worth living. If this girl had waited for several years, she would have had a different child, to whom she would have given a better start in life.

Our analogue to this case is:

11 See note 5, *supra*, at p. 352.

> A woman chooses to have a child through cloning. Because she chooses to conceive in this way, she gives the child a bad start in life. Though this will have bad effects throughout the child's life, his or her life will, predictably, be worth living. If this woman had chosen to procreate by alternative means, she would have had a different child, to whom she would have given a better start in life.
>
> In both cases, two courses of action are open to the prospective mother. In criticising these women's pursuit of the first option available ... people might claim that each mother's decision will probably be worse for *her child*. However, as Parfit notes ... neither decision can be worse for the particular children born; *the alternative for both of them was never to have existed at all*.[12]

What is argued for on the basis of the non-identity problem is therefore the proposition that:

> If some act A is a necessary condition for a person P to come into existence, then P cannot legitimately complain that A was performed, as long as P has a life which is not so bad that it is not not-worth-living.

What Kind of Identity?

What kind of analysis of personal identity does the use of the non-identity problem in reproductive ethics imply? The initial plausibility of Parfit's argument rests on the assumption that two fertilised eggs that are radically genetically different because they arise from the union of different sperm and eggs must also give rise to different persons. This seems to point to a genetic analysis of personal (?) identity, at least up to the point of personhood, where some other kind of personal identity takes over.

But is genetic identity really necessary for personal identity? Parfit, who famously denies any 'deep further fact' explanation of personal identity,[13] cannot hold that, because genetics would be exactly such a deep further fact. It might also be possible for me to be instantiated in another medium, for instance in a future super-computer, and if we can make sense of that thought we should also be able to make sense of the idea that I could be instantiated in another genetically different biological organism. The super-computer we just imagined might, for instance be a self-renewing organic entity. If I was transferred to a different medium, I would still be me, even though I would not be numerically identical to my old self. It is therefore not logically necessary that there cannot be personal identity between two genetically different human organisms. It may be necessary in terms of current, contingent features of human embodiment, but that is different from logical necessity.

---

12 See note 6, *supra*, at p. 119 (emphasis in original).

13 See note 5, *supra*, at p. 262.

Some Complicating Examples

Let us look at some examples of possible modes of reproduction that complicates the simple non-identity claim outlined above.

The first example is foetal reduction in the context of multi-foetal pregnancies. In pregnancies with three or more foetuses the chance of the birth of at least one child that survives the neonatal period increases if one or more of the foetuses are killed *in utero.*[14] Let us imagine that I am the only surviving child of a case of multi-foetal pregnancy with initially five foetuses reduced by foetal reduction to a singleton pregnancy.[15] Could I validly complain about the fact that foetal reduction was performed, and that I do now not have any contemporaneous siblings, or not as many contemporaneous siblings as I would like? One way of looking at this question would be to say that although foetal reduction increased my chance of being born, it was not absolutely necessary, i.e. I could have been born even if foetal reduction had not taken place, even if the chance of my survival would have been very low, or I could have been born if one, two or three instead of four of my sibling foetuses had been killed. I therefore do seem to have a valid complaint, if I believe that my lack of contemporaneous siblings have harmed me.[16] So there is at least one type of reproductive technology that is unaffected by the non-identity problem. A further complication for the application of the non-identity problem to reproductive matters occurs in the context of assisted reproductive technologies when an embryo has already been created *ex utero*.

Let us imagine the following scenario. A woman can choose to implant an embryo either this month or the next month. If she implants the embryo it will go to term and is likely to be born between 38 and 42 weeks of gestation. At the moment she has a disease that will harm the embryo, albeit only slightly, but it can be cleared up if she waits a month. Since it is the same embryo, the child which is born will be genetically the same whatever she chooses, and since the two expected periods of birth overlap (i.e. the child might be born on the same day whatever she chooses) there seems to be good reason to claim that whatever she chooses she would produce one and the same child; and that it is this child she has harmed if she chooses not to wait a month with implantation. But if that is true, that child would be identical to the child she produced if she waited two months, which would be identical to the child she produced if she waited three months and so on. Since identity is a transitive relation, this indicates that all of these possible children are identical to the first child – the child she would have if she implanted the embryo now. According to this line

14 Chescheir, N.C., 'Outcomes of multifetal pregnancy reductions', (2004) 47(1) *Clinics in Obstetrics and Gynecology*, 134-145. Lewi, L., Jani, J. and Deprest, J., 'Invasive antenatal interventions in complicated multiple pregnancies', (2005) 32(1) *Obstetrics and Gynecology Clinics of North America*, 105-126.

15 The numbers here do not matter for the argument. It would, for instance, work just as well if I was one out of two surviving children from a reduction of four foetuses.

16 Being an only child myself I tend to believe that such a complaint is not very firmly grounded, but it is not obviously incoherent.

of argument there would thus be harm to the child if the embryo was implanted at a non-optimal time, even though this child (i.e. the child born at a certain time) was only born because implantation took place when it did.

If we want to deny this conclusion we would have to assert that, counterfactually, genetically identical children born at different times from the implantation of one and the same embryos are in fact different persons.[17] That assertion could be backed by the consideration, often put forward in the context of discussions of reproductive cloning, that two genetically identical persons can turn out to be very different if they are exposed to different environments, and that that is sufficient for them not to be the same person. But as we will see below, that analysis of personal identity in terms of psychological and/or physiological characteristics instead of genetic characteristics in itself has significant and problematic consequences.

The Personal Non-identity Problem

Many philosophers who agree with the analysis of the non-identity problem outlined above, at the same time defend a theory of moral status that connects moral status to personhood. The details of exactly what attributes an individual needs to have to be a person differ among personhood theorists, but they all agree that some higher mental states like self-awareness are necessary for personhood.[18] They are thus, for instance, able to argue that abortion on demand is morally unproblematic because it does not involve the killing of a person but only of a human non-person. Actions that affect human individuals before they become persons are only morally important if the individuals affected later become persons and are at that time positively or negatively affected by the prior action.[19] If I act in a way which is harmful towards a pre-personal human individual, but that individual never becomes a person, then I have not harmed him or her. Based on this analysis John Harris is, for instance, able to argue that if I clone myself, but make sure that the clone's higher brain functions

---

17 In discussion following presentations of earlier versions of this paper people have claimed that I would be a different person if I was born one day later than I was actually born, and when pressed have seemed to commit themselves to the view that I would have been another person even if I had been born only minutes earlier or later. I find this proposition completely implausible.

18 Glover, J., *Causing Deaths and Saving Lives*, Harmondsworth, Penguin Books, 1977. Kuhse, H. and Singer, P., *Should the Baby Live*?, Oxford, Oxford University Press, 1985. Singer, P., *Practical Ethics* (2nd ed), Cambridge, Cambridge University Press, 1993. Harris, J., *The Value of Life*, London, Routledge & Kegan Paul, 1985. Harris, J., *Wonderwoman and Superman – The Ethics of Human Biotechnology*, Oxford, Oxford University Press, 1992. Rachels, J., *The End of Life*, Oxford, Oxford University Press, 1986. Tooley, M., *Abortion and Infanticide*, Oxford, Oxford University Press, 1985.

19 For a criticism of this view see Persson, I., 'Harming the Non-Conscious', (1999) 13(3/4) *Bioethics*, 294-305.

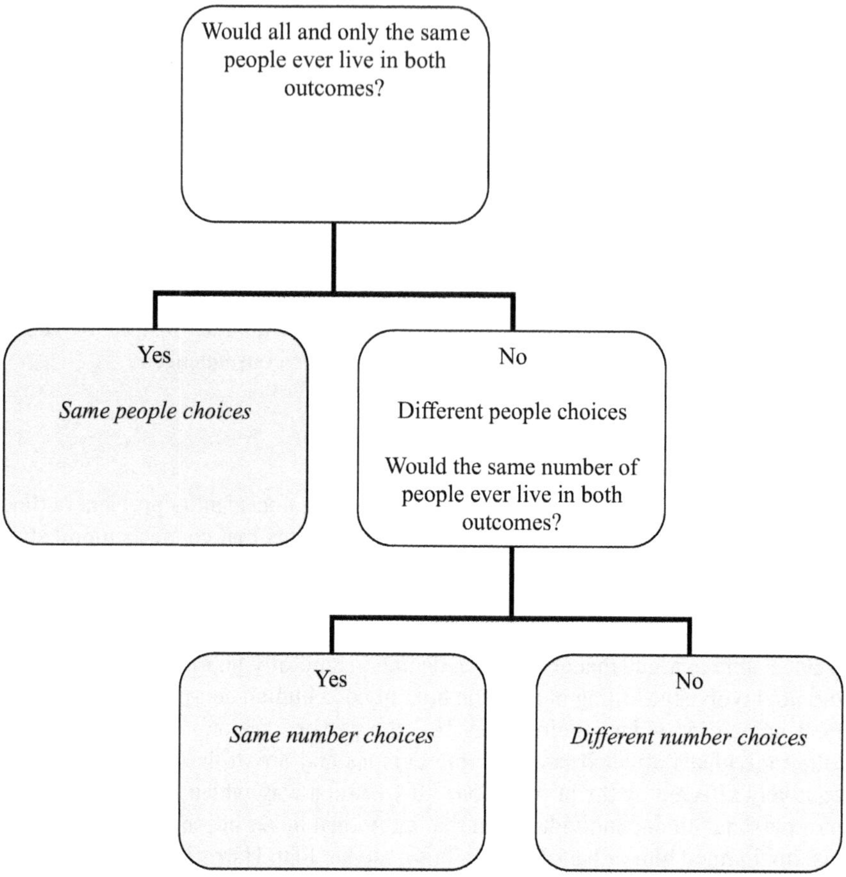

Figure 25.1

are destroyed early in foetal life, then there is in principle nothing wrong with letting the clone mature to adult size and use it as an organ bank.[20]

In his analysis of the non-identity problem Parfit produces the following schema of the possible choices in a situation where our actions affect future people (Figure 25.1)

This schema is, however, ambiguous with regard to the left-hand section of 'same people choices', since we can conceive of closely parallel worlds where the same individuals exist but as different persons. Even though genetic identity is a necessary condition for personal identity in humans it is not a sufficient condition.[21]

---

20 Harris, J., *The Value of Life*, *op cit.*, note 19, at p. 124.

21 In the present context we can allow ourselves to ignore the complications caused by the further arguments made by Parfit aimed at showing that personal identity may not depend on any necessary further fact (including genetic constitution) but only on psychological

The category of 'same people choices' can therefore be divided into 'same persons choices' and 'different persons choices'. We can, for instance, consider cases like the following:

> Melanie has conceived a foetus which is now 8 weeks old.[22] A pill is made available to her that will cause her foetus severe brain damage by removing 50 per cent of its potential for intelligence. The pill will not cause the foetus or the resulting child any pain or physical discomfort. Convinced by the analysis of the non-identity problem she has discussed with her philosopher friends she flips a coin to decide whether or not to take the pill. Whether or not she takes the pill, she is absolutely committed to bringing the child to term.

In this scenario there are two possible outcomes. Either child A is brought into being with unaltered intelligence, or child B is brought into being with 50 per cent of the intelligence of child A but with the same genetic constitution.[23] Whatever Melanie chooses as the result of tossing the coin the same human individual will be brought into the world (i.e. it will be a 'same people choice'), but it is highly implausible to claim *that the same person will emerge.* Given the differential in intelligence, the correct analysis seems to be that child A and child B will develop a mental life which is so different that already at the time when they become persons they will be two different persons.[24] In our everyday talk about personality and personal identity we are quite used to expressions like 'after the stroke he became a totally different person', and in the present context such language seems even more appropriate since child A and child B share no common experiences prior to the intervention. It thus seems that Melanie does nothing wrong if she tosses the coin and takes the pill. If she takes the pill she brings into the world a person who would not otherwise have been brought into the world, a person who has a life which is worth living, and a person who is presumably happy that he or she, and not the possible more intelligent inhabitant of the same body, was chosen to be brought into existence. Her motives are not bad either; they are actually fairly honourable in that she tries to apply the analysis of several well-recognised moral philosophers in her own life.

This conclusion does, however, seem highly counter intuitive. If Melanie takes the pill we must surely be able to say that she harms and/or wrongs the person who will come into existence? One possible option would be to follow the analysis proposed by John Harris. He suggests that we can analyse a 'harmed condition' as the condition which obtains wherever someone is in a disabling or hurtful condition,

---

continuity. In the case of human persons under present circumstances genetic identity is a necessary condition for personal identity.

22 The foetus is thus not yet sentient, and not a person on any of the standard personhood theories.

23 A real life analogy to this hypothetical scenario is the continuum from total alcohol abstinence during pregnancy to an alcohol intake that produces foetal alcohol syndrome.

24 If this scenario is not convincing then it can without problems be exchanged for scenarios where the pill produces severe anti-social personality disorder (previously called 'psychopathy') or some other major psychological change.

and that we can further claim that X has been harmed by Y if X is in a condition that is harmed and Y is responsible for X being in that condition.[25] On this analysis, Harris would presumably say that Melanie harms child B if she takes the pill. In a discussion of wrongful life cases he thus concludes:

> What then is the wrong of wrongful life? It can be wrong to create an individual in a harmed condition even where the individual is benefited thereby. The wrong will be the wrong of bringing avoidable suffering into the world, of choosing deliberately to increase unnecessarily the amount of harm or suffering in the world or of choosing a world with more suffering rather than one with less.[26]

Here it is important to note that although Harris would presumably think that Melanie had *harmed* child B, he would not think that she had *wronged* child B. Child B would have no valid grievance against its mother – the only valid grievance would be that which other inhabitants of the world could put forward because Melanie had caused the world to be in a worse state than if she had refrained from taking the pill and child A had been brought into the world. Seen from the perspective of child B what Harris' analysis thus leaves us with is wrongless harmdoing.[27, 28]

Harris' analysis and the standard analysis of Melanie's case outlined above also share a problem which can be brought out if we turn to consider that Melanie's case actually belongs to a continuum of cases as illustrated in Figure 25.2.[29]

At one end of the continuum we have Melanie1 who takes a tablet which reduces the intelligence of her child by 1 percent, our Melanie is actually Melanie50, and at the other end of the continuum we have Melanie100 whose tablet simply produces a child without any cognitive abilities. On both Harris' analysis and the standard analysis Melanie1 has both harmed and wronged her child. Her child is born with an impairment that could have been avoided, and the person it will become has a legitimate grievance against Melanie1. At some point down the continuum of cases the situation suddenly changes. If the harm done to the brain of the foetus is sufficient to make it into a different person when it matures, the standard analysis

25 In the cloning paper by Burley and Harris referred to *supra*, Harris does however seem not to use this analysis of harming.

26 Harris, J., *Wonderwoman and Superman*, *op cit.*, note 19, at p. 90.

27 The literature contains many discussions of harmless wrongdoing, but wrongless harmdoing has received much less attention, presumably because most authors would see such a category as bordering on the conceptually incoherent.

28 A further problem with this analysis is that it seems to locate the ethical complaint in the wrong place, by locating the harm done to the state of the world, and not to the person who has been harmed. It is truly bizarre that the only complaint child B has against Melanie in this situation is the same complaint that everyone else has, i.e. that she has made the world slightly worse than it would otherwise be.

29 This continuum is in some ways similar to one discussed by Ingmar Persson in which we gradually remove neurons from the brains of a foetus. Persson presents his example in a paper concerned with ascription of harm to non-conscious entities, and argues for quite different conclusions than the ones presented here. See note 19, *supra*.

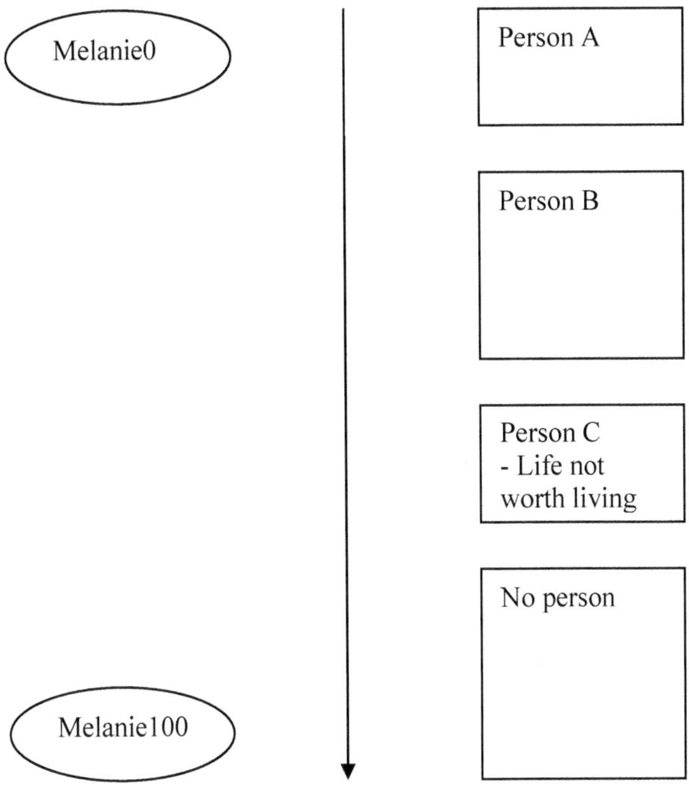

Figure 25.2

tells us that the person has neither been harmed nor wronged and the Harris analysis that the person has been harmed but not wronged. The child of Melanie50 therefore has no legitimate grievance on either analysis. Even further down the continuum the situation changes once again. If the harm done to the foetus is so severe that it becomes a person with a life not worth living it has again been both harmed and wronged. And at the bottom end of the continuum we have yet another reversal. If the harm done to the brain of the foetus is sufficient to ensure that it will never become a person both Harris' and the standard analysis leads to the result that the resulting child has neither been harmed nor wronged, since these categories only pertain to persons.[30]

We thus have the very strange situation that even though we have a clear continuum of harm done to the brain of Melanie's foetus there are two points on this continuum where she can get off the moral hook of being an evil person simply by doing more harm! If we thus imagine Melanie to be somebody who desires to have

30 Remember that the harm we are discussing is cognitive harm, not pain or discomfort.

a child which will forever be dependent on her, but not so helpless that it does not recognise its own dependency (i.e. if we imagine Melanie to be a truly evil person with a truly evil set of motives), then what she should do is to pick the pill which will destroy exactly so much of the brain of her foetus that it becomes a different person than the one it would have become if she had not taken any tablet. If she manages to pull this off she will not only not have wronged her child, she will have brought somebody into the world who would not otherwise have been brought into the world, and who should therefore be thankful to Melanie for this good deed!

A possible response to this criticism could be to propose an analysis within a possible worlds/branching time framework. On such an analysis, what we should do is to compare the state of the world in the possible world created by Melanie1-100 respectively with that created if she does not take the pill (Melanie0).[31] Here it seems justified to claim that all the possible worlds created are worse when compared to the one containing Melanie0, and that their degree of badness tracks the degree of harm done by the different tablets. This might initially seem to be a welcome conclusion, and we may be willing to overlook that this analysis is of no help in deciding whether or not any of the individuals in these worlds have a valid claim against Melanie. There is, furthermore, an additional remaining problem which is caused by the fact that the comparison has so far only been done in terms of the similar individuals living in each of the parallel worlds. On the present analysis the worst of all these worlds is the world containing Melanie100 and her child. If we compare the world of Melanie0 and the world of Melanie100 there is no doubt that the state of Melanie0's child compared to the state of Melanie100's child entails that the first world is substantially better. But both John Harris, and the proponents of the standard non-identity analysis, must vigorously deny this conclusion. Even if the same number of individuals exists in the two worlds, and even if they are actually the same individuals, these philosophers will claim that the two worlds are incomparable in this direct way, because they contain a different number of persons. As was mentioned above they see what Melanie100 does as morally innocuous, and – if her child is used for some good (and non-painful) purpose – perhaps even morally commendable. And they reach this conclusion because they focus so intently on harms to persons only. But as soon as that move is made, they have to admit that Melanie50 has not harmed her child either, because had she not taken the pill some other child would have been born.

Wrongful Life and Wrongful Birth

What are the implications of the analysis above for the approach to wrongful life and wrongful birth litigation? One obvious implication is that at least one of the

31 This analysis could be seen as one possible 'quantitative' extension of John Harris' analysis of harming. If I harm somebody by being responsible for their being in a harmful condition, then it seems reasonable to say that the magnitude of harm depends on the severity of the harmful condition.

reasons given for denying wrongful life claims is considerably weaker than is usually assumed. Accepting the argument that existence is almost always preferable to non-existence and that a complainant therefore cannot be said to have been harmed by being born in a disabled state, as Stephenson LJ seems to do in the leading English case of *McKay v. Essex Area Health Authority*,[32] creates, as we have seen above, as many problems as it solves. It leaves the door wide open for a whole range of harmful reproductive practices. It is clearly the case that a person can be harmed by being born in a disabled state, and it is furthermore the case that the person born in such a condition will also in some instances have been wronged by the person or persons who inflicted the harm if they owed a duty of care. The fact that we may for social policy reasons, or because of a high valuation of the right to reproductive freedom, allow parents – and in particular mothers – to harm and wrong their embryos and foetuses without incurring legal liability, does not show that they do not harm and wrong them. There seem to be no comparable social policy reasons for excluding wrongful life claims against healthcare professionals or their employers.

What then about wrongful birth? Mason has argued convincingly that the current approach to wrongful birth cases concerning healthy children is incompatible with an orthodox approach to tort law.[33] It is clearly the case that having a child when you did not want to have one can cause financial hardship and that in some cases this outcome is caused by the negligent action of a healthcare professional. Parents should therefore be able to obtain compensation for the unwanted costs that have been imposed on them.

From the point of view of an orthodox Parfitian analysis of the non-identity problem, current UK jurisprudence disallowing wrongful birth cases is, however, paradoxically correct. Any act which brings a person into the world with a life that is worth living, and does not at the same time decrease the quality of other peoples' lives so much that the net welfare gain becomes negative, makes the world a better world and is therefore a morally commendable act. It would, therefore, be perverse to require a doctor to pay compensation, just because he had been causally involved in making the world a better world.

This seems to me to be just one more reason to be wary of the apparent theoretical elegance and wide argumentative reach of the non-identity problem.

32 *McKay v. Essex Area Health Authority* [1982] QB 1166.

33 Mason, J.K., 'From Dundee to Darlington: An End to the *McFarlane* Line?', *op cit.*, note 4.

Chapter 26

Life-Prolonging Treatment and Patients' Legal Rights

Loane Skene

A patient's 'right' to decide what treatment he or she wants in the final stages of life is especially topical at present, in the wake of Terri Schiavo's case[1] in the United States and the recent judgment of the Court of Appeal in the United Kingdom in *Burke v. The General Medical Council*.[2] It is commonly said that patients have the right to autonomy and that therefore they are entitled to decide what treatment they will or will not have. However, the reference to a patient's 'autonomy' in this context conceals a fundamental misconception concerning the rights that patients legally have.

It is true that the law has increasingly acknowledged and given effect to patients' autonomy, including the right to make their own medical decisions, but only when the choice to be made is between one of a number of options offered by their medical carers. Competent, adult patients are clearly legally entitled to refuse treatment they do not want, or to choose to wait and see whether their condition improves without treatment. There have been many cases over the years in which this principle has been stated by the courts, usually when deciding what information a doctor must provide in order to enable a patient to give 'informed consent' to undergo a medical procedure.[3] In Australia, a patient's right to refuse treatment has also been specifically stated in legislation,[4] which in some states, also entitles patients to appoint an agent to refuse treatment on their behalf if they are not themselves competent to refuse that treatment at a later time.[5]

---

1 The various court applications and findings are well summarised by Annas, G, '"Culture of Life" Politics at the bedside – the case of Terri Schiavo', (2005) 352 (16) *NEJM*,1710-1715.

2 *Burke v. General Medical Council*, [2005] EWCA Civ 1003; appeal from decision at first instance: *Burke, R (on the application of) v. The General Medical Council*, [2004] EWHC 1879 (Admin).

3 Skene, L. and Smallwood, R., 'Informed Consent: Lessons from the Antipodes', (2002) 324 *British Medical Journal*, 39-41, available at: bmj.com/cgi/content/full/324/7328/39 at 25 May 2005.

4 Medical Treatment Act 1988 (Vic) Part 2.

5 Medical Treatment Act 1988 (Vic) Part 2, Consent to Medical Treatment and Palliative Care Act 1995 (SA) s 7; Powers of Attorney Act 1998 (QLD) ss 35(2)(b), 36(2).

What has not been said – because it is not the law – is that patients are entitled to *require* that they must be given particular treatment. In this respect, I have argued in earlier papers,[6] and the Court of Appeal has now ruled to similar effect, that Munby J was in error in his view of the meaning of patients' autonomy in *Burke* at first instance.[7] Munby J said that patients not only have a 'right to be protected *from* treatment … which will result in dying in avoidably distressing circumstances' (i.e. a right to refuse treatment) but also a 'right to be protected from … a *lack* of treatment in such cases'[8] (i.e. a right to demand treatment, or at least 'routine' care); and that in the UK, that right may be enforced under the European Convention on Human Rights.[9]

In taking this view, Munby J regarded 'the right to be protected from treatment' as one of the 'dignity interests' protected by Article 8 of the Convention and added the 'right to be protected … from a *lack* of treatment, which will result in one dying in avoidably distressing circumstances' as another such interest.[10] Munby J said that 'The personal autonomy protected by Article 8 means that in principle it is for the competent patient, and not his doctor, to decide what treatment *should* or *should not* be given'.[11] In the context of Munby J's judgment, this appears to be a choice that is not limited to one of the options offered by the doctors, but to be at large. In my view, the patient is legally entitled to choose the first (an option offered by the doctor), but not the second (the patient's own preference). The reason is that patients have never been legally entitled to demand particular treatment. The treatment that is appropriate for a particular patient is a matter of clinical judgment, for the doctor to decide. For example, I cannot require my doctor to undertake a bilateral mastectomy for me because I am concerned about the possibility of developing breast cancer. The doctor will assess whether that procedure is appropriate, given my family history or other risk factors. If the doctor makes that assessment and offers me the choice of surgery, radiotherapy or chemotherapy, I can then choose which of those 'available options' to pursue and ask the doctor to take that course. That is fundamentally different from

6 Skene, L., 'Disputes about the withdrawal of treatment: The role of the courts', (2004) 32 (4) *J of Law, Med and Ethics*, 701-6; Skene, L., 'Withholding and withdrawing treatment in South Australia when patients, parents or guardians insist that treatment must be continued', (2004) 24(2) *Adelaide Law Rev*, (in press); Skene, L., 'Terminally ill infants, parents and the courts', (2005) 24(4) *Medicine and Law*, (in press); Skene, L., 'The *Schiavo* and *Korp* cases: conceptualising end of life decision making', (2005) *Journal of Law and Medicine*, (in press).

7 Note 2, *supra*.

8 *Burke*, note 2, *supra*, para 64 (emphasis added). See also his ultimate conclusion that it is for the patient to decide 'where his best interests lie, as to what life-prolonging treatment he *should* or should not have': para 116, point (11) (emphasis added).

9 Incorporated into UK law by the Human Rights Act 1998.

10 *Burke*, note 2 *supra*, para 213(i) (emphasis added).

11 *Burke*, note 2 *supra*, para 213(n) (his emphasis).

my legal right to refuse treatment, even if the doctor recommends it. That right is absolute, not dependent on the doctor's opinion of what is best for me.[12]

In support of his decision, Munby J cited a number of judicial statements that, in his view, supported a principle that patients have a right to choose the treatment they want, at least when a procedure is 'routine' like artificial feeding. However, I believe that, in stating the judicial authority on which he relied in support of that proposition, Munby J wrongly elided judicial statements about a patient's right to refuse treatment with other statements that might seem on their surface to suggest that autonomy means also the right to require treatment to be provided, but can be seen on closer examination not to have been applied in that way in any of the cases. Munby J did not acknowledge the distinction between the two types of statement in his judgment. Yet the difference between them is fundamental.

Consider the following examples of the second type of statement (the patient's 'right' to demand particular treatment) quoted by Munby J. As he said, Lord Goff said in *Bland* that 'Respect must be given to the *wishes of the patient*'.[13] And Lord Scarman referred in *Sidaway* to 'the patient's right to *make his own decision*'.[14] Cardozo J iterated in *Schloendorff v. Society of New York Hospital*, a patient's 'right to determine *what shall be done* with his own body'.[15] However, when these statements are read in the context of the cases in which they were made, it is clear that the respective judges meant that a patient can choose one of a number of available options, not whatever treatment the patient wants.

In *Bland*, the issue was whether it was lawful to withdraw life-sustaining treatment from a patient in a persistent vegetative state. It was about people (the patient's family and the medical carers), refusing or deciding not to proceed with life-prolonging treatment.

In *Sidaway* and *Schloendorff*, the issue was the information to be given to a patient in order for the patient to make an informed choice about whether to agree to treatment recommended by the doctor – another aspect of the right to refuse treatment. The inference underlying the principle of informed consent is that the patient, if fully informed about a proposed procedure, especially potential risks, might choose not to proceed with it. This is clear when one analyses cases of 'alleged negligent

---

12 Patients may in some circumstances have a legal right to *routine care*. For example, where a person has been accepted as a patient by a doctor or hospital, there is then a duty to take 'reasonable' care imposed by the law of tort (negligence) and the law of contract. It is also possible for such a duty to arise if an expectation is raised that care will be provided, for example by a hospital sign 'Emergency services'. However, the services to be provided are still determined by the clinical judgment of the doctors. The patient cannot require that a particular service must be provided. Whether artificial nutrition and hydration are 'routine' will depend on the facts in each case (Munby J thought that they did fall within the concept of routine care).

13 *Airedale NHS Trust v. Bland*, [1997] AC 789, 826, at p 864 (emphasis added).

14 *Sidaway v. Board of Governors of the Bethlem Royal Hospital and the Maudsley Hospital*, [1985] AC 871, at p. 882 (emphasis added).

15 (1914) 105 NE 92, at p. 93 (emphasis added).

non-disclosure'. Their crux is whether a doctor should be required to compensate a patient for injuries following a medical procedure, even if the doctor performed the procedure with due care and skill, because the doctor did not tell the patient in advance about a 'material risk'.[16] The patient's argument is that, if told about that risk, s/he would not have agreed to the procedure and so would not have suffered the injury. One main issue in such cases is causation. If informed of the risk, would the patient in fact have refused the procedure, or would the patient have agreed to proceed in any event, now saying with the benefit of hindsight that he or she would not have agreed to it?[17] Throughout the case, the issue is one of accepting or refusing treatment that the doctor has recommended. It is not whether the patient is entitled to a particular type of treatment against medical advice.

Thus, the judicial authority cited by Munby J to show that patients are entitled to choose whatever treatment they want (at least where the treatment is 'routine') can be seen upon closer examination not to support such a proposition. Moreover, the falsity of this proposition is apparent when one considers the law from another perspective. There are many cases that indicate that life-prolonging treatment may be lawfully withdrawn when doctors consider that it is not in the patient's best interests to continue to provide it. The ground on which such treatment is withdrawn is futility, not patient autonomy. Consider these examples.

In *Bland*, the judges of the House of Lords unanimously (though in separate judgments) agreed that it was not in the patient's best interests to continue to be artificially fed – and to be subjected to the other invasive and undignified procedures that care of such patients requires – when he had no hope of recovery. The *Bland* case has been followed in later cases in England.[18] Similarly, in the United States, the New Jersey Supreme Court held in the case of Karen Ann Quinlan that it was lawful to withdraw treatment when there was 'no reasonable possibility of a patient returning to a cognitive sapient state';[19] and in the case of Nancy Cruzan, the US

---

16 Compare *Rogers v. Whitaker*, (1992) 175 CLR 479, at p. 490.

17 Compare *Rosenberg v. Percival*, (2001) 205 CLR 434, at p. 441.

18 See *Re J (a minor) (medical treatment)*, [1990] 3 All ER 930, in which the court would not order intensive care for a child who suffered severe brain injury after a fall and the mother's application was refused; *Re C (A minor)* (1997) 40 BMLR 31, where Orthodox Jewish parents believed that life should always be preserved, the court would not order that treatment be given; *A National Health Service v. D*, [2000] 2 FLR 677, at p. 686, in which the English High Court accepted unanimous medical opinion from three paediatricians that mechanical ventilation and the processes of intensive care were not in the best interests of a 19-month-old child who was severely disabled (he had irreversible and worsening lung disease, heart failure, hepatic and renal dysfunction; life expectancy one year at most). The court made the declaration (at p. 678) that was sought by the NHS Trust responsible for the child's care, and also by the Official Solicitor, but opposed by the parents: In the event of the child suffering 'a respiratory and/or cardiac failure and/or arrest,' it would be lawful to treat him with only palliative care. The case of Charlotte Wyatt, recently before the courts again, resulted in a similar order.

19 *In Re Quinlan*, 70 NJ 10, 355 A. 2d 647 (1976).

Supreme Court endorsed the withdrawal of tube feeding from another woman in a persistent vegetative state.[20] In Terri Schiavo's case, nearly 20 judges took a similar view over a seven-year period in a number of courts extending to the US Supreme Court.[21]

In Australia, the case law is the same. Bland's case was approved as Victorian law in the case known as *BWV*.[22] That involved an elderly woman with Pick's disease, a form of dementia, who was being kept alive with artificial feeding and hydration (a 'PEG' tube), like Terri Schiavo. Both the Victorian Civil and Administrative Tribunal and the Supreme Court of Victoria held that it was lawful to withdraw that feeding and to allow her to die. Artificial feeding was categorised as 'medical treatment' that could be refused under the Medical Treatment Act 1988 (Vic), either by a patient (if competent to do so), or by an agent or guardian using a 'Refusal of Treatment Certificate' form under the Act. Also, artificial feeding was ruled not to fall within the definition of 'palliative care', which cannot be refused under the Act. This ruling involved a finding that PEG feeding is outside the scope of the 'reasonable provision of food and water', which does fall within the definition of 'palliative care'. Other cases have come before the guardianship tribunal in Queensland that have also led to treatment being withheld or withdrawn. In *Re RWG*, the Queensland tribunal held that a 'no CPR' order was lawful for a 73-year-old man with acquired brain disorder;[23] and in *Re MC*, the tribunal upheld the withdrawal of artificial feeding from an 80-year-old woman in a persistent vegetative state.[24]

It should be noted that in many of these cases family members agreed that treatment should be withdrawn (that occurred in *Bland* and *BWV*, for example). That was not, of course, the case with Terri Schiavo. However, the wishes of family members are not determinative if it is futile to continue treatment in a particular case. This is clear from the case law. In a New South Wales case decided last year, the case of *Messiha*, treatment – including artificial ventilation and feeding – was withdrawn from a 75-year-old man with severe hypoxic brain damage after cardiac arrest despite family objections.[25] The judge (Justice Howie) said that courts are not making a 'value judgment of the life of the patient' in such cases or 'disregard[ing]

---

20 *Cruzan v. Director, Missouri Department of Health*, 497 US 261 (1990). The court said in that case that treatment could be withdrawn if there was 'clear and convincing evidence' that the patient would refuse it if she could speak for herself. However, it is not essential that the family must consent in order for treatment to be lawfully withdrawn. As Professor John Robertson observed: 'Doctrines of futility have sometimes allowed doctors and hospitals to refuse or withdraw treatment even though the family insists on continuing it': Robertson, J., '*Schiavo* and Its (In)significance', (March 2005) *University of Texas Public Law & Legal Theory*, Research Paper Series No. 72, at p. 8.

21 See Annas, note 1, *supra*.

22 *BWV*, [2003] VCAT 121 (28 February 2003); *Gardner; re BWV*, [2003] VSC 173 (29 May 2003).

23 [2000] QGAAT 2.

24 [2003] GAAT 13.

25 *Messiha (by his tutor) v. South East Health*, [2004] NSWSC 1061.

the wishes of the family'.[26] The question is whether the court is satisfied that medical staff agree that withdrawing treatment is 'in the welfare and interest of the patient' and that question 'is principally a matter for the expertise of professional medical practitioners'.[27] Similarly, in another New South Wales case, *Northridge*, Justice O'Keefe clearly accepted that courts could authorise the withdrawal of treatment despite family objection (though, on the facts, he did not make such an order in that case).[28] Justice O'Keefe said that the 'usual relief' where courts authorise the withdrawal of treatment, is 'by way of a declaration that "the responsible medical practitioners ... may lawfully discontinue all life sustaining treatment and medical support measures, (including ventilation, nutrition and hydration by artificial means) designed to keep (the patient) alive in (his or her) existing permanent vegetative state"'.[29]

The Australian law is also evident in guidelines recently published by the NSW Department of Health.[30] These Guidelines envisage withdrawal of artificial hydration and nutrition as 'a treatment limitation decision that may be made in accordance with these guidelines';[31] and acknowledge that treatment may be withdrawn even if family members object.[32] The National Health and Medical Council has developed a document to assist in the diagnosis of persistent vegetative state, now called Post-coma unresponsiveness (Vegetative State), but the document does not have the status of formal guidelines.[33]

---

26 *Ibid.*, para 25.

27 *Ibid.*

28 *Northridge v. Central Sydney Area Health Service*, [2000] NSWLR 1241 para 110; see also para 111, referring to Practice Note.

29 *Ibid.*, para 110.

30 NSW Department of Health, *Guidelines for End-of-life Care and Decision Making*, 2005.

31 *Ibid.*, at p. 13, para 7.4. The Guidelines note that 'artificial hydration and nutrition is an intervention with its own possible burdens and discomfort, for example, those related to having tubes in situ or regularly replaced'.

32 *Ibid.*, at p. 9, para 6.3 ('Inappropriate requests for continuing treatment'), 6.5 ('Options for resolving disagreement'). The Guidelines list a court application (initiated by either medical carers or family members) as the final step. The cases of *Messiha*, note 25 above, and *Northridge*, note 28 above, are authority for the power of the court to make a declaration that treatment may be lawfully withdrawn; and in *Messiha*, in particular, that a declaration can be made even if the patient's family object. The diagrammatic management plan in the Guidelines (at p. 7) suggests that, after court intervention, 'consensus' is reached; this seems to me unduly hopeful. The bottom line is that a court can sanction the withdrawal of treatment however much the family object.

33 NHMRC, 'Post-coma unresponsiveness (Vegetative State): A clinical framework for diagnosis', 18 Dec 2003, available at: http://www7.health.gov.au/nhmrc/publications/synopses/hpr23syn.htm. This document constitutes, as it states, a 'framework of considerations for diagnosis of Post-coma unresponsiveness'; but it should not be regarded as having the status of formal guidelines, which do not yet exist. The document is intended to be informative. It does not prescribe procedures to be followed, or time limits, for establishing a diagnosis.

It can be seen therefore that the decision whether treatment, or a particular type of treatment, is appropriate for a patient is one of clinical judgment, to be made by the doctor, on the basis of the patient's 'best interests'. It is not to be made by the patient or family members. It is true that, in determining the patient's best interests, doctors may sometimes take into account what is known of the patient's wishes;[34] and in American jurisprudence, the patient's wishes are in some cases a paramount factor in determining his or her best interests, under the 'substituted judgment' test.[35] But the situation is different when the patient has a terminal condition and is not expected to recover consciousness. As Lord Goff observed in *Bland* (after rejecting the American test of substituted judgment as not part of English law):

> ... where the question is whether life support should be withheld from a PVS patient, it is difficult to see how the personality of the patient can be relevant ...[36]

That is, even if it may be relevant in some cases to consider a patient's willingness to accept a severely limited life in preference to being allowed to die when deciding about continuing treatment,[37] it is not relevant if the patient is never likely to regain consciousness. If the patient may become aware of his or her circumstances, it may be proper to take into account the patient's view of a 'life worth living'. But if the patient will not have that opportunity, the patient's wishes for continued treatment (and *a fortiori* the family's wishes) are neither determinative nor relevant, save insofar as the family may have some 'comfort ... if they believe ... that the patient would not have wished his life to be artificially prolonged if he was totally unconscious and there was no hope of improvement in his condition'.[38] Treatment may be lawfully withheld where medical opinion is that it would be 'futile' to continue life-prolonging treatment, regardless of the wishes of the patient or the patient's family. Once the case is categorised as one in which the patient has not

---

34 In Victoria, that is, in fact, required under the legislation; see Guardianship and Administration Act 1986 (Vic) s 38 (definition of 'best interests'); *Medical Treatment Act*, s 5B(2)(b) discussed by Skene, L. 'The *Schiavo* case: could it happen here?' (unpublished), under which it is, in effect, not possible for the Public Advocate or a patient's guardian or agent to refuse treatment on behalf of a patient under the Medical Treatment Act if the patient's prior wish to refuse treatment is not known.

35 The substituted judgment test was neatly stated by Lord Goff in *Bland*, note 13 above, at All ER p. 872 '[I]n the absence of clear and convincing evidence of the patient's wishes, the surrogate decision-maker has to implement as far as possible the decision which the incompetent patient would make if he was competent'.

36 *Id.*

37 See the cases in which courts have accepted such an argument on 'human rights' grounds: L. Skene, 'Withholding and withdrawing treatment in South Australia when patients, parents or guardians insist that treatment must be continued'. (2004) 24(2) *Adelaide Law Review* (in print).

38 *Bland*, note 13 *supra*, at All ER p. 872 per Lord Goff.

earlier refused treatment, either specifically or by implication,[39] then the patient's wishes are no longer determinative.

The recent decision of the Court of Appeal in *Burke*,[40] which was handed down as this chapter went to press, has confirmed this principle. The Court said that Munby J's 'erudition and industry are self-evidently on display throughout [the] 225 pages [of his judgment]' but that 'much of the judge's industry is misplaced' and it would be 'inappropriate to leave the judgment to be seized on and dissected by lawyers seeking supportive material for future cases'.[41] The statements from the Court of Appeal that are most on point for the purpose of the present chapter are the following. Patients do have a 'paramount right to refuse treatment' but 'the corollary does not ... follow'.[42] The judgment continues: 'Autonomy and the right of self determination do not entitle the patient to insist on receiving a particular medical treatment regardless of the nature of the treatment'.[43] Medical staff may have a legal duty to provide treatment but that arises from their relationship with the patient, not from the patient's directions regarding treatment and the duty is not absolute; treatment can be lawfully withdrawn where a competent patient refuses treatment and also 'where the patient is incompetent and it is not considered [by the patient's clinicians] to be in the best interests of the patient to be artificially kept alive'.[44]

The appellant, Mr Burke, did not in fact fall into either of these categories. He is a competent patient who, despite the pain and distress of his condition, wishes to be kept alive and to be assured in advance that that will occur. The Court stated that, in such a case, the hospital would be obliged to continue 'reasonable steps to keep the patient alive'.[45] This principle seems *prima facie* inconsistent with my argument that patients are not legally entitled to require that they be given any treatment contrary to clinical judgment. However, it is clear from the Court of Appeal's judgment that the duty to provide reasonable treatment arises from the relationship with the patient

---

39 Whether personally or by appointing an agent to refuse on the patient's behalf where that is permitted by legislation; that is not allowed by common law.

40 Note 2, *supra*.

41 *Ibid.*, at para 24.

42 *Ibid.*, at para 31.

43 *Id.*

44 *Ibid.*, paras 31-3.

45 *Ibid.*, para 34. The Court indeed went further, suggesting that the deliberate withdrawal of artificial nutrition and hydration (ANH) in the face of a competent patient's expressed wish for it to be continued would amount to murder (paras 34, 53) and also a breach of the Convention (para 39). The statement regarding murder seems in my view open to question, especially if the principle extends beyond ANH. If any continued treatment is considered by the medical carers to be futile or 'contra-indicated' (compare paras 54-5), there is no legal duty to continue it (*Bland*); the patient's wishes cannot change that principle. The criminality of an act or omission causing death has always been determined independently of the victim's wish for death to be expedited; consent is no defence to murder. The statement in the judgment seems to me a concession to Mr Burke personally in the context of his own circumstances (compare para 83).

at common law (the hospital having accepted the patient into its care); and what is 'reasonable' is a clinical decision. The judgment clearly covers the continuance of artificial nutrition and hydration (ANH) at the request of a competent patient but 'reasonable' treatment may not extend to surgery requested by the patient, or ongoing artificial respiration, or even, perhaps, the initiation of ANH that has not yet been instituted.

In conclusion, therefore, it can be seen that the numerous judgments in the *Schiavo* case and the recent judgment of the Court of Appeal in *Burke* clearly demonstrate that patients have a legal right to refuse medical treatment but not to require it to be provided against clinical advice. For this reason, advance directives will be conclusive only when a patient is refusing treatment. If a patient is keen for life-prolonging treatment to be initiated or continued in the final stages of life, the patient's wishes may be considered in determining what is in the patient's best interests but they will not be determinative. The only, very limited, legal right that a competent patient may have to continued treatment is to 'reasonable steps' such as ANH that have already been initiated. The duty to provide treatment of that kind, if it exists, arises from the hospital-patient relationship and not from the patient's wish for the treatment. Beyond this limited situation, courts will not compel clinicians and hospitals to provide treatment that they do not consider to be in the patient's best interests and there is no legal obligation on medical carers to seek court authority before withholding or withdrawing treatment.[46]

46 *Burke*, note 2, *supra*, para 70.

Chapter 27

From *Bland* to *Burke*: The Law and Politics of Assisted Nutrition and Hydration

Sheila A.M. McLean

Introduction

The recent debate on the provision or withholding of artificial or assisted nutrition and hydration (ANH) was ignited by the case of Oliver Leslie Burke, which will be considered in more depth later. However, although the case itself is controversial and complex, it has arguably been decided without context. In what follows, some attempt will be made to contextualise ANH and to show that a case such as *Burke* was always likely to be raised given the manner in which ANH has come to be perceived in law and medicine. That is, it is the location of ANH firmly within the realm of medical treatment which was the genesis of Mr Burke's action. Despite this, the judges considering this action singularly failed to address this question which, it will be argued, is actually at the heart of this matter.

ANH in Context

It might be thought to be common sense that nutrition and hydration are not medical matters; rather they amount to no more than basic care. Certainly, if one has responsibility for another person, to deprive them of food and water would be a criminal offence; murder, if the person subsequently dies as a result.[1] Equally, in most situations in hospital, where a clear duty of care to patients exists, failure to provide food and water would theoretically be a criminal offence.[2]

Of course, ANH might be distinguished from the standard provision of food and water because it is not delivered in the same way. Thus, it might be said, there is a difference between people eating and drinking for themselves and people who require the assistance of medical staff to receive nutrition and hydration. Two issues, however, arise from this. First, there are many people who require assistance in receiving nutrition, yet we provide it anyway; indeed, failure to do so would be

1 *R v. Senior* [1899] 1 QB 283.

2 But see *R v. Arthur* (1981) 12 BMLR 1.

tantamount to murder if the person dies. In respect of the decision in the case of *R v. Arthur*[3] to withhold nutrition and hydration from a Down's Syndrome child, *Mason and McCall Smith's Medical Ethics* say 'to take a such a life is to make a social rather than a medical decision – the fact that it was taken by a doctor rather than a member of the public should be irrelevant'.[4]

Second, merely because medical personnel are involved in, for example, inserting the tube which delivers the ANH and ensuring that the supply is uninterrupted, this does not necessarily mean that it becomes a medical issue. If, for example, lawyers were trained to do this – as undoubtedly they could be – it would not become a 'legal' matter. Thus, the mere fact that nutrition and hydration are delivered by artificial means is insufficient to make it any more of a clinical matter than is the routine provision of food in a hospital.[5] While the insertion of a nasograstric tube requires a degree of skill, it has already been suggested that other, non-medical, personnel could be trained to do this. The fact that something is generally done by someone with medical expertise does not necessarily make it medical. Indeed, ANH has been described as 'relatively simple and straightforward and a routine staple of day-to-day medical practice in hospitals up and down the land ...'.[6]

This matters because, once categorised as medical treatment rather than basic care, the question as to its provision or not is judged by different standards. Whereas my failure to feed my child – no matter what the reason – would amount to a criminal offence, special rules exist when events, actions or omissions are deemed to be medical rather than more broadly social.[7] The behaviour of doctors is judged in large part by the now-modified *Bolam* test,[8] derived from the case of *Bolam v. Friern Hospital Management Committee.*[9] Therefore, the test applied when ANH is under consideration is not the rightness or wrongness of depriving someone of nutrition and hydration; rather, it becomes what would a reasonable doctor do in the circumstances? This test has been widely criticised,[10] and as has been noted, it has undergone some modification over the decades since it was decided. Nonetheless, there remains a reliance on acceptable or responsible medical behaviour, as judged theoretically by the law but in practice substantially by doctors themselves, which

3 *Supra cit.*

4 *Mason and McCall Smith's Law and Medical Ethics*, (7th ed) Oxford, Oxford University Press, 2006, p. 547, para 16.23.

5 For further discussion, see McLean, S.A.M., 'Is there a legal threat to medicine?', *Journal of the Voluntary Euthanasia Society of Scotland*, Special Edition, September 1993.

6 *R (on the application of Burke) v. General Medical Council*, (2004) 79 BMLR 126, per Mr Justice Munby, at p. 140.

7 See, for example, the case of *R v. Arthur, supra cit.*

8 See for example, the cases of *Bolitho v. City and Hackney Health Authority*, (1997) 39 BMLR 1; *Pearce v. United Bristol Healthcare NHS Trust*, (1999) 48 BMLR 118.

9 [1957] 2 All ER 118.

10 See, for example, McLean, S.A.M., *A Patient's Right to Know: Information Disclosure, the Doctor and the Law*, Aldershot, Dartmouth, 1989 (Paperback 1995); *Mason and McCall Smith's Law and Medical Ethics, supra cit.*

disguises the value-laden nature of the decision itself. The presumption that once something can be called 'medical' it becomes value-free is one which can and should be resisted, yet it is one that, as we will see, has apparently become common currency in our courts of law.[11]

Airedale NHS Trust v. Bland[12]

Although the non-provision of nourishment had already been considered in a UK court in the case of *R v. Arthur*,[13] it was the case of Anthony Bland that focussed critical attention on ANH. Whereas in the *Arthur* case, the doctor decided against even providing assisted nutrition and hydration, in the *Bland* case it was already in place. The question was whether or not it could lawfully be removed.

It will be recalled that Tony Bland was a young man injured in a disaster at a football ground. He was subsequently diagnosed as being in a persistent (now permanent) vegetative state (PVS). Accurate diagnosis of this condition means that the person concerned can breathe on his own, but has essentially no higher brain function. In essence, he will never be aware of his circumstances and although existence can be maintained for many years in some cases, there is apparently no prospect of recovery. In other words, as Lord Goff put it in the House of Lords, the patient exists in a state equivalent to a 'living death'.[14] In order to maintain a patient in this situation, it will be necessary to provide ANH as the patient clearly is unable to feed himself. It will also probably be necessary to provide other services, such as antibiotics, which are clearly medical in nature, but the question as to whether or not ANH is medical treatment is crucial to the outcome for the patient.

Management of patients in this situation is not simple. On the one hand, provision of ANH can sustain life for some time; on the other, few people would choose to live in such a condition. Moreover, although we are normally assured that resources should never be involved in life and death decisions it is impossible to avoid consideration of whether or not maintaining this 'living death' is in fact a sensible use of resources which seem destined never to meet the demands placed upon them. The crux of the question, then, hinges on how we are to judge the provision of ANH? If it is basic care, then it is clear that it must be provided, unless we are prepared to say that we sanction the deliberate judgment that a person's life is not worth living; that s/he would be as well off, if not better off, dead. This is undoubtedly a difficult pill to swallow, but as will be suggested *infra*, it is arguably what *in fact* we are doing. If, however, ANH is medical treatment then, as we have seen, its provision or withdrawal will be judged against different standards which, it will be argued, obfuscate the reality of what is going on.

---

11 For further discussion, see McLean, S.A.M., *Old Law, New Medicine*, London, Rivers Oram/Pandora, 1999.

12 *Airedale NHS Trust v. Bland*, (1993) 12 BMLR 64.

13 *Supra cit.*

14 *Supra*, note 14, at p. 111.

The inclusion of ANH within the medical model is a direct consequence of the *Bland* judgment, which enabled – perhaps encouraged – the General Medical Council (GMC) to include ANH in its guidance on managing life-prolonging measures.[15] Before addressing the GMC guidelines, it is important to evaluate the basis on which Their Lordships in this case were persuaded that ANH was indeed medical treatment rather than basic care. For Lord Keith, the decision fell to be measured in this way:

> This was coupled with the argument that feeding by means of nasogastric tube was not medical treatment at all, but simply feeding indistinguishable from feeding by normal means. I am of the opinion that regard should be had to the whole regime, including the artificial feeding, which at present keeps Anthony Bland alive. That regime amounts to medical treatment and care, and it is incorrect to direct attention exclusively to the fact that nourishment is being provided. In any event, the administration of nourishment by the means adopted involves the application of a medical technique.[16]

For him, then, the fact that ANH was part of the whole of the care being provided was sufficient for it to be categorised as medical. However, it must be asked whether this is a robust assertion. Part of the care of a patient in PVS will also include, for example, washing him. Are we to presume therefore that this simple, respectful, task is medical treatment, and that its provision or withholding can and should be judged on a medical rather than a social basis; on the basis of clinical considerations rather than common decency?

For Lord Goff, the question was even more easily answered:

> There is overwhelming evidence that, in the medical profession, artificial feeding is regarded as a form of medical treatment; and, even if it is not strictly medical treatment, it must form part of the medical care of the patient.[17]

If anything, arguably this is an even more dubious basis on which to conclude, particularly since the consequences for the patient are potentially so serious. That is, to suggest that because doctors *think* ANH is medical treatment it must be so, is to surrender the moral and ethical debate to clinicians, who are no better than anyone else at making such decisions, and is to expand the discrete area of expertise to which they may lay claim. As Lord Browne-Wilkinson said, '... behind the questions of law lie moral, ethical, medical and practical issues of fundamental importance to society'.[18] Indeed, as Lord Mustill pointed out, what was actually happening was that '... the authority of the state, through the medium of the court, is being invoked to permit one group of its citizens to terminate the life of another'.[19]

---

15 *Withholding and Withdrawing Life-prolonging Treatments: Good Practice in Decision-making*, London, GMC, 2002.

16 *Supra*, note 14, at p. 106.

17 *Ibid*., at p. 117.

18 *Ibid*., at p. 124.

19 *Ibid*., at p. 131.

If there is any doubt about the significance of categorising ANH as medical treatment, it must surely be assuaged by the way in which the *Bland* decision was reached. Having satisfied themselves that ANH is medical treatment, most of Their Lordships were able to retreat to more familiar decision-making territory. Lord Goff, for example, said:

> … I cannot see that medical treatment is appropriate or requisite simply to prolong a patient's life when such treatment has no therapeutic purpose of any kind, as where it is futile because the patient is unconscious and there is no prospect of any improvement in his condition.[20]

This sentiment was largely echoed by Lord Browne-Wilkinson, who said:

> In my judgment it must follow from this that, if there comes a stage where the responsible doctor comes to the reasonable conclusion (which accords with the views of a responsible body of medical opinion) that further continuance of an intrusive life support system is not in the best interests of the patient, he can no longer lawfully continue that life support system: to do so would constitute the crime of battery and the tort of trespass to the person. Therefore he cannot be in breach of any duty to maintain the patient's life. Therefore he is not guilty of murder by omission.[21]

Thus, the fact that ANH was categorised as medical treatment rather than basic care was sufficient to reduce the stringency of the tests used to measure its 'rightness' or 'wrongness'. Basic ethical principles – for example the sanctity of life or even respect for persons – give way to the professional judgment of the healthcare team. It is clear, of course, that the sanctity of life principle is not always dominant in court decisions, although it is constantly referred to. For example, In *Re H*,[22] a case concerning a severely brain damaged woman who was not technically in a PVS, the court said:

> The sanctity of life is of vital importance. It is not, however, paramount and … I am satisfied that it is in the best interests of this patient that the life sustaining treatment … should be brought to a conclusion.[23]

The point, however, is that when the sanctity of life principle is not paramount, this is generally because either the patient has refused treatment or it cannot be said to be in the best interests of the patient. This latter is a judgment which transcends the medical and should not therefore be based on what doctors would normally do, or even what doctors believe is the right thing to do. Yet, in the *Bland* judgment, Lord Browne-Wilkinson was clear that the ultimate decision as to benefits or best interests was for doctors, saying:

---

20 *Ibid.*, at p. 116.

21 *Ibid.*, at p. 129.

22 *Re H (adult: incompetent)*, (1997) 38 BMLR 11.

23 *Ibid.*, at p. 16.

> Only if the doctors responsible for his care hold the view that, though he is aware of nothing, there is some benefit to him in staying alive, would there be anything to indicate that it is for his benefit to continue the invasive medical care.[24]

The GMC Guidance[25]

Following the *Bland* judgment, the GMC issued guidance to doctors on the cessation of life-prolonging treatment, including ANH. As these were at the heart of Mr Burke's case, they are worth referring to in some detail. Specifically on the subject of ANH the guidelines run as follows:

> Decisions involving artificial nutrition or hydration may be particularly difficult and/or contentious. In part this is because the benefits and burdens of either nutrition or hydration may not be well known and involve difficult assessments of the patient. For example, patients in the later stages of a progressive or severely disabling condition, where their body systems begin to shut down, may increasingly lose interest in food or drink. For some patients not taking nutrition or hydration may be part of the natural dying process. Problems in making assessments can arise because some patients may under-report their symptoms, while perceptions may differ between doctors, members of the health care team and those close to a patient, about the presence or severity of symptoms such as pain.[26]

The guidance continues:

> In the face of such uncertainties, there may be concern about the possibility that a patient who is unconscious or semi-conscious, and whose wishes cannot be determined, might experience distressing symptoms and complications or otherwise be suffering, because their needs for nutrition or hydration are not being met. Alternatively there may be concern that attempts to meet the patient's needs may cause avoidable suffering. For some people there may be emotional difficulties in deciding not to provide what they see as basic nurture for the patient.[27]
>
> In view of these considerations, it is essential that doctors ensure that those involved in making the decision are provided with clear and up to date information about what is known of the benefits, burdens and risks of providing nutrition and hydration through artificial means, and information about the basis on which the particular patient's needs have been assessed. It is also essential that doctors making decisions about artificial nutrition and hydration take careful account of the principles of good practice set out in this guidance.[28]

---

24 *Supra*, note 14, at p. 130.

25 *Withholding and Withdrawing Life-prolonging Treatments: Good Practice in Decision-making*, London, GMC, 2002.

26 *Ibid.*, para 22.

27 *Ibid.*, para 23.

28 *Ibid.*, para 24.

Noting that a competent patient has a right to make his or her own decisions about the acceptability of treatment, the guidance affirms that:

> Adult competent patients have the right to decide how much weight to attach to the benefits, burdens, risks, and the overall acceptability of any treatment. They have the right to refuse treatment even where refusal may result in harm to themselves or in their own death, and doctors are legally bound to respect their decision. Adult patients who have the capacity to make their own decision can express their wishes about future treatment in an advance statement.[29]

However, for the patient in PVS this general right to make autonomous – even life-threatening – treatment decisions is inapplicable and it will be left to others to speculate, and ultimately decide, on what amounts to the best way forward. The fact that the sanctity of life principle does not always predominate leaves scope for decisions that effectively mean that it will be deemed not to be in a person's interests to survive. Making that decision a predominantly or purely clinical one means that – despite what the guidance says – it will probably inevitably reflect the views of the doctors concerned as to the quality of that person's life. Moreover, as was Mr Burke's concern, an individual's own position on the provision of life-sustaining treatment may be disregarded when that person is no longer able to express it. This is despite the robust statement of Sir Thomas Bingham MR in the case of *Frenchay Healthcare NHS Trust v. S*[30] where he said:

> It is, I think, important that there should not be a belief that what the doctor says is in the patient's best interest is the patient's best interest. For my part I would certainly reserve to the court the ultimate power and duty to review the doctor's decision in the light of all the facts.[31]

Of course, ideally the patient's own wishes would be those which inform any decisions. Although the guidance notes that a person can prepare an advance statement of wishes which – if valid and applicable in the circumstances – will effectively bind the doctor, this has always been assumed only to apply to the refusal of life-sustaining treatment, not its provision. Because the decision as to whether or not to withhold or withdraw 'treatment' is now clearly categorised as a medical one, the patient can control only that aspect of the decision which depends on his consent. Thus, to force treatment on an unwilling patient (or one who has expressly rejected it in an advance directive) would be to assault that patient.[32] It is accepted that patients cannot force doctors to provide treatment that is regarded as futile,[33] unduly burdensome or without benefit. Each of these raises separate but similar questions.

---

29 *Ibid.*, para 13.

30 (1994) 17 BMLR 156.

31 *Ibid.*, at p. 164.

32 See *Re C (adult: refusal of treatment)*, (1994) 15 BMLR 77; *Ms B v. An NHS Hospital Trust*, (2002) 65 BMLR 149

33 However this is defined.

For example, even if we accept that ANH is medical treatment, can treatment *in fact* be burdensome if the person is unable to experience it? On the other hand, if – as we are constantly told – life is always a benefit, how can the provision of 'treatment' be said to be a benefit? Finally, can ANH be described as futile?

The purpose of ANH arguably is to keep the patient alive. It is not directly related in PVS cases, or cases where the person is in the process of dying, to effecting a cure. However, irrespective of the quality or length of the life ANH can sustain, its provision is certainly not futile, as it achieves precisely what it is intended to: that is, it keeps the patient alive. Equally, if it is not normally regarded as being unduly burdensome in other cases, it must be asked why it should be so regarded for the patient at the end of life. The answer must surely be that what is actually being evaluated – by doctors and perhaps relatives – is the perceived quality of the patient's life. This may be inevitable – even unobjectionable – but it is in no obvious way a medical decision.

The Burke Judgments

Oliver Leslie Burke has a degenerative condition known as cerebellar ataxia. In time, his condition will predictably deteriorate to the point where – prior to becoming comatose – he will be unable to perform ordinary bodily functions by himself and will need assistance in every aspect of his life, such as obtaining nutrition and hydration. Despite this he will be able to think, and to appreciate his surroundings. Mr Burke was concerned that the terms of the GMC's guidelines might result in him being deprived of nutrition and hydration, and that he would suffer the prolonged and distressing dying process which that deprivation would cause. Accordingly, he challenged the lawfulness of certain parts of the guidance, claiming that they infringed on his human rights as guaranteed by the European Convention on Human Rights which was incorporated into UK law by the Human Rights Act 1998.[34]

At the first hearing of the case,[35] Munby J was satisfied that sections of the guidance were in breach of his rights and found largely in Mr Burke's favour. Munby's judgment is extremely long and ranges over a wide range of issues, a source of some criticism from the Court of Appeal when it subsequently heard this case,[36] and it is not possible to consider it in the depth it undoubtedly deserves. However, there are some aspects of his judgment that are of particular interest for this discussion. First, he repeated that the starting point should always be a presumption in favour of saving life, but also acknowledged that this is not always the preferable outcome, saying '… the starting point … must be the very strong presumption in favour of taking all steps which will prolong life. Save in exceptional circumstances, or where

34 *R (on the application of Burke) v. General Medical Council*, (2004) 79 BMLR 126.
35 *R (on the application of Burke) v. General Medical Council*, (2004) 79 BMLR 126.
36 *Burke v. GMC*, [2005] EWCA Civ 1003 (28 July 2005).

the patient is dying, the best interests of the patient will normally require such steps to be taken'.[37]

From his perspective, it followed that if a patient wanted to continue receiving treatment, in this case ANH, it was for him and him alone to make that decision, at least for as long as he is aware of what is happening. Article 3 of the Convention (prohibition on cruel and inhumane treatment) and Article 8 (broadly the right to self-determination) would be engaged were people to be denied treatment, at least until the point at which the patient was no longer self-aware. As he said, however:

> ... it is one thing to say that the effect of art 8 and art 3 is to require the continuation of ANH for a patient who wants it, who retains some awareness of his surroundings and predicament and who therefore continues to be exposed to the possibility of acute mental and physical suffering. It is a very different thing to assert that art 8, whether alone or in conjunction with art 3, requires the continuation in *all* circumstances of ANH during the final hours of a dying and comatose patient. In my judgment it does not. Nor does art 2[38] [Article 2 is the right to life article].

Thus, in Mr Burke's circumstances, permitting a medical decision to withdraw or withhold ANH when he was able to experience this would be to breach some of his human rights. Munby also, however, seemed potentially to contradict his previously quoted statement when he argued that it could be a breach of his Article 3 right to do so even if he was unable to experience it. In this he challenged the earlier judgment of Dame Elizabeth Butler-Sloss in the case of *NHS Trust A v. M* and *NHS Trust B v. H* which had indicated that a person had to be able to experience the degrading treatment before Article 3 could be engaged.[39] For Munby:

> ... however unconscious or unaware of ill-treatment a particular incompetent adult or a baby may be, treatment which has the effect on those who witness it of degrading the individual may come within art 3. Otherwise ... the Convention's emphasis on the protection of the vulnerable may be circumvented.[40]

Underpinning Munby's position was the fundamental rejection of the dominance of medical decision making in life and death matters, although – perhaps strangely – he did not address the question central to this argument; that is, whether or not ANH was properly conceptualised as medical treatment. Indirectly, however, he did so by couching the question from the basis of who would be the appropriate decision-makers, saying:

---

37 *Supra*, note 14, at p. 163.

38 *Ibid.*, at p. 184.

39 58 BMLR 87. More recently this position was confirmed in *NHS Trust v. I*, [2003] EWHC 2243.

40 *Supra*, note 14, at p. 177.

> … the decision as to what is in fact in the patient's best interests is not for the doctor: it is for the patient if competent or, if the patient is incompetent and the matter comes to court, for the judge.[41]

However, in a somewhat snippy judgment the Court of Appeal showed some impatience both with the length of Munby's judgment and with its content. In addition, the Court was unhappy that Munby had allowed the court to be used as 'a general advice centre'.[42] It was also somewhat suspicious of the motivation for the raising of the case in the first place, saying:

> The manner and circumstances in which these proceedings were commenced suggest that he was persuaded to advance a claim for judicial review by persons who wished to challenge aspects of the GMC Guidance which had no relevance to a man in Mr Burke's condition.[43]

Before turning to the central argument, the Court of Appeal also identified three areas which had been given weight in Munby's judgment and about which they were concerned; namely, patients' rights to choose specific treatments, the situation where life-sustaining treatment can be withdrawn from an incompetent patient and the question of whether or not court approval is needed before such a withdrawal.[44] The Court was concerned about these aspects of the earlier judgment because they seemed to go beyond what was required to consider Mr Burke's circumstances.

In reaching its conclusion to overturn Munby's decision that parts of the GMC guidelines were unlawful,[45] the Court nonetheless conceded that 'the facts of the individual case may make it difficult to decide whether the duty to keep the patient alive persists'.[46] The duty to provide ANH was, it said not absolute, and the exceptions were described as being:

> (1) where the competent patient refuses to receive ANH and (2) where the patient is not competent and it is not considered to be in the best interests of the patient to be artificially kept alive.[47]

Recognising that the second category has been the more difficult to interpret, the Court nonetheless indicated that this was not problematic in Mr Burke's case, saying:

> No authority lends the slightest countenance to the suggestion that the duty on the doctors to take reasonable steps to keep the patient alive in such circumstances may not persist.

---

41 *Ibid.*, at pp. 159-160.

42 *Supra*, note 38, para 21.

43 *Ibid.*, para 14.

44 *Ibid.*, para 48.

45 *Ibid.*, para 47: '…we do not consider that, insofar as the Guidance relates to Mr Burke's predicament, there was any ground for declaring it unlawful.'

46 *Ibid.*, para 33.

47 *Id.*

> Indeed, it seems to us that for a doctor deliberately to interrupt life-prolonging treatment in the face of a competent patient's expressed wish to be kept alive, with the intention of thereby terminating the patient's life, would leave the doctor with no answer to a charge of murder.[48]

Central to Munby's judgment was the concept that a patient has a right to choose what treatments should be made available, although he did concede that doctors could not be forced to provide treatment that they regarded as futile or unduly burdensome.[49] However, the Court of Appeal conceptualised patient choice in a different way, declaring it to be 'no more than a reflection of the fact that it is the doctor's duty to provide a treatment the he considers to be in the interests of the patient and that the patient is prepared to accept'.[50]

It must be said that this is a rather weak description of a right to choose, and certainly is not one to we would normally subscribe. Recognition of the right to make healthcare choices has grown in strength over the years, so that it is often seen as independent of clinical decisions. For example, the right to choose to decline even life-saving[51] or life-sustaining[52] medical treatment would clearly in some cases offend the clinical view of what is in the best interests of the patient, yet it trumps clinical judgments. Instead, as a consequence of the Court of Appeal's characterisation of the right to choose, it became clear that medical judgment predominates. For the Court of Appeal:

> Where life depends upon the continued provision of ANH there can be no question of the supply of ANH not being clinically indicated *unless a clinical decision has been taken that the life in question should come to an end*[53] (emphasis added).

This overt declaration that doctors may decide that a life should come to an end is unusual. Generally courts go to great lengths to avoid characterising non-treatment decisions in this way by, however disingenuously, declaring that the court does not sanction the taking of a life; rather, it simply pronounces on whether or not it is in a patient's best interests to have their life sustained. This distinction, which has always been suspect, did not apparently commend itself to the Court of Appeal, whose honesty is to be commended, even if – taken to its logical conclusion – it would turn current law on its head.

Clinical decision making in these circumstances, therefore, could trump the decisions of patients, even although the GMC's own guidelines make it clear that such decisions 'may be particularly difficult and/or contentious'[54] because 'the benefits and burdens of either nutrition or hydration may not be well known and

48 *Ibid.*, para 34.
49 *Supra*, note 14, at p. 191.
50 *Supra*, note 38, para 51.
51 *Re C (adult: refusal of treatment)*, (1994) 15 BMLR 77.
52 *Ms B v. An NHS Hospital Trust*, (2002) 65 BMLR 149.
53 *Supra*, note 38, para 53.
54 *Ibid.*, para 22.

involve difficult assessments of the patient'.[55] Unsurprisingly, the Court of Appeal judgment was welcomed by the CMC,[56] although it was greeted with less enthusiasm by the Disability Rights Commission whose Chairman said:

> Many disabled people fear that some doctors make negative, stereotypical assumptions about their quality of life. This ruling will not allay many of their fears. If you become incompetent someone else can still decide what is burdensome and what is in your best interests.[57]

ANH: Law and Politics

What the *Burke* judgments have achieved, then, is the further entrenchment in law of the notion that ANH is indeed medical treatment. Thus, the decision about whether or not it should be provided is one that sits firmly within the medical professionals' competence, which – it has been argued – has continued to expand to include matters which are only tangentially medical. Kennedy, for example, has said that 'the scope of the alleged unique competence of the doctor has become as wide, as imprecise and as flexible as the meanings given to the notions of health and ill-health.[58] It must surely be correct that doctors should not be forced to provide treatment which they believe will either not help, or at worst will hurt, their patients. It was also accepted by the Court of Appeal that sometimes the delivery of ANH can indeed be unpleasant as well as futile. The question, however, is whether, in cases where it is not, it should be withdrawn against the express wishes of the patient, even if s/he is no longer competent but has expressed the desire before lapsing into incompetence that it should be continued. Indeed, even where it is unpleasant, if the patient asks for its continuance, surely this suggests that s/he is willing to accept this unpleasantness in order to stay alive? Further, if ANH were continued beyond the point at which the patient was unable to experience the unpleasantness, how can this be used as a justification for removing it?

As has already been argued, much of what we regard as basic care – such as, for example, wiping patients' faces – will be continued irrespective of the condition of the patient. To do any less would be completely to ignore the respect that is due even to the terminally ill or comatose. Although this task falls within the clinical management of the patient, its provision is regarded as necessary and is not categorised as 'medical'. What, then, differentiates ANH? It cannot be that it is delivered as part of the whole medical management of the patient, because this

---

55 *Id.*

56 Available at: http://www.gmcpressoffice.org.uk/apps/news/latest/print.php?key=181 accessed on 08/08/05.

57 Available at: http://www.drc-gb.org/newsroom/newsdetails.asp?id=833&section=1 accessed on 08/08/05.

58 Kennedy, I., *Treat Me Rights: Essays in Medical Law and Ethics*, Oxford, Clarendon Press, 1988 (reprinted in 1994), at p. 23.

would apply to other ways in which the patient is treated, but which will continue to be provided. It cannot be that it is delivered by a healthcare professional, who has the right to refuse to provide futile treatment, since ANH is no more futile than face washing; that is, both achieve their intended outcome.

In fact, what differentiates ANH from other care that might be delivered irrespective of the patient's prognosis or condition is that it has been – without any real argument – characterised as medical treatment. This may have been convenient, but it arguably should have been given more consideration, because the consequences are potentially important for patients. Both of the *Burke* judgments indicated that, once Mr Burke becomes unaware of his situation, it would be permissible to remove ANH. This is dependent on ANH being seen as medical treatment rather than basic care, which will be continued until death. The presumption, as was the case in *Bland*, was that at this stage the matter becomes clinical, not personal. The individual has lost the capacity to be self-aware or self-directing and others must decide whether he should live or die. However, even if we can accept this, it ignores the possibility that s/he will live in distress *now* in contemplation of death being brought about deliberately and in a manner to which s/he clearly objects, even if s/he is unaware of it when it happens. Munby's insistence that Article 3 rights extend even to those who are no longer aware of the degradation that may accompany their death must have raised the hopes of those with particular concern about the treatment of people at the end of their lives. That this was not directly endorsed by the Court of Appeal will doubtless generate concern.

So far, it has been argued that it is the categorisation of ANH as medical treatment which leads to a conclusion which is either illogical or disrespectful. However, it is plausible that even more lies behind the Appeal Court's judgment than meets the eye.

In a commentary on the first hearing of this case, Mason and Laurie point to the fact that Munby's judgment could not in logic be constrained to ANH.[59] If ANH is medical treatment, and if the patient had the right to require ANH (at least until he is unconscious and in the final stages of the process of dying), then, they argue, this must apply to all end of life care. If this is not what is intended, they continue, Munby gave 'arguably insufficient emphasis ... to the reasons why and how we should distinguish between ANH as *basic care* and other forms of treatment'.[60] In fact, as I have suggested, it was not just that the analysis was inadequate; essentially, as in the Court of Appeal, it was entirely absent.

Failure to make any such distinction means that the decision must be scrutinised in the same way as would be other decisions about healthcare resources and their best or most appropriate uses. Indeed, in supporting the GMC's appeal against Munby's judgment, a lawyer for the Health Secretary, Patricia Hewitt indicated that '[t]he

59 Mason, J.K. and Laurie, G.T., 'Personal autonomy and the right to treatment: A note on *R (on the application of Burke) v. General Medical Council*', *Edin L.R.*, Vol 9, pp. 123-132 (2005).

60 *Loc cit.*, at p. 131.

National Health Service should not have to give life-prolonging treatment to every patient who demands it because that would mean a crippling waste of resources'.[61] However, the prolongation of the provision of ANH is unlikely to bankrupt the NHS in circumstances such as those experienced by Mr Burke, and others like him. Since he would in any event be given ANH – as was made clear in both hearings of his case – until he had very little time left to live, it cannot surely be said that its continued provision until the end would be excessively expensive. It would, however – at least for Mr Burke – be respectful of him and his wishes.

Of course, in some cases, such as a person in PVS, the provision of ANH might be required for many years, and this would be a strain on already tight resources. There are, however, other ways of managing this situation without declaring ANH to be medical treatment. Patients in PVS will almost certainly at some stage require the provision of services, such as antibiotics, which indubitably *are* medical treatments. If it can be agreed to be appropriate that medical treatment can, in certain circumstances, be withdrawn or withheld, then surely the patient could be managed in this way? If, as is clear, the aim is to bring about the patient's death, their very vulnerability will make that possible, without having to deny them the essentials of life.

Because, however, ANH is agreed to be medical treatment, any suggestion that the views of patients should be determinative would mean that *all* treatment which they request should be provided. This would undoubtedly have grave resource-based consequences for the health service. Mason and Laurie suggest, however, that Munby did not need to have gone so far as to make this sweeping generalisation, saying:

> The same position could have been reached via a dignity-based analysis, by arguing for example, that to remove such basic care as feeding and hydration is – objectively assessed – an affront to human dignity, and that a continuing *obligation* to provide such care is required.[62]

With respect, however, this was arguably not a course of action available to Munby (or to the judges in the Court of Appeal). The *Bland* case made it clear that ANH *is* medical treatment; as such, the decision whether or not to provide it falls within a medicalised analysis of care provision, as set out specifically in the GMC guidelines. The precedent is set. It would not have been possible for a judge at first instance to stand the law as described in the House of Lords on its head. Intellectually, of course, the argument from respect for persons can be made – as is attempted in this chapter – but it is effectively not available to the courts.

In the meantime, other cases continue to emerge where doctors wish not to provide treatment which the patient wants to receive,[63] and a series of post-*Bland*

61 Statement available at: http://www.timesonine.co.uk/newspaper/0,,173-1618268,00.html accessed on 19/05/05.

62 Mason and Laurie, *loc cit.*, at p. 132.

63 See the case of 'Mr A', discussed at length in *The Herald*, 17/08/05.

cases have widened the range of those for whom non-provision of ANH has been held to be lawful.[64]

Conclusion

The characterisation of ANH as medical treatment has, as could surely have been anticipated, had profound consequences. Capitulation to the medical view of what they are doing has led to a situation in which the basics of life can be removed with the explicit aim of ending that life. There are two major concerns about this. First, if we accept Munby's interpretation of the intended protection of Article 3 of the Convention on Human Rights – and I submit that we should – it is difficult not to characterise death by dehydration as falling within its prohibition on degrading treatment. Second, for patients like Mr Burke, no account was seemingly taken of the *current* effect on him of the knowledge that he may well die in a way to which he has a specific objection.

For the patient in PVS, continuing ANH may prolong life for many years, and may indeed be an expensive and ultimately useless waste of resources, unless preserving all life at any cost is the principle underpinning our society and our law. Clearly, it is not, and many would object to any suggestion that ANH should be continued in hopeless cases such as this. However, managing a patient in PVS will generally require more than this; for example, the provision of antibiotics consequent on the episodic infections to which people in this situation are subject. Failure to offer this kind of treatment would likely also result in death, but offends less acutely those who maintain that food and water are basic care; not medical treatment. If the intention, as it clearly was, was to bring about Anthony Bland's death, this could almost certainly have been achieved in ways other than the reclassification of food and water from basic care to medical treatment.

It is tempting to postulate that two issues were significant here. First, the courts are reluctant ever to agree that they sanction steps to bring about a death knowingly and intentionally. Indeed, some of Their Lordships in the *Bland* case preferred to conceptualise what was happening as nature taking its course. This intellectual sleight of hand ignored the fact that in itself PVS is not a terminal condition. In fact, what was happening was that the Court handed to the doctors the right to bring about the death of the patient. Therefore, to avoid allegations that this was in fact euthanasia, a second step became necessary; namely, to 'neutralise' the event by declaring it to be a matter of professional clinical judgment.

Medical practitioners all too often are confronted with difficult choices, some of which will result in the death of their patient. They are not, it is argued here, assisted by the inappropriate handing over to them of the kinds of decisions which relate

---

64 See, for example, *Re D*, (1997) 38 BMLR 1, *Re G (adult incompetent: withdrawal of treatment*, (2001) 65 BMLR 6.

more to ethical and legal matters than to the purely clinical.[65] Disentangling nutrition and hydration from the clinical arena may have a cost in resource terms; failure to do so has a cost in terms of humanity. Arguably, we should prioritise the latter over the former.

65 For further discussion, see McLean, S.A.M., *Old Law, New Medicine*, London, Rivers Oram/Pandora, 1999.

Chapter 28

Euthanasia as a Human Right

Tom Campbell

Introduction

The core arguments over the legalisation of euthanasia do not seem to have changed much over the 30 years or so that that Ken Mason has contributed to the discussion of this contentious issue.[1] A recent London revival of Brian Clark's play 'Whose Life is it Anyway?', concerning the personal reflections and resistance to official medical and legal orthodoxies on the part of a paralysed but fully conscious woman, is as starkly relevant as it was when first performed in 1978. Self-determination, now more frequently referred to as 'autonomy', remains pitted against the culturally entrenched prohibition on killing innocent persons, with both sides drawing different conclusions from the often miserable plight of the unfortunate persons involved.

Majority opinion in most developed countries supports some more proactive way of managing the dying process than leaving people to die 'naturally', supplemented by the ('unnatural?') administration of opiates,[2] but it is thwarted politically by rightly cautious judiciaries unwilling to depart on their own authority from the traditional prohibition of intentional killing,[3] and by a general reluctance of elected representatives to take on organised medical and religious opinion.[4] In consequence we remain stuck, officially, with healthcare regimes that permit only the withholding or withdrawal of treatment (sometimes including artificial feeding)

---

1 See Mason, J.K., 'Death and Dying: One Step at a Time?', in McLean, S.A.M. (ed), *Death, Dying and the Law*, Dartmouth, 1996: 161-178; Mason, J.K. and Mulligan, D., 'Euthanasia by Stages', 347 *Lancet*, 1996: 810-11; Mason, J.K., McCall Smith, R.A. and Laurie, G.T., *Law and Medical Ethics* (6th ed), London, Butterworths, 2002.

2 Thus, in Australia, Morgan Poll Finding No 2768, 78 per cent of respondents were in favour of doctors being able to give patients a lethal dose if required by a hopelessly ill patient in great pain.

3 See *Pretty v. The United Kingdom* (appln no 2346/02): available at: http://www.echr.coe.inf.

4 Rare exceptions include the Netherlands; in the US, Oregon's Death with Dignity Act (1994) and, in Australia, the Northern Territory, where the Legislative Assembly, after prolonged public debate, passed into law by a majority of 13 votes to 12, the Rights of the Terminally Ill Act 1995 (NT), only to have it overturned by a private member's bill in the Federal Parliament in 1997. For the Netherlands, see de Haan, J., 'The New Dutch Law on Euthanasia', 10 *Medical Law Review*, 2002, 57-75.

and the use of pain-killing drugs that may be or may not be effective and may or may not ('unintentionally') hasten the death of those involved, an official system that is mercifully moderated by the unofficial practice of a significant minority of healthcare professionals, often in connivance with distressed relatives, who take positive moves to end the lives of those in ghastly situations when there is no effective treatment to cure their ailment and nothing they can do for themselves to end their painful or pointless existences.[5]

This brief and somewhat polemical analysis fails to capture the complex variety of medical scenarios that occur on a daily basis mainly in, but also outside, hospitals, and the diverse mix of conflicting ideologies that confront each other over the samples of personal horrors that surface in legal cases from time to time.[6] The variables involved include the nature of the diagnosis, the prognosis in the light of available treatments, the imminence of death, the present and foreseeable quality of life of the person, the extent and nature of the pain and suffering of the person, the degree to which that can be controlled, and the effect that palliates have on the intellectual and emotional capacities of the sick person, the person's personal values, relationships and beliefs and the resources available to be deployed. There are major morally relevant differences between, for instance: (1) fully conscious but permanently physically paralysed young persons suffering only in consequence of their paralysis, (2) elderly demented people with painful and distressing symptoms but no prospect of an early death, and (3) fully conscious people who know that they and their family are facing a fraught process in which they will die a painful death that can be alleviated, only marginally, by means of mentally incapacitating medicines and (4) people in persistent vegetative states whose biological lives may be prolonged indefinitely. Nevertheless, each of these scenarios shares the common factor that in each case current criminal laws rule out a particular option which is relevant to their circumstances: intentionally bringing about the death of the person concerned, by actively assisting in the suicide of the patient (medically assisted suicide) or by the intentional killing of the persons involved (active euthanasia). I will call this the euthanasia option.

The absence of the euthanasia option undoubtedly results in a great deal of unnecessary suffering, which in some cases is simply horrendous ('undignified' is too weak a term) and, in other cases, deprives people of their preferred mode of exiting this life before their quality of life deteriorates to a level they find unacceptable. Why

5 See, for instance, Ginger, P. and Kuhse, H., 'Doctors' practices and attitudes regarding voluntary euthanasia', 148 *Medical Journal of Australia*, 1988, 623-27. Medical practitioners who quite openly practice voluntary euthanasia are rarely prosecuted and even more rarely convicted (but see *R. v. Cox*, [1992] 12 BMLR 38).

6 For instance, Karen Quinlan (*In the matter of Karen Anne Quinlan*, 355 A 2d 647 (1976) NJ SC); Elizabeth Bouvia (*Bouvia v. Superior Court*, 225 California Reporter 297, T App 1986); Nancy Cruzan (*Cruzan v. Director, Missouri Department of Health*, 497 US 261 (1990); Anthony Bland (*Airedale NHS Trust v. Bland*, [1993] 1 All ER 821, HL); Diane Pretty (*R. v. DPP*, [2002] 1 All ER 1, HL); Sue Rodriguez (*Rodriguez v. British Columbia A-G*, (1993) 82 BCLP (2d) 273).

then has there been so little progress in resolving these issues? Philosophers tell us that our inherited moral frameworks are ill adapted to this and many other issues relating to the life and death of humans and other conscious beings and need radical revision if we are to adapt to medical and moral advances. Psychologists tell us that our way of dealing with our awareness of mortality is to suppress thoughts of death and dying, thus explaining our failure to confront the reality of our own demise and our unpardonable neglect of those who are going through the process, particularly when they are elderly and/or incompetent. We simply do not want to know. Political scientists tell us that there are powerful and intense minorities within medical and religious establishments that have the bargaining or voting power to block progressive political decision making on such issues. Lawyers tell us that it is not possible to formulate legislation that can permit the euthanasia option while guarding against abuse of that option by greedy or uncaring relatives, cost-conscious hospital managers and ageist, paternalistic or weary doctors making unacceptable decisions about what sort of life is worth living. On the other hand, increasingly, thoughtful people, especially those with distressing experiences of seeing others go through the process of dying, fear that they themselves may have to go through a terminal illness or process of mental and physical deterioration within a health system in which the combination of economic and legal limits can lead to unnecessary suffering and dreadful neglect of their wishes and interests. And few people are happy with the current compromise over permanently comatose but biologically living persons who are allowed to die of hunger and/or dehydration.

My, mainly philosophical and inevitably selective, contribution to this debate is to offer some analysis of the nature of the arguments standardly presented for and against the euthanasia option from the perspective of human rights. I am not concerned with the legal arguments put forward in courts about the proper interpretation of current human rights law, but with the nature of the moral arguments about what these legal rights ought to be. I suggest that the debate about euthanasia as a human right has (unnecessarily) led to an overemphasis on pro-euthanasia arguments based on autonomy and on anti-euthanasia arguments based on the 'right to life'. Both positions underrate the essentially humanitarian considerations that, in my view, form the prime basis for seeing the euthanasia option as a distinct human right.

This fits well enough, I think, with Ken Mason's sceptical attitude towards absolutist autonomy claims,[7] his dislike of rhetorical affirmations of 'the sanctity of life', and his recent comment on the case of Mrs Pretty, to the effect that her interests were sacrificed for the benefit of others.[8] I do not suggest, however, that he will agree with my general thesis that there should be legislative provision to permit the euthanasia option to feature routinely in end-of-life decision making. However, since

7 Mason, 'Death and Dying: One Step at a Time?', p. 162: 'The principle of patient autonomy, for example, cannot be seen as an absolute. It can only exist within the overall framework of the individual case …'.

8 For this, see the forthcoming (7th) edition of Mason, McCall Smith and Laurie, *op cit.*

the developments Mason hopes for have not transpired, it may be time to reconsider his gradualist strategy and consider adopting legislative changes that directly address the provision of an effective remedy for the tragic abuse of a small but significant number of people who are denied the opportunity to end their lives in situations that have become unacceptable to them or to those who have their interests at heart. I share his opinion that too much emphasis is placed on the significance of autonomy in this and other medical settings, but I question whether his gradualist approach to euthanasia is adequate to the task of bringing about the necessary cultural and legal changes required, and I disagree with his belief that medical professionals should not be involved in implementing more active forms of euthanasia. Indeed, I consider that to be effective the euthanasia option must be available as a normal part of the services available within the complex settings of individual patient care.[9]

This is not a development that we can or should look to attain by means of human rights litigation. Judiciaries are very properly limited by the historical understanding of conventions, charters and bills of rights on the basis of which legal decisions are often nowadays made. Legislators, on the other hand, are able, and have a duty, to draw on the moral discourse of human rights to formulate specific legislation for democratic debate and decision making.

Consequentialist Arguments Against Euthanasia

This chapter cannot provide a comprehensive survey of euthanasia argument and attempts only the beginning of an analysis of the arguments involved from a human rights perspective. Its limited aim is to promote consideration of what weight we should give to the competing considerations cited in the standard arguments. By classifying some arguments as human rights-based and others as being, for instance, consequentialist, or deriving from public goods, we may be in a better position to decide which considerations should be determinative of the outcome of the debate. In general, it is to be expected that human rights arguments should be given special weight and normally trump other considerations, particularly where the focus is on protecting the major interests of minorities against the lesser interests of larger groups.

Analysing arguments for and against euthanasia from a human rights perspective directs us to the nature and force of human rights rationales. What is the distinctive content and function of human rights discourse, and are they indeed necessarily overriding? Reflection on the euthanasia debate may help to clarify these complex and difficult questions. In this regard, I focus on the function of human rights in standing up for and seeking to protect the interests of vulnerable minorities, in the sense of smaller aggregates of persons whose interests conflict with those of larger

---

9 Myers, D.W. and Mason, J.K., 'Physician Assisted Suicide: A Second View from Mid-Atlantic', 28 *Anglo-American Law Review* 1999, 265-286. For an excellent discussion of this issue see Otlowski, M., *Voluntary Euthanasia and the Common Law*, Oxford University Press 2000, at 459-493.

aggregates or powerful minorities. From this angle, the question of whether or not legally to permit euthanasia is a human rights issue in so far as the assumed interests of majorities or powerful minorities groups tend to override the greater interests of minorities who are not in a position to protect these interests. It follows that, if we accept the moral force of the arguments in support of such minority interests, it is appropriate to draw on human rights discourse to argue for legislative change to further the minority interests that would otherwise be subordinated to public policies that protect the lesser interests of other, and larger, groups.[10]

Reviewing euthanasia arguments from this point of view reveals that the strongest arguments against legalising the euthanasia option are largely directed at preserving social benefits, such as enhancing general respect for human life, shielding populations from anxiety engendered by the legitimation of medically procured killing, and promoting a positive social image of medical practice that is acceptable to the medical profession and the majority of their clients. In the case against euthanasia, all of these social benefits are permitted to outweigh the interests of that minority of persons whose lives have such negative value that it is reasonable for them (or, if they are not competent, for others) to elect their deaths, including the right to call on others, who are suitably qualified and involved in their care, to bring about this eventuality and the interests of that, perhaps small, minority whose dying involves severe pain that current medical treatments is unable to alleviate.[11] It is the neglect of these profound personal interests as experienced by what may be a relatively small minority of the human race that arguably renders the prohibition of, or failure to provide, the euthanasia option a violation of human rights, a paradigm example of the lesser interests of majorities or powerful minorities being allowed to override the greater interests of vulnerable minorities.

No comprehensive categorisation is attempted here, but there are several anti-euthanasia arguments that appear evidently consequentialist and some that are overtly utilitarian in that the consequences involved are those of maximising pleasure and minimising pain.[12]

These anti-euthanasia arguments draw attention to:

1. The alarming consequences the existence of the euthanasia option would have for those who would not wish to use it and fear that it would be chosen for them. The key value here seems to be the peace of mind of the population

10 For the classic contemporary statement of this contention see Dworkin, R.M., *Taking Rights Seriously*, London, Duckworth, 1978.

11 See Battin, M.P., *The Least Worst Death*, Oxford, Oxford University Press 1994, pp. 33-39.

12 Instead of sampling the vast literature on this topic, I have selected these rationales from those which feature in the Market Research Services (MRS) Poll of Public Opinion, May 1995, commissioned by the Coalition Against Euthanasia of the Northern Territory prior to the passage of the Rights of the Terminally Ill Act 1995.

generally and in particular all those who are facing debilitating terminal illnesses (The 'patient morale' argument).
2. The adverse impact on healthcare generally arising from the changed values and motivations of the medical profession and healthcare workers, whose commitment is traditionally to the preservation of life and the relief of suffering. To even allow for the euthanasia option would be detrimental to these two key prerequisites of the general happiness (The 'health outcomes' argument).
3. The diversion of scarce resources from the provision of pain relief and psychological support that features centrally in the care of those who are dying, as in the hospice movement, thus increasing rather than decreasing the suffering associated with dying (The 'palliative care' argument).
4. The increasing likelihood that medical care will be used as a cover for the morally unjustified taking of life, by removing the legal sanctions that are currently provided by the blanket criminalisation of murder (The 'slippery slope' argument).

Each of these considerations deserves close and serious attention. Here I only note their consequentialist form, and the fact that they are used to trump the more personal and intense interest of that minority of persons who have to suffer because there is no euthanasia option available. The 'patient morale' argument assumes that we should protect people in general from possible unease arising from their knowledge that euthanasia is an option that might be suggested to or for them. The 'health outcomes' argument is a speculative assertion about the impact that the implementation of the euthanasia option would have on the attitudes of health carers, hence reducing the quality of outcomes for patients in general. The 'palliative care' argument looks to the wellbeing of another minority, also often experiencing distressing circumstances. Nevertheless, its focus is on the benefits to the wider group that flow from holding back from meeting the needs of a minority of that minority who might themselves be in need of palliative care. Finally, the 'slippery slope' argument is an overtly consequentialist arguments about the beneficial effects of deterrence and absolute moral rules in reducing unjustified homicide.[13]

To this may be added evidence that the interests of this vulnerable minority are subordinated to the opinions and lesser interests of other, more powerful, minorities. There are some anti-euthanasia arguments that may be categorised in this way, such as the impact that the duty to administer the euthanasia option would have on the autonomy, moral integrity, and (not usually articulated) the financial interests of medical professionals (The 'medical autonomy' argument[14]). Then there is the less

13 Recent research indicated that there is no evidence that such results do follow liberalisation of euthanasia laws. See Smith, S.W., 'Evidence for the Practical Slippery Slope in the Debate on Physician Assisted Suicide and Euthanasia', 13 *Medical Law Review*, 2005: 17-44.

14 Mason has some sympathy for this thesis. See Mason, *loc cit.* (1996), p. 165.

direct, but important, impact of religious pressure groups, with intense preferences about how others should behave that can have a decisive electoral influence on the conduct of politicians, who object to any watering down of the prohibition of the taking of any innocent human life (The 'pro-life' argument).

It may be that, once this line of analysis is brought to our attention, the apparently equal balance of arguments for and against the euthanasia option is decisively tipped in favour of legitimating the (already common) practice of voluntary and non-voluntary (but not involuntary) euthanasia. The strongest arguments against euthanasia are majoritarian ones in the sense that the appeal to majority or larger group interests; the balancing arguments in its favour are minority rights ones, in that they pinpoint the fundamental interests of a vulnerable minority. Rejecting the euthanasia option is putting too little weight on important minority interests and too much weight on the less intense interests of majorities. This sets the scene for claiming that euthanasia ought to be a human right, thus overriding the significant but less imperative interests of majorities and powerful minorities.

Human Rights Arguments and the Euthanasia Option

Presenting the case for euthanasia in terms of a human right to euthanasia (in certain circumstances) is capable of many different interpretations. Several alternatives suggest themselves. I consider three of them: the 'pro-choice', the humanitarian and the right to life.

Pro-choice

On this interpretation of the right to euthanasia, it is the ideal of liberty which requires that each individual should have control over their own lives, subject only to the protection of others from the direct harm caused by such choices. No sphere is more evidently within this realm of 'privacy' than the life and healthcare of the individual.

This is the consideration that tends to dominate the human rights discourse of those in favour of euthanasia. Euthanasia is to be considered a matter of individual choice. Whose life, or death, is it anyway?[15] This model is particularly germane to the fully conscious paralytic and the competent person facing a progressively grim future. It is certainly one of the most powerful rationales in the armoury of the euthanasia advocate. There is something quite appalling in the state preventing someone who is in such a situation but is unable to bring about their own death by enlisting the help of others who can carry out the process humanely and reliably.

However, as Ken Mason points out, the autonomy argument has many limitations in medical contexts in which the preconditions of autonomy are not adequately

15 Jackson, E., 'Whose Death is it Anyway?', 57 *Current Legal Problems*, 2004, 408-435.

present.[16] Emphasising autonomy may be harmful to the cause of non-competent sufferers who are unable to choose their treatment, yet who make up a significant proportion of those for whom death is a reasonable option, even although it is not one that they are in a position to choose for themselves. The plight of this group could to an extent, but only partially, be overcome by advance directives, or living wills, or powers of attorney. Currently such devices are available to permit, in some circumstances, the withholding or withdrawal of treatment (which does not adequately address the euthanasia option), but not to legitimate assisted 'suicide', so that they do not eliminate the prospect of being left to die a natural but nasty death.

Moreover, a purely autonomy based argument is clearly too weak to produce the absolutist claims made under its banner to the effect that a person is always entitled to choose their own death and have such assistance as they need in procuring that death. Choice is very important for human beings, partly for its own sake, and even more for the power it gives us to protect and promote those things about which we care. But it is not always an overriding factor, even in relation to self-regarding conduct.[17] This is recognised in such limited quasi-euthanasia legislation as has been enacted, where the right to choose death is restricted to those who are near death and experiencing unacceptable or unbearable suffering. In other words, the choice is acceptable only if it is a reasonable choice and a reasonable choice is one that does not impair the basic interests of the chooser, as identified by others. Choice is accepted as important in the context of euthanasia because of what it enables the individual to achieve, namely the cessation of an objectively unacceptable existence, not simply because it is the satisfaction of a preference.

Of course, we do go beyond this in giving some weight to the exercise of choice as an end in itself. Thus, in this context, we accept that people should be legally entitled to end their own lives for any or no reason. However such a right has none of the urgency and potency that we associate with the right of suffering persons in great distress and pain to kill themselves. And we certainly do not consider that anyone who, absent such circumstances, chooses to die should have a right to assistance in so doing.

16 Mason, 'Death and Dying: One Step at a Time', p. 165.

17 An interesting question is whether it is sufficient to justify a right to be kept alive through artificial feeding, as Leslie Burke sought to claim as a legal right within the UK health system. This distressing case of a man with cerebellar ataxia, a degenerative brain condition, is unlikely to have arisen without the fear and abhorrence arising from the practice of withdrawing artificial feeding so that people die of malnutrition. Of course, this does not happen where the carers believe that the patient will experience suffering, but it is understandable that a person facing a degenerative condition might want to be protected against this eventuality. Similar questions relating to a non-competent person arose in the case of Terri Schiavo. The undoubtedly difficult choices involved in such cases are exacerbated by the use of the passive euthanasia option.

Humanity

Accepting that even a small percentage of those who are dying do so in extreme pain and with great suffering that cannot be relieved by any available therapeutic medicines or treatments, we can readily accept that there ought to be a right to die in such circumstances, a right that correlates with the duty of everyone to allow such persons to kill themselves, if necessary with the help of specified others, or, in cases of incapacity, have the killing initiated and carried out for them. Relieving extreme suffering must be one of the strongest reasons for ascribing such duties to those capable of relieving that suffering, hence the affirmation of a universal right to the relief of pain, if necessary by being killed.

Philosophers sometimes seek to reduce human rights rationales to the defence and exercise of autonomy.[18] Pleasure and pain are seen as qualities treasured by those who tend to infringe rights. They have their place in the good life but not in the determination of rights and duties, at least, not fundamental rights and duties. Thus, not being tortured is a human right because it undermines autonomy – not because it hurts. Social and economic rights are seen as necessary conditions of autonomy, not as ways to avoid hunger, suffering, sickness and death as evils in themselves. However, while autonomy has great intrinsic value, and perhaps even greater instrumental value, it does not exhaust the reasons for establishing universal rights with overriding correlative duties.

Spelling out the implications of the humanitarian aspect of human rights discourse is a complex business with few absolutes as outcomes. If both the autonomy and the suffering of individuals provide foundations for universal overriding rights, it by no means easy to accommodate the two values or to identify the relevant correlative duties. But in the context of euthanasia, bringing in the humanitarian dimension does open the way for an overriding right to medically assisted suicide when a competent person in unrelievable pain is in the care of health services and seeks this service. It also renders much less problematic non-voluntary (as distinct from involuntary) euthanasia for incompetent sufferers with little or no prospect of recovering their capacity for autonomy. This does not mean that by bringing pain and suffering into the rationales for human rights we are excising autonomy in those cases where a person chooses to remain in pain, either because they prefer this to death or because they wish to remain able to communicate with their friends and relatives and die what they see as a 'dignified' death in charge of their faculties rather than comatosed for the purpose of pain relief.

This will seem too radical for some. By relying on autonomy alone, advocates of 'voluntary euthanasia' are able to resist the slippery slope allegation by saying that the euthanasia in question does not involve the incompetent let alone the competent, but unwilling, choice of the person. Once we allow the option of active

18 Griffin, J., 'Discrepancies Between the Best Philosophical Account of Human Rights and the International law of Human Rights', 101 *Proceedings of the Aristotelian Society*, 2001, 1-26.

euthanasia for humanitarian reasons it is a relatively easy moral step from voluntary to non-voluntary euthanasia but not, as some say, to involuntary euthanasia – that is euthanasia against the will of the person concerned. This is an important matter, for otherwise, by excluding non-voluntary euthanasia, we fail to address the plight of the suffering incompetent. This is not to endorse the moral form of the slippery slope argument, but to insist that there is no slippage involved in applying humanitarian considerations to justify the practice of non-voluntary euthanasia.[19]

The 'Right to Life'

Quite different consequences follow if we explore a third way of approaching the 'right to die', namely through the thesis that this follows from the 'right to life'. It may be argued that, if a person has the right to life it follows as a matter of logic that the person has the right to die. To have a right means that I am entitled to have or do something but allows not only the waiving of that right but the right not to have or do that something.

This is a fallacious argument in that only some rights are 'option' rights in the sense that they their correlative duties can be called in or waived at the request of the right-bearer.[20]

The euthanasia option cannot be logically deduced from the right to life. Indeed, as currently understood, in law, the right to life excludes the euthanasia option, since it correlates with the duty to preserve life.

However, neither is it necessary to interpret the right to life in terms of what is usually referred to as the 'sanctity of life'. Excluding religious interpretations of the sanctity of life along the lines that life is given by God and may not, therefore, be taken away by anybody but God (the assumption being that God does not operate through human beings in this regard), I will take 'the sanctity of life' to mean a combination of three claims: (1) that there is an absolute right not to be killed, (2) that there is no entitlement to waive that right, and (3) that there is a duty not to kill oneself.

So understood, the 'right to life' must be viewed as involving a prohibition of the euthanasia option. Indeed, it seems to be a glaring exception to my thesis that the strongest anti-euthanasia arguments are consequentialist in form. It is indeed a knockout argument against involuntary euthanasia. However, I would argue that this version of the right to life is not a strong argument if it is taken to ascribe to human beings an absolute right that cannot be waived or overridden in any circumstances.

If the argument is that God has given life and only God can, therefore, take it away, then the right in question is God's, not ours (although the duties fall on

---

19 See Kuhse, H., 'Why Killing is Not Always Worse – and Sometimes Better – than Letting Die', in Kuhse, H. and Singer, P. (eds), *Bioethics: An Introduction*, Oxford, Blackwell, 1999, 236-52.

20 It was tried, unsuccessfully, in *R (Pretty) v. DPP*, [2002] 1 All ER 1, HL, at p. 7 and in the European Court of Human Rights in *Pretty v. United Kingdom*, (2002) 66 BMLR 147.

all other beings capable of killing). If it is a secular right, directed to protecting the interests of the right-holder, than it is the right-holders right to waive that right when they believe it in their interests so to do. Further such a right does not have any purchase and does not apply if the individuals concerned have no interests (as when they are permanently lacking in any consciousness), or when it is not in their interests to continue living (as in the case of unrelievable severe pain).

Indeed, it is not difficult to demonstrate that there are lots of moral intuitions licensing exceptions to absolutist prohibitions as regarding the taking of life, the waiving of the right to life and suicide. Moreover, many other human rights, such as the right to free speech, are firmly and primarily grounded in consequentialist reasoning. Sanctity of life intuitions are also undermined by calling into question not the general, but the particular, application of the useful and important distinction between acts and omissions. Healthcare is one of those contexts in which there is often no moral relevance in the distinction between acts and omissions *per se* because of the assumed duty of health professionals to assist actively in promoting the wellbeing of those in their care. There is, therefore, no need to place significant weight on the medically artificial and increasingly indefensible distinction between active and passive euthanasia – a distinction that is abused by its use in defending the awful practice of leaving people to die in unrelievable pain or killing them (sorry, letting them die) through the withholding or withdrawal of nutrition. Reflection on the reality of death and dying as it is experienced by a minority of persons provides plenty of counter-intuitions to those associated with the abstract notion of the sanctity of (human) life. These counter intuitions are based on the value of autonomy and on the disvalue of suffering, both of which give rise to moral obligations stringent enough and sufficiently universal in their application to ground human rights claims to active euthanasia.

The Medical Role

Recognising that one of the powerful minorities opposing the euthanasia option is constituted by health professionals, the acceptance of euthanasia as a human right calls into question the strategy for reshaping assisted suicide and passive euthanasia practice through gradual reforms led my medical practitioners drawing on their clinical experience. The radical change of outlook required to implement a human right to euthanasia requires the validation that can be provided only by a political decision of the majority. Further, I disagree with Mason's early argument that, while there may be a case for permitting assisted suicide,[21] we should be seeking to keep healthcare professionals out of more interventionist forms of active euthanasia for fear of undermining their important medical ethos which commits

21 Mason, 'Death and Dying: One Step at a Time', pp. 164-169. Compare Meyers, D.W. and Mason, J.K., 'Physician Assisted Suicide: A Second View from Mid-Atlantic', 28 *Anglo-American Law Review*, 1999, 265-86.

them to the preservation of human life.[22] This I take to be a combination of the consequentialist 'health outcome' and the 'medical autonomy' arguments outlined above. The suggestion is that the advantages of some forms of active euthanasia could be achieved through mercy killing that does not involve health professionals caring for the persons concerned.

The, perhaps unfortunate, fact is that dying has become a medicalised process, that normally occurs in hospitals, making it impossible for the healthcare system to opt out of a phase of life that occurs within their domain. Moreover, as Mason himself insists, the decisions in question are particular ones about particular people, not a separate category of cases that can be diverted from health professionals.[23] Euthanasia should not have to require opting out of the medical system with the considerable wellbeing risks that such a course of action entails. Rather euthanasia requires to be articulated as one option amongst other options that the expertise of the healthcare system should bring to bear on the care of individual patients.

Further, the criteria for legalised euthanasia must include such matters as prognosis, prospects of pain relief, and humane methods of killing, that require medical knowledge and experience to apply correctly. Even more important, it is vital that euthanasia decisions are taken in full cognisance and authentication of the situation of each individual, something that is not entirely, but which must necessarily include, medical appraisal. And it is also clear that the process of actively assisting suicide or terminating life must be carried out in a humane and effective way and this must require medical supervision. Any justified legitimation of the euthanasia option must locate it in the context of the medical alternatives and require the co-operation of healthcare professionals.

This need not involve all intensive care and palliative care specialists offering and carrying out such treatments any more than all gynaecologists and obstetricians offering and carrying out abortions, but it does require the healthcare system to ensure that it is an option available to all patients. Conscientious exemption from participating in euthanasia can readily be available for healthcare professionals for whom this is an unacceptable practice, as long as this does not jeopardise the universal availability of the option to all those who may be in need of it. However, if we are dealing here with a defence of the human rights of those facing an unpalatable dying, then, in general terms, the greater interests of the right-holders must take precedence over the less morally less fundamental matter of protecting the preferences of health professionals.

Conclusion

Does it really matter if the arguments over euthanasia are or are not human rights arguments? This depends on what follows rhetorically and institutionally. If a human

22 This line of thought is lucidly considered and rejected in Rachels, J., *The End of Life: Euthanasia and Morality*, Oxford, Oxford University Press, 1986, 118-29.

23 Mason, 'Death and Dying: One Step at a Time', p. 166.

rights argument is one that overrides others, then it is, of course, very important, although there is a risk of circular reasoning in that we will be inclined to say that any overriding moral consideration is, *ipso facto*, a human rights argument. But at least all of this fixes our attention on what the paramount considerations are with respect to any particular issue.

I certainly do not want to expand the *corpus* of human rights if this means that their interpretation and development is dependent on a judiciary with the power to override legislation in virtue of its views as to what constitutes a human right. That is no way to settle the matter in a democracy, even if politicians are reluctant to take a lead in this sphere. However, there are other important functions for human rights discourse. One of these is to set the priorities for legislative action. Human rights abuses demand attention and cannot be put to one side as too difficult, too controversial or too expensive.

Another function of the discourse of human rights draws attention to those minorities who tend to be overlooked in the process of democratic politics, either because they fall below the radar of majority opinion, or because there are powerful forces stacked up against them. It is mainly in this respect that I consider it illuminating and valuable to regard the euthanasia option as a human right, provided this is interpreted as unleashing both autonomy and humanitarian reasons for determining the form and content of that right.

This is not a utilitarian argument for a human right in the sense that it depends on arguing that the greatest happiness of the greatest number will be enhanced by the reduction of suffering that euthanasia makes possible. That may be an argument for euthanasia, but not what I take to be a human rights-based argument. The human rights rational is focussed on the fact that the lesser interests of the majority (fear of involuntary euthanasia, the consequences of changing the traditional medical ethos, etc.) should not be allowed to trump the greater interests of those who are in grave need of the euthanasia option.

Euthanasia is a topic of such sensitivity and conflict that any robust contribution to the debate will raise the ire and disgust of some, especially where non-voluntary euthanasia is on the agenda. It is to the great credit of Ken Mason that he has made important contributions to this and many other contentious topics in medical law and ethics with such good humour and informed common sense. I offer these reflections on some of this important work in the hope that we follow his example, albeit arriving at rather different conclusions.

Chapter 29

The Futility of Opposing the Legalisation of Non-voluntary and Voluntary Euthanasia

Len Doyal

'(Fiction) of use to justice? Exactly as swindling is to trade' Jeremy Bentham[1]

The Scottish Enlightenment generated important insights on the role of emotion in moral judgment. When Hume argued that 'reason is and ought to be the slave of the passions' he included moral reason and the social customs and psychological reinforcement that inform it.[2] There is much of value in emphasising the role of both culture and intuition in moral thought. As regards culture, sensitisation to moral plurality has led to less dogmatism and more dialogue between conflicting moral traditions. And despite obvious problems with moral intuitionism, moral philosophers have found it difficult to exclude it entirely from their arguments (e.g. Rawl's concept of reflective equilibrium).[3] The work of Professor Kenyon Mason in medical law and ethics represents all that is best in the tradition of Scottish Enlightenment – clear argument that tries to find an appropriate balance between reason and the emotional and professional needs of both patients and healthcare providers.

The strengths in Mason's approach make his book with Professor Alexander McCall Smith and latterly with Dr Graeme Laurie – *Law and Medical Ethics* (LME) – the best in the field.[4] While there are other fine expositions of medical law, none attempt to integrate it with serious moral reflection in the manner of LME. Because the book has incrementally evolved over several editions, it is a treasure trove of the recent history of medical law and ethics in the UK, whose authors have managed to sustain a surprisingly consistent – and always readable – approach to legal and moral reasoning about medicine.[5] However, there are difficulties with some of their moral

---

1 Bentham, J., Works, J. Bowring (ed), Edinburgh, Simpkin Marshall, 1843. Vol. 7. p. 283. Dr. Miran Epstein pointed out this reference to me.

2 Hume, D., *Treatise of Human Nature*, Garden City, New York, Dolphin Books, 1961, p. 375.

3 Rawls, J., *A Theory of Justice* (2nd ed), Cambridge, MA, Harvard University Press, 1999.

4 Mason, J.K., McCall Smith, R.A. and Laurie, G.T., *Law and Medical Ethics* (6th ed), London, Butterworths, 2002 (hereafter LME).

conclusions. Sometimes, the authors place too much trust in the 'passions' (as per Hume) of healthcare professionals and their regulators.

This chapter will examine some of the moral problems to which such trust can lead in relation to debates about the legalisation of euthanasia. The focus of the chapter will be a critique of their analysis of non-voluntary active euthanasia (NVAE). Voluntary active euthanasia (VAE) gets much more attention in public debate. This is somewhat surprising given the number of severely incompetent patients who die slowly each year through decisions not to provide or to withdraw life-sustaining treatment (withdrawal of treatment decisions) – with death foreseen as the certain or almost certain outcome.[6] Indeed, there is good reason to believe that sometimes the human suffering that might be relieved from NVAE is greater, since patients may suffer but lack the competence to understand why.It will be argued that with appropriate regulation, NVAE can be morally justified and should be legalised and that since this is so, it must also be true for VAE and physician-assisted suicide (PAS).

Dr Smith, Nurse Jones and Miss Adams

For the sake of clinical relevance and, hopefully a little fun, imagine a real clinical case and the doctors and nurses – the healthcare team (HCT) – managing it. Miss Adams is 50, and eight months ago suffered a severe stroke. She has no close relatives. So extensive is her brain damage that the HCT agree that she will never again be self-aware, be able to engage in self-directed activity or have the capacity for any meaningful social interaction. However, she is not in a permanent vegetative state and appears to have primitive levels of sentience in the context of sleep-wake cycles. Dr Smith is Miss Adams' neurologist and responsible for her care. One month ago, because of her deteriorating respiratory function, she was placed on a ventilator where she remains. Sporadically, and despite appropriate medication, Miss Adams seems through the noises that she makes to be uncomfortable at best and in pain at worst. Dr Smith and the HCT conclude that she should be taken off her ventilator, foreseeing that this will almost certainly lead to her death.

Dr Smith was trained at a major teaching hospital where he received a good education in ethics and law applied to medicine. His text book was LME and he

5 Since LME is such a fine bibliographical resource for the problem at hand, there is little point in here repeating standard references to all of the arguments to be considered. The primary focus of references will remain on the merits of the text of LME itself. While the content of LME will be accepted as an approximation of Mason's own views, it is clear from some of his other publications that this is not always quite true. When other publications indicate differences of emphasis or approach, this will be indicated.

6 Although such estimates are problematic because so many countries do not keep accurate data, those that do exist suggest that significant percentages of total deaths occur as a result of withdrawal of treatment decisions. See: Parliamentary Assembly, 'Assistance to patients at the end of life', Council of Europe, Doc.10455, 2005: 8-9.

has continued to buy new editions. As a neurologist, Dr Smith has previously had patients like Miss Adams and not found their clinical management particularly troubling. He has been involved in many withdrawal of treatment decisions and has used LME as a guide – especially the chapters on 'medical futility'. He knows, for example, that such decisions – including the suspension of nutrition and hydration – can be justified when patients are terribly brain damaged and it is agreed by the HCT either that:

- while the patient retains some sentience, their life will – in effect – be 'demonstrably awful' by virtue of the effects of their neurological damage (e.g. no potential for self-directed activity or social interaction) and any suffering that they may also experience;[7]
- the patient is so brain damaged that they will be forever unconscious and in a permanent vegetative state (PVS) and the court agrees.[8]

He understands that the legal case that best represents the first category is *Re J* and the second category the case of *Airedale NHS Trust v. Bland*[9] (*Bland*). Following the authors of LME, he accepts that the provision of life sustaining treatment is 'medically futile' in these circumstances because it is 'non-productive' and 'cannot provide a minimum likelihood or quality of benefit'.[10] Therefore, Smith does not feel that switching off Miss Adams' ventilator is in any way problematic.

So far so good. But surprisingly, Miss Adams' respiratory function improves. Indeed, she breathes on her own for one and a half more weeks. With heavy hearts, the HCT decides that enough is enough. Now they will make sure that Miss Adams will not potentially suffer for much longer. They agree to withdraw her medically administered hydration and nutrition. The most senior nurse, Lesley Jones, consults LME, also one of her favourite texts. While most of the case law on the withdrawal of dehydration and nutrition concerns PVS, the authors appear confident that, '... the approach adopted by the courts in *Re J* could properly be applied to the withdrawal of feeding (or other vital treatment) from severely damaged adult patients'.[11] LME points out that the identical position is adopted in the guidance from the British Medical Association (BMA), particularly with reference to severe dementia and strokes.[12] After further consultation with the hospital's legal department, Miss

7 LME, at p. 479, para 16.29; pp.1500-591, paras 6.88-90.

8 *Ibid.*, at pp. 507-508, para 17.9.

9 *Re J (a minor) (wardship: medical treatment)*, [1991] Fam 33; *Airedale NHS Trust v. Bland*, [1993] 1 All ER 821.

10 LME, at p. 473, para 16.10. Also see p. 551, para 18.58, along with Schneidermand, L.J. and Jecker, N.S., 'Futility in Practice', (1993) 153 *Arch Intern Med*, 437-441.

11 LME, at p. 522, para 17.51.

12 British Medical Association, *Withholding and Withdrawing Life-prolonging Medical Treatment: Guidance for Decision Makers* (2nd ed), 2001, paras 21.4, 22.

Adams' feeding tube is removed in the expectation that she could take up well over one week to die.

That evening, Dr Smith has trouble sleeping. Coincidentally, that same day, the beloved family dog ended her increasingly painful battle with cancer by being 'put to sleep' by a local vet. Everyone involved believes that this was the only humane course of action because the dog could no longer do the kinds of things that make a dog's life worth living – in a very important sense, she could no longer be 'a dog'. Dr Smith's insomnia starts when he makes comparisons between the plight of his dog and Miss Adams. She too has permanently lost all of the attributes – reason, choice, ability to communicate, self-awareness, awareness of others – that make human life worth living. And on top of this she seems to be suffering in ways that are both unpredictable and difficult to control medically.

The next morning, Dr Smith phones Nurse Jones – a long standing and close colleague. He confesses his concern. Nurse Jones agrees, saying only, 'About time, someone said it!' For the HCT to be forced to watch Miss Adams die slowly from lack of water and food seems profoundly wrong when everyone knows that her life can be ended quickly and painlessly. Yet as good students of LME, Smith and Jones also know that any form of intentional killing is illegal. The authors quote Devlin J, 'While motive is irrelevant, intention is all-important. If a doctor intends to kill, he is as liable to prosecution (for murder) as is the layman'. This is so whether '… life is cut short by weeks or months … or years'.[13] As law-abiding citizens, Smith and Jones take this seriously. However, they would like to use the case of Miss Adams to discuss with clinical colleagues whether or not the law concerning euthanasia should be changed. The hospital management agrees to a grand round for this purpose the following week. Funds are provided to photocopy the relevant chapters of LME which are to form the basis of the discussion.

The First Grand Round: To Kill or Not To Kill?

At the beginning of the meeting, Dr Smith outlines Miss Adams' case. After one week, she is still alive. He describes the concern that he and Nurse Jones have about their decision that will lead to her certain death but only in ways that may cause her to suffer. 'I know that legally we can't just end her life now,' he says, 'but why not? What is the moral point of allowing it to continue?'

The first to speak in response is Dr Scott, Head of Haematology. He argues that Smith and Jones are clinically doing the right thing and that they should take comfort from the moral difference between not providing Miss Adams with life-sustaining treatment and actively killing her. He points out that their first decision – to discontinue artificial ventilation – can clearly not be equated with killing her since she is still alive. Scott agrees, however, that this argument becomes more complicated when death is the foreseen and certain result, as is the case with the withdrawal of hydration and nutrition. Here, the decision to omit to save the patient's life appears to

13 LME, at p. 531, para 18.9.

be inseparable from an intent to kill her as she is clearly being dehydrated and starved to death. Turning to Smith and Jones, Scott says, 'I do understand how confusing it is that there appears to be no logical difference between action and omission and indeed the authors of LME appear to agree that there is none. But I don't care what logic tells us. It was decided in *Bland* that withdrawing hydration and nutrition is an omission. And I bet that most of us here would agree that emotionally there just *is* an obvious difference between standing back and watching death happen and doing something to cause it.'[14] Waving his tattered photocopy of the relevant chapters from LME, he claims that the authors defend emotional and moral intuition in the face of such apparent inconsistency. He reads it aloud:

> Doctors who engage in passive euthanasia need … the comfort of thinking they are not actually killing their patients. A sophisticated morality will recognise such human needs … (and) … The act/omission distinction plays an important role in the preservation of a near-absolute prohibition of killing.[15]

Murmurs of approval follow Dr Scott's intervention. At this point, Dr Stable – a consultant paediatrician – speaks up. He suggests that that Smith and Jones are being arrogant in thinking that healthcare professionals should ever judge the worth of another human life. Stable argues that when doctors claim that they are withdrawing life saving treatment in the best interest of a patient, it should only be because such treatment will no longer be of clinical benefit. What doctors must not do is to purport to decide that a patient's life is no longer worth living. In support of this position, Stable points out that LME appears to say says much the same thing, although rather than 'benefit', the authors use the language of 'purpose' or 'medical futility'. He goes on, 'We shouldn't be making judgments about the value of a patient as a person – any more than we do when we decide not to prescribe antibiotics for a viral infection.'

Then Stable turns to the law, quoting from LME on withdrawal of hydration and nutrition in *Bland*:

> All the opinions stressed that it was not a matter of it being in the best interest of the patient to die but rather that it was not in his best interests to treat him so as to prolong his life in circumstances where 'no affirmative benefit' could be derived from the treatment.[16]

As regards his own specialisation, he hammers this point home by reference to BMA guidance, as cited by LME, which states:

---

14 *Bland*, at p. 509, para 17.12.

15 LME, at pp. 498-499, para 16.84: p. 548, para 18.50. The authors appear to align themselves with these views in reference 88, on p. 548, and elsewhere.

16 *Ibid.*, at p. 510, para 17.14.

> When a decision is reached to withhold or withdraw a particular treatment, it is the value of the treatment which is being assessed, not the value of the child – the overall objective of providing benefit does not change.[17]

Stable also points out that the latest BMA guidance is even more explicit on this question.[18] He adds, 'The Catholic Church and the BMA agree. This helps me emotionally when I make withdrawal of treatment decisions for my young patients.'

Then Dr Benedict, a palliative care consultant, leaps in. He agrees with all of Dr Stable's arguments. However, he believes that Smith and Jones are morally confused in even more important ways. If they have decided to withdraw life-sustaining treatment intending that Miss Adams should die, this action is both illegal and immoral. Benedict goes on, 'Smith and Jones have a perfectly good justification for not keeping Miss Adams alive: to relieve her suffering for the reasons that Dr Stable has just outlined. But that does not make intentional killing acceptable here any more than it does when we administer high doses of morphine in palliative care.' Benedict argues that in making non-treatment decisions, doctors should train themselves to keep the intention to relieve suffering separate from the intention to kill.[19] He argues that the good consequences of such decisions (the relief of suffering) easily outweigh the bad consequences (the potential death of the patient). Turning again to LME as a source, Benedict describes the legal basis of the doctrine of double effect. The authors quote Lord Goff, among others:

> ... a doctor may, when caring for a patient who is dying of cancer, lawfully administer painkilling drugs despite the fact the he knows that an incidental effect of that application will be to abbreviate the patient's life.[20]

According to Benedict, the authors of LME support this prohibition of active killing because it, 'could have the effect of blunting the respect which we accord to human life'.[21]

Dr Rain, a consultant cardiologist, agrees, claiming that legalisation of euthanasia would lead to a slippery slope with incompetent people being inappropriately killed. According to Rain, this is precisely what has happened in the Netherlands. He reminds everyone that the discussion in LME about slippery slopes is primarily about VAE and Physician Assisted Suicide (PAS). The authors cite evidence that some Dutch doctors have not strictly abided by the law and that this indicates that the legalisation of any form of medical killing will be problematic. Rain reads, '[s]uch failures suggest that administrative or internal medical control of the practice is

17 LME, at p. 501, para 6.92.

18 British Medical Association, *Medical Ethics Today* (2nd ed), London, British Medical Journal Press, 2004, pp. 353-4, 392.

19 Gillon, R. 'Foreseeing is not necessarily the same thing as intending', *BMJ*, 1999, 318:1431-1432.

20 LME, at p. 558, para. 18.77.

21 *Ibid.*, at p. 548, para 18.50.

unlikely to prevent abuses … and … [t]his might provide grounds for asserting that it becomes far more difficult to control the practice once an absolute prohibition against killing is removed'.[22] Rain agrees, maintaining that such difficulty is even more probable in situations where incompetent patients lack the autonomy to make their own wishes known. Interestingly, he is willing to admit that there may be exceptional circumstances where doctors understandably feel compelled to help patients die. However, he accepts the argument put forward in LME that it is better for them to depend on the leniency of the courts than to argue for the legalisation of such acts.[23] Rain concludes, 'I agree that the medical profession must retain a proper emphasis on the duty to protect life. As it is so eloquently put in LME with respect to the care of children, "… the spectre of the paediatrician armed with a lethal syringe … is quite unacceptable."'[24]

By this point, the one thing on which everyone in the grand round can agree is that Dr Smith and Nurse Jones should have a chance to answer their critics at next week's meeting. This allows them to review their arguments over a glass of wine and their well thumbed copies of LME. Unfortunately, the more carefully they read, the more problems they discover.

Dr. Smith and Nurse Adams Reply

The next Grand Round is very well attended and Dr Smith and Nurse Jones decide to divide their response between them. In the meantime, Miss Adams has finally died.

Dr Smith begins by rejecting as illogical and morally incoherent Dr Scott's argument in support of the act/omission distinction. He says that it is true that a failure to act with the foresight that death will be the consequence may not be the moral equivalent of active killing – for example, failing to fly immediately to Niger with food to save one unknown child is not morally equivalent to going there and selecting a child whom one then actively kills. But this argument does not apply to a doctor with a recognised duty of care to protect the life and health of a specific person. Smith says that the authors of LME would agree, quoting Lord Mustill, '… a person may be criminally liable for the consequences of an omission if he stands in such a relation to the victim that he is under a duty to act'.[25] Thus a paediatrician in A&E who watches a treatable child die might face a murder charge. Morally, the same argument applies. For example, to watch a child drown when she could easily be saved is morally equivalent to actively killing her.[26] Smith concludes on the basis of these arguments that there is no morally sustainable distinction between his own

22 *Ibid.*, at pp. 533-534, para 18.16.

23 *Ibid.*, at pp. 546-547, para 18.46.

24 *Ibid.*, at pp. 498-499, para 16.84.

25 *Ibid.*, at p. 549, para 18.52.

26 Rachaels, J., 'Active and passive euthanasia', *New England Journal of Medicine*, 1975, 292: 78-80. Also see Kuhse, H., 'Why killing is not always worse – and sometimes better – than letting die', *Cambridge Quarterly of Healthcare Ethics*, 1998, 7: 371-4.

decision to starve and dehydrate Miss Adams to death and painlessly killing her with respect and care. Indeed, a rapid death is morally preferable to a slow one because there is no chance of further suffering or indignity.

But things are not as simple as they seem. Referring again to his copy of LME, Smith reminds his colleagues that despite the previous judgment of Lord Mustill in *Bland*, the Law Lords – as Dr Stable already indicated – rejected the equivalence between act and omission, even though they agreed that there 'was no moral or logical difference' between the two.[27] Why should this be so? Smith suggests that the answer can only be that the judges might wish to create such legal fiction for reasons of public policy rather than concern about the welfare of individual patients. Quoting again from the authors of LME:

> ... the distinction reflects a widely held moral intuition which, even if it involves inconsistency, allows for the practical conduct of day to day moral life. Morality, like the law, needs to be rooted in daily experience. Doctors who engage in passive euthanasia need ... the comfort of thinking that they are not actually killing their patients.[28]

Smith was born and grew up in South Africa prior to democracy and he is surprised that the authors have such a cavalier view of irrationality in moral life. 'Once reason is rejected, how is an unjust and immoral consensus to be questioned?', Smith asks the audience. 'In any case', he goes on, 'my moral intuition and, according to opinion polls, that of the majority of the people and many doctors in the UK, is that doctors should be allowed to end the lives of patients like Miss Adams quickly and without suffering.[29] I also feel strongly that no matter how lenient courts have been in the face of active killing by doctors, they should not be expected in these circumstances to face criminal charges for doing what they believe to be right.'

Nurse Jones then takes over and directs her arguments to Dr Stable. She rejects his claims that non-treatment decisions can be isolated from prior judgments about the value of patients' lives and whether or not they would be better off dead. Jones asks a simple question, 'Would it ever be acceptable to withdraw life-sustaining treatment from patients who, as LME puts it, stand "a reasonable chance of recovery?"'[30] She maintains that the answer must be 'no' and a murder charge might follow. 'So' Jones goes on, 'the most morally important difference between Miss Adams and patients with a better prognosis cannot be that in one case medical treatment will work and in

27 LME, at p. 509, para 17.12. For and even more clear statement of the degree to which Professor Mason is perfectly clear about the moral and logical absurdities of the act/omission distinction in the context of withdrawal of hydration and nutrition, see Laurie, G.T. and Mason, J.K., 'Negative treatment of vulnerable patients: euthanasia by any other name?', *The Juridical Review*, 2000, Part 3: 159-178.

28 LME, at p. 548, para 18.50.

29 House of Lords, *Select Committee on the Assisted Dying for the Terminally Ill Bill* (Vol.1) (2005): 75-79, 31-2. See also, Wise, J., 'Public supports euthanasia for most desperate cases', *BMJ*, 1996, 313:1423.

30 LME, at pp. 558-559, para 18.77.

the other it will not. Had Miss Adams been given artificial nutrition and hydration, it would have worked – in the sense that she would have benefited from living longer than she did. Why didn't we allow her this benefit? It can only be because all of us involved with her care had already agreed that she could not benefit from staying alive or that it was productive for her to do so.' Jones then argues that Dr. Stable may have misunderstood the authors of LME who are aware – unlike the British Medical Association! – that in these circumstances a judgment of no therapeutic benefit is tantamount to the judgment that Miss Adams' life itself is of no further benefit for her.[31] The belief that they think otherwise may be based on their continued use of the language of 'medical futility' or 'non-productivity in relation to withdrawal of treatment decisions'.[32,33] Ultimately, the authors argue that the best way to take the decision to kill out of the hands of doctors, and thus to resolve the tangles that not doing so creates, is to find another way of morally and legally grounding withdrawal of treatment decisions so that doctors are not deemed to be responsible for them and therefore for NVAE, if this is what such decisions logically amount to. The authors are clear that they believe that to impute responsibility to doctors in these circumstances would be a disaster.[34]

Jones takes a quick sip of her tea and asks, 'How might this be done? The solution of the authors of LME is "substituted judgment", the assumption that withdrawal of treatment is what PVS or *Re J* type patients would have wanted for themselves.' She explains that the authors are clear that this assumption is reasonable since no one competent to refuse treatment would wish to be kept alive with such serious brain damage.[35] 'Unfortunately, it would seem,' Jones expands, 'that to avoid the legal fiction that doctors do not make judgments about the value of the lives of PVS and *Re J* type patients, the authors of LME have embraced yet another such fiction. The fact is that unless there is some form of advance directive or other hard evidence to guide us, we simply do not know what someone like Miss Adams and patients like her would have wanted. Indeed, for all we know, she may have wished to continue to be treated in the hope of a miracle. After all, many competent patients already demand the continuation of life-sustaining treatment with precisely such hope in mind. Therefore, why should we make a contrary assumption in our substituted judgment?' Jones argues that if we do so, it must be because it has already been decided that further life provides no benefit or value and that, therefore, no competent person would choose it. 'Seen in this way,' Jones says, 'to appeal to substituted judgment to justify withdrawal of treatment is to do no more than reiterate the judgment that these lives are not worth living. Indeed, using substituted judgment, why should we not also assume that the same person we are accepting would want not to be kept

31 *Ibid.*, at p. 518, para 17.42. Again, for an even more clear statement of the issue by Professor Mason, see Laurie and Mason, *loc cit.*

32 LME, at p. 473, para 16.10.

33 *Ibid.*, at pp. 562-563, para 18.89.

34 *Ibid.*, at p. 568, para 18.102.

35 *Ibid.*, at pp. 518-519, para 17.43; p. 520, para 17.47.

alive would also want a death as quick, dignified and comfortable as possible?' By this time, Dr Stable is looking distinctly uncomfortable.

Visibly frustrated, Dr Benedict jumps back in, saying: 'Look. As I said last week, the key issue in all of this is not about any of these things. It's about the doctor's intent. Decisions to withdraw treatment which conform to appropriate clinical criteria will still be illegal if their aim is to kill rather than to relieve suffering. It is the double effect argument that remains crucial here; the law should be respected!'

It is now Dr Smith's turn to be impatient. He argues that no one is suggesting that the law should be broken. What he and Jones have tried to demonstrate is that the law is logically and morally incoherent and should be changed. 'I think,' Smith says, 'that we have shown how and why decisions to withdraw treatment that is of no benefit are always based on prior decisions that the patient's life is itself no longer worth living. It must follow that death is a moral good for them. If so, where is the moral wrong in intending that they should die? Claiming that the intention to relieve suffering is the only acceptable motive when withdrawal decisions are made, simply begs the question of the moral wrongness or rightness of intentional killing.' Smith draws the conclusion that in this sense, the double effect argument is not an argument at all but an assertion of moral and often religious dogma.[36] 'And if it is not morally wrong to intend the death of patients for whom withdrawal decisions have been made, why should it be wrong to further benefit them through deliberately and with great respect killing them quickly?'

Taking the argument still further, Smith says, 'Once we all agreed that it was clinically appropriate to withdraw hydration and nutrition from Miss Adams, it would have been professionally unacceptable for me keep this from happening on the grounds that I had suddenly realised that I was no longer clear about my own intentions. It is the patient's interest and dignity and not my perception of my own virtue that is most important!'[37] Many of the nurses smiled knowingly and nodded in agreement but Dr Benedict is still unhappy. 'This is all fine and good but we could get round these problems through good palliative care where intentional killing is never required.' Smith replies, 'I respect your expertise but the standard of excellence that you set is only available to a minority of NHS patients.[38] I can see that you are here with some of your colleagues from oncology and you know as well as I that the needs of patients like Miss Adams are not going to be a priority for any of you. We all agree that all patients should have access to effective pain relief

36 Doyal, L. and Doyal, L., 'Why active and physician assisted suicide should be legalised', *BMJ*, 2001, 323: 1079-1080.

37 Doyal, L., 'The moral character of clinicians or the best interests of patients', *BMJ*, 1999, 318: 1432-1433.

38 For example, in 2003, there were four paediatric palliative care consultants in the UK. See, Hutchinson, F., King, N. and Hain, R.D.W., 'Terminal care in paediatrics: where are we now?', *Postgraduate Medical Journal*, 2003, 79: 566-568. More generally, see: House of Lords Select Committee on the Assisted Dying for the Terminally Ill Bill (Vol.1) (2005):33-36. Shortages elsewhere have been widely reported.

when they need it. However, why should scarce specialist resources that competent patients desperately need be wasted on patients who cannot comprehend the nature of their suffering, who will not benefit from further life but who would benefit from a quick and painless death?' Like Dr Stable, Dr Benedict also looks unhappy but says nothing more.

Nurse Jones now begins to conclude her response to their critics. She returns to Dr Rain's argument about slippery slopes and the moral and medical disaster that the legalisation of euthanasia in Holland supposedly demonstrates. Jones rejects Rain's argument because she rejects his evidence. 'So what do we know?,' she asks, 'the Dutch refer to all deaths involving what we have been calling acts and omissions as 'medical decisions at the end of life ... (MDELs) ... but "euthanasia" only refers to voluntary active euthanasia. In 1995, around 20 per cent of total deaths within each year were the result of withdrawal of treatment and 19 per cent from the administration of opioids. VAE accounted for around 2.5 per cent of total deaths. Add physician-assisted suicide and the figure remains well under 3 per cent.'[39] Jones then points out that by 2001, there had been no increase above these figures; the situation had stabilised.[40] She goes on, 'We know that withdrawal of treatment decisions and the use of potentially dangerous doses of morphine to relieve pain are also taken in other hospitals throughout the world. But we have few systematic studies of this area of medical practice – not to mention covert active involuntary or voluntary euthanasia. It is interesting that the only reason we know so much about MDELs in Holland is because this area of clinical life is more publicly regulated and healthcare professionals are supposed to classify and report them accordingly.'

'So,' Jones asks, 'have we got any evidence to support Dr Rain's view that legalisation in Holland of voluntary active euthanasia has led to worrying levels of involuntary active euthanasia?' She explains that while Dutch doctors do actively take the lives of PVS and *Re J* type patients, it is difficult to know exact numbers. This is because even though doctors have some scope for such actions in the best interests of patients, especially when relatives are in agreement, their legal status is still somewhat unclear. For this reason, professional disclosure is not as good as it is with other MDELs, including VAE. Evidence gathered in other ways, however, suggest that NVAE accounts perhaps accounts for just 1 per cent of deaths, although this figure may be somewhat higher when non-reporting is taken into account.[41] With a PowerPoint slide she earlier prepared, Jones goes on to show how that the number of such deaths in Holland still appears to be less than in some countries where voluntary euthanasia has not been legalised.[42] For example, Australia, appears

---

39 Griffiths, J., Bood, A. and Weyers, H., *Euthanasia and Law in the Netherlands*, Amsterdam, Amsterdam University Press, 1998, at pp. 197-257. Also see note 36, *supra*, House of Lords, at p. 61.

40 See 'Assistance to patients at the end of life', Council of Europe, *supra*.

41 See Griffiths, *et al*., *op cit*.; see also Hutchison, *et al*., *loc cit*.; House of Lords Select Committee report, *supra cit*., at p. 61.

42 See 'Assistance to patients at the end of life', Council of Europe, *supra*.

to have considerably higher rates of non voluntary euthanasia than Holland, despite the fact that all forms of euthanasia are illegal there. For example, one famous study indicates that '… while (approximately) 30 per cent of all Australian deaths were preceded by an action or omission explicitly intended to end the patient's life, in only 4 per cent was the decision taken in response to an explicit request from the patient.'[43] The situation in Belgium was similar, one of the probable reasons for its legalisation there.[44] 'Certainly,' Jones adds, 'the standard of care for those for whom life-sustaining treatment can no longer benefit appears no worse in Holland than in other European countries for which we have limited evidence.'

'Of course, although we do have some important information about the behaviour and attitudes of UK doctors, we have no really clear idea of what is going on in the UK. For all we know, there could be even more NVAE here than in Australia, including both the active killing that Dr Smith and I have argued can be morally justified and other killing that cannot. Indeed, this is almost certainly so if we agree, as at least the authors of LME at times appear to, that morally and logically when hydration and nutrition are removed from patients, this *is* NVAE![45] This means that we when people express fears that if euthanasia were legalised in the UK, the situation might become as bad as it is in Holland, their evidence base is highly suspect to say the least. The fact is that fears that were expressed about the legalisation of active euthanasia in Holland for incompetent patients have not been borne out. The situation there is not out of control and has no appearance of being so.[46] Dr Smith and I believe that the same situation would prevail in the UK if our laws were similar to those in Holland.'

At this point, a visiting Dutch doctor intervenes and smiles saying, 'In Holland, when we hear British colleagues predict terrible consequences that might occur in your country were you to adopt our euthanasia laws, the name Shipman comes irresistibly to mind! Take care to make your regulations even better than ours.'

The audience responds with a mixture of sheepish laughter and embarrassed silence. Nurse Jones then admits that her ethical deliberations of the last week have led her to have some degree of frustration with the authors of LME, the book that has served her well in so many ways. She points out that the authors can see the importance of enabling legislation to clarify the legal status of withdrawal of treatment decisions, 'However they won't go further than this,' she says, 'again,

43 Kuhse, H., Singer, P., Baume, P., Clark, M. and Rickard, M., 'End-of-life decisions in Australian medical practice', *Medical Journal of Australia*, 1997, 166: 191.

44 Deliens, L., Mortier, F., Bilsen, J., Cosyns, M., vander Stichele, R., Vanoverloop, J. and Engels, K., 'End-of-life decicisions in medical practice in Flanders, Belgium: a nationwide survey', *The Lancet*, 2000; 356: 1806.

45 See Laurie and Mason, *loc cit*.

46 See Griffiths, *et al*., *op cit*. The entire book is an excellent argument to this effect. Notably, the House of Lords Select Committee, *supra cit*., did not argue to the contrary, although legitimate concerns were expressed about reporting which the Committee was told the Dutch recognised and were in the process of correcting.

they seem to be convinced that unless clinicians are encouraged to believe the fiction that they are intellectually and emotionally removed from the causation of death in withdrawal of treatment decisions, they may become confused about their "role".'[47] 'But,' Jones says, 'where is the evidence of this, especially since in the case of withdrawal of hydration and nutrition such personal disassociation is almost impossible?' Jones suggests to the audience that legalisation will in fact be more likely to increase the moral sensitivity of doctors to the suffering of patients like Miss Adams, to strengthen their courage to do what is right for them and to be sure that they are doing so according to acceptable rules. She also points out that various surveys have shown that the majority of the public wants such help at the end of life to be available.[48]

At this point, the second grand round has to end. It is thought inappropriate to take a vote on who agreed and disagree with Dr Smith and Nurse Jones. However, it is clear that everyone accepts that the issue of non-voluntary active euthanasia is more morally complex that they had originally thought and it seems that Smith and Jones have persuaded some to change their minds.

Discussion: Lessons for the Debate About Active Voluntary Euthanasia and Physician-assisted Suicide

If the arguments for the legalisation of NVAE proposed by Smith and Jones were more widely accepted, this would spell good news for competent and seriously ill patients who find life so unbearable that they wish to be painlessly killed. Against the background of the duty of care, suppose that we can agree that that when incompetent patients now have life-sustaining treatment withdrawn it can only legitimately be because their doctors have already made decisions that their lives are not worth living. Yet we have seen that there is no logical or moral difference between act and omission as regards such patients. Morally, therefore, some doctors are in reality actively and appropriately killing their patients in this way every day, whatever their intentions and however quickly death occurs. These same doctors – in collaboration with the HCT – should also have the legal right to intervene to ensure a quick and human death for PVS and *Re J* type patients. Moreover, suppose that a competent patient is suffering in ways that they believe to be both permanent and intolerable and it is clear that they themselves no longer believe that there is any benefit to living. Why should they not be able to make the same decisions about a quick death for themselves that doctors should be able to make for permanently incompetent patients? Why should voluntary active euthanasia also not be legalised?

Unfortunately, most of the arguments put forward by Smith and Jones are rejected by medical and legal orthodoxy in the UK and to a large degree by the authors of LME. They do accept the right of competent patients to refuse life-sustaining

47 LME, at pp. 538-539, para 18.25. The reference here is specifically to PAS, although the authors would clearly apply it to all forms of active euthanasia.

48 See Wise, *loc cit.*

treatment (although even here the authors have concerns, especially about the moral status of advance directives).[49] But this leaves competent patients who are seriously ill with stark choices if they believe that death is in their best interest. If they are not capable of taking their own lives (e.g. because they are paralysed) all they can do is refuse treatment and face the prospect of a potentially slow and undignified death, along with sometimes unpredictable amounts of suffering. On the other hand, if they are able physically to kill themselves but have no access to lethal drugs, a failed attempted suicide may lead to even more indignity and suffering for them and their families.

Why should any competent patient who cannot kill themselves be placed in this position? What is the moral good of forcing them to have a slow death, if they wish otherwise? Depicted on the cover of the most recent edition of LME is the well known case of ventilator dependent Ms B which again confirmed the legal right of patients to refuse life-saving treatment.[50] However, after doing so, she then took four weeks to die.[51] Mrs B may have wanted this extra time because of further choices she wanted to make before she died. However, if she had made it clear that she did not wish to live any longer, her interests would have best been served if a sympathetic doctor agreed to end her life quickly. While it is clear that the authors of LME reject this option, at the same time they also recognise the absurdity of the act/omission distinction:

> The main practical difference ... [as regards a patient like Mrs B] ... must lie in the immediacy and the certainty of death when the respirator is turned off; the care team is, effectively, being asked to suffocate their patient ... and this ... surely pulls the carpet from under those who would identify 'switching off' as an omission.[52]

What we are left with, therefore, is the argument that it *is* morally acceptable for doctors to be able to act to kill patients at their own request – provided that as a consequence they do not die too quickly!

How do the authors justify such a surprising position? It is not because they are unaware of the legal fictions which have been discussed in this chapter but due to their fears about the social consequences of these fictions being banished from the law and from professional regulation. Their primary reason for supporting the continuing legal ban on VAE is the extension of the slippery slope argument. They state, '[l]egalising active euthanasia compromises the duty of the state to protect its subjects and the integrity of the medical profession ...'.[53] Yet as has been shown with respect to NVAE, there is there is no convincing evidence to support their case. Such evidence would have to show that in countries where VAE is legally practiced,

49 LME, pp. 551-555, paras 18.59-18.67.

50 *Re B (adult: refusal of medical treatment)*, [2002] 65 BMLR 149.

51 LME, at pp. 541-542, para 18.33.

52 *Ibid.*, at p. 561, paras 18.83-18.84.

53 *Ibid.*, at p. 568, para 18.102.

there is a poorer standard of medical care for the relevant cohort of patients than in countries where this is not so. This evidence just doesn't exist.[54] What we do know is that some doctors in the UK are also practising all forms of euthanasia, albeit covertly.[55] Therefore, as was the case with NVAE, it is quite wrong for opponents of VAE to criticise the Dutch on the basis of good published evidence made possible by their legalisation, when the critics have no accurate understanding of the related behaviour of doctors in their own countries. Indeed, the effective regulation that legalisation makes possible may well promote the moral values associated with being a good doctor and avoiding whatever slippery slopes that may be present through non-legalisation (e.g. poor regulation and injustice).

What about the legalisation of PAS? Here, the presentation in LME of arguments for and against is more balanced but less specified than the discussion of VAE. This is perhaps unsurprising, in light of Professor Mason's own declared support of legalisation in highly specific circumstances (e.g. progressive neurological disorder).[56] Given their own criticism of the act/omission distinction in relation to cases like *Re B*, it would be surprising if the authors wished to draw an overly sharp moral distinction between PAS and Ms B's competent request for assistance to end her life by turning off her ventilator. Yet it has to be said that in LME itself, the picture remains confused. The book carefully documents how the law will not countenance the equation of refusals of life-sustaining treatment as suicide, thus legally protecting doctors who make such decisions. But ultimately the authors of LME reject legalisation, although recognising that the arguments are 'finely balanced'.[57] The justification, as usual, is '... at the end of the day, there may be strong pragmatic reasons for the view that the medical profession simply should not involve itself in actions which confuse its role'.[58] Equally, there are the usual concerns that increasing the potential that PAS might create pressure on vulnerable persons to ask for assistance when they really do not want it.

Yet again, however, there is no convincing evidence that the legalisation of PAS leads to the increased exploitation of the vulnerable, although it is the case that some potentially vulnerable people fear that this might happen. For example, PAS has been legalised in Oregon with no obvious decline in moral standards or significant evidence of coercion, any more than in Holland.[59] In the former, the three primary

---

54 Smith, S., 'Evidence for the practical slippery slope in the debate on physician-assisted suicide and euthanasia', *Medical Law Review*, 2005, 13: 2005.

55 House of Lords Select Committee, *supra cit.*, at pp. 31-32. While many opinion polls support the view that some covert AE and PAS must be occurring in the UK, the BMA and the GMC in their deposition tried to play this down, incredibly because of non-reporting. See also, LME, at pp. 537-538, para 18.23.

56 Mason, J.K. and Mulligan, D., 'Euthanasia by stages', *Lancet*, 1996;347:810-11.

57 LME, at 543, para 18.37.

58 *Ibid.*, at p. 539, para 18.25.

59 State of Oregon, Death with Dignity Act, 1994.

reasons consistently given for wanting to end life are fear of losing autonomy, loss of dignity and decreasing ability to engage in enjoyable activities.[60] Admittedly, it is also true that a lesser but still significant number ask for assistance because they 'fear being a burden'. However, because such fears are so linked to the objective and personal impact of the other three variables, this makes it difficult to cite them as direct evidence of coercion on its own right. What is important is persistent regulatory diligence. Thus in their arguments, the authors have given unequal priority to the fears of *potential* patients at one end of a hypothetical slippery slope who may become vulnerable and fear coercion over the wishes of *actual* patients on the other end of a real slippery slope who for obvious reasons believe their lives are no longer worth living, wish for help in ending them and cannot get it. That the authors can support such inequality is made even more strange by the inclusion in the text of the following quote from Cory J:

> Dying is an integral part of living ... It follows that the right to die with dignity should be as well protected as is any other aspect to the right to life. State prohibitions that would force a dreadful death on a rational but incapacitated terminally ill patient are an affront to human dignity.[61]

Why didn't Professor Mason stick to his guns? Is it because if the argument of Cory J is convincing in relation to PAS, say for patients with motor neurone disease, it must be so for patients requesting VAE and for NVAE for patients who need similar help but cannot ask for it?

Conclusion

It has been argued that despite the many merits of LME, including a fine exposition of the law concerning non-voluntary and voluntary euthanasia, the authors offer no convincing moral arguments against the legalisation of either – provided, of course, both are rigorously regulated. Instead, they minimise the importance of what they themselves recognise as rational analysis in favour of what is more or less described as a professional culture of irrationality – of legal fiction – that they believe works in support of the public good.[62] However, they offer no convincing evidence why this should be the case. The comparative evidence that is available does not corroborate the slippery slopes – as opposed to a few slips – on which the authors' conservatism about euthanasia rests and it is telling that one of the finest expositions of why this is so is not referred to in the text.[63] What should be remembered is that at any given time, professional cultures – indeed, all cultures – will embrace irrationalities which

---

60 Oregon Department of Human Services, *Sixth Annual Report on Oregon's Death with Dignity Act*, Department of Human Services, 2004, p. 14.

61 LME, at p. 543, para 18.37; (1993) 107 DLR (4th) 342, at p. 413.

62 LME, at pp. 567-568, para 18.101.

63 See Griffiths, *et al.*, *op cit.*

call for challenge. Historically, Professor Mason has played an important role in resisting one: a sometimes crude overemphasis on respect for autonomy in medicine when it is clear that autonomy itself can hugely vary and that there are obvious circumstances where it does not supersede individual or public interests. It is a pity that he and his colleagues have not extended that same academic rigour to their moral analysis of euthanasia, especially since they are all aware of the problem of attempting to assess the correctness of a moral argument to the 'passions' of a vote.[64]

Still, LME has become an evolving reflection of the evolution of the healthcare professions over the last 15 years. I live in hope that, consistent with the traditions of the Scottish Enlightenment, the increasing 'passions' among the medical profession about the reasonableness of legalising euthanasia will in some future edition of LME be taken more seriously. At least in part, Professor Mason has himself shown the way forward with his support for enabling legislation as regards particular end of life decisions.[65] Meantime, and returning to Dr Smith's family dog, those who continue their opposition to legalisation on the basis of current legal and professional passions perhaps lose sight of the degree to which these can cloud the capacity to exercise appropriate care and concern for both incompetent and competent patients for whom life has become intolerable. As Professor Emily Jackson has recently and so perfectly put it:

> Far from representing a unique opportunity for abuse of vulnerable patients, legalised euthanasia would be subject to a strict regulatory framework which would offer far more rigorous protection than is currently the case when doctors take decisions that shorten their patients' lives. The general prohibition on doctors killing their patients would remain intact, but we would acknowledge that an exceptionless rule which forces some people to endure a death that we would not inflict on a pet hamster is cruel and morally indefensible.[66]

Amen to that!

Acknowledgement

Many thanks to Professor Lesley Doyal for her help and support

---

64 LME, at p. 538, para 18.24.

65 Mason, J.K., 'Death and dying: one step at a time', in McLean, S.A.M., *Death, Dying and the Law*, Aldershot, Dartmouth, 1996, pp. 161-178.

66 Jackson, E., 'Whose death is it anyway: euthanasia and the medical profession', *Current Legal Problems*, 2004, 57: 414-442. Aside from being a superb analysis of the many of the issues discussed in this paper, Professor Jackson's paper is also an excellent bibliographical resource for further reference, especially in relation to contemporary debates about voluntary euthanasia.

Chapter 30

Defending the Council of Europe's Opposition to Euthanasia[1]

John Keown

Introduction

In the ongoing international debate about the legalisation of euthanasia a significant point of reference has been the recommendation against legalisation passed in 1999 by the Parliamentary Assembly of the Council of Europe.[2] Recommendation 1418 urged member states 'to respect and protect the dignity of terminally ill or dying persons in all respects'.[3] To this end it recommended a trio of means:

- recognising and protecting a terminally ill or dying person's right to comprehensive palliative care ...;
- protecting the terminally ill or dying person's right to self-determination ...;
- upholding the prohibition against intentionally taking the life of terminally ill or dying persons.[4]

In relation to this third means it added:

- recognising that the right to life, especially with regard to a terminally ill or dying person, is guaranteed by the member states, in accordance with Article 2 of the European Convention on Human Rights which states that 'no one shall be deprived of his life intentionally'.[5]

---

1 A version of this chapter appears in German as 'Pro und Contra Euthanasie: Die Parlamentarische Versammlung des Europarates verwirft den Marty-Report', in Hans Thomas (ed) *Ärztliche Freiheit und Berufsethos*, Dettelbach, J.H. Roell, 2005. I am grateful to Dr Thomas for his agreement that the original English version be published in this *festschrift*.

2 Protection of the human rights and dignity of the terminally ill and the dying, Council of Europe, Recommendation 1418 (1999) http://assembly.coe.int/Documents/AdoptedText/ta99/erec1418.html. The Council of Europe, which should not be confused with the European Union, was established in 1949 in order *inter alia* to defend human rights.

3 *Ibid.*, at para 9.

4 *Id.*

5 *Id.*

More recently, moves have been made to revise the Council's position. In September 2003 a Report – *Euthanasia* – was passed by a narrow majority of the Council's Social, Health and Family Affairs Committee.[6] The Report comprised a Draft Resolution (of nine paragraphs) and an Explanatory Memorandum (of 63 paragraphs). The Memorandum was written by Mr Dick Marty, a 'radical-liberal' member of the Parliamentary Assembly and the Committee's Rapporteur. In April 2004 the Parliamentary Assembly voted to send the report back to the Social, Health and Family Affairs Committee for reconsideration.[7] A revised report was produced in February 2005.[8] This chapter will consider these reports in turn.

The Marty Report (2003)

The Report's Reasoning and Recommendations

The Report stated that some doctors practised active, voluntary euthanasia on, or assisted in suicide, terminally ill patients who experienced 'constant, unbearable pain and suffering without hope of any improvement'.[9] It added that this practice was usually 'confined to the shadows of discretion or secrecy', that decisions could be taken in an arbitrary manner, that pressures from the family could be more pernicious 'if exercised in the dark and beyond any procedures or control' and that it was 'this reality' that carried 'the greatest risk of abuse'.[10] Further, penal and professional sanctions were very rare. Hence, there was a 'striking divergence' between law and practice and this gap had to be reconciled if respect for the rule of law was to be maintained.[11] The closure of this gap was one reason, it claimed, why legislation was passed in 2002 in the Netherlands and in Belgium to permit voluntary euthanasia subject to 'rigorously regulated and controlled conditions'. Such legislation was designed:

> to bring such practices out of the grey area of uncertainty and potential abuse by establishing strict and transparent procedures, mechanisms and criteria which doctors and nursing staff have to observe in their decision-making.[12]

---

6 *Euthanasia*, Report of the Social, Health and Family Affairs Committee of the Council of Europe, 10th September 2003 (Doc. 9898): http://assembly.coe.int/Documents/WorkingDocs/Doc03/EDOC9898.htm (hereafter 'Marty I').

7 http://www.coe.int/NewsSearchInternetNewsSearchDateKW.asp?lmLangue=1&qrNewsExpMonth=4&qrNewsExpYear=2004&KW=marty&Submit=Go.

8 *Assistance to Patients at End of Life*, Report of the Social, Health and Family Affairs Committee, 9th February 2005 (Dec. 10455) http://assembly.coe.int/Documents/WorkingDocs/Doc05/EDOC10455.htm (hereafter 'Marty II').

9 Marty I (Draft Resolution) para 1.

10 *Ibid.*, at para 2.

11 *Ibid.*, at para 3.

12 *Ibid.*, at para 4.

Further, it was difficult to distinguish ethically between active voluntary euthanasia and the withholding or withdrawal of life-sustaining treatment when it was known that as a result the patient would die sooner, which the Report described as 'passive euthanasia'.[13] The Report went on:

> Nobody has the right to impose on the terminally-ill and the dying the obligation to live out their life in unbearable suffering and anguish where they themselves have persistently expressed the wish to end it.[14]

Its argument continued that we now respected 'a person's choice to take their own life' and avoided making value judgments about it, a development which could in no way be interpreted as a devaluation of human life. Moreover, palliative care could not take away unbearable pain and suffering in all cases and, in any event, the issues went beyond the alleviation of pain:

> the degree of patients' own suffering, including mental anguish and loss of dignity that they feel, is something that only they can assess. Individuals suffering in the same situation may take different end-of-life decisions, but each human being's choice is deserving of respect.[15]

In light of the above considerations the Draft Resolution recommended that member states:

- collect and analyse empirical evidence about end-of-life decisions ...;
- promote public discussion of such evidence ...;
- promote comparative analysis taking into account in particular the results of the legislation in the Netherlands and Belgium 'notably their effects on practice in the matter of euthanasia' and, in the light of the evidence and public discussion;
- consider whether legislation should be envisaged, where it has not already been introduced, to exempt from prosecution doctors who agree to help terminally ill patients undergoing constant, unbearable pain and suffering without hope of any improvement in their condition, to end their lives at their persistent, voluntary and well-considered request, subject to prescribed rigorous and transparent conditions and procedures.[16]

Some Criticisms

The Report was flawed, not least because it repeatedly overstated the arguments for legalisation and downplayed or ignored the arguments against.

---

13 *Ibid.*, at para 5.
14 *Ibid.*, at para 7.
15 *Ibid.*, at para 8.
16 *Ibid.*, at para 9.

Arguments Advanced by the Report

(a) The rule of law

The Report claimed that the rule of law supported legalisation. However, just as the opening paragraph of Recommendation 1418 noted that it is the vocation of the Council of Europe 'to protect the dignity of all human beings and the rights which stem therefrom' so too the rule of law affords protection to all citizens, recognising their fundamental equality-in-dignity. Just as no-one is above the law so no-one is beneath the law. A law permitting voluntary euthanasia would, for the first time, allow certain private citizens to kill other private citizens on the basis of the arbitrary judgment, historically denied in Western law and medical ethics, that they would be better off dead. In short, the rule of law, to which the arbitrary exercise of power is repugnant, not least the power of life and death, surely tells not for but against legalisation.

(b) 'Closing the gap'

The argument that there is a 'striking divergence' between the law and medical practice and that the gap must be closed if respect for the rule of law is to be maintained is unconvincing. First, the assertion that there is a 'striking' discrepancy between law and practice is controversial. Obtaining reliable data on the incidence of the offences of murder and assisted suicide by medical practitioners is, not surprisingly, difficult. The surveys cited by the Report allegedly demonstrating a 'striking' discrepancy in countries where euthanasia and assisted suicide are illegal must be read with caution. For example, the Report pointed out that according to a survey of UK doctors[17] almost 60 per cent replied that they had been asked to hasten death and 32 per cent had complied. These are not insubstantial figures. However, they require some qualification. The 60 per cent includes 14 per cent who were asked to let the patient die 'through deliberate inaction' which the survey defined as 'passive euthanasia'. And the 32 per cent who said they had taken active steps to end a patient's life represented only 9 per cent of all of the doctors who had been sent a questionnaire. Nor did the survey ask how often euthanasia had been performed. Moreover, unlike the three comprehensive surveys into end-of-life decision making in the Netherlands which have been carried out by Professor van der Maas *et al.* since 1991, the UK survey, as its definition of 'passive euthanasia' indicates, did not consistently define 'euthanasia' in terms of the *intentional* hastening of death, which may have led to some confusion. Nor did the UK survey involve interviews with doctors, something which van der Maas found important in clarifying the thinking of his respondents in distinguishing euthanasia from other end-of-life decisions.[18] Further, another UK

17 Ward, B.J. and Tate, P.A., 'Attitudes among NHS doctors to requests for euthanasia', (1994) 308 *BMJ*, 1332.

18 Keown, J., *Euthanasia, Ethics and Public Policy*, Cambridge, Cambridge University Press, 2002, at p. 94 n. 22. The three surveys are van der Maas, P.J., van Delden, J.M.M. and Pijnenborg, L., *Medische beslissingen rond het levenseinde. Het onderzoek voor de Commissie onderzoek medische praktijk inzake euthanasia*, The Hague, SDU Uitgeverij Plantijnstraat,

survey, commissioned by the BBC and involving a sample of health professionals twice as large as the survey cited by the Report, disclosed that only 4 per cent had assisted suicide, either by providing drugs or advice.[19] Similarly, a US survey found that only 6 per cent of physicians there had performed euthanasia or assisted suicide, the author of the survey concluding that it was a 'rare' event.[20] More recently, a large survey of UK doctors concluded that the proportion of deaths from euthanasia and assisted suicide is 'extremely low'.[21]

Secondly, even if there *were* a serious discrepancy between the law and practice of voluntary euthanasia it would not follow that the gap should be narrowed by relaxing the law. Many criminal laws are regularly broken. Some prohibitions, such as the law against possessing hard drugs, are frequently breached without detection but it does not follow that the law should therefore be relaxed to accommodate those who snort cocaine. The Report seemed simply to assume that if voluntary euthanasia was practised it should therefore be condoned.[22] But what if, as much evidence suggests,[23] voluntary euthanasia is carried out on patients whose autonomy is compromised by clinical depression or whose suffering could be alleviated by palliative care? In other words, why did the Report seem to assume that the problem with the alleged gap between the criminal law and medical practice lay with the former rather than the latter, that the law was bad and the practice good? Was Dr Kevorkian a model of good medical practice? Of the 69 people he assisted in suicide

---

1991; van der Wal, G. and van der Maas, P.J., *Euthanasie en andere medische beslissingen rond het levenseinde. De praktijk en de meldingsprocedure*, The Hague, SDU Uitgevers, 1996; van der Wal, G., van der Heide, A., Onwuteaka-Philipsen, B.D. and van der Maas, P.J., *Medische besluitvorming aan het einde van het leven: De praktijk en de toetsingprocedure euthanasiae*, Utrecht, De Tijdstroom, 2003. For an analysis of the first two surveys see Keown, J., *op cit.*, Part III. For an analysis of the third see Fenigsen, R., 'Dutch euthanasia: the new government ordered survey', (2004) 20 *Issues in Law and Medicine*, 73.

19 McLean, S.A.M. and Britton, A., *Sometimes a Small Victory*, (1996) Appendix III, table 17, at pp. 31-2.

20 Meier, D.E. *et al.*, 'A National Survey of Physician-Assisted Suicide and Euthanasia in the United States', (1998) 338 *N Engl J Med*, 1193.

21 Clive Seale, 'National survey of end-of-life decisions made by UK medical practitioners' (2006) 20 *Palliative Medicine*, 3 at 6.

22 Revealingly, the Draft Resolution did not propose that in the light of whatever evidence might emerge from studies into the incidence of euthanasia there should be a review of various options, including improving the provision of quality palliative care and/or tighter enforcement of the criminal law. It proposed solely that member states consider legalising euthanasia. That this appeared to be the Report's not too skillfully hidden agenda was also suggested by its underlying argument in principle for reform. For: if there is a right to voluntary euthanasia why should it not be recognised by law whatever the evidence about its current incidence?

23 See generally, New York State Task Force on Life and the Law, *When Death is Sought: Assisted Suicide and Euthanasia in the Medical Context*, Albany, Health Education Services, 1994; Keown, J., *op cit.*

only a quarter were terminally ill.[24] Why assume that the law should accommodate Kevorkians in practice rather than in prison?

Thirdly, if the law against voluntary euthanasia is occasionally broken, so too is the law against non-voluntary euthanasia (both in jurisdictions where, like the UK and US, voluntary euthanasia is illegal and in jurisdictions, notably the Netherlands, where it is legally permitted). If the Report believed the gap between the law and practice of voluntary euthanasia militated in favour of legalisation, then why not the gap between the law and practice of non-voluntary euthanasia?

Fourthly, relaxing the law to allow euthanasia to be performed in certain circumstances would not mean that euthanasia would be performed only in those circumstances. Legislative proposals for regulating euthanasia typically set out procedural requirements aimed at *monitoring* the practice of euthanasia; they do not seek to *prohibit* the practice of euthanasia which fails to satisfy those requirements. In other words the potential for abuse, for breaking the law against murder and assisted suicide, remains. Indeed, it may well be that legalising euthanasia in certain circumstances would result in euthanasia in other circumstances being regarded by the criminal justice system as less, not more, serious; a lower, not a higher priority. It is noteworthy that in the Netherlands *very* few doctors have been prosecuted for breaching the requirements for lawful euthanasia and that those doctors who have been convicted of murder have typically been dealt with by the courts with striking leniency.

Finally, advocates of legalisation often allege that in countries where voluntary euthanasia is illegal there is a higher incidence of *non*-voluntary euthanasia than in countries where voluntary euthanasia is lawful and that legalising voluntary euthanasia would reduce the incidence of non-voluntary euthanasia. Euthanasia advocates argue that doctors are currently 'forced' to practice non-voluntary euthanasia precisely because voluntary euthanasia is unlawful. This is unpersuasive. If voluntary euthanasia is unlawful then so too is non-voluntary euthanasia. How can the same prohibition which deters them from performing the former encourage them to perform the latter? Legalising voluntary euthanasia, far from discouraging the non-voluntary variety, would surely do the opposite. For it would send out a signal that killing patients, at their request, can benefit them. Many doctors would then reasonably ask why patients should be denied this benefit merely because they are unable to request it.

(c) The Dutch experience

The Report implicitly endorsed the Dutch and Belgian legislation. It described the procedures prescribed by the legislation as 'strict and transparent' and claimed that the Dutch surveys have shown that 'close monitoring' is possible. There is a problem with this: the Dutch surveys have shown precisely the opposite.

---

24 Roscoe, L., Malphurs, J., Dragovic, L. and Cohen, D., 'Dr. Jack Kevorkian and Cases of Euthanasia in Oakland County, Michigan, 1990-1998', (2000) 343 *New England Journal of Medicine*, 1735-6 (Correspondence).

For example, the so-called 'strict and transparent procedures' in the Dutch legislation (which essentially enshrine guidelines which have been in operation since 1984 when the Dutch Supreme Court first declared voluntary euthanasia lawful) include a requirement for doctors to report all cases to the authorities. The three Dutch surveys carried out by Professor van der Maas *et al.* have demonstrated that *a clear majority of cases has been covered up by doctors.*[25] In other words, in the bulk of cases there has not even been an opportunity for control. Even in relation to the minority of cases which *has* been reported the report is filed by the doctors, who are hardly likely to disclose that they have breached the guidelines. The surveys have indicated, moreover, that failure to report is by no means the only important requirement which has been widely ignored, with virtual impunity, by Dutch doctors. In breach of the requirement of an 'explicit request' by the patient thousands of Dutch patients (mainly, but not exclusively, incompetent) have been intentionally killed without request. Indeed, the survey authors have remarked that *it is the responsibility of patients to make it clear if they do not want to be euthanised should they become incompetent.*[26] So much, then, for euthanasia being confined to those who explicitly request it. Mr Marty cited these surveys[27] but made no mention of this revealing remark nor of many of the surveys' other disturbing revelations. Again, the conspicuous failure of the Dutch regulatory mechanisms over the past 20 years has been repeatedly demonstrated by commentators of whose work Marty seems oblivious.[28] Also notably absent from the Report is any reference to the serious

25 Keown, J. *op cit.*, at pp. 113, 132; Richard Fenigsen, R., *loc cit.*, at pp. 73, 77.

26 Dr Richard Fenigsen translates the relevant passage on page 201 (lines 22-27) of the third survey (van der Wal, G., van der Heide, A., Onwuteaka-Philipsen, B.D. and van der Maas, P.J, *op cit.*) as follows:

'Due consideration should be give to the question how termination of life without explicit request can be prevented. It should be the responsibility of the patients, (their) next of kin, the doctors, the nurses, and the management, to clarify, well in advance, orally and in writing what are the wishes of the patient concerning the end of his life; for example, as a statement of will or as advance care planning.'

['Het verdient overweging om na te gaan op welke wijze levensbeeindigend handelen zonder uitdrukkelijk verzoek kan worden voorkomen. Hier ligt een veraantwoordelijkheid voor patienten, naasten, artsen, verpleging en management, om vroegtijdig, mondeling en schriftelijk, duidelijkheid te creeren over de wensen van de patient met betrekking tot diens levenseinde, bijvoorbeeld door middel van wilsverklaringen en advance care planning.'] I am grateful to Dr Fenigsen for this translation (Personal communication, 31st January 2005).

27 Marty I (Explanatory Memorandum) at paras 20-24.

28 See, for example, Gomez, C.F., *Regulating Death: Euthanasia and the Case of the Netherlands*, New York, Free Press, 1991; Hendin, H., *Seduced by Death: Doctors, Patients and Assisted Suicide*, New York, W.W. Norton 1998; Keown, J., *op cit.* The focus in this chapter is on the Dutch rather than the Belgian experience, partly because Dutch law has approved euthanasia for much longer (and there is accordingly more evidence about Dutch practice) and partly because the Belgian law largely emulates the Dutch law.

concerns which have been expressed, not least about the non-voluntary euthanasia of disabled newborns, by the UN Human Rights Committee.[29]

In short, there is indeed a 'striking divergence', but it is between the law and the practice of euthanasia in the Netherlands. Another gap, hardly less striking, is that between the reality of Dutch practice and its representation by the Marty Report.

(d) Changing attitudes toward suicide

The Report also presented a contentious interpretation of changing attitudes to suicide. In England, for example, the decriminalisation of suicide by the Suicide Act 1961 reflected, as the Government of the time made abundantly clear,[30] not a condonation of suicide but a realisation that criminal punishment was an inappropriate way of dealing with the suicidal. As Lord Bingham confirmed in the *Pretty* case, in which the House of Lords rejected an alleged right to assisted suicide, the Suicide Act 1961 conferred no right on anyone to commit suicide.[31]

(e) Public opinion

The Report claimed that public opinion polls show a majority in favour of legalisation. Such polls must, however, be read with no little reserve. A report commissioned by the House of Lords Select Committee on the Assisted Dying for the Terminally Ill Bill concluded that research conducted hitherto into public and health sector attitudes to the legalisation of euthanasia was:

> limited in value and cannot be accepted at face value as an authentic account of opinion within the United Kingdom. The subject matter is extremely complex and sensitive and therefore very challenging for anyone attempting to gain a meaningful understanding of opinion.[32]

It added:

---

29 See paras 5-6, available at: http://www.unhchr.ch/tbs/doc.nsf/(Symbol)/CCPR.CO.72.NET.En?Opendocument.

30 Keown, J., *op cit.*, at pp. 64-66.

31 *Regina (Pretty) v. Director of Public Prosecutions (Secretary of State for the Home Department Intervening)*, [2002] 3 WLR 1598. His Lordship stated (at paragraph [35]): 'Suicide itself (and with it attempted suicide) was decriminalised because recognition of the common law offence was not thought to act as a deterrent, because it cast an unwarranted stigma on innocent members of the suicide's family and because it led to the distasteful result that patients recovering in hospital from a failed suicide attempt were prosecuted, in effect, for their lack of success. But while the 1961 Act abrogated the rule of law whereby it was a crime for a person to commit (or attempt to commit) suicide, it conferred no right on anyone to do so. Had that been its object there would have been no justification for penalising by a potentially very long term of imprisonment one who aided, abetted, counselled or procured the exercise or attempted exercise by another of that right. The policy of the law remained firmly adverse to suicide, as section 2(1) makes clear.'

32 *Report of the House of Lords Select Committee on the Assisted Dying for the Terminally Ill Bill*, HL Paper 86-I (2005), para 232.

> This is particularly the case with regard to the attitudes of the general public, whose real views on euthanasia are clearly obscured by a lack of information on the subject and by the lack of opportunity to reflect in an informed way upon the implications of any change in the law for themselves and for society.[33]

In any event, even if the Marty Report's claim were true it could hardly be allowed to dictate law and public policy any more than a finding that a majority of people favour capital punishment.

(f) Equating euthanasia with non-treatment

The Report's equation of 'euthanasia' with the withdrawal of life-sustaining treatment when the shortening of life is foreseen, which it described as 'passive euthanasia', is misleading. The Report defined 'euthanasia' as:

> any medical act intended to end a patient's life at his or her persistent, carefully considered and voluntary request in order to relieve unbearable suffering.[34]

How, then, can the withdrawal of treatment when the doctor merely *foresees* that it will shorten life count, on the Report's own definition, as 'euthanasia'? For one thing, it is doubtful whether withdrawal, and particularly withholding, can properly be characterised as an 'act'.[35] For another, even if there were foresight of death it would not follow that there was also an intention to end life. For the report to conflate these two forms of conduct, which there are cogent ethical reasons to regard as distinct, invites confusion. Moreover, by defining 'euthanasia' as 'active, voluntary euthanasia' the Report adopted the controversially narrow Dutch definition. One danger of this definition is that it can be used (as it has been in the Netherlands) to deflect discussion of non-voluntary and involuntary euthanasia on the ground that they are not 'euthanasia' and therefore lie outside the boundaries of the euthanasia debate.

(g) Misrepresenting the case against euthanasia

The Report stated that opponents of legalisation reject the claim that:

> each individual, out of respect for his or her dignity and value, has a right to take decisions concerning his or her own life and death in accordance with his or her own values and beliefs, as long as no harm is done to others, and not to have these imposed.[36]

It would have been less misleading to have stated that opponents of euthanasia, while supporting the right of patients to make a wide range of decisions concerning their medical treatment, reject *one* decision as being incompatible with the patient's

33 *Id.*

34 Marty I (Explanatory Memorandum) at para 8.

35 Yet Marty boldly asserted that withdrawal is 'an act of commission, if ever there was one'. *Ibid.*, at para 59.

36 *Ibid.*, at para 55.

dignity and value: the decision to be intentionally killed, or to be helped to commit suicide. Moreover, to prohibit that choice does not deny the patient's dignity but affirms it, just as disallowing some other choices a person may want to make, such as to be executed rather than be imprisoned or enslaved rather than free, equally respects his or her inalienable dignity. The fact that, through depression or pain or loneliness, some patients may lose sight of their worth is no argument for endorsing their misguided judgment that their life is no longer worth living. Were the law to allow patients to be intentionally killed by their doctors the law would be accepting that there are two categories of patients: those whose lives are worth living and those who are better off dead. What signal, moreover, would that send out to the sick, the elderly, the disabled and the dying?

The Report went on to imply that opponents of euthanasia are imposing on the terminally ill 'the obligation to live out their life in unbearable suffering and anguish ...'.[37] On the contrary, many of the leading opponents of euthanasia, such as the late Dame Cicely Saunders, foundress of the hospice movement, have devoted their lives to the alleviation of suffering and anguish. The standard case against euthanasia recognises the right of patients to refuse treatments because they are futile or too burdensome, and to be treated with palliative drugs, even if it is foreseen that death will come sooner. It does *not* hold that life should be preserved at all costs; that is a cheap caricature.

Counter-arguments Not Met The Report glossed over several important counter-arguments. For example, it mentioned but nowhere rebutted the counter-argument that legalising voluntary euthanasia leads as a matter of practice and of logic to non-voluntary euthanasia. This counter-argument runs that the slide will occur as a matter of practice because 'safeguards' to prevent it cannot be made effective and as a matter of logic because the case for voluntary euthanasia for the terminally ill contains the seeds of its own extension to those who are not terminally ill or to those who cannot request it. The failure of 'safeguards' as a matter of practice is amply demonstrated by the Dutch experience. That experience also illustrates the force of the logical 'slippery slope', which is a product of the unresolved tension in the argument for voluntary euthanasia between patient autonomy and patient welfare.

(a) Respect for patient autonomy

The Report stated that opponents of euthanasia dismissed 'the individual's right to take decisions concerning his or her own life and death in accordance with his or her own beliefs and values, as long as no harm is done to others'.[38] It concluded that consideration should be given to exempt from prosecution doctors who agree to help 'terminally-ill patients undergoing constant, unbearable pain and suffering without

37 *Ibid.*, at para 56.

38 *Ibid.*, at para 62.

hope of any improvement in their condition, to end their lives at their persistent, voluntary and well-considered request …'.[39]

If, however, there is a right to make decisions concerning life and death in accordance with one's own values and beliefs, why should euthanasia not be available to *any* autonomous person who believes for whatever reason (terminal illness, chronic physical or mental illness, 'tiredness of life', bereavement, divorce, unemployment …) that their life is no longer 'worth living'? By imposing conditions such as 'terminal illness' on candidates for euthanasia why was the Report not denying each individual's 'right to take decisions concerning his or her own life and death in accordance with his or her own values and beliefs'? Interestingly, the former Dutch Health Minister, Mrs Borst, a leading defender of the Dutch euthanasia regime, has stated that she thinks the elderly should be able to obtain suicide pills which they could take if they simply felt 'tired of living'.[40] Mr Marty could not claim to be unaware her viewpoint: it was pointed out by the author in his response to Mrs Borst's speech at a hearing on euthanasia held by his Committee in Paris in 2002.[41]

(b) Respect for patient welfare: the life 'not worth living'

No responsible doctor would kill a patient merely because the patient requested it, however autonomously, any more than a responsible doctor would amputate a healthy leg just because the patient requested it. Indeed, in the Netherlands doctors refuse many autonomous requests for euthanasia. The doctor grants the request only if the *doctor* judges that the patient is right in thinking that death would be a benefit. But if the doctor thinks he or she can make this judgment (that the patient would be better off dead) in relation to a patient who asks for euthanasia, why cannot the doctor make that decision in relation to a patient in the same situation who is unable to request it? In other words, if death would benefit the patient why should it be denied the patient merely because of incompetence? Illustrating the force of this counter-argument, in 1996 two Dutch Courts of Appeal, adapting the reasoning previously used by the courts to justify voluntary euthanasia, held it lawful for doctors to give lethal injections to disabled babies.[42] More recently, the public prosecution service has endorsed guidelines, passed by the Dutch Paediatric Society, permitting non-voluntary euthanasia of certain neonates.[43]

(c) Expert committees

Mr Marty's Explanatory Memorandum concluded:

---

39 *Ibid.*, (Draft Resolution) at para 9(iv)

40 CNN.COM/WORLD 14th April 2001.

41 A hearing which, like the Report, was unbalanced: invited speakers in favour of legalisation markedly outnumbered those against.

42 Jochemsen, J., 'Dutch Court Decisions on Nonvoluntary Euthanasia Critically Reviewed', (1998) 13(4) *Issues Law Med*, 447.

43 Sheldon, T., 'Dutch doctors adopt guidelines on mercy killing of newborns', (2005) 331 *BMJ*, 126.

> As a lawyer and a legislator, I note that all over the world, doctors are ending the lives of patients, often in secrecy and with a sense of guilt. The law seems to want to ignore this fact of life, whereas it ought to have the courage to address it. Decriminalising euthanasia, rather than keeping the ban, might enable us to better supervise it and also prevent it.[44]

Mr Marty seemed unaware that around the world the case for legalising voluntary euthanasia has been considered by 'lawyers and legislators' time and again and that they have, with few exceptions, rejected that case. He omitted even to mention important reports such as that of the New York State Task Force (1994) whose members, both pro- and anti-euthanasia in principle, unanimously rejected legalisation on the ground that it would be socially disastrous.[45]

The Marty Report appeared in September 2003. It was scathingly criticised by the Council's Committee on Legal Affairs and Human Rights later that month.[46] Mr Kevin McNamara, this Committee's Rapporteur, called in his Explanatory Memorandum for the Parliamentary Assembly to reaffirm Recommendation 1418 rather than to adopt the Marty Report.[47] The Marty Report was debated in April 2004 by the Parliamentary Assembly.[48] The Assembly decided not to vote on the text and charged the Social, Health and Family Affairs Committee to prepare a new text bringing together the widely diverging viewpoints expressed in the debate. In February 2005, the Committee produced a revised report.

Marty Revised (2005)

The revised Report comprised a Draft Resolution of six paragraphs and an Explanatory Memorandum by Mr Marty running to 51 paragraphs and four Appendices (outlining respectively the law in the Netherlands, Belgium, Switzerland and proposed legislation in France).[49] The revised Draft Resolution was noticeably more conservative than the original. The original's focus on euthanasia, including its explicit recommendation that member states consider the legalisation of euthanasia, was replaced by an emphasis on the promotion of palliative care and on the prevention of euthanasia in secret. However, not least when read in the light of the

---

44 Marty I (Explanatory Memorandum) at para 62.

45 See note 23, *supra*.

46 *Euthanasia. An Opinion by the Committee on Legal Affairs and Human Rights*, (23rd September 2003) Doc 9923 Rapporteur: Mr Kevin McNamara, United Kingdom, Socialist Group (Hereafter 'Legal Opinion'): http://assembly.coe.int/Documents/WorkingDocs/Doc03/EDOC9923.htm.

47 Legal Opinion (Explanatory Memorandum) para 4.

48 Available at: http://www.coe.int/NewsSearch/InternetNewsSearch.asp?KW=marty+&lmLangue=1&Submit=Search&L=.

49 *Assistance to Patients at End of Life*, Report of the Social, Health and Family Affairs Committee, 9th February 2005 (Doc. 10455): http://assembly.coe.int/Documents/WorkingDocs/Doc05/EDOC10455.htm (Hereafter 'Marty II').

accompanying revised Explanatory Memorandum (which was by contrast barely amended), the revised Draft Resolution remained open to serious objection.

The Revised Draft Resolution

The more conservative tone of the Report was reflected in its change of title, from *Euthanasia* to *Assistance to Patients at End of Life*. Moreover, its opening paragraph affirmed that it was 'important and necessary' to reaffirm the 'fundamental principle' in Recommendation 1418 of protecting the dignity and rights of all human beings. The paragraph continued:

> The Assembly takes this opportunity to reiterate its unwavering belief that this principle means, inter alia, that it is forbidden to cause someone's death deliberately.[50]

However, the remainder of the Draft Resolution proceeded, by leaving open the option of legalising euthanasia, to saw off the branch on which this reaffirmation sat. No sooner had the first paragraph of the Draft Resolution reaffirmed Recommendation 1418's opposition to intentional killing than paragraph two stated that the Assembly could not ignore certain facts, such as that the Netherlands and Belgium had enacted laws which permitted euthanasia; that Bills to legalise it had been introduced in 'numerous' other countries; that in several countries opinion polls suggested a majority favoured legalisation; and that euthanasia was practised in countries where it was illegal 'in proportions well in excess of what was previously believed'. Further undermining the Draft Resolution's stated opposition to intentional killing, paragraph three stated that euthanasia was a 'very delicate' issue which touched on the 'moral, religious and cultural values of our societies' and that it therefore followed that the solution to the problem 'cannot be the same for all countries'. It was 'essential' that these 'different sensitivities' be respected 'while reiterating the inviolable principle that human rights and dignity must be respected'.

Paragraph four recommended that member states should implement a genuine policy of assistance to patients at the end of life which did not cause them to want to die, as by promoting palliative care (including care in their own homes) and the avoidance of superfluous treatment. However, paragraph five proposed that 'greater transparency' be achieved so as to reduce as far as possible the practice of euthanasia 'in secret or in a legal vacuum' and that procedures be introduced, where they did not already exist, clearly defining the responsibilities of medical and nursing staff and ensuring the traceability of all decisions, thus facilitating effective monitoring. That the Draft Resolution was open to the legalisation of euthanasia became even clearer in paragraph six which reiterated that in view of the 'diversity of cultural and religious sensitivities' among member states it was 'hardly possible to recommend a universal model for all to follow' and that member states should analyse the Dutch and Belgian experience and relevant Bills currently being discussed in other

---

50 Marty II (Draft Resolution) at para 1.

countries and should 'prevent euthanasia from developing in a shroud of secrecy because of legal uncertainties or outdated norms'.[51] Not, note, to prevent euthanasia from developing, but to prevent euthanasia from developing in secrecy.

In short, the Draft Resolution's first paragraph was progressively undermined by its subsequent paragraphs. Moreover, neither the report nor the accompanying Draft Explanatory Memorandum pointed out why, if euthanasia was a 'very delicate' issue which touched on the 'moral, religious and cultural values of our societies' it therefore followed that the solution to the problem could not be the same for all countries. Until very recently, it *has* been the same and, with few exceptions, still is. And is not capital punishment an issue which also touches on moral and cultural values but which is nevertheless prohibited by the Council of Europe?

The Draft Resolution's suggestion that euthanasia is practised in secret because of 'legal uncertainties and outdated norms' rings hollow. Leaving aside that we are not told what these 'uncertainties' are, nor the norms are 'outdated', nor how they together promote secret euthanasia, the undisputed reality is that the legal norms in the Netherlands, which are of recent vintage, have conspicuously failed to prevent the practice of euthanasia in secret. That the revised Report remained sympathetic to the legalisation of euthanasia, despite its opening paragraph, becomes even clearer when the revised Draft Resolution is read in the light of the revised Explanatory Memorandum.

The Revised Explanatory Memorandum

As has been noted, the revised Draft Resolution was more conservative in tone than its original version. Not so the revised Explanatory Memorandum (again drafted by Mr Marty) which remained little more than a crude polemic for legalisation.[52] Given that the revised version is vulnerable to the same objections levelled above at the original version, little remains to be said. Three additional points, however, may be made.

First, the revised Memorandum criticised 'the silence in which this issue is more often than not enshrouded'[53] and announced that a 'long-repressed debate' had now been launched in several countries.[54] Mr Marty's understanding of the history of the subject is no sounder than his grasp of its other dimensions. The truth of the matter is that the legalisation of euthanasia has been debated since the nineteenth century. Bills were introduced in the US from the early twentieth century and in the UK

51 *Ibid.*, at para 6(v).

52 In his conclusions Mr Marty commented that the answer to the questions he raised about patient autonomy, dignity and the practice of secret euthanasia should 'not necessarily' be the legalisation of euthanasia, at least as a solution applicable to all members states. (*ibid.*, explanatory memorandum, at para 49). It seems clear, however, that 'not necessarily' for 'everyone' did not mean 'not' for 'anyone'.

53 *Ibid.*, at para 12.

54 *Ibid.*, at para 49.

from the 1930s.[55] The debate has intensified over the last twenty years, not least as a result of the decision of the Dutch Supreme Court in 1984 to permit voluntary euthanasia. The intensification has been reflected by the publication of reports of expert bodies such as the New York State Task Force in 1994[56] and the House of Lords Select Committees in 1994[57] and 2005,[58] by widespread media coverage of the issue (illustrated by the Diane Pretty case[59]) and the voluminous academic literature on the subject. So much, then, for the debate being 'long-repressed'.

A second point concerns the revised Memorandum's claim, in relation to the Netherlands and Belgium, that '[t]he initial indications would not seem to point to any increase in the number of cases of euthanasia or any other types of abuse'.[60] The reality of the matter is that there was a substantial increase in the number of cases in the Netherlands between 1990 and 1995 and that cases of unchecked abuse, from the practice of euthanasia without request to non-reporting, have been numerous.

A third point concerns the persistence of errors in the revised Memorandum even though they had been exposed by the Legal Affairs and Human Rights Committee. For example, this Committee (rightly) concluded that the Dutch euthanasia surveys had demonstrated: 'a disturbingly high incidence of euthanasia ... without the patient's explicit request and an equally disturbing failure by medical practitioners to report euthanasia cases to the proper regulatory authority'.[61] Mr Marty's revised Memorandum did not respond to such objections and persisted in its misrepresentation of the Dutch experience.[62] Similarly, the Legal Affairs Committee urged that the withholding or withdrawal of treatment because, for example, its burdens outweighed its benefits 'should not be confused with voluntary active euthanasia or physician assisted suicide where the intention is to accelerate or cause death by withholding or withdrawing treatment'.[63] Again without meeting this objection, the revised Memorandum maintained its controversial definition of withholding or withdrawing life-support as 'passive euthanasia'. Indeed, it even compounded matters by asserting that 'euthanasia' was commonly practised and supported this with a comment by the French Health Minister that many life-support machines were switched off every year! The Minister was further quoted as saying that an end should be brought to this 'unacceptable hypocrisy'.[64] There is, of course, no hypocrisy in prohibiting intentional killing while allowing the withholding or withdrawal of treatment which

---

55 Emanuel, E.K., 'The History of Euthanasia Debates in the United States and Britain', (1994) 121 (10) *Annals of Internal Medicine*, 793.

56 See note 23, *supra*.

57 *Report of the House of Lords Select Committee on Medical Ethics*, HL Paper 21-I (1994).

58 See note 32, *supra*.

59 *Pretty v. United Kingdom* (2002) 66 BMLR 147, EctHR.

60 Marty II (Explanatory Memorandum) at para 51.

61 Legal Opinion (Conclusions of the Committee) Amendment D.

62 Marty II (Explanatory Memorandum) at paras 26-30; 51.

63 Legal Opinion (Conclusions of the Committee) Amendment E.

64 Marty II (Explanatory Memorandum) at para 48 fn. 15.

is futile or too burdensome. Indeed, it may strike the reader as remarkable that a Report which affirmed the prohibition on intentional killing while paving the way for its legalisation should have accused the present law of hypocrisy.

Conclusion

The core argument informing the Marty Report – that because euthanasia takes place illegally the Council of Europe should, in the light of empirical evidence, consider legalising it so as to 'bring it out into the open' where it could be better 'controlled' – has been undermined by the evidence from the Netherlands. This is hardly surprising: if some doctors are prepared, when voluntary euthanasia is illegal, to ignore the law of murder which prohibits it why should they be expected, when it has been legalised, to observe the guidelines which permit it? And, as the Dutch slide down euthanasia's 'slippery slope' confirms, once the rhetorical mask of autonomy is stripped away the true face of euthanasia is revealed: the judgment that certain patients are better off dead. The Marty Report, in its original and revised versions, is an exercise in failed cosmetic surgery. Indeed, it read less like an informed report from a Council of Europe Committee and more like a propaganda pamphlet from a euthanasia pressure-group.

On 27th April 2005 the Parliamentary Assembly voted by 138 votes to 26 (with 5 abstentions) to reject the Marty Report.[65]

65 Available at: http://www.coe.int/NewsSearch/InternetNewsSearchDateKW.asp?lmLangue=1&qrNewsExpMonth=04&qrNewsExpYear=2005&KW=marty&Submit=Go. On 12th May 2006 the House of Lords rejected a Bill to legalise physician-assisted suicide which had been considered by a Select Committee of the House (see note 32, supra). For a critique of the Bill see John Keown, *Considering Physician-Assisted Suicide: An Evaluation of Lord Joffe's Assisted Dying for the Terminally Ill Bill* (2006) (available at: www.carenotkilling.org)

Chapter 31

Newborn Screening for Sickle Cell Disease: Socio-Ethical Implications

Denise Avard, Linda Kharaboyan and Bartha Knoppers

Introduction

Newborn screening is now integrated into routine neonatal practice in many parts of the world, and the overall ethical acceptability of newborn screening programmes is well recognised.[1] Although the procedure corresponds in essence to genetic screening, it is seldom referred to as such and is often categorised as a public health disease prevention programme aimed at early detection and treatment of asymptomatic newborns affected by specific treatable disorders. Accordingly, the overall ethical issues that have been dealt with extensively in the context of medical genetics, such as the principle of autonomy and the requirement for informed decision making, have been considered less significant with regard to publicly mandated newborn screening, because these newborn public health programmes are believed to be implemented in the interests of children and therefore override the need for an explicit or written informed consent.[2] The WHO considers that newborn screening should be mandatory if early diagnosis and treatment will benefit the newborn.[3]

As scientific and genetic technologies advance, classical newborn screening programmes aimed at detecting only preventable diseases are now being revisited and expanded. In some countries, they are being redesigned to include new disorders which are not in total compliance with the long-established WHO criteria of conditions suitable for screening.[4] Using the same blood sample collected to screen for classical disorders like phenylketonuria (PKU) and congenital hypothyroidism,

1 Kerruish, N.J. and, Robertson, S.P., 'Newborn Screening: New Developments, New Dilemmas', (2005) 31 *J. Med. Ethics*, 393-8.

2 Laberge, C., Kharaboyan, L. and Avard, D., 'Newborn Screening, Banking, and Consent', (2004) 2(3) *GenEdit*, available at: http://www.humgen.umontreal.ca/int/GE/en/2004-3.pdf.

3 World Health Organization (WHO), *Proposed International Guidelines on Ethical Issues in Medical Genetics and Genetic Services*, Geneva, December 15 and 16, 1997, available at: http://whqlibdoc.who.int/hq/1998/WHO_HGN_GL_ETH_98.1.pdf (accessed 05/15/06).

4 Wilson, J. and Jungner, G., *Principles and Practice of Screening for Disease*, Geneva, World Health Organization (Public Health Paper), 1968.

laboratories are now able to examine DNA and test newborn bloodspots for conditions which are still untreatable, to identify a genetic predisposition not manifested until adulthood, to indicate genetic susceptibility to common multifactorial diseases and, finally, to reveal incidental results such as carrier status for both treatable diseases and untreatable conditions.

There are many disorders currently being considered for inclusion in newborn screening programmes, such as inborn errors of metabolism,[5] cystic fibrosis,[6] muscular dystrophy[7] and Type I diabetes.[8] Here we will focus on one illustrative example: newborn screening for sickle cell diseases (SCD). Sickle cell disease is an example of a genetic condition that is considered a global health problem. Increasingly, industrialised countries are integrating sickle cell disease into their newborn screening programmes.[9] Screening for SCD can occur during the prenatal or neonatal period. In this chapter we will focus on neonatal screening.

Although sickle cell disease can be treated through early detection and supportive therapies, neonatal screening for sickle cell disease is controversial and raises new challenges. Screening programmes provide clinical advantages, but there is also the risk of harm. In particular, there are three socio-ethical issues we would like to explore. First, as a result of neonatal screening and without having requested the information, we can identify carriers of the sickle cell trait at a time when concern about carrier status may not be a priority. Second, there are a number of approaches to neonatal screening for SCD. For example, infants can be screened on a selective basis (only high-risk infants) or by using a universal approach (all newborns). The issue of whether a programme screening for SCD should be universal or selective raises concerns about equity, the risk of discrimination and cost. Third, given the trend to promote community engagement, and the mounting pressure from advocacy groups to expand newborn screening programs, a decision to introduce newborn screening for SCD must proceed with careful consideration of the relevant ethical and social issues. This chapter does not discuss SCD newborn screening as part of the overall newborn screening programme or whether it should be integrated with the current neonatal screening programmes.

In the first part of this chapter, we will examine the rationale for sickle cell screening, including background, prevalence and program description. This will be followed by a discussion of ethical and social issues, such as the identification

---

5 Seymour, C.A., Thomason, M.J., Chalmers, R.A., *et al.*, 'Newborn Screening for Inborn Errors of Metabolism: A Systematic Review', (1997) I *Health Technology Assessment*.

6 Wald, N.J. and Morris, J.K., 'Neonatal Screening for Cystic Fibrosis', (1998) 316 *BMJ*, 404-405.

7 Parsons, E.P., Bradley, D.M. and Clarke, A.J., 'Newborn Screening for Duchenne Muscular Dystrophy', (2003) 88 *Arch. Dis. Child*, 91-92.

8 Bennett, J.S., Baughcum, A.E., Carmichael, S.K., She, J.X. and Schatz, D.A., 'Maternal Anxiety Associated with Newborn Genetic Screening for Type 1 Diabetes', (2004) 27 *Diabetes Care*, 392-7.

9 Weatherall, D.J. and Clegg, J.B., 'Inherited Haemoglobin Disorders: An Increasing Global Health Problem', (2001) 79 *Bulletin of the World Health Organization*, 704-12.

of carriers, the constraints of using a selective or a universal approach for such programmes, and the pressures exerted on decision makers by advocacy groups.

The Rationale for Neonatal Screening of Sickle Cell Disease

Background

Sickle cell disease (SCD) consists of a group of life-threatening, genetically inherited disorders, characterised by large amounts of abnormal haemoglobin in the red blood cells. Most infants with SCD are healthy at birth and become symptomatic later, in infancy or childhood. Affected infants generally present clinically during infancy or early childhood with painful swelling of the hands and feet (dactylitis), pneumococcal sepsis or meningitis, severe anaemia and acute spleen enlargement, acute chest syndrome, pallor, jaundice or splenomegaly.[10] The long-term consequences of SCD include chronic organ damage, such as degeneration of the kidneys, bones and joints, and chronic pain and disability, which compromise quality of life. These persons live under the possibility of early sudden death related to the disease[11] and the lifespan varies between 42 years for males and 46 years for females.[12]

With the exception of bone marrow or stem cell transplantation, only available for a limited number of patients with compatible donors, there is currently no definitive cure for SCD.[13] Nevertheless, improvements in the medical care of children with SCD have increased their life expectancy and studies have shown that prognosis for patients has improved considerably through early diagnosis and treatment such as the early use of prophylactic penicillin and ongoing effective management of infections in children with the condition.[14]

Prevalence

The disease mostly affects people whose ancestors are from Africa but is also prevalent in people of Mediterranean, Caribbean, South and Central American,

10 American Academy of Pediatrics (AAP), 'Health Supervision for Children with Sickle Cell Disease – Policy Statement', (2002) 109(3) *Pediatrics*, 526-35.

11 Thomas, V.J. and Taylor, L.M., 'The psychosocial experience of people with sickle cell disease and its impact on quality of life: Qualitative findings from focus groups', (2002) 7 *British Journal of Health Psychology*, 345-63.

12 Quinn, C.T., Rogers, Z.R., Buchanan, G.R., 'Survival of children with sickle cell disease', (2004) 103(11) *Blood*, 4023-7; Platt, O.S., Brambilla, D.J., Rosse, W.F., Milner, P.F., Castro, O., Steinberg, M.H., *et al.*, 'Mortality in sickle cell disease: Life expectancy and risk factors for early death', (1994) 330 *New England Journal of Medicine*, 1639-43.

13 Weatherall, Clegg, *loc cit.*

14 Ballas, S.K., 'Sickle Cell Disease: Clinical Management', (1998) 11 *Clinical Haematology*, 185-214.

Middle Eastern and Indian ancestry.[15] The population at risk of SCD in Canada is unknown, and there are no available statistics to show whether there has been an increase in sickle cell disease in Canada over recent years as a result of increased migration.[16] Estimates indicate that, in the United Kingdom, the prevalence of sickle cell disease and other haemoglobinopathies (genetically inherited disorders of haemoglobin) amongst newborns is now higher (1:2380) than cystic fibrosis (1:2500),[17] a disease that is predominantly prevalent in Caucasian populations[18] and that has received much more attention than SCD.[19]

Types of Screening Programmes

Newborn screening aims to identify affected infants and begin preventive treatment before disease manifestation. Outside of Canada (e.g. in the US, the UK and France), newborn screening for sickle cell disease has generally been accepted as an effective intervention. However, an important drawback is the lack of consistent policies for SCD screening.[20] For example, Wertz reported that in the United States, where programmes for sickle cell anaemia screening exist, differences exist among primary care physicians in the commitment to, and acceptability of, screening of all newborns, with 71 per cent of paediatricians, 46 per cent of obstetricians, and 40 per cent of family practitioners agreeing that at risk groups should be screened.[21]

Neonatal screening programmes can be offered universally or selectively. Universal screening is generally considered a routine public health intervention offered to the entire newborn population or to all pregnant women. In fact, universal neonatal screening for SCD has been implemented in most of the United States[22] and in all of England as of April 2005.[23] In contrast to universal screening, selective or targeted screening concentrates on subpopulations with the aim of identifying high-risk infants and, indirectly, of identifying high-risk parents to offer them the opportunity of screening in future pregnancies.

15 American Academy of Pediatrics, *supra*, note 10.

16 D. Soulières, hematologist, personal communication.

17 Streetly, A., *Policy Decision for Implementing Neonatal Screening for Sickle Cell Disease*, NHS Sickle & Thalassaemia Screening Programme, 2002.

18 Parsons, Bradley, *supra cit.*, note 7.

19 Kmietowicz, Z., 'Screening for Sickle Cell Disease and Thalassaemia Saving Lives', (2004) 329 *BMJ*, 69.

20 Streetly, A., 'A National Screening Policy for Sickle Cell Disease and Thalassaemia Major for the United Kingdom', (2000) 320 *BMJ*, 1353-4.

21 Wertz, D., 'Ethical Issues in Pediatric Genetics', (1998) 6 *Health Law Journal*, 3-42.

22 National Newborn Screening and Genetics Resource Center (NNSGRC), *U.S. National Screening Status Report*, Austin, May 2, 2006, http://genes-r-us.uthscsa.edu/nbsdisorders.pdf (accessed on 05/15/06).

23 NHS Sickle Cell and Thalassaemia Screening Programme, *Policy for Newborn Screening*, London, July 2004, http://www-phm.umds.ac.uk/haemscreening/Documents/NewbornScreeningPolicy.pdf (accessed on 04/08/04).

The decision whether to adopt a universal or selective strategy rests with public health authorities and involves complex arguments about the risk of discrimination, equity, and cost-effectiveness.[24] Although deciding on a screening approach is not an easy task, long-standing principles have been established to guide policy-makers in their decision making.

Perhaps the most cited source of screening criteria are the 1968 Wilson and Jungner principles of early disease detection.[25] Essentially, they prescribe that conditions that are screened for should present an important health problem (i.e. be relatively prevalent); that an acceptable treatment be available to treat the screened condition; that facilities for diagnosis and treatment be widely available; that the cost (including diagnosing and treating patients) be economically balanced in relation to possible expenditure on medical care as a whole; and that diagnosed patients benefit from timely follow-up services.

A condition that complies with the above criteria is suitable for universal newborn screening. Although there is no definitive cure for SCD, it does fit the 1968 criteria: increased survival and health development of children with the condition is largely attributed to neonatal screening with prompt prophylactic penicillin treatment and to the effective management of infections.[26,27,28] Because of this, the establishment of a newborn screening programme for sickle cell disease has been described as justifiable and unquestionable.[29] Accordingly, since the publication of the NIH consensus statement on mandatory newborn screening for haemoglobinopathies in 1987,[30] 48 American states as well as the District of Columbia have implemented universal newborn screening programmes for SCD.[31] Moreover, as of April 2005, all babies in England are being screened for SCD as part of the centralised newborn programme, which screens for phenylketonuria (PKU) and congenital hypothyroidism.

---

24 Aspinall, P.J., Dyson, S.M. and Anionwu, E., 'The Feasibility of Using Ethnicity as a Primary Tool for Antenatal Selective Screening for Sickle Cell Disorders: Pointers from Research Evidence', (2003) 56 *Social Science & Medicine*, 285-97.

25 Wilson, Jungner, *supra cit.*, note 4.

26 Zeuner, D., Ades, A.E., Karnon, J., Brown, J., Dezateux, C. and Aninowu, E.N., 'Antenatal and Neonatal Haemoglobinopathy Screening in the UK: Review and Economic Analysis', (1999) 3(11) *Health Technology Asessment.*

27 Davis, S.C., Cronin, E., Gill, M., Greengross, P., Hickman, M. and Normand, C. 'Screening for Sickle Cell and Thalassaemia: A Systematic Review with Supplementary Research', (2000) 4(3) *Health Technology Assessment.*

28 NIH Consensus Development Program, *Newborn Screening for Sickle Cell Disease and Other Hemoglobinopathies: National Institutes of Health Consensus Development Conference Statement*, April 6-8, 1987, http://consensus.nih.gov/cons/061/061_statement.htm (accessed on 05/15/06).

29 Streetly, *supra cit.*, note 20.

30 Consensus Conference, 'Newborn Screening for Sickle Cell Disease and Other Hemoglobinopathies', (1987) 258 *JAMA*, 1205-9.

31 National Newborn Screening and Genetics Resource Center, *supra cit.*, note 22.

In instances where the disease is not prevalent in all regions or in all spheres of the population, authorities might opt for a targeted approach instead of a universal screening programme. For example, France has chosen to offer SCD screening to all high-risk infants[32] by adopting a targeted screening approach in metropolitan areas, where infants are offered sickle cell screening if they fall under one of the 5 criteria defined by the Association Française pour le Dépistage et la Prévention des Handicaps de l'Enfant.[33] The five criteria are as follows: (1) if one of the two parents is originally from a country where the incidence of SCD is significant; (2) if one of the parents is from one of the above countries and the other is from Asia; (3) if the mother is at risk and the father is not known; (4) if a parent suffers from a haemoglobin disorder or is aware of any family history in this regard; and (5) if there is any doubt with regard to the four previous points. A concern with this approach is that some infants belonging to high-risk groups may be difficult to identify.[34] Following the introduction of the SCD screening programme there is evidence that early sudden death for children born with SCD is rare. However, follow-up studies of the long-term impact on reducing morbidity and mortality are lacking.[35]

Due to global migration, it is estimated that immigrants from visible minorities account for 11.2 per cent of the Canadian population.[36] The greatest concentration of visible minorities is in large urban areas, with nearly 42 per cent living in Toronto, 18 per cent in Vancouver and 13 per cent in Montreal.[37] Within the province of Quebec, Montreal is home to 92 per cent of the ethnic groups (from areas like the Caribbean, French Antilles and northern Africa) as well as immigrants from Arab/West Asian countries.[38] Therefore, a high concentration of SCD carriers or patients is likely in major Canadian cities. However, in the absence of a screening programme of neonates for SCD, in Montreal and elsewhere, small selective programmes, initiated only by individual clinicians, currently operate in Montreal.[39] In Toronto, a presentation to 'The Commission on the Future of Health Care in Canada' draws

---

32 Briard, M.L., 'Le dépistage néonatal de la drépanocytose en métropole', (2000) 39 *La Dépêche*.

33 Association française pour le Dépistage et la Prévention des Handicaps de l'Enfant, *Guide pratiques pour les professionnels de santé – Le dépistage néonatal*, March 2001.

34 Cronin, E.K., Normand, C., Henthorn, J.S., Hickman, M. and Davies, S.C., 'Costing model for neonatal screening and diagnosis of haemoglobinopathies', (1998) 79 *Arch. Dis. Child. Fetal Neonatal Ed.*, F161-7.

35 Farriaux, J.-P., 'Le dépistage néonatal de la drépanocytose' (2003) *Ann Biol Clin*, 61: 376-8.

36 Compiled from the 2001 Statistics Canada Census website.

37 Statistics Canada, '1996 Census: Ethnic Origin, Visible Minorities', *The Daily Tuesday*, February 17, 1998: http://www.statcan.ca/Daily/English/980217/d980217.htm (accessed 05/15/06).

38 *Id.*

39 Edgar Delvin, personal communication.

attention to the need for guidelines, education and training regarding sickle cell disease.[40]

Socio-ethical Concerns Related to Screening for SCD in Newborn Screening Programmes

Classical newborn screening usually occurs in the absence of explicit written parental consent.[41] However, for every one affected child, haemoglobin electrophoresis also identifies around 50 carriers[42] who require follow up because their parents may be at risk and therefore in need of genetic counselling. While withholding carrier information from parents is unacceptable, no consent to knowledge of carrier status is obtained prior to screening. If consent was required, some believe that parental refusal could jeopardise the overall preventive goals of newborn screening.[43] Policymakers must face the difficult issue of carrier information when deciding whether or not to include the disease in universal newborn screening panels. A second dilemma decision makers face is determining the type of screening programme most appropriate for a certain population given the constraints of costs and the selective profiling on the basis of ethnicity. A final issue that will be discussed pertains to the pressures exerted by patient advocacy groups to include new diseases in the universal newborn screening programme.

The Identification of Carriers and Incidental Results

Perhaps the most critical issue related to the implementation of a universal SCD screening program is that, in addition to finding affected newborns, disease screening also identifies carriers.[44] Detection of the sickle cell trait in newborns can offer opportunities for extended family testing and genetic counselling to parents for

---

40 Sickle Cell Parents' Support Group (prepared by Anne C.D. Clarke), 'Presentation to the Commission on the Future of Health Care in Canada: The Care and Treatment of Canada's Multi-Racial Population', 28 May 2002.

41 Avard, D. and Knoppers, B.M., 'Screening and Children Policy Issues for the New Millenium', (2001) 2(3) *ISUMA*, 46-57.

42 Council of Regional Networks for Genetics Services (CORN), 'US Newborn Screening System Guidelines II: Follow-up of Children, Diagnosis, Management, and Evaluation', (2000) 137(4) *J. Pediatrics*, S1.

43 Stewart, R., Oliver, S., 'What is known about communication with parents about newborn bloodspot screening?', UK Newborn Screening Programme Centre, London, May 2003: http://www.newbornscreening-bloodspot.org.uk (accessed 05/15/06).

44 Screening for sickle cell syndromes is unique because both homozygotes and heterozygotes may be detected during screening. Indeed approximately 50 infants who are carriers of haemoglobin variants are identified for every one individual who is detected with sickle cell disease. See Council of Regional Networks for Genetic Services, *Guidelines for Follow-up of Carriers of Hemoglobin Variants Detected by Newborn Screening*, Texas, September 10, 1995.

future reproductive choices: if an infant is a carrier, one or both parents are carriers. This information is useful to parents if they do not know their carrier status.

However, identifying carriers raises a number of ethical dilemmas for the family. First, while identification of carriers may be beneficial for the parents, birth is generally considered a poor time for communicating carrier screening information. Moreover, this information is of minimal benefit to the child; indeed, it may not be useful until the child reaches adolescence or reproductive age. There is no certainty that the genetic information will reach the child in an understandable form and at the appropriate time for the benefits to accrue: i.e. during adolescence or adulthood.[45] Additional disadvantages of knowing carrier status include alteration of self-esteem,[46] impact on a family's perception of the child,[47] lack of choice to be tested,[48] increased anxiety,[49] blaming oneself for the condition and possible discrimination against the child in education, insurance and employment.[50]

Past experiences have demonstrated that, in the absence of proper public education and parental counselling, confusion about the significance of carrying the common sickle cell trait (about 1 in 12 African Americans are carriers[51]) and the rare sickle cell anaemia (with a frequency of 1 in 600) has led to discrimination and stigmatisation.[52] Consequently, with the establishment of a newborn SCD program, the detection of carriers (both parents and children) should be accompanied by adequate counselling. Furthermore, the information provided during the screening programme and follow-up should specifically describe the characteristics of carrier screening.

While identification of carrier status has no implication whatsoever for the health or the medical care of the newborn, it increases parents' knowledge of haemoglobin variants so that they will not confuse benign states with the disease. It can also help identify and counsel couples with the sickle cell trait who are at risk of having other children with sickle cell disease. However, providing information to parents

---

45 McCabe, L.L. and McCabe, E.R.B., 'Genetic Screening: Carriers and Affected Individuals', (2004) 5 *Annual Reviews Genomics Human Genetics*, 57-69.

46 Working Party of the Clinical Genetics Society (A. Clarke, Chairman), 'The Genetic Testing of Children', (1994) 31 *J. Med Genet.*, 785-97.

47 American Society of Human Genetics, American College of Medical Genetics (ASHG/ACMG), 'Points to Consider: Ethical, Legal and Psychological Implications of Genetic Testing in Children and Adolescents', (1995) 57 *Am. J. Hum. Gen.*, 1233-41.

48 Wertz, D.C., Fanos, J.H. and Reilly, P.R., 'Genetic Testing for Children and Adolescents. Who Decides?', (1994) 272 *JAMA*, 875-81.

49 Working Party of the Clinical Genetics Society, *supra cit.*, note 46.

50 Working Party of the Clinical Genetics Society, *supra cit.*, note 46; American society of Human Genetics, American College of Medical Genetics, *supra cit.*, note 47.

51 From the American Sickle Cell Association website: http://www.ascaa.org/comm.htm.

52 Farriaux, J.P. and Dhondt, J.-L. (eds), *New Horizons in Neonatal Screening*, Excerpta Medica, Amsterdam, 1994; Knoppers, B.M. and Laberge, C.M. (eds), *Genetic Screening: From Newborns to DNA Typing*, Excerpta Medica, Amsterdam, 1990.

for decision making is secondary to the primary reason for neonatal screening.[53] In short, where screening can detect a treatable disease and at the same time reveal carrier status, the recommendations are that parents be advised of this possibility before the test and that results be given to the parents, in combination with any necessary counselling.[54]

Informing, educating and counselling families of carriers identified by newborn screening are major challenges from a logistical perspective; adequate funding is needed for comprehensive educational programme care. As mentioned earlier, a universal newborn screening programme would potentially identify thousands of carriers who require primary health care workers to provide counselling.[55] There are few studies that report on the way health services are organised for children with SCD or for carriers of the SC trait.[56] In fact, very little is known about who informs parents about SC screening, whether information is provided before or after screening, what expertise the health providers have, or what type of information is provided and in what form. We also do not know what happens to carriers of the SC trait: are parents informed? Are they offered counselling? Are parents and other family members offered screening to determine if they are carriers? Who ensures that the child is told upon reaching adolescence?

The long-term use of carrier status information impacts on consent issues. Many official policies concerning carrier status strongly advise against notifying the child, particularly because of the relative absence of programmes to support counselling.[57] Not only does this mean that the child has been tested without his or her consent, but he or she is also effectively denied relevant reproductive information.

Certain questions must be answered before implementing universal screening programmes capable of detecting carriers. For instance, should screening be conducted without prior consent, seeing as it can yield genetic information which some parents would prefer not knowing? How and under what circumstances should information about the sickle cell trait be conveyed to parents? Is it ethically justifiable not to inform parents if their child is a carrier of the sickle cell trait? Is it ethically acceptable to screen newborns when adequate education and counselling cannot be provided? If SCD screening is implemented, how will it affect newborn screening for treatable conditions?

---

53 Council of Regional Networks for Genetic Services, *supra*, note 44.

54 British Medical Association, *Human Genetics Choice and Responsibility*, London, Oxford University Press, 1998, p. 100.

55 World Health Organisation (WHO), *Control of Hereditary Disease – Report of a WHO Scientific Group*, Geneva, 1996.

56 See Goldbloom, R.B., 'Screening for Hemoglobinopathies in Canada', in Canadian Task Force on the Periodic Health Examination, *Canadian Guide to Clinical Preventive Health Care*, Ottawa, Health Canada, 1994; Yorke, D., Mitchell, J., *et al.*, 'Newborn screening for sickle cell and other hemoglobinopathies: a Canadian pilot study', (1992) 15(4) *Clin. Invest. Med.*, 376-83.

57 Lane, P.A., 'Issues Regarding Identification of Hemoglobinopathy Carriers by Neonatal Screening', (1998) 15 *Genetic Drift* (Newsletter).

If SCD screening is conducted, parents will need to be given information about various subjects: for example, the significance of results and their right to accept or decline SCD screening or notification should they prefer not knowing about carrier status.

The Constraints of Using Ethnicity as a Primary Tool for Selective Screening

Race and geographical origin constitute a significant factor in the incidence of SCD. The disease mostly affects people whose ancestors are from Africa, India, the Mediterranean, the Caribbean, South and Central America and Middle Eastern countries. However, in multicultural, melting-pot societies, it may become difficult to determine individuals' ethnicity or origin simply by looking at their skin colour. While resource-based arguments suggest that a targeted approach (selecting certain infants on the basis of race and ethnicity) for SCD screening is most efficient, the consensus view, based on practical experience in the UK,[58] and the US experience in the state of Georgia,[59] is that universal screening of all newborns for SCD is preferable. Programmes that screen in only specific high-risk segments of a population tend to miss individuals who are inaccurately registered. Because the benefits of screening for SCD are so compelling, leaving the selection based on ethnic and racial groups to the discretion of individual physicians or health care facilities has been abandoned in the United States[60] and in the United Kingdom.[61] Indeed, since SCD occurs among a wide range of ethnic and racial groups, efforts at targeting specific high-risk groups for newborn screening inevitably miss some affected infants because of difficulties in properly assigning race or ethnic origin during the prenatal period or in the newborn nursery.[62] Professional assessment of the mother's race is often wrong.[63]

Defining the screened population is a controversial topic in haemoglobinopathy screening. Guidelines and reviews of screening programmes have been published by various agencies around the world. Some have recommended universal screening for all newborns, while others have suggested that screening strategies, whether universal or selective, should depend on the proportion of high-risk individuals in a community.[64] One of the problems with targeted screening lies in the difficulty of identifying and selecting individuals. For instance, investigators in Georgia, US, compared the number of black newborns screened for haemoglobinopathies

58 Sassi, F., Archard, L. and Le Grand, J., 'Equity vs Efficiency: A Dilemma for the NHS', (2001) 323 *BMJ*, 762-3; Panepinto, J.A., Magid, D., Rewers, M..J. and Lane, P.A., 'Universal Versus Targeted Screening of Infants for Sickle Cell Disease: A Cost-Effectiveness Analysis', (2000) 136 *J. Pediatrics*, 201-8.

59 Harris, M.S. and Eckman, J.R., 'Georgia's Experience with Newborn Screening: 1981-1985', (1989) 83 (suppl.) *Pediatrics*, 858-60.

60 NIH Consensus Development Program, *supra cit.*, note 28.

61 NHS Sickle Cell and Thalassaemia Screening Programme, *supra cit.*, note 23.

62 Goldbloom, *supra cit.*, note 56.

63 Wertz, *supra cit.*, note 21.

64 Goldbloom, *supra cit.*, note 56.

between 1981 and 1985 with black birth figures for the same period, and estimated that approximately 20 per cent of black newborns were not screened.[65] Results of a study of universal screening in multiethnic California also indicated that an approach of targeting certain groups in that state would have missed at least 10 per cent of those whose sickle cell disease was actually diagnosed at birth.[66] Indeed, the US experience suggests that adequate targeting strategies are difficult to define and the criteria used to identify ethnic origin in relation to risk of sickle carrier status are likely to vary between and within countries, thus making the generalisability of such analyses difficult to interpret.[67]

Critics of the targeted approach have also raised the issue of the cost of determining race and ethnicity in the newborn nursery.[68] Another criticism is that a selective approach could be seen as discriminatory.[69] Before implementing a newborn screening programme for SCD, policy makers will need to consider whether universal screening in a given area constitutes a rational policy.

Political Pressure by Advocacy Groups

Newborn screening for PKU, developed in the 1960s, originated with the work of Robert Guthrie, a highly motivated parent who had a son with mental retardation and a niece with PKU.[70] He helped organise parents to lobby their governments to establish newborn screening programmes. Similarly, parents today continue to press for screening programmes.[71]

Partnership and public consultation have become important tools in policy development because they increase legitimacy and improve transparency in the policy development process. A review of the literature on public consultation and involvement shows that public involvement in policy development is no longer limited

65 Harris, Eckman, *supra cit.*, note 59.

66 Shafer, F.E., Lorey, F., Cunningham, G.C., Klumpp, C., Vichinsky, E. and Lubin, B., 'Newborn Screening for Sickle Cell Disease: 4 Years of Experience from California's Newborn Screening Program', (1996) 18(1) *J. Pediatr. Hematol. Oncol.*, 36-41.

67 Lees, C.M., Davies, S. and Dezateux, C., 'Neonatal Screening for Sickle Cell Disease (Cochrane Review)', in *The Cochrane Library*, Issue 3, Chichester, UK, John Wiley & Sons, 2004.

68 Lane, J.R. and Eckman, P.A., 'Cost-effectiveness of Neonatal Screening for Sickle Cell Disease', (1992) 120(1) *J. Pediatrics*, 162-3; Cronin, Normand, Henthorn, Hickman, Davies, *supra cit.*, note 34.

69 Sassi, Archard, LeGrand, *supra cit.*, note 58.

70 McCabe and McCabe, *supra cit.*, note 45.

71 Guthrie, P., 'Pressure Mounts to Expand Screening of US Newborns', (2005) 173(1) *JAMC*, 22; See March of Dimes: https://www.marchofdimes.com; See also Genetics Interest Group: http://www.gig.org.uk; Eggertson, L., 'Canada Lags on Newborn Screening', (2005) 173 *CMAJ*, 23; Gillot, J., 'Childhood Testing for Carrier Status: the Perspective of the Genetic Interest Group', in Clarke, A. (ed), *The Genetic Testing Children*, Oxford, Bios Scientific Publishers, 1998, p. 97.

to the reactions to particular services or products.[72] As early as 1986, the Ottawa Charter[73] emphasised the importance of public health and promotion and greater consultation with the public. The belief is that the result of involving communities of users, the public, and health professionals will be greater harmonisation and successful implementation of an initiative or programme. The partnership of parents and health professionals will encourage the dissemination of balanced information.[74] These steps need encouragement, and many drawbacks to effective implementation exist: there are wide gaps in knowledge, language barriers, cultural differences, and economic issues, and there are also time constraints.[75]

What is known about the views and experience of families and health professionals? For example, the public needs to understand the difference between carrier status and clinical diagnosis.[76] There is insufficient information about family values and expectations with regard to SCD screening. It is important to consult high-risk populations to understand if identified infants are being enrolled in a programme for treatment and care, if certain types of services or programs are deemed necessary to prevent the birth of children with the disease, and if there is a need for community education, couples counselling, and/or carrier screening to all high-risk populations of childbearing age.

Research on other screening programmes suggests that the perspectives of health professionals differ from those of parents. According to a survey by Wertz on topics relevant to the genetics of paediatrics, the views of parents and primary care physicians differ significantly. Increasingly, parents do not accept a paternalistic approach but rather believe that nothing should be withheld from them.[77]

Furthermore, there is an inadequate number of certified counsellors to respond to the need for support.[78] While medical care personnel are increasingly exposed to genetics, difficulties in the interpretation of DNA reports raise important educational challenges. There are also concerns about resources available to establish newborn follow-up and trait counselling programs. For example, in the USA,[79] counselling of

---

72 Butler, A., *Consumer Participation in Australian Primary Care: A Literature Review*, Australia, National Resource Centre for Consumer Participation in Health, 2002.

73 1st International Conference on Health Promotion, *Ottawa Charter*, Ottawa, November 1986.

74 National Health and Medical Research Council and Consumers' Health Forum of Australia, *Statement on Consumer and Community Participation in Health and Medical Research*, Australia, 2001.

75 Hamlett, P.A., 'Technology Theory and Deliberative Democracy', (2003) 28(1) *Science Technology and Human Values*, 112-140.

76 McCabe and McCabe, *supra cit.*, note 45.

77 Wertz, *supra cit.*, note 21.

78 Task Force on Life and the Law, 'Genetic Testing and Screening in the Age of Genomic Medicine', New York, November 2000, http://www.health.state.ny.us/nysdoh/taskfce/screening.htm (accessed 05/15/06).

79 Day, S.W., Brunson, G.E. and Wang, W.C., 'Successful newborn sickle cell trait counselling program using health department nurses', (1997) 23 *Pediatric Nurse*, 557-61.

families with infants with a trait is either very limited in scope or non-existent and with little follow-up facilities. Follow-up of SCD is often fragmented and acceptance of counselling is low.[80]

Finally, in the care of carrier status, there is uncertainty about how best to inform parents about the diagnosis of the sickle cell trait in the newborn.[81] The possible benefits for the child are educational and useful only when the child is older. However, it is unclear whether informing parents is beneficial to the child and how best to inform parents. Hence, focusing more on the needs, wants and opinions of parents is key to facilitating participation and to helping with the presentation of information materials.

Conclusion

Neonatal screening for SCD allows early diagnosis and therefore early treatment and education. However, such a screening programme must take into consideration a number of socio-ethical concerns.

We presented three main socio-ethical concerns with respect to SCD neonatal screening. First, the need to address the difficulties raised by revealing carrier status; second, whether neonatal screening should be selective or universal; and third, the need to address the role of consumer groups if screening is to reach its promise of predictive and preventive aspects.

Neonatal screening can detect most high-risk infants, but what should be communicated about carrier status? Ultimately, the identification of carriers calls for a re-examination of classical newborn screening consent procedures. How to do this without affecting or harming the newborn screening programme for immediately treatable conditions is the central issue. Deciding to screen for SCD and identifying carriers raise wider questions regarding parents' rights to refuse newborn screening for sickle cell diseases. Consequently, newborn screening for SCD cannot be carried out in the same manner as screening for treatable conditions occurs today because of the ethical issues related to carrier identification in the former. Informed consent with a clear understanding of the potential social and psychological harms is a key ethical issue. Considering the possible 'harm' of SCD consent process on classical screening programs, should SCD be universal or selective?

There is a difference of opinion about whether SCD screening should be selective or universal, and there is even less consensus on whether or how ethnicity or race should be used in selective screening programmes for sickle cell disorders. Experts debate whether it should be decided on the basis of proportion of the population from ethnic minorities, whether it is cost-effective without the risk of reduced

80 Kladny, B., Gettig, E.A. and Krishnamurti, L., 'Systematic follow-up and case management of the abnormal newborn screen can improve acceptance of genetic counselling for sickle cell or other hemoglobinopathy traits', (2005) 7 *Genetics in Medicine*, 139-42.

81 P.T. Rowley, 'Parental Receptivity to Neonatal Sickle Trait Identification', (1989) *Pediatrics*, 891-3.

effectiveness, and whether there is risk of discrimination. The best way to address this dilemma is to improve available data on cases of SCD, carrier rates and by using standardised instruments for collecting ethnicity data.[82] Neonatal programs have the ability to identify newborns with SCD and identify carriers of the SC trait. Estimates indicate that about half of all infants in the UK who are carriers have mothers who are carriers.[83] Some say that it is more economical to ask women about their ethnic origin and offer screening only to those with genetic backgrounds in areas where the disorder is highly prevalent. Others suggest that such policies miss a significant number of affected cases because the screening criteria might be inadequate and inconsistently applied.

Finally, how can we best involve the parents? Obviously, there is a need for appropriate information and counselling prior to screening and for appropriate resources as well as for adequate follow-up services. This should be combined with educational programmes and resources. Public interest in sickle cell disease has prevailed since Robert Guthrie's initiative in the 1960s. The involvement of ethno-cultural groups and their representatives in assessing the risks and benefits of neonatal screening for sickle cell is needed. Generally, recommendations regarding such a programme are derived from professionals or bioethicists and the voice of parents – consumers – is rarely heard at the discussion table.[84] The drive towards more equal partnerships in decision making in health programmes implies the need to promote and initiate dialogue with parents on a range of these socio-ethical issues.

Despite the socio-ethical quandaries of carrier identification, targeted versus universal approaches, and, in part, because of the experience of pressure from parents, newborn screening programmes for sickle cell disease have been introduced in numerous countries. Based on lessons from the past, it is important that genetic counsellors in sickle cell screening programmes discuss the confidentiality of results and the potential for genetic discrimination by life and medical insurance companies with families, to ensure that they understand the significance of carrier identification. It is also vital that policy makers provide proper public education so that discriminatory practices do not take place.

Perhaps a novel way to change the contours of the debate would be to take the best interests of the child approach. Where, when, and how can those interests be ensured? Though many answers to our research questions are still lacking and the social constraints of resources or failures such as discrimination are important political and systemic issues, to answer SCD questions, the rights and interests of the child should be paramount.

---

82 Hickman, M., Modell, B., Greengross, P., Chapman, C., Layton, M., Falconer, S. and Davies, S.C., 'Mapping the Prevalence of Sickle Cell and Beta Thalassaemia in England: Estimating and Validating Ethnic-specific Rates', (1999) 104 *Br. J. Haematol.*, 860-7.

83 NHS Sickle Cell and Thalassaemia Screening Programme, *supra cit.*, note 23.

84 Wertz, D.C. and Gregg, R., 'Genetics services in a social, ethical and policy context: a collaboration between consumers and providers', (2000) 26 *Journal of Medical Ethics*, 261-5.

Acknowledgements

The authors thank the following individuals for providing suggestions and support in preparing this chapter: A. Saginur, E. Levesque. This study was supported by Valorisation Recherche Québec.

Chapter 32

The 'Do No Harm' Principle and the Genetic Revolution in New Zealand

Mark Henaghan[1]

Genetic medicine has the potential to do much good for society. A survey of New Zealand general medical practitioners[2] showed that they used genetic tests for a range of disorders such as Haemochromatosis, Thrombophilia, Cystic Fibrosis, Huntington's Disease, Myotonic Dystrophy, Turner's Syndrome, Factor V Leiden, Fragile X Syndrome, Prader-Willi Syndrome and Thalassemia.[3]

---

1 Thank you to Kirsty Dobbs for research assistance, Karen Warrington for producing the final manuscript and Richman Wee for his comments on a draft.

2 White, S. and McLeod, D., *Genetic Testing: A Survey of New Zealand General Practitioners' Knowledge and Current Practice*, prepared for the National Health Committee, March 2003.

3 Following descriptions are based on the Online Mendelian Inheritance in Man (Genetic Disease Database – www.ncbi.nlm.nih/gov/entrez/query.fcgi?db=OMIM).

Haemochromatosis (also Hemochromatosis) – There are at least five recognised types of Haemochromatosis, which can be characterised by minimal to severe iron overloading (due to defects in iron metabolism). It is one of the most treatable genetic disorders if detected early (by simple venesection – a procedure similar to blood donation – where blood is removed until iron levels are reduced to normal levels). In an untreated patient, iron store levels keep rising which can have the following consequences; cirrhosis of the liver, heart disease, diabetes, endocrine and sexual dysfunction and arthritis.

Thrombophilia – Thrombophilia is the broad term used to encapsulate a group of conditions in which there is an increased tendency for excessive clotting in the blood (which can lead to deep vein thrombosis (DVT), heart attacks, embolisms and strokes. Episodes of thrombophilia may occur as an isolated event or as a repeated event. In those people where thrombophilia has a genetic basis events are more likely to be repeated (however presence of the mutated gene may not result in an event of thrombophilia). *Factor V Leiden* is one specific type of thrombophilia.

Cystic Fibrosis – Cystic fibrosis is a life threatening disorder that causes severe lung damage and nutritional deficiencies due to a mutation in the cystic fibrosis gene. The mutation affects cells that produce mucus, sweat, saliva and digestive juices; these secretions become thick and sticky, causing severe congestion. The most dangerous consequence of cystic fibrosis is respiratory failure.

Huntington's Disease – Huntington's Disease is a genetic disorder that causes degeneration of brain cells resulting in uncontrolled movements, loss of intellectual capacity and emotional

These are diseases with high penetrance but low prevalence in the community. For example, Professor Stephen Robertson, of the Medical School at Otago University, has determined the cause of OPD2 (Otopalatodigital syndrome type 2)[4] through the discovery of gain of function mutations in the gene encoding filamin A. Filamin A is a widely expressed protein that plays an important role in the cytoskeleton of humans. In the Maori kindred used to localise the mutations, the disease was seen as a 'makutu' (a curse). The family had suffered the deaths of several male descendents afflicted by the syndrome. The mutations in filamin A (in all four disorders) result in a range of congenital malformations. In this particular family the severity of the congential malformations culminated in perinatal death. The identification of the genetic basis of OPD2 has been described as the 'lifting of the makutu'.[5] For this family, there is now the hope of continuing the male line through the use of reproductive technologies to avoid the transmission of the disease.

---

disturbance. The disease is passed from parent to child; each child of a Huntington parent has a 50 per cent chance of inheriting the gene and getting the disease.

Myotonic Dystrophy – Myotonic (Muscular) Dystrophy is the most common form of adult muscular dystrophy characterised by a progressive, selective pattern of muscle wasting and weakening. Myotonic dystrophy has been labelled multisystemic as it has the ability to affect a wide range of organs and tissues, in addition to the voluntary muscle system.

Turner's Syndrome – Turner's Syndrome is a result of the loss of a sex chromosome in women. It affects approximately 1/2500 female live births worldwide. It results in a broad range of features, from major heart defects to minor cosmetic issues. The majority of patients present with short stature and loss of ovarian function (although the severity of such problems is variable).

Fragile X Syndrome – Fragile X Syndrome is the most commonly inherited form of mental retardation. Symptoms, such as developmental delay, speech delay, short attention span, temper and autistic like behaviours, appear at a very young age. It is a result of a defect on the X chromosome and affects males more severely than females.

Prader-Willi Sydrome – Prader-Willi Syndrome is a complex genetic disorder that results in a range of features: short stature, mental retardation, learning disabilities, incomplete sexual development, low muscle tone, and an involuntary urge to eat constantly (which often leads to obesity). This syndrome is associated with an abnormality on chromosome 15.

Thalassemia – Thalassemia results from the defective synthesis of haemoglobin (a protein in the blood that carries oxygen). It describes a group of disorders that range from barely detectable abnormality to severe or fatal anemia.

4 Robertson *et al.* identified localised mutations in the filamin A gene that led to 'a broad range of congenital malformations ... in four X-linked human disorders: otopalatodigital syndrome types 1 and 2, frontometaphyseal dysplasta and Melnock-Needles syndrome'. Robertson, S.P., Twigg, S.R.F., Sutherland-Smith, A.J., *et al.*, 'Localised mutations in the gene encoding the cytoskeletal protein filamin A cause diverse malformations in humans', *Nature Genetics*, (2003) 33: 487-488, at p. 487.

5 The 'Lifting of the Makutu', documentary screened on Television New Zealand (TVNZ), February 28 2005, highlighted the significance for the families of Professor Robertson's work.

There is potential for genomics[6] to help explain the causes of, and how best to respond to, chronic conditions which are widespread in the community such as cancer, diabetes, heart disease and depression. Lawrence Gostin when opening a workshop on the *Implications of Genomics for Public Health* said:

> What if genetic knowledge was used not only to benefit individual patients, but to benefit whole populations? What if genomics could help illuminate the critical interactions that science has been trying to understand for decades, those dynamics between inner characteristics and such things as diet, the environment and behaviour? This would truly be a revolution in public health and we may be on the cusp of this revolution.[7]

The title of this book has its origins in the philosopher Hippocrates. In his work *Epidemics*, Hippocrates instructed the physician to 'make habit of two things – to help or at least to do no harm'.[8] Today, when doctors take the Hippocratic Oath, they swear to adopt a regimen 'for the benefits of the patients according to my ability and judgment, and not for their hurt or any wrong'.[9]

Beauchamp and Childress[10] argue that the duty to do no harm is a negative duty (by comparison with the positive duty of beneficence). It is a duty to prevent harms that would not have happened but for exposure to the healthcare setting. The duty began at a time when the patient was an object of concern rather than a subject in her or his own right. The physician of the Hippocratic era has been described as 'a craftsman whose effectiveness depended ... on ... tailoring his art to the individual patient in his or her circumstances'.[11]

The patient is now seen as a subject able to decide and act in her or his own best interests after the risks and benefits of the procedure have been explained. Genetic medicine, like all medicine, has risks and benefits as well as the known and unknown. The complex interaction between genetic design and the environment means that it is not always possible to be categorical about the risks and benefits. Patients who are

---

6 Genomics means the study of the entire human genome. Genomics explores not only the action of single genes but also the interactions of multiple genes with each other and the environment.

7 Hernadez, L. (ed), *Committee on Genomics and the Public's Health in the 21st Century Board on Health Promotion and Disease Prevention*, The National Academics Press, Washington DC, Oct 7-8 2004, at p. 2, available at: http://www.nap.edu.

8 'Epidemics I', in *Hippocrates* (Translation WHS Jones, Loeb Classical Library), Cambridge, MA: Harvard University Press, 1923-1988, vol. 1, p. 165.

9 The Hippocratic Oath. Modern formulations of the principle are: The Geneva Convention Code of Medical Ethics (as adopted by the World Medical Association in 1949) – 'The health of my patient will be my first consideration'; The International Code of Medical Ethics – 'A physician shall act only in the patient's interest when providing medical care ...'; New Zealand Medical Association, Code of Ethics – '1. Consider the health and well-being of the patient to be your first priority'.

10 *Principles of Biomedical Ethics*, (1989) Oxford University Press, New York.

11 Sharpe, V.A. and Faden, A.I., *Medical Harm: Historical, Conceptual and Ethical Dimensions of Iatrogenic Illness*, United Kingdom, Cambridge University Press, 1998, 37.

ill are more likely to hear the benefits rather than the risks. The newness of genetic medical techniques, depending on how they are seen, can raise community concerns as can any medical breakthrough, such as heart transplants and in vitro fertilisation technology.

In the case of heart transplants, concerns were raised about the 'unnaturality'[12] of the transplant of one human's heart to another. Perhaps this ethical concern was augmented by the fact that a heart is associated with the most intimate of human feelings. People objected to what they perceived as the possible loss of identity when such an organ was removed. Concerns also existed as to the safety of the procedure, given its novelty.

In the case of IVF, many observers labelled Louise Brown, the first baby born through IVF technology in 1978, a 'test tube baby' – something from beyond nature. Jeremy Riftkin, a staunch opponent of IVF, suggested that the child might be psychologically 'monstrous':

> What are the psychological implications of growing up as a specimen sheltered not by a warm womb but by steel and glass, belonging to no one but the lab technician who joined together the sperm and the egg? In a world already populated experiencing people with identity crisis, what the personal identity of a test-tube baby?[13]

Who should decide, and how should it be decided, whether genetic medicine may do harm to an individual or a community as a whole? This chapter shows that the decisions in New Zealand are made partly by prescriptive legislation[14] but mostly by a committee structure whereby one committee designs the guidelines and another committee applies them.[15] As the committees will be appointed by government, they will be controlled by government. There is some room for public input but by and large the committees will be guided by general principles and their own collective conscience. The system is similar to the one that has operated for assisted reproduction technologies for some time in New Zealand.[16] From a politician's point of view the system has the advantage of delegating difficult questions, where there are conflicting moral visions, to committees. This is a very New Zealand solution, given that it is a country which thrives on a plethora of committees, whether they be to make decisions about education in schools or the allocation of health resources. The danger of this approach is that the committee making the policy is not at the sharp end of having to apply it, as, for example, the HFEA authority is in the United Kingdom.

---

12 Mannermaa, M., *Biosociety and the Human Being*, a report prepared for the National Technology Agency of Finland, April 2003.

13 Riftkin, J., *The Biotech Century: Harnessing the Gene and Remaking the World*, New York, Penguin Putnam, 1998.

14 Human Assisted Reproductive Technology Act 2004 (known as the HART Act).

15 Set up by the Human Assisted Reproductive Technology Act 2004.

16 There has been no legislatively designed structure until the 2004 HART Act.

The Human Fertilisation and Embryology Act 1990 in the United Kingdom was well ahead of its time. It set up a comprehensive licensing structure and a publicly accountable authority which make decisions and policy. One lesson from the United Kingdom experience of the Human Fertilisation and Embryology Act 1990 is that in fast developing areas of medicine it is not possible to have a legislative blueprint which foresees all possible medical advances. Professor Sheila McLean said in 2003 when commenting on the Human Fertilisation and Embryology Act that 'the growing range of topics which have reached the UK courts and the exponential growth of development, seems likely to mandate revision [of the 1990 Act] sooner rather than later'.[17] For example, the creation of an embryo by cell nuclear replacement,[18] tissue typing for saviour siblings, and the use of pre-implantation genetic diagnosis,[19] the use of donor sperm and treatment after separation of the parties[20] and what happens to frozen embryos after parties separate and disagree over implantation[21] were all issues not foreseen in 1990.[22] The New Zealand approach, by comparison, is lightweight in terms of substantive content, leaving it mostly to the process of committee decision making by consensus. Fundamental issues of knowledge within the medical profession of the new genetic technologies, integration of them into the public health system and their accessibility to the general public are left out of the regulatory structure. As Professor Mason[23] observed in 1988 there has been a 'remarkable shift' from the Hippocratic position. The new reality is based on the 'differential allocation of resources – whether on financial, logistic or simply emotional grounds' with the emphasis on the 'relative quality of the lives of others competing for those resources'.[24] Genetic medicine comes at a price; principles need to be in place to guide who will have access to it.

By way of comparison, in the field of genetic modification in the environment New Zealand has had much more comprehensive public debate, public awareness and legislation.

---

17 McLean, S.A.M., 'Issues in Assisted Reproduction – The UK Experience', in *Raising the Standards*, New Zealand Law Society 2003, 209-222, available at: http://www.lawyers.education.org.nz.

18 *R (Quintavalle) v. Secretary of State for Health*, [2003] 2 AC 687.

19 *R (on the application of Quintavalle) v. Human Fertilisation and Embryology Authority*, [2005] 2 FCR 135.

20 In *re R (A child) (IVF: paternity of child)*, [2003] 2 WLR 1485.

21 *Evans v. Amicus Healthcare Ltd*, [2004 3 WLR 681.

22 The House of Commons Science and Technology Committee, *Human Reproductive Technologies and the Law*, (24 March 2005) HC 7-1. This Report considered changes which might be needed in the 1990 legislation. The Department of Health is presently conducting its own inquiry.

23 Mason, J.K., *Human Life and Medical Practice*, Edinburgh University Press 1988, 4.

24 Mason, *op cit*.

The Do No Harm Approach Applied to the Genetic Revolution in the Environment

New Zealand is a nuclear free zone known for its high quality, disease-free dairy, beef and lamb products. Farming accounts for 4.8 per cent of the country's gross domestic product compared to 0.9 per cent in the UK and 1.4 per cent in the US. With a clean green image at stake it is not surprising that the guiding principle is one of precaution. The Hazardous Substances and New Organisms Act 1996[25] (HSNO) is based on a set of core principles. Fundamental to the Act is consideration of the effects of a hazardous substance or a new organism on the health and safety of people, and on the New Zealand environment. The underlying mandate is the 'need for caution in managing the adverse effects where there is scientific and technological uncertainty about those effects'.[26]

The HSNO Act establishes a new statutory body, the Environmental Risk Management Authority (ERMA), to assess and develop controls for the importation, manufacture, development and release within New Zealand of hazardous substances and new organisms. ERMA is intended as a 'one stop shop' for the evaluation and control of environmental risks through a single process based on a consistent set of objectives. The Act provides a basis for the public to have an input into making decisions on approvals and for taking Mäori concern and international agreements into account.

The next step in New Zealand's response to genetically modified organisms was the establishment of the Royal Commission on Genetic Modification. The Royal Commission was an independent body established in 2000 by an Order in Council dated the 8th of May 2000.

While the Royal Commission was conducting its inquiry, a voluntary moratorium was implemented by the Hon Pete Hodgson, Minister for Research, Science and Technology. The voluntary moratorium on genetic modification research during the Royal Commission's inquiry into genetic modification was designed to keep New Zealand's future options open. The Royal Commission reported on 27 July 2001. Its major conclusion was that New Zealand should adopt a strategy of preserving opportunities and proceed to use genetic modification selectively and with appropriate care. In drawing this conclusion it explicitly rejected the idea of a New Zealand free of all genetically modified material at one extreme and the option of unrestricted use of genetic modification at the other:

---

25 HSNO for short. Prior to the enactment of the HSNO Act, the importation (into New Zealand) and the manufacture of hazardous substances and new organisms was regulated by a plethora of statutory regimes (Explosives Act 1957, Dangerous Goods Act 1974, Toxic Substances Act 1979, Pesticides Act 1979, Animal Remedies Act 1967, Plants Act 1970, Animals Act 1967 and the Biosecurity Act 1993). More importantly, the development of genetically modified organisms was not covered by legislation at all.

26 Section 7, HSNO Act 1996.

> There are aspects of genetic modification we consider positive and useful and hence to have an important place in New Zealand's future in certain defined situations. We also want to maintain non-genetic modification options as effective choices. We favour a strategy of preserving opportunities and proceeding selectively with appropriate care. [27]

Stephen Herrera in the 2005 Technology Review[28] describes New Zealand's approach to genetically modified organisms as 'a transparent, enforceable, publicly accessible, and scientifically robust regulatory framework'.[29] The public is able to voice concerns about any genetically modified organism project and the government must address those concerns before the application is granted. Once an application is approved the law protects biotechnology firms that meet the standards and their field trials cannot be subverted by civil suits to prevent them.

Several field trials of genetically modified trees, onions and dairy cows have been approved. The 'do no harm principle' is the clear legislative basis for the genetic revolution as it applies to the environment.

The 'Do What the Committee Decides' Approach to the Genetic Revolution as it Applies to Humans

There is less legislative sense of direction when it comes to the genetic revolution in medicine in New Zealand. In 2001 it was noted that:

> There are many unknowns in this rapidly developing area of human medicine. We can't be certain of the real potential of the technologies and who may benefit, and we don't know how much of a risk they present to our society. What we can be certain of however, is the fact that these sorts of technologies will develop and evolve in ways that we can't predict ... This situation presents a real challenge to societies and governments. What sort of controls will allow us to realise the benefits of new technologies, yet will also safeguard us from their abuses? What sort of controls are flexible enough to stay current in the face of rapidly developing technology, yet also provide the sort of precautionary approach that society wants? [30]

As from 30 October 2003[31] a definition of human cells has been added to the Hazardous Substances and New Organisms Act 1996 to include human reproductive and embryonic cells. 'Human cells' – (a) means human cells, human cell lines, or human tissues that are being grown or maintained outside the human body; and

---

27 Report of the Royal Commission on Genetic Modification: http://www.mfe.govt.nz/publications/organisms/royal-commission-gm/index.html. See chapter 13: Major Conclusion: Preserving opportunities, paragraph 3.

28 'New Zealand: Green Haven for Biotech', [2005] *Technology Review*, 28-30.

29 *Ibid.*, at p. 30.

30 Ministerial Report, *New Reproductive Technologies: Implications for Legislation*, Hon. Pete Hodgson (Minister of Research, Science and Technology), 7 May 2001.

31 Section 4(1) HSNO Amendment Act 2003 (2003 No 54).

(b) includes human reproductive cells or embryonic cells that are grown or maintained outside the human body.

At present, work on genetic modification of cells is overseen by the Gene Technology Committee. This Committee was set up by the Health Research Council which is responsible for distributing about NZ $60M a year for health research. The Health Research Council has authority under s 27 of the Health Research Council Act to set up such a committee to provide advice. The Health Research Council has published a document entitled *Processes and Guidelines for Application for Approval of Proposals Involving Administration of Gene Products to Human Subjects in New Zealand.*[32] The criteria for approval are:

- whether there is sufficient evidence from laboratory and experimental studies in animals to allow a trial in humans to proceed;
- whether the proposed trial will provide a clinical benefit and scientifically useful information, particularly in relation to safety and efficacy;
- whether there is adequate information on the safety and toxicity of the materials to allow them to be used in trials in humans;
- whether the investigators have the qualification, experience and track record to conduct the proposed trial;
- whether the investigators have conducted appropriate risk assessment of their proposed procedures.[33]

The Gene Technology Committee is made up of 15 scientists who oversee the scientific validity of proposed gene research. There is no current avenue for ethical scrutiny or for public input into the Committee's decisions.

The only major legislation in New Zealand which deals directly with genetic medicine is legislation designed to deal with assisted reproduction – the beginnings of life. The Human Assisted Reproductive Technology Act 2004 (HART Act) views the following activities as socially and morally harmful and prohibits them outright:

- The selection of an in vitro embryo for implantation into a human being on the basis of the sex of the embryo.
- The performance of any procedure, or the provision, prescription, administration of any thing so as to increase the probability that a human embryo will be of a particular sex (there is a defence to the above two prohibitions if the act was performed to prevent or treat a genetic disorder).
- The commercial supply of human embryos or gametes.
- The artificial formation, for reproductive purposes, of a cloned embryo (a cloned embryo is not formed by splitting on one or more occasions).

---

32 Health Research Council, Wellington (2002).

33 See Peart, N., McCrimmon, F. and Dawson, J., 'Clinical Trials', in Dawson, J. and Peart, N. (eds), *The Law of Research*, University of Otago Press (2003) 175-195 for a full discussion of clinical trials in New Zealand.

- The artificial formation, for reproductive purposes, of a hybrid embryo.
- The implantation into a human being of a cloned embryo.
- The implantation into a human being of an animal gamete or embryo.
- The implantation into a human being of a hybrid embryo.
- The implantation into an animal of a human gamete or embryo.
- The implantation into an animal of a hybrid embryo.
- The implantation into a human being of a genetically modified gamete, human embryo or hybrid embryo.
- The implantation into a human being of gametes derived from a foetus, or an embryo that has been formed from a gamete or gametes derived from a foetus.[34]

A cloned embryo is defined as a human embryo that is a genetic copy (whether identical or not) of a living or dead human being,[35] a stillborn child, a human embryo or a human foetus.

The banned list is not based on any major public outcries about potential harm to society as the moratorium on genetic modification in the environment was. The main themes running through the prohibition are concerns about hybrid creations either with animals or other humans and the cloning of embryos. The exceptions expressed in the banned list all have the theme of therapeutic benefit.

The key policy making body in the HART Act is the Advisory Committee.[36] This Committee is appointed by the Minister of Health, which is an indication that the matter is seen as one of health rather than human rights where the Minister of Justice would be the appointer. The Committee is made up of reproductive specialists in practice and research, ethicists, consumers of assisted reproduction, Mäori (the indigenous people of New Zealand) perspectives, lawyers and the Commissioner for Children or her representative. At least half the Committee must be lay persons which means they are not involved as health practitioners or in health research. The Committee is required to report to the Minister of Health on the controversial issues of cloning, hybrids, genetic modification such as germ line therapy and pre-implantation genetic diagnosis. The Committee is also charged to produce guidelines on assisted reproduction procedures and research. Transparency is attempted by a requirement that the agenda and minutes of the Committee meetings must be published on the Internet. The public can have input through responses to discussion papers and through public meetings where oral submissions can be made. When guidelines are issued they are to be published on the Internet and the Minister of Health is required to present them to Parliament. Whilst the outcomes are public the deliberations themselves are not.

34 Section 8 HART Act 2004.
35 Section 5 HART Act 2004.
36 Subsection 32-42 HART Act 2004.

Professors Mason, McCall Smith and Laurie in *Law and Medical Ethics*[37] show the complexity of the arguments on germ line therapy. They contend that it is difficult to distinguish between eugenically motivated or enhancement germ line manipulation on the one hand and truly therapeutic intervention on the other. The authors observe that 'science's bad record in keeping to a narrow, acceptable track record lends some force to the arguments of those who would prevent such meddling altogether'.[38] They wisely conclude that 'it certainly seems to us to be one of those subjects which would only be acceptable following wide and informed public discussion'.[39] There is no such mechanism for informed public discussion in the current New Zealand framework.

In their deliberations the Committee is required to be guided by the following principles:

- The health and wellbeing of children born as a result of the performance of an assisted reproductive procedure or an established procedure should be an important consideration in all decisions about the procedure.
- The human health, safety and dignity of present and future generations should be preserved and promoted.
- While all persons are affected by assisted reproductive procedures and established procedures, women, more than men, are directly and significantly affected by their application, and the health and wellbeing of women must be protected in the use of these procedures.
- No assisted reproductive procedure should be performed on an individual and no human reproductive research should be conducted on an individual unless the individual has made an informed choice and given informed consent.
- Donor offspring should be made aware of their genetic origins and be able to access information about those origins.
- The needs, values and beliefs of Mäori should be considered and treated with respect.
- The different ethical, spiritual and cultural perspectives in society should be considered and treated with respect. [40]

There is no specific mention of harm in the principles or the analysis of risks and benefits which is the primary focus of the HSNO legislation. Informed consent becomes a token gesture if there is not rigorous scientific analysis of the risks and benefits of a particular procedure. The term 'health' in the guidelines should be implied to include scientific harms and benefits.

---

37 (4th ed), London, Butterworths, 1994.

38 *Ibid.*, at p. 146.

39 *Ibid.*, at p. 146.

40 Section 4 HART Act 5 2004.

The applier of the guidelines for assisted reproductive procedures[41] and research[42] is an ethics committee. The prime focus of such a committee will be the committee's own views and conscience as to what ethical values they believe are important in the particular case. A case that went to the Courts in Quebec shows that ethics committees may need to have knowledge beyond that of ethics. In *Weiss v. Soloman*,[43] a Quebec man's family successfully sued an ethics committee after the man died following an angiogram used to assess the possible side effects of a drug (which was being trialled) designed to reduce retinal oedema. The dead man had a heart condition which put him at risk and which the ethics committee did not warn him about. The Court ruled that the committee should have had this knowledge and warned the man even though at the time there was no literature relating angiograms to cardiac arrest. This decision suggested that ethics committees need to be experts in all areas of the research they are dealing with. This is a high standard, but in evolving areas of medical research it may well be the appropriate standard. In New Zealand it may be more difficult to hold ethics committees accountable by the use of litigation. Under New Zealand's accident compensation legislation[44] it is not possible to sue for personal injury, negligence or medical misadventure. Therefore those who suffer injury because of the unreasonable behaviour of an ethics committee will not be able to bring civil action in New Zealand.

Apart from already established procedures, it is illegal in New Zealand to perform procedures or engage in research without ethics committee approval.[45]

A Current Working Example – Regulation of Preimplantation Genetic Diagnosis

Until the Advisory Committee is set up the HART Act enables the Minister of Health to approve guidelines developed as interim guidelines for up to three years after the legislation has been passed.[46] The National Ethics Committee on Assisted Human Reproduction (NECAHR) has published guidelines on preimplantation genetic diagnosis (PGD).

---

41 Defined as the creation of an embryo, the storage, manipulation and use of gametes and embryos, the use of embryo cells and the implantation of gametes and embryos, s 5 HART Act 2004.

42 Defined as research that uses or creates a human gamete, a human embryo or by a hybrid embryo, s 5 HART Act 2004.

43 [1989] 48 CCLJ 280.

44 Accident Compensation Act 1972, 1982. Accident Rehabilitation and Compensation Insurance Act 1992. Injury Prevention, Rehabilitation and Compensation Act 2001.

45 Section 16 HART Act 2004.

46 Section 83 HART Act 2004.

The guidelines emphasise that PGD can only be carried out where there is a 'serious impairment' to the resultant individual.[47] The problem is who determines the level of impairment. The guidelines provide that 'it is the responsibility of PGD providers, in collaboration with a genetic counsellor, to ascertain whether a familial disorder is likely to be serious in offspring of a particular couple considering PGD'.[48] By way of contrast, the Human Fertilisation and Embryology Authority[49] in the UK has included in its latest Code of Practice (2003) a more comprehensive list of factors which should be taken into account in the decision of whether to use preimplantation genetic diagnosis treatment. These are:

- the view of those seeking treatment of the condition;
- their previous reproductive experience;
- the likely degree of suffering associated with the condition;
- the availability of effective therapy or management now and in the future;
- the speed of degeneration in progressive disorders;
- the extent of any intellectual impairment;
- the extent of social support available and
- the family circumstances of the people seeking treatment.[50]

The perception of the risk by those seeking treatment is an important factor, and the Code says that 'the seriousness of the condition is expected to be a matter for discussion between the people seeking treatment and the clinical team'.[51] The issue of harm is to be decided collaboratively and not solely by the medical team, as the NECAHR guidelines currently stand.

The NECAHR guidelines provide that sex determination for familial sex-linked disorders may be carried out where:

(i) no specific test for the disorder is available; and
(ii) there is a high risk of serious abnormality; and
(iii) the option of prenatal testing alone is unacceptable to the couple.[52]

47 Principle one of the Guidelines on Preimplantation Genetic Diagnosis prepared by the National Ethics Committee on Assisted Human Reproduction, March 2005, and since designated as interim ACART guidelines under s83 of the HART Act 2004 available at http://www.necahr.govt.nz/guidelines.htm.

48 *Id.*

49 Human Fertilisation and Embryology Authority Code of Practice (6th ed), (2003) available at: http://www.hfea.gov.uk/HFEAGuidance.

50 *Id.*

51 *Id.*

52 Draft National Ethics Committee on Assisted Human reproduction, 2005, *loc cit.*

The prohibition on the use of sex selection where there is a specific test is not medically or ethically justifiable. There is evidence[53] that when a genetic disease is directly associated with a gender it is easier to test for gender and choose the gender that will not have the disorder than to analyse the embryo for the condition itself. This will not create a 'backdoor' selection of male embryos over female ones because of the two hundred or so known sex-linked diseases (ranging in severity from colour blindness to haemophilia and Duchenne's Muscular Dystrophy) most only affect males.[54]

The NECAHR guidelines provide that PGD for the purpose of HLA tissue typing may be undertaken but only if approval is given by NECAHR on a case by case basis. This will only be provided where:

> The affected child has a gene disorder which has been identified within a family. There must be a 'serious impairment' because of the gene disorder.[55]

By contrast, other countries state a higher threshold. In Sweden[56] it must be an 'hereditary disease leading to premature death for which no treatment or cure is possible'. In France[57] it must be a particularly severe genetic disorder, known to be incurable at the time of diagnosis.

Second, there must be a 25-50 per cent risk that the embryos created are affected by the particular genetic disorder within the family.[58] There are no conditions which presently have a 50-99 per cent risk. All other possibilities for treatment and sources of tissue for the affected child must have been explored.[59] The intended must be a sibling of the potential child.[60] The expressed intention must be to take only

53 See discussion in the report by the Working Party on the Protection of the Human Embryo and Fetus (CDBI-CO-GT3) prepared for the Steering Committee on Bioethics, *The Protection of the Human Embryo In Vitro* (June 2003), p. 35.

54 HFEA, *Sex Selection: Choice and Responsibility in Human Reproduction* (2002), p. 9. X-linked disorders may be either X-linked dominant or X-linked recessive inheritance. Since a female has two X chromosomes, whereas a male has only one, X-linked recessive inheritance affects males almost exclusively. X-linked dominant condition can affect either male or females, although females are more mildly affected.

55 See NECAHR guidelines, *loc cit.*

56 See Law No 115 of March 14, 1991 and Instructions by the Ministry of Health and for Social Affairs on Prenatal and PGD (described in Comité Consultatif National d'Ethique pour les sciences de la vie et de la santé (CCNE), Reflections Concerning an Extension of Preimplantation Genetic Diagnosis, Opinion No 72 (July 4, 2002).

57 See discussion in Plachot, M. and Cohen, J., 'Regulations for Preimplantation Genetic Diagnosis in France', *Journal of Assisted Reproduction and Genetics*, (2004) 21, No 1, p. 5.

58 Principle two NECAHR Guidelines, *loc cit.*

59 Principle three NECAHR Guidelines, *loc cit.*

60 Principle three NECAHR Guidelines, *loc cit.*

cord blood for purposes of treatment, and not other tissue or organs.[61] Additional counselling will be provided to the couple undergoing treatment.[62]

The problem with these guidelines is that they do not cover a child who has a 'sporadic' rather than hereditary condition. Charlie Whitaker in the United Kingdom was just such a child.[63] He suffered from a rare form of anaemia where the bone marrow produces few red blood cells. Charlie was pale, had an irregular heartbeat and heart murmurs. Charlie got irritable and tired and fainted a lot. His condition needed intensive therapy such as painful, day-long blood transfusions and daily injections of life-saving drugs. There was no cure, but bone marrow transplants give a 90 per cent chance of recovery. If Charlie's parents could have another child whose tissue matched Charlie's, then this child's cells could help Charlie's body to create red blood cells. The chance of his parents having another baby with the disease are no greater than those parents in the general population (5 to 7 per million live births). The embryos created by Charlie's parents were not likely to have the same defect as Charlie. The requirement that there be a 25-50 per cent risk that the embryos to be implanted carry the disease would not be met. Because there is no 'benefit' to the embryos from testing, permission would be denied, yet if those embryos were to be tested and found to have a disorder they would be destroyed or used for research. Is it really a 'benefit' to be destroyed? The embryos that 'benefit' are those that do not have a genetic disorder and are then implanted. Whilst the House of Lords in *R (Quintavalle) v. HFEA*[64] required that embryos be at risk of the condition affecting the child, Lord Phillips MR did emphasise that it makes 'little sense' not to reap the benefits of embryo research. In 2004, the Human Fertilisation and Embryology Authority reversed its previous position on PGD with HLA tissue typing, paving the way for it to accept applications, such as the one in Charlie Whitaker's case.[65]

The NECAHR guidelines prohibit using PGD to select for a similar genetic abnormality to that which one of the parents has. The assumption is that it would be detrimental to the welfare of the child to do so. A blanket prohibition assumes that all genetic abnormality would lower quality of life whereas quality of life is a relative term which is better decided on a case by case basis. Emerging research[66] is challenging views of what is and what is not a disability.

The NECAHR guidelines are weak on the cost and accessibility of preimplantation genetic diagnosis. NECAHR's consultation document states that funding of PGD is to be left up to the government. Until 2006 costs for PGD are not met by the healthcare

61 Principle four NECAHR Guidelines, *loc cit.*

62 Principle five NECAHR Guidelines, *loc cit.*

63 See http://bbc.co.uk/1/hi/health/2167792.stm. The Whitakers obtained the appropriate treatment in the United States and a son was born to them in 2003.

64 [2003] Lloyd's Rep Med 294.

65 CH(04)05-04/08/04. Available at: http://www.hfea.gov.uk/HFEAGuidance/ChairsLettersArchive/2003-2004, accessed on 22/09/05.

66 Wertz, D., 'Drawing Lines: Note for Policy Makers', in Parens, E., and Asch, A. (eds), *Pre-Natal Testing and Disability Rights*, Washington, DC, Georgetown University Press, 2000, 261-287.

budget. New Zealanders had to go to Melbourne to have the procedure carried out. Questions of equity and rights of access are fundamental and prior to issues of the ethical acceptability of the techniques themselves. It is not ethically acceptable to allow the services only to those who can afford them. NECAHR should make it a precondition that there is equal ability to access PGD services.

The Real Harm – Lack of Practitioner Knowledge of Genetic Procedures

In 2003[67] a survey of New Zealand general practitioners was carried out to assess the current practice of general practitioners in relation to genetic testing. The practitioners were given three case vignettes on breast cancer, cystic fibrosis and Huntington's Disease to assess. In the breast cancer vignette only 15.4 per cent of the practitioners indicated that they would refer the patient to genetic services and only 1.6 per cent would order a test. The practitioners were then told that the patient had a genetic test and the result showed she had a mutation in the BRCAI gene. Only 3 per cent of the general practitioners felt confident to discuss the test information and the chances of her risk of developing cancer.

The next case involved cystic fibrosis, where the patient's sister had died of the disorder. The chance of the patient being a carrier of cystic fibrosis is 66 per cent. Only 8.6 per cent of the general practitioners identified this. The general practitioners were asked about the risks to the patient's child if the patient had a genetic test and the result for cystic fibrosis was negative and the patient did not know about her dead sister's mutation status. The risk would be lower but still significant as the sister may have at least one unknown mutation. Only 1.2 per cent of the general practitioners identified the risk as significant and 35.4 per cent were unsure.

In the Huntington's Disease case, 45.2 per cent indicated the wrong genetic test for the disorder even though the Huntington's Disease genetic test is one of the top ten genetic tests utilised word wide. Of the general practitioners 46.6 per cent reported that they had not received any training in clinical genetics. Many of the general practitioners commented that they lacked knowledge of genetic testing, genetic theory, the appropriateness of different tests, the extent to which tests can be accessed and the reliability of tests.

In this context, the statutory and ethical frameworks appear as side issues and distractions from the real harm which is a lack of knowledge and desire to use genetic medicine for the common good.

67 White, S. and McLeod, D., 'Genetic Testing: A Survey of New Zealand General Practitioners' Knowledge and Current Practice', prepared for the National Health Committee, March 2003.

Conclusion

New Zealanders are very proud of their environment. The laws put in place to protect the environment from unforeseen consequences of genetic modification have a strong precautionary element of doing no harm, a vigorous scientific testing process and clear room for public input into the issue. New Zealanders appear to value their health less. The legal structures for the advancement of genetic medicine are piecemeal and lack any clear unitary message. There is no clear process for evaluating the benefits and risks of genetic medicine. There is no principle of ensuring equitable access to genetic medicine or for ensuring that the benefits of genetic medicine become part of the public health system. Such a haphazard directionless approach is likely to do much more harm than good.[68]

68 The New Zealand Law Foundation has awarded a large charitable grant to a team of Otago University researchers, led by Professor Mark Henaghan and Professor Donald Evans, to work in collaboration with Professor Sheila McLean of Glasgow University and Professor Mildred Cho from Stanford University, to develop a comprehensive regulatory framework on genetic medicine for New Zealand. See www.otago.ac.nz/law/genome.

Chapter 33

Cloning, Zoning and the Harm Principle

Roger Brownsword[1]

Introduction

Pluralistic communities – where fundamental values are disputed, or where there is disagreement as to the weight to be accorded to such values – are not designed for regulatory convenience. As the House of Commons Science and Technology Committee put the point in its controversial report on *Human Reproductive Technologies and the Law*:[2]

> We accept that [in] a society that is both multi-faith and largely secular, there is never going to be consensus on … the role of the state in reproductive decision-making. There are no demonstrably 'right' answers to the complex ethical, moral and political equations involved … We recognise the difficulty of achieving consensus between protagonists in opposing camps.[3]

Under such conditions, unless regulatees are either not politically engaged or are simply prepared to trust the judgments of regulators, the capacity of the regulatory system will be put to the test – or, at any rate, in the absence of happenstance consensus or convergence of views, this will be so. For, where there are fundamental value differences and where disputants take their differences seriously, how are particular regulatory positions to be defended? Moreover, as regulatory regimes aspire to extend

---

1 A version of this paper was given as a CMLE Lecture at King's College London in March 2005. I am grateful to Jonathan Glover, Tom Campbell, and others who participated on that occasion. Needless to say, the usual caveats apply.

2 HC 7-1, Science and Technology Committee, *Human Reproductive Technologies and the Law* (Fifth Report of Session 2004-05) (London: TSO, 24 March, 2005). Ironically, the Report was judged newsworthy not simply for its permissive recommendations (especially concerning sex selection) but also for the fact that the Committee, with its quest for consensus, was actually divided down the middle, 5 of the 11 members disagreeing with the Report: see HC 491, Science and Technology Committee, *Inquiry into Human Reproductive Technologies and the Law*, (Eighth Special Report of Session 2004-05) (London: TSO, 29 March, 2005) Annex A.

3 *Ibid.*, at para 46.

across national boundaries, claiming regional or even international jurisdiction, the problems posed by pluralistic communities seem even more intractable.[4]

The regulation of cloning is a case in point.[5] So far as human reproductive cloning is concerned, we have convergence: pluralism notwithstanding, it is agreed that cloning humans with reproductive intent is immoral (indeed, a crime against humanity) and that it should be prohibited. By contrast, we have deep pluralist divisions in relation to therapeutic cloning and human embryonic stem cell research. Within nation states (even within the permissive United Kingdom, for example) there are serious differences of view; moving out to larger regulatory arenas, we find in both Europe and the United States a patchwork of regulatory positions; and, at the United Nations, members have struggled to agree upon a suitably anodyne form of words that will accommodate their deepest differences – an unconvincing majority eventually adopting a Declaration that prohibits 'all forms of human cloning inasmuch as they are incompatible with human dignity and the protection of human life'.[6]

In the face of these difficulties, a turn to proceduralism (to defensible regulatory processes if not to consensually supported outcomes) beckons.[7] However, before we do this, we should assess the regulative potential of the venerable principle that, whatever else, we should do no harm to others (*primum non nocere*).[8] As an internal regulative standard, this principle would limit the legitimate outcomes of democratic decision making: only if a local regulatory position on cloning were compatible with the (no) harm principle would it pass muster. Similarly, as an external regulative standard, the principle would place a limit on subsidiarity: within their own zone of regulatory competence, local regulators would be permitted to give effect to the local evaluation of cloning but only so long as this caused no harm outside the zone. Under this approach, a patchwork of regulatory positions applying to various human

4 Compare the excellent discussion in Plomer A., *The Law and Ethics of Medical Research – International Bioethics and Human Rights*, London, Cavendish, 2005, especially chs 1 and 2. See, too, Brownsword R., 'What the World Needs Now: Techno-Regulation, Human Rights and Human Dignity', in Brownsword R. (ed), *Human Rights* (Volume IV of *Global Governance and the Quest for Justice*), Oxford, Hart, 2004, at p. 203.

5 See, further, Brownsword, R., 'Stem Cells and Cloning: Where the Regulatory Consensus Fails', (2005) 39 *New England Law Review*, 535-571.

6 The General Assembly adopted the United Nations Declaration on Human Cloning, 84 voting in favour, 34 against, and with 38 abstentions (see UN press release GA/10333 (March 8, 2005)). For the prior recommendation made by the Legal Committee, see UN press release GA/L/3271 (February 18, 2005).

7 See Brownsword, R., 'Regulating Human Genetics: New Dilemmas for a New Millennium', (2004) 12 *Medical Law Review*, 14; and Beyleveld, D. and Brownsword, R., *Consent in the Law*, Oxford: Hart, 2006, ch. 10.

8 Compare the qualified libertarian approach of the Science and Technology Committee, note 1, *supra*. Put shortly, the Committee seeks to forge consensus around the principle that the State should not interfere with reproductive freedom provided that the exercise of such freedom occasions no demonstrable harm to others or to society.

cloning procedures and purposes would not necessarily be symptomatic of regulatory discomfort. Far from it – each regulatory zone would be encouraged to articulate its own local view on cloning; and the task of super-regulators would simply be to ensure that the regulatory positions struck in each zone were not harmful to others.

The purpose of this chapter is to take a harder look at this idea of the harm principle as a regulative standard for pluralistic communities, using cloning as the test case. The argument and analysis is in three parts.

The first part sketches a particular kind of pluralism, a three-way disagreement that a community has about fundamental values (the 'bioethical triangle' as I term it).[9] The three key values here – values consistently reflected in the universalising work of the UNESCO International Bioethics Committee – are human welfare, human rights and human dignity.

In the second part, recalling the two perennial problems associated with any regulative principle that is formulated in terms of harm to others, the crucial questions are: what counts as 'harm'; and who counts as an 'other'? Is a cloned child 'harmed'? Is a 100-cell human embryo an 'other'? It is suggested that, in pluralistic communities, there are competing conceptions of the harm principle and, concomitantly, rival interpretations of the key elements of 'harm' and 'other'. These problems, it should be emphasised, are no mere footnote caveats to an otherwise unproblematic liberal principle; these are problems that strike right at the heart of any claim to neutrality that we might advance on behalf of the (no) harm principle.[10]

If the harm principle cannot be employed in a neutral fashion as an internal regulative standard, are its prospects any better as an external regulative standard? In the third part of the discussion, it is suggested that, in this external regulatory role, too, the neutrality of the harm principle is compromised. Moreover, even if a measure of conscientious exemption is recognised, so that local opponents of cloning are not required to contribute financially towards regional or international research initiatives, the (no) harm principle still falls short of being a compelling justification for permissive regulatory positions.

In conclusion, while the (no) harm principle is an important reminder that we should always strive to do the right thing (morally speaking), under conditions of pluralism there are competing accounts of what precisely we must and must not do if we are to do the right thing. In consequence, the principle is compromised as a neutral regulative principle. So far as the regulation of cloning is concerned, zoning

---

9 See, e.g., Brownsword, R., 'Three Bioethical Approaches: A Triangle to be Squared', paper given at international conference organised by Sasakawa Peace Foundation, Tokyo, September 2004, available at: www.ipgenethics.org/conference/transcript/session3.doc; also, see *loc cit.*, note 5, *supra*.

10 Compare Human Genetics Commission, *Profiling the Newborn: A Prospective Gene Technology?*, (March, 2005) para 3.28 for questions concerning 'the issue of how the concept of harm is to be understood in the context of the acquisition of individual genetic profiles. Clearly, simply acquiring the raw information cannot be physically injurious, but do we consider an interpretation of it that may result in unjustified anxiety, false reassurance or unwarranted expenditure harmful?'

might well be the model for both the present and the future. However, this will not be a regulatory patchwork harmoniously co-ordinated by a neutral harm principle; rather, then as now, it will be a patchwork that reflects the regulatory *real-politik* as particular values or particular compromises emerge as working standards for divided communities.

Cloning and a Particular Kind of Pluralism

Pluralism comes in many different forms. The kind of pluralism presupposed in this discussion is by no means exceptional – indeed, it is precisely the setting that UNESCO consistently assumes when it declares that the international community should strive to avail itself of the benefits of new technologies (such as cloning technologies) while always fully respecting human rights and human dignity. This triangulates as a utilitarian stream of thinking (dedicated to maximising human wealth, health and happiness), a rights-led human rights perspective (founded on respect for the inalienable and intrinsic dignity of humans) and a duty-driven dignitarian view. Having sketched this triangle, particularly its dignitarian elements, we can consider how it bears on views relating to human reproductive cloning and then human therapeutic cloning.

Pluralism and the Bioethical Triangle

Neither utilitarian nor human rights thinking requires any introduction. By now, we are all familiar with the tension between utilitarian promotion of the general good and the constraints imposed if individual rights are to be taken seriously. Where human rights has made its mark, it is axiomatic that best practice demands careful attention to free and informed consent, that the capacity for autonomous decision making should be respected, that privacy and confidentiality should be protected, and so on.

Arguing against both the utilitarians and the human rights theorists, there is now a determined alliance of dignitarian views This perspective condemns any practice, process or product – human reproductive cloning, therapeutic cloning and stem cell research using human embryos being prime examples – which it judges to compromise human dignity. Such condemnation (by reference to human dignity) operates as a 'conversation stopper';[11] but the dignitarians are not troubled – to say that something violates human dignity is the ultimate condemnation. The

11 See Birnbacher, D., 'Do Modern Reproductive Technologies Violate Human Dignity?', in Hildt, E. and Mieth, D. (eds), *In Vitro Fertilisation in the 1990s*, Aldershot, Ashgate, 1998, 325-333. Compare Nuffield Council on Bioethics, *Genetically Modified Crops: the Ethical and Social Issues*, London, 1999, at p. 96 (those who contend that genetic modification is intrinsically wrong or unnatural present views that 'have something of an "unarguable" quality, inasmuch as no amount of information, explanation or rationalisation would move a person with such views from their position').

emergence of the new dignitarian view creates a genuinely triangular contest, the dignitarians disagreeing as much with the utilitarians as they do with the human rights constituency – with the former because they do not think that consequences, even entirely 'beneficial' consequences (that is, 'beneficial' relative to a utilitarian standard), are determinative; and with the latter because they do not think that informed consent cures the compromising of human dignity.

Somewhat confusingly, human dignity is a key idea in two corners of this three-way contest.[12] The idea that we should disallow a practice because human dignity is compromised is not a prominent feature of utilitarian thinking. With the human rights constituency, however, matters could scarcely be more different. Human rights theorists believe that the entire apparatus of human rights is premised on the principle of respect for human dignity – and, indeed, this very premise is written into the historic human rights instruments of the mid twentieth century.[13] In the dignitarian corner, too, respect for human dignity is fundamental but not as the underpinning of human rights and individual autonomy. Drawing on a mixture of Kantian, Catholic and communitarian credos, this constituency registers its discomfort with various aspects of new technology by contending that human dignity is compromised.

In the light of this pluralism, how do we account for the views generally held about cloning, reproductive and therapeutic?

Pluralism and Human Reproductive Cloning

If there is a regulatory consensus about anything in bioethics and biolaw, it is that human reproductive cloning is unethical and that it should be prohibited.[14] All 191 member states of the United Nations (notwithstanding their failure to agree upon the terms in which the prohibition should be expressed) so hold. Even in the United Kingdom, there was a panic when it was thought that the law might (inadvertently) permit human reproductive cloning – a panic that was calmed only when legislation was rushed through to make it a serious criminal offence to place in a woman 'a human embryo which has been created otherwise than by fertilisation'.[15]

---

12 See Beyleveld, D. and Brownsword, R., *Human Dignity in Bioethics and Biolaw*, Oxford, Oxford University Press, 2001.

13 See, Brownsword, R., 'Bioethics Today, Bioethics Tomorrow: Stem Cell Research and the "Dignitarian Alliance"', (2003) 17 *Notre Dame Journal of Law, Ethics and Public Policy*, 15-51.

14 See, e.g., Article 1(1) of the Additional Protocol to the Council of Europe's Convention on Human Rights and Biomedicine, Oviedo, 4.IV.1997 (the Protocol is dated 12.I.1998 (at Paris)); and Article 11 of the UNESCO Universal Declaration on the Human Genome and Human Rights, adopted by the General Conference of UNESCO at its 29th session on November 11, 1997, and endorsed by the United Nations General Assembly on December 9, 1998 (see Resolution A/RES/53/152).

15 Section 1(1) of the Human Reproductive Cloning Act 2001. For the background, see Brownsword, R., 'Stem Cells, Superman, and the Report of the Select Committee', (2002) 65 *Modern Law Review*, 568-587.

Relative to the bioethical triangle, some of the thinking that opposes human reproductive cloning is distinctly utilitarian, reflecting concerns about safety and risk (without any overwhelming offsetting benefit). As Alan Colman put it, if human reproductive cloning were to be attempted, it 'would quite likely join thalidomide in the teratogenic hall of infamy'.[16] We might also detect a utilitarian approach in arguments that raise concerns about damage to the emotional and psychic welfare of the child – as in worries about the creation of confusion and ambiguity in familial relationships.[17]

From a human rights perspective, too, human reproductive cloning looks problematic. Thus, when (in March 1997) the European Parliament called for a ban on human reproductive cloning, the preamble to the resolution stated that:

> the cloning ... of human beings cannot under any circumstances be justified or tolerated by any society, because it is a serious violation of fundamental human rights and is contrary to the principle of equality of human beings, as it permits a eugenic and racist selection of the human race ...

If called upon to make the charge more precise, human rights theorists might argue that cloning is liable to be abused creating a threat to individuality or the sense of an independent self,[18] and interfering with an agent's right to an open future.[19]

It is from the dignitarians, however, that we have the bluntest and the most unqualified condemnation of human reproductive cloning. Quite simply, cloning is viewed as an unnatural intervention in the human reproductive process and a straightforward compromising of human dignity.[20]

Pluralism notwithstanding, then, we hear a chorus of voices, secular and religious, pro-life and pro-choice, not only condemning human reproductive cloning but settling for nothing short of complete prohibition.[21] Nevertheless, the consensus

---

16 Colman, A., 'Why Human Cloning Should not be Attempted', in Burley, J. (ed), *The Genetic Revolution and Human Rights*, Oxford, Oxford University Press, 1999, 14-18, p. 16.

17 This consideration was highlighted, e.g., by the House of Lords Select Committee in its report on *Stem Cell Research*, London, HMSO, 2002, HL Paper 83(i) (Report), Appendix 6 (Reproductive Cloning) para 6.

18 Compare, e.g., Andrews, L.B., 'Is There a Right to Clone? Constitutional Challenges to Bans on Human Cloning', (1998) 11 *Harvard Journal of Law and Technology*, 643; and Deech, R., 'Cloning and Public Policy', in Burley, *op cit.*, at p. 95.

19 See Davis, D.S., 'Genetic Dilemmas and the Child's Right to an Open Future', (1997) 28 *Rutgers Law Journal*, 549, esp at 561-567.

20 Cf, e.g., Santorum, R., 'The New Culture of Life: Promoting Responsible and Appropriate Medical Research', (2003) 17 *Notre Dame Journal of Law, Ethics and Public Policy*, 151-156, at pp. 154-155 ('America has never been a nation of strict utilitarianism ... And it is critical that we seek a responsible policy framework that will protect and enhance human dignity').

21 Compare Kunich, J.C., 'The Naked Clone', (2002-2003) 91 *Kentucky Law Journal*, 1.

against human reproductive cloning is less deeply rooted than it seems; what we have is a happenstance convergence of essentially oppositional bioethical constituencies drawn together by the contingencies of the moment.[22]

Cloning and Cloning Consider the following two distinctions. First, there is a distinction between (micro) cloning just one person as opposed to (macro) cloning many persons, groups, classes or even whole populations. Secondly, there is a three-way distinction between cloning for genetic connection, cloning for genetic compatibility, and cloning for genetic characteristics. In the first case, the cloners simply want to maintain a genetic lineage (regardless of its particular genetic make-up); in the second case, lineage is not enough, it is the genetic compatibility of the clone with the cloner that matters – for example, a person with leukaemia wishes to clone herself in order to produce a tissue compatible clone to serve as a bone marrow donor;[23] and, in the third case, it is the substantive genetic specification that matters not its pedigree.[24] To repeat, for dignitarians, such distinctions are immaterial; human reproductive cloning, whether micro or macro, whether for connection or for compatibility or for characteristics, compromises human dignity and it needs to be prohibited – period. However, for utilitarian and human rights theorists, these distinctions are not to be dismissed so quickly.

A number of commentators have suggested that, if reproductive cloning were to become a safe and reliable procedure, then it might be regarded as a legitimate supplement to existing reproductive technologies.[25] For example, why not make this option available to a couple whose gametes are not usable and who wish to have a genetically related child; or, again, why not permit parents who have lost their only child, say a much-loved daughter, to clone a child that is as full a replacement as is genetically possible? Lawrence Wu puts the argument on utilitarian grounds.[26]

> [Micro cloning] can perform a valuable service for many in an area of fundamental concern – having children – and it does not cause any tangible harm that science is incapable of perfecting away and that caring parents are incapable of loving away.

---

22 For a nice example of 'consensus by convergence', see the Report of the California Advisory Committee on Human Cloning, *Cloning Californians?*, Sacramento, CA, January 11, 2002. The many arguments against human reproductive cloning are listed in Part IIB of the Report.

23 See, too, Chester, R., 'Cloning for Human Reproduction: One American Perspective', (2001) 23 *Sydney Law Review*, 319, 339.

24 Compare, Robertson, J.A., 'Liberty, Identity, and Human Cloning', (1997-98) 76 *Texas Law Review*, 1371.

25 See, e.g., Harris, J., 'Clones, Genes, and Human Rights', in Burley, J. (ed), *op cit.*, 61 at pp. 86-88; and Robertson, *loc cit.*

26 Wu, L., 'Family Planning Through Human Cloning: Is There a Fundamental Right?', (1998) 98 *Columbia Law Review*, 1461, at p. 1514.

However, it might also be put on grounds of human rights and, in particular, the right of reproductive autonomy (albeit hotly contested).[27] Dan Brock, for example, concludes that the right 'presumptively includes both a right to select the means of reproduction, as well as a right to determine what kind of children to have, by use of human cloning'.[28] Granted, this right is only presumptive. However, it is very broadly articulated and some human rights theorists might favour limiting it to cloning for genetic connection, thereby disabling it from running on to include cloning for genetic compatibility (cases of the saviour sibling kind looking suspect perhaps) or for genetic characteristics (this being the more problematic case).

Nevertheless, utilitarians and human rights theorists alike would have reasons to pause. First, even if the technology were reliable, there might be a concern that the certification of applicants for micro-cloning reproductive services would be ineffective.[29] From a human rights perspective, it would be imperative to ensure that, in practice, the reproductive technology was not employed in such a way that cloned children were denied the opportunity of having a life with an open future.[30] As Cass Sunstein has cautioned, it will not do for people to treat 'their children-to-be as means, with prearranged agendas, rather than as ends, to seek their own path'.[31] Moreover, so long as there are various characteristics and dispositions (for example, being a good talker or a good listener) that are not readily classifiable as legitimate or illegitimate selections, so long as there is no bright line to be drawn between 'negative' and 'positive' cloning, a precautionary approach seems advisable.

Secondly, there is also a much more subtle concern that might worry human rights theorists, namely that licensing micro cloning for genetic characteristics might change the culture of reproduction in a way that, in the longer run, would be deleterious to a flourishing community of rights. To treat children as commodities seems to be a further step towards consumption and markets; and, quite possibly, it would change the terms of the relationship between parents and children.[32] To say

27 Against a fundamental constitutional right to engage in either reproductive or therapeutic cloning, see Sunstein, C., 'Is There a Constitutional Right to Clone?', (2002) 53 *Hastings Law Journal*, 987. By contrast, Wu, note 26, *supra*, argues that a fundamental right to reproductive autonomy extends to a negative right against State prohibition blocking access to cloning technologies.

28 Brock, D., 'Cloning Human Beings: An Assessment of the Ethical Issues Pro and Con', in Nussbaum, M.C. and Sunstein, C.R. (eds), *Clones and Clones: Facts and Fantasies about Human Cloning*, New York and London: W.W. Norton & Company, 1998, 141, p. 145.

29 For a sophisticated discussion of how selective regulation of human reproductive cloning might prove counter-productive or ineffective, see *Cloning Californians?*, Part IIB(5), note 22, *supra*.

30 See Davis, note 19, *supra*, especially pp. 561-567 (arguing that a reflexive application of autonomy values will set limits to parents' reproductive autonomy).

31 Note 27, *supra*, p. 1000.

32 The 'saviour sibling' cases already raise questions of this kind; cf Brownsword, R., 'Reproductive Opportunities and Regulatory Challenges', (2004) 67 *Modern Law Review*, 304-321. For some hints as to how this idea might be developed in relation to micro-reproductive

that this would not be a change for the better, in the sense that it would diminish the pleasure of parenting is not the point; the question is whether it would undermine the conditions that enable rights-holders to make sense of their rights and responsibilities, as well as to come to terms with their own identities.[33]

Macro Cloning Turning from *micro* cloning to *macro* cloning, a utilitarian would want to be assured that the loss of genetic diversity implicated in such a project would not unintentionally render humans less resistant to disease; and utilitarians would also want to be confident that the impact of such a large-scale intervention really would produce a better balance of utility than alternatives – after all, we have been here before, both with the best of intentions and the worst of intentions, in both fact and fiction.[34] Again, though, until human reproductive cloning technology is reliable, there are overwhelming reasons for the utilitarian to advocate restraint.

A fortiori, human rights theorists will be nervous about any proposal for macro cloning. If programmes of mass cloning are designed to produce utility maximising societies, we can guarantee that this will be at the price of sacrificing individual rights. These large-scale exercises in social engineering inevitably prioritise the grander social objectives, individuals are not taken seriously, and humans are exploited while their rights are violated. This is not a path that any sensible human rights theorist can entertain.

On this analysis, if human reproductive cloning techniques were reliable, human rights theorists might be tempted to license micro cloning (certainly where its purpose was for genetic connection) and, in this, they would be supported by utilitarians (provided that this did not have negative implications for the regulatory position concerning therapeutic cloning or for the broader reputation of the scientific community, and the like). However, human rights theorists surely would unite with the dignitarians in opposing any enthusiasm that utilitarians might display for macro cloning. The case that needs much further reflection is that of micro cloning for genetic characteristics.

Pluralism and Therapeutic Cloning

When we turn to the regulation of so-called 'therapeutic cloning', or allied procedures involving the isolation and manipulation of human embryonic stem cells, there

---

cloning, see Radin, M.J., 'Cloning and Commodification', (2002) 53 *Hastings Law Journal*, 1123.

33 Trying to make sense of the idea of the corrosion of a rights-supporting context is not easy. However, for suggestive discussions, see Dworkin, R., *Sovereign Virtue*, Cambridge, Mass., Harvard University Press, 2000, Ch. 13; Habermas, J., *The Future of Human Nature*, Cambridge, Polity Press, 2003; and, McKibben, B., *Enough: Genetic Engineering and the End of Human Nature*, London, Bloomsbury, 2003.

34 See, e.g., Glover, J., 'Eugenics and Genetic Manipulation', in Burley (ed), *op cit.*, at p. 101; and Ryan, A., 'Eugenics and Genetic Manipulation', *loc cit.*, at p. 125. Famously in fiction, see Aldous Huxley, *Brave New World*, London, Chatto and Windus Ltd, 1932.

is little sign of, or hope for, a consensus. In some jurisdictions, there are outright prohibitions; in others, the position is permissive but heavily qualified (for example, restricting researchers to the use of supernumerary human embryos); in others, the regulation is relatively liberal (notably that in the United Kingdom); and, in yet others, we find prohibition at one level co-existing with permission at another.[35] How are we to account for the bioethical divisions that underlie these very different regulatory positions?

The reason for such diversity is that the ethical hot-spot is now the treatment (and destruction) of human embryos, not the possibility of attempts at human reproductive cloning going wrong or being abused. With the exception of dignitarian bioethics – which holds constantly to the view that human cloning, whether for reproductive or therapeutic purposes, compromises human dignity and, thus, should be prohibited[36] – this changes the ethical calculation; and, with that, the bioethical and regulatory consensus breaks down.

Dignitarian condemnation aside, the general perception of therapeutic cloning and stem cell research is that this is a field of very considerable medical significance, that (even allowing for the hype) it is conceivable that there could be major benefits resulting from this kind of research. For both utilitarians and human rights theorists, this is a positive consideration. On the negative side, there seem to be no real counter-weights: provided that it is believed that terminated embryos neither suffer nor have rights, and provided that those who donate eggs or embryos do so on the basis of free and informed consent, all is well. If there are precautionary arguments about longer-term disutility or indirect damage to rights-holders, the burden of persuasion has yet to be discharged. If there is a risk here, it seems to be that people perhaps live longer or that, thanks to stem cell treatments for Parkinson's and Alzheimer's disease, the quality of life for large classes of elderly people is considerably improved. While such developments might have important economic consequences, as well as consequences for the allocation of public healthcare resources, it surely would be perverse for either utilitarians or human rights theorists to put such possibilities into their deficit columns.

Translating these ethical judgments – the dignitarian apart – into preferred regulatory positions is more complex. Assuming that therapeutic cloning and human embryonic stem cell research are to be permitted, regulators might hedge their

35 For a helpful review of the regulatory scene in Europe, see Halliday, S., 'A Comparative Approach to the Regulation of Human Embryonic Stem Cell Research in Europe', (2004) 12 *Medical Law Review*, 40-69; and, for the US, see Peterson, S.E., 'A Comprehensive National Policy to Stop Human Cloning: An Analysis of the Human Cloning Prohibition Act of 2001 with Recommendations for Federal and State Legislatures', (2003) 17 *Notre Dame Journal of Law, Ethics and Public Policy*, 217.

36 Although, if dignitarians oppose reproductive cloning as an unnatural intervention, should they not welcome the termination of a cloned embryo? But, then, how would this sit with the dignitarian objection to the use of human embryos as research tools, where the point is not so much the non-natural nature of the exercise as the instrumentalisation of humanity? Presumably, in the case of therapeutic cloning, two wrongs do not make a right.

permission in various ways – for example, by restricting the class of embryos to be available for such research, or by refusing to allow embryos to be specifically created for research, or by imposing pre-conditions relating to the necessity and proportionality of the use of embryos. Such restrictions, even if intuitively plausible, do not actually make a great deal of sense from a utilitarian and/or human rights perspective. However, this is not the place to pursue this point.[37] For, it is time to move on to the harm principle.

Contested Conceptions of the Harm Principle

Even in pluralistic communities, there will be widespread support for the axiom that we should do no harm to others. After all, in any moral community, one of the constitutive ideals is that the interests of others should be respected; being other-regarding is part of what it means to adopt a moral viewpoint.

Accordingly, in private dealings, we should try to avoid causing harm to others; and, as John Stuart Mill famously argued, in freedom-loving societies, it provides guidance to regulators.[38] Stated in one way, the (no) harm principle is that regulators should respect the sovereignty of individual choice where acts are not harmful to others; turning the coin over, the principle is that regulators should not restrict freedom unless the actions to be restricted are harmful to others (this being a necessary if not sufficient condition for legitimate restriction).

So far, so good? Alas not, because where the moral viewpoint is given competing content by a plurality of particular versions of morality, the harm principle begs all the important questions. Whether in relation to private or public dealings, the principle is not neutral: its regulative application turns on how the notion of 'harm' and the category of 'others' are interpreted; and these key ideas only take on a specific meaning once they are interpreted through the lens of a particular angle of the bioethical triangle.[39]

Before we articulate the competing interpretations that are yielded by pluralism, we should nip in the bud any suggestion that common sense answers to these critical interpretative questions will be supplied by the local conventions of language or by the intuitions of ordinary people. Under conditions of pluralism, value differences will already insinuate themselves into the way people use the word 'harm' or who they count intuitively as being a relevant 'other', and so on. If Mill knew that common sense was for the common man, today's regulators know that the reasonable man is something of a chameleon.[40] What is reasonable, or right-thinking, or reflective of the moral high ground, is relative to the particular part of pluralism that is taken as criterial.

---

37 See further, *op cit.*, note 5, *supra.*

38 Mill, J.S., 'On Liberty', in J.S. Mill, *Utilitarianism*, London, Fontana Press, 1962 (edited by Mary Warnock).

39 Compare Plomer, note 4, *supra.*

40 Compare Lord Hope's remarks in *Chester v. Afshar*, [2004] UKHL 41, para 83.

The Utilitarian Reading of the Harm Principle

Following a utilitarian approach, 'harm' is largely equated with the stuff of disutility: that is to say, pain and suffering, distress, anxiety, the frustration of plans and non-satisfaction of preferences, and the like. As for 'others', quite simply, they are those beings who are capable of experiencing just this kind of pain and suffering.

Applying the harm principle, so understood, to reproductive human cloning, utilitarians will support prohibition so long as the procedure is unsafe and, thus, capable of generating various types of disutility. Should reproductive cloning become a safe and reliable procedure, and should it prove to be less disruptive of familial relations than some fear, utilitarians might find that they are running out of reasons to maintain their opposition. Of course, those who (for non-utilitarian reasons) are distressed by reproductive human cloning will pose some awkward questions for utilitarian-minded regulators – in response to which, they might simply disregard such distress as irrational or, following the spirit of Mill, judge that the price of freedom is that the preferences of some will have to be overridden.

Applying the same approach to therapeutic cloning, utilitarians will see no objection to terminating the development of a 100-cell human embryo. At that stage of embryonic development, the prevailing wisdom is that there is no possibility of pain and suffering being experienced. The embryo, to be sure, is a potential other; but, at the relevant time, it is not yet in that category and so it is not capable of being harmed.

The Human Rights Reading of the Harm Principle

In its most robust and distinctive form, human rights theory interprets 'harm' by reference to the set of human rights, including both negative and positive rights within this set, and views such rights under a will or choice theory. It is the presupposition of will theory that gives informed consent its integrated role in human rights thinking, the rights-holder being able to authorise actions that would, consent apart, involve a violation of rights. It follows that, given this approach, it is human 'rights-holders' who are the relevant 'others'.

From such a perspective, human reproductive cloning is to be opposed where it threatens the wellbeing of rights-holders (as it might if cloning procedures issue in the birth of damaged children) or where the autonomy of rights-holders is compromised – hence the intense concerns about cloning for characteristics and the closing off of an open future.

As for therapeutic cloning, while human rights theorists might disagree about the stage at which foetal or neonatal life attains rights-holding status (if at all), no will theorist would argue that a 100-cell human embryo is a *paradigmatic* rights-holder. For there is, at this stage, a very long way to go before the embryo is capable of actively participating in a community of rights. Accordingly, in the absence of extreme precaution or arguments that are indicative of indirect risk to (unproblematic) rights-holders, the harm principle offers no reason to prohibit therapeutic cloning.

One such indirect argument, it will be recalled, concerns the corrosion of the conditions that are presupposed by a community of rights-respecting agents. Without collapsing into simple dignitarian conservativism, the implication is that members of communities of rights have responsibilities that go beyond their individual obligations to one another and their collective support for public goods; they are, so to speak, stewards of the cultural conditions that support a particular way of life and they owe it not only to one another, but also to future generations, to pass on sustainable conditions. Such an idea definitely merits further consideration; but whether it has any purchase in relation to therapeutic cloning remains to be seen.

The Dignitarian Reading of the Harm Principle

For dignitarians, 'harm' is understood as any act that compromises human dignity; and 'others' are understood individually, collectively, and inclusively as members of the community. So understood, the harm principle demands that human reproductive cloning should be prohibited because, even if a clonee is not harmed in any sense that would be recognised by utilitarian or human rights standards, this directly compromises human dignity. As for therapeutic cloning, the embryo is definitely an 'other', it is instrumentalised, and this is a procedure that is harmful – human dignity is violated.

Let us take stock. First, under conditions of pluralism, there will be different views about the regulation of reproductive and therapeutic cloning of humans. Secondly, outside the convergence that we currently have in relation to human reproductive cloning, regulators will not be able to take up positions that enjoy the support of the full plurality. Thirdly, any attempt to defend a particular regulatory position by reference to a supposedly neutral harm principle will come apart as soon as pressure is applied to the key concepts of 'harm' and 'other'. Fourthly, once this pressure is applied, the regulatory veneer will fall away to disclose the elements of the plurality that actually underlie the regulatory position. But, even if it will not work as an internal regulative principle, might the (no) harm principle serve as an external regulative standard? This is our next question.

Cloning and Regulatory Zoning

Let us suppose that the harm principle is proposed as an external regulative standard on the following terms. First, the super-regulator for the regional or international community will not prescribe a particular community-wide regulatory position; there will be no community-wide rule prohibiting, permitting or requiring cloning of various kinds. Each local regulator will be authorised to declare its own regulatory position to apply within its sphere of competence. Secondly, the only limit on local regulators is that the position that they take must not have external adverse effects, causing harm to other regulators or their regulatees. Each regulatory zone enjoys regulatory autonomy but only so far as this is consistent with the (no) harm principle. And, thirdly, recognising that some (notably dignitarians) oppose all forms of human cloning as a matter of conscience, no one will be required to act or contribute to regional activities that offend their conscience. So, for example, where a particular zone prohibits, say, therapeutic cloning, and where it does so on grounds of conscience, then that zone will be exempted from making financial contribution to any regional research initiatives that involve therapeutic cloning.

In support of this approach, it will be argued that it facilitates peaceful co-existence by allowing for, say, the Green Zone to permit any form of cloning while, at the same time, allowing for, say, the Red Zone to prohibit all forms of cloning (with various shades of Green and Red in between). The Greens can say to the Reds, 'We do not insist on you taking a permissive approach; how you regulate your zone is your business – at any rate, so long as you do not violate the harm principle'. And, conversely, the Reds can say to the Greens, 'We do not insist on you taking a prohibitive approach; how you regulate your zone is your business – at any rate, so long as you do not violate the harm principle'. This is not just a rhetorical possibility – echoes of this kind of thinking are to be heard in the explanatory statements made by member states, particularly those that take a permissive approach to therapeutic cloning, regretting the failure to achieve consensus at the United Nations.[41]

Is this the answer? Is this where the harm principle is rescued as a neutral regulative principle? Alas, it is not. For, scaling up the regulatory ambition does not scale down the problems that we have seen with the principle. Under conditions of pluralism, different zones will (as we have assumed) adopt rather different regulatory positions. We will have a patchwork. And, within that patchwork, the position and perspective of the dignitarian Red Zone most clearly highlights the limitations of the proposed regional approach.

Let us suppose that the Reds do not accept the legitimating regional rhetoric; they do not accept that they are not being harmed by the permissive approach of the Green Zone. True, it is not as though Green clones are crossing the borders into the Red Zone like airborne GMOs that interfere with non-GMO agriculture. Nor is it the fact that the availability of cloning facilities in the Green Zone invites an element of cloning tourism on the part of disaffected persons who live in the Red Zone (although there might be something in this). No, the objection from the Red Zone is, quite simply, that they are harmed by very fact that cloning takes place in the Green Zone: human dignity is compromised and that is the only harm that counts.

Quite clearly, it will not do to respond that the Reds have a funny idea of 'harm', one that does not accord with the understanding of those in the Green Zone, or possibly of the regional regulators themselves. Once this is said, the game is up: it is an admission that the harm principle is not neutral and that, in practice, the regional regulators read harm in the way that utilitarians or, possibly, human rights theorists do.

41 See note 6, *supra* (particularly the statements by the Republic of Korea, the United Kingdom, Singapore, China and Sweden).

Nevertheless, is there not another justificatory tack? This argues that, within the region, the Reds are authorised to set their own (prohibitory) local regulatory terms; and, moreover, that in deference to their dignitarian views they have been granted a special exemption under the conscience clause. Under conditions of pluralism, what more can the Reds reasonably demand? As a strategy for rubbing along at regional level, this has some attraction; and, quite possibly, 'reasonable' Reds will recognise that they cannot realistically ask for further concession or influence. However, if the Reds 'unreasonably' demand more, what might they say?

First, they might assert that, while some supra-regulatory allowance for subsidiarity is unobjectionable, where human dignity is at stake a zoning approach simply will not do. For a region to be a real community, a community-wide rule must be set and that rule must bind all members within the protective and inclusive terms of dignitarian thinking. It follows that, wherever cloning takes place in the community (including in the Green Zone), there is damage to human dignity, harm is done, and the harm is felt by dignitarians even in the Red Zone.

Secondly, because the obvious response to the first assertion is that the conditions of pluralism militate against privileging dignitarian thinking, the Reds might be moved to suggest that their dignitarian morality is superior to its rivals. If the Reds so contend, then they can hardly object to dignitarianism being double-checked for its right to be respected as at least an *equal* (let alone a *privileged*) constituent of the plurality. If such an examination reveals dignitarianism as a hotch-potch of inconsistent judgments held together only by the overarching claim that human dignity should not be compromised, regulators might think twice. Even if regulators are not convinced that reasons can be given for privileging either the utilitarian or the human rights strands of the plurality,[42] they might judge that the dignitarians have yet to give reasons for even being included within the plurality.

Conclusion

There is probably more than one moral to be taken from this story, not least about the non-negotiability of human dignity. However, the one that I want to highlight is simply that the (no) harm principle is no more neutral as a regional regulative principle than it is as a basis for setting local regulatory standards. This is not to say that the harm principle is not of importance. Far from it, even under conditions of pluralism, it expresses a commitment to a moral way of life. The difficulty is that, within the plurality, there is more than one such way of life.

As we have seen, under conditions of pluralism, many will agree that human reproductive cloning should be prohibited and there will be divided views about the right regulatory approach to therapeutic cloning. In regional regulatory regimes, these local differences are played out on a larger stage. However, these are not simply

42 To avoid any misunderstanding, though, I should say that I would argue that some version of human rights thinking has much better prospects than utilitarianism.

particular cases of consensus and dissensus. These views flow directly from the three key value perspectives that make up the conditions of pluralism.

Faced with such conditions, regulators might be advised to turn to procedural strategies, inviting regulatees to respect the regulatory regime because of the fair and open processes that have been adopted to generate the regulatory outputs. However, before giving up on a material justification, regulators might glimpse a hope in the harm principle, which seems to be common ground in the plurality. Such a hope, though, is bound to be dashed; for, the key elements of the regulative principle (the notion of 'harm' itself and the interpretation of 'other') are necessarily viewed in quite different ways by the rival perspectives of pluralism.

Finally, regulators operate on the basis of both hope and expectation. Their hope, as the German representative said, when explaining Germany's vote in favour of the recommendation made by the United Nations Legal Committee, is that 'the current system of anarchy over human cloning [will] be overcome … and that consensus [will] again be possible'.[43] However, under conditions of regional pluralism, the expectation must be rather different. Here, zoned co-existence (which is surely several steps up from anarchy) might be the best that we can achieve in practice; but we would be misleading ourselves if we thought, first, that this is where the harm principle points and, then, that the same principle can be applied neutrally to keep co-existence within acceptable limits.

43 See UN press release GA/L/3271 (February 18, 2005).

Chapter 34

Exposing Harm: The Erasure of Animal Bodies in Healthcare Law

Marie Fox

Introduction

This chapter addresses the nature of harm and how healthcare law is blind to certain forms of harm, in the context of exploring how biotechnologies utilise animal bodies. My aim is three-fold – to demonstrate how law and bioethics may selectively manipulate or downplay the notion of harm, to uncover the harm inflicted on animals in the name of human health, and to argue that healthcare lawyers should foreground the notion of harm, which has been relatively unexplored in contrast to the attention focused on other bioethical concepts, such as autonomy or dignity.[1]

Of course, in many respects, heath care law, like other branches of law, is unable to avoid the question of harm and, particularly, the ways in which law can offer redress for harm caused by healthcare professionals. However, as Joanne Conaghan has noted, because of lawyers' tendency to focus on the issue of compensation, 'the concept of harm is not one upon which people frequently dwell. Harm is widely assumed to be self evident'.[2] Thus, law's function in redressing harms is viewed as relatively uncontentious, seeming to stem, in the case of healthcare, from the fundamental and uncontroversial ethical injunction of non maleficence.[3] Yet, when one considers the diverse range of harms with which healthcare law is currently confronted, it becomes clear that the notion of harm is much more contested than is generally assumed in the medico-ethical literature. Harms traditionally acknowledged

1 See, for instance, Morgan, D., *Issues in Health Care Law*, London, Cavendish, 2000; Beyleveld, D. and Brownsword, R., *Human Dignity in Bioethics and Biolaw*, Oxford, OUP, 2002.

2 Conaghan, J., 'Law, Harm and Redress: A Feminist Perspective', (2002) 22 *Legal Studies*, 319-339.

3 For those who espouse the orthodoxy of the 'four principles' approach to medical ethics (see e.g. Beauchamp, T. and Childress, J., *Principles of Biomedical Ethics*, (5th ed) Oxford, OUP, 2001; Gillon, R. *Philosophical Medical Ethics*, Chichester, John Wiley & Sons, 1985) it is notable that this principle of non maleficence or refraining from causing harm has attracted much less critical attention than other principles, notably that of protecting autonomy, where the complexities of the concept and its relation to legal doctrines, such as informed consent, are evident.

by law, such as direct interference with a human being's bodily integrity occasioned by non consensual interventions or enrolment in unethical clinical trials, may be relatively straightforward. Yet, in recent years more nebulous harms have attracted legal attention, as law attempts to deal with wrongs occasioned by invasions of privacy, or the unauthorised retention of organs or tissue, or is faced with assessing whether the birth of a healthy but unwanted child may be properly adjudged a harm. Still more problematic is the issue of whether law can impose accountability for harms caused by systemic failures in the delivery of healthcare, such as the recent controversy over the MRSA 'superbug' in hospitals or the failure to offer services on the grounds of limited resources. Moreover, as healthcare lawyers increasingly engage in forms of risk analysis they are confronted with the quantifiability of still more speculative future harms.

Given such examples, in this chapter I wish to follow Robin West in arguing that more work needs to be done on the conceptual foundations of harm. She suggests that the influence of jurisprudential movements, such as law and economics, has resulted in a channeling of attention towards regulatory concepts such as cost, which are more readily quantifiable than harm.[4] As she contends, rather than marginalising harm, legal scholarship should be more attentive to defining it:

> while we have a good deal of jurisprudential scholarship on what might be called the 'instrumental' premise of law – that law is basically an instrument for the redress of harms – we have very little understanding of what might be called the necessary 'hedonic' foundations of that instrumentalism – what harm is, what harms we suffer, and how we come to know about them.[5]

In this chapter I seek to explore the diverse range of harms inflicted on animals by new biotechnologies. I argue that these should become a central preoccupation of bioethicists and lawyers, rather than being disregarded in calculating whether such technologies should be sanctioned for human use, and, if so, how they should be regulated. This exercise would serve to make us more conscious of law's power to define what is and is not harm. My particular focus is on how healthcare lawyers disregard the ethical problems posed by new forms of human intervention in animal lives to produce transgenic animals. However, encouraged by the conceptual fluidity of harm, I argue that the notion of what counts as legally harmful may be refashioned in order to accommodate such new forms of harm. In the conclusion I wish to suggest tentatively that this may be an area where it is strategically useful to advocate legal reform on behalf of animals, as well as a topic which offers ways to re-think how we teach and conceptualise healthcare law.

---

4 West, R., *Caring for Justice*, New York, New York University Press, 1997, at p. 165.

5 *Ibid.*, at p. 95.

The Socio-Legal Construction of Harm to Bodies

It has become commonplace in critical legal scholarship to note the importance of naming harms in order for them receive legal recognition, thus facilitating redress for victims or survivors of such harms. Perhaps the most telling illustration pertains to sexual harassment. Although it was not until the mid 1970s that Anglo-American courts and tribunals first countenanced sexual harassment cases,[6] this was indicative only of the fact that the behaviour had no name, and thus no remedy in law; not that it did not exist as a harm.[7] Many other examples of how harms were neglected historically may be derived from within healthcare law. Thus, for decades health professionals disregarded evidence of sexual abuse of children, at least partly due to a prevalent assumption that parents simply would not abuse their children in this way. Only the outbreak of a series of high profile scandals, resulting in public inquiries into the deaths of children at the hands of their families, prompted investigation into the nature and scale of child sexual and physical abuse,[8] and alerted health professionals to their role in contesting this form of harm. This example demonstrates the dangers in relying on 'common sense' perceptions of what harm is, and illustrates Carol Smart's contention that 'harm' is not 'a transcendental notion which is automatically knowable and recognisable at any moment in history'.[9] Similarly, it is only since the 1990s that ethico-legal attention has begun to focus on the pain that may be experienced (often without anaesthesia) by newborn babies in the context either of treating or inflicting non therapeutic procedures on them.[10] The uncovering of such harms validates West's important insight that because women (and children) have been culturally subordinated in patriarchal societies, law has historically 'not included the harms suffered distinctively or disproportionately by women' since 'the "harms" we are all equally protected from (or compensated for) are, largely, those harms which men suffer'.[11] Instead, she suggests that law consistently trivialises, ignores, legitimates and minimises harms sustained mainly by women, such as

---

6 See for instance, in the UK, *Strathclyde RC v. Porcelli*, (1986) IRLR 134 and in the US the Supreme Court decision in *Meritor Savings Bank, FSB v. Vinson*, 477 U.S. 57 (1986).

7 See MacKinnon, C., *Sexual Harassment of Working Women*, New Haven, Yale University Press, 1979 and 'Sexual Harassment: Its First Decade in Court', in her *Feminism Unmodified: Discourses on Life and Law*, 1987, Cambridge MA: Harvard University Press, pp. 103-116.

8 See Porter, R., 'Children and the Concept of Harm', in Hillyard, P., *et al.* (eds), *Beyond Criminology: Taking Harm Seriously*, London, Pluto Press, 2004, pp. 236-50.

9 Smart, C., 'A History of Ambivalence and Conflict in the Discursive Construction of the 'Child Victim' of Sexual Abuse', (1999) 8 *Social and Legal Studies*, 391-406, at p. 392.

10 See Alderson, P., *et al.*, 'The Participation Rights of Premature Babies', (2005) 13 *International Journal of Children's Rights*, 31-50; Fox, M. and Thomson, M., 'Short Changed: The Law and Ethics of Male Circumcision', (2005) 13 *International Journal of Children's Rights*, 161-181.

11 See note 4, *supra*, at p. 9.

domestic or sexual violence.[12] As West notes, because of legal culture's legitimising power, harms which it fails to recognise effectively disappear:

> The consequence, then, is that for those legimated harms, the victim not only has no legal recourse but also has to seriously question whether she has been harmed at all ... Legal culture in this way serves to legitimate not only the specific harm but also the hierarchic distributions of rights and powers that facilitated its occurrence.[13]

Drawing on West's insights I suggest that, since speciesism is even more deeply embedded in our legal culture than sexism,[14] it is no surprise that law is still more blind to harms inflicted on animals. In scientific training, laboratory animals are constructed as disposable research tools,[15] while in legal terms we are not inclined to see redress as appropriate to animals, who are deemed legal objects rather than subjects with standing.[16] If, as West argues, we have difficulty in seeing many of the harms inflicted on women because of law's gender bias, harms to animals will be still less visible. Yet, it is important to expose such harms to ethico-legal scrutiny, since, as Conaghan has argued:

> Virtually all of life's vicissitudes – birth, death, illness, work, family breakdown – are now located in a minefield of legal wrongs and remedies whilst, in our everyday lives – as doctors, teachers, builders, parents, volunteers we must endlessly adjust our conduct to avoid inflicting legal harm on others.[17]

Healthcare law is certainly centrally implicated in dealing both with life's 'messiness' and the question of who precisely constitute the 'others' to whom we owe ethical obligations. Although I do not wish to rehearse here the thorny issue of whether animals are persons or what constitutes personhood,[18] I argue that the continued refusal to recognise animal harm is problematic, given the increasing readiness of lawyers and courts to acknowledge harms to 'marginal' humans like premature

12 *Ibid.*, at pp. 113, 134, 146, 164.

13 *Ibid.*, at p. 151.

14 See Fox, M., 'Re-thinking Kinship: Law's Construction of the Animal Body', (2004) 57 *Current Legal Problems*, 469-93, at pp. 485-9.

15 See Birke, L., *Feminism, Animals and Science: The Naming of the Shrew*, Buckingham, Open University Press, 1994. Significantly in its recent report the Nuffield Council on Bioethics point to the innate conservativism of scientists working in fields such as experimental physiology and biology who may be unable to see the value of replacing animal models in research – Nuffield Council on Bioethics, *The Ethics of Research Involving Animals*, London, 2005, para 11.30.

16 Animals' lack of legal standing is, of course, intimately connected to their status as property in law – see Francione, G., *Animals as Property*, Harvard University Press, 1985.

17 See note 2, at p. 323.

18 See, for example, Harris, J., *The Value of Life: An Introduction to Medical Ethics*, London, Routledge & Kegan Paul, 1985.

babies, foetuses or embryos,[19] where many of the same issues surrounding denial of harm have prevailed in the past. Moreover this acknowledgement of harm to marginal humans is occurring at a juncture where humans are devising new ways in which to exploit animals for our ends and consuming more animal bodies in the process. I turn now to consider how harm to animals passes unnoticed in ethico-legal accounts of these practices.

Biotechnologies and the Invisibility of Harm

While many philosophers have addressed the harms that animals suffer in the name of medical science,[20] and some lawyers have sought to contest law's role in perpetuating such harms,[21] these critiques have made virtually no impact on the terrain of healthcare law. In the major healthcare texts, the ethics of inflicting animal harm is omitted from a consideration of the ethico-legal provisions governing enrolment in clinical trials, notwithstanding the suffering and deaths of countless animals that such research entails.[22] In healthcare law journals and edited collections the animal subject is similarly absent – usually cropping up only where it is impossible to obscure entirely the question of animal exploitation. As I have argued elsewhere, it is only in the case of xeno technologies, where the very prominent use of animal bodies makes it impossible for healthcare lawyers to evade how humans use other animals, that the ethics of the practice is explicitly addressed.[23] Yet, even in this context, animal suffering is routinely minimised and many of the ways in which animals are sacrificed are glossed over. Thus, not only does xenotransplantation

19 See, for instance, Fovargue, S. and Miola, J., 'Policing Pregnancy: Implications of the Attorney-General's Reference (No 3 of 1994)', (1998) 6 *Medical Law Review*, 265-96; Fox, M., 'Cyborgs, Commodities or Pre-persons? The Legal Construction of Embryo Bodies', (2000) 8 *Health Care Analysis*, 171-189. Given that the human embryo is undoubtedly less sentient, less conscious and not yet part of a social network in any meaningful sense, I would argue that embryo research poses many fewer ethico-legal problems than research on animals.

20 See, e.g., from a variety of different philosophical perspectives, Singer, P., *Animal Liberation*, New York, Random House, 1975 (2nd ed 1995), Regan, T., *The Case for Animal Rights*, Berkeley, University of California Press, 1984; Clarke, S. *The Moral Status of Animals*, Oxford, OUP, 1984; Adams, C., *Neither Man nor Beast: Feminism and the Defense of Animals*, New York, Continuum, 1994.

21 See note 16, *supra*; Wise, S., *Drawing the Line: Science and the Case for Animal Rights*, Cambridge, Mass., Perseus Books, 2002; Radford, M., *Animal Welfare Law in Britain*, Oxford, OUP, 2001.

22 Although the concept of pain is not straightforward – see, for instance, Scarry, E., *The Body in Pain: The Making and Unmaking of the World*, Oxford, OUP, 1985 – especially where it is inflicted on one who is unable to articulate it, I shall assume that is uncontroversial that the mammals who are subject to the sort of procedures detailed below feel pain (I deal below with the issue of how we can empathise with animal pain).

23 Fox, M., 'Reconfiguring the Animal/Human Boundary: the impact of xeno technologies', (2005) 31 *Liverpool Law Review*, 149-67.

require animals (currently pigs) to 'donate' tissue or organs, thereby seeming to require the systematic breeding of yet more pigs for human use, it also requires that primates stand in for human recipients in clinical trials until such time as it may be deemed sufficiently safe for clinical trials involving humans to begin.[24] Prior to the trials currently taking place, experiments will have been carried out on 'lesser' animal 'models', such as rodents.[25] In addition to these direct harms inflicted by animal experimentation, the 'donor' animals used will be transgenic – i.e. animals genetically engineered with human genes in order to avoid the problem of hyperacute rejection in human recipients. As I argue below, such interferences with the mouse genome should be considered a major ethico-legal problem in itself. Moreover, donor animals must be bred in sterile conditions and denied social contact with other animals, thus adding to the stress already suffered by laboratory animals.[26] Given this multiple consumption of animals by xeno technologies, and the ways in which their newly fashioned bodies and body parts trouble the human/animal dichotomy, it is not surprising that healthcare lawyers and ethicists are forced to address the ethics of animal use in this context. Yet, significantly, in the risk calculations which xenotransplantation prompts,[27] the focus is overwhelmingly on the speculative costs of viral outbreaks to humans (whether individuals or global populations) whereas the concrete evidence of various forms of harm to animals is downplayed. It should also be noted that those pharmaceutical companies which sponsor research in xeno technologies and stand to make enormous profits from 'successful' outcomes have vested interests in downplaying such costs and are prepared to litigate aggressively in order to prevent such evidence of animal suffering from entering the public domain.[28] Again a consideration of such issues is not considered to fall within the proper domain of healthcare law.

---

24 Indeed, this continuing research on primates represents a significant, but usually unremarked, drawback to proposals that we should impose a moratorium on human trials until they can be deemed sufficiently safe, since primates will continue to be used as surrogate recipients in the meantime.

25 See British Union for the Abolition of Vivisection, *Designer Mice: A BUAV special report into the use of mice in genetic experiments*, London, undated.

26 The Nuffield Council on Bioethics notes the impact of laboratory animals' environment in cages or pens, where they will spend most of their time, upon welfare and suggests the inadequacy of current UK regulations by noting that 'For example, rats are social animals that, in the wild have large home ranges, eat a varied diet and exhibit a range of complex behaviours. Yet according to current guidelines for laboratory animals, two adult rats can be kept for the whole of their life in a cage with a floor area of 700cm^2 (the size of a large shoe box)' – see note 15, *supra*, at para 12.13

27 See Welsh, I. and Evans, R., 'Xenotransplantation, Risk, Regulation and Surveillance: Social and Technological Dimensions of Change', *New Genetics and Society*, 18:2/3 (1999), pp. 197-217; Brown, N. and Michael, M. 'Risky Creatures: Institutional Species Boundary Change in Biotechnology Regulation', *Health, Risk & Society*, 4 (2002) 207-22.

28 *Imutran Ltd v. Uncaged Campaigns*, (Ch.Div) [2001] 2 All ER 358.

In the case of other biotechnologies, the animal harm and sacrifice entailed is more completely ignored. For instance, the debates which preceded the banning of human reproductive cloning in the UK,[29] were notable for the absence of any discussion of the problems occasioned by animal cloning, while those defences of human cloning which have plausibly countered conventional arguments against it have been equally silent on the vast animal suffering this technology entails.[30] In more established reproductive technologies, such as donor insemination and *in vitro* fertilisation, the role played by experiments in breeding animals for the farming and racing industries has been rendered still more obscure. Aside from some early feminist critiques of reproductive technologies, which have been marginalised in recent debates, little attention has been paid to the interesting parallels in the ways in which women and animals have been objectified and rendered the experimental object of reproductive research.[31]

The Creation of Transgenic Animals

In this section I want to foreground the use of transgenic animals to argue that the suffering which this technology creates is, in itself, worthy of ethico-legal attention.[32] Transgenic animals are created through recombinant-DNA technology which enables the genetic material of more than one organism or species to be combined. When the gene of choice is expressed in the recipient animal it will be carried through subsequent offspring in the germline.[33] In this respect the creation of transgenic animals is qualitatively different from earlier selective breeding techniques which have also caused significant animal suffering. As D'Silva notes:

---

29 Human Reproductive Cloning Act 2001.

30 See Harris, J., *On Cloning*, London, Routledge, 2004; 'Goodbye Dolly? The Ethics of Human Cloning', (1997) 23 *Journal of Medical Ethics*, 353-60.

31 See, for instance, Corea, G., *The Mother Machine: Reproductive Technologies from Artificial Insemination to Artificial Wombs*, London, The Women's Press, 1988, chapters 4-6 noting how animal breeding is a precursor of human technology and suggesting that it alerted men to the idea of controlling women's reproduction: 'Although, today, the language men employ in speaking of use of reproductive technology on women differs from that employed in speaking of its use on animals... [w]omen and animals remain part of nature to be controlled and subjugated' (at p. 313). See also, Corea, G., 'Egg Snatchers', Murphy, J., 'Egg Farming and Women's Future' and Murphy, J., 'From Mice to Men', all in Arditti, R., *et al.* (eds), *Test-tube Women: What Future for Motherhood?*, London, Pandora Press, 1984.

32 It should be noted that the silence attending the harms of animal genetic engineering is echoed in other disciplines. A recent book, arguing that sentient animals have moral status but not rights, omits any discussion of transgenic animals or biotechnology, although a chapter is devoted to 'Science and Suffering' – Hills, A., *Do Animals Have Rights?*, Cambridge, Icon Books, 2005.

33 See note 25, *supra*, at pp. 26-36 for a discussion of different mechanisms for accomplishing transgenesis.

> Genetic selection has given us crippled chickens, painfully lame cows, turkeys unable to breed, pigs and chickens that die from heart failure in their infancy – no wonder the concerned welfarist takes a decidedly cautious view of a new technology which can create in a year what may have taken selective breeders decades to achieve.[34]

As noted above, transgenic animals play a pivotal role in facilitating xeno technologies, and they have a variety of other uses in clinical research. Firstly, they enable scientists to study biological function development involving the operation of genes, as selected genes can be introduced, removed or blocked. Secondly, they function as disease models. A 'disease gene' (usually human) is manufactured and inserted into the genome of an animal (usually a mouse) in order to permit an examination of the working of hereditary human genetic diseases. The Harvard onco-mouse, which was genetically engineered to develop cancer and became the first animal to be made the subject of a patent in the US and the EU, is an example of this type. Other mice have been engineered with obesity genes, impaired or absent immune systems, cleft palate deformities and chronic liver disease. Thirdly, transgenic animals are used as models in toxicological testing – genetically altered mice are more finely tuned 'research tools' than conventional mice, as they may be rendered especially susceptible to carcinogens or other toxins. Finally, transgenic mice may be used as 'pharm' animals whose genes are manipulated to express important medical proteins or pharmaceuticals in milk, blood or urine. Following experimental work in mice, the technology has been transferred to genetically modified farm animals like sheep, goats and cows.[35]

Although it is sometimes asserted that these developments benefit animal species,[36] it is clear that such modifications are overwhelmingly pursued in order to benefit humans or for commercial gain. Yet they have attracted little legal scrutiny although they fit somewhat uneasily into the existing legal regulatory scheme under the Animals (Scientific Procedures) Act 1986 (A(SP)A). Since the legislation predates these technologies it is not surprising that a lack of regulatory fit is evident here, as in so many areas of healthcare law. However, because the Act adopts the broader term 'procedure' as opposed to 'experiment', it covers a range of animal use, including the breeding of transgenic animals and animals suffering from harmful genetic defects, even if they are not used subsequently in experimental procedures. This does at least have the merit of ensuring that licences are required for breeding and

---

34 D'Silva, J., 'Campaigning against transgenic technology', in Holland, A. and Johnson, A. (eds), *Animal Biotechnology and Ethics*, London, Chapman & Hall, 1998, at p. 93.

35 For more detail on these uses and their limitations see note 25, *supra*, at pp. 47-87 and Rollin, B., *The Frankenstein Syndrome: Ethical and Social Issues in the Genetic Engineering of Animals*, Cambridge, CUP, 1995.

36 See, for instance, Koopman, J., 'The Patentability of Transgenic Animals in the United States of America and the European Union: A Proposal for Harmonization', (2002-3) 13 *Fordham Intell. Prop., Media & Ent. L.J.*, 103-204, at p. 115.

use of transgenic animals.[37] However, as with more conventional animal research, in deciding whether a licence should be granted to produce, breed or use genetically modified animals, the legislation requires the Animal Procedures Committee (APC) to weigh putative benefits against the likely adverse effect on the research animals, and it is necessary that there should be no alternatives.[38] The British Union for the Abolition of Vivisection (BUAV) suggest that theoretically both criteria should be difficult to satisfy, but contend that in practice:

> It would appear that both of these considerations are seemingly overlooked in granting ... licences. It is doubtful, therefore, whether informed and rigorous cost-benefit analyses are regularly undertaken when licences for animal genetic modification are applied for. This is especially so for those areas where fundamental research is planned which is considered to be of little value to the potential elaboration of human diseases.[39]

The creation of transgenic animals thus constitutes a particular example of how, in animal research, the correspondence of law's viewpoint with that of the human experimenter has a tendency to result in animal interests losing out in the cost-benefit analysis which determines the legal permissibility of research.[40] In part I would argue that this is attributable to researchers' lack of empathy with the experimental animal, which represents an important philosophical obstacle to attempts to place harm to animals on the legal and political agenda. Ever since Descartes' infamous pronouncement in the sixteenth century that animals were without minds and unable to feel pain, scepticism about animal pain has plagued discussion of this topic. Certainly, most commentators now accept that vertebrate mammals feel pain:

> Physiologically, some animals, especially higher mammals have similar central nervous systems to us, and they respond as we do when they are in the kind of circumstances in which we would feel pain: their blood pressure rises, their pulse rates increase, their pupils dilate, glands in their brain secrete chemicals that we know act as painkillers.[41]

However, it remains contentious how pain and its impact on animal welfare are to be assessed. Thus, the recent Nuffield Council Report on the ethics of using animals in clinical research starts promisingly by identifying harm as a central feature of its

37 The 1986 Act established a statutory body – the Animal Procedures Committee (APC) – to oversee the operation of the Act and license animal researchers, research projects and persons in charge of 'designated establishments' where research or breeding is carried out.

38 See Animals (Scientific Procedures) Act 1986, s 5a, 5(6).

39 See note 25, *supra*, at p. 4.

40 The cost-benefit analysis underpinning the Act has recently been reviewed by the APC – see Animal Procedures Committee, *Review of the Cost-benefit Assessment in the Use of Animals in Research*, London, 2003. For further discussion of the limitations of the 1986 Act see Fox, M., 'Animal Rights and Wrongs: Medical Ethics and the Killing of Non-human Animals', in Lee, R. and Morgan, D. (eds), *Death Rites: Law and Ethics as the End of Life*, London, Routledge, 1994.

41 See note 32, *supra*, at pp. 38-9.

inquiry.[42] It concedes that '[a]ll research licensed in the UK under the A(SP)A has the potential to cause pain, suffering, distress or lasting harm to the animals used', and that the objective should be the elimination of this harm:

> A world in which the important benefits of such research could be achieved without causing pain, suffering distress, lasting harm or death to animal involved in research must be the ultimate goal.[43]

Yet, notwithstanding such sentiments, a subsequent chapter of the Report questions whether the concept of harm, which is usually applied to humans, can be meaningfully applied to research animals.[44] It identifies 'philosophical problems' with assessing animal welfare, which essentially are reducible to the question of whether we can ever adopt the animal's perspective. Thus, it highlights the difficulty of getting 'inside the mind' of an animal to be sure that behaviours which we perceive as signs of pain or suffering truly reflect these states', and notes that attempts to do so may involve an invalid anthropomorphic ascription of a human disposition to animal actions.[45] Yet, as Robin Attfield has contended:

> readiness to take non-human interests seriously ... does not involve attempting to enter into the subjectivity of animals, any more that a concern for other people involves telepathy. Nor does it involve imagining what it is like to be the creature in question ... there are many interests which do not turn on consciousness, and which are thus at least as manifest to an observer as to the creature in question.[46]

West has argued that an inability to share the experiences of others also afflicts the thinking of those she terms 'empathetically impotent' economists and lawyers who point to the inability of an observer to make 'interpersonal comparisons of utility'.[47] The consequence of such thinking, as she notes, is that 'since we can't in any meaningful way "know" the subjective hedonic lives of others we must, if we wish to maximise their subjective well being, rely on objectively knowable proxies'.[48] By contrast, she argues that lawyers should adopt a more empathic understanding of the wrongs suffered by others and contest the erasure of emotions and subjectivity. I would suggest that this is particularly important for biolaw, since, as David Cooper has argued, intuitive emotional responses to biotechnologies should not be dismissed as irrational. Rather 'by reflecting on these responses ... we come to see what is wrong, and distinctively so, with producing "oncomice", "transgenic hybrids" and

42 See note 15, *supra*, at p. xviii.

43 *Id.*

44 *Ibid.*, at para 4.2.

45 *Ibid.*, at para 4.4.

46 Attfield, R., 'Genetic Engineering: Can Unnatural Kinds be Wronged?', in note 34 *supra*, at p. 206.

47 See West, R., 'Economic Man and Literary Woman: One Contrast', (1988) 39 *Mercer Law Review*, 867-78.

48 See note 4, *supra*, at p. 172.

so on'.[49] In this regard the Nuffield Report also displays positive signs. Hence, while it is excessively concerned to refute charges of subjectivity and anthropomorphism, to a limited extent it does depart from a wholly objective test of animal welfare/ harm, proposing that human inability to experience the world from the particular animal's perspective 'is mostly irrelevant with regard to assessing pain and suffering in laboratory animals'.[50] It advocates use of a 'critical anthropomorphic' approach in the assessment of animal welfare, which requires 'the critical use of humane experience to recognise and alleviate animal suffering by combining one's perception of a particular animal's situation with what can be determined by more objective science-based observations'.[51] However, the problem with such science-based observations is that they are likely to entail a continuing bias towards the use of traditional models such as the mouse. Thus, in relation to mouse cognition and pain the report states:

> Pain pathways ... extend to other areas of the cortex, known as the association cortex, the great expansion of which is unique to humans and certain other primates ... These areas are virtually non-existent in the brains of rodents ... this finding suggests that animals such as mice, which lack similarly developed brain structures, may be very unlikely to experience suffering resulting from pain in a similar way, although they do suffer pain itself. Therefore, evidence about differences in the way in which pain is embedded in the brains of different animals supports the view that care is required when ascribing states such as suffering to mice.[52]

Again this betrays how the human, and animals who most closely resemble the human, are made the measure of all suffering, while the variability of animal experiences is seized upon to mimimise ethical responsibility for, or empathy with, the suffering of 'lesser animals' like rodents. As the BUAV note, 'being small and commonly perceived as "pest" animals the suffering and distress that might be triggered in mice, confined and already suffering from the various effects of transgenesis or mutagenesis, may be easily overlooked or dismissed'.[53] The downplaying of such harms can be seen when the Nuffield report examines the welfare implications of using mice as disease models. In relation to cancer models, for instance, welfare implications are dismissed in a single sentence – 'With regard to animal welfare,

49 Cooper, D.E., 'Intervention, Humility and Animal Integrity', in note 34 *supra* at p. 147. See also Clark, S. 'Intrinsic Criticisms of Biotechnological Critique', in Olderberg, D. (ed), *Human Lives*, London, Macmillan, 1995.

50 See note 15, *supra*, at para 4.6.

51 *Id.* For more detail see Morton, D.B., Burghardt, G. and Smith, J.A., 'Critical Anthropomorphism, Animal Suffering and the Ecological Context', 20 (1990) *Hastings Center Report on Animals, Science and Ethics*, 20 (1990) 13-39.

52 See note 15, *supra*, at para 4.16.

53 See note 25, *supra*, at p. 13.

mouse models of cancer usually demonstrate an increased incidence of tumours and an increased morbidity that will require careful monitoring'.[54]

This contrasts with accounts of animal suffering outlined in an early critique by Gill Langley, who details suffering caused by factors such as oncogenes causing tumors in unexpected places where 'they may not be detected before they cause substantial pain and distress'.[55] She contends that the technology is inherently unpredictable, with at least seven poorly understood factors generating random outcomes and immense potential for animal suffering:

> Genetic manipulation affects the most fundamental but immensely complex processes of cells and tissues. These processes are so poorly understood and controlled that genetic manipulation produces physical abnormalities which can cause pain and distress to many animals.[56]

Moreover, because of our incomplete knowledge of these processes, it seems to be generally accepted that assessing the welfare implications of these transgenic animals is more complex than for 'normal' laboratory animals. As an Animal Procedures Committee report has noted, 'comprehensive information on the welfare implications of particular strains of GM animals is not ... readily available from public sources'.[57] This raises the concern that animals may suffer in ways not readily detectable by the sorts of scientific criteria which Nuffield and other commentators[58] deem part of adequate welfare assessments.

In addition to animal suffering, the other major ethical problem is the escalation in the number of animals which must be bred and subsequently discarded in order to produce 'the particular desired transgenic object of genetic engineering'.[59] While the success of animal welfare campaigns in the 1970s and 1980s had led to reductions in the number of animal procedures, as testing for cosmetic substances was phased out, and some of the most notorious toxicity testing refined,[60] the 1990s witnessed the first overall increase in registered animal procedures since the mid 1970s because

---

54 See note 15, *supra*, at para 7.9. This is somewhat ironic in view of its later recommendation that the APC should publish fuller details of animal suffering in the research it licenses – see note 83, *infra*.

55 Langley, G., 'A Critical View of the Use of Genetically Engineered Animals in the Laboratory', in Wheale, P. and McNally, R. (eds), *Animal Genetic Engineering: Of Pigs, Oncomice and Men*, London, Pluto, 1995, pp. 184-193, at p. 188. See also note 15 at p. 1.

56 *Id.*

57 Animal Procedures Committee, *Report on Biotechnology*, London, 2001, para. 49.

58 Broom, D.M., 'The effects of biotechnology on animal welfare', in note 34 *supra*, at p. 70.

59 See note 55 *supra*, at pp. 189-90.

60 For instance, in the UK, Home Office guidance has restricted the use of the Draize test which involves placing the substance to be tested for toxicity into the eyes of live conscious rabbits, and no longer permits animal testing for cosmetic products – see statement by the Secretary of State for the Home Department, House of Commons, Hansard written answers for 16 Jan 2001, cited in BUAV, see note 25, *supra*, at box. 11.2.

production and use of transgenic animals had become research 'flavour of the day'.[61] Advocates of biotechnology claim that engineering animal disease models will eventually reduce the number of animals used, since 'the use of more genetically uniform or inbred stocks, if appropriate to the particular experiment, may reduce variation and therefore allow the use of fewer animals'.[62] However, in the short term it has been responsible for an unprecedented increase in the number of animals used in scientific experiments. The ten years from 1991-2001 witnessed a 1017 per cent rise in the number of transgenic animals used in experiments,[63] and in 2003 764,000 procedures involved transgenic animals (97 per cent of them mice) accounting for over a quarter of all procedures in that year.[64] The sheer scale of animal bodies consumed by genetic engineering is partly because it has proven a massively inefficient way of producing the desired characteristics in animals. As the BUAV report notes:

> It is becoming clear that the exact location of each gene is vital to its proper function within the chromosome – the shotgun approach to transgenesis may therefore be wholly unsuited to producing a fully functional transgene and may explain some of the dreadful waste of life entailed by transgenesis.[65]

Similarly, the Nuffield Council found that the wastage of animals in the genetic modification processes was a core concern for respondents.[66] A related problem was the risk of duplication of harmful procedures in producing transgenic animals.[67] Yet, the rush to patent transgenic animals suggests that considerable incentives exist for such research to continue. The Nuffield report estimates that:

> over the next two decades 300,000 new genetic lines of mice could be created, and expectations are that the total number of mice that are expected to be used in mutagenesis and phenotyping studies are of the order of several million each year in the UK alone. [Furthermore] … large numbers of animals are used to produce and maintain each line of GM animals.[68]

It notes that over 3,000 mouse mutant lines are believed to be currently available and that 'mouse clinics' are being built around the world to analyse them.[69] Not only

61 See note 55, *supra*, at p. 190.

62 See note 15, *supra*, at para 12.4.

63 See note 25, *supra*, at p. 6.

64 Home Office, *Statistics of Scientific Procedures on Living Animal Great Britain 2003*, Norwich, HMSO, 2004.

65 See note 25, *supra*, at p. 18.

66 See note 15, *supra*, Appendix 5, at p. 306.

67 *Ibid*., at paras 15.71-15.75, Nuffield noted that international databases were a useful mechanism for archiving and distributing information on genetically modified animals.

68 *Ibid*., at para 15.7, 'The number of animals currently required to establish an individual genetic line carrying a particular mutation currently ranges from 50 to several hundred' – *ibid*., at para 7.15.

69 *Ibid*., at paras 7.5-7.6.

do such technologies fuel the commodification as well as the modification of these animals, but the requirement that inventions be 'novel' in order to attract patent protection serves to compound the lack of openness and visibility which already shrouds animal research. Moreover, while mice constitute the vast majority of transgenic animals since they are immensely adaptable subjects,[70] it is also politically expedient to experiment on rodents to avoid the public outcry that would greet such experiments were they performed on primates, cats or dogs. Thus, although transgenic animals certainly function to blur the human/animal boundary, it is equally true that they blur the boundary between animals and things and are thus more easily constructed as commodities. In this way, the erasure of harms to transgenic mice is more complete than for other animals, and they are even less likely than other animals to be construed as worthy of the attention of healthcare law.

Conclusion

As Conaghan contends '[t]he notion of harm implies some element of social recognition; as such, it is fluid and contentious, shifting and changing over time'.[71] This fluidity offers an opportunity to call attention to new forms of harm. Thus, notwithstanding the 'unknowability' of harm, I would endorse the calls of West and other feminist scholars for a legal ethics that is more attentive to the experiences and harms of others in our society. While their arguments are limited to human societies, I would suggest that it is unacceptably speciesist to limit our empathy to our human kin. In tailoring mice to human ends in increasingly invasive ways we acquire special ethical responsibility to them, quite apart from those we owe to mice in general, whose societies are linked with ours in complex ways.[72] Speciesism and our consequent acceptance of a clear dichotomy between humans and other animals is the major obstacle to acknowledging the harm we cause these creatures. Like scientists who 'manufacture' these animals, and officials and judges who grant patents to their 'inventors',[73] our species bias leads us to view these mice as human inventions rather than our sentient kin. However, as the human/animal binary becomes increasingly untenable when we modify animals with human genes and attempt to transfer their body parts to ours, law has to work increasingly hard to maintain the species boundary.[74] Yet law could also be co-opted to contest the reduction of animals to research material, and to challenge dominant understandings that because such abuse takes place on the sanctified terrain of scientific medicine

70 See Haraway, D., *Modest Witness@Second_Millennium.FemaleMan_Meets_OncoMouse [tm]*, New York, Routledge, 1996, pp. 78-85, on the adaptability of rodents.

71 See note 2, *supra*, at p. 322.

72 As the BUAV notes, 'In the wild they spread through human trading and settlement – our presence in the world invariably being shared with mice' – see note 25, *supra*, at p. 11.

73 See for instance, Jones, T.A., 'Patenting Transgenic Animals: When the Cat's Away, the Mice Will Play', (1992-3) 12 *Vermont Law Review*, 875-923.

74 See note 23, *supra*.

it is legitimate or inevitably represents 'progress'.[75] Hillyard and Tombs have noted that 'defining what constitutes harm is a productive and positive process'.[76] By illustrating how harms are differentially constructed or disregarded when animal bodies are concerned, law can be forced to recognise animal suffering, just as it has had to grudgingly acknowledge harms inflicted on the bodies of women or children.[77]

Of course such efforts face the counter argument that to weigh animal suffering adequately in cost-benefit analyses will likely cause some research to be ruled out as morally unacceptable, thereby potentially harming humans. Yet, as Margot Brazier has argued of embryo experimentation, such harms as may be occasioned by the loss of projected benefits of research are speculative when compared to the harm inflicted on the research subject. [78] Hence, no one can have a right that such research is conducted. Additionally, I am concerned to challenge the polarisation that frequently characterises debates about animal versus human interests. Far from being diametrically opposed, animal and human interests often coincide. Thus, when considering xeno technologies, if the various forms of animal suffering they occasion were taken seriously and aligned with human interests in avoiding new cross species infections, that might convince policy makers to abandon xeno research. This would free up resources for other initiatives and lend impetus to law reform efforts which aim to avoid wastage of viable human organs.[79] Similarly, as animal protection groups have argued, the outlawing of transgenic experiments may not seriously hamper productive medical research, given reservations about the transferability of such research to human patients, particularly in the case of multifactorial genetic diseases like diabetes or Alzheimer's.[80]

Although in my view such arguments point to the need to outlaw these forms of harmful research, this seems an area where less radical law reform can be strategically useful. Thus, I would concur with Broom that current legislation should be amended specifically to regulate transgenic animals. He proposes that we adopt the Netherlands

---

75 Jeffrey Burkhardt notes the tendency in the discourse of biotechnology and its reporting to present all innovations as 'advances' to which challenges are irrational – see 'The Inevitability of Biotechnology? Ethics and the Scientific Attitude', in note 34, *supra*, at p. 123.

76 Hillyard, P. and Tombs, S., 'Introduction', in note 8, *supra*.

77 In this paper I have been concerned to identify tangible harms in terms of harms and suffering to animal bodies, but important and less tangible harms also exist pertaining to animal 'telos' and human authorship of animal bodies. See, for instance, Holland, A. and Johnson, A., 'Introduction', in note 34, *supra*; Rifkind, J., *Algeny*, New York, Viking Press, 1983, Fox, M., 'Transgenic Animals: Ethical and Animal Welfare Concerns', in Wheale, P. and McNally, R. (eds), *The Bio-Revolution: Cornucopia or Pandora's Box?*, London, Pluto, 1990.

78 Brazier, M., 'Embryos Rights: Abortion and Research', in Freeman, M. (ed), *Medicine, Ethics and Law*, London, Stevens, 1998.

79 See, for instance, Harris, J., 'Organ Procurement: Dead Interests, Living Needs', (2003) 29 *Journal of Medical Ethics*, 130-34.

80 See note 25, *supra*, at pp. 50-68.

approach of using transgenic animals only where specific permission is granted.[81] He also argues that UK legislation should expressly provide that commercial profit is insufficient justification for modifying an animal so that its welfare is poor and:

> stipulate that no genetically modified or treated animal should be permitted to be used commercially until comprehensive studies of the welfare of the animal have been carried out during two generations and continuing for their maximum commercial life.[82]

Another uncontentious, but valuable, legal reform would adopt the Nuffield Council's recommendation that fuller information be made available about the types of procedures to which animals are subjected and the suffering which they experience. Specifically, Nuffield notes that the severity banding used in the granting of licences, according to which animal suffering can be classified as 'substantial', 'moderate', 'mild' or 'unclassified' is not especially meaningful. They propose that clearer information be provided regarding the duration and nature of animal suffering inflicted over the course of the project licence, and that account be taken of the impact on welfare of the research animals' environment.[83] Nuffield also stresses the necessity for retroactive information about the actual suffering experienced, as opposed to the researcher's estimate of average animal suffering at the beginning of the project.[84] As the Report notes:

> Constructive debate would be facilitated by the provision of clear information about the full implications of research involving animals in terms of the kind, numbers and species of animals used, as well as the pain, suffering and distress to which they can be subjected.[85]

Although I am generally inclined to skepticism about the value of law reform strategies aimed at improving animal welfare, in this particular context such reforms would help reduce the number of wasteful experiments, render visible the harm we inflict upon animals, and highlight harms peculiar to transgenic animals, thus serving to minimise animal suffering in the short term and to lend impetus to moves for the abolition of animal genetic engineering in the longer term. As West has highlighted, and the examples above demonstrate, an important linkage exists between naming harm and law reform. Although in West's words, I see such reforms as serving 'to give substantive content to the concept of harm [and] to articulate what … the law could do to minimise those harms',[86] simultaneously I would urge that we should be alert to the perils of engaging in law reform. By specifically legislating for transgenic animals we are in many respects legitimating what is and may be done to them. Moreover, as the Nuffield Report has noted:

---

81 See, note 58, *supra*, at p. 80.

82 *Ibid.*, at p. 70.

83 See note 15, *supra*, at paras 1525-15.34.

84 *Id.*

85 *Ibid.*, at p. 20.

86 See note 2, *supra*, at p. 176.

> Regulation can act as an emotional screen between the researcher and animal, possibly encouraging the researcher to believe that simply to conform to regulations is to act in a moral way.[87]

For this reason it is necessary that law reform strategies should go hand in hand with educative attempts. Lawyers and ethicists have a role to play in influencing the curriculum to place the issue of animal harm, and indeed harm in general, more firmly at the centre of the healthcare agenda. Burkhardt has argued that for the ethics of animal welfare to be taken seriously 'fundamental changes in the scientific attitude would be necessary' and that 'moral or ethical education of young scientists and students would … be key'.[88] His observation is equally applicable to changing the legal mindset. We need to disrupt the boundaries of what is deemed the 'proper' concern of medical law by making the issues of harm and the power to define it central to the agenda of modern healthcare law. In so doing we not only highlight the animal suffering which medical science can cause but help reframe the concept of harm to make it more relevant to our biotechnological or post human era.

Acknowledgements

I would like to acknowledge the helpful comments of Sheila McLean and the support of the AHRC Research Centre for Law, Gender and Sexuality.

87 See note 15, *supra*, at para 15.14.

88 See, note 75 *supra*, at p. 130.

Chapter 35

Is the Gender Recognition Act 2004 as Important as It Seems?[1]

Kenneth McK. Norrie

Introduction

Gender matters. However much the law strives for equal opportunities and outlaws sex discrimination, society remains gendered and so does the law. The assumed fact of gender will frequently determine how the law responds to particular persons or the circumstances they find themselves in or the relationships they enter into. This is so in a variety of areas of law, but perhaps most obviously in determining the validity of recognised and state-sanctioned conjugal relationships (that is to say marriage and civil partnership). Given the wide importance of gender, it is somewhat surprising that Parliament has never seen the need to lay down any criteria for the determination of an individual's gender. This is not to be explained on the basis that, until at any rate the development of gender reassignment surgery, gender is always certain, for the problem of the hermaphrodite has been exercising legal commentators for almost two millennia.[2] It is, however, the ability of modern medical practice to respond in a practical way to the needs of transsexuals that has created an environment in which neither the courts nor the legislature can ignore either gender itself or individuals who seek to change from one to the other.

The Pre-2004 Transgender Cases

The story of George Jamieson, who became April Ashley and married the Hon Arthur Corbett, is well-known, as is Ormrod J's judgment annulling the marriage in the seminal case that followed.[3] Ormrod J, a judge chosen to hear the case because of his medical as well as legal background, made two crucial findings: (i) that there were

1 Helpful comments on an earlier draft of this chapter were made by Dr Stephen Whittle, Head of the Graduate School of Law, Manchester Metropolitan University and these are gratefully acknowledged. The argument presented here is mine, however, and not his. Responsibility for remaining errors is (of course) mine alone.

2 See D. 1, v, 10; Grotius, *Jurisprudence of Holland*, I, iii, 6; Sanchez, *De Sancto Matrimonii*, cvi, 380; Paulus, D, xxii, 5, 15.

3 *Corbett v. Corbett*, [1971] P 83.

four factors to be taken into account in determining a person's gender: chromosomal, gonadal, genital and psychological and (ii) that when the first three are congruent at birth then that determines a person's gender for the rest of their life. Though a first instance decision, it dominated the law of England (and was assumed to reflect the law of Scotland) for over three decades, setting the rule not only in its own context (validity of marriage) but also in other areas of law such as the criminal law[4] and employment discrimination law.[5] Regular challenges to the *Corbett* rule were made in the European Court of Human Rights, on the basis that the UK's position was inconsistent with the European Convention on Human Rights' (ECHR) Article 8 right to private life and the Article 12 right to marry and found a family[6] and, until 2002, these challenges were consistently rejected by the European Court (albeit with an ever-decreasing majority). Also at around that time the domestic English courts faced the most sustained challenge to the rule in *Corbett* since that decision, in a case which raised exactly the same issue, in the same context, if in rather more benign circumstances.

In *Bellinger v. Bellinger* the judge at first instance refused to grant a declaration of validity of a marriage between Mr and Mrs Bellinger, the latter having undergone gender reassignment surgery before a ceremony of marriage 20 years previously. The Court of Appeal refused the appeal and refused also to overrule *Corbett*, on the ground that to do so would involve a major change of the law which it is properly for Parliament rather than the court to make.[7] There was, however, a strong dissenting judgment from Thorpe LJ which, three months later, was founded upon by Chisholm J in the Family Court of Australia in *Kevin and Jennifer v. Attorney General*[8] where the claim was to all intents and purposes exactly the same. Chisholm J explained how *Corbett* had been based on scientific propositions that could not stand in light of understandings developed since 1970 and on social perceptions that were, even on their own terms, no more than unreasoned assertions. Nine months after *Kevin and Jennifer*, the European Court in *Goodwin v. United Kingdom*[9] also rejected *Corbett* (and their own previous jurisprudence on the issue), on the basis that it was

4 *R v. Tan*, [1983] QB 1053, which involved a conviction for a gender-specific crime. This case was not followed in Australia: *R v. Harris and McGuiness*, (1988) 17 NSWLR 158.

5 *White v. British Sugar Corporation*, [1977] IRLR 121 (now overruled: see n. 39 below).

6 *Rees v. United Kingdom*, [1986] 9 EHRR 56; *Cossey v. United Kingdom*, (1990) 13 EHRR 622; *Sheffield & Horsham v. United Kingdom*, (1998) 27 EHRR 163; *X, Y and Z v. United Kingdom*, (1997) 24 EHRR 143. An in-depth analysis of the ECHR cases is to be found in Reed, R., 'Transsexuals and European Human Rights Law', in Graupner, H. and Tahmindjis, P. (eds), *Sexuality and Human Rights: A Global Perspective*, New York, Haworth Press, 2005.

7 [2002] 2 WLR 411. See Norrie, K. McK., 'Family Law Update', (2001) 6 *SLPQ*, 237.

8 [2001] Fam CA 1074.

9 (2002) 35 EHRR 18.

indeed inconsistent with both Articles 8 and 12 of the ECHR, and seven months after *Goodwin* Chisholm J's judgment in *Kevin* was upheld by the Full Court of the Family Court of Australia[10] (albeit on different grounds). Less than two months after that, the House of Lords handed down their decision in *Bellinger.*[11] To the surprise of many, the House of Lords did not follow Thorpe LJ's dissent and reinterpret English law in a way that was consistent with the ECHR. Rather, they held that *Corbett* represented the true state of English law and that legislative rather than judicial change was the only possible route to ECHR consistency. Three months later, and on the first anniversary of the European Court's decision in *Goodwin,* the British Government published a draft Bill designed to reverse the rule in *Corbett* and *Bellinger*. The Gender Recognition Act 2004 came into force in April 2005.

The Gender Recognition Act 2004 and the Nature of Transsexualism

This Act allows individuals to apply to a Gender Recognition Panel, for the granting of a 'Gender Recognition Certificate',[12] on the granting of which the applicant's gender becomes 'the acquired gender',[13] subject to certain exceptions to be discussed later. The Panel is obliged to grant the Certificate if the applicant has or has had gender dysphoria, has lived in the acquired gender for at least two years, and intends to continue to do so for the rest of his or her life.[14] As such, the Panel's decision is one of fact rather than judgment. There is no requirement for surgical or any other form of medical treatment before an application may be made or a Certificate granted. A married person, or a person in a civil partnership, is not entitled to a Gender Recognition Certificate but may apply for an interim Gender Recognition Certificate,[15] which allows for the speedy dissolution of their marriage or civil partnership:[16] on such dissolution the divorce court will issue a full Gender Recognition Certificate[17] which itself will entitle the parties to re-establish their legal relationship with their ex-spouse or ex-civil partner as, respectively, a civil partnership or a marriage.

Though it is clear that the Act is designed to reverse the rule in *Corbett* and *Bellinger*, the requirement to satisfy the European Convention on Human Rights has meant that it goes very much further than simply allowing transgendered persons to marry in their new gender. It is, however, not immediately apparent either how

10 [2003] Fam CA 94.

11 [2003] UKHL 21, [2003] 2 All ER 593.

12 Gender Recognition Act 2004, s 1.

13 *Ibid.*, s 9.

14 *Ibid.*, s 2.

15 *Ibid.*, s 4(3) as amended by s 250 of the Civil Partnership Act 2004.

16 Gender Recognition Act 2004, sched 2, amending s 12 of the Matrimonial Causes Act 1973 for England and Wales, s 1 of the Divorce (Scotland) Act 1976 for Scotland, and art 14 of the Matrimonial Causes (Northern Ireland) Order 1978 for Northern Ireland.

17 Gender Recognition Act 2004, s 5.

far the Act goes or, as we will see, the extent to which it remains necessary to rely on its terms. These matters depend, at least partly, upon the mischief that the Act is designed to address, and the key to understanding what that mischief is lies in long-established judicial attitudes to the very nature of transsexualism, which remain of crucial importance. In *Corbett* the medical evidence variously described April Ashley as 'a male homosexual transsexualist', 'a castrated male' and 'an intersex'.[18] Ormrod J described transsexuals as persons with 'an extremely powerful urge to become a member of the opposite sex', who suffer psychologically 'but do not respond favourably to psychological treatment'.[19] This is reflected in the description offered by Lord Nicholls in *Bellinger*:

> Transsexual people are born with the anatomy of a person of one sex but with an unshakeable belief or feeling that they are persons of the opposite sex. They experience themselves as being of the opposite sex ... The aetiology of this condition remains uncertain. It is now generally recognised as a psychiatric disorder.[20]

These passages show that both Ormrod J and Lord Nicholls see gender dysphoria as a disorder of the mind: they regard it as axiomatic that for persons in whom there is a gender disparity between the body and the mind it is *self-evidently* the mind and not the body that is suffering the disorder and that surgery or medical intervention is appropriate only because psychological intervention is ineffective. Yet whoever is 'generally recognising' this assertion, it is not transsexual people, who are much more likely to regard the abnormality as being one of the body[21] – it is their body that is wrong rather than their mind, with the result that surgery or medical intervention is appropriate in its own terms, which is to ensure that their body is altered to reflect the reality of their mind. The supposition that transsexualism is a disorder of the mind allows the judges to make a more crucial assertion: that surgery to alter the body may well harmonise the body with the mind but it neither cures transsexualism nor gives the patient the 'right' or 'true' body. Reflecting Ormrod J's language of the 'artificial vagina' that April Ashley possessed,[22] Lord Nicholls describes gender reassignment as follows:

> For men [surgery] may mean castration or inversion of the penis to create a false vagina. For women it may mean a mastectomy, hysterectomy or creation of a false penis by phalloplasty.[23]

The surgery, in other words, is designed not to reflect reality or fact, but to falsify the patient's body as a way of ameliorating (but not curing) the disorder of the mind. It is

---

18 [1971] P 83, at p. 99.

19 *Ibid.*, at p. 98.

20 [2003] UKHL 21, at para 7.

21 Recognised by Baronness Hale in *A v. Chief Constable of West Yorkshire Police*, [2004] UKHL 21, at para 26.

22 [1971] P, at p. 98.

23 [2003] UKHL 21, per Lord Nicholls at para 40.

but second best to a cure, which would be altering the mind rather than the body. '[t]he purpose of these operations [castration, amputation of the penis and construction of an artificial vagina]' declared Ormrod J in *Corbett* 'is, of course, to help to relieve the patient's symptoms and to assist in the management of their disorder; it is not to change their sex'.[24] In *Bellinger* Lord Nicholls uses virtually the same language: 'the aim of the surgery is to make the individual feel more comfortable with his or her body, *not to "turn a man into a woman" or vice versa*'[25] (emphasis added). Lord Hope is to the same effect:

> The essence of the problem, as I see it, lies in the impossibility of changing completely the sex which individuals acquire when they are born ... (M)edical science is unable, in its present state, to complete the process. It cannot turn a man into a woman or turn a woman into a man. That is not what the treatment seeks to do after all, although it is described as gender reassignment surgery.[26]

If medical science is unable to do this, then the law cannot do so either, and the Gender Recognition Act 2004 is, therefore, of limited scope – it does not turn a man into a woman, nor does it tackle the 'impossibility' of changing sex. Rather, it merely permits individuals to be treated for the purposes of the law *as if* they belonged to the gender that they live their lives in rather than the gender that they (in reality) remain. Put shortly, the Act creates a legal fiction which allows the law to ignore for most purposes the individual's real gender.

Gender Reassignment and Marriage

The explanation for this insistence on immutability of 'real' gender lies, I suggest, in the perceived need for absolute certainty within the context in which *Corbett* and *Bellinger* arose; that is to say marriage.[27] Ormrod J denied that April Ashley was a woman because, with a merely artificial vagina, she could not naturally perform 'the essential role of a woman in marriage'[28] and that 'having regard to the essentially heterosexual character of the relationship which is called marriage, the criteria [for determining gender in that context] must ... be biological'.[29] Lord Hope and Lord Nicholls similarly hold that the meaning of the words 'male' and 'female' within the context of marriage must refer back to the role that men and women usually play in procreation: they assume (as the European Court does not[30]) that procreation

24 [1971] P, at p. 98.

25 [2003] UKHL 21, at para 41

26 *Ibid.*, at para 57.

27 In the words of Baronness Hale in *A v. Chief Constable of West Yorkshire Police*, [2004] UKHL 21, at para 51: 'Marriage is still a status good against the world in which clarity and consistency are vital'.

28 [1971] P, at p. 106.

29 *Id.*

30 *Goodwin v. United Kingdom*, (2002) 35 EHRR 18, at para 98.

and marriage are inherently *and necessarily* connected, with the result that 'male' and 'female' in marriage law are words referring not so much to gender roles as procreative potential. Lord Hope says:

> Of course it is not given to every man or every woman to have, or to want to have, children. But the ability to reproduce one's own kind lies at the heart of all creation, and the single characteristic which invariably distinguishes the adult male from the adult female throughout the animal kingdom is the part which each sex plays in the act of reproduction. When Parliament uses the words 'male' and 'female' in section 11(c) of the [Matrimonial Causes Act 1973] it must be taken to have used those words in the sense which they normally would have when they are used to describe a person's sex, even though they are plainly capable of including men and women who happen to be infertile or are past the age of childbearing.[31]

There is no question but that there is a clear difference in the factual role that each gender plays in the natural process of reproduction, but it is a leap of logic to assume from this that these roles require to be replicated in the legal institution of marriage. For it should not be forgotten that marriage is a legal construct rather than a natural state of being. Animals who mate for life, like swans, mate, they do not marry; bull walruses with harems of cows are *not* polygamists. Yet Lord Nicholls is quite deliberate in drawing what he perceives as an essential link between procreation and marriage. He defines gender, for the purposes of marriage, as involving a general capacity to reproduce, since the primary *raison d'être* of marriage was, for many centuries, reproduction.[32] The fact that modern society no longer sees marriage in this way was one of the major reasons why the Family Court of Australia felt able to depart from the *Corbett* precedent,[33] but Lord Nicholls is altogether unwilling to go so far. He states merely that 'for a long time now the emphasis has been different. Variously expressed, there is much more emphasis now on the "mutual society, help and comfort that the one ought to have of the other"'.[34] However, even when marriage was the primary social environment in which procreation took place, it never followed that individual marriages required to be procreative in intent or potential: the infertile can marry validly, as can those who deliberately take steps to avoid reproduction. The House of Lords itself over 50 years ago accepted that consummation could validate a marriage even when steps were positively taken to avoid procreation.[35] Since individual marriages do not require to be procreative, it is illogical to define gender for the purposes of marriage in terms of procreative potential. In reality, *Bellinger* represents a judicial fear, not of those who are lacking

31 [2003] UKHL 21, at para 64.

32 *Ibid.*, at para 46.

33 *Re Kevin and Jennifer*, *supra cit.*, at para 153.

34 [2003] UKHL 21, at para 46.

35 *Baxter v. Baxter*, 1948 AC 274, in which it was held that the wearing of a condom does not prevent consummation. The very asking of the question illustrates graphically just how artificial and technical the concept of marriage is.

'all the equipment' (in Lord Hope's unfortunate phrase[36]), but that marriage will lose its opposite-sex character. If gender reassignment surgery does not in reality turn a man into a woman but that 'man' is permitted to marry a man, then the very nature of marriage is altered – it is opened up to same-sex couples (so long as one of the men has had his penis chopped off first). Lord Hope let the mask slip with a remarkable misinterpretation of the result in *Goodwin v. UK*. He says this '[The] problem would be solved if it were possible for a transsexual to marry a person of the *same* sex, which is indeed what the European Court of Human Rights has now held should be the position in *Goodwin*'.[37] The European Court held no such thing. Recognising a change of gender actually allows marriage to remain opposite-sex, but only if gender is recognised as being as much a legal construct as marriage itself. Lord Hope's slip is explained by his underlying belief that, whatever the law says, a person's 'true' gender remains defined by the body he or she was born with. Dressed up as a requirement for procreative potential, the true message of *Bellinger* is that while the law may evolve in such a way that a person's legal gender can change, a person's true gender (and thereby the opposite-sex nature of the legal institution of marriage) remains immutable.

Gender Reassignment in Other Contexts

It needs always to be remembered that Ormrod J in *Corbett* was careful to limit his conclusions to their own context, and though there is no need in logic to follow these conclusions in areas other than marriage, subsequent cases assumed that there was.[38] Nothing in the House of Lords decision in *Bellinger* suggests an application of that case wider than marriage and the heavy reliance on the nature of marriage and on the interpretation of the particular marriage statute in question suggests strongly that, at the very least, different arguments would need to be deployed in different contexts if the same conclusion is to be reached. In fact, shortly after *Bellinger*, the same court held that a different conclusion was possible – indeed required – in different circumstances, with the result that a person was for the first time in the United Kingdom legally recognised as belonging to their new gender. This, even before the coming into effect of the Gender Recognition Act 2004.

A v. Chief Constable of West Yorkshire Police[39] involved a male to female transsexual who had had her application to become a police officer rejected on the basis of her transsexuality. To discriminate in employment against a person because of their transgender status has for some time now been recognised as being contrary to the Sex Discrimination Act 1975,[40] but the Chief Constable sought to rely on

36 [2003] UKHL 21 at para 57.

37 *Ibid.*, at para 69, emphasis added.

38 See notes 4 and 5, *supra.*

39 [2004] UKHL 21.

40 *P v. S and Cornwall County Council*, [1996] 1 ECR 2143, [1996] 2 CMLR 247; *KB v. National Health Service Pensions Agency* [2004] IRLR 240.

the defence that being of one gender or the other was a 'genuine occupational qualification' for the police force, as a result of statutory rules requiring that when the police undertake intimate body searches only male police officers may search males and only female police officers may search females.

The House of Lords was unanimous in rejecting this defence, on the ground that it would have been within the operational control of the Chief Constable to exempt Ms A from carrying out such searches at all. This would have been a more proportionate response to the situation than the outright refusal to employ her. More crucially, it held[41] that the words 'woman' and 'man' in the Sex Discrimination Act 1975 do not refer, in that context, to procreative ability (even if imaginary) but rather must be read 'as referring to the acquired gender of a post-operative transsexual who is visually and for all practical purposes indistinguishable from non-transsexual members of that gender'.[42] In reaching that conclusion the Court relied heavily on the European Court of Justice's interpretation of the Equal Treatment Directive[43] and in particular its decision in *P v. S & Cornwall County Council*,[44] described by Lord Nicholls as 'the sheet-anchor of Ms A's case'.[45] A narrow application of *A v. West Yorkshire Police* would limit it to equal treatment cases, but the decision is actually much wider. Their Lordships rejected the crucial finding in *Corbett* and endorsed in *Bellinger* that legal gender is determined at birth and cannot thereafter be altered: it was this finding that had allowed the *Corbett* rule to be extended beyond the narrow confines of marriage. A wider *ratio* of *A v. West Yorkshire Police* is that gender can only be determined by an identification of the best way to further the policy of the particular statute in question. In *A v. West Yorkshire Police* that policy was 'to afford protection to the dignity and privacy of those being searched in a situation where they may well be peculiarly vulnerable'.[46] This was achieved by accepting that the applicant belonged to her new gender, *even without the enactment of the Gender Recognition Act*. This means that the definition of 'male' and 'female' might be different depending upon the issue – the same person may be male for one purpose (say, following *Bellinger*, marriage) and female for another (following *A v. West Yorkshire Police*, performing intimate body searches).

This is not a limited or academic point. Even after the coming into force of the Gender Recognition Act 2004, there will be individuals who have not sought, are in the process of seeking, or are not eligible to obtain, a Gender Recognition Certificate, but who are living their lives in the other gender to that in which they were brought up. A person may not have lived in the new gender for two years; an individual may have sound reasons for not wishing to bring a successful marriage to an end; the individual may be too young to access the Act; or the question may arise after

41 Lord Rodger of Earlsferry dissenting.

42 [2004] UKHL 21, per Lord Bingham, at para 11.

43 76/207/EEC.

44 [1996] 1 ECR 2143, [1996] 2 CMLR 247.

45 [2004] UKHL 21, at para 10.

46 Per Lord Rodger, at para 19.

the death of the transsexual person. With every gender-specific legal rule the court faced with a transsexual person who does not (or does not yet or never did) possess a Gender Recognition Certificate will have to ask whether the real purpose of the statute is achieved by recognising or by refusing recognition of the new gender. *Corbett* and *Bellinger* relied heavily on procreative potential to deny recognition; *A v. West Yorkshire Police* relied heavily on the Equal Treatment Directive to allow recognition. But there is no middle way between recognition and non-recognition in any one situation and the question becomes which approach is likely to be adopted in contexts other than equal treatment and marriage. I suggest that the underlying rationale in *Corbett* and *Bellinger* is inherently narrow (procreative potential) while the underlying rationale in *A v. West Yorkshire Police* (furthering the policy of the statute) is inherently wide, with the result that it will now be difficult to deny recognition of the new gender for the purpose of any rule to which procreation can be shown to be entirely irrelevant. The Gender Recognition Act becomes, therefore, of much more limited scope than at first sight appears. We may test this by applying *Bellinger* and *A v. West Yorkshire Police* to a number of different gender-specific statutory provisions: whenever the former applies the Act must be used to effect a gender change, but when the latter applies the Act may be avoided.

One such statutory provision is the rule in the Children (Scotland) Act 1995 that a Children's Hearing (the tribunal in Scotland charged with making decisions in respect of child offenders and neglected children) shall be composed of a panel of three members, at least one of whom is a man and at least one of whom is a woman.[47] Procreative potential is self-evidently not relevant to the ability of a panel member to make appropriate decisions as to the welfare of a child. If a person who has changed sex is to all intents and purposes indistinguishable in his or her acquired gender from a person born into that gender, then the new gender ought to be accepted even without, or before the granting of, a Gender Recognition Certificate. In that way, the social policy behind the legislative rule (ensuring that each child who appears before a hearing can relate in gender terms to at least one of the decision makers) is thereby achieved.

Another gender-specific rule is contained in the Human Fertilisation and Embryology Act 1990, whereby the male partner of a woman who gives birth after infertility treatment shall be deemed to be the father of the child.[48] In *X, Y and Z v. United Kingdom*[49] the European Court held that the refusal to accept that a female to male transsexual could be regarded as a 'man' for this purpose was not contrary to the Article 8 right to family life. The point of the rule in the 1990 Act is to confer paternity on a man who *is not and cannot be* the natural father. The rule, in other words, is *engaged* by lack of procreative potential, so that very lack cannot be used to deny the rule's application in particular circumstances: *Bellinger* is therefore of no relevance. The aim of the 1990 Act appears to be to ensure that children born

47 Children (Scotland) Act 1995, s 39(5).

48 Human Fertilisation and Embryology Act 1990, s 28(3).

49 (1997) 24 EHRR 143.

following infertility treatment have fathers in both the legal and the social sense. It might well be argued that since the applicant in *X, Y and Z* adopts the social role of father (confirmed by the granting to him of parental responsibility) and since recognition of his legal fatherhood would allow the statutory purpose to be achieved, the effect of applying the wide interpretation of *A v. West Yorkshire Police* suggested above will be to put in doubt the continued authority of *X, Y and Z v. United Kingdom*.

Again, the Civil Partnership Act 2004 creates an institution for same-sex couples – equivalent in most respects to marriage. It is, however, limited in availability to couples who are of the same sex and is therefore, at least relationally, every bit as gender-specific as marriage. The question is this: Can a male to female transsexual enter into a civil partnership with a female in the absence of a Gender Recognition Certificate? In other words, is gender, for the purposes of civil partnership, determined by the marriage rule in *Bellinger* or by the social rule in *A v. West Yorkshire Police*? The initial temptation would be to say that since civil partnership is designed to replicate marriage the same rule should apply. However, it is a mistake to see civil partnership as replicating marriage. The legislature was very careful to maintain a number of differences, most of them relating to conjugal sexual activity and parenthood.[50] These were the very issues that determined the approach in *Bellinger* but they are quite deliberately not relevant for civil partnership. And if procreative potential is at the heart of *Bellinger*, its irrelevance to civil partnership could not be more clear.[51] So we must try to identify a purpose behind the gender-specificity in the rules for civil partnership other than any relating to sexual activity. If the purpose of the same-sex requirement in the Civil Partnership Act is to clearly differentiate that institution from marriage, and to reinforce the opposite-sex nature of the institution of marriage, then this is, in fact, achieved more readily by recognising than by denying the validity of a civil partnership entered into by two persons who lead their lives and present to the world as a couple of the same gender, notwithstanding that one of them used to be of the opposite gender. The fear in *Bellinger*, as we have seen, was fundamentally the fear of same-sex marriage. This fear would be realised, at least outwardly, by insisting that a transsexual person retains their original gender, thereby requiring that person to enter into a marriage with a person who is the same gender as that in which the transsexual person now presents to the world, rather than a civil partnership. An argument against this might be that the Gender Recognition Act provides a ready means by which a transsexual can seek recognition of his or her new gender and that to rely upon the wide interpretation of *A v. West Yorkshire Police* is to avoid this statutory mechanism. But there is nothing in the Gender Recognition Act, or in *A v. West Yorkshire Police*, that *requires* the use of the statutory procedure.

50 In relation to the Scottish differences between marriage and civil partnership, see Norrie, K. McK., 'What the Civil Partnership Act 2004 Does Not Do', 2005 *SLT (News)*, 35-40.

51 Same-sex couples can and do nurture children together, but they do not and cannot procreate together.

The Act nowhere provides, as it could easily have done, that recognition of a new gender can be achieved *only* by the statutory process. And that process might not be available: for example a civil partnership may be entered into from the age of 16, but a Gender Recognition Certificate cannot be applied for until the person is 18.[52]

A rather more difficult question concerns those areas explicitly excluded from the operation of the Gender Recognition Act. On the granting of a Gender Recognition Certificate, the acquired gender is recognised for all purposes other than the stated exceptions, but the Act does not explicitly state that the new sex is not recognised – merely that the Gender Recognition Certificate does not have effect in the stated circumstances. So the question arises whether *A v. West Yorkshire Police* could be used to provide recognition in such circumstances. One exception is parental status[53] but that, being a matter of procreation, is likely to be governed if not by the Act then by *Bellinger*. Another exception to the effect of the Gender Recognition Certificate is succession to titles of honour.[54] Again, because of the centuries-old assumptions upon which legitimacy for this purpose is based (primogeniture and blood-link) any argument based on *A v. West Yorkshire Police* is likely to fail. Entitlement to take part in gender-limited sporting events may be prohibited or restricted notwithstanding the possession of a Gender Recognition Certificate, but only if this is 'necessary to secure (a) fair competition or (b) the safety of competitors'.[55] If such restriction is not so necessary, then the Gender Recognition Certificate must be given effect to; and if a Certificate is not possessed then applying the wide rationale in *A v. West Yorkshire Police* suggests that recognition of the new gender must be allowed in those sports in which no competitive advantage is obtained by having the physical attributes of the other gender (bowls, croquet and the like).

Perhaps most difficult of all are the gender-specific offences. A Gender Recognition Certificate does not have effect in this context.[56] So a male to female transsexual who holds a Gender Recognition Certificate can be convicted of being a male living off the earnings of a prostitute; a female to male transsexual can be raped but a male to female transsexual cannot be.[57] An argument based on the social utility of these (socially useless[58]) rules may well be precluded by the very fact that Parliament has chosen to retain them and to provide that they are unaffected by the statutory Gender Recognition Certificate. If so, the courts may well feel obliged to hold that they are

52 Gender Recognition Act 2004, s 1(1).

53 2004 Act, s 12.

54 2004 Act, s 16.

55 2004 Act, s 19. See *Richards v. United States Tennis Association*, 400 NYS 2d 267 (1977).

56 2004 Act, s 20.

57 Unless statute makes that offence non-gender-specific, as it has done in England but not in Scotland.

58 Interestingly, Baroness Hale in *A v. West Yorkshire Police*, at para 52 suggested that it was to avoid this very nonsense that the Court of Appeal in *R v. Tan*, [1983] QB 1953 'found it convenient' to follow *Corbett* to ensure that the male to female transsexual in that case could be convicted of the gender-specific offence of living off the earnings of a prostitute.

unaffected by a non-statutory change of gender via *A v. West Yorkshire Police*. It is submitted, however, that this is to read more effect into the 2004 Act than its terms provide, for as we have seen the Act does not explicitly exclude gender recognition by means other than the statutory process. The ideal solution to this problem is, of course, to render the criminal law entirely gender neutral, but until that is done transsexuals may be unable to obtain the benefits (or to avoid the disadvantages) of the gender in which they actually live their lives.

Conclusion

The Gender Recognition Act 2004 was fought for over the course of three decades. Its passing was rightly seen as a great victory for the transgender community, and for the human rights of equality and dignity. Especially after *Bellinger* it was seen as a dramatic metamorphosis in the UK's attitudes to gender and gender roles. But if the full implications of *A v. West Yorkshire Police* are as described above and its wide rationale were adopted in areas beyond equal treatment then the effect of the 2004 Act is limited to marriage and, perhaps, re-registration of birth certificates. Having shown willful wrong-headedness in *Bellinger*,[59] the House of Lords redeemed itself very shortly thereafter in *A v. West Yorkshire Police*. The earlier case made the Act inevitable, while the latter case rendered it for many purposes unnecessary.

59 A more detailed analysis of that case may be found in Norrie. K. McK., '*Bellinger v. Bellinger*, the House of Lords and the Gender Recognition Bill', (2004) 8 *Edin LR*, 93-99.

Chapter 36

The Positive Side of Healthcare Rights

Christopher Newdick[1]

Introduction

In the early years of the National Health Service many needy patients may have regarded access to care more as a privilege than a right. The notion of 'professional perfectionism'[2] dominated the NHS, in which government claimed little direct influence over the medical profession. This period of medico-political consensus produced a largely paternalistic profession treating largely passive patients unlikely to claim specific access to health resources. Not only patients and NHS managers, but the courts too were wholly deferential and uncritical of the manner in which the Service was organised and run. Indeed, even up to 1990, only three cases had claimed rights to NHS welfare – each of which failed on the ground that the area was inappropriate for judicial involvement.[3]

Let us reflect on where we are now. First, the deference that characterised the NHS in its early years has evaporated. This change is not unique to the NHS, but its impact on healthcare is significant. Until the 1970s we were inclined to regard as exceptional the results of public enquiries critical of the NHS. Today, however, in the wake of the inquiry into deaths of children at Bristol Royal Infirmary,[4] the murders committed by Harold Shipman,[5] the carelessness of Rodney Ledward,[6] and the

---

1 With the usual caveat, I thank my colleagues Professor Chris Hilson and Martha-Marie Kleinhans for their assistance with this chapter.

2 See Klein, R., *The New Politics of the NHS* (4th ed), Harlow, Prentice Hall, 2001, at p. 28.

3 See *R v. Secretary of State, ex p Hincks*, (1980) 1 BMLR 93; *R v. Secretary of State, ex p Walker*, (1987) 3 BMLR 32 and *R v. Central Birmingham HA, ex p Collier* (1988, unreported). Of course, claims to compensation in the law of negligence were becoming common.

4 *Learning from Bristol: The Report of the Public Inquiry into Children's Heart Surgery at the Bristol Royal Infirmary, 1984-95* (Cm. 5207, 2001).

5 *Harold Shipman's Clinical Practice 1974-1998*, available at: www.doh.gov.uk/hshipmanpractice/shipman.pdf.

6 *The Inquiry into Quality and Practice within the NHS Arising from the Actions of Rodney Ledward* (Department of Health, 2001).

retention of organs at Alder Hey Hospital,[7] government and the public have become critical of the NHS and demanded systemic change to its organisation. The authority of the General Medical Council has been reduced and a raft of new supervisory and regulatory bodies have been created to reassure us that the medical profession is behaving properly.[8] Such an environment encourages a different attitude which is more likely to generate claims against doctors and the NHS as a whole.

Second, the introduction of market forces to the NHS in 1991 has been pursued with enthusiasm by the Labour government.[9] Markets, it is said, tend to drive quality up and costs down, but they also change patients' perceptions of their place in the NHS. When patients are treated as 'consumers', with the right to choose when and where they will be treated,[10] hospitals will naturally compete with one another, sensitive to their position in the performance league tables. (Indeed, whereas the original 'internal' market was limited to NHS hospitals, today's NHS encourages private healthcare to compete with the NHS.[11]) Government has responded to public pressure for improvements in the NHS by introducing principles broadly similar to those in the high street and, in doing so, encouraged amongst patients a consumerist sense of rights.

Third, government now plays a very visible role in healthcare. Of course, it avoids any discussion of the hard choices required by NHS managers when finite resources fail to accommodate patient demand. On the other hand, as the healthcare debate becomes both more voluble and sensitive, party politics makes large and sometimes unachievable promises for the NHS. Professor Sir Ian Kennedy has criticised the way in which 'Politics' has misrepresented the capacity of the NHS to respond to patient demand. In his *Bristol Report* he condemned successive governments for making unsustainable claims for the NHS which were not capable of being met on the resources made available, and then of blaming doctors, nurses and NHS managers when patients' expectations were disappointed.[12] Over many years, the net impact has been to drive up expectations and, by the failure to fund the NHS in a way that accommodates demand, encourage the making of claims to healthcare rights.

---

7 *AB v. Leeds Teaching Hospital NHS Trust*, [2004] EWHC 644.

8 See generally, Newdick, C., *Who Should We Treat? – Rights, Rationing and Resources in the NHS*, Oxford University Press, 2005, ch. 8.

9 Although the emphasis is less marked in Scotland. Comparing waiting times in England and Scotland, the Prime Minister, Tony Blair, has said that better performance in England is due to market forces, see *The Scotsman*, 20 April 2005.

10 *Choose and Book – Patient's Choice of Hospital and Booked Appointment* (Department of Health, 2004), *Patient Choice – Guidance for PCTs, NHS Trusts and SHAs on offering choice of where they are treated* (Department of Health, 2003), *Choose and Book – Patient's Choice of Hospital and Booked Appointment* (Department of Health, 2004).

11 See Kmietowicz, Z., 'Private Sector Operations to Rise from 4% to 11% of Total', (2005) 330 *British Medical Journal*, 1165.

12 *Learning from Bristol: The Report of the Public Inquiry into Children's Heart Surgery at the Bristol Royal Infirmary, 1984-95* (Cm. 5207, 2001) 57, para 31.

In these ways the notion of 'rights' and expectations to healthcare have expanded rapidly over the past 15 years or so, a process which has been consolidated by the Human Rights Act 1998. Rights celebrate the status of the individual. They are at their least complicated when they insulate the person from unwarranted intrusion by public authority; when they protect negative freedom to be let alone. But healthcare rights also raise a different question of *positive* rights: rights to benefit from another.[13] How does rights theory permit public authorities to balance *competing* claims to finite resources and promote *community* interests? Within a regime of scarce resources this prompts questions such as: what are the fundamental objectives of the NHS? [14] Should they be *utilitarian* and designed to maximise health gain for the greatest number, or *egalitarian* – to reduce health inequality in the community? Alternatively, should *clinical* solutions focus on those most in *need*, or on those most likely to *benefit* from treatment?[15] How should health authorities balance the claims of paediatric, orthopaedic and geriatric patients; or access to cancer, cardiac, or fertility care; whether care should be provided in hospital, or in the community; or whether more should be spent on preventive, acute or chronic care? Inherent in each question is the tension between clinical, economic, ethical and political judgments, and the sometimes conflicting interests of individuals and the community as a whole.

Attempts have been made to devise comprehensive theories on which to respond to these matters.[16] In truth, however, the enterprise is in search of a holy grail. Priority setting involves judgment which defies objective, or algorithmic analysis.[17]

> The debate about priorities will never finally be resolved. Nor should we expect a final resolution. As medical technology, the economic and demographic environment, and social attitudes change, so almost certainly will our priorities.[18]

The real challenge is to understand the decision-making *process*, how decisions are made, within what framework of values and by whom – patients, 'citizens', doctors, politicians, or judges?[19] The following, therefore, explores the nature of the rights

---

13 The distinction is not without its difficulties in political theory. See Berlin I., *Four Essays on Liberty*, Oxford University Press, 1975 and Plant, R., *Modern Political Thought*, Oxford, Blackwells, 1991, ch. 7.

14 See Daniels, N., 'Four Unsolved Rationing Problems: A Challenge', (1994) 24 *Hastings Center Report*, (no. 4) 27-29.

15 Most notably see the cost-benefit theory of the Quality Adjusted Life Year (QALY), discussed by Newdick, C., *op cit.*, ch. 2.

16 See New, B., 'Defining a Package of Healthcare Services the NHS is Responsible for – The Case for', (1997) 314 *British Medical Journal*, 503-505.

17 See generally Klein, R. and Redmayne, S., *Managing Scarcity – Priority Setting and Rationing in the National Health Service*, Buckingham, Open University Press, 1996.

18 Klein, R., 'Dimensions in Rationing: Who Should Do What?', in *Rationing in Action*, London, BMA, 1994, at p. 103.

19 See generally Daniels, N. and Sabin, J., *Setting Limits Fairly – Can We Learn to Share Medical Resources?*, Oxford University Press, 2002.

claimed and the differing ways in which those claims confer tangible benefits on patients. In doing so, it emphasises the 'positive' side of the rights equation in the NHS. Clarity in this area enables patients, doctors and most of all government to measure the promises made in this sensitive area against a yardstick which balances the rights and responsibilities of individuals and NHS institutions. Bearing in mind Professor Sir Ian Kennedy's criticism, it increases transparency in the debate and reduces the likelihood of misinterpretation and misunderstanding. With this in mind, this chapter will discuss a matrix on which rights may be claimed by distinguishing: (1) NHS 'targets' and healthcare rights, (2) private and public rights, (3) negative and positive rights and (4) procedural and substantive rights.

NHS 'Targets' and Healthcare Rights

The 'rights' in question in this discussion concern those recognised in law and enforceable in the courts. We should note, however, that many of the promises made by government are not intended to create enforceable rights and duties.[20] Government always seeks to enlarge access to treatment and one response is to make generic promises for the NHS by means of waiting time 'targets' imposed on NHS managers. For example the *Patient's Charter*, introduced by the Conservatives under John Major in 1996, promised to reduce waiting times. They have been used ever since as a device to reassure patients, encourage NHS managers and enable government to claim success. Recent amongst these promises is the policy in England of *Choose and Book*[21] in which the government has undertaken that patients requiring admission to hospital will be seen within specified waiting times and be offered a choice of four hospitals. However, such a target is unlikely to confer enforceable rights on patients.

On the other hand, targets do have an indirect impact on access to NHS care. Despite their aspirational, non-legal, nature, they play an important role in the performance-management of NHS managers. They may not confer direct rights upon patients, but NHS managers are put under severe pressure to achieve them; indeed, they are often referred to in the NHS as 'P.45 issues' because senior managers risk losing their jobs if they fail to meet them. Although they insulate NHS bodies from litigation, they also give the centre powerful levers to encourage greater activity. Their disadvantage is that they tempt Secretaries of State to make promises for the NHS which may not be achievable on the resources available; indeed, the threat

---

20 See e.g., *Danns v. Department of Health*, (1995) 25 BMLR 121, at p. 130. Exceptionally, sufficiently specific promises may give rise to legitimate expectations, see Steele, I. 'Substantive Expectations: Striking the Right Balance', (2005) 121 *L.Q.R*,. 300 for an illuminating discussion.

21 *Choose and Book – Patient's Choice of Hospital and Booked Appointment*, Department of Health, 2004.

of sanctions for failure has tempted NHS managers to distort the figures simply to achieve centrally imposed targets.[22]

Leaving aside these aspirational, or 'target' duties, we now turn to the matrix of enforceable rights on which claims may be based.

Private and Public Rights

The nature of the rights and obligations that arise between parties can be described on a spectrum distinguishing *private* and *public* rights.[23] At one end of the spectrum, private parties are entirely free to formulate their own private legal relationships with one another without hindrance from government. The clearest example of unrestricted private rights of this nature exists in the making of many (but not all) wills and contracts. I am at liberty to leave my estate to whomsoever I please without regard to the needs of those who might benefit from my benefaction. So too in contract, subject to the laws on illegality and unfair contract terms, parties are free to agree to their own terms whether or not they are sensible.[24] In principle the contract is enforceable irrespective of its impact on the other party, or indeed, on the public interest. I may enforce my private rights under a pension policy, notwithstanding that my claim will have adverse consequences for many other beneficiaries of the same fund.[25]

Within the contemporary 'mixed economy' of NHS care, many private companies provide services to NHS patients under contracts with NHS bodies. Private contractors are directly engaged in the promotion of *public* objectives. Nevertheless, private providers of public services are entitled to enforce their private rights notwithstanding their impact on the public interest. The position is explained in *R v. Northumbrian Water Ltd, ex p Newcastle and North Tyneside HA*.[26] The respondent private company undertook to provide water for public consumption. However, it refused to fluoridate the supply, notwithstanding that all parties agreed that it would be in the interest of children's dental health to do so. It said that such a course could lead to complaints from those who objected in principle to the policy, or from litigants claiming they

---

22 *Inappropriate Adjustments to NHS Waiting Lists*, House of Commons Public Accounts Committee, 46th Report, Session 2001-02. See also *Waiting List Accuracy: Assessing the Accuracy of Waiting List Information in NHS Hospitals*, Audit Commission, 2003.

23 But not as black and white concepts, see Shue, H., *Basic Rights: Subsistence, Affluence and US Foreign Policy*, Princeton UP, 1980 discussed in Mowbray, A., *The Development of Positive Rights Under the ECHR*, Oxford, Hart Press, 2003, at pp. 222-25.

24 See *White and Carter v. McGregor*, [1962] AC 413, at p. 430 per Lord Reid. For exceptional influences of public law principles on private parties see Beatson, J., 'Public Law Influences in Contract Law', in Beatson, J. and Friedmann, D. (eds), *Good Faith and Fault in Contract Law*, Oxford University Press, 1995, discussing especially fiduciary contracts and the powers of private regulatory bodies.

25 See *Equitable Life Assurance Society v. Hyman*, [2000] 3 All ER 961.

26 [1999] Env. LR 715.

had been damaged by it. Rejecting the application for judicial review of the refusal, the Divisional Court held that the company was entitled to take an entirely *private* view of its responsibilities and to put the interests of its shareholders first. Thus, within the confines of its contract, a private company is entitled to promote its own interests notwithstanding its impact on the public interest.

Compare the position of *public* bodies responsible for providing, or arranging healthcare. Bodies created by statute have no existence independent of the statutes by which they have been created. They have no common law rights of their own because their powers are granted solely by statute.[27] Their statutory duties may give rise to rights in respect of others; which I will call 'public' rights. Health Boards and Primary Care Trusts, for example, have two salient statutory duties; first to 'promote a comprehensive health service'[28] and second, a duty not to exceed the finite financial allocations made to them.[29] There is no power to modify these obligations, or to charge patients for the services provided, or to exclude some patients with expensive demands. Significantly, these rights are not normally owed to individuals but to the community as a whole. Obviously, given the finite resources made available to them, additional investment in one part of the service may mean disinvestment from another. Hard choices between deserving patients are inevitable. For this reason, by contrast to the 'absolute' private rights discussed above, public rights are often relative, in the sense that competing claims have to be weighed and balanced and a judgment exercised as to relative merits.[30]

This makes another point, although it is not expressed in the NHS legislation. Whereas private rights may seek to promote the liberty of the individual, 'public' rights often promote another concern valued by modern democracies, that of *equality between* individuals because they promote the good of the community as a whole. How should this delicate and unenviable function be performed? The following considers how the balance between these hard choices should be struck.

Negative and Positive Rights

Let us further refine the distinction between private and public rights by creating a matrix which also distinguishes *negative* and *positive* rights.

Negative rights seek to protect the individual from interference. They may arise by private agreement (say in a landlord's covenant of quiet enjoyment in a lease), or by standards imposed on individuals by common law, for example, rights in the law of

27 See Law, J in *R v. Somerset CC, ex p Fewings*, [1995] 1 All ER 513, 524. Of course, these powers may include the entering of private contracts (e.g. of employment or procurement).

28 See National Health Service (Scotland) Act 1978, s 1 and the National Health Service Act 1977, s 1.

29 National Health Service (Scotland) Act 1978, s 85A and National Health Service Act 1977, s 97(1).

30 *R v. N and E Devon HA, ex p Coughlan*, [1999] Lloyds Rep Med 306, paras 23-25.

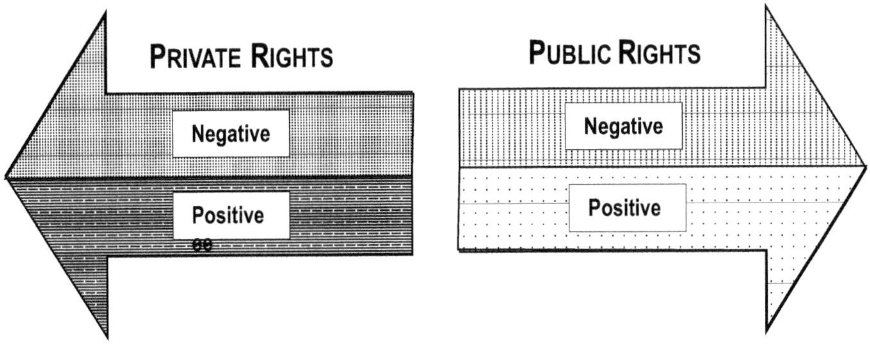

Figure 36.1 Private and Public, Negative and Positive Rights

negligence, the law of confidentiality and informed consent. Between private parties, they may be thought of as *negative/private* rights. Equally, negative rights may arise by virtue of the statutory duties imposed upon *public* authorities. Many of the public rights enshrined in the European Convention are negative in the sense that they protect the right to be let alone (and are sometimes called *civil* rights), for example freedom of speech, freedom of assembly and association, the right to private and family life and freedom from discrimination. Their advantage from a public welfare perspective is that they are relatively inexpensive to maintain. Of course, rights to a fair trial and security of the person necessarily require an apparatus to guarantee them, such as a system of independent judiciary and an impartial executive, but their costs are within the reach of industrialised nations. Rights of this nature, which are the responsibility of the State to protect, arise in the *negative/public* corner of the matrix.

By contrast, *positive* rights confer some tangible or economic benefit. The purpose of many *private*, commercial agreements is precisely to confer positive rights on the parties, including contractual rights to compensation for breach (for example within contracts for health insurance). Rights of this nature may be referred to as *positive/private* rights. In the NHS, however, the notion of *positive/public* rights of access to NHS care is important (also referred to as *social*, or *economic* rights). NHS resource allocation concerns positive rights of access to care and it is in this area of the matrix that most difficulty arises.[31] The positive/public rights of one individual, or group, cannot be considered in isolation from the rights of others. The European Court of Human Rights is concerned that, since the member states do not all share the same gross domestic product, care must be taken to ensure that rights recognised in one country are enforceable throughout. As it has said in the context of the duty to safeguard the right to life under Article 2:

31 But see *R v. N and E Devon HA, ex p Coughlan*, [1999] Lloyds Rep Med 306 on the duty owed to patients receiving long-term care in nursing homes.

> Bearing in mind ... the operational choices which must be made in terms of priorities and resources, the scope of the positive obligation must be interpreted in a way which does not impose an impossible or disproportionate burden on the authorities.[32]

Also, in the *positive/public* quadrant of the rights matrix, courts are poorly equipped to make distributive judgments. They have no expertise and, in an area of such political sensitivity, no democratic authority to do so. But to say the courts should hesitate in this corner of the matrix is not to say that positive/public rights confer no enforceable rights at all. This requires a further distinction between *procedural* and *substantive* rights.[33]

Procedural and Substantive Rights

By what mechanisms can positive rights be enforced? Positive claims to resources may be made within a framework of procedural or substantive rights. Procedural rights guarantee access to procedures alone; their purpose is not to provide access to resources. By contrast, substantive rights create enforceable rights of access to specific resources. Each may equally arise within *private* rights (compare for example, the *procedural* right to a fair hearing prior to dismissal from a contract of employment, to the *substantive* right to compensation arising from breach of contract). Here, however, we are concerned with the *public* end of the spectrum and with the responses of the courts to claims to positive/public rights.

Let us discuss procedural rights first, followed by substantive rights.

Procedural Rights

Procedural rights enable the courts to avoid becoming embroiled in substantive matters of this nature, over which they are ill equipped to adjudicate, whilst at the same time demanding minimum standards of propriety in the decision making process. They guarantee an appropriate procedure only. Crucial to the nature of the right, therefore, is the intensity of the scrutiny with which the court will review the decision. If the review is too weak, it will undermine the claim and defeat the existence of the right. If it is too intense, it may erode the authority and effectiveness of the statutory decision maker and frustrate the will of Parliament. What trends have emerged in the common law with respect to procedural rights? We distinguish the relatively weak scrutiny that existed up to 1997,[34] followed by the more intense review that developed thereafter.

---

32 *Keenan v. United Kingdom*, (2001) 33 EHRR 913, para 90.

33 The distinction applies equally within *private* rights, but is most significant in connection with access to healthcare.

34 The changed attitude is demonstrated by *R v. N. Derbyshire HA, ex p Fisher*, [1997] 8 Med LR 327.

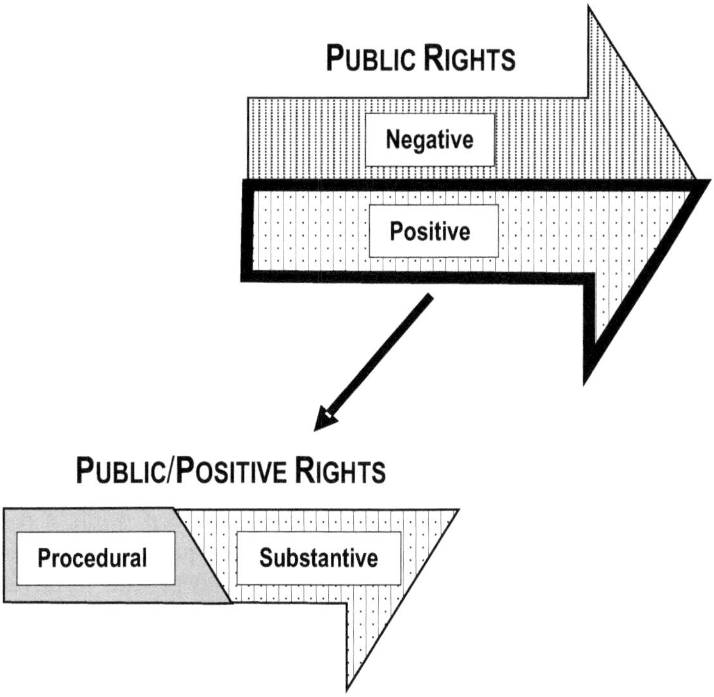

Figure 36.2 Public Negative and Positive Rights

Weak Procedural Scrutiny until 1997 Weak scrutiny permits decision makers such a breadth of discretion that it provides insufficient incentive to ensure that the basis of their decisions are rational, fair and consistent. For example in *R v. Birmingham HA, ex p Collier*,[35] a four-year-old boy required urgent cardiac surgery. His consultant placed him at the top of his list of priority cases and yet the operation was cancelled time and again. The condition was acute and life-threatening (in the absence of treatment). An application for judicial review of the reasons for the refusal to treat the boy was refused because 'this court is in no position to judge the allocation of resources by this authority'.[36] The court refused even to enquire why such a case could not be referred to another hospital. The degree of scrutiny of the decision was so feeble that managers might have felt free to make whatever decision they pleased with little regard to the interest of the patient concerned. Such latitude, without further explanation or accountability, is unlikely to generate trust and confidence in the NHS.

35 Unreported, Court of Appeal, 1988.
36 *Id.*

Intense Scrutiny Thereafter By the late 1990s the courts had developed more robust scrutiny of resource allocation decisions. In *R v. NW Lancashire HA, ex p A. D. & G*,[37] for example, three applicants for transsexual surgery were refused funding for their care. They sought judicial review of the decision on the ground that the merits of their case had not been properly considered. The Court of Appeal upheld their case and quashed the decision. It confirmed that substantive matters of resource allocation were for those appointed to the task and not for the courts. On the other hand, it was sensitive to the danger that health authority decisions of this nature could become chaotic unless a consistent procedural framework of values was available for guidance. The defect in the decision was not its conclusion, but the manner in which the decision had been reached. It was legitimate to place transsexual applicants lower in the order of priorities than others requiring (say) life-saving treatment, but the process would be subject to close review to ensure fairness and consistency between patients. In addition, provision should have been made to enable those with exceptional needs to have the merits of their claims subject to special consideration.[38]

The advantage of this 'strong', procedural right is that, while it provides no guarantee of treatment, it forces public authorities to provide cogent reasons for the unenviable decisions required of them and enables patients to understand the difficult decisions that arise.[39] In sum, greater transparency is more likely to generate confidence in the system.

Substantive Rights

By contrast, substantive rights generate specific access to resources. We have noted the courts' reluctance to involve themselves in this area; nevertheless, human rights legislation will tend to encourage substantive rights to healthcare. For example, in *D v. United Kingdom*,[40] the European Court of Human Rights required medical care to be provided indefinitely to an overseas visitor from St Kitts who had been convicted and imprisoned for attempting to smuggle cocaine into the UK. The applicant had been diagnosed with HIV/AIDS after his arrival in the UK and, as a prisoner in one of HM Prisons, was entitled to receive care as an NHS patient. However, at the end of the prison sentence the right ends and the Secretary of State sought to deport him from the UK. The Court agreed that his deportation would be in breach of Article 3. He required treatment which could not be provided in St Kitts. Were he to be returned there, he would inevitably die in inhuman and degrading circumstances.

---

37 (2000) 53 BMLR 148.

38 For such a case, see *R (ota F) v. Oxfordshire Mental Healthcare NHS Trust*, (2002) EWHC 535 in which it was said the procedure should not be 'judicialised'.

39 Although there is also a risk of anodyne reasoning which obscures the real motivations for decision-making, see de Smith, A., Lord Woolf and Jowell. J., *Judicial Review of Administrative Action*, London, Sweet and Maxwell, 1995, para 9-045.

40 (1998) 42 EHRR 149.

Exceptionally, given that he was in the terminal stages of the disease and his treatment had commenced in the UK he was entitled to remain and continue to be cared for in the UK.

Similarly, the Supreme Court of Canada has decided that deaf patients have rights to sign interpreters in every hospital in order to guarantee effective communication with hospital staff.[41] Such a right is necessary to ensure that deaf patients enjoy equal rights of access to hospital care. On the other hand, reversing the Court of Appeal of British Columbia, it has denied a right of access to Lovaas treatment to autistic children.[42] The treatment is one of very few to show signs of improving the condition. Nevertheless, it remains of uncertain clinical value. The temptation for courts to involve themselves with positive/public rights is problematic. Obviously, courts focus on the merits of individuals. However, they should understand that, within finite financial allocations, the specific allocation of resources to some will tend to reduce the funds available to others. Yet the court is blind to their competing demands. This point was made in the Court of Appeal by Balcombe LJ, who said:

> I would stress the absolute undesirability of the court making an order which may have the effect of compelling a doctor or health authority to make available scarce resources (both human and material) to a particular child, without knowing whether or not there are other patients to whom those resources might more advantageously be devoted.[43]

This persuasively suggests that intervention of the sort undertaken in *D v. United Kingdom* should be resisted unless the court has evidence of the 'opportunity costs' of the impact of its decision upon others and is satisfied, not just that its own sense of priority is superior to that of those appointed to decide such matters, but that the latter is insupportable.[44] Successful cases of judicial review should refer the decision back to the decision maker for reconsideration, but should normally stop short of diverting resources to particular patients.

Although the courts will not normally allocate scarce healthcare resources, they may be inclined to persuade those responsible for doing so. In *Simms*,[45] for example, the applicants suffered potentially fatal neuro-degenerative disorders caused by Cruetzfeld-Jacob disease. Their doctors proposed a new, costly and untested treatment but the hospital ethics committee was concerned as to the merits of treating patients

---

41 *Eldridge v. British Columbia (Attorney General)*, (1997) 151 DLR (4th) 577. This might be considered to be a *procedural* (rather than substantive) claim since it sought only equal *access* to hospital care (rather than specific health resources).

42 *Auton v. British Columbia*, [2004] 3 SCR 657.

43 *Re J*, [1992] 4 All ER 614, 625. Precisely this point has been made in the housing context in *R v. Bristol Corporation, ex p. Hendy*, [1974] 1 All ER 1047, 1051 per Scarman LJ.

44 *D* was not followed in *N v. Secretary of State for the Home Department*, [2005] UKHL 31 in which a patient suffering from AIDS was amenable to deportation because, unlike D, she was receiving treatment and not in the terminal stages of the disease. Lord Hope described the distinction as 'disingenuous' (at para 53).

45 [2003] 1 All ER 669.

in this way. In the desperate circumstances of the case, the court considered that it would be lawful to use the treatment, notwithstanding its uncertain effects. Note, however, the pressure exerted by the court on the hospital to provide the treatment. Reflecting on the misgivings of the ethics committee, the court said that 'it would be an unbelievably cruel blow to have the High Court say Yes to the treatment and the two committees of the hospital to say No'.[46] Accordingly, the court recommended that, if the ethics committees rejected the application, the Department of Health should take responsibility for the case. Unsurprisingly, this was sufficient to secure treatment for the patients.

But an expression of judicial preference is very different from mandating that particular care be provided. Courts should never direct how scarce resources should be spent on untested treatments, particularly when they have no evidence of their costs or impact on the care available to others. Were they to be inclined to do so on the 'rescue principle' that every last effort should be made to save a patient's life, many patients who were amenable to effective care might find priority being diverted to others to support treatment of uncertain value.[47] Such a response to individual need would not generate maximum community benefit.

Conclusion

Given their 'polycentric' nature, courts cannot balance substantive demands in cases of this nature. But could health authorities develop criteria capable of doing so? The PCTs in Berkshire have developed a particular response to the more demanding procedural environment by creating a Priorities Committee working within an Ethical Framework.[48] The Committee has no statutory identity and so provides only guidance to PCTs. The framework is expressed in terms of generic, non-specific principles against which particular treatments are tested in the light of their clinical evidence. Inevitably, the decision-making process leaves room for differences of opinion and the exercise of discretion. Could additional clarity be attempted?

Such an enterprise is being undertaken in New Zealand which has attempted to devise a 'scoring system' for allocating resources. Unsurprisingly, perhaps, the solution is more *technocratic* than Berkshire's Ethical Framework, but its intention is to promote equal access to care on the basis of clinical need. Clinical Priority Assessment Criteria (CPAC) seek to prioritise patients for elective secondary or tertiary treatment according to numerical scores awarded by clinicians, based on need and ability to benefit. The advantage of the system is the way in which it openly

---

46 *Ibid.*, paras. 70 and 72.

47 The problem is especially acute in relation to 'orphan drugs' which have received accelerated licensing approval on the basis that they show promise in relation to conditions which affect less that 5 in 10,000 patients. Clearly, given the commercial demand for orphan drugs, their manufacturing costs are likely to be extremely high yet their clinical effectiveness may remain largely unproven.

48 www.berkshire.nhs.uk/priorities/policies/pdf/ab_ethical_framework.pdf.

connects patient need with government funding. Thus, the score required by patients to achieve access to care may be higher or lower depending on a financial threshold (FT) which is determined according to the level of funding made available. Patients with total CPAC scores equal to, or higher than, the FT are booked to receive surgery within six months of their CPAC assessment. Patients with scores just beneath the FT but deemed clinically in need of surgery, or likely to deteriorate to such an extent they are likely to meet the FT in the next year or two, are placed on an Active Care and Review list for regular review. The remainder are referred back to primary, general practitioner, care without obtaining access to hospital. Those not admitted because of having insufficient points can make a direct connection between access and public authority commitment to care.

The system is at its most persuasive in particular medical specialties (for example opthalmology)[49] where doctors can assess patient need against a reasonably objective, pre-determined numerical score. In reality, of course, the process of scoring is often less than wholly objective because doctors may award different scores to identical patients. Also the system is less cogent when comparisons are made between different types of clinical condition.[50] How can one compare on a common scale the relative needs of (say) opthalmic, orthopaedic or geriatric patients? I doubt whether such a uniform slide-rule could ever be discovered. Never the less, CPAC offers a glimpse of future decision making.[51] Similar approaches are being considered in the UK[52] and it seems likely that some such a system will be implemented here. In time argument will arise as to the legal status of these scoring systems. With the increased precision of such systems, do they create *procedural* rights only, or should patients who achieve scores above the FT enjoy *substantive* rights to care? No doubt, the answer will depend on the nature of the scoring system, legitimate expectations and the consequences for other patients.[53]

Pressure to recognise substantive rights to care is likely to increase.[54] At the same time, however, we need to bear in mind the rights of those who find it difficult to attract popular support, notably, chronically ill and elderly patients and those with long-term mental illness. In the absence of reliable priority scoring systems against which differing groups of patients can be assessed, there is a danger of resources

---

49 See Hadorn, A. and Holmes, A., 'The New Zealand Priority Criteria Project', (1997) 314 *British Medical Journal*, 131.

50 See Derrett, S., Paul, C., Herbison P. and Williams, H., 'Evaluation of Explicit Prioritisation for Elective Surgery: a Prospective Study', (2002) 7 *J. Health Services Research and Policy*, (Supplement 1) 14, noting limitations of the system.

51 See generally, *CPAC Evaluation Project – Descriptive Study*, Ministry of Health, New Zealand, 2002.

52 See the tentative views in the draft paper *What's the Score in Orthopaedics*, NHS Modernisation Agency, 2003.

53 Litigation in New Zealand is yet to resolve the question in respect of CPAC.

54 Even the European Court of Justice has introduced substantive healthcare rights under the principle of freedom of movement of (public) services. See the Court of Appeal's misgivings in *R (Watts) v. Bedfordshire PCT*, [2004] 77 BMLR 26.

being diverted to articulate, or popular, pressure groups. Until such a common substantive measure becomes available, *strong procedural* rights are likely to be the fairest method of making decisions of this kind. Equally, the many hundreds of local health boards and primary care trusts face the daunting task of devising fair and reasonable local criteria to protect procedural rights; and the response of each could be very different.

In principle, the Department of Health should lead the debate as to how this process should develop by encouraging health authorities to develop consistent priorities policies. In practice, however, government refuses to acknowledge that hard choices are required in the NHS. If party politics obstructs central guidance in this matter, health authorities should collaborate with one another under their own initiative to devise consistent, transparent and robust priorities policies, well informed by public opinion. Such a collaboration is being pursued in Berkshire, Oxfordshire and Buckinghamshire by the creation of the *Thames Valley Ethical Framework* to guide the PCTs in each county. Whatever the impetus, there is an urgent need to clarify patients' procedural rights within the NHS against a realistic appreciation of the hard choices required of it.

Chapter 37

In Defence of Doctors

Vivienne Harpwood

> Where then, does the doctor stand today in relation to society? To some extent, and perhaps increasingly, he is a servant of the public, a public which is, moreover, widely – though perhaps not always well – informed on medical matters. The competent patient's inalienable rights to understand his treatment and to accept or refuse it are now well established and society is conditioned to distrust professional paternalism. The talk today is of 'producers and consumers' and the ambience of the supermarket is one that introduces its own stresses and strains.[1]

Introduction

The above statement, made in the 2002 edition of *Law and Medical Ethics* under the co-authorship of Ken Mason, identifying some of the pressures on doctors today, sets the scene for the discussion in this chapter, which seeks not to justify medical mistakes, nor to excuse malpractice, but to place in context the role of the doctor in modern society and to explain some of the difficulties faced by members of a profession that has been much criticised and is more highly regulated than any other. The chapter concludes with an attempt to suggest some tentative solutions that might offer a balanced approach to the positions of doctors and patients.[2]

It is not difficult instantly to identify a wide range of factors with the potential to increase occupational stress for members of the medical professions.[3] Many of these pressures have been increasing since the major NHS reforms introduced in 1990. A large number of pressures are the result of the attempts of successive governments to reduce the cost of providing healthcare to an increasingly ageing population, for example by requiring authorisation of the use of certain treatments through the National Institute for Clinical Excellence. Other regulatory frameworks have been designed with a view, at least in part, to reducing the cost of clinical negligence

1 Mason, J.K., McCall Smith, R.A. and Laurie, G.T., *Law and Medical Ethics* (6th ed), London, Butterworths, 2002.

2 I am grateful to Edwin Egede for his able assistance with the research for this chapter.

3 At least 18 bodies with powers to investigate GPs are listed by David Roberts on http://www.countrydoctor.co.uk.

litigation.[4] More recent years have witnessed the imposition of heavy burdens of additional regulation, often imposed in the course of *ad hoc* responses to serious medical malpractice scandals such as those that occurred in the course of paediatric cardiac care in Bristol.[5] In a different but related context, the Courts have recently responded to demands by patients and the Government[6] for greater autonomy and choice in their treatment by endorsing the need for patients to be better informed about risks and side effects of medical treatment.[7] Developments in the structure of healthcare and initiatives produced by successive governments are too numerous to cover in depth in this account, but it is not difficult to demonstrate that there can be few professions that so are constantly subjected to change as that of the doctor.

All of these developments have contributed to the tensions under which doctors are now required to work. There have been concerns among clinicians about the pace of change, about major issues such as working hours, unemployment, fear of physical violence, rapid technological developments, the implementation of new legislation, potential litigation or professional discipline and repeated reorganisation of health services – all of which are claimed to have had a significant impact on stress levels in the healthcare professions. Inadequate resources and the constant need to meet government targets have also been cited by NHS employees as major inducers of stress.[8]

The Growing Criticism of Doctors

It is well recognised that the Bristol Royal Infirmary (BRI) Inquiry Report was highly critical of the medical profession as a whole and of a culture in healthcare that was not peculiar to Bristol.[9] Doctors have been much criticised in the media, and the influence of the media on governments and the public is incalculable.[10] The media influence on public understanding of health issues is a major cause for concern. One example of a disproportionate media response to a scientific dilemma was the

4 For example, The Health Act 1999, which created the Commission for Health Improvement, now The Healthcare Commission.

5 *Learning from Bristol: the report of the public inquiry into children's heart surgery at the Bristol Royal Infirmary 1984-95*, available at: http://www.bristol-inquiry.org.uk/final_report.index.htm.

6 See for example, *Creating a Patient-led NHS – delivering the NHS Improvement plan*, 2005 available at: http://www.dh.uk/assetRoot/04/10/65/07/04106507.

7 *Chester v. Afshar*, [2004] 4 All E.R. 587.

8 Wyatt, J., 'Time to Take Action', *Journal of Heath Management*, December 2003/January 2004, Institute of Health Management.

9 Section 2, Chapter 25 deals with issues directly concerning the GMC including those surrounding clinical audit, appraisal, revalidation, various aspects of medical education training, ensuring that doctors maintain professional competence throughout their working lives, and aspects of professional discipline.

10 See Tony Blair's speech to the Institute of Public Policy and Research (IPPR) May 26th 2005.

reporting of a supposed link between autism and the MMR single vaccination, which began media scare-mongering that made the public believe, despite the weight of evidence to the contrary, that a well-established method of vaccination was unsafe.

The healthcare professions in general, their regulators, and doctors in particular, have been subjected to a barrage of criticism in the course of recent inquiries into malpractice scandals. It was through the media that the situation involving paediatric heart surgery in Bristol was first exposed. Media reports of the events that led to the BRI Inquiry contain unremitting criticism of the doctors and other healthcare professionals involved, as do contemporary commentaries on the Inquiry itself. Many of Sir Ian Kennedy's indictments of the doctors concerned have generated criticisms that have tainted the medical profession in general, after the deaths and serious injuries suffered by so many children as a result of medical malpractice. His comments ranged from criticism concerning poor organisation, failure of communication and lack of leadership, to that surrounding the 'club culture' and failure to put patients at the centre of care.

In a related vein, the Report of The Shipman Inquiry,[11] chaired by Dame Janet Smith, was highly critical of the GMC, the body responsible for regulating doctors. Harold Shipman was convicted of 15 murders in 2000, but the Inquiry concluded that he had probably killed at least 200 more patients during his career. Part of the remit of the Inquiry was to consider how this had happened, and to make recommendations as to how patients could be protected from such events occurring again. The Fifth Report issues a scathing indictment of the past practices and procedures of General Medical Council (GMC), the doctors' disciplinary body, and makes recommendations about further changes that are needed in the way that doctors are regulated. Many of Dame Janet's criticisms have been cited in the media. The following comment by a solicitor who represented the families of many of Shipman's victims appeared in the *Guardian* newspaper:[12]

> Blunders, loopholes, shortcomings and cover-ups were exposed by Dame Janet Smith's public inquiry ... Doctors have become accustomed to believing that they deserve privileged treatment.

More recently the controversy surrounding the evidence given by Sir Roy Meadow and other paediatric expert witnesses in child abuse and murder trials has created a storm of critical comment, with the result that many doctors are reluctant to appear as expert witnesses in court proceedings.[13] The GMC concluded that Sir Roy Meadow had 'abused his position as a doctor' and 'seriously undermined'[14] the position of

---

11 Available at: http://www.the-shipman-inquiry.org.uk/5r.

12 Alexander, A., 'Where is the political will to save us from bad doctors?', *The Guardian*, 19 April 2005.

13 The Royal College of Paediatrics and Child Health has claimed that in England one third of districts are without a paediatrician specialising in child protection – *The Times*, 15 March 2004.

14 General Medical Council, Fitness to Practice Determination, 15 July 2005.

doctors giving expert medical evidence in legal proceedings by citing misleading statistics in his evidence given during the trial of Sally Clark in 1999 for murdering her two sons, Christopher and Harry. Doctors' organisations argue that the GMC ruling that Sir Roy Meadow be struck off the medical register will have serious repercussions for the recruitment of paediatricians wishing to specialise in child protection. Despite this very serious situation, during the appeal process and before the GMC hearing, Sir Roy Meadow was unable to comment in his own defence despite the inevitable adverse press coverage he was receiving. He was bound by medical confidentiality and by the rules of the court. He has since argued that his vilification amounted to a trial by the media and that the disciplinary proceedings before the GMC may well have been influenced by adverse statements made about him in the media. As one commentator pointed out, this had the inevitable effect of giving his critics a dominant position in the debate.[15] In fact, his name was almost never mentioned in the media without the epithet 'the discredited' even before the final sanction was imposed on him.[16]

These are but a few examples of many instances of adverse criticism in the media concerning alleged medical malpractice. Doctors themselves have expressed concerns about the critical light in which the news media portrays them, and about the way in which the misdeeds of a few individuals can tarnish the reputation of the profession as a whole. One questionnaire survey[17] sent to doctors who qualified between 1993 and 2000 yielded many comments on this issue. Among them:

> The media demonises the medical profession – seizing upon the occasional failure (of course these must be addressed) to condemn the entire profession.
>
> Media attitudes and seemingly constant negative criticism are having a significant effect on morale of doctors around me.

Institutional Changes in Healthcare

Structural reforms have been a feature of the NHS for almost two decades. There have been around twenty major changes in the way in which healthcare is delivered and regulated over the past twenty or more years.[18] The NHS has been in a virtually perpetual state of reform and reorganisation for so long that there appears to be constant upheaval. Many of the reforms are the result of attempts to marshal finite resources within an ever growing health service that is pledged to be free at the point of delivery. The BRI Inquiry Final Report emphasises that:

---

15 Gooderham, P., 'Complaints About Medical Expert Witnesses in the United Kingdom', 2004 *Med. Law. International*, vol 6 No 4, 297-325.

16 This point was made by his MP, David Curry in 'Cot-death professor: campaign against me puts children at risk', *The Independent*, 8 May 2004, cited in Gooderham, *loc cit.*

17 Goldacre, M.J., Evans, J. and Lambert, T.W., 'Media Criticism of Doctors: Review of UK Junior Doctors' concerns Raised in Surveys', *BMJ*, 2003;326;629-630.

18 For a detailed account see Lewis, R. and Gilliam, S., 'Back to the Market: Yet More Reform to the NHS', *International J. Health Services*, Vol 33, No 1, 77-84.

> The fact that the NHS is, in essence, a value-driven, politically sensitive enterprise, means that it is always changing. It has never been free of the tinkering which shifting views on the proper role of the public and private sector and on levels of taxation inevitably bring to bear. But the 1980s and 1990s were somewhat special in both the pace and nature of the changes which took place.[19]

Ironically, the BRI Inquiry itself accelerated the pace of change through its recommendations, increasing the pressure on those working in the NHS.

Another writer commented:[20]

> The advocates of every new reform argue that it will make the NHS more efficient or effective, save money or produce more or better patient care ... By the time that the researchers have painstakingly documented and measured progress and assessed the impact of one set of reforms, the next wave of organisational change is already upon us.[21]

Market incentives in healthcare were introduced by the Thatcher administration, and have in turn been reduced and re-invigorated by more recent administrations.[22] One recent comment made on yet another set of proposed reforms is particularly apt:

> Doctors and nurses are wearied by the quickening pace of organisational changes that appear to have solved nothing. They do not 'own these reforms'. The new guidance appears to redefine the very nature of the NHS ... Both within and without observers may wonder whether the NHS is about to be reformed out of all recognition.[23]

Clinicians have worked under the regimes of the NHS Trusts, Health Authorities and – for some now – Foundation Hospitals. They have learned to cope with Non-executive Directors and Chairmen as well as executive boards. They are told what treatments are approved, and their professional discretion is eroded by edicts from their employers and the Government about affordable and appropriate therapies that they should employ. Doctors must familiarise themselves with guidelines issued by NICE, some of which may not coincide with instructions from their managers or their own professional judgement. Drugs that have been approved by NICE are funded by commissioners of healthcare, but it is generally recognised that NICE is working at a slower pace than cutting-edge researchers. This leads to dilemmas for clinicians who are aware that more effective drugs exist than those sanctioned by NICE and who wish to prescribe accordingly, on the basis of clinical need. Tensions between management and clinicians are heightened by the fact that Trust Boards

---

19 *BRI Inquiry Report*, *supra cit.*, chapter 4, at p. 50, para 2.

20 Walshe, K., 'Foundation Hospitals: a new direction for NHS Reform', *J R Soc Med*, 2003; 96: 106-110.

21 *Ibid.*, at p. 109.

22 Secretary of State for Health, *The NHS Plan: A Plan for Investment, a Plan for Reform*, CM 4818-I The Stationery Office, London 2000.

23 Lewis, R. and Gilliam, S., *loc. cit.*

carry ultimate responsibility for any financial overspend, and are reluctant to allow spending on high cost drugs which are not recommended by NICE.

This situation is illustrated by the highly publicised[24] national controversy that has arisen over Herceptin, a drug that has only been approved by NICE to prolong survival in the one in five women with advanced breast cancer who carry a genetic flaw producing a protein known as HER2. The same drug has been shown in clinical trials[25] to be highly beneficial for patients in the early stages of the disease. There are concerns that there will be delays in approving the drug for the treatment of this second group of women, and that there may be a postcode lottery over who can receive the treatment, which is very expensive. The drug must be assessed by NICE in a process which is likely to take a year, and then the decision whether to fund treatment will lie with Primary Care Trusts which, as commissioners, will need to decide whether this is possible from a cost perspective when set against the potential loss to other patients and services that need to be commissioned. To treat around 45 women with the drug would add approximately £1m to the budget of a Trust,[26, 27] and there would be few Trusts which would be comfortable about permitting such a large overspend. Clinicians who are required by the developing common law on consent to treatment to inform patients of these issues require high levels of support from their managers – support which is not always available, despite the intense public pressure engendered by dramatic media reports.

Structural reforms have also included the increasing devolution of healthcare systems within the UK, leading to a bewildering plethora of disparate regulation which directly contradicts the Government's commitment to 'end post-code prescribing'. NHS organisations with virtually identical functions are given different names in different regions. Doctors and patients in England, Wales, Scotland and Northern Ireland, and even those responsible for the administration of healthcare within each region, are uncertain as to what is happening elsewhere in the UK. This situation can lead to particular difficulties for doctors and patients who relocate within the UK, and for Trusts located in regional borders, whose staff are understandably confused over different approaches to healthcare provision. For example some NHS Trusts in England commission services from NHS bodies in Wales. Significant confusion arises over differences in funding, (in England there is payment by results whereas in Wales there is not); differences in year-on-year inflationary uplift; different approaches to waiting lists; differences in the star-rating system; differences in definitions of

---

24 See Revill, J., *The Observer*, 22 May 2005.

25 Professor Ian Smith, of the Royal Marsden Hospital in London, the lead UK investigator of the latest study, which involved 500 UK patients, described the news about Herceptin as an historic development in the treatment of breast cancer, *The Times*, 24 May 2005.

26 I am grateful to Dr Malcolm Adams of Velindre NHS Trust for supplying me with these estimates.

27 The Court of Appeal decided in April 2006, after this chapter was written, that a patient was entitled to be treated with Herceptin before it had been approved by NICE - *Rogers v Swindon NHS Primary Care NHS Trust* [2006] EWCA Civ 397.

patient populations; differences in prescription charges (free prescriptions in Wales for people aged under 25 and, currently, a £3 charge to be reduced to nil for everyone else who is not on benefit in Wales).

Doctors have, over the past decade or so, been introduced to clinical governance, risk management and compulsory training in the form of continuous professional development. The implementation of clinical governance and the associated burden of administration for doctors and NHS managers have resulted in additional pressures being placed upon them, and increasing requirements for documentation, regular reporting and compulsory audit have increased occupational stress on doctors. They are now required to undergo annual appraisals, and their work is subjected to regular inspections by the Healthcare Commission. They are constantly bombarded by barrages of government documentation explaining how proposed reforms are to be 'delivered'. Many of these developments are accompanied by a range of jargon, and doctors are expected to familiarise themselves with a new vocabulary formulated for the most part by civil servants, involving various meanings of the words 'standards', 'quality requirements', 'benchmarks', 'criteria', 'targets', 'guidelines', 'protocols', treatment plans', 'clinical networks', 'pathways of care' and 'quality assurance' to name but a few of the phrases listed in various glossaries to government documents.[28] Doctors are required to absorb information about new systems for reporting critical incidents, and to come to terms with the requirements of the National Patient Safety Agency. They are given set targets and can expect to see the results of their efforts and even their personal records publicised in national tables which reveal the success or otherwise of their endeavours.

As Chris Ham has observed, it is important to engage clinicians in order to generate real improvements in healthcare delivery, yet many radical reforms have failed to meet expectations:

> Improvement of the performance of healthcare depends first and foremost on making a difference to the experience of patients and service users, which in turn hinges on changing the day-to-day decisions of doctors, nurses and other staff.[29]

In yet another new development the year 1996 saw the introduction of the new NHS Complaints System, which has been reformed since that date on more than one occasion. The Healthcare Commissioner, whose role was extended in the same year,[30] has overseen a wide range of developments but there still appears to be little

28 Many of these words are listed in the randomly selected glossy brochure entitled *Healthcare Standards for Wales: Making the Connections Designed for Life*, 2005 NHS Wales.

29 Ham, C., 'Improving the Performance of Health Services: The Role of Clinical Leadership', 2003, *The Lancet*, vol 361, 1978-1980, at p. 1980.

30 The Healthcare Commissioners Act 1996, for a commentary see Harpwood, V., 'The Healthcare Commissioner: An Extended Role in the 'New' NHS', 1996 *European Jo Healthcare*, vol 4, 72-89.

real understanding among healthcare professionals about why people complain or how best to respond to complaints.[31]

Paradoxically, some of the measures introduced to provide better protection for patients are placing increasing demands on doctors and could be counter-productive in the longer term. Thus, for example, the pressure to reduce waiting times for treatment is made more burdensome for healthcare professionals by the need to ensure that each patient receives more time for consultation during the consent process.

Surprisingly, after the Government's investment in the development of new Medical Schools, another source of anxiety for doctors has recently been identified. Junior doctors now face unemployment and are considering leaving the profession according the BMA.[32]

Legislative Changes

Doctors are expected to recognise, to assimilate, to understand and in some instances to apply a raft of complex legislation which directly or indirectly affects their work. Among the recent legislative reforms which have a direct affect on medical practice are The Mental Capacity Act 2005, The Health Service Commissioners Act 1996, the Data Protection Acts 1995 and 1998, the Freedom of Information Act 2000, the Health Act 1999, the Human Rights Act 1998, the Disability Discrimination Acts 1995 and 2005, the National Health Service Reform and Health Care Professions Act 2002, The Human Fertilisation and Embryology Act 1990, the Public Interest (Disclosure) Act 1998, the Health and Safety at Work etc Act 1974 to name but a few. European directives have been implemented in relation to many areas of healthcare delivery. Many statutes are accompanied by a complex and detailed framework of secondary legislation which can be difficult to interpret, and which is enforced or supervised by regulatory bodies. Doctors are expected to cope with the implementation of new rules and regulatory frameworks despite having virtually no training on new legislation, and while also being expected to cope with heavy workloads and stringent targets. Although training is regarded as part of continuous professional development in the context of clinical governance, few doctors have received instruction on, for example, the impact of the Human Rights Act on their professional practice.[33] In any event, there are few doctors who are able to take time away from clinical practice to learn about such developments.

31 Mulcahy, L., *Disputing Doctors: The Socio-Dynamics of Complaints about Medical Care*, Maidenhead, Open University Press, 2003.

32 BBC News, 28 July 2005.

33 Exceptionally, Specialist Registrars in Wales are required to undertake training in law and ethics.

Regulatory Bodies

Numerous regulatory bodies have been established in recent years to oversee the delivery of healthcare, and the work of NHS organisations and staff. Many of these organisations have been given additional or modified roles and have changed their titles and acronyms over the years – factors which add to the confusion for doctors. To the cynical clinician NICE, CHI, HFEA, MDA, MHRA, NCAA, NPSA, NHSLA are simply evidence of a rash of 'initiativitis' by successive governments. Moreover, during the past two decades numerous quangos with remits that affect doctors have appeared and disappeared, at great cost to the taxpayer.

In addition to these organisations, doctors who make professional errors face questioning in the course of public inquiries, hospital inquiries, Coroners' inquests, the NHS complaints system, civil litigation, criminal prosecutions and disciplinary action by the General Medical Council.

Suspensions of doctors by their employers for various forms of incompetence and malpractice, often at heavy cost to the public purse, have been a serious cause for concern over the many years. Despite guidance issued by the Chief Medical Officer the problem continues to demoralise the profession as a whole.[34] These and other reviewing procedures require meetings and the production of paperwork and divert doctors' time from patient care.

Professional Monitoring and Discipline

Even before the reports of the BRI and Shipman Inquiries there was a large body of literature that was highly critical of the GMC and its handling of the regulation and discipline of doctors.[35] However, it was the reports of these two Inquiries which provided the strongest possible impetus for numerous changes in the NHS, and had a particular impact on professional regulation and discipline, resulting in proposals to change the way in which failing doctors are dealt with by the GMC. Although some of the recommendations have now been acted upon, doctors still face criticism because of the general view that the body that disciplines them is not independent of the profession. It has been argued that the GMC is even at odds with itself in its consultation document *Protecting Patients: A Summary Consultative Document*, behaving like 'a body that seems to be trying to accommodate the conflicting

---

34 National Audit Office, *The Management of Suspensions of Clinical Staff in NHS Hospital and Ambulance Trusts*, 2003 HC 1143.

35 See for example, Smith, R.G., *Medical Discipline. The Professional Conduct Jurisdiction of the General Medical Council*, Oxford, Clarendon Press 1994 at pp. 1858-1990; Gladstone, D. (ed), Johnson, J., Pickering W.G., Salter, B. and Stacey, M., *Regulating Doctors* (2000), London, Institute for the Study of Civil Society; Kennedy, I., *The Unmasking of Medicine*, London, Allen and Unwin, 1981.

demands of its different stakeholders rather than brokering clear and bold changes in the interests of the public'.[36]

In its response to the Chief Medical Officer's review of clinical performance and medical regulation following the Shipman Inquiry, the BMA[37] supported the principle of revalidation – checks at regular intervals on doctors in order to demonstrate that they should continue to hold a licence to practise. Doctors greatly fear disciplinary action by the GMC and the ultimate sanction of being struck off the medical register, and are aware of the heightening disciplinary culture, yet they are still unclear as to what form revalidation procedures will take. The valid point is made by the BMA that clinicians might well find that they will be forced to spend less time on patient care if regulation is too burdensome, emphasising that doctors are concerned that new systems for revalidation will be time consuming and over-bearing.

> Any arrangement put in place should not introduce an onerous workload or have intimidating undertones as it may pose a threat to recruitment and retention and would potentially encourage early retirement amongst older doctors. [38]

Further threats are perceived by doctors who believe that the GMC operates a blame culture. The BMA warns of the need to avoid disincentives to doctors to take on high-risk procedures or patients, or to practice innovatively and points out that some people employed by public bodies act in ways which are highly risk-averse because they fear disciplinary action and litigation.

Outside the GMC the work of individual doctors is monitored in a variety of different ways, among them audit, which is now compulsory, the well-established system of Confidential Inquiries, clinical governance processes and compulsory annual complaints reviews. From a psychological perspective, the work of the National Clinical Assessment Authority (NCAA) has been hailed as a better approach to dealing with problem doctors than the draconian GMC stance. The NCCA quickly identifies errant doctors at an early stage and institutes remedial training in the absence of a blame culture, while the threat of the GMC simply imposes fear and paralysis.[39]

---

36 Dewar, S. and Finlayson, B., *Reforming the GMC*, (2001) *BMJ*; 322: 689-690, at p. 689.

37 BMA Press release, 20 May 2005.

38 The BMA response to the CMO's review on maintaining high standards of professional practice can be found on the BMA website at: http://www.bma.org.uk/ap.nsf/Content/cmoresponse.

39 Osborne, J., *Regulating Doctors: Should We Swallow Dame Janet's Medicine?*, 2005 *BMJ*, 330: 546; see also Irvine, D., 'GMC and the Future of Revalidation: Patients, Professionalism and Revalidation', 2005 *BMJ*, 330:1265, at p. 1265.

Technological Developments

The speed with which technology in medicine is developing is breath-taking, and progresses at an exponential rate. New medical devices and procedures are appearing regularly, new techniques are being developed, and vital breakthroughs in diagnostic procedures and treatments are announced every year. For example, very premature babies who would in earlier generations have died, are now surviving as a result of new technologies, and difficult choices must be made when their survival depends on intrusive and sometimes painful treatment. Doctors today, across a range of medical specialties, are faced with ethical, practical and legal dilemmas on a regular basis. Their decisions are questioned by the media and sometimes in the courts. On some occasions the customary privacy and anonymity afforded to patients and their carers is waived in order to for them to gain public sympathy through publicity.[40]

Doctors wishing to conduct clinical trials feel hampered by the weight of new regulations introduced as a result of the implementation of the EU Directive on Clinical Trials.[41] As intelligent and conscientious professionals, with a need to explore the risks and benefits of proposed new treatments many believe that their professional development is being stifled.

New techniques in computing need to be mastered by doctors both in relation to technical scientific processes and also in relation to patients' records. Although doctors are not alone among professionals in the need to acquire computing skills, the nature of their work demands special sensitivity and care, and a particular knowledge of complex legal issues surrounding data protection and security, adding yet another pressure to the agenda. Patients who are able to access information on the internet are also placing pressure on doctors by demanding particular treatments and creating the need for doctors to spend additional time providing explanations and clarifying misunderstandings and misconceptions about treatment options and medical conditions.

Societal Pressures

The complex nature of modern society has increased the pressures on doctors. While political developments such as devolution, regulation and the introduction of monitoring require day to day changes in working conditions, national and international crises call for time to be set aside by doctors for emergency planning outside the usual work routine.

People in general are more aware of their rights as consumers in modern society, and the respect accorded to doctors by earlier generations is no longer much in evidence. It is believed that the so-called compensation culture in modern society places doctors in fear of litigation and allegedly causes them to practice

40 See, for example, *Wyatt v. Portsmouth NHS Trust*, [2005] EWHC 693 (Fam).

41 Dir 2001/20/EC Clinical Trials Directive.

defensively,[42] though hard evidence of this can be difficult to find. The number of clinical claims against the NHS rose steadily throughout the last two decades of the twentieth century,[43] and in 2002-2003 they reached their highest recorded levels. It is difficult to obtain precise information on the current level of claims because of the devolved nature of healthcare in the UK and because no single organisation collates the final figure for all claims against GPs, hospital doctors and those working outside the NHS. However, in 2005, Tony Blair was anxious to impart the message that the number of claims against public bodies, including doctors has fallen. He pointed out that it is a fact that between 2000 and 2005 the number of accident claims fell by 5.3 per cent, and that during the same period, accident claims against local authorities, schools, volunteering organisations and other public sector bodies fell by 7.5 per cent. The costs of tort claims in the UK in 2000 were 0.6 per cent of GDP, which is the lowest of any developed nation except Denmark. In that same year the cost of all tort litigation in the UK as a percentage of GDP was less than a third of that in the US.[44]

According to the Lord Chancellor, a wide spectrum of factors is thought to have contributed to the compensation culture, among them the media influence, the system of recovery with prospects of high costs and lengthy delays that makes inflated settlements preferable; inaccurate expectations by claimants about what the litigation system will produce; the misleading of the public by advertisements in hospital waiting rooms, suggesting that patients who do not recover quickly might want to consult a solicitor; the fact that in some hospitals there are solicitors' offices next to the flower shop in the hospital itself; and the growth of claims farmers who have fostered the attitude that people who are injured should try to turn injury into money. In Lord Irvine's view, the 'loud voice of compensation' can sometimes drown out the quieter voice of balance and reason.[45]

As long as the threat of litigation remains, even the best doctors will feel uneasy and sense the much vaunted 'dagger at the doctor's back'.[46]

The drive towards patient autonomy has added further pressures in the healthcare context and more demands on doctors' time. The European Charter of Patients' Rights,[47] although not yet incorporated into UK law, is evidence of a trend across Europe in favour of patient autonomy. Among the fourteen rights listed in the Charter are the right to information, the right to consent, the right to freedom of choice and the right to respect for patients' time. Policy in Government and in the courts in the UK is now very much slanted towards the empowerment of patients. Countless statements have been made by those in authority about putting patients at the centre

---

42 Lord Falconer, in a speech to the IPPR, 26 May 2005.

43 See McHale, J., 'Medical Malpractice in England – Current Trends', *2003 European Jo Health Law*, 1:135-151.

44 Speech to the IPPR, *supra cit.*

45 Speech to the IPPR, *supra cit.*

46 per Lord Denning in *Hatcher v. Black, The Times*, 2 July 1954.

47 Basis Document, Rome 2002, available at: http://www.activecitizenship.net/health/European_Charter.

of healthcare. This concept is not new, having been a commitment at the inception of the NHS, but it is now being heavily promoted in government literature. To take one of a number of recent examples, in *Creating a Patient-led NHS,*[48] the government argues that:

> Wherever possible, the NHS should offer choices of services and treatment. Information services need to be supported by well-trained staff who can help people make more sense of the information, make choices and access the system.[49]

There are more and more initiatives aimed at patient and public involvement in healthcare decision making and participation in healthcare organisations. The public is consulted more than ever before on healthcare issues as a direct result of recommendations in the BRI Inquiry Report. While these initiatives are greatly to be welcomed, they do place greater time-constraints on clinicians who are already expected to meet fixed targets in other direction.

The Response of the Courts: New Developments in Case Law

The cultural change in favour of greater involvement of patients in decisions about their care has been absorbed at last by the courts. In *Chester v. Afshar*[50] the House of Lords went further than ever before in recognising the importance of patient autonomy in the context of consent to treatment. Lord Hope examined the leading cases in the UK and other jurisdictions, and several academic opinions, and emphasised that the function of the law is to protect the patient's right to choose. Lord Walker took a similar stance, arguing that advice by the doctor is the very foundation of a patient's consent to treatment:

> In a decision which may have a profound effect on her health and well-being a patient is entitled to information and advice about possible alternatives or variant treatments.[51]

Lord Steyn made the following statement:

> A patient's right to an appropriate warning from a surgeon when faced with surgery ought normatively to be regarded as an important right which must be given effective protection whenever possible.[52]

Even the dissenting speeches contained strongly statements in favour of autonomy. Lord Bingham stated categorically that medical paternalism 'no longer rules', and:

48 *NHS Confederation Briefing Paper*, 2005 NHS Confederation.

49 *Ibid.*, para 5.

50 [2004] 4 All E.R. 587.

51 *Ibid.*, para 98.

52 *Ibid.*, para 17.

> The patient's right to be appropriately warned is an important right, which few doctors in the current legal and social climate would consciously or deliberately avoid.[53]

However, Lord Bingham found against the patient because in his view the law should not seek to reinforce the right of a patient to receive information by providing the opportunity 'for the payment of very large damages by a defendant whose violation of that right is shown not to have worsened the physical condition of the claimant'.[54]

Lord Steyn's statement sums up the juridical basis of the approach:

> On a broader basis, I am glad to have arrived at the conclusion that the claimant is entitled in law to succeed. The result is in accord with one of the most basic aspirations of the law, namely to right wrongs. Moreover, the decision … reflects the reasonable expectations of the public in contemporary society.[55]

The implications of this decision for hard-pressed clinicians are far-reaching. Clinical governance and risk management will need to embrace the principle established by this ruling, creating yet more paperwork and generating the need for training of all relevant staff on consent. The Department of Health has yet to update its Reference Guide to Consent in the light of the new developments. Pressure to reduce waiting lists and times, the new consultant's contracts and reductions in the working hours of junior doctors in accordance with the European Working Time Directive, as well as the new GP contract and new consultants' contracts, mean that less time is available for doctors to spend with patients. It is necessary for adequate time to be devoted to each patient to facilitate free and informed choices about treatment in the light of all possible options. Although it is important that patients should be free to make informed choices about the treatment, more time devoted to the consenting process will inevitably mean that healthcare professionals are placed under even greater stress.

Occupational Stress in the NHS

There has been a recent spate of successful litigation in the UK in respect of psychiatric injury suffered as a result of stress at work,[56] and there is a growing culture of stress awareness in the UK in all occupational settings. The first claim made by a doctor for work stress was *Johnstone v. Bloomsbury Health Authority*.[57] It involved a claim by a junior doctor for damages arising from psychiatric illness caused by working excessively long hours. That claim was settled out of court but it

53 *Ibid.*, para 9.
54 *Ibid.*, para 25.
55 *Ibid.*, para 5.
56 Following the case of *Barber v. Somerset County Council*, [2004] IRLR 475 HL.
57 *Johnstone v. Bloomsbury Health Authority*, [1991] All IRLR 118.

was soon followed by a number of successful claims for work stress by employees of public bodies.[58]

The Health and Safety Executive defines stress as 'the adverse reaction people have to excessive pressures or other types of demands placed upon them'.[59] It is too simplistic to attribute the perceived increase in work-related stress in healthcare entirely to the catalogue of changed working conditions, societal pressures and new regulatory or administrative frameworks, and it must be recognised that in almost every respect employees in civilised societies have far safer and more amenable working conditions than ever before in the course of history, thanks to modern health and safety legislation. What has changed in recent years is that there has developed a greater awareness than ever before of occupational stress. The need to conquer occupational stress can perhaps be regarded as the final frontier in the struggle to ensure safe working environments, and governments are considering how to respond to it.

Although some degree of pressure might be regarded as beneficial in providing the stimulus and incentive to hard work, there is a distinction between acceptable work pressure, and stress that is the result of excessive pressure at work, the result of which is recognised stress-related illness. Recognised causes of stress include poor communications between management and staff, strained work relationships, excessive workloads, job insecurity, long working hours, role ambiguity, harassment, bullying and violence.

In the context of the working environment in healthcare, there have been numerous suggestions that doctors are now subjected to greater stress than ever before, as a result of many of these identifiable pressures, and these have been supported to some extent by research findings. If sickness absence generally is an indication of stress levels, it is significant that the public sector has the highest level of sickness absence, currently put at 10.7 working days per employee. Still more significant is that in the NHS there is a sickness rate of around 11.6 days per employee.[60]

The work ethos and culture in the NHS, coupled with external factors associated with increased patient and government expectations, are likely causes of occupational stress among doctors. Research has led to the suggestion that barriers to managing workplace stress exist in the healthcare setting[61] and that it is regarded by managers as a low priority. Data produced in 2001 by Neurolink,[62] an organisation consisting of independent mental health experts, in a survey of multidisciplinary health professionals, indicated that 96 per cent of respondents considered that occupational

58 Cf *Walker v. Northumberland County Council*, 1995 ICR 702, QB.

59 Regarded as an acceptable definition by the Court of Appeal in *Sutherland v. Hatton*, [2002] EWCA Civ 76, part 2, para 7.

60 Chartered Institute of Personal and Development, *Employee Absence 2204 – A Survey of Management Policy and Practice*, July 2004.

61 Cox, T. and Griffiths, A., *Interventions to Control Stress in the Health Service*, London, Health and Safety Executive, 1997.

62 Cited in Wyatt, J., 'Stress Management', *Institute of Health Management Journal*, June 2001 available at: http://www.ihm.org.uk.

stress in the NHS was increasing and that 94 per cent believed that occupational stress was compromising NHS performance. Of the surveyed, 94 per cent believed that stress was causing increased levels of absenteeism and 95 per cent believed that occupational stress was causing healthcare workers to leave the NHS. Also, 84 per cent claimed that the stress levels within their own work agenda were increasing, and 82 per cent of respondents said that work stress had affected their family or their relationships with their colleagues. The highest impact on level of stress was thought by respondents to be related to repeated policy initiatives and to their administrative workload.

A survey by the Health and Safety Executive[63] in 2002 revealed that healthcare professionals were twice as likely to suffer stress in comparison with 2,000 standard occupational groups, and a Healthcare Commission survey of NHS staff in England, carried out in 2003 and responded to by 203,911 staff, indicated that 37 per cent of staff had experienced harassment, bullying or abuse at work; 15 per cent had reported physical violence in the last 12 months and 39 per cent said that they had been suffering from work-related stress in the previous year.

Work related stress is allegedly at the heart of reports that there are many doctors considering leaving the profession. One study after another of the views of doctors has revealed that they are seriously disillusioned. A national survey involving 42,360 GPs, conducted by the British Medical Association in 1991,[64] even before new targets and further regulatory measures were introduced, disclosed that a quarter of GPs were seriously considering leaving the profession within five years, and that 48 per cent hoped to retire before the age of 60. Of the respondents, 80 per cent claimed that they were suffering from excessive stress at work, and 93 per cent thought that fewer patients and longer consultation times were necessary to meet the demands of proper patient care. Also, 46 per cent of the GPs in the survey indicated that they would not recommend the profession to a newly qualified doctor. And 80 per cent thought that hospital care had declined. It is still too early to determine whether the newly introduced GP contract, designed to address some of these concerns, has achieved better morale among GPs.

A survey for the Health Service Journal in 2001 revealed 62 per cent of consultant surgeons intended to retire early, and 100 per cent of consultant paediatricians surveyed were intending to seek early retirement from the NHS,[65] blaming excessive stress.

In 2004, another study[66] of 4,221 doctors, of whom 2,727 responded, indicated that of 1,047 junior doctors who were considering staying in medicine but practising

---

63 Health and Safety Executive, cited by Morgan Cole Solicitors in Lecture, *Managing Stress in the Workplace*, 23 April 2004.

64 *The Guardian*, 12 October 2001.

65 Cited in Wyatt, J., 'Stress Management', *Institute of Health Management Journal*, June 2001, available at: http://www.ihm.org.uk.

66 Moss, P.J., Lambert, T.W., Goldacre, M.J. and Lee, P., 'Reasons for Considering Leaving UK Medicine: Questionnaire Study of Junior Doctors' Comments', 2004, *BMJ*, doi:10.1136/bmj.38247.594769.AE, October 2004.

outside the UK, 41 per cent offered as their reasons matters concerning working conditions. Of the 279 doctors who were considering relinquishing medicine altogether, 75 per cent gave working conditions as their reason. Dissatisfaction with NHS working conditions should, over time, be reduced in accordance with the European Working Time Directive[67] and the 'New Deal'[68] initiative, but there are still problems in relation to the reduction in working hours for junior doctors in order to ensure compliance as a result of recent reforms in the training of senior house officers.

Occupational stress claims involving psychiatric injury are increasing in number in the NHS. Stress levels in female doctors have been recognised as high for some time,[69] and the extensive and rapid change in the NHS since 1990 has been blamed for the feelings of loss of control and demoralisation perceived by some members of the profession.[70] Doctors were listed in 1995 as carrying a suicide risk that was 72 per cent higher than that of the general population.[71] However, while a group of researchers in 2001 pointed out the need to monitor the increased risk of suicide in female doctors in the UK in comparison with that of the general population,[72] they noted that in male doctors the risk was lower than in the population as a whole. It would be interesting to speculate about the gender-based reasons that might account for this disparity.

Numerous suggestions have been made as to the reasons for the increased stress claimed by NHS employees. Wyatt, for example, suggests that rising patient expectations are responsible, together with a lack of support during periods of change, and the imposition of targets without proper consultation. She blames cultural and psychological distances between managers and doctors, and serious weaknesses in the infrastructure of healthcare organisations as factors that have contributed to workplace stress in the NHS.[73]

---

67 1993/014/EC and Department of Health, *Guidance on Working Patterns for Junior Doctors*, London 2002 availabale at: http://www.dh.gov.uk/assetRoot/04/06/63/04066366.

68 NHS Management Executive, *Junior Doctors: The New Deal*, London: Department of Health, 1991.

69 'Stress in Female Doctors', *Women in Management Review*, Vol 12, No 8, 1997, 325-344.

70 See for example, the work of Sutherland, V. and Cooper, C.L., 'Identifying Distress Among General Practitioners: Predictors of Psychological Ill-health and Job Satisfaction', *Social Science Medicine*, Vol 37, 575-81.

71 McKevitt, C., *et al.*, *Doctors' Health Needs for Services*, London, Nuffield, 1995.

72 Hawton, K., Clements, A., Sakarovitch, C., Simkin, S. and Deeks, J.J., 'Suicide in Doctors: A Study of Risk According to Gender, Seniority and Speciality in Medical Practitioners in England and Wales 1979-95', *J. Epidemio. Community Health*, 2001; 55; 296-300.

73 Wyatt, J., 'Stress Management', *Institute of Health Management Journal*, June 2001 available at: http://www.ihm.org.uk.

Conclusion

There can seldom be simple solutions to complex problems. It may be possible to devise compromises that will ensure that the balance is redressed to enable doctors to work more effectively to meet the needs of patients in the modern professional setting. These solutions include the fostering of a better understanding between doctors and patients by clear statements of the rights and responsibilities of both groups; better training for doctors in communicating effectively with patients; discussions between the Government and the media on the best way to ensure responsible reporting of health news without compromising press freedom; reducing the number of Government 'initiatives' aimed at promoting efficiency in healthcare, to give the healthcare professions a respite at least for a while from interference with their professional discretion; ensuring that doctors are fully supported by management when essential changes are introduced in their working environments; reducing enforced accountability on doctors in order to achieve the correct balance between trust and accountability;[74] placing a stronger emphasis on the need for patients as individuals to take responsibility for their own lives; reducing the problems inherent in the current litigation system by introducing the promised Compensation Bill and NHS Redress Bill[75] and by promoting a 'blame free culture' as in encouraged by the NPSA and as was recommended by the BRI Inquiry Report – although this has been greeted with cynicism in many quarters; informing doctors fully of new legislation and case-law developments that directly affect their work and their relationships with patients; facilitating the consent process by allowing more time for each patient (clearly a resource issue), allowing systems as opposed to individuals to take the blame for medical errors, by encouraging the imposition of primary liability on healthcare organisations, as opposed to vicarious liability which identifies individual error; ensuring that the system for disciplining doctors is independent of the profession in order to maintain public credibility; monitoring patterns of stress at work in the healthcare professions and involving the Trade Unions in this process.

It is impossible given the constraints of space, to explore any of these issues in depth, but it is worth mentioning one important matter by way of conclusion. The emphasis in the UK to date has been on the duties and responsibilities of doctors, with little reference to corresponding responsibilities of patients. Other jurisdictions have embraced the concept of patients' responsibilities and it is possible to find many statements of patients' responsibilities in the US, even in the brochures given to patients on entering hospital for treatment.[76] When the restructuring of the US

74 This point was made in the 2004 Reith Lectures by Onora O'Neill when she argued: 'Efforts to prevent the abuse of trust are gigantic, relentless and expensive; their results are less than perfect.' She contended that there is a need for a proper balance to be achieved between trust, transparency and accountability.

75 See the Queen's Speech 17 May 2005.

76 For example the literature given to patients entering Central DuPage Hospital states that doctors and patients are partners in the healthcare team and lists the responsibilities that both owe to each other.

healthcare system was planned in 1997, the President's Advisory Commission on Consumer Protection and Quality in the Health Care Industry drafted a Consumer Bill of Rights and Responsibilities.[77] This document contained a detailed statement of what doctors and patients could expect of one another. Consumer (patient) responsibilities included those of taking responsibility for maximising healthy habits, such as exercising, not smoking and eating a healthy diet; becoming involved in specific healthcare decisions; working collaboratively with healthcare providers in developing and carrying out agreed-upon treatment plans; disclosing relevant information and clearly communicating wants and needs – to name but a few.

Despite the criticisms that have been made of doctors in recent years, an opinion poll conducted by MORI in 2005 revealed that patients still have great regard for the medical profession. Medical scandals leave the respect accorded to doctors by the public intact despite adverse publicity from the Shipman, Ledward, Neale, Alder Hey and Bristol scandals. The MORI poll, the results of which were announced in March 2005 found that more than 91 per cent of the public trust doctors to tell the truth. This is a higher rating than that given to any other professional group included in the poll.[78] In 2003 MORI conducted a survey of politicians' attitudes to doctors and discovered that 74 per cent thought that doctors are patient-focused, committed (92 per cent), and hard-working (87 per cent).[79]

A survey conducted in the year 2000 indicated that among doctors themselves there is an unwillingness to criticise colleagues for inadequate work, and that despite the apparent increase in critical media coverage, most doctors believe that there has been no deterioration in professional standards, that there have always been problems in the profession and that the media is exaggerating the problem.[80]

These attitudes suggest that some solutions lie with doctors and patients themselves. Meanwhile – pity the poor doctor!

---

77 Available at: http://www.hcqualitycommission.gov.

78 For the public poll, MORI Social Research Institute interviewed a representative quota sample of 2,000 adults aged 15+ in 193 sampling points across Great Britain, via omnibus methodology. Interviews were conducted face to face, in home, from 17-21 February 2005, using computer assisted personal interviewing. This data has been weighted to the known profile of UK populations.

79 MORI, 18 February, 2003, available at: http://www.mori.com/polls/2003/bma.

80 2000 Medix UK plc.

For Product Safety Concerns and Information please contact our EU representative GPSR@taylorandfrancis.com Taylor & Francis Verlag GmbH, Kaufingerstraße 24, 80331 München, Germany

Batch number: 10725973

Printed by Printforce, the Netherlands